Attitudes towards Sexuality in Judaism and Christianity
in the Hellenistic Greco-Roman Era

Enoch, Levi, and Jubilees on Sexuality

The Dead Sea Scrolls on Sexuality

The Pseudepigrapha on Sexuality

Philo, Josephus, and the Testaments on Sexuality

PHILO, JOSEPHUS, AND THE TESTAMENTS
on
SEXUALITY

*Attitudes towards Sexuality in
the Writings of Philo and Josephus and in
the Testaments of the Twelve Patriarchs*

William Loader

WILLIAM B. EERDMANS PUBLISHING COMPANY
GRAND RAPIDS, MICHIGAN

© 2011 William Loader
All rights reserved

Published 2011 by
Wm. B. Eerdmans Publishing Co.
2140 Oak Industrial Drive N.E., Grand Rapids, Michigan 49505

Printed in the United States of America

16 15 14 13 12 11   7 6 5 4 3 2 1

Library of Congress Cataloging-in-Publication Data

Loader, William R. G., 1944-
Philo, Josephus, and the Testaments on sexuality: attitudes towards sexuality in the writings
of Philo and Josephus and in the Testaments of the Twelve Patriarchs / William Loader.
p.   cm. — (Attitudes towards sexuality in Judaism and Christianity
in the Hellenistic Greco-Roman era)
Includes bibliographical references (p.   ) and indexes.
ISBN 978-0-8028-6641-7 (pbk.: alk. paper)
1. Philo, of Alexandria. 2. Josephus, Flavius. 3. Sex — Religious aspects — Judaism.
4. Sex — Religious aspects — Christianity. 5. Sex in the Bible.
6. Bible. O.T. — Criticism, interpretation, etc.
I. Title.
B689.Z7L63 2011
296.3'8 — dc23
2011019093

www.eerdmans.com

Contents

Acknowledgments	xii
Introduction	1

PART ONE

ATTITUDES TOWARDS SEXUALITY IN THE WRITINGS OF PHILO OF ALEXANDRIA   2

1.1	Introduction: Issues in Reading Philo on Sexuality	2
1.2	Man and Woman: Beginning from Genesis 1 – 3	10
	1.2.1 The Creation of Human Beings	11
	1.2.1.1 Image, Genus, and Moulded from Clay	11
	1.2.1.2 "Male and Female"	15
	1.2.1.3 "Let us make"	16
	1.2.1.4 Potentially Good	17
	1.2.1.5 The Garden of Virtues	20
	1.2.1.6 Conclusion	21
	1.2.2 Woman and Man	21
	1.2.2.1 The Creation of Woman (Gen 2:20-24)	21
	1.2.2.1.1 The Creation of Woman in "On Creation"	21

1.2.2.1.2	The Creation of Woman in "Questions and Answers on Genesis"	26
1.2.2.1.3	The Creation of Woman in "Allegorical Interpretation" and Beyond	29
1.2.2.1.4	Conclusion	30
1.2.2.2	Women and Gender Roles	31
1.2.2.3	Male and Female Identity	34
1.2.2.4	Male and Female in Human Psychology: Mind, Senses, Passions	41
1.2.2.5	Woman in Perspective: A Summary Assessment	45
1.2.2.6	Sex	56
1.2.2.6.1	Pleasure in Procreation	56
1.2.2.6.2	Sex only for Procreation	61
1.2.3	The Danger of Pleasure (Gen 2:25 [3:1] – 3:6)	66
1.2.3.1	The Snake of Pleasure	66
1.2.3.1.1	The Snake of Pleasure in "On Creation"	66
1.2.3.1.2	The Snake of Pleasure in "Questions and Answers on Genesis"	71
1.2.3.1.2	The Snake of Pleasure in "Allegorical Interpretation" and Beyond	72
1.2.3.2	Dangers of Sexual Pleasure Elsewhere	76
1.2.3.3	Eliminating Sexual Passion?	84
1.2.3.4	Control and Moderation of Sexual Passion	91
1.2.3.5	Sexual Asceticism and the Therapeutae/Therapeutrides	100
1.2.4	Life Beyond the Garden (Gen 3:14 – 4:1)	110
1.2.4.1	The Consequences of Failure	110
1.2.4.1.1	The Consequences of Failure in "On Creation"	110
1.2.4.1.2	The Consequences of Failure in "Questions and Answers on Genesis"	111
1.2.4.1.3	The Consequences of Failure in "Allegorical Commentary" and Beyond	111
1.2.4.1.4	Conclusion	116
1.2.4.2	Conception, Childbirth, and Human Biology	117
1.2.4.3	Household Management	125
1.2.4.4	Death and Hope	128
1.2.4.5	Sexual Intercourse as Symbol of the Soul's Relationships	136
1.3	Sexual Allusions and Images Beyond Genesis 1 – 3	141
1.3.1.	Significant Motifs Generated by Genesis 4 – 11	141
1.3.1.1	Cain	141
1.3.1.2	The Enochs	142

1.3.1.3	The Angels' Sex with Women	143
1.3.1.4	Noah	144
1.3.1.4.1	Noah's Ark	144
1.3.1.4.2	Noah's Name	144
1.3.1.4.3	Noah and Agricultural Imagery	144
1.3.1.4.4	Noah and Drunkenness	145
1.3.1.4.5	Noah and Nakedness	146
1.3.1.5	Babel	147
1.3.2	Significant Motifs Generated by Genesis 12 – 50	147
1.3.2.1	Abraham	148
1.3.2.1.1	Abraham's Migration	148
1.3.2.1.2	Abraham and Sarah	149
1.3.2.1.3	Abraham, Sarah, and Hagar	153
1.3.2.1.4	Abraham and Sarah, Pharaoh and Abimelech	155
1.3.2.2	Sodom and Lot	156
1.3.2.2.1	Sodom's Sins	156
1.3.2.2.2	Lot's Wife and Daughters	157
1.3.2.2.3	Lot, Abraham, and the Kings	159
1.3.2.3.	Isaac and Rebecca	159
1.3.2.4.	Jacob and Esau	162
1.3.2.5.	Leah and Rachel	163
1.3.2.6.	Joseph	166
1.3.2.6.1	Joseph in the Positive	166
1.3.2.6.2	Joseph in Question	168
1.3.2.6.3	Joseph and the Eunuchs	173
1.3.2.7.	Dinah	174
1.3.2.8.	Tamar and Judah	177
1.3.2.9.	Reuben	179
1.3.3	Significant Motifs Generated by the Story of Moses and Exodus	180
1.3.3.1	Moses	180
1.3.3.1.1	Moses in Mos. 1	180
1.3.3.1.2	Moses Beyond Mos. 1	181
1.3.3.2	The Exodus	183
1.3.3.2.1	The Departure from Egypt	183
1.3.3.2.2	Marah, Manna, and the Golden Bull	184
1.3.3.3	Midianites, Moabites, and Phinehas	185
1.4	Sexual Issues in Philo's Exposition of Law	188
1.4.1	Adultery and Associated Issues	188
1.4.1.1	Adultery in "On the Decalogue"	188

1.4.1.2		Adultery in Special Laws and Elsewhere	190
1.4.1.3		Laws treated under the Heading of the Prohibition of Adultery	193
	1.4.1.3.1	Incest	193
	1.4.1.3.2	Intermarriage	195
	1.4.1.3.3	Remarriage of a Divorced Wife	199
	1.4.1.3.4	Intercourse during Menstruation	201
	1.4.1.3.5	Intercourse with Sterile Women	202
	1.4.1.3.6	Pederasty and Same-Sex Intercourse	204
	1.4.1.3.7	Bestiality	217
	1.4.1.3.8	Prostitution	218
	1.4.1.3.9	Accusations of Adultery	224
	1.4.1.3.10	Rape of a Widow or Divorcee and Seduction or Rape of an Unmarried, Unbetrothed Woman	225
	1.4.1.3.11	Intercourse with a Woman Espoused to be Married to Another	227
	1.4.1.3.12	Accusations that One's Wife was not a Virgin at Marriage	228

1.4.2   Beyond the Prohibition of Adultery and Associated Laws   229
   1.4.2.1   Circumcision   229
   1.4.2.2   Laws treated under the Headings of the First Five Commandments   231
      1.4.2.2.1   The First Two Commandments: Worship and Idolatry   231
      1.4.2.2.2   The Third Commandment: Vows   237
      1.4.2.2.3   The Fourth Commandment: Sabbath   238
      1.4.2.2.4   The Fifth Commandment: Honouring Parents   242
   1.4.2.3   Laws treated under the Headings of the Last Four Commandments   243
      1.4.2.3.1   The Seventh Commandment: Killing   243
      1.4.2.3.2   The Tenth Commandment: Coveting   246
1.4.3   Legal Provisions Beyond the Decalogue and Special Laws   249
1.4.4   Conclusion   251

1.5   Conclusion   252

PART TWO

ATTITUDES TOWARDS SEXUALITY IN THE WRITINGS OF JOSEPHUS — 259

2.1　Introduction: Issues in Reading Josephus on Sexuality — 259

2.2　Narratives Pertinent to Issues of Sexuality — 265
  2.2.1　The Creation Account — 265
  2.2.2　From Cain to Noah — 270
  2.2.3　Abraham — 271
    2.2.3.1　Abraham and Sarah in Egypt — 271
    2.2.3.2　Sodom, Lot, and his Daughters — 273
    2.2.3.3　Abraham, Sarah, and Abimelech — 275
  2.2.4　Isaac and Rebecca — 276
  2.2.5　Esau, Jacob and Rachel — 278
  2.2.6　Dinah — 280
  2.2.7　Joseph — 282
  2.2.8　Moses and the Exodus — 285
    2.2.8.1　Moses and his Marriages — 285
    2.2.8.2　The Midianite Women — 286
  2.2.9　The Period of the Judges — 287
    2.2.9.1　Rahab — 287
    2.2.9.2　The Rape at Gibeah — 287
    2.2.9.3　Deborah and Jephthah — 289
    2.2.9.4　Manoah and his Wife — 290
    2.2.9.5　Samson — 291
    2.2.9.6　Ruth — 292
  2.2.10　The Period of the Kings — 294
    2.2.10.1　David — 294
    2.2.10.2　The Rape of Tamar — 297
    2.2.10.3　Solomon — 297
  2.2.11　Exile and the Return — 299
    2.2.11.1　Darius' Bodyguards — 299
    2.2.11.2　Ezra and Intermarriage — 299
    2.2.11.3　Manasseh and Intermarriage — 301
    2.2.11.4　Esther — 301
  2.2.12　The Early Hasmonean Period — 303
    2.2.12.1　The Tobiad Romance — 303
    2.2.12.2　John Hyrcanus, Alexander Janneus, and Salome Alexandra — 304

2.2.13	Herod	305
2.2.13.1	The Marriage of Herod and Mariamme	305
2.2.13.2	Herod, Antony, and Cleopatra	306
2.2.13.2.1	Antony's Sexual Predation	306
2.2.13.2.2	Herod's Love and Fear of Mariamme: First Story	307
2.2.13.2.3	Herod and Cleopatra	308
2.2.13.3	Herod, Caesar, and Mariamme	309
2.2.13.3.1	Herod's Love and Fear of Mariamme: Second Story	309
2.2.13.3.2	Herod and Mariamme's Execution	310
2.2.13.4	Herod and Further Sexual Adventures	312
2.2.13.4.1	Herod and Mariamme 2, Daughter of Simon	312
2.2.13.4.2	Pheroras and the Female Slave	313
2.2.13.4.3	Salome and Syllaeus	314
2.2.13.4.4	Herod, Aristobulus, and the Eunuchs	315
2.2.14	Tales from Parthia and Rome	316
2.2.14.1	Phraates and the Italian Female Slave	316
2.2.14.2	Mundus, Paulina, and the Priests of Isis	316
2.2.14.3	Anilaeus and Asinaeus	317
2.2.15	Herodian Marriages	318
2.2.15.1	Antipas and Herodias	318
2.2.15.2	Later Herodian Marriages	318
2.3	Laws and Related Issues	321
2.3.1	The Law Given at Sinai	321
2.3.2	The Law Reviewed before Moses' Farewell	323
2.3.3	The Law in Against Apion	328
2.3.4.	The Essenes and Celibacy	334
2.4	Reviewing Josephus on Sexuality	339
2.4.1	Prisoners, Slaves, and Sexual Abuse	339
2.4.2	Marriages	343
2.4.3	Intermarriage	345
2.4.4	Incest	348
2.4.5	Adultery	349
2.4.6	Female Virginity	350
2.4.7	Divorce and Remarriage	350
2.4.8	Prostitution	352
2.4.9	Same-Sex Intercourse	353
2.4.10	Other Prohibitions (Bestiality, Infanticide, Abortion), Fertility Enhancement and Love Potions	355
2.4.11	Purity Provisions	356

2.4.12	*Women*	357
2.4.13	*Sexual Love*	361
2.5	Conclusion	365

PART THREE

ATTITUDES TOWARDS SEXUALITY IN THE TESTAMENTS OF THE TWELVE PATRIARCHS 368

3.1	Introduction	368
3.2	Testament of Reuben	371
3.3	Testament of Simeon	391
3.4	Testament of Levi	392
3.5	Testament of Judah	400
3.6	Testament of Issachar	411
3.7	Testament of Zebulon	414
3.8	Testament of Dan	414
3.9	Testament of Naphtali	415
3.10	Testament of Gad	420
3.11	Testament of Asher	420
3.12	Testament of Joseph	421
3.13	Testament of Benjamin	425
3.14	Conclusion	427

Conclusion	436
Bibliography	438
Index of Modern Authors	457
Index of Ancient Sources	460

Acknowledgments

This book is the fourth volume to emerge from my research on attitudes towards sexuality in Judaism and Christianity of the Hellenistic Greco-Roman era, a five year project funded through an Australian Professorial Fellowship from the Australian Research Council, 2005-2010. Murdoch University has provided me with invaluable infrastructure support, not least through the inter-library loans scheme which has found obscure literature for me from all over the world. Without the advantage of electronic resources such research would never have been possible, especially not in such an isolated city as Perth in Western Australia.

I especially thank my colleagues on the other side of Australia, David Runia and James McLaren, of Melbourne, who very kindly read and commented on penultimate drafts of the sections on Philo and Josephus, respectively. As usual with this kind of research I find myself greatly indebted to all who have laboured on these texts before me, most of whom I know only by name, but many of whom I have met, and seek to honour them in the best way possible: by engaging their work. As in previous volumes this investigation works closely with the primary texts, in this case, with three major bodies of writing, and retains the broad focus on matters pertaining to sexuality. This volume completes the work on early Jewish literature. The final volume will address the New Testament literature on sexuality.

I am again particularly grateful to Mary J. Marshall for her careful proofreading and, beyond that, her conscientiousness in laboriously checking my citations. I also express my appreciation to William B. Eerdmans Jr for his support and encouragement, and for his willingness to publish the results of this research.

Introduction

This investigation forms part of a larger project of research on attitudes towards sexuality in Judaism and Christianity in the Hellenistic Greco-Roman era. As in the previous volumes, sexuality is understood in the broad sense of matters pertaining to sexuality rather than in the more defined sense which we find in discussion of sexual orientation and sexual theory. The first volume dealt with the early Enoch literature, *Aramaic Levi Document*, and *Jubilees*,[1] the second, with the Dead Sea Scrolls,[2] the third, with Pseudepigrapha,[3] but including also works such as Ben Sira and Theodotus. This, the fourth volume, deals with the extensive writings of Philo and Josephus, and also the *Testaments of the Twelve Patriarchs*, which, while in its present form is a product of second century Christianity, includes also Jewish tradition and has much in common with the philosophical perpective of Philo and Josephus.

Each set of writings has its own introduction.

Unless otherwise indicated, biblical citations are from *New Revised Standard Version (NRSV)* (Hebrew Bible and New Testament), or *NETS* (Septuagint).[4] Where I offer my own or modified translation I indicate that with an asterisk.

---

[1] William Loader, *Enoch, Levi, and Jubilees on Sexuality: Attitudes towards Sexuality in the Early Enoch Literature, the Aramaic Levi Document, and the Book of Jubilees* (Grand Rapids: Eerdmans, 2007).

[2] William Loader, *The Dead Sea Scrolls on Sexuality: Attitudes towards Sexuality in Sectarian and Related Literature at Qumran* (Grand Rapids: Eerdmans, 2009).

[3] William Loader, *The Pseudepigrapha on Sexuality: Attitudes towards Sexuality in Apocalypses, Testaments, Legends, Wisdom, and Related Literature* (Grand Rapids: Eerdmans, forthcoming).

[4] Albert Pietersma and Benjamin G. Wright, ed. *A New English Translation of the Septuagint* (Oxford: Oxford University Press, 2007).

PART ONE

Attitudes towards Sexuality in the Writings of Philo of Alexandria

1.1 Introduction: Issues in Reading Philo on Sexuality

Philo of Alexandria (ca. 20 B.C.E – 50 C.E.) provides us with a rich resource for understanding attitudes towards sexuality in Alexandria in the early first century C.E., or at least of his own. For he was not simply another Jew in Alexandria, but a highly educated one, in both Jewish and Greco-Roman culture, and well-connected to leading circles of his time, indeed, through his own family, where his brother and nephew held influential positions in both the commercial and political world.[1] His brother, Alexander, ran a lucrative import-export business and had connections with Agrippa 1 and the imperial family. Philo's nephew, Tiberius, Alexander's son, was even more prominent, holding governorships in Judea, Syria, and Egypt and was chief of staff for Titus in suppressing the Jewish revolt of 66-70 C.E. Philo belonged therefore to a Jewish elite, who both enjoyed the privileges of Roman Alexandria and had to cope with increasing turbulence and deterioration in relations with Rome, on the one hand, and both the Greek and Egyptian populace of Alexandria, on the other. With regard to his attitude to matters sexual we must,

---

[1] For a detailed discussion of Philo's family and his social and political context see Daniel R. Schwartz, "Philo, His Family and His Times," in *The Cambridge Companion to Philo* (ed. Adam Kamesar; Cambridge: Cambridge University Press, 2009) 9-31; Kenneth Schenck, *A Brief Guide to Philo* (Louisville: Westminster John Knox, 2005) 9-14, 29-48; Peder Borgen, *Philo of Alexandria: An Exegete for his Time* (NovTSup 86; Leiden: Brill, 1997; Atlanta: SBL, 2005) 14-45.

therefore, take into account his privileged context, which could assume wealthy households and well-educated men and, it seems, also many women, and varying degrees of familiarity not only with Jewish thought, but also with streams of Hellenistic culture and philosophy of the time, including the challenge to make the case for oneself and others that properly educated Jews could hold their heads high in the social and intellectual world of the time.[2]

The comparatively immense body of Philo's writings[3] confronts the researcher with special challenges, not least in presenting findings. Whereas in most analyses of attitudes towards sexuality I have sought to follow as far as possible the sequence of the text before drawing together conclusions in a summary, this is simply unrealistic with Philo because of the number of the writings and their extent. A topical approach which draws together themes from all of the literature is to some extent unavoidable. In embarking on such an endeavour I will seek nevertheless to give as much attention as possible to the flow of contexts. This is especially important in dealing with Philo because sometimes the same or similar motifs appear in a number of contexts, which at times result in somewhat different shades and slants of meaning. It is further complicated by the fact that while in expositions Philo generally follows the thread of the biblical narrative, he frequently digresses to consider tangential material. Further, at times signalled by him but at times not, Philo engages the material at two levels, literal and allegorical, so that statements made for instance about male and female in the latter must be assessed on the extent to which they also reflect his attitudes towards sexuality or whether they are so much shaped for allegorical exposition that no useful information can be gained. Here I find no general rule, so that each instance must be weighed separately.

Beyond this, Philo's compositions will have been completed over an extended period of time, so that we need at least to entertain the possibility that his thought may have changed or developed in that process over time. Unfortunately it is not possible to date individual works, although there is broad agreement that there are different sets of writings, which, at times Philo, himself, helps us to recognise, belong to an ordered sequence. There are three main bodies of expositional material. *The Exposition of the Law*, 12 tractates, begins with creation in Genesis and concludes with rewards and punishments, which include a vision of the future. A full five tractates deal directly with matters of Law, supplemented by a tractate on Virtues. The other half, beside the opening and closing tractates, consist of an

---

[2] For the view that he may have been of priestly descent see Schwartz, "Philo, His Family and His Times," who cites the disparaging comments in *Spec.* 1.24 about bastard stock (11).

[3] For a general introduction see James R. Royse, "The Works of Philo," *The Cambridge Companion to Philo* (ed. Adam Kamesar; Cambridge: Cambridge University Press, 2009) 32-64; Schenk, *Brief Guide*, 14-23.

account of the Law as embodied and lived out in the patriarchs, though two of these, *On Isaac* and *On Jacob* have not survived.

The *Allegorical Commentary*, on the one hand, attends more closely to detail in its exposition of most of Genesis, but, on the other, focuses primarily on allegorical exposition. It encompasses 26 tractates of which probably seven have not survived. Beside these two major collections two tractates (or sets of tractates) have survived in Armenian: *Questions and Answers* on Genesis and on Exodus, which address various select details of the biblical text and also have a strong emphasis on allegorical exposition. In addition to these three collections are historical works, two related to the political crisis of the late 30s, *Against Flaccus* and *On the Embassy to Gaius*, and accounts of Jewish law in the fragmentary *Hypothetica* and of the Therapeutae in *On the Contemplative Life*, with a further five works which have not survived. Five philosophical works have survived, at least in part, and beside these we have a two volume treatment, *Life of Moses*, similar in focus to the *Exposition*.

I provide a full list of all tractates referred to with both their Latin and English names in the Index. Within the body of the discussion I shall refer to tractates using the abbreviated Latin title. Philo's works are conveniently available in the twelve volumes of the Loeb Classical Library,[4] providing English translations of the critical Greek text of Cohn Wendland[5] and of the Armenian of *Questions and Answers*. Unless otherwise indicated I cite the Loeb translation.

The most extensive treatment of sexuality in Philo remains the pioneering work of Richard A. Baer.[6] He argued that the polarity male-female belonged for Philo to the irrational soul of human beings, whereas the rational is neither male nor female but asexual. Philo employs the polarity also differently to speak of progress as forsaking the irrational for the rational, where male represents the rational and female, the irrational. Baer notes that the allegorical use is inextricably intertwined with Philo's view of real woman.[7] He also identifies tension between Philo's positive statements about the composite created human being, including sense-perception, the passions, and even pleasure, and the much more common denigration of the latter three. According to his analysis, *Opif.* 151-152 "indicates that the sin of the first man was the result of sexual desire", and

---

[4] F. H. Colson, G. H. Whittaker (and R. Marcus), *Philo in Ten Volumes (and Two Supplementary Volumes)* (12 vols.; LCL; London: Heinemann; Cambridge MA: Harvard University Press, 1929–62).

[5] L. Cohn and P. Wendland, *Philonis Alexandrini opera quae supersunt* (Berlin: Reimer, 1896-1914). I have also consulted Peder Borgen, Kåre Fuglseth, Roald Skarsten, *The Works of Philo: Greek Texts with Morphology* (Logos Research Systems, 2005).

[6] Richard L. Baer, *Philo's Use of the Categories Male and Female:* ALGHJ 3 (Leiden: Brill, 1970).

[7] Baer, *Male and Female*, 41.

while he notes that apart from that "Philo does not specifically mention sexual desire as that which caused the first man to sin",[8] he nevertheless suspects that it is implied in Philo's attacks on pleasure.[9]

In her discussion of women in Philo, which she astutely describes as "an attempt to search Philo's writing for answers to questions that I am convinced he never asked ... a subject that was incidental to his main concern,"[10] Dorothy Sly seeks to go beyond the unresolved tension which Baer identified. She argues that for Philo womanhood, that is, the life of a woman between puberty and menopause, was defiled and corrupted by sexual intercourse.[11] Though she acknowledges that "Philo never makes such a statement directly" she argues that "his association of words leads to that conclusion".[12] This assessment of Philo's view of sexual intercourse enables her to explain Philo's allegorical use of virginity. Women's sexuality, "simply by virtue of being woman", becomes man's downfall.[13] Sly has no doubt that "Philo sees the 'fall' as sexual. The serpent represents pleasure, and the most intense pleasure Philo knows is that experienced by a man in intercourse. In *Op*.152 he states explicitly that sexual desire is the cause".[14] She then differentiates between the sexually aggressive woman, "a powerful danger" to men,[15] women who are primarily a danger to themselves like Lot's wife,[16] and worthy women. These acceptable women serves men's interests, obedient and subservient to their husbands, as noble, freeborn women whose sexuality is restrained, appealing to Augustan values of the day.[17] Mary Rose D'Angelo argues this in detail, noting Philo's employment of εὐσέβεια in a way that reflects "the Roman virtue *pietas*", with its emphasis on the proper disposition not only toward God/the gods but everyone, "parents and children, spouse and siblings, but also patrons, clients, city and nation, including dependents and authorities of every degree up to and including the emperor".[18]

Sly notes that Philo is "less concerned with absolutes than with relative positions. Lower forms (designated as feminine, passive, inferior) need not be

---

[8] Baer, *Male and Female*, 37.

[9] Baer, *Male and Female*, 38 n.1.

[10] Dorothy Sly, *Philo's Perception of Women* (BJS 209; Atlanta: Scholars Press, 1990).

[11] Sly, *Philo's Perception of Women*, 72, 77-81.

[12] Sly, *Philo's Perception of Women*, 80.

[13] Sly, *Philo's Perception of Women*, 108.

[14] Sly, *Philo's Perception of Women*, 109.

[15] Sly, *Philo's Perception of Women*, 115.

[16] Sly, *Philo's Perception of Women*, 118.

[17] Sly, *Philo's Perception of Women*, 154, 160, 173, 180, 199.

[18] Mary Rose D'Angelo, "Gender and Geopolitics in the Work of Philo of Alexandria: Jewish Piety and Imperial Family Values," in *Mapping Gender in Ancient Religious Discourses* (ed. Todd Penner and Caroline Vander Stichele; BIS 84; Leiden: Brill, 2007) 63-88, 71.

eliminated or crushed, but, rather, controlled. On the interpersonal level, woman need not be degraded or even ostentatiously put in her place. She need simply be subject to male command and male interest".[19] Similarly she argues that "Philo's calls for quitting the body are rhetorical, and that the theme of his work is control of the lower elements rather than separation or elimination".[20] This might call into question her assertion that engagement in sexual intercourse remains necessarily defiling and corrupting. There is tension between her model of restrained sexuality and sex as defiling, which is not resolved by limiting it to procreation, but has to do in part with how one reads Philo's statements about pleasure.

Some studies address attitudes to sexuality directly, Horowitz, arguing that Philo diverged from rabbinic tradition by portraying the first sexual union as "a departure from man's previous clinging to God",[21] and Boyarin, contrasting rabbinic affirmation with Philo's negation of human sexuality on the basis of Hellenistic dualism.[22] Discussing women, Wegner concluded that "Philo's depiction of the female character owes far more to Greek ideas, mediated through Hellenistic culture, than to the Jewish Scripture he inherited from his ancestors".[23] In response above all to Boyarin, whose reading he sees as imposing a gnostic framework onto Philo, Winston highlights Philo's very positive assessment of all creation as evidence of excellence.[24] He draws attention, as had Sly, to the importance of evaluating Philo's rhetoric. Noting Philo's sometimes negative language about the body as a plotter against the soul and as a corpse, he writes, "This Platonic rhetoric, in which Philo sometimes revels, does not necessarily commit him to a severe downgrading or hatred of the body as such".[25] He also challenges overly simplistic readings of Plato and the Stoics which ignore the range of positive and negative images, for instance in Plato between the *Timaeus* and *Phaedo* or among statements by Epictetus.[26] "It is essential to decide in each

---

[19] Sly, *Philo's Perception of Women*, 184.

[20] Sly, *Philo's Perception of Women*, 220.

[21] Maryanne Cline Horowitz, "The Image of God in Man—Is Woman Included?" *HTR* 72 (1979) 175-206, 192.

[22] Daniel Boyarin, *Carnal Israel: Reading Sex in Talmudic Culture* (Berkeley: University of California Press, 1993) 78-80.

[23] Judith Romney Wegner, "Philo's Portrayal of Women: Hebraic or Hellenic?" in *"Women Like This": New Perspectives on Jewish Women in the Greco-Roman Period* (ed. A. J. Levine; Atlanta: Scholars, 1991) 41-66, 65.

[24] David Winston, "Philo and the Rabbis on Sex and the Body," in *The Ancestral Philosophy, Hellenistic Philosophy in Second Temple Judaism: Essays of David Winston* (ed. Gregory E. Sterling; BJS 331; SPM 4; Providence: Brown University Press, 2001) 199-219, 201.

[25] Winston, "Philo and the Rabbis," 206.

[26] Winston, "Philo and the Rabbis," 208-10. See also Kathy L. Gaca, *The Making of Fornication: Eros, Ethics, and Political Reform in Greek Philosophy and Early Christianity*

case whether the author's apparent devalorization of the body is largely rhetorical, for the sake of moral emphasis, or whether it reflects an inflexibly dark view of the body".[27] He also challenges the suggestion that Philo has reduced sex to mere functionality for the purpose of procreation, noting "that it can be the occasion for genuine love and mutuality is thus intimately connected to this positive evaluation of the material world",[28] and writing of the key text of man and woman's first encounter in *Opif.* 151-152:

> Philo's description of Adam's initial encounter with Eve is clearly idyllic and touchingly romantic. It highlights the feelings of love and fellowship and the couple's hope of future offspring. Moreover, it is explicitly stated that it was not their tender desire for one another in itself, but rather the bodily pleasure that it naturally begot that became the source of potential wrongs and lawless deeds.[29]

Gaca places Philo's discussion of sexuality in the context of Hellenistic Judaism's concerns with desire based on the tenth commandment, as apostasy from God, and on Platonic assessment of sexual desire as the most potent evil.[30] That includes a correlation between sexual desire and desire for too much food and drink,[31] so that Philo can claim that "the prohibited types of animal flesh, such as pork, are particularly laced with an aphrodisiac surplus (*Spec* 4.100-18)".[32] For Philo, then, "the sexual and other physical appetites are inherently bad because their inborn proclivity to be unrestrained is also a proclivity to transgress God's will as written in the Pentateuch".[33] Contrary to Plato, for whom "appetitive sexual desire is valuable within reason and beneficial when exercised to the necessary degree required for good health," for Philo "it has no redeeming merit because there cannot possibly be any merit in wanting to act contrary to God's will".[34] Thus she sees Philo portraying sexual desire as "inherently wicked and its primary

---

(Berkeley: University of California Press, 2003), who notes that both Seneca and Musonius Rufus, the Roman Stoics, appear to stand under the influence of the later Neopythagoreans like Charondas and Ocellus, which has led to the widespread misconception that procreationism was a Stoic tenet, whereas their stance is rather an exception and certainly different from earlier Stoics and also from later ones (61, 97, 111-14).

[27] Winston, "Philo and the Rabbis," 210.
[28] Winston, "Philo and the Rabbis," 214.
[29] Winston, "Philo and the Rabbis," 215.
[30] Gaca, *Making of Fornication*, 193.
[31] Gaca, *Making of Fornication*, 195.
[32] Gaca, *Making of Fornication*, 196.
[33] Gaca, *Making of Fornication*, 197-98.
[34] Gaca, *Making of Fornication*, 198-99.

yearning is to break away from the regulatory confines of the Pentateuch".[35] While Philo frequently uses Stoic terminology, his concern is different from theirs which is about impairment of reason, whereas for Philo it is about disobeying God.[36] Thus "though Philo draws upon the Stoics and Plato to articulate this notion of soul fornication, neither the Stoics nor Plato would recognize Philo's religious sexual ethic as their own, for Philo presupposes the Pentateuch and its didactic metaphor of spiritual fornication".[37] Accordingly, "for Philo, by contrast, Aphrodite as Pleasure is not a genuine goddess who merits reverence, as she was for the Greeks. She is the cosmic madam of religiously alienating sexual desire".[38] Gaca sees Philo drawing on the later Pythagorean tradition represented by Charondas and Ocellus, whom he cites in *Aet.* 12, "who likewise maintain that sexual relations can only be rightly for procreation or reprehensibly for pleasure".[39] She then goes on to note that for Philo "sexual activity for pleasure rather than for procreation is apostasy only in circumstances where the Pentateuch outlaws it on a literal level or stigmatizes it as an abomination" whereas "if husbands make love with their wives for non-reproductive pleasure, he recommends the regimen of Moses' dietary laws, not death, for this class of sexual offenders".[40] Gaca assumes a consistently negative stance on the part of Philo towards sexual pleasure.

One of the chief difficulties in discussing Philo's range of statements pertaining to sexuality derives from his allegorical method, where maleness and femaleness, and male and female traits, many of them socially conditioned, serve purposes which may have nothing directly to do with sexual behaviour at all. While Baer and Sly noted that the literal and allegorical are inextricably intertwined, Sharon Lea Mattila has advanced the discussion by employing the distinction between sexuality and gender.[41] It enables her to show that both men and women have a rational element (usually depicted as male in gender)[42] and to speak of "a kind of gender gradient underlying much of Philo's thought, whose positive ('male') and negative ('female') poles are consistently defined, and whose predominant feature is hierarchy".[43] Both men and women can move up or down

---

[35] Gaca, *Making of Fornication*, 199.

[36] Gaca, *Making of Fornication*, 201.

[37] Gaca, *Making of Fornication*, 202.

[38] Gaca, *Making of Fornication*, 203.

[39] Gaca, *Making of Fornication*, 205.

[40] Gaca, *Making of Fornication*, 215.

[41] Sharon Lea Mattila, "Wisdom, Sense Perception, Nature, and Philo's Gender Gradient," *HTR* (1996) 103-29. See also Colleen M. Conway, "Gender and Divine Relativity in Philo of Alexandria," *JSJ* 34 (2003) 471-91.

[42] Mattila, "Wisdom, Sense Perception, Nature," 104-105.

[43] Mattila, "Wisdom, Sense Perception, Nature," 106.

the gradient, though "there is no question that for Philo, the biological fact of being a woman does naturally pull one down toward the negative end of the gradient".[44] Rather than being Philo's innovation, it more likely reflects, she argues, the accepted understanding of his intellectual environment.[45] She notes that "Philo is aware that the human soul cannot extricate itself totally from its body and material environment"[46] and depicts "reconciliation and harmony between mind and sense perception" as desirable.[47]

Investigation of Philo's attitudes towards sexuality needs to take into account a range of issues, many of which have emerged in research thus far. Sly's comments are salutary that we are asking questions about something which Philo did not directly address. An atomistic collection of texts sorted by theme simply will not do, not to speak of forcing them into a coherent system. Philo can take a biblical text and interpret it quite differently in different contexts. In the *Allegorical Commentary*, where literal interpretation is minimal, and to some degree in *Questions and Answers*, where allegorising is more prominent, we can expect stronger negative comments on sexuality than in the *Exposition of the Laws*, where a substantial amount of the discussion, but by no means all, remains at a literal level. The degree to which metaphorical employment of male-female and literal concern with maleness and femaleness are intertwined or can be distinguished is a constant issue. Gender issues are not the same as sexual issues, but nor are they separate, especially when they have a clearly biological basis. We shall need to take into account the extent to which Philo's gender gradient also reflects an ontology of what it literally means to be man or woman. While forced syntheses deny diversity, sometimes diversities may be more apparent than real. This is particularly the case where one might cite totally negative assessments of sense-perception, the passions, and even pleasure as absolute statements, which seem in direct contradiction to positive statements. Sometimes the juxtaposition of both in a single context helps us see that absolute formulations frequently serve rhetorical emphasis and are misunderstood if taken at face value. Context is particularly important in determining meaning in Philo.

Ideally an investigation should entail something like a commentary on each work. Such has been the foundation for the current study, but neither space nor reader patience permits us writing such a work, since so much in Philo's writings consists of variations on a few central themes, not least in allegorical expositions, where the method is well suited to interpreters who can use it to say what they

---

[44] Mattila, "Wisdom, Sense Perception, Nature," 107; similarly Conway, "Gender and Divine Relativity," 480.

[45] Mattila, "Wisdom, Sense Perception, Nature," 112; similarly Conway, "Gender and Divine Relativity," 482.

[46] Mattila, "Wisdom, Sense Perception, Nature," 115.

[47] Mattila, "Wisdom, Sense Perception, Nature," 117.

want to say, almost from any text. Philo leads us down a garden path, as it were, not part of a formal grid but following the terrain of the biblical story and with many side paths which connect us to earlier and later stages of the main route and many favourite stopping places. As a compromise between a topical and contextual approach which follows the sequence of each writing, I shall roughly follow the order of the biblical narrative, beginning with the creation stories, then treating the images which emerge from the stories from Cain to Moses, concluding with a discussion of laws. This matches to some extent Philo's own approach in the *Exposition*, which, as he explains, covers "the creation of the world ... history, and ... legislation" (*Praem.* 1-3). It has the advantage for us that we can draw on parallel treatments of Genesis and Exodus among Philo's works and that by beginning with creation we already deal with fundamental issues, such as Philo's anthropology and psychology, which then inform his subsequent expositions. Thus from Genesis 1 – 3, we move to Philo's treatment of a range of figures and events in the rest of Genesis and beyond, before turning to laws, where we follow Philo's own lead in the *Decalogue* and *Special Laws* of dealing with them within the framework of the Decalogue. A brief concluding chapter will then summarise the findings.

1.2   Man and Woman: Beginning from Genesis 1 – 3

We begin our analysis by considering Philo's treatment of the creation narratives in the three main exegetical commentaries, the *Exposition of the Law*, the *Questions and Answers*, and the *Allegorical Commentary*, and related material from elsewhere in each. In his expositions of the creation stories we find most of the major themes pertaining to sexuality. Of these commentaries only the *Exposition* in *Opif.* takes us right back to the beginning with Genesis 1. There Philo begins by setting his discussion in the context of lawgivers, portraying the Genesis creation narrative as an appropriate introduction to what is the theme of the commentary series as a whole, namely exposition of how people are to live in the world. Underlying this is the notion that, as he puts it, "the world is in harmony with the Law, and the Law with the world, and that the man who observes the law is constituted thereby a loyal citizen of the world, regulating his doings by the purpose and will of Nature, in accordance with which the entire world itself also is administered" (*Opif.* 3). This is good Stoicism,[48] but also good Judaism, in the

---

[48] David T. Runia, *On the Creation of the Cosmos according to Moses: Introduction, Translation and Commentary* (Leiden : Brill, 2001), writes: "The conception of cosmic law and the citizenship of the world is strongly indebted to Stoic philosophy, but had become by Philo's time a widespread and popular philosophical theme by no means confined to the Stoic school" (333).

sense that it affirms the world of creation and implies that to live in harmony with the world and live in harmony with divine law are one and the same.[49] What that means concretely, and in particular in relation to sexuality, will be determined by how Philo understands the constitution of human beings and how they were made.

1.2.1 The Creation of Human Beings

1.2.1.1 Image, Genus, and Moulded from Clay (Gen 1:27; 2:7)

In *Opif.* Philo makes clear that creation of the incorporeal ideas, after which all manifestations in the real world are patterned, reflecting Philo's espousal of Platonism, took place in the beginning on the first day (*Opif.* 29-35; Gen 1:1-5). This enables him then to explain the creations of the other five days as a sequence (rather than a temporal scheme) in which ideas became *genera*. As a result, when he comes to the sixth day, though not noting it as such, he declares that "to crown all he made man" (*Opif.* 65; cf. already 25), and again: "to crown all, as we have said before, He made man, and bestowed on him mind (νοῦν) *par excellence*, life-principle of the life-principle itself" (*Opif.* 66). According to Philo, human origins, from mere semen, "so poor a thing as seed", to the full grown person, mirror the creation of all creatures, from simple, inferior creatures to the best, human beings (*Opif.* 68). While he emphasises the great difference in quality between lower and higher forms, they are all God's creation and by implication good. Then in *Opif.* 69 he alludes to Gen 1:26: "Moses tells that man was created after the image of God and after his likeness" (Gen 1:26), explaining that "it is in respect of the Mind, the sovereign element of the soul (τὸν τῆς ψυχῆς ἡγεμόνα νοῦν), that the word 'image' is used; for after the pattern of a single Mind, even the Mind of the Universe as an archetype, the mind in each of those who successively came

---

[49] On the complex understanding of the Law in Philo see John W. Martens, *One God, One Law: Philo of Alexandria on the Mosaic and Greco-Roman Law* (Studies in Philo of Alexandria and Mediterranean Antiquity 2; Leiden: Brill, 2003), who emphasises Philo's adaptation of Greco-Roman categories. "He alters 'unwritten law' to signify one who follows the law of nature and who becomes its embodiment. The 'living law' comes to mean not only one who is king, but the one who follows the law of nature. These forms of law find their content in the law of nature" and it is found in the Law of Moses (101). See also Hindy Najman, "A Written Copy of the Law of Nature: An Unthinkable Paradox?" *SPA* 15 (2003) 54-63; Hindy Najman, "The Law of Nature and the Authority of Mosaic Law," *SPA* 11 (1999) 55-73; and earlier Valentin Nikiprowetzky, *Le commentaire de l'Écriture chez Philon d'Alexandrie: Son caractère et sa portée. Observations philologiques* (ALGHJ 11; Leiden: Brill, 1977) 117-55.

into being was moulded" (cf. also *Opif.* 25; *Somn.* 1.74). The rational aspect, mind, relates to the body, according to *Opif.* 69, as does God to the world. Staying with Gen 1:26 he picks up the words, "Let us make" (ποιήσωμεν) to explain human vulnerability to evil as not deriving from God (*Opif.* 72-75), a matter to which we return below.

He then employs the word γένος, used in the preceding context of Genesis LXX for kinds of animals (Gen 1:11, 12, 21, 24, 25), to speak of the man made according to Gen 1:26-27 as γένος: "And when Moses called the genus (τὸ γένος) 'man,' quite admirably did he distinguish its species (εἴδη), adding that it had been created 'male and female'," (*Opif.* 76).[50] This receives immediate qualification: "and this though its individual members had not yet taken shape. For the primary species (τὰ προσεχέστατα τῶν εἰδῶν) are in the genus (γένει) to begin with, and reveal themselves as in a mirror to those who have the faculty of keen vision" (*Opif.* 76). This excludes any notion of androgyny, for it reduces male and female here to potential or pattern within a *genus*.[51] Philo next addresses why man was created last, offering three reasons: because everything was ready for him, because it showed that God would provide for him, and because the last and first match each other, heaven "the most perfect of imperishable objects" and man "the noblest of things earthborn" (*Opif.* 82); and finally, he adds: because it set up man to rule over all below heavenly beings (*Opif.* 83-88).

After an extensive extrapolation on the seventh day, Philo returns to Gen 2:4, 5, which he takes as referring again to the creation of "the incorporeal ideas present only to the mind" (*Opif.* 129), and to Gen 2:6, which inspires a description of earth as mother nature (*Opif.* 133). He then comes to Gen 2:7, declaring:

> By this also he shows very clearly that there is a vast difference between the man thus formed and the man that came into existence earlier after the image of God: for the man so formed is an object of sense-perception partaking already of such or such quality, consisting of body and soul, man or woman, by nature mortal (ὁ μὲν γὰρ διαπλασθεὶς αἰσθητὸς ἤδη μετέχων ποιότητος, ἐκ σώματος καὶ ψυχῆς συνεστώς, ἀνὴρ ἢ γυνή, φύσει θνητός); while he that was after the (Divine) image was an idea or type or seal, an object of thought (only), incorporeal, neither male nor female, by nature incorruptible (ὁ δὲ κατὰ τὴν εἰκόνα ἰδέα τις ἢ γένος ἢ

---

[50] Baer, *Male and Female*, observes: "He speaks of 'genus' and 'species' not only because of the frequent occurrence of the expression κατὰ γένος in Gen. 1, but also because these terms are part of the philosophical vocabulary with which he approaches Scripture" (34).

[51] Cf. Verna E. F. Harrison, "The Allegorization of Gender: Plato and Philo on Spiritual Childbearing," in *Asceticism*, (ed. Vincent L. Wimbusch and Richard Valantasis; New York: Oxford University Press, 1995) 520-34, 528-29.

σφραγίς, νοητός, ἀσώματος, οὔτ' ἄρρεν οὔτε θῆλυ, ἄφθαρτος φύσει). (*Opif.* 134)

While the description of the former figure as as ἰδέα τις ἢ γένος ἢ σφραγίς ("idea or type or seal") and ἀσώματος ("incorporeal") might suggest the Platonic *idea* of a human being, already created by implication on the first day (Gen 1:1-5), the allusion is most naturally understood as referring to the *genus* which he identified in Gen 1:27. Mention of the image and of male and female supports this. Some, however, do suggest that Philo is here reading Gen 1:27 differently from in *Opif.* 76, namely as referring to the Platonic idea,[52] and doing so perhaps under influence of Alexandrian exegetical tradition, which he will have adopted here without bringing it into harmony with what he has said earlier.[53] Alternatively, we should read it on the assumption that in alluding to Gen 1:27 Philo is, indeed, picking up what he was saying in *Opif.* 76, and then either referring just to its mind[54] or to the figure as a whole.[55] One might see Philo's words ἰδέα τις ἢ γένος (lit. "a kind of idea or *genus*") as deliberately distinguishing the figure as *genus* and kind of idea from the pure idea. Against limiting it to the mind, Runia notes, "it would be a mistake ... simply to identify the *nous* in §69 with the 'invisible' in §135. Not only does the distinction between the generic and the individual have to be added, but the former state is what the latter must aspire to attain".[56] He argues that it is best to take "'the human being after the image' as the 'ideal' person, i.e. an idealization of human nature in terms of the intellect", though he acknowledges that "this admittedly leaves the question of the relation to the Idea of humankind and the intellect of rational soul of empirical humankind somewhat up in the air", adding that "we can put the blame on Philo for this lack of clarity".[57]

While much of the debate is beyond the scope of our investigation, the allusion to male and female is clearly relevant to our theme. The figure as a whole,

---

[52] Nikiprowetzky, *Commentaire*, 65; Winston, "Philo and the Rabbis," 211.

[53] Thomas H. Tobin, *The Creation of Man: Philo and the History of Interpretation* (CBQMS 14; Washington: CBA, 1983) 126; Gregory E. Sterling, "'The Jewish Philosophy': The Presence of Hellenistic Philosophy in Jewish Exegesis in the Second Temple Period," in *Ancient Judaism in its Hellenistic Context* (ed. Carol Bakhos; JSJSup 95; Leiden: Brill, 2005) 131-53, 141, 146; Gregory E. Sterling, "'Wisdom among the Perfect': Creation Traditions in Alexandrian Judaism and Corinthian Christianity," *NovT* 37 (1995) 355-84, 362-63.

[54] Baer, *Male and Female*, 30; similarly David T. Runia, *Philo of Alexandria and the Timaeus of Plato* (Philosophia Antiqua 44; Leiden: Brill, 1986) 335.

[55] Runia, *Creation*, 323.

[56] Runia, *Creation*, 324.

[57] Runia, *Creation*, 323.

as *genus*, embodied the two options, male or female but was neither; the figure of Gen 2:7, is either male or female and of mixed substance, "body and soul" and "by nature mortal". Certainly the contrast between the two serves not to demean the composite human being "made up of earthly substance and of Divine breath" (*Opif.* 135), but to differentiate them. We return below to significance of male and female in relation to the former.

We turn first to the parallel accounts, at least on Genesis 2, in *QG* and the *Allegorical Commentary*. In the former Philo appears to express the relation between the two texts more simply, explaining: "the moulded man is the sense-perceptible man and a likeness of the intelligible type" (*QG* 1.4).[58] Similarly in the *Allegorical Commentary* he elaborates: "There are two types of men; the one a heavenly man (οὐράνιος ἄνθρωπος), the other an earthly (γήϊνος). The heavenly man, being made after the image of God, is altogether without part or lot incorruptible and terrestrial substance; but the earthly one was compacted out of the matter scattered here and there, which Moses calls 'clay'" (*Leg.* 1.31; see also 2.4). Philo explains that "as the face is the dominant element in the body, so is the mind the dominant element of the soul (ψυχῆς ἡγεμονικόν ἐστιν ὁ νοῦς): into this only does God breathe (ἐμπνεῖ), whereas He does not see fit to do so with the other parts, whether senses or organs of utterance and of reproduction" (*Leg.* 1.39).

The mind, then, into which God breathed, is immortal. The rest of the soul, namely the body with its senses and passions, including sexual passions, is mortal. Having introduced the two types of men, Philo can however then write: "The one then that was made according to the original has his sphere not only in the planting of virtues but is also their tiller and guardian, and that means that he is mindful of all that he heard and practised in his training; but the 'moulded' man neither tills the virtues nor guards them, but is only introduced to the truths by the rich bounty of God, presently to be an exile from virtue" (*Leg.* 1.54). This creates some tension because Philo here wants the former to be a model, so even speaks of its training, though really this figure is to be seen as perfect and complete in itself, the heavenly man. Philo clearly assumes a Platonic distinction between the idea and the reality, but also a distinction between a person's current state and the ideal that they can become, and uses the biblical material to make this point in diverse ways,

---

[58] So David M. Hay, "Philo's Anthropology, the Spiritual Regimen of the Therapeutae, and a Possible Connection with Corinth," in *Philo und das Neue Testament: Wechselseitige Wahrnehmungen: 1. Internationales Symposium zum Corpus Judaeo-Hellenisticum 1.-4. Mai 2003* (ed. Roland Deines and Karl Wilhelm Niebuhr; Tübingen: Mohr Siebeck, 2004) 127-42, 130, who also notes 1.8, where he shows that he is using other exegetes when he interprets Gen 1:27 as depicting man as idea and as needing no instruction (131).

which may include sometimes using both Gen 1:27 and 2:7 to refer to human reality and potential.[59]

A similar flexibility in dealing with these texts is evident elsewhere in the *Allegorical Commentary*. Thus in *Her.*, while expounding Lev 17:11 (the soul of every flesh is the blood), he contrasts two souls, one living by the flesh and its desires, and the other by reason and divine in-breathing, alluding to Gen 2:7 (54-57). In *Plant.* he cites God's breathing on man the breath of life in Gen 2:7 to argue that "it cannot but be that he that receives is made in the likeness of Him Who sends forth the breath", "made after the Image of God", understood as fashioned "after the image of the Archetype, the Word" (*Plant.* 19-20). The underlying assumption appears to be that the moulded man has his body with its senses and passions made from earth's substance and his mind inbreathed by God. As Runia notes of Gen 1:27 and 2:7, "in many texts Philo tends to reconcile the two accounts to a large degree; cf. *Spec.* 1.171; *Virt.* 203-205; *Det.* 80-86; *Plant.* 18-20; *Her.* 56. In *Mut.* 223 Philo indicates that theologically he has a preference for the Platonizing image-relation rather than the Stoicizing part-whole relation. But both have a biblical foundation".[60] We can now turn to the specific issue of how Philo interprets male and female in Gen 1:27.

1.2.1.2 "Male and Female"

In describing the *genus* figure as "neither male nor female" (*Opif.* 134), Philo appears to imply that it is asexual, in the sense of representing potential to be realised in the species.[61] As noted above, nothing suggests that he sees the figure as bisexual, that is, androgynous.[62] Indeed, Philo may be deliberately warding off

---

[59] Runia, *Philo and the Timaeus*, notes: "When not engaged in giving a detailed running commentary on the double account of man's creation, he prefers to present a relatively straightforward interpretation. On the sixth day both the 'true man' (pure mind) and man as σύνθετον (mixture of rational and irrational) are created" (335).

[60] Runia, *Creation*, 324; cf. also Baer, *Male and Female*, 24-26; Tobin, *Creation of Man*, 20-21; Sterling, "Jewish Philosophy," 147. See also Hay, "Philo's Anthropology," who provides a table showing the diverse range of interpretations which Philo gives (132-33). He concludes: "Thus we find tensions or contradictions in Philo's various statements about the creation of humanity in Genesis 1 and 2. Plainly he was guided or constrained in what he said by his sense of obligation to explain the details of the biblical narratives, by his awareness of what other exegetes had said about them, and by a desire which he shared with some of those exegetes to interpret the scriptures in relation to Greek philosophy, especially Platonic philosophy" (135).

[61] Baer, *Male and Female*, 88.

[62] Cf. Charles Harold Dodd, *The Bible and the Greeks* (London: Hodder and Stoughton, 1935) 151.

the myth of androgyny.[63] Elsewhere he writes of what he portrays as the fanciful myth of androgyny as propounded by Aristophanes in Plato's *Symposium* as designed to mandate illicit love (*Contempl.* 63). That does not stop him, however, from employing its imagery, even here in *Opif.* (151; cf. also *Her.* 164; *QG* 1.25), but for Philo the dividing which it assumes refers to the divine surgery on Adam according to Gen 2:21, not to the anger of Zeus. Similarly in the *Allegorical Commentary* Philo writes of the *genus*: "having first fashioned man as a genus, in which the prophet says that there is the male and the female genus, He afterwards makes Adam, the finished form or species" (*Leg.* 2.13). In *Her.* he is then quite explicit: "'God made man,' he says, 'made him after the image of God. Male and female He made' – not now 'him' but 'them'. He concludes with the plural, thus connecting with the genus mankind the species which had been divided, as I said, by equality" (*Her.* 164). The asexual character of Philo's treatment of Gen 1:27 in *Opif.* 134, but also when it is seen as pointing to individuated realisation, as in *Her.* 164, is, in addition, not to be understood as positing an ideal where the sexual is to be abandoned, an ideological ground for celibacy. Philo never uses it in this way. Rather his concern appears to be simply to make sense of treating Gen 1:27 as identifying a *genus* of what was to come about.

The allusion to male and female in association with the image of God in Gen 1:27 might have evoked the notion that the original of the image, the Logos or God, also embodied male and female, but, here, too, Philo entertains no such notion. On the other hand, to identify the image, the logos, and God as asexual[64] is not the same thing as saying that they are a-gendered. As Mattila has convincingly shown, Philo assumes a hierarchy of being according to which male values and roles are superior[65] and shows himself to be very aware of this in the language he uses of God.

1.2.1.3 "Let us make"

As noted above, the plural reference, "Let us make" (ποιήσωμεν) in Gen 1:26 enables Philo to explain how imperfections crept into human being (*Opif.* 72-75).

---

[63] Baer, *Male and Female*, 35.

[64] Cf. Baer, *Male and Female*, who writes: "The male-female polarity in Philo's writings is part of the mortal sphere of the created world. It does not function on a cosmic scale, particularly in the drama of creation, as it does in many of the Gnostic systems" (19; similarly 65).

[65] Mattila, "Wisdom, Sense Perception." She writes "of a kind of gender gradient underlying much of Philo's thought, whose positive ('male') and negative ('female') poles are consistently defined, and whose predominant feature is hierarchy" (106), emphasising "that the 'male' and 'female' poles of this gradient are gender-linked; they are not sexually determined" (106).

Similarly in *Conf.* Philo notes that "man is practically the only being who having knowledge of good and evil often chooses the worst" (*Conf.* 178). He goes on to explain: "Thus it was meet and right that when man was formed, God should assign a share in the work to His lieutenants, as He does with the words, 'let *us* make men,' that so man's right actions might be attributable to God, but his sins to others ... He delegated the forming of this part to His inferiors" (*Conf.* 179). The same thought is expressed also in *Fug.* prompted by Jacob's reference to God and the Angel as helping him in Gen 48:15-16 (*Fug.* 67-72), where he concludes: "a plurality of makers produce man so-called, one that has an admixture of sense-perception ... for the words, 'let us make man' point to him in whom an irrational and rational nature are woven together" (*Fug.* 71-72; similarly *Mut.* 30-31).

This might easily have been treated as grounds for seeing the body and material creation as something deserving no respect or even as evil, such as in gnostic thought. Against this Baer rightly notes that Philo speaks of helpers only in relation to human beings, not to the rest of creation.[66] Philo's account is also different from Plato's in the *Timaeus* (42D2-4), under whose influence he stands here.[67] There the demiurge, having created only the rational soul, assigned the task of creating the rest of the mortal *genera* to the young gods, then retired (*Tim.* 42e 5-6). In Philo God remains involved, to the extent that, in contrast to Plato where "God creates the rational soul, his subordinates the irrational soul and the body; in Philo it is by no means clear exactly what is made by whom".[68]

1.2.1.4 Potentially Good

The combined nature of the moulded man creates a potential for evil, but is not evil in itself. In *Opif.* Philo speaks of this man as beautiful and good (*Opif.* 135, 139) and depicts the clay as nothing but the best since it served to be the dwelling of the image of God (*Opif.* 137).[69] "That first man, earth-born (γηγενής), ancestor of our whole race", Philo explains, "was made, as it appears to me, most excellent in each part of his being, in both soul and body" (*Opif.* 136).[70] Whatever else Philo

---

[66] Baer, *Male and Female*, 66-76; cf. J. Fossum, "Gen. 1,26 and 2,7 in Judaism, Samaritanism, and Gnosticism," *JSJ* 16 (1985) 202-39, 208; and see the critical discussion in Birger A. Pearson, "Philo and Gnosticism," ANRW II.21.1, 295-342. See also Runia, *Creation*, 238.

[67] See Runia, *Creation*, 237; Runia, *Philo and the Timaeus*, 242-49.

[68] Runia, *Creation*, 237.

[69] Only here does Philo speak of the body as a temple – so Runia, *Creation*, 335.

[70] Runia, *Creation*, notes that "by using the term γηγενής Philo invites comparison with the theme of the 'earth-born' in Greek mythology and ethnography" (334). Cf. also Wis 7:1. It may well reflect the LXX which uses γῆ in Gen 2:7 and 3:19-20. On this see

may say later and elsewhere, his comments here affirm excellence in God's creation of the human being and that includes his sexuality, here, male.[71] Runia writes of the "very positive evaluation of the human body" in *Opif.* 136-147 as "striking in the light of Philo's frequent inclination to a platonizing devaluation of the corporeal".[72] Observing that in the *Timaeus* Plato also "gives a very positive portrayal" (87C-89C), Runia comments that "we should note that the terms in which Philo expresses this bodily excellence in §138 are more Greek than Jewish".[73] Even though Philo notes that the pristine beauty is diminished in the copies (*Opif.* 141-142), the goodness of this creation clearly applies not just to the first specimen of humanity.[74] Overall this being was made to be at home in the universe and its ordinances (*Opif.* 143-144, 146-147) and to reflect traces of kinship to the divine (*Opif.* 145-146). Earlier in *Opif.* he writes of the human being made for philosophy, "the contemplation of the heavenly existences", lacking also "none of the means of living and of living well (τὸ ζῆν καὶ τὸ εὖ ζῆν)" (*Opif.* 77). Similarly in *Spec.* 2 he comments about "the creation of the world" that "its earliest inhabitants, children of earth in the first or second generation, must have used the gifts of the universe in their unperverted state before pleasure had got the mastery" (*Spec.* 2.160) and that our goal should be "as far as possible to assimilate our present-day life to that of the distant past" (*Spec.* 2.160).

In his review of "those passages in Philo that reflect his attitude towards the created world" Baer observes that, "it is striking to note that, on the whole, the *Exposition* reflects a far more consistently positive orientation towards creation than does the *Allegory of the Laws* or the *Questions and Answers*".[75] He accounts for this by the fact that in the *Exposition* "the actual content of the Old Testament

---

William Loader, *The Septuagint, Sexuality, and the New Testament: Case Studies on the Impact of the LXX on Philo and the New Testament* (Grand Rapids: Eerdmans, 2004) 48.

[71] Baer, *Male and Female*, "Philo clearly attributes nobility and excellence to the first man in the totality of his being and not just to his rational soul" (36). See also p. 89.

[72] Runia, *Creation*, 322. On the major importance of Philo's affirmation of God's creation for Philo as a Jew and its underlying influence on all his discussions, see already Walther Völker. *Fortschritt und Vollendung bei Philon von Alexandrien: Eine Studie zur Geschichte der Frömmigkeit* (TU 49.1; Leipzig: Hinrichs, 1938) 85, 88, not least in treatment of the passions (136).

[73] Runia, *Creation*, 332.

[74] As Baer, *Male and Female*, notes, "Philo, in his interpretation of the Genesis account of the creation and fall of man, is not simply speaking about what happened in the distant past but about man as he is today, is clear from the conclusion of this section of Op. Mund.", citing *Opif.* 170 (35). Similarly Runia, *Creation*, writes: "Adam is thus not only the first human being, but he typifies what human life can be like at its best, i.e. before the fall from grace, and what it is very often like now, i.e. a descent into passion and sin" (18).

[75] Baer, *Male and Female*, 95. Similarly Völker, *Fortschritt und Vollendung*, 89.

exercised greater influence in Philo's thinking than was the case in Leg. All. and throughout the *Allegory*", and similarly in *Questions and Answers* where "the real thrust of the writing is found in the allegorical amplifications".[76] On the other hand, he argues, Philo never completely ignores that "this world, including man's body, is God's creation".[77]

The notion of potential for evil but also for good does however comes to expression at a number of points in the *Allegorical Commentary*, including in its reflections in the context of creation. Thus in *Leg.* in one of his many uses of Plato's image of the charioteer and his two horses, Philo writes: "when the two, the high-spirited and the lustful, are guided by the reasoning faculty as horses by their driver, then justice emerges" (*Leg.* 1.72), but injustice, when passions get hold of the reins (*Leg.* 1.73). The assumption is that good order is possible and "the high-spirited and the lustful", including sexual desire, have their proper place. We shall return to this image below in discussing Philo's psychology. Of human beings of the moulded type he writes in *Leg.* 2, that linked to their minds "in closest fellowship, are senses, passions, vices, ten thousand other presences" (*Leg.* 2.4). Both "sense and the passions are helpers of the soul and come after the soul" (*Leg.* 2.5), passions not least, "for pleasure and desire contribute to the permanence of our kind" (*Leg.* 2.8).[78] They, including sexual passion and desire, also have the potential for destructiveness, one of Philo's major themes.

As Baer observes of such texts, "man's irrational soul and the material world are seen as potentially but not absolutely evil. Man becomes involved in moral evil not simply because he is σῶμα and αἴσθησις as well as νοῦς but because of a distorted relationship between the lower and higher parts of his being".[79] He concludes: "sense-perception, the body, and even passion, when under the rightful dominion of the mind, contribute to man's total well-being and are not morally blameworthy. Yet, when not fully subject to mind, they can completely thwart the

---

[76] Baer, *Male and Female*, 95.

[77] Baer, *Male and Female*, 95.

[78] On this see David Winston, "Philo of Alexandria on the Rational and Irrational Emotions," in *Passions and Moral Progress in Greco-Roman Thought* (ed. John T. Fitzgerald; London: Routledge, 2008) 201-20, who notes in relation to this passage that "The view that the passions are an important and indispensable component of human nature and therefore cannot be eliminated is a Peripatetic position ..., apparently also the view of Poseidonius, who aimed not at the eradication of the irrational elements, but at their submission to reason" (212); similarly A. Le Boulluec, "La place des concepts philosophiques dans la réflexion de Philon sur le plaisir," in *Philon d'Alexandrie et le langage de la philosophie, Monothéismes et Philosophie* (ed. Carlos Lévy; Turnhout: Brepols, 1998) 129-52, 145.

[79] Baer, *Male and Female*, 91.

higher aspirations of the soul."[80] This has important implications for evaluating Philo's attitude towards sexuality and its associated passion and pleasure.

1.2.1.5 The Garden of Virtues

Philo portrays the garden into which this man is introduced as a garden of virtues. In *Opif.*, where he reverses the order of Genesis and introduces it after the creation of woman, Philo writes: "In the divine park or pleasuance all plants are endowed with soul or reason, bearing the virtues for fruit, and beside these insight and discernment that never fail, by which things fair and ugly are recognized, and life free from disease, and incorruption, and all that is of a like nature" (*Opif.* 153), going on to conclude, "this description is, I think, intended symbolically rather than literally" (*Opif.* 154) and represents the soul amid the virtues (*Opif.* 155).

In *QG* Philo similarly interprets the garden as the place of the soul's virtues (*QG* 1.6, 8), which it identifies with the rivers. Thus Gihon, for instance, represents moderation "because it labours with regard to food and drink, and produces the various pleasures of the belly and those parts which are below the belly" (*QG* 1.12). According to his depiction in the *Allegorical Commentary*, not only is the heavenly man its resident, who "has his sphere not only in the planting of virtues but is also their tiller and guardian", but also "the 'moulded' man", who "neither tills the virtues nor guards them, but is only introduced to the truths by the rich bounty of God, presently, to be an exile from virtue" (*Leg.* 1.54; cf. also 1.57). Here Philo also sees the rivers as symbols. He identifies the Tigris with "self-mastery", comparing "desire, with which self-mastery is occupied, to a tiger, the animal least capable of being tamed" (*Leg.* 1.69), almost certainly sexual desire as the most difficult to control, the "lustful part", located in the abdomen (*Leg.* 1.70, 71). In the garden of virtues it is in control. The notion of the garden as a symbol of the place of virtues occurs also in *Conf.* 61; similarly *Plant.* 38; and *Migr.* which speaks of the tree of life as "planted in the midst of the Garden, even Goodness with the particular virtues and the doings which accord with them to be its bodyguard" (*Migr.* 37; cf. also 35-36). Philo can also claim that Eden had no wild animals, in contrast to the ark into which all entered, alluding to the dangerous passions (*Plant.* 43). In *Cher.* he expounds the name, Eden, as "delight", which, he explains, is "not the weak and wanton sort, which the brute passion pleasure brings, but that sense of profound content and joy, which knows not toil or trouble" (*Cher.* 12). At both a literal and allegorical level Philo appears to assume that the potential was there for good to remain and to be restored, but also for its demise and thus for expulsion from the garden.

---

[80] Baer, *Male and Female*, 91.

1.2.1.6 Conclusion

Our discussion thus far has considered Philo's expositions of Gen 1:1 – 2:15, with particular attention to Gen 1:27 and 2:7. He employs the latter two in diverse ways. He does not appear to read the former as depicting androgyny. While he uses "Let us make" to sustain his theodicy, nothing indicates that he sees the creation as in any sense worthless or human beings as inherently bad, though their creation of mixed substance makes them inherently vulnerable. These general comments apply therefore also to human sexuality. Philo assumes hierarchy within creation, but none of it is bad in itself.

1.2.2 Woman and Man

Philo knows that woman also belongs to God's good creation, but sees her advent as the source of major problems. This is even more so because he employs the categories male and female allegorically to propound the psychology which underlies his ethical and spiritual exhortations. Thus relation of mind to body in an individual parallels the relation of man to woman, and provides also the basis for allegorical analogies in which relating to one's irrational being is described as relating to the female. Within this section we consider, therefore, both the literal creation of woman and Philo's allegorical use of it, including in his psychology, and conclude with a consideration of the place of sexual pleasure and the role of sexual intercourse. First we turn to the actual creation of woman beside man and their first encounter.

1.2.2.1 The Creation of Woman (Gen 2:20-24)

1.2.2.1.1 The Creation of Woman in "On Creation"

As noted above, in *Opif.* Philo postpones the detail about the garden till after the creation of woman. He also omits detail about woman as helper (cf. Gen 2:18, 20) and simply declares: "But since no created thing is constant, and things mortal are necessarily liable to changes and reverses, it could not but be that the first man too should experience some ill fortune. And woman becomes for him the beginning of blameworthy life (ἀρχὴ δὲ τῆς ὑπαιτίου ζωῆς αὐτῷ γίνεται γυνή)" (*Opif.* 151). Placing γυνή ("woman") at the conclusion of the sentence, enhances the focus on woman.[81] While Philo continues with reference to the man's solitariness: "he went on growing like to the world and like God" (*Opif.* 151), "a remarkable

---

[81] Runia, *Creation*, 356.

formulation of the *homoiôsis* doctrine", like *Tim.* 30c-31b, perhaps also "an ethical, or perhaps even a mystical, ideal" (cf. also Wis 10:1),[82] as something now to be lost, woman and sexuality were "required for the survival and perpetuation of the species".[83] Accordingly, Philo explains:

> When the woman too had been made (ἐπλάσθη), beholding a figure like his own and a kindred form (ἀδελφὸν εἶδος καὶ συγγενῆ μορφὴν), he was gladdened by the sight, and approached and greeted her (ἠσμένισε τῇ θέᾳ καὶ προσιὼν ἠσπάζετο). She, seeing no living thing more like herself than he, is filled with glee and shamefastly returns his greeting (γάνυταί τε καὶ ἀντιπροσφθέγγεται μετ' αἰδοῦς). Love (ἔρως) supervenes, brings together and fits into one the divided halves, as it were, of a single living creature, and sets up in each of them a desire for fellowship [intercourse] with the other with a view to the production of their like (πόθον ἐνιδρυσάμενος ἑκατέρῳ τῆς πρὸς θάτερον κοινωνίας εἰς τὴν τοῦ ὁμοίου γένεσιν). And this desire begat likewise bodily pleasure (ὁ δὲ πόθος οὗτος καὶ τὴν τῶν σωμάτων ἡδονὴν ἐγέννησεν), that pleasure which is the beginning of wrongs and violation of law (ἥτις ἐστὶν ἀδικημάτων καὶ παρανομημάτων ἀρχή), the pleasure for the sake of which men[84] bring on themselves (δι' ἣν ὑπαλλάττονται) the life of mortality and wretchedness in lieu of that of immortality and bliss. (151-152)

Philo reduces woman's actual creation to brief mention in a subordinate clause: "When the woman too had been made", which prompts Runia to comment: "It seems as if Philo is disinclined to write the straightforward words 'and then God created woman'".[85] Here Philo also employs the verb ἐπλάσθη (cf. *Opif.* 153 διαπλασθείσης), not used in Gen 2:21-25, but previously used in Gen 2:7. This has the "effect of relating the creation of woman to the fundamental anthropological text of Gen 2:7".[86] The omissions noted above, of reference to the

---

[82] So Runia, *Creation*, 356.

[83] Runia, *Creation*, 355. "Why does Philo introduce a comparison between man's idealized existence before the creation of woman and his compromised life thereafter?" asks Runia (361), if not to imply something negative about women along the lines of the *Timaeus*.

[84] Runia, *Creation*: "Furthermore, in the context of her book and its explicit distinction between man's and woman's role in sex, it was unwise for Sly to take over the LCL translation 'men bring on themselves,' since the third person verb clearly refers to the first man and the first woman. They descended into misery together" (360).

[85] Runia, *Creation*, 354. Cf. also Baer, *Male and Female*, who writes: "Philo gives no one answer as to how and when the first woman was created, nor does he appear to be particularly interested in this question" (88).

[86] Runia, *Creation*, 357.

garden and a helper, enhance this juxtaposition. Treating it "as the turning point in the fortunes of humankind involves a drastic adaptation of the biblical narrative".[87]

Accordingly, many have read the entire passage negatively. Thus van den Hoek finds playful negativity here in Philo: "At times he is ironic, at other times comic: man has to *enjoy* the pleasure of misfortune, but what a dubious pleasure it is! He drops his jaw, *gazing at* his new counterpart and *enjoying* what he sees. Some priggish overtones are not missing either: it is with the proper respect that Philo has her respond to his greetings, and their being together is after all for the purpose of procreation".[88] Or with Runia one might see here the "musings, somewhat reminiscent of a crusty old bachelor",[89] though he does not read this as totally negative. Sly's paraphrase is negative: "When Adam and Eve see one another, *eros* intervenes, sets up desire, and begets 'bodily pleasure, that pleasure for the sake of which men bring on themselves the life of mortality and wretchedness in lieu of that of immortality and bliss'".[90] This reflects her assumption that Philo shares the view that sexual intercourse is both defiling and corrupting,[91] which she accordingly misreads into this text. Baer also reads the text

---

[87] Runia, *Creation*, 354.

[88] Annewies van den Hoek, "Endowed with Reason or Glued to the Senses: Philo's Thought on Adam and Eve," in *The Creation of Man and Woman: Interpretations of the Biblical Narratives in Jewish and Christian Traditions* (Themes in Biblical Narrative: Jewish and Christian Traditions I; ed. G. P. Luttikhuizen; Leiden: Brill, 2000) 63-75, 72.

[89] Runia, *Creation*, 357. He sees in "had to enjoy" (Greek) a "light-hearted touch" (356).

[90] Sly, *Philo's Perception of Women*, 109. She adds: "There is no doubt then that uncontrolled womanhood is the occasion for the first sin of man" (109). On this Runia, *Creation*, writes: "A comparison of Sly's paraphrase and quote with the original reveals that she has somewhat tendentiously coalesced the text in such a way that Philo's implicit distinction between legitimate desire (for sex in order to procreate) and illegitimate desire (for pleasure) is obscured. For Philo only the latter has pernicious results" (360).

[91] Sly, *Philo's Perception of Women*, 72, 77-78, 81. Thus she writes: "Philo (and his community, if he is interpreting their actions accurately) considered the sexual act to some degree defiling. In his writing, the defilement appears to attach itself permanently to women. Although Philo never makes such a statement directly, his association of words leads to that conclusion" (80), though she regularly reflects some tension around these claims, as here with the words, "although Philo never makes such a statement directly", and, for instance: "True, he does not transfer their allegorical virginity to their literal stories" (73-74) and must acknowledge, that her "obvious inference ... that Philo associates defilement with woman, i.e. with the sexually active female ... is never, however, stated directly. Philo makes the connection implicitly, not explicitly" (81). She claims that "an unarticulated revulsion against womanhood is revealed in his association of words, that is, of 'virgin' with 'undefiled,' especially on the allegorical level" (82). She can transfer this to literal women partly on the basis of her assumption that "it is impossible to separate the theoretical statements from their application to the human situation" (43).

negatively: "Op. Mund. 151-52 indicates that the sin of the first man was the result of sexual desire".[92] By contrast, responding to Boyarin, who declares, "The very coming into being of woman is already the Fall",[93] Winston hails "Philo's description of Adam's initial encounter with Eve" as "clearly idyllic and touchingly romantic. It highlights the feelings of love and fellowship and the couple's hope of future offspring". He continues: "Moreover, it is explicitly stated that it was not their tender desire for one another in itself, but rather the bodily pleasure that it naturally begot that became the source of potential wrongs and lawless deeds".[94]

Noting that "the interpretation of this passage, though central to Philo's purpose in writing the entire treatise, is rather difficult",[95] brought about, he suggests, by Philo himself, Runia cautions care in deciphering its meaning: "Philo does not say that sexual desire is the beginning of all evil. Sexual desire is fine if directed towards procreation. But it can easily lead to the desire for physical pleasure, and that is what causes human downfall. Philo's views have often been not properly understood".[96] Thus he affirms Winston's depiction of the positive aspects of the sexual encounter.[97] Indeed, only the last sentence in the passage is negative. Sexual desire produces bodily pleasure and such pleasure is the cause of mortality and wretchedness. As we shall see below, the issue is not really pleasure in itself but misplaced pleasure and pleasure-seeking in contrast to the pleasure, including sexual pleasure, which accompanies what is good and right. The latter surely includes, as here, being "gladdened" at the sight of beauty (including sexual attractiveness), "glee", "love", and "desire for intercourse", leading to procreation. Runia notes the focus on "bodily or physical appearance", which serves

---

[92] Baer, *Male and Female*, 37. Similarly Horowitz, "Image of God": "Philo saw the union of first man with woman as a departure from man's previous clinging to God" (192). "Sexuality is attributed to the female, and her creation, which aroused desires for bodily pleasure in the first man, was the beginning of evil (Op. mund. 58.151-52)" (192). See also Cristina Termini, "Philo's Thought within the Context of Middle Judaism," *The Cambridge Companion to Philo* (ed. Adam Kamesar; Cambridge: Cambridge University Press, 2009) 95-103, who in relation to *Opif.* 151-152, writes: "Here we find the growing suspicion of human sexuality that is common in Middle Judaism in general" (105).

[93] Boyarin, *Carnal Israel*, 79, whose reading of Philo, Winston, "Philo and the Rabbis," describes as "virtually Gnostic" (201 n.8).

[94] Winston, "Philo and the Rabbis," 215. Drawing on Winston's response to Boyarin's sharp contrast between Philo and the rabbis, Runia, *Creation*, concludes: "It is a gross over-simplification to conclude that Philo, Hellenistic Judaism and Christianity are fatally tainted with Platonic views on body-soul dualism, whereas rabbinic Judaism develops biblical views entirely unaffected by Greek philosophy (cf. 59)" (361).

[95] Runia, *Creation*, 354.

[96] Runia, *Creation*, 355.

[97] Runia, *Creation*, 357.

differentiation between the two, but also Philo's emphasis on the female as "more affected by bodily and physical matters than the male ... the foundation for the allegory of man as mind and woman as sense-perception".[98] To this point "so far Philo has given a wholly positive account of the relation between the sexes".[99]

Woman is by implication a positive addition, as one would expect, given Philo's adherence to the biblical account of her divine creation, which Philo nowhere denies, but her creation, like the creation of the moulded man and his senses and passions, created the potential for evil. Qualified in that sense, "woman becomes for him the beginning of blameworthy life" (*Opif.* 151). The pleasure of sexual intercourse, which has its proper place according to Philo in sexual intercourse for procreation, can become a goal in itself. Then, as the strongest of all lures of pleasure, it generates a whole range of evils (similarly *T. Reub.* 2:8).[100] One needs therefore to distinguish carefully between potential and actual. Creation of woman opened new realities, including sexual union and sexual pleasure, meant to promote propagation of the species, but detached from that context and pursued for pleasure alone, desire for sexual intercourse and so sexual pleasure become an enemy. Accordingly for these two, understood as man and wife, as Runia observes, "Philo is happy to grant them love and desire for sexual relations leading to the birth of children. The problem is that this desire (πόθος) can easily be perverted into desire for pleasure, i.e. sexual gratification. That, for Philo, is the starting-point of wickedness and a life of misery".[101]

Philo does not depict this first sexual encounter between the man and the woman as sin or a fall. As Runia notes, "Philo does not give the impression of regarding the descent into wickedness as a 'fall from grace,' i.e. a single event which might not have happened, but rather as a structural feature of the world of becoming".[102] In addition, they do not become mortal as a result of an act, but are so because of their mixed composition of immortal soul and mortal body, though to choose pleasure (especially sexual pleasure) as one's goal is to choose mortal rather than immortal life. Again, as Runia observes, "the goal should be to regain the perfection of the first human being, who, we recall, lived in total accord with the law of nature ... The radical reversal of their lives, from immortality and bliss to mortality and toil, is not primarily a historical event, i.e. 'the fall,' but rather elucidates a fundamental structural aspect of human existence".[103]

---

[98] Runia, *Creation*, 357.
[99] Runia, *Creation*, 358.
[100] On this see pp. 404-406 below.
[101] Runia, *Creation*, 358.
[102] Runia, *Creation*, 356.
[103] Runia, *Creation*, 24. Similarly: "Is the reversal of human fortune something which unfortunately happened in the beginning, or is it simply part and parcel of human existence?

Sly takes up the description of the woman responding with *aidōs*, which she rightly notes, is "not the shame of awareness of good and evil (Gen 2:25; cf. Leg 3.65f), for it occurs before the temptation".[104] She goes on to argue that it is best understood as "'appropriately' or 'as a woman ought.' Eve meets her master, she greets him as a woman ought, i.e. deferentially". She then claims: "Because the expression occurs here gratuitously, Philo clearly is making a statement about woman's place".[105] This may be so, but given Philo's regular concern with proper and improper sexual behaviour, it seems to me more likely to indicate that in the encounter she did not flaunt herself like a prostitute.[106]

Runia points to the influence here on Philo of Plato's *Timaeus*, where similarly woman "appears on the scene after man and that her arrival means the beginning of love (ἔρως), which leads to the birth of children (*Tim.* 91a-d)" and notes the allusion in fitting two halves together to "Plato's playful theory on the origins of love put forward by the comic poet Aristophanes in the *Symposium*" (*Symp.* 189-193).[107] "For Philo the allusion is an attractive way of expressing the powerful attraction that love brings about".[108] On the other hand, he observes, "Philo's connection of *erôs* with physical pleasure and the descent into wickedness represents a severer view than we find in Plato. Indeed, when looked at in detail, Philo's attitude to sexuality bears little resemblance to that of Plato".[109] Philo's emphasis on propagation, "to produce a being similar to themselves" (*Opif.* 152), "departs from the Symposium account, which for obvious reasons does not emphasize the aspect of reproduction, but comes closer to the *Timaeus* (cf. esp. 91d)".[110]

1.2.2.1.2 The Creation of Woman in "Questions and Answers on Genesis"

In *QG* Philo is typically concerned not with woman, but with using the account of woman's creation to describe the relationship between the rational and irrational in

---

In spite of the protological context of the account, the latter seems nearer to what Philo intends" (363).

[104] Sly, *Philo's Perception of Women*, 205.

[105] Sly, *Philo's Perception of Women*, 205. Cf. also van den Hoek's reference above to "priggish overtones" ("Endowed with Reason," 72).

[106] Cf. Runia, *Creation*, who writes: "I would suggest that Philo is importing into the scene what he regards as ideal womanly behaviour, and this involves an appropriately modest response to the man's overture" (357).

[107] Runia, *Creation*, 355, 357. Runia, *Philo and the Timaeus*, 346. See also Baer, *Male and Female*, 38.

[108] Runia, *Creation*, 358.

[109] Runia, *Creation*, 355.

[110] Runia, *Creation*, 358.

human beings, so that only incidentally does it reveal particular information about his understanding of man and woman. In *QG* on Gen 2:18 we find love affirmed when he writes: "to every one of those who come together in the partnership of love the saying of Pythagoras can be applied, that 'a lover is indeed another self'" (*QG* 1.17). We also find Philo interpreting Gen 2:21-22 using Plato's myth: "the lawgiver says that woman was made from the side of man, intimating that woman is a half of a man's body" (*QG* 1.25), a detail which he then employs to account for the different days of purification after childbirth for male and female, 40 days and 80 days (*QG* 1.25). His main concern, however, is allegorical meaning. Accordingly, he writes: "man is a symbol of mind, and his side is a single sense-faculty. And the sense-perception of a very changeable reason is symbolized by woman" (*QG* 1.25). Then we read in his comment on God's building the woman (Gen 2:22):

> The harmonious coming together of man and woman and their consummation is figuratively a house. And everything which is without a woman is imperfect and homeless. For to man are entrusted the public affairs of the state; while to a woman the affairs of the home are proper. The lack of her is ruin, but her being near at hand constitutes household management. (*QG* 1.26)

This strikingly positive statement affirms women, but within the typical familial structures of the time where women carried responsibility for managing the domestic household.[111] In response to the question why according to Gen 2:21 woman was formed from the side of man and not from the ground like man, Philo then proffers four reasons:

> First, because woman is not equal in honour with man. Second, ... because those who take wives who have passed their prime are to be criticized for destroying the laws of nature. Third, he wishes that man should take care of woman as of a very necessary part of him; but woman, in return, should serve him as a whole. Fourth, he counsels man figuratively to take care of woman as of a daughter, and a woman to honour man as a father. And this is proper; for woman changes her habitation from her family to her husband. (*QG* 1.27)

While the first reasserts the usual hierarchy, the second places sexual intercourse for procreation at the heart of the relationship and the third places value on the man's caring for the woman as a necessary part of himself and her serving him. This parallels the author's understanding of the role of the irrational and the

---

[111] Winston, "Philo and the Rabbis," writes: "Philo's position is not so different from that of the Stoics in general who believed that while the main aim of marriage was procreation, this did not exclude the making of a life in common with the concomitant intimacy and mutual love", citing *Spec.* 1.138 (212) and *QG* 1.26 (213).

rational within a person. As there with the irrational, so here, the woman is valued and in that context sexual intercourse is valued (though only for procreation). The fourth reason reflects both the usual large discrepancy in age between men and their wives and the inequality which was assumed. As Philo explains, the husband takes over from the father and so she should show "the honour which she showed those who begot her. For man has a wife entrusted to him as a deposit from her parents but woman (takes a husband) by law" (*QG* 1.27).

Philo goes on in *QG*, commenting on Gen 2:23, to affirm beauty, including sexual attractiveness (a "lovely vision .. this most shapely and very charming creature!") (*QG* 1.28). He makes out of γυνή an etymology which enables him to claim: "The woman is called the power of giving birth with fecundity, and truly so; either because after receiving the seed, she conceives and gives birth; or, as the prophet says, because she came from man, not through spirit nor through seed, like those after him, but by a kind of mediate nature, just as a shoot is taken from a vine for growing another vine" (*QG* 1.28). In this way Philo salvages something from the failure of the LXX to reproduce the איש אשה (*ish-ishshah*; man-woman) pun of Gen 2:23 by interpreting the LXX's γυνή ("woman") as deriving from γεννάω ("to give birth"). [112]

He then explains Gen 2:24, a man's leaving his parents (not the usual pattern), thus: "Most excellent and careful was it not to say that the woman should leave her parents and be joined to her husband – for the audacity is bolder than the nature of woman – but that for the sake of woman man is to do this. Since with a very ready and prompt impulse he is brought to a concord of knowledge. Being possessed and foreseeing the future, he controls and stills his desires, being fitted to his spouse alone as if to a bridle" (*QG* 1.29). The words, "with a very ready and prompt impulse he is brought to a concord of knowledge", may be using sexual intercourse as a metaphor for the mind relating to the body and controlling it. But Philo probably sees a match also at the literal level, so that its import intends that consummation be followed by marital sexual fidelity. It is important to see that Philo is here affirming sexual relations. The literal is probably also present in his further allusion to Gen 2:24 in the words: "when Scripture says that the two are one flesh, it indicates something very tangible and sense-perceptible, in which there is suffering and sensual pleasure, that they may rejoice in, and be pained by, and feel the same things, and much more, may think the same things" (*QG* 1.29). Clearly sexual pleasure has a positive place here as by implication have women.

---

[112] On this see Loader, *Septuagint*, 65.

1.2.2.1.3 The Creation of Woman in "Allegorical Interpretation" and Beyond

In *Leg.* Philo's focus is even more on an allegorical exposition. Notwithstanding his affirmation in *Leg.* 2.5-9 of passions as helpers, reflecting allegorical interpretation of woman being made as helper for man (Gen 2:18, 20), Philo is primarily concerned with the dangers they present. More clearly developing the allegorical understanding, *Leg.* acknowledges of Gen 2:21: "How could anyone admit that a woman, or a human being at all, came into existence out of a man's side?" (*Leg.* 2.19), and so looks for deeper meaning, identifying "side" as "strength" (*Leg.* 2.21) and sense-perception being created when the mind is asleep (*Leg.* 2.25). Accordingly, Philo explains, "he adds the words, 'He built it to be a woman', proving by this that the most proper and exact name for sense-perception is 'woman'. For just as the man shows himself in activity and the woman in passivity, so the province of the mind is activity, and that of the perceptive sense passivity, as in woman" (*Leg.* 2.38). The "now" (νῦν), preserved in Gen 2:23 LXX, is then the basis for declaring that only the mind knows future and past, the senses only the present (*Leg.* 2.42-43).

Later in *Leg.* Philo can interpret Gen 2:24 quite negatively when applying it allegorically: "For the sake of sense-perception the Mind, when it has become her slave, abandons both God the Father of the universe, and God's excellence and wisdom, the Mother of all things, and cleaves to and becomes one with sense-perception so that the two become one flesh and one experience" (*Leg.* 2.49). He then cites Levi as representing the correct option, now using Gen 2:24 positively: "This man forsakes father and mother, his mind and material body, for the sake of having as his portion the one God, 'for the Lord Himself is his portion'," citing Deut 10:9 (*Leg.* 2.51). The negative application of Gen 2:24 is found also in *Gig.* 65: "But the sons of earth have turned the steps of the mind out of the path of reason and transmuted it into the lifeless and inert nature of the flesh. For 'the two became one flesh' as says the lawgiver. Thus they have debased the coin of truest metal and deserted from their post, left a place that was better for a worse, a place amid their own people for a place amid their foes".

Philo is similarly heavily allegorical in *Cher.* when he writes that mind once existed on its own. "It was but half the perfect soul, lacking the power whereby it is the nature of bodies to be perceived, a mere unhappy section bereft of its mate without the support of the sense-perceiving organs" (*Cher.* 59). "God then, wishing to provide the Mind with perception of material as well as immaterial things, thought to complete the soul by weaving into the part first made the other section, which he called by the general name of 'woman' and the proper name of 'Eve', thus symbolizing sense" (*Cher.* 60). This was positive and the senses got to work (*Cher.* 62). Given his statements elsewhere, this can probably be taken to reflect also a positive valuing of woman at a literal level. Thus a little earlier in the same work he wrote: "Man and Woman, male and female of the human race, in the course of nature come together to hold intercourse for the procreation of children" (*Cher.* 43). Citing *Cher.* 109-112, Winston, writes: "Philo sees in the loving interdependence of all things in the universe a token of the all-pervading harmony that reveals its perfection",[113] concluding "Philo's view that marriage is more than merely a procreative necessity and that it can be the occasion for genuine love and mutuality is thus intimately connected to this positive evaluation of the material world".[114] In *Her.* Philo writes: "Of the mortal He made two portions, one of which He named men, the other women" (*Her.* 139) and later emphasises a degree of equality, at least in relation to procreation: "Equality too divided the human being into man and woman, two sections unequal indeed in strength, but quite equal as regards what was nature's urgent purpose, the reproduction of themselves in a third person" (*Her.* 164).

1.2.2.1.4 Conclusion

There appears to be some consistency in Philo's understanding of Gen 2:20-24, at least with regard to how he relates the passage to woman and sexuality. Sexual encounter, including the passion and pleasure associated with it, appears to be something positive and affirmed by God as the means of procreation.[115] Philo does not reduce that meeting to the level of robotic functionality, but at least in *Opif.* 151-152 allows signs of pleasure without censure. As we shall see the "robotic" may pertain to Abraham and Hagar, not, however to Abraham and Sarah: "For with the concubine the embrace was a bodily one for the sake of begetting children. But with the wife the union was one of the soul harmonized to heavenly love" (*QG* 3.21).[116] The very possibility which joins pleasure and procreation also leaves open what Philo sees as its abuse, namely seeking pleasure, and sexual pleasure in particular, for its own sake, so that the advent of woman also amounted to the advent of a false option, but it was never the only option with her. Neither woman nor sexual intercourse with its accompanying passion and pleasure is itself evil. The allegories which equate woman and sense-perception, while implying women's inferiority and vulnerability to be swayed through the senses to follow

---

[113] Winston, "Philo and the Rabbis," 213.

[114] Winston, "Philo and the Rabbis," 214.

[115] Cf. Runia, *Creation*, who writes: "We should note also that Moses is negative about sexual passion, but not about sexuality itself. It is required for the continuation of the species" (24).

[116] On this see Samuel Belkin, *Philo and the Oral Law: The Philonic Interpretation of Biblical Law in Relation to the Palestinian Halakah* (Cambridge, Mass.: Harvard University Press, 1940) 220.

Man and Woman: Beginning from Genesis 1 – 3 31

the wrong option, confirm the basic insight, that Philo sees both as works of God's creation.

1.2.2.2 Women and Gender Roles

When we turn to Philo's understanding of women beyond his exposition of Gen 2:20-24, we face the similar complication that Philo is sometimes making observations directly about women, but at other times using male and female allegorically but in a way that nevertheless betrays his view of women in the literal world. Philo assumes gender roles, which he applies at both the literal and metaphorical level. We shall return below to the extent to which his gendered metaphors make problems for him. Here we are concerned with literal women.

Clearly Philo sees some gender roles as biologically determined. Thus he declares: "Men could not contest with women, nor women with men, the functions which fitly belong only to the other sex. If women should affect the practices of men, or men attempt those of women, they will in each case be held to belie their sex and win an ill name thereby" (*Sacr.* 100). He then explains: "To sow and beget belongs to the man and is his peculiar excellence, and no woman could attain to it. Again welfare in child-bearing is a good thing belonging to women, but the nature of man admits not of it" (*Sacr.* 101; similarly *QG* 3.18). The roles of each are affirmed.

His interpretation of Gen 3:16 provides some warrant for these differences. Thus we read:

> The woman incurred the violent woes of travail-pangs, and the griefs which come one after another all through the remainder of life. Chief among them are all those that have to do with children at birth and in their bringing up, in sickness and in health, in good fortune and evil fortune. In the next place she tasted deprivation of liberty, and the authority of the husband at her side, whose commands she must perforce obey. The man, in his turn, incurred labours and distress in the unceasing sweat of his brow to gain the necessaries of life. He was without those good things which the earth had been taught to bear of itself independently of all skill in the husbandman. (*Opif.* 167)

These roles play an important part in Philo's allegories related to virginity, sexual intercourse, conception, pregnancy, giving birth and nurture (see 1.4.5 below).

Philo hails Sarah as embodying the ideal wife. She

> showed her wifely love ... by sharing with him the severance from his kinsfolk, by bearing without hesitation the departure from her homeland, the continual and unceasing wanderings on a foreign soil and privation in famine, and by the campaigns in which she accompanied him. Everywhere and always she was at his side, ... his true partner in life and life's events, resolved to share alike the good and ill. She did not,

like some other women, run away from mishaps and lie ready to pounce on pieces of good luck, but accepted her portion of both with all alacrity as the fit and proper test of a wedded wife. (*Abr.* 245-246)

Male headship of the household is assumed, so that Philo writes: "When a man is united and associated with his wife, and a father with his sons, there is no need for several names, but only of the first one" just the man's (*QG* 2.26). Similarly, he reports that in Mosaic law "wives must be in servitude to their husbands, a servitude not imposed by violent ill-treatment but promoting obedience in all things" (*Hypoth.* 7.3) and "the husband seems competent to transmit knowledge of the laws to his wife, the father to his children, the master to his slaves" (*Hypoth.* 7.14; similarly Josephus *Ap.* 2.201). "For in a wise man's house no one is slow in showing kindness; but women and men, slaves and free, are full of zeal to do service to their guests" (*Abr.* 109), described later as a "household, like a well ordered crew, ... obedient to a single call from him who steered them like a pilot" (*Abr.* 116). As Sly has shown, Philo consistently revises the literal image of those biblical women he deems acceptable to bring them into conformity with his ideal of what constitutes a respectable woman in good standing in the Jewish community. She illustrates this by her analysis of Philo's depictions of a number of key women. Of Sarah she writes: "The overall effect is to make Sarah more self-effacing than she appears in the Bible, but by this altered behaviour she also conforms more closely to Philo's ideal of a wife"; [117] of Rebecca: "The motives of modesty and veneration on which the literal Rebecca acted are characteristic of Philo's model wife, and are his own addition to Scripture".[118] Thus "on the occasions when he allows them to emerge as real women, their virtues always pale beside their husbands', and discordant wills are harmonized".[119] "Acceptable women operate within a framework prescribed by men, and in their actions they defer to men".[120]

The same is true in relation to the wider social sphere, where Philo declares:

For since it saw as clearly, as if they were outlines on a flat surface, how unlike the bodily shapes of man and woman are, and that each of the two has a different life assigned to it, to the one a domestic, to the other a civic life, it judged it well in other matters too to prescribe rules all of which though not directly made by nature were the

---

[117] Sly, *Philo's Perception of Women*, 150.
[118] Sly, *Philo's Perception of Women*, 155.
[119] Sly, *Philo's Perception of Women*, 180.
[120] Sly, *Philo's Perception of Women*, 178.

outcome of wise reflection and in accordance with nature" (*Virt.* 19; similarly *Anim.* 11.1).[121]

In this Philo is assuming the defined roles for women of his time. These are not in themselves negative statements about women, except when women step outside their roles. This is clear from the following:

> Market-places and council-halls and law-courts and gatherings and meetings where a large number of people are assembled, and open-air life with full scope for discussion and action – all these are suitable to men both in war and peace. The women are best suited to the indoor life which never strays from the house, within which the middle door is taken by the maidens as their boundary, and the outer door by those who have reached full womanhood. (*Spec.* 3.169).

As Sly notes, "clearly, this prescription could be followed only in families wealthy enough to afford household help that would free the wife from running ordinary errands",[122] so that Philo is either unaware of how most ordinary women lived or is "straining for an ideal that never existed except in the minds of a few men".[123] She suggests that his statements are probably based on an idealised understanding of Greek society and that "his view of it was derived from the literature, which itself may have presented an idealized picture".[124] D'Angelo notes that Philo's Alexandria would have come under considerable pressure as a result of Augustan laws on marriage and Augustan promotion of Roman *pietas*.[125] She notes that in Philo εὐσέβεια is becoming "the Roman virtue *pietas*, which combines devotion to deity with familial love, affection and responsibility, as well as the display of the appropriate disposition and duty toward all to whom one is related: not only parents and children, spouse and siblings, but also patrons, clients, city and nation, including dependents and authorities of every degree up to and including the emperor".[126] Niehoff similarly notes that the notion of women's seclusion was a Roman idea, expressed, for instance, by Seneca about his aunt in

---

[121] On Alexander in *Anim.* 11.1 as "a defender of women's rights" see Abraham Terian, *Philonis Alexandrini De Animalibus: The Armenian Text with an Introduction, Translation, and Commentary* (SHJ 1; Chico: Scholars, 1981) 123.

[122] Sly, *Philo's Perception of Women*, 197.

[123] Sly, *Philo's Perception of Women*, 198.

[124] Sly, *Philo's Perception of Women*, 198.

[125] D'Angelo, "Gender and Geopolitics," 70. "The social tensions that resulted from the Roman imposition of these distinctions were felt throughout the province, but appear to have been particularly acute in Alexandria" (70).

[126] D'Angelo, "Gender and Geopolitics," 71. "Even where Philo makes no explicit appeal to the Roman order, his use of εὐσέβεια appears to be formulated in response to the gendered protocols of imperial family values" (75).

Egypt (Seneca *Helv.* 19.6) and stood in contrast to Egyptian norms: "The image of this woman perfectly corroborated Seneca's general advocation of manly self-restraint. Philo shared his position. He wanted Jewish women to play a similar role as Seneca's idealized aunt".[127]

From this perspective Philo draws strict consequences:

> the government of the greater is assigned to men under the name of statesmanship, that of the lesser, known as household management, to women. A woman then, should not be a busybody, meddling with matters outside her household concerns, but should seek a life of seclusion. She should not shew herself off like a vagrant in the streets before the eyes of other men, except when she has to go to the temple, and even then she should take pains to go, not when the market is full, but when most people have gone home, and so like a free-born lady worthy of the name, with everything quiet around her, make her oblations and offer her prayers to avert the evil and gain the good. The audacity of women who when men are exchanging angry words or blows hasten to join in, under the pretext of assisting their husbands in the fray, is reprehensible and shameless in a high degree. (*Spec.* 3 170-172)

He then alludes to the biblical command prohibiting a woman from grabbing the genitals of her husband's opponent in a dispute (*Spec.* 3.175-176). In contrast to such shamelessness Philo idealises the Therapeutae, whose meeting room was divided with a wall 3-4 cubits high: "This arrangement serves two purposes; the modesty becoming to the female sex is preserved, while the women sitting within ear-shot can easily follow what is said since there is nothing to obstruct the voice of the speaker" (*Contempl.* 33). We return to discuss their unique situation below (1.3.5).

Philo's notions of appropriate roles in real life, as well as in his related allegorical expositions, are rooted in his understanding of male and female identity.

1.2.2.3 Male and Female Identity

Philo's statements frequently reflect particular understandings not only of gender roles but also of the nature of what it means to be male and female, again, applied at both a literal and metaphorical level. The differences come through in a wide variety of contexts. Thus in explaining the difference between male and female sacrifices he declares: "the male is more complete, more dominant than the female,

---

[127] Maren Niehoff, *Philo on Jewish Identity and Culture* (TSAJ 86; Tübingen : Mohr Siebeck, 2001) 105. See earlier Isaac Heinemann, *Philons Griechische und Jüdische Bildung: Kulturgleichende Untersuchungen zu Philons Darstellung der Jüdischen Gesetze* (Hildesheim: Olms, 1973) who notes that Philo's view stands in tension with both Egyptian and Jewish understandings of women's roles (240).

closer akin to causal activity, for the female is incomplete and in subjection and belongs to the category of the passive rather than the active" (*Spec.* 1.200; similarly 228, 233; 2.32-34; *QE* 1.7; *Leg.* 2.38; *Deo* 3). In Philo's numerology male is odd and female even (*Spec.* 2.58; *QG* 2 13-14). In reflecting on the number six he writes: "We may say that it is in its nature both male and female, and is a result of the distinctive power of either. For among things that are it is the odd that is male, and the even female" (*Opif.* 13). This indirectly affirms, of course the rightful place of both male and female. In *QG* Philo similarly relates the difference between male and female to the structure of the universe: "It was necessary to honour man with pure and unshadowed light, but woman, since she was a mixture, with night and darkness and a mixed mass. Therefore in the constitution of the universe, the (numerical) oddness of the masculine number composed of unity produces squares, but the feminine even number, composed of two, produces oblongs" (*QG* 2.14). This may reflect belief that women are also of lesser worthy substance. These contrasts are not Philo's invention but derive from the Pythagorean tables of opposites as preserved by Aristotle, *Metaph.* A 5, 986a25.[128]

Likewise Philo writes that "Nature is feminine in a material sense, and proves on investigation to be solely suffering and passive rather than active" (*QG* 3.3). Women are depicted as passive rather than active (*QE* 1.8; *QG* 3.13), weak (*Anim.* 11.1), and less suited for war (*Mos.* 1.8), whereas men are strong and can act "'courageously' which is more commonly called 'being manly'" (*QE* 2.112). There are exceptions who prove the rule, such as Julia Augusta, of whom Philo writes: "For the judgements of women as a rule are weaker and do not apprehend any mental conception apart from what their senses perceive. But she excelled all her sex in this as in everything else, for the purity of the training she received supplementing nature and practice gave virility to her reasoning power ..." (*Legat.* 319-320); or, negatively: "A wife has great power to paralyse and seduce her husband and particularly if she is a wanton, for her guilty conscience increases her wheedling" (*Legat.* 39).

To be sluggish is to be "womanish" (*Abr.* 150); he associates "womanish" and "relaxed by softness" (*QG* 2.49; cf. also *Cher.* 82: "like womanish folk, nerveless and unstrung, flagging ere the struggle begin, with all our spiritual forces relaxed, sink into utter prostration"). According to Philo "the female clings to all that is born and perishes" (*Spec.* 3.178). In lists of what is positive and strong Philo lists the male, but among the lifeless, incomplete, diseased, enslaved, he includes the female (*Leg.* 2.97). Women are "endowed by nature with little sense" (*Prob.* 117).

---

[128] Runia, *Creation*, 127. See earlier Genevieve Lloyd, *The Man of Reason: "Male" and "Female" in Western Philosophy* (2d ed.; London: Routledge, 1995) 3, 25; and Wegner, "Philo's Portrayal of Women," who writes: "Philo's statements on biological science, 'male' and 'female' principles, and 'masculine' and feminine' attributes offer overwhelming evidence that he modelled his work closely on Greek authorities" (51).

As representative of "the weak feminine passion of sense-perception" (*Leg.* 3.11) she "has no capacity derived from herself to receive reproof" (*Leg.* 3.50). "Pre-eminence always pertains to the masculine, and the feminine always comes short of and is lesser than it", so that God, too, is be thought of as masculine and Wisdom necessarily as feminine (*Fug.* 51), though paradoxically also spoken of as masculine. Naturally for Philo, and to some degree reflecting also the biblical culture, only males are therefore called to pilgrimage three times a year (*Leg.* 3.11; Deut 16:16).

Confusion of roles is particularly serious according to Philo. "There is no greater impiety than to ascribe to the passive element the power of the active principle" (*Spec.* 3.180). Thus he notes that the Law "considered that in such matters the true man should maintain his masculinity, particularly in his clothes, which as he always wears them day and night ought to have nothing to suggest unmanliness. In the same way he trained the woman to decency of adornment and forbade her to assume the dress of a man, with the further object of guarding against the mannish-woman as much as the womanish-man" (*Virt.* 20-21) and earlier: "it lays down rules even about the kind of garment which should be worn. It strictly forbids a man to assume a woman's garb, in order that no trace, no merest shadow of the female, should attach to him to spoil his masculinity" (*Virt.* 18). Here we see not only the importance of differentiation, but clear indication that the male is superior to the female. Men are more bold than women; thus "most excellent and careful was it not to say that the woman should leave her parents and be joined to her husband – for the audacity is bolder than the nature of woman – but that for the sake of woman man is to do this" (*QG* 1.29).

More seriously, "woman is more accustomed to be deceived than man. For his judgment, like his body, is masculine and is capable of dissolving or destroying the designs of deception; but the judgment of woman is more feminine, and because of softness she easily gives way and is taken in by plausible falsehoods which resemble the truth" (*QG* 1.33); similarly: "woman is of a nature to be deceived rather than to reflect greatly" (*QG* 1.46). Eve then becomes the exemplar; she was the first to touch the fruit: "it was fitting that man should rule over immortality and everything good, but woman over death and everything vile" (*QG* 1.37). Similarly he says of her that "she was the beginning of evil and led him (man) into a life of vileness" (*QG* 1.45). Accordingly when men "turn away and stray out of the course which leads to virtue, sense-perception, the woman inherent in their nature, makes them stray still more, and forces them to run aground" (*Somn.* 1.246). Philo clearly sees women as potentially more open to deception and therefore potentially dangerous: "For the majority of wars, and those the greatest, have arisen through amours and adulteries and the deceits of women, which have consumed the greatest and choicest part of the Greek race and the barbarian also, and destroyed the youth of their cities" (*Ios.* 56). By contrast the high priest is a symbol of one who has left the woman of sense-perception behind: "But the high priest is blameless, perfect, the husband of a virgin, who, strange paradox, never becomes a woman, but rather has forsaken that womanhood through the company of her husband. And not only is he a husband, able to sow the seed of undefiled and virgin thoughts, but a father also of holy intelligences" (*Somn.* 2.185).

Similarly, he claims, that women are more readily likely to go along with customs, rather than develop independence of thought and so more appropriately represent a lower level of learning: "I suggest, then, that the father is reason, masculine, perfect, right reason and the mother the lower learning of the schools, with its regular course or round of instruction" (*Ebr.* 33). This spirit "bows down to the opinions of the multitude and undergoes all manner of transformations in conformity with the ever-varying aspirations of human life" (*Ebr.* 36). It makes women a danger to statesmen in tempting them to go along with multitude (*Ios.* 64-65). "Indeed, custom is the rule of the weaker and more effeminate soul. For nature is of men, and to follow nature is the mark of a strong and truly masculine reason" (*Ebr.* 55).

In employing allegory Philo speaks of the female sex as "irrational and akin to bestial passions, fear, sorrow, pleasure and desire" (*QG* 4.15) and interprets the allusion to Sarah, that in her "there ceased to be ... the ways of women" as indicating the path of the true learner as one of abandoning the female (*QG* 4.15; similarly *Ebr.* 59-60). He even interprets the incident at Sodom as indicative that the wise man is prepared to surrender his daughters, that is the feminine, in the interest of keeping the masculine mind unharmed (*QG* 4.38). "For progress is indeed nothing else than the giving up of the female gender by changing into the male, since the female gender is material, passive, corporeal and sense-perceptible, while the male is active, rational, incorporeal and more akin to mind and thought" (*QE* 1.8). Philo writes of the sons of Abraham's concubine: "those of inferior descent are certainly to be called female and unvirile, for which reason they are little admired as great ones" (*QG* 4.148). The same point is made in *Gig.*:

> Again, the spiritual offspring of the unjust is never in any case male: the offspring of men whose thoughts are unmanly, nerveless and emasculate by nature are female. Such do not plant a tree of virtue whose fruit must needs be true-born and excellent, only trees of vices and passions, whose off-shoots are feminine ... This is why we are told that these men begat daughters, while none of them is said to have begotten a son. For since just Noah who follows the right, the perfect and truly masculine reason, begets males, the injustice of the multitude appears as the parent of females only" (*Gig.* 4-5)

By contrast Lot "was the parent of daughters only and could rear no male or perfect growth within his soul" (*Ebr.* 164). Similarly in *Sacr.* he writes that "the female offspring of the soul is vice and passion, that emasculating influence which affects us in each of our pursuits. The male offspring is health of soul and virtue, by which we are stimulated and strengthened" (*Sacr.* 103; cf. also *QG* 4.148).

At times he produces allegorical explanations which appear to do away with the feminine entirely as in his statement about the Sabbath as given the name 'virgin' and 'motherless' as "begotten by the father of the universe alone, the ideal form of the male sex with nothing of the female. It is the manliest and doughtiest of numbers, well gifted by nature for sovereignty and leadership" (*Spec.* 2.56); similarly "motherless, exempt from female parentage, begotten by the Father alone, without begetting, brought to the birth, yet not carried in the womb ... ever virgin, neither born of a mother nor a mother herself, neither bred from corruption nor doomed to suffer corruption" (*Mos.* 2.210).[129] Philo says something similar of virtue:

> virtue as in truth being motherless, and having no part in the female sex but being sown only by the Father of all, who needs no material substance for His generation. But the virtue of the virtuous man has the rights of both sister and wife, of a sister because there is one Father for both, Who begot all things, and of a wife because everything that comes about through conjugation is called 'wife'. And so, the righteous man is a consort of righteousness, the ignorant man of ignorance, the sincere man of sincerity, the pious man of piety, and, in a word, the wise man of wisdom" (*QG* 4.68; similarly *Her.* 62: "Not so was it with Virtue or Sarah, for male descent is the sole claim of her, who is the motherless ruling principle of things, begotten of her father alone, even God the Father of all").

On the other hand, at times Philo employs sexual imagery to speak of the soul's intercourse with God, which thus affirms both male and female: "if God returns to the soul, and the soul returns to Him, He immediately shows it to be filled with joy, the name of which is feminine, while its nature is masculine" (*QG* 4.18). Similarly he writes that "the righteous man is a consort of righteousness, the ignorant man of ignorance, the sincere man of sincerity, the pious man of piety, and, in a word, the wide man of wisdom" (*QG* 4.68). The employment of such sexual imagery, which we discuss in greater detail below (1.4.5), appears to reflect

---

[129] Commenting on the connection between 7 and the goddess Nike in *Opif.* 100, Runia, *Creation*, notes that "it was standard Pythagorean practice to identify numbers with various divinities of the Greek pantheon" (273). While Philo does not vouch for it as his words λόγος ἔχει ("is said to") indicate (*Opif.* 100), "the comparison or identification of the hebdomad with the goddess (though never explicitly named) is found in no less than 10 Philonic passages" (273). Runia points to the list in Horst Moehring, "Arithmology as an Exegetical Tool in the Writings of Philo of Alexandria," in *The School of Moses: Studies in Philo and Hellenistic Religion: In Memory of Horst R. Moehring* (ed. John Peter Kenney; BJS 304; SPM 1; Atlanta : Scholars, 1995) 141-76, 156.

a basically positive attitude towards women and sexual intercourse with them in the right relationship and for the right purpose (procreation). Philo notes that "when a man comes in contact with a woman, he marks the virgin as a woman" (*QE* 2.3) in order to contrast with woman paradoxically becoming a virgin when she espouses the virtues, but not in a way that denies the validity of the literal. In *QG* 3 he is quite explicit:

> And the greatest desire is that of intercourse between man and woman, since it forms the beginning of a great thing, procreation, and brings about in the progenitors a great desire toward their progeny, for it is rather natural to be very fond of, and tender toward, them. And it indicates the cutting off not only of excessive desires but also of arrogance and great evil and such habits" (*QG* 3.48)

The "cutting off" which he sees circumcision symbolising, is not rejection of sexual intercourse but of the excess to which love of sexual intercourse can lead. Thus here too affirmation of sexual intercourse also implies affirmation of women.

While some statements give the impression that Philo sees no place for the feminine in one who aspires to wisdom and so depicts Sarah as leaving behind the ways of women, he can also praise Leah: "I admire all-virtuous Leah" (*Migr.* 95).

> She aims at being favourably regarded, thinking praise due to her not only from thoughts masculine and truly manly, by which the nature that has no blemish and truth impervious to bribes is held in honour, but also from those which are more feminine, which are wholly at the mercy of appearances and powerless to understand anything presented to contemplation outside them. (*Migr.* 95).

His interest here is primarily symbolic as is clear from his application: "It is characteristic of a perfect soul to aspire both to be and to be thought to be, and to take pains not only to have a good reputation in the men's quarters, but to receive the praises of the women's as well" (*Migr.* 96). On the other hand it prompts him to make some positive statements which must also have literal meaning: "It was for this reason that Moses gave in charge not to men only but to women also to provide the sacred appointments of the Tabernacle" (*Migr.* 97; similarly *Mos.* 2.137). But he soon slips back into allegory: "These, in whose eyes Leah, that is virtue, desires to be honoured are citizen women and worthy of their citizenship" (*Migr.* 99) and "it is best, then, that the array of women, that is of the senses, in the soul, should be propitiated as well as that of the men, that is of our several thoughts" (*Migr.* 100). This is so typical.

Conclusion

It is clear therefore from both his direct and indirect statements that Philo considers women inferior to men in a number of respects. They include physical and intellectual strength. The weakness also entails a greater emotional attachment to people and things. Accordingly Philo understands this as the basis why women should not be engaged in political leadership, but should remain in the domestic sphere. Already from the statements considered it is clear that Philo identifies women with the sensual, which he can describe as the irrational, in contrast to mind as the rational. We shall see that despite occasional statements which might suggest otherwise, Philo does not advocate doing away with the senses any more than he advocates doing away with women. Male and female belong to being human as it belongs to creation and is symbolised for Philo in the number six, a coupling of the odd and even in the very structure of reality (*Opif.* 13-14). There Philo also implies that woman's make-up is different: "It was necessary to honour man with pure and unshadowed light, but woman, since she was a mixture, with night and darkness and a mixed mass" (*QG* 2.14) and relates this to her being even and not odd. Mind needs to control passions which make their approach through the senses:

> Pleasure does not venture to bring her wiles and deceptions to bear on the man, but on the woman, and by her means on him. This is a telling and well-made point: for in us mind corresponds to man, the senses to woman; and pleasure encounters and holds parley with the senses first, and through them cheats with her quackeries the sovereign mind itself. (*Opif.* 165)

His approach is well represented in the following:

> The soul has, as it were, a dwelling, partly men's quarters, partly women's quarters. Now for the men there is a place where properly dwell the masculine thoughts (that) are wise, sound, just, prudent, pious, filled with freedom and boldness, and kin to wisdom. And the women's quarters are a place where womanly opinions go about and dwell, being followers of the female sex. And the female sex is irrational and akin to bestial passions, fear, sorrow, pleasure and desire, from which ensue incurable weaknesses and indescribable diseases. He who is conquered by these is unhappy, while he who controls them is happy. And longing for and desiring this happiness, and seizing a certain time to be able to escape from terrible and unbearable sorrow, which is (what is meant by) 'there ceased to be the ways of women' – this clearly belongs to minds full of Law, which resemble the male sex and overcome passions and rise above all sense-pleasure and desire and are without sorrow and fear and, if one must speak the truth, without passion, not zealously practising apathy, for this would be ungrateful and shameless and akin to arrogance and reckless boldness, but that which is consistent

with the argument given, (namely) cutting the mind off from disturbing and confusing passions (*QG* 4.15)

In the same way he assumes it appropriate that men control women, who not only lack perspective, but are also more vulnerable to being deceived and led astray. Thus, from Philo's perspective, it is not only the woman who sets out to seduce who poses a danger for men. Woman as more prone to the irrational already poses a danger. For all that, women belong in Philo's world, in Philo's understanding of the household, and ideally serve as partners to men, quiet, submissive, and modest, and bearers of their children. To deny them, as to advocate apathy, is arrogant and apparently unrealistic. The issue is control.

If there is some ambiguity in identifying Philo's attitudes towards women and a need to clarify the extent of rejection and affirmation, this is even more so the case with his statements about human beings in themselves, in particular, about the mind, the senses, and the passions, to which sexual desire belongs. These are so closely related to Philo's understanding and employment of gender categories that they are appropriately treated here. As the passage just cited shows, Philo's understanding of women informs his psychology, and his psychology, in turn, informs his view of women.

1.2.2.4 *Male and Female in Human Psychology: Mind, Senses, Passions*

Philo's understanding of the make up of human beings is usually embedded in his expositions and exhortations calling for their self-management. At times, however, he pauses to explain. A standard element in his explanations derives from Stoic psychology. Accordingly, beside the mind (νοῦς) the soul has seven parts: five senses (αἰσθήσεις) and two faculties (ὄργανα) (*Opif.* 62-66; 117; *Abr.* 236; *QG* 1.7; 2.12; 3.4; 4.110; *QE* 2.97; *Leg.* 1.11; *Det.* 168; *Agr.* 30; cf. also *T. Reub.* 2:1 – 3:9). The senses are sight, hearing, taste, smell, and touch, described in *Plant.* as like trees in the body (*Plant.* 29). The faculties are speech (φωνητήριον) and generation (γόνιμον), that is, the ability to procreate through sexual intercourse. Sometimes he omits the generative aspect altogether as in *Abr.* 29 (probably because he wanted the seventh and mind to coincide) and in the long exposition in *Somn.* 1.25-37; or he lists it as an eighth (*Aet.* 97; cf. also *QG* 1.57).

Philo can also speak of speak of three parts of the soul, following Platonic psychology: "one part that is the seat of reason (τὸ μὲν λογικόν), another that is the seat of high spirit (τὸ δὲ θυμικόν), and another that is the seat of desire (τὸ δὲ ἐπιθυμητικόν)" (*Leg.* 1.70; similarly 3.115; *Virt.* 13).[130] He then identifies

---

[130] On Plato's tripartite model and Philo's adaptation of it, including its images, see Runia, *Philo and the Timaeus*, 301-11; Winston, "Emotions," 201-202.

their location: "the head is the place and abode of the reasonable part, the breast of the passionate part, the abdomen of the lustful part" (*Leg.* 1.70).[131] To each is attached a virtue: "prudence (ἐπιστήμην) to the reasonable part, for it belongs to reason to have knowledge of things we ought to do and of the things we ought not; courage (ἀνδρείαν) to the passionate part; and self-mastery (σωφροσύνην) to the lustful part" (*Leg.* 1.70). In *Leg.* 3.115 he employs Plato's tripartite model and assigns the senses to the rational part of the soul.[132] Runia notes that other authors such as Cicero, the Platonists, Albinus and Galen, and the commentator Calcidius, treated the Platonic imagery similarly and that Philo's was "by no means an original adaptation, but shows dependence on the way the *Timaeus* was traditionally read".[133] Most commonly Philo operates, in effect with a bipartite model of the soul: rational and irrational. Runia notes that "in Middle Platonism the bipartite division of the soul into a rational and irrational part was standard dogma".[134]

---

[131] On locating the mind in the head Runia, *Creation*, notes that "in Philo's time there was an unresolved controversy between the followers of Aristotle and the Stoa, who regarded the heart as the location of the directive part, and followers of Plato, who placed it in the head. Philo tends to follow the Platonic line, but at *Spec.* 1.213 and *Sacr.* 136 he states that the Mosaic view is unclear" (336).

[132] On this see Mattila, "Wisdom, Sense Perception, Nature," who writes: "This is a decidedly 'male' image of the senses and one which casts them into a role that is almost the antithesis of the role they play elsewhere in Philo. Yet this anomalous portrait occurs in quite a few places and is too striking to ignore" (118).

[133] Runia, *Philo and the Timaeus*, 267. See also Winston, "Emotions," 202.

[134] Runia, *Philo and the Timaeus*, 263, similarly pp. 305, 468. He observes: "Philo's mixture of Platonism and Stoicism on the subject of the πάθη accurately reflects developments in the history of philosophy", pointing to Poseidonius' rejection of the unitary notion of the soul of the old Stoa and return to Platonic tripartite model – amounting to bipartite solution (301). See also Winston, "Emotions," 202; Carlos Lévi, "Philo's Ethics," in *The Cambridge Companion to Philo* (ed. Adam Kamesar; Cambridge: Cambridge University Press, 2009) 146-71, 155-59, who notes that Philo freely reworks Stoic concepts in a Platonic sense, at times even using them to incorporate ideas "foreign to Stoicism and even in contradiction with it" (156); and Gretchen Reydams-Schils, "Philo of Alexandria on Stoic and Platonist Psycho-Physiology: The Socratic Higher Ground," in *Philo of Alexandria and Post-Aristotelian Philosophy* (ed. Francesca Alesse; SPA 5; Leiden: Brill, 2008) 169-95, who sets out schematically the models found in Philo: the soul/body distinction; mind versus the senses and the passions; the Stoic model of the soul; the Platonic model of the soul; and mixed cases (175-87). She concludes: "A return to the Socratic position of a struggle between soul and body, which interferes with the proper functioning of reason, allows Philo to avoid controversies between different groups of philosophers, controversies that have become firmly entrenched in the doxographical material Philo would have used". "This in turn allows him to use the psychological model, whether Platonist, Stoic, or a mixed version, that suits his exegetical purpose best in any

In addition Philo speaks of the passions, sometimes listing these, as in Stoicism, as four: pleasure, fear, pain, and desire (*Ios.* 79; *Opif.* 79; *Decal.* 142-145; *Spec.* 2.30, 157; *QG* 4.15; *Prob.* 18, 159; *Leg.* 3.113; *Conf.* 52). At times he goes beyond these, for instance, when he writes of "fear or anger, or grief or pleasure, or any other passion" (*Deus* 71). Of the four main passions, pleasure and desire are closely related and Philo applies both to sexual passion. He frequently identifies them, using the Platonic framework, as the passions of the belly and, as he often puts it, the area "below the belly",[135] meaning the sexual genitalia: "insatiable lusts of the belly, inflame also the lusts seated below it (τὰς ὑπὸ γαστέρα)" (*Spec.* 1.192; *Leg.* 3.114; *Deus* 15); "the pleasures of the belly and the parts below it" (ὑπογαστρίους) (*Spec.* 2.163; *Mos.* 2.23-24; *QG* 1.12; *Sacr.* 49; *Fug.* 35); "the delights of the belly and the organs below it (τῶν μετὰ γαστέρα)" (*Virt.* 182); "an unlocked tongue or insatiate greed of belly, or in uncontrolled lasciviousness of the lower-lying parts (τῶν ὑπογαστρίων)" (*Somn.* 2.147; similarly *Virt.* 208; see also *Spec.* 2.195; *Mos.* 1.28).[136]

While most of the time Philo is warning against what these passions, especially sexual desire, can do – and so they appear negative, a theme to which we return below – he can speak of all of these aspects also in positive or at least neutral terms.[137] Thus of the five senses and the two faculties he can write: "These are all pure in a virtuous man and by nature are feminine when they belong to the irrational species, but (when they belong to) a good possessor, they are masculine" (*QG* 2.12). In *Leg.* he uses the image of women as helpers (Gen 2:18, 20) to argue that "sense and the passions are helpers of the soul and come after the soul" (*Leg.* 2.5). Accordingly, he writes: "We have to say, then, that sense-perception comes under the head neither of bad nor of good things, but is an intermediate thing common to a wise man and a fool, and when it finds itself in a fool it proves bad,

---

given context" (190). "Both the Platonist and the Stoic models are at the service of scriptural exegesis for Philo" (193).

[135] A. Peter Booth, "The Voice of the Serpent: Philo's Epicureanism," in *Hellenization Revisited: Shaping a Christian Response within the Greco-Roman World* (ed. Wendy E. Helleman; Lanham: University Press of America, 1994) 159-72, notes that "Philo's frequent reference to pleasure, in terms of 'the belly and the parts below,' is a commonplace of *anti-Epicurean* literature in antiquity" (165).

[136] David E. Aune, "Mastery of the Passions: Philo, 4 Maccabees and Earliest Christianity," in *Hellenization Revisited: Shaping a Christian Response within the Greco-Roman World* (ed. Wendy E. Helleman; Lanham: University Press of America, 1994) 125-58, writes: "Philo's treatment of the passions can best be described as a blending of Platonic psychology with Stoic moral theory, which is then used for interpreting the Bible and defending the Jewish faith" (126).

[137] On this see Baer, *Male and Female*, 90; Winston, "Emotions," 212.

when in a sensible man, good" (*Leg.* 3.67). Similarly in *Det.* he writes: "These seven in a wise man's soul are found to be pure and undefiled, and herein deserving of honour, but in the soul of a foolish man unclean and polluted" (*Det.* 169). There he identifies their active and passive roles neutrally as male and female:

> Each of the seven faculties shows itself in one way as male, in another way as female; for since it is either in restraint or in motion, in restraint when at rest in sleep, in motion when now awake and active – when regarded under the aspect of restraint and inaction, it is called female owing to its having been reduced to passivity; when looked at under the aspect of movement and employment of force, being thought of as in action, it is described as male. (*Det.* 172)

He concludes: "Thus in the wise man the seven faculties are evidently clean, but by the law of contraries, in the worthless man all exposed to punishment" (*Det.* 173). Elsewhere he depicts them as female and belonging to irrational parts of the soul, in contrast to mind, which were produced by God's helpers, and so vulnerable and fallible, though not in themselves evil.[138] As Runia notes, Philo's psychology "does effectively convey the Platonic viewpoint that, when the soul descends into the body, it requires αἴσθησις and a moderate dose of παθήματα, so that συναμφότερον (87e5) can live out its allotted period".[139] Reviewing the many texts which affirm the senses, Baer concludes: "In the texts just examined man's irrational soul and the material world are seen as potentially but not absolutely evil. Man becomes involved in moral evil not simply because he is σῶμα and αἴσθησις as well as νοῦς but because of a distorted relationship between the lower and higher parts of his being".[140] Similarly Wilson writes:

> The self must exert its male, active authority over irrational desire in the same way that God rules the world or a man rules his household. It must also realize its female, receptive capacities in communion with the divine just as Sophia joins with God to

---

[138] Cf. Aune, "Mastery of the Passions": "The result of Philo's Platonic-Stoic synthesis is that the 'high-spirited' and 'lustful' portions of the soul (as well as the corresponding parts of the body—the chest, stomach, and what lies below the stomach) are by nature irrational and diseased" (126).

[139] Runia, *Philo and the Timaeus*, 265; similarly, speaking of the body as a corpse: "it needs the irrational part in order to be adequately adapted to the necessities and contingencies of the body" (469) and of the passions: "Among these the most commonly mentioned are fear, desire (including hunger, thirst, sexual lust), cowardice, pain and pleasure. In order to lead a good life man's aim must be to moderate these πάθη, convert them to εὐπάθεια, or perhaps even eliminate them altogether" (469).

[140] Baer, *Male and Female*, 90.

create the world or the chaste Therapeutrides join with God to help bring their virtuous community into being.[141]

He goes on to note that:

> In developing this particular psychic ideal, with its nexus of active and passive, it would appear that Philo is not altogether anomalous, but actually participates in a wide-ranging and variously negotiated concept of ancient anthropology, according to which human wholeness entails the actualization of both "masculine" and "feminine" faculties in a mutually supportive and transformative process.[142]

Philo's employment, especially of Stoic categories like *apatheia*, could easily lead to the conclusion that Philo espouses the denial of passions altogether, including, therefore, sexual passion. We shall return to that issue below (1.2.3.3). First we come back to Philo's understanding of woman which can now be considered in the light of what we have discussed thus far, including his psychology.

1.2.2.5 Woman in Perspective: A Summary Assessment

Understanding Philo's view of woman entails weighing not only what he describes as the ideal but also his depiction of roles and traits, especially as he used them in his extensive allegories. Does, for instance, Philo's psychology, and the therapy or soteriology it serves, apply equally to men and women? How far does the value system based on this differentiation in such allegory of the soul reach? Does abandonment of the female in the soul imply something negative or defiled about women in a literal sense? Is then the ultimate goal male celibacy?[143] Is there any room for women at all?

In this section we draw on observations in the material considered thus far and to some extent presuppose much that is still to come, but in ways which also introduce the basis for the following discussions. An appropriate starting point is to note that Philo believes in creation, including the creation of humankind, which he celebrates as exhibiting God's excellence in creation and describes as not only

---

[141] Walter T. Wilson, "Sin as Sex and Sex with Sin: The Anthropology of James 1:12-15," *HTR* 95 (2002) 147-68, 157. He writes: "The telos of spiritual development, then, is neither masculinity as such nor femininity as such, but 'a kind of androgyny of the soul' that restores humankind's primal, undifferentiated state and brings the activity of the soul's male-female polarity into alignment with the interpersonal and metaphysical realities to which it belongs" (157).

[142] Wilson, "Sin as Sex," 157.

[143] This issue arises in Philo's idealistic depiction of the Therapeutae which we discuss separately below (1.3.5).

ideal but also as worth taking as a model or goal.[144] While his praise of creation precedes his account of the formation of woman, nothing indicates that woman should be excluded from this positive evaluation.[145] More importantly, God formed woman. The fact that God was accompanied by helpers in creating humankind enables Philo to account for potential evil, but that is as applicable to the man as it is to the woman.

Clearly Philo does not treat the woman as simply a second human being. To the solitary man there is not only the addition of another human being, but three further factors of crucial significance: the ending of his solo-existence, considered by Philo as comparable to God's; the appearance of a different kind of human being, female; and the issue of how the two should relate. Philo is quite clear about the fact that solo-existence was unrealistic for mortal humankind if it is to survive. With regard to the woman, despite obvious differences, he nowhere suggests that woman's psychological constitution is fundamentally different from the man's. That is, she, too, is appropriately described as having seven faculties, the five senses, speech, and organs related to generation; or three aspects, mind, high-spirit, and passion.[146] While Philo never says so explicitly, she, too, may be depicted as mind riding the chariot, and needing to control the reins. This remains

---

[144] Winston, "Philo and Rabbis," notes that "the few Philonic statements that apparently denigrate bodily training all occur in passages contrasting the unholy contests that the Greek states held in their triennial festivals with the truly sacred contests for the winning of virtue and take up a motif made popular by the Cynic/Stoic diatribe" (208).

[145] Cf. Boyarin, *Carnal Israel*: "The very coming into being of woman is already the Fall" (79). Winston, "Philo and Rabbis," rightly protests: "To attribute to Philo, as Boyarin does, the view that God's creation of woman/sense-perception is unwelcome to him would stand on its head Philo's firm and confident conviction that all that God has created, without exception, is evidence of His absolute perfection and excellence" (201) and amounts to virtually gnostic reading of Philo (201 n. 8).

[146] Writing of Philo's gendered allegory of the soul in *Opif.* 165-166, Runia, *Creation*, writes: "It does not divide humanity into two groups, for as he states here explicitly, the allegory applies to us all. (I see no reason to assume that Philo is writing for men only). 'Male' and 'female' represent a kind of psychological imagery that can help explain the workings of the soul. The schematic nature of the allegory is lost if one regards Eve as 'the archetypal female,' as Sly (1990, 109) does. For Philo Eve is the embodiment of archetypal female characteristics." (381-82). He is citing Sly, *Philo's Perception of Women*. See also Mattila, "Wisdom, Sense Perception, Nature," who notes that "Philo does not, however, deny women, merely by virtue of their sex, the capacity to attain to the rational, 'male' virtues to which men can attain. Neither are men, merely by virtue of their sex, denied the capacity to plunge down into the deepest recesses of the irrational or 'female'" (107).

true despite Philo's being "thoroughly androcentric"[147] reflected in his almost always focussing on men.[148]

As we shall see, Philo depicts the relating of the man and woman as including sexual response to each other. This he portrays as something positive, and as conducive and designed solely for the purpose of bringing about propagation of the species through sexual intercourse. The responses, clearly physical, involve bodily pleasure. This is not a fall[149] or failure, but as appropriate as eating and drinking if properly directed and not in excess.[150] Things go wrong where eating and drinking are to excess (and eating and drinking the wrong things) and where sexual desire loses procreation as its goal and seeks fulfilment for its own sake, and also chooses the wrong object for its affection.[151] The mythology of the snake, which we discuss below, primarily symbolises the allure of pleasure for its own sake and in excess. The potential for wrongdoing is thus present for both man and woman.

This picture is, however, incomplete, because Philo makes differentiations between man and woman and these go beyond the obvious, namely, their organs and roles related to procreation.[152] Philo clearly believes in other significant differences, including in physical strength, but also in mental ability, not least in the ability to manage what comes to them through the senses, and especially the

---

[147] Winston, "Philo and the Rabbis, 216.

[148] Sly, *Philo's Perception of Women*: "Unless Philo is in a situation where he is forced to notice women as people, his tendency is to operate in a male world" (63). Conway, "Gender and Divine Relativity," probably goes too far when she argues that in relation to ascent and descent of the gender scale Philo "conceives of this only for the man" (480). This ignores Philo's significant women.

[149] Cf. Sly, *Philo's Perception of Women*, who writes: "There is little doubt that in both cases Philo sees the 'fall' as sexual. The serpent represents pleasure, and the most intense pleasure Philo knows is that experienced by a man in intercourse" (109).

[150] Cf. Sly, *Philo's Perception of Women*, who sees sexual intercourse negatively and declares "that for Philo the only truly, inescapably sexual person is *gynē*" (99). On the contrary the man, too, is sexual and has an obligation under God's natural law to engage in sexual intercourse for procreation.

[151] Gaca, *Making of Fornication*, writes: "Human beings must keep their appetites under rational guard by curbing their wild sexual desire through restricting the intake of food and drink" (195).

[152] Wegner, "Philo's Portrayal of Women," writes: "The only context in which he treats the sexes with relative impartiality is when acknowledging the indispensability of both for reproduction" (*Her.* 164) (50). On Philo's espousal of widespread assumptions about men and women Sly, *Philo's Perception of Women*, comments: "Anthropologists have observed that the relating of woman to body and nature, and of man to mind and culture, and the concomitant belief in male superiority, have been common to all cultures. Philo appears to be voicing a universal tendency" (100-101).

passions. The material considered above makes it clear that Philo shared widely held views which depicted woman as passive, male as active, woman as inferior, male as superior, and so forth.[153] Of particular significance is Philo's conviction that women are less capable of dealing with the dangers confronting both men and women from the passions. Such assessment will derive in part from the social context where men were usually at least ten years older than their wives and where men were beset with much greater concerns about protecting daughters than they were with protecting sons.

It obviously made sense, then, for Philo, when applying male female imagery to human psychology to identify mind, the rational, as male and the senses, the irrational, as female.[154] As Baer notes "The use of man to symbolize νοῦς and woman αἴσθησις is found throughout Philo's writings and is the main device by which he relates the creation narratives to man's present situation".[155] This generates considerable complexity because we now have both men and women with parts designated male and female. It becomes even more complex because Philo brings to his understanding not only perceptions about different abilities between men and women with respect especially to their minds, but also different social roles. A woman's male mind needs to be exercised with socially acceptable female roles and to manage her female irrational aspects accordingly, and a man's

---

[153] Sly, *Philo's Perception of Women*, observes by way of summary of what she goes on to demonstrate in detail: "Philo expresses value judgments by noting significance in the gender of words, by playing on etymological connections, and by attributing masculine and feminine qualities to his philosophical terms. In all instances, masculinity and maleness signify superiority, and femininity and femaleness inferiority. These value judgments pervade his work in such a way that it is impossible to separate the theoretical statements from their application to the human situation" (43).

[154] Sly, *Philo's Perception of Women*, comments "because he associates the weaker qualities with sense-perception and has arbitrarily designated them female, he speaks as though these predominate in each individual woman" (96). This suggests a movement in the opposite direction, from allegory to reality. It is likely that the allegorical and the literal were mutually reinforcing, while it will have been prejudices at the literal level which were the main source for the development of the allegory and not vice versa. As Mattila, "Wisdom, Sense Perception, Nature," notes, however, the "female" is not the only image which Philo uses for sense-perception. She notes that in *Leg.* 3.115 he employs Plato's tripartite model and assigns the senses to the rational part of the soul (119).

[155] Baer, *Male and Female*, 39. He writes: "Female terminology occurs more frequently and receives noticeably greater emphasis in those instances where Philo describes man's irrational soul in strongly pejorative terms than in passages where he evaluates the irrational soul in neutral or positive terms. Indeed, it is precisely by exploiting the female terminology of the Biblical text that Philo most clearly expresses his depreciation of the irrational soul and of the perishable realm of creation" (40).

male mind needs to be exercised with socially acceptable male roles and to manage his female irrational accordingly.[156]

Given her inferior ability to exercise such management, a woman poses a greater danger to a man in this respect than another man. Given a man's sexual response to a woman, this danger is further enhanced. Philo assumes that the converse is not the case, namely that a man is a sexual danger to a woman, because he does not apparently consider that female sexual urge is as strong as a man's (*QG* 3.47) and probably assumes also that it is passive. There are, therefore, grounds, given Philo's understanding, for his treating women as a potential danger, both to men[157] and to themselves,[158] and therefore for his stance of believing that they should be controlled.[159] Thus social control of real women is then a relatively neat match with the need to control one's own inner feminine, irrational soul. This need not amount to hatred of women any more than it need produce hatred of one's own irrational self. Philo does not appear to have chosen either of these options.[160] He believes all of humankind is God's creation, while at the same time embracing a gender hierarchy of his time, which clearly understood women as inferior.[161]

---

[156] Sly, *Philo's Perception of Women*, comments, "Just as sense-perceptions and mind in the individual have their own proper function based on fixed characteristics, so do woman and man in an inter-personal relationship" (95). "Eve, sense-perception, is intended to be a helper to Adam, mind, but if he does not exercise sufficient control over her, she will be influenced by his enemy, the passion pleasure, into causing harm to the two of them" (103).

[157] This need not be sexual. Thus Sly, *Philo's Perception of Women*, points to Miriam's insubordination (119-120).

[158] Sly, *Philo's Perception of Women*, observes that in some instances the focus is on women as a danger not to men, but to themselves, citing Lot's wife (118).

[159] According to Sly, *Philo's Perception of Women*, with regard to women, Philo "does not credit, or burden, them with sexual accountability" (108). This is true to the extent that Philo assumes their inferior capacity to manage passions and that therefore men should control them. On the other hand, Philo does not exempt them from accountability altogether and has no hesitation in depicting seductresses as inculpated in wrongdoing. His illustration of the Midianite women, who represent "sexually aggressive woman as a powerful danger" (115) is a case in point.

[160] Mattila, "Wisdom, Sense Perception, Nature," notes that in Philo's image of growth "the flesh does not become pure mind; the earthly 'female' does not dissolve itself into the disembodied perfection of the 'male'. Instead, the 'female' blends and merges with the 'male'. She is 'made manly' – she does not become 'male'" (117). She observes that "the desire for reconciliation and harmony between mind and sense perception finds its most vivid expression in Philo's description of the choir by the seashore in Exodus 15" (117), citing *Agr.* 80-81.

[161] Mattila, "Wisdom, Sense Perception, Nature," notes that "this suggests that the hierarchy has little to say about any personal misogyny on Philo's part" (112). On Philo's

Yet he frequently speaks in most disparaging terms of both: the inner feminine irrational and women.[162] He is particularly scathing wherever sense-perception has come to rule mind, instead of vice versa, both within women and men, and through women, frequently using the image of the seductress at both a literal and symbolic level.[163] As Baer observes:

> This pejorative use of female terminology to describe man's irrational soul and the created world is found throughout Philo's writings. It is particularly frequent in Leg. All. and Quaest. in Gen. His depreciation of actual woman and of female sense-perception are frequently so closely entwined that no clear separation between the two can be made. Philo's usual practice is to speak disparagingly of actual woman on the basis of the literal meaning of a text and then to allegorize the passage in terms of sense-perception. But nowhere are these two foci really far apart, for it is precisely Philo's depreciation of woman that permits him to use her as a symbol of sense-perception and the material world which leads in turn to a further devaluation of woman. It is certainly not coincidental that he emphasizes the female nature of sense-perception predominantly in those instances where his evaluation of sense-perception is decidedly negative.[164]

His stance seriously discriminates against women,[165] but, of course, he would argue, on good grounds. However, provided women behave appropriately, they are, on the contrary, to be highly valued.[166] Sly hypothesises, surely correctly,

---

consistency with his cultural context see also Conway, "Gender and Divine Relativity," who notes that if anything different it is his constant linking to state of the soul (482).

[162] Sly, *Philo's Perception of Women*, observes that Philo's very negative comments about wives in discussing Essene celibacy derive not from the Essenes but his own negative perspective (207).

[163] Sly, *Philo's Perception of Women*, writes: "Thus, it appears that when Philo is considering women on the human level, he divides them into two classes, i.e., noble, freeborn women, and slavish harlots. Leah and Rachel represent these two extremes" (173; similarly 171).

[164] Baer, *Male and Female*, 40.

[165] As Lloyd, *Man of Reason*, notes, "That woman symbolically represents the non-rational aspects of human nature does not of itself carry the implication that women are irrational, but it is precisely his pejorative attitude to women that enables Philo's allegories to function as they do. Philo's use of male-female symbolism and his depreciation both of actual women and of sense-perception are so closely intertwined that often no clear separation can be made between them" (25).

[166] As Lloyd, *Man of Reason*, observes, "This version of moral progress is not meant to exclude actual women, but it calls on them to set aside those character traits which are supposed to characterize them as female" (27). cf. Dorothy Sly, "Philo's Practical Application of Dikaiosynē," *SBLSem* (1991) 298-308, who argues unconvincingly that

"that there is a group of women who are acceptable to Philo. They may appear to exercise independence, like Miriam and her 'best' women. But they are operating within a framework prescribed by men, and in their actions they defer to men".[167] They include also the Hebrew midwives, and those who help furnish the tabernacle. On description of the latter she writes: "We see in this extended passage that good women act with apparent initiative and freedom, indeed more than Scripture affords them, but always in the role prescribed by men, and in a manner that enhances the male activity".[168] She also goes on to show that Philo treats the wives of the patriarchs as models of submission.[169] Of Sarah and Rebecca she writes: "Philo takes advantage of their popular images to mold them into the likeness of his ideal wife, obedient and deferential to her husband".[170]

The appropriateness of women allowing themselves to be controlled, is an understanding reinforced by the biblical injunction in Gen 3:16, but for Philo, grounded in their being, their creation, and so to serve the interests of men.[171] His social context refines that further in terms of not only bearing children for the household but managing it and not stepping outside those roles into areas where men, with their superior physical and mental strength, are more appropriately active. Such is the basis of the harmony between man and woman which he espouses, perhaps even to appeal to the society of his day,[172] but it is not equality.[173] According to Sly, in relation to the place of women, "Philo believed

---

according to Philo "women, homosexuals and slaves either do not possess, or do not use, reason" (300).

[167] Sly, *Philo's Perception of Women*, 122; similarly 130.

[168] Sly, *Philo's Perception of Women*, 125.

[169] Sly, *Philo's Perception of Women*, 154-55.

[170] Sly, *Philo's Perception of Women*, 160. "The point of contact between the matriarchs of Scripture and the 'good' women whom we studied earlier is the description *asteia te kai astē*. Such a one is a real person, a woman, yet one who had earned Philo's admiration, like the virgin. She takes the place in society that is prescribed for her, and exercises freedom within its constraints. the purpose of her action and her existence is to contribute to the well-being of man. When the matriarchs of Scripture are presented as women, they are made to fit this description" (178).

[171] So Sly, *Philo's Perception of Women*, who writes: "Those persons who are present as women fall into groups, depending upon whether they are useful or dangerous to good men." (180).

[172] So Sly, *Philo's Perception of Women*, who writes: "I suspect that Philo's lip-service to women in the *Exposition* is indicative of a desire to portray Judaism as relevant to the age" (189).

[173] So Sly, *Philo's Perception of Women*, who notes for instance that in Philo's "idyllic picture of the male and female working in harmony as they are intended" the two choirs, led

that the hope for present society was to return to the standards of a better age derived from his reading and enhanced by his imagination. This was the Golden Age of Greece combined with the period of the patriarchs".[174]

The male gendered superior values of greater wisdom and ability to manage reach far beyond Philo's understanding of humanity.[175] They inform his understanding of God, who has to be portrayed as male in that sense.[176] As noted above, Philo's reading of Gen 1:27 as indicating that that man was neither male nor female appears designed not to say something about an asexuality in God, but to indicate that the genus embodied both, but was necessarily neither, since only in making individual human beings would that potential be realised.[177] While God is not male or female in that sense, Philo clearly attributes masculine traits to God, because masculine values are by nature superior. The superiority of such values finds its way down the ladder of being, where at every point the superior has to be masculine and inferior feminine.[178] As Mattila observes, "unlike his approach to some of his other philosophical assumptions, Philo never seems to feel the slightest need to defend his gender hierarchy. ... this gradient was probably

---

by Moses and Miriam, there is no question of equality of rank, since Moses appoints Miriam (122).

[174] Sly, *Philo's Perception of Women*, 222.

[175] So Sly, *Philo's Perception of Women*, who writes: "Philo presupposes that there is a natural difference between the sexes, and that this difference should and does permeate all aspects of being" (179).

[176] Baer, *Male and Female*, speaks of this as different from the male-female polarity of the sense-perceptible realm, so that here "male refers to that realm which is intrinsically asexual, i.e. the sphere of nous, the Logos, and ultimately God himself. It is in accord with the second usage that Philo is able to describe God as male in Fug 51" (49; similarly 65). As Mattila, "Wisdom, Sense Perception, Nature," rightly notes, Baer "does not name this pattern as the gender polarity that it is – a 'male'–'female' polarity pervading Philo's writings that functions very much on a cosmic scale" (105). "What results appears to be a logical incongruity. That which is asexual, Philo perceives as 'male' – a concept which by definition should have at least some relation to a sexual category. As has long been recognized in feminist criticism, however, sex and gender are not necessarily logically connected" (105). "Given that the gradient is hierarchical, and τὸ ὄν is envisaged as being higher than the gradient's 'male' pinnacle, the transcendent God may even be said to be more 'male' than 'male', or 'ultramale'" (126).

[177] Cf. Conway, "Gender and Divine Relativity," who argues that "For Philo, the phrase means something closer to 'not divided into male and female, but united as completely masculine'" (490).

[178] On the chain of being see Sly, *Philo's Perception of Women*, who notes that there even pleasure has a place (105-106), but especially Mattila, "Wisdom, Sense Perception, Nature," (106).

infused so deeply into the popular philosophy of his environment that it would have been equivalent to what we today would accept as 'scientific fact'."[179]

This creates some slight anomalies which Philo takes in his stride. It means, for instance, that Wisdom, Sophia, a female image, must be seen as male when impregnating the mind of human beings (who are inferior), and that mind must in turn be female.[180] Further down the scale it means that men can make their inner feminine irrational male, when they bring it under control, thus in that sense leaving the feminine behind, and, more dramatically, women can also be deemed male by doing the same.[181] Here Philo sometimes employs, instead, the distinction between woman and virgin, setting virgin and post-menopausal women at a higher level than other women.[182] Sly sees here a differentiation which implies abhorrence of such womanhood,[183] but this does not appear to be the case. As she, herself, acknowledges, some of Philo's very good women are wives who bear offspring and are nowhere despised for that. When she writes, "By turning Biblical women into virgins, Philo shows two apparently contradictory tendencies. He enhances the status of these woman by elevating them to virginity, but he negates their personal individuality by having them absorbed by their husbands",[184] this assumes a matching value at the literal level. Yet it is too strong to describe Philo as negating personal individuality at the literal level. Certainly, however, "when Philo treats of them on the human level, he downplays their initiative and moulds them into submissive helpmates".[185] The problem with matching allegorical and literal is well illustrated by her own concession when she writes that making these women virgins "enables him ... to present the great heroes of Israel's past as sexually restrained, since their wives are, allegorically at least, virgins".[186] The slight mismatch is appropriate: "restrained"? Yes, but not celibate. As she

---

[179] Mattila, "Wisdom, Sense Perception, Nature," 112.

[180] On Philo's sensitivity to the daringness of this image, which he accordingly designates a "mystery", see the discussion in Sly, *Philo's Perception of Women*, 133-37, and the discussion in 1.4.6 below. See also Mattila, "Wisdom, Sense Perception, Nature," 109.

[181] Baer, *Male and Female*, comments: "In view of Philo's strongly disparaging attitude towards woman and the female as well as his glorification of the male, but more particularly in the light of his identification of the female with sense-perception and the material world, and the male with the rational soul, it is not surprising to find that progress in the moral and religious life involves forsaking the realm of the female. Although Philo does not himself use the exact expression, this process might well be described by the phrase 'becoming male'" (45).

[182] Sly, *Philo's Perception of Women*, 71-72.

[183] Sly, *Philo's Perception of Women*, 72, 77-78, 81, 145.

[184] Sly, *Philo's Perception of Women*, 131; similarly 145.

[185] Sly, *Philo's Perception of Women*, 146; similarly 154.

[186] Sly, *Philo's Perception of Women*, 132.

acknowledges in relation to the patriarchs' allegedly not knowing their wives: "It appears to be primarily for allegorical purposes that Philo attaches importance to the fact that Scripture does not explicitly say that the patriarchs 'knew' their wives"[187] and goes on to show that Philo believes they obviously did.[188] Sly's problematic merging of both levels is evident in her comment: "In these marriages the wives remain virgins, and therefore, according to Philo's understanding of the word, not women at all. For a woman is one who has been defiled and corrupted by a man, but God's consorts suffer no such pollution".[189] Would Philo really consider Sarah as defiled by Abraham? Similarly mismatching she writes: "they are rendered by Philo as perpetual virgins, thus representing an impossible dream for Jewish women, destined by biology and custom to a life of 'defilement' and 'corruption'".[190]

As Runia observes, "Philo's true attitude to women was one of ambivalence – perhaps even cognitive dissonance – rather than the misogyny that seems to inform most of his theoretical statements about the female".[191] The comment on virgins does however reflect a widespread social view which places a higher value on virgins, including in a literal monetary sense. In this usage "virgin" and "male" become almost interchangeable ways of describing a woman's status as having brought sense-perception to heel.[192] Paradoxically a man who does the same may be described as "male" and making his female irrational male, but, where the focus is on his relationship to God or Wisdom, who have called him to such control, he is designated a "virgin", impregnated by divine seed which produces virtuous offspring.[193]

---

[187] Sly, *Philo's Perception of Women*, 138.

[188] Sly, *Philo's Perception of Women*, 139-40.

[189] Sly, *Philo's Perception of Women*, 145.

[190] Sly, *Philo's Perception of Women*, 145.

[191] Runia, *Creation*, 360. Petra von Gemünden and Pierre Magne de la Croix, "La femme passionnelle et l'homme rationnel? Un chapitre de psychologie historique," *Bib* 78 (1997) 457-80, note that sometimes Philo can speak negatively of the feminine but positively of women, such as of the matriarchs (470-71), sometimes the reverse (472-73).

[192] On this see Baer, *Male and Female*, 51. Similarly on *Cher.* 50 Sly, *Philo's Perception of Women*, remarks: "A close examination of Philo's wording in this passage shows that although the virgin is functionally female (as the partner of God), she is qualitatively equivalent to male. She can be unmanned—turned into a woman" (137-38). Mattila, "Wisdom, Sense Perception, Nature," goes beyond this to claim: "Both Baer and Dorothy Sly have interpreted 'virgin' and 'male' to be soteriologically equivalent in Philo. In essence, however, their identity runs deeper; the 'virgin' is, in fact, far more 'male' than 'female'" (106). This makes sense in the light of the overall gender hierarchy to which she draws attention.

[193] So Baer, *Male and Female*, 54-55.

In all such distinctions it is important to weigh carefully Philo's rhetorical tone. Where his focus is on the danger from unruly passions, he can designate the irrational which mediates them in the harshest terms, so that one could easily conclude that he advocates the complete annihilation of the source as evil – which might include any passion, but especially sexual desire, all pleasure, including sexual pleasure, one's own irrational soul and also women.[194] Fortunately on a number of occasions Philo supplements his absolutes with relativising comment in ways that allow us to see that he is not constantly making extreme and contradictory statements, but that they must be read in the context of his thought system as a whole.[195] As Winston notes, we meet similar issues of absolute rhetoric and relative meaning in both the Stoic and Platonic statements about the body.[196]

Sexual intercourse plays a major role in Philo's depictions of what are appropriate relations between figures on the gender gradient, generating a host of confusing images, which each have their logic when understood within Philo's system of thought. We discuss these separately below (1.2.4.5). Male, female, and sexual union, are fundamental to his thought and clearly highly valued by him when in right alignment serving the right purpose. Each has its place. For woman, that is the highly valued role of serving the interests of a husband in complete submission, bearing children for the household, and following his lead.

In what follows we turn to another of the foundational elements in Philo's thought which arises from his exposition of the creation of woman, namely, sexual intercourse, in particular, sexual pleasure and sexual passion. In the context of discussing the snake we then consider its dangers as part of the threat and the constant conflict which the passions pose for the mind, conveyed through the senses, and what Philo understands as appropriate response.

---

[194] Gaca, *Making of Fornication*, reflects this misreading when she claims that for Philo "the sexual and other physical appetites are inherently bad because their inborn proclivity to be unrestrained is also a proclivity to transgress God's will as written in the Pentateuch" (198). This flies in the face of *Opif.* 151, for instance. It is then a distortion when she writes that "Philo's Tenth Commandment is innovative as a Decalogue rule because it valorizes sexual desire as the main source of all wickedness" (198), that "sexual desire is inherently wicked and its primary yearning is to break away from the regulatory confines of the Pentateuch" (199), and writes of it as "the inborn appetite to defy the Lord ... inherently culpable" (200), though the sexual application of the tenth commandment as illicit sexual desire is not to be denied.

[195] Similarly Sly, *Philo's Perception of Women*, 184, 220; Winston, "Philo and the Rabbis," 206.

[196] Winston, "Philo and the Rabbis," 208-11. See further on this in section 1.3.3 below.

1.2.2.6 Sex

1.2.2.6.1 Pleasure in Procreation

We noted above how in *Opif.* Philo introduces the creation of woman negatively at first: "woman becomes for him the beginning of blameworthy life" (*Opif.* 151), but in what follows highlights also the positive in his retelling of Gen 2:23: "beholding a figure like his own and a kindred form, he was gladdened by the sight, and approached and greeted her. She, seeing no living thing more like herself than he, is filled with glee and shamefastly returns his greeting" (*Opif.* 151-152). He continues: "Love supervenes, brings together and fits into one the divided halves, as it were, of a single living creature, and sets up in each of them a desire for fellowship [intercourse] with the other with a view to the production of their like" (*Opif.* 152). This is unmistakably positive in affirming sexual passion ("love", "desire for intercourse with the other") and pleasure ("glee"), in the context of sexual intercourse for the purpose of procreation. Thus, further on, he extrapolates on pleasure, including sexual pleasure, as something positive for human beings:

> And certainly the first approaches of the male to the female have pleasure (ἡδονήν) to guide and conduct them, and it is through pleasure that begetting and the coming of life is brought about (αἵ τε σποραὶ καὶ γενέσεις διὰ ταύτης συνίστανται), and the offspring is naturally at home with nothing sooner than pleasure (τά τε γεννώμενα οὐδενὶ πρῶτον οἰκειοῦσθαι πέφυκεν ἢ ταύτῃ), delighting in it and feeling distress at pain its contrary. (*Opif.* 161)

Philo brings this comment in the context of explaining that the speaking snake is an allegory of the "ten thousand champions and defenders" of pleasure, who "dare to spread the doctrine that she has assumed universal sovereignty over small and great, and that no one whatever is exempt therefrom" (*Opif.* 160), an allusion to Epicurean philosophy as understood by its critics, but there is no need on these grounds to dismiss all that is said here (see the discussion in 1.2.3.1.1 below).

While pleasure can very quickly cease to be ethically neutral, as he tells us endlessly, it remains his basic assumption that pleasure has an important role to play, especially "in a marriage where the union is brought about by pleasure (γάμος δέ, ὃν μὲν ἁρμόζεται ἡδονή)" (*Abr.* 100). In this he may well reflect the view that heightened pleasure enhances conception.[197] Indirectly we see an affirmation of pleasure in sexual intercourse also in his explanation of

---

[197] On this see William Loader, *The Dead Sea Scrolls on Sexuality: Attitudes towards Sexuality in Sectarian and Related Literature at Qumran* (Grand Rapids: Eerdmans, 2009), esp. in relation to 1QapGen ar/1Q20 2.9-10, 14-16 (290).

circumcision, which notes that "among the love-lures of pleasure the palm is held by the mating of man and woman (τὰ νικητήρια φέρεται τῶν ἐν ἡδοναῖς φίλτρων ἡ ἀνδρὸς πρὸς γυναῖκα συνουσία)" and that circumcision is "the figure of the excision of excessive and superfluous pleasure (περιττῆς ἐκτομὴν καὶ πλεοναζούσης ἡδονῆς), not only of one pleasure, but of all the other pleasures signified by one, and that the most imperious (δία μιᾶς τῆς βιασκιτωτάτης καὶ τῶν ἄλλων ἀπασῶν)" (*Spec.* 1.9). The issue is not pleasure, but its excess. The same is true of the remarkable statement in *Spec.* 3.9, warning about sex with one's own wife, when "natural pleasure", clearly affirmed, becomes excess. As Niehoff notes in discussing *Spec.* 3.8-9, "Philo acknowledges the satisfaction of hunger and sexual desire as 'a pleasure in accordance with nature'" and "consequently suggests that pleasure becomes a moral issue when excess is involved".[198] As Ellis observes, Philo's expositions of law on defiling a virgin in *Spec.* 3.65-70 and on false accusations about a wife's virginity in 79-81 assume a positive place for fulfilment of sexual desire in appropriate contexts.[199] The latter accuses the wrongdoers that they "retain no conjugal affection for their wives" (οἰκεῖον ἐπὶ ταῖς γαμεταῖς πάθος) (*Spec.* 3.80). "The proper passion of which Philo speaks apparently consists at least partly of sexual desire. Here, then, Philo speaks approvingly of a man's sexual desire for his wife".[200] Similarly in *Virt.* 112 in discussing captive women Philo speaks approvingly of marriage for love: "After this, live with her as your lawful wife, because holiness requires that she who is to enter a husband's bed, not as a hired harlot, trafficking her youthful bloom, but either for love of her mate or for the birth of children, should be admitted to the rights of full wedlock as her due". Ellis suggests that this is "an apparent departure from his procreationist stance".[201] More likely Philo sees the two as necessarily linked.

Philo's positive stance towards sexual intercourse for procreation, including with pleasure may be reflected in his statement of preference in *Decal.* 110, where he describes three kinds of people: those who live by the passions, those who love only God and do not relate to the body, and those who do both but keep balance

---

[198] So also Niehoff, *Philo on Jewish Identity*, 95. Commenting on the impact of adultery according to Philo she writes: "The excess of pleasure is thus judged from a distinctly social perspective. In this context Philo does not dwell on the inherent wickedness of pleasure. He is rather concerned with its right measure which will ensure order and harmony in the individual person as well as in society at large" (96).

[199] J. Edward Ellis, *Paul and Ancient Views of Sexual Desire: Paul's Sexual Ethics in 1 Thessalonians 4, 1 Corinthians 7 and Romans 1* (LNTS 354; London: T&T Clark, 2007) 90.

[200] Ellis, *Sexual Desire*, 91.

[201] So Ellis, *Sexual Desire*, writes: "Here Philo, in an apparent departure from his procreationist stance, speaks of love as a legitimate motivation for sexual intercourse" (91).

and control. Philo prefers the latter. This might indicate a level of disapproval of those in the second category who might on those grounds promote celibacy. We return to this issue in discussing celibacy and asceticism below (1.2.3.5).

In *QG* Philo similarly begins by flagging the negative: "Generation, as the arguments of philosophers go, is the beginning of corruption" (*QG* 1.10), but generation, and the sexual desire to generate, is not in itself corruption. Thus he treats Gen 2:23 positively: the man has "a lovely vision ... this most shapely and very charming creature!" (*QG* 1.28), going on to link her designation as γυνή to her reproductive role: "The woman is called the power of giving birth with fecundity" (*QG* 1.28). Thus he continues: "But when Scripture says that the two are one flesh, it indicates something very tangible and sense-perceptible, in which there is suffering and sensual pleasure, that they may rejoice in, and be pained by, and feel the same things, and much more, may think the same things" (*QG* 1.29). These positive details are subsumed beneath his primary agenda of speaking of the mind's relation to the senses, but they are not to be denied. In *QG*, interpreting the fig leaves, he refers to "the genitals" positively as "instruments of greater things" (*QG* 1.41).

In *QG* 3 Philo makes similar comments about circumcision to those noted above in *Spec.* 1.9, commenting that "the greatest desire is that of intercourse between man and woman, since it forms the beginning of a great thing, procreation, and brings about in the progenitors a great desire toward their progeny" and circumcision "indicates the cutting off not only of excessive desires but also of arrogance and great evil and such habits" (*QG* 3.48). Again pleasure in sexual intercourse for procreation is thus affirmed, only its excess censured. Similarly in *QG* 4 Philo writes: "It is necessary to receive enjoyment of love and affection from a wife and to fulfil the law concerning the rearing of children" (*QG* 4.154). As the context suggests, that includes the pleasure of sexual intercourse.

Speaking of the ark as representing the body he writes: "since the ark is symbolically the body, the covering of the body must be thought of as whatever protects and preserves it and closely guards its power, (namely) pleasure. For by pleasure it is truly preserved and sustained in measure and in accordance with nature, just as it is disintegrated by pain" (*QG* 2.46). This will include the pleasure of food, but probably also include the role of sexual pleasure in procreation. He goes on to interpret "going in", entering the ark, as "the non-begetting of seed" and "going out" as "generation" (*QG* 2.49). Accordingly he writes: "When they went out, it was as married couples, the father together with his wife, and then the several sons, each with his wife" and that "those who went in should abstain from intercourse with their wives, and that when they went out, they should sow seed in accordance with nature" (*QG* 2.49). His rationale for the distinction is that "it would have been inept for them now, while the living were perishing, to beget those who were not (yet) in existence and to be snared and surfeited at an unseasonable hour with sensual pleasure". Philo sees no place for sexual pleasure apart from procreational sex. "To go to bed with your wives is the part of those seeking and desiring sexual satisfaction" (*QG* 2.49). Then he continues: "But after (the flood) had ceased and come to an end and they had been saved from the evil, He again instructed them through the order (of their leaving the ark) to hasten to procreate, by specifying not that men (should go out) with men nor women with women but females with males" (*QG* 2.49). In this we see Philo's characteristic stance: sexual intercourse for pleasure without prospect of progeny, even with one's own wife, and also same-sex relations, men with men or women with women, are wrong and contrary to nature; sexual intercourse for procreation between husbands and wives and with pleasure is affirmed. In an incidental way in *QE* 2 Philo affirms sexual love: "For just as a lover puts aside all other things and hastens to his desire, so also does one who hungers and thirsts for knowledge ..." (*QE* 2.13).

In the *Allegorical Commentary* Philo employs the image of women as "helpers" to depict the proper role of the senses and passions (*Leg.* 2.5) and despite his negative slant on Gen 2:24, can use it positively of Levi, as noted above. The positive stance is also surprisingly present in his initial depiction of the snake in *Leg.*, which we shall be considering when discussing pleasure as danger. Thus he explains: "Two things, mind and bodily sense, having already come into being, and these being in nakedness after the manner that has been set forth, it was necessary that there should be a third subsistence, namely pleasure (ἡδονήν), to bring both together to the apprehension of the objects of mental and of bodily perception" (*Leg.* 2.71). In itself this explanation does not bedevil pleasure, as one might have expected, but explains it is a necessary component of human existence. "Who was it that brought them together save a third, a bond of love and desire (δεσμὸς τρίτος ἔρωτος καὶ ἐπιθυμίας), under the rule and dominion of pleasure (ἀρχούσης καὶ δυναστευούσης ἡδονῆς), to which the prophet gave the figurative name of a serpent?" (*Leg.* 2.72). In fact pleasure is made by God: "first He made mind, the man, for mind is most venerable in a human being, then bodily sense, the woman, then after them in the third place pleasure (ἡδονήν)" (*Leg.* 2.73). This potentially neutral description continues in what follows where Philo explains the suitability of the gliding serpent to represent pleasure: "To begin with it takes its gliding course in five ways, for pleasures (ἡδοναί) are occasioned by sight and by hearing and by taste and by smell and by touch; but those connected with sexual intercourse prove themselves the most violent of all in their intensity (γίνονται δὲ αἱ σφοδρόταται καὶ σύντονοι αἱ περὶ τὰς γυναῖκας ὁμιλίαι), and this is the method ordained by Nature for the reproduction of the type" (*Leg.* 2.74). Neither sexual intercourse nor its pleasure is being condemned here; on the contrary they belong to what is "ordained by Nature" and so follows divine will. It is important then not to read into Philo the equation of the serpent with the devil or Satan.

The positive beginning and possibility of sense and passion, including, therefore, sexual passion and pleasure, regularly come to expression elsewhere in the *Allegorical Commentary*, despite being outnumbered by the warnings of danger. As Philo affirms a place for women, so he affirms the role of the senses. Thus in *Cher.* he speaks of "half the perfect soul" needing "the sense-perceiving organs" as a mate (*Cher.* 59), "weaving into the part first made the other section" (*Cher.* 60). Writing of God's rule in *Cher.* Philo explains: "combining all things He claimed the sovereignty of all for Himself; to His subjects he assigned the use and enjoyment of themselves and each other" (ἀπόλαυσιν ἔνειμε τοῖς ὑπηκόοις ἑαυτῶν τε καὶ ἀλλήλων) (*Cher.* 113). The latter, "enjoyment of themselves and each other", is an important affirmation of appropriate pleasure and Philo may well include sexual intercourse for procreation in such enjoyment. His exposition of the law exempting the newly married man from war (Deut 20:5-7) affirms the latter's desire for sexual intercourse, though Philo is more concerned with allegory (*Agr.* 148, 153; cf. also *Virt.* 28-31). Similarly Philo notes that Abimelech sees Isaac and Rebecca enjoying "merriment" together (*Plant.* 169; Gen 26:8). This may remain at the symbolic level but could also affirm their play, most likely understood as sexual. In *Migr.* he writes of the travels of traders, including their leaving behind what Philo positively describes as "the pleasure too great for words which we take in wife and children and in all else that is our own" (*Migr.* 217).

Despite his many warnings about the dangers of pleasure, not least sexual pleasure and passion for it, the evidence is substantial that Philo views sexual pleasure and desire in the right context positively.[202] That context is very carefully defined and repeatedly emphasised.

---

[202] So, for instance, Graziano Ranocchia, "Moses against the Egyptian: The Anti-Epicurean Polemic in Philo," in *Philo of Alexandria and Post-Aristotelian Philosophy* (ed. Francesca Alesse; SPA 5; Leiden: Brill, 2008) 75-102, who writes: "Even legitimate or natural pleasures (ἡ κατὰ φύσιν), like those of the table or conjugal love, are blameworthy when (but only when) they are sought intemperately, because 'it is through pleasure (δι' ἡδονήν) that we commit evil'" (93). He rejects the view of Booth "that Philo makes no distinction between this kind of pleasure and the impure pleasure of pederasts and prostitutes. The mere fact that he recognises the existence of natural pleasures that are legitimate if enjoyed with moderation, is sufficient to refute it" (93). Cf. Booth, "Voice of the Serpent," 165. He goes on, however, to claim that for Philo "Even carnal pleasure, conceived as a necessary physiological means for the reproduction of mankind (which is self-evident), is no more than a necessary evil, a bitter and inevitable fruit of amorous desire" (94). I believe this generalises beyond the evidence. On Philo's distinctive contribution of portraying pleasure as an entity in itself and using it to explain the presence

1.2.2.6.2 Sex only for Procreation

Before we consider the dangers of pleasure, which in Philo far outnumber mention of its positive role, we first note Philo's emphasis on procreation as the sole ground for sexual intercourse and so as alone justifying desire for it and pleasure in it. A number of texts already alluded to above underline it, such as *Opif.* 152 which speaks of "a desire for fellowship [intercourse] with the other with a view to the production of their like (πόθον ἐνιδρυσάμενος ἑκατέρῳ τῆς πρὸς θάτερον κοινωνίας εἰς τὴν τοῦ ὁμοίου γένεσιν). Similarly in offering Hagar to Abraham, Sarah comments: "the purpose for which we ourselves came together and for which nature formed the union of man and wife, the birth of children, has not been fulfilled" (οὗ δὲ χάριν καὶ αὐτοὶ συνεληλύθαμεν καὶ ἡ φύσις τὴν ἀνδρὸς καὶ γυναικὸς ἡρμόσατο κοινωνίαν, τέκνων γένεσις οὐκ ἔστιν) (*Abr.* 248). Accordingly, Philo has her declare that she "shall have no jealousy of another woman, whom you will take not for unreasoning lust (δι' ἐπιθυμίαν ἄλογον) but in fulfilment of nature's inevitable law. And therefore I shall not be backward to lead to you a bride who will supply what is lacking in myself" (*Abr.* 249-250), in Philo's view, for functional intercourse not for pleasure. Thus, Philo reports, Abraham "took the mate whom she had approved and kept her till she had borne a child, or, as the surest version of the story runs, only till she became pregnant, and when this occurred not long after he abstained from her through his natural continence and the honour which he paid to his lawful spouse" (*Abr.* 253). This may imply he advocates sexual abstinence generally during pregnancy, but more likely relates only to Hagar because of her status.

Directly addressing the passions, Philo declares in *Mos.* 1 "For on his belly he bestowed no more than the necessary tributes which nature has appointed, and as for the pleasures that have their seat below (τῶν τε ὑπογαστρίων ἡδονῶν), save for the lawful begetting of children, they passed altogether even out of his memory" (*Mos.* 1.28). In *Spec.* 1 he explains that marriage laws "are intended to promote the generation of children" (*Spec.* 1.112) and in *Spec.* 3 charges those involved with infanticide of therefore engaging in intercourse just for "love of pleasure": "For they are pleasure-lovers when they mate with their wives, not to procreate children and perpetuate the race, but like pigs and goats in quest of the enjoyment which such intercourse gives" (*Spec.* 3.113). In *Virt.* he writes that Abraham "the father of many children, begotten of three wives, not for indulgence in pleasure but in the hope of multiplying the race" (*Virt.* 207). Similarly in *Praem.*, speaking of future suffering he writes of people seeing "the women whom

---

of evil, see Boulluec, "Plaisir," 135, and on Philo's positive appreciation of sexual pleasure, pp. 143-45.

they took in lawful wedlock for the procreation of true-born children, chaste domestic loving wives" (*Praem.* 139).

We noted above that in discussing the image of going in and out of the ark Philo expresses disapproval of intercourse with one's wife if not for procreation (*QG* 2.49). He comments similarly in discussing Abraham's requiring Isaac to place his hand under his thigh (Gen 24:2): "Being about to bind him by an oath concerning the betrothal, he bids him place his hand close to the place of generation, including a pure association and an unpolluted marriage, not having sensual pleasure as its end but the procreation of legitimate children" (*QG* 4.86), again emphasising sex not without pleasure, but only for procreation. He then reports of Isaac's marriage: "For at this time it was not for the sake of irrational sensual pleasure or with eagerness that he had intercourse with his wife but for the sake of begetting legitimate children, (and so) it was wholly appropriate that he should undertake marriage when the number of his years was the same as the number of days of the embryo in the womb" (*QG* 4.154).

In the *Allegorical Commentary* he writes that man and woman "in the course of nature come together to hold intercourse for the procreation of children" (*Cher.* 43). In *Her.* he notes that men and women are "quite equal as regards what was nature's urgent purpose, the reproduction of themselves in a third person" (*Her.* 164). In *Congr.* Philo protects his daring image of the mind's intercourse by explaining: "In the present discussion, we must eliminate all bodily unions or intercourse which has pleasure as its object. What is meant is a mating of mind with virtue. Mind desires to have children by virtue, and, if it cannot do so at once, is instructed to espouse virtue's handmaid, the lower instruction" (*Congr.* 12). Citing only intercourse which has pleasure as its object seems a little strange when he appears to mean all literal intercourse, but it may be that he simply assumes that sexual intercourse and pleasure properly (and usually) belong together. Philo would doubtless assent to his nephew's words upholding animals as models: "The females succumb to mounting only for the purpose of impregnation; then they run away from the males, fulfilling the law of nature which has found out the corruption that results from the male joining the female in sexual indulgence" (*Anim.* 48).[203]

As Ellis observes, "procreationism does not necessarily involve a negative view of sexual desire".[204] Not all marriages are to be reduced to the functionality of Abraham's marriage to Hagar, his marriage with Sarah a clear counter-instance. Nevertheless as many have noted, Philo lays heavy emphasis, as we have seen, on procreation. Gaca notes that "Philo accepts Plato's theory of the irrational physical

---

[203] For a similar assumption about superior restraint on the part of animals see Terian, "*De Animalibus*,"161, who cites Plutarch *Mor.* 988F-991D.

[204] Ellis, *Sexual Desire*, 88.

appetites as well as his position that the sexual appetite is the most domineering and recalcitrant of the lot".[205] She also makes the point that while Philo uses Stoic terminology, his concerns are informed by a Jewish Platonic perspective, where desire and sexual desire, in particular, flouts the tenth commandment and so defies God.[206] Perhaps a more differentiated perspective would identify not sexual desire in itself, but illicit sexual desire, wherever it is in excess and misdirected, including towards self-fulfilment and not procreation, as contravening the tenth commandment. She then observes that "though Philo draws upon the Stoics and Plato to articulate this notion of soul fornication, neither the Stoics nor Plato would recognize Philo's religious sexual ethic as their own, for Philo presupposes the Pentateuch and its didactic metaphor of spiritual fornication".[207] In contrast to their acknowledgment of Aphrodite, she observes, "for Philo ... Aphrodite as Pleasure is not a genuine goddess who merits reverence, as she was for the Greeks. She is the cosmic madam of religiously alienating sexual desire".[208] Referring then to Philo's insistence on sexual intercourse only for procreation, Gaca writes that "Philo belongs fully to the later Pythagorean tradition of Ocellus and Charondas, who likewise maintain that sexual relations can only be rightly for procreation or reprehensibly for pleasure".[209] She notes that "Philo's thought shows other Pythagorean tendencies as well, such as his conviction that overeating or eating the wrong foods makes one oversexed", though, as she points out, for Philo the additional factor is the divine command.[210]

In discussing Philo's approach to laws she argues that Philo "does not grant that sexual activity constitutes rebellion against God simply by occurring for pleasure rather than for reproduction. He distinguishes two degrees of sexual wickedness".[211] These are "defying God through formally rebellious sexual activity, such as adultery, male homoerotic relations, and reconciled marriages of

---

[205] Gaca, *Making of Fornication*, 195. "Contrary to reason, they are insatiable in their primary desires for too much sexual pleasure, food, and drink" (195).

[206] Gaca, *Making of Fornication*, 200-201. In discussing laws she then notes that Philo "distinguishes two degrees of sexual wickedness" in relation to sexual intercourse rather than procreation (214). "Sexual activity for pleasure rather than for procreation is apostasy only in circumstances where the Pentateuch outlaws it on a literal level or stigmatizes it as an abomination" (215).

[207] Gaca, *Making of Fornication*, 202.

[208] Gaca, *Making of Fornication*, 203.

[209] Gaca, *Making of Fornication*, 205. Winston, "Philo and the Rabbis," notes that among the Stoics Musonius "appears to be the only one who explicitly prohibits nonprocreative intercourse even within marriage (κἂν ἐν γάμῳ ᾖ)" (217). See also Runia, *Creation*, 358.

[210] Gaca, *Making of Fornication*, 206.

[211] Gaca, *Making of Fornication*, 214.

the sort Philo abhors."[212] Noting the difference between these laws which require the death penalty and those that do not, she speaks of an "incomplete assimilation of Pythagorean procreationism" and observes that "sexual activity for pleasure rather than for procreation is apostasy only in circumstances where the Pentateuch outlaws it on a literal level or stigmatizes it as an abomination".[213] Otherwise "if husbands make love with their wives for non-reproductive pleasure, he recommends the regimen of Moses' dietary laws, not death, for this class of sexual offenders" (citing *Spec.* 3.9; 4.96-97).[214]

In commenting on Gaca's reference to Pythagorean influence Niehoff points out that Pythagorean sources "prohibited any sexual act not specifically aimed at procreation and enjoined men to direct their thoughts during orgasm to that overall aim. Philo, however, does not seem to have embraced such extreme ideals".[215] She notes that "unlike the Pythagoreans and later Babylonian rabbis, Philo was not concerned with the life-containing potency of the sperm itself. He rather objected to sexual relations that were devoid of any procreational context and thus served only to satisfy physical pleasures".[216] Thus on sex during menstruation, where Philo was "translating distinctly ritual notions into general ideals of sexual morality ... he obviously opposed sex wherever there was no chance of conception". "This may," she adds, "say little about a couple's conduct during the remaining periods",[217] and concludes:

> It is highly significant that he, unlike the more Pythagorean Musonius, makes no general statement about the 'unjust and unlawful' nature of any sexual act which is not specifically directed to procreation. It would thus appear that the married couple was left in peace by Philo during all the days of the month that the woman was not directly bleeding.[218]

---

[212] Gaca, *Making of Fornication*, 214-15.

[213] Gaca, *Making of Fornication*, 215. On those not requiring the death penalty she points to the laws about rape of an unbetrothed virgin or a widow or divorcee (*Spec.* 3.64, 65-71) (212-13).

[214] Gaca, *Making of Fornication*, 215.

[215] Niehoff, *Philo on Jewish Identity*, 100.

[216] Niehoff, *Philo on Jewish Identity*, 100. Similarly Holger Szesnat, "'Pretty Boys' in Philo's De Vita Contemplativa," *SPA* 10 (1998) 87-107, who writes: "In cases of *sexual pleasure* ... Philo is so negative that he seems to be calling for a complete eradication of such pleasure (eg. *Leg.* 3.68; *Spec.* 1.8). It is only the duty of procreation that makes it necessary to control such sexual pleasure, as opposed to eradicating it completely (eg. *Mos* 1.28-29)" (93).

[217] Niehoff, *Philo on Jewish Identity*, 100.

[218] Niehoff, *Philo on Jewish Identity*, 100-101.

> He thus insists on the general possibility of procreation as a criterion for legitimizing sex ... the procreative purpose, however, only sets the general framework for sexuality and does not govern every sexual act.[219]

Niehoff notes Philo's apparent willingness to accept continuing marriage (and by implication sexual intercourse) in cases where a marriage turns out to be infertile and does not require its dissolution.[220]

> Consistent with these views, Philo never expresses concern for the individual sexual act as such. Unlike the Pythagoreans, he neither prescribes how it should be performed nor does he tell the male what to think while copulating. He did not embrace the Pythagorean belief that 'wretched offspring' comes from intercourse 'that fails to be temperate and purposeful'. [citing Iambl *Vit Pyth* 211] On the contrary, Philo even admits that it is through pleasure that 'begetting and the coming of life is brought about' (Opif. 161). Sexual pleasure was thus acknowledged as long as it was not divorced from the overall purpose of procreation.[221]

Accordingly, we see in Philo a combination of aspects which determine his approach to sexual intercourse, including its pleasure and desire for it. It is clear that he sees its purpose as procreation and its place in marriage and condemns desire for the pleasure of sexual intercourse for any other purpose. While one may treat his tolerance of marriages continuing which happen to be or have become infertile as an aberration, it is more likely that it reflects an affirmation of love and affection in marriage, to which he often alludes and which in this case he does not want to deny. Niehoff may well be right, however, that we should not envisage that Philo would have insisted that couples monitor the days of the woman's fertility and abstain from sex otherwise. To some degree this is an issue seen quite differently in our own age of effective contraception and proper understanding of the fertility cycle. Philo will have applied his insistence on procreation within a framework of a much less informed understanding, probably on the basis that he saw marital love expressed in sexual intimacy and commitment to the goals of procreation as in harmony except where (as he assumes) men become sex-crazed and have no other interest than to find sexual pleasure.

Philo's positive attitude towards sexual passion and pleasure in the context of procreation in marriage also finds indirect confirmation in his many exhortations which call for control and moderation of the passions, to which we turn below, rather than their banishment. But first we return to the Genesis text where the snake also symbolises what is negative about the passions.

---

[219] Niehoff, *Philo on Jewish Identity*, 101.

[220] Niehoff, *Philo on Jewish Identity*, 101.

[221] Niehoff, *Philo on Jewish Identity*, 101-102. She also notes that Philo nowhere commends long periods of abstinence like the Pythagoreans (102).

1.2.3 The Danger of Pleasure (Gen 2:25 [3:1] – 3:6)

1.2.3.1 The Snake of Pleasure

1.2.3.1.1 The Snake of Pleasure in "On Creation"

While in *Opif.* Philo identifies woman as "the beginning of a blameworthy life" (*Opif.* 151) and initially expounds this in the context of their delight in sexual intercourse and the inordinate lusting for that pleasure which ensued, the Genesis account portrays the first human failure as taking place in the encounter with the snake in the choice to eat forbidden fruit. Philo also embraces this account, first noting that the garden was itself a place of pleasure, its plants "endowed with soul or reason, bearing the virtues for fruit, and beside these insight and discernment" (*Opif.* 153). As noted above, he treats it symbolically. "Moses evidently signifies by the pleasuance the ruling power of the soul which is full of countless opinions, as it might be of plants; and by the tree of life he signifies reverence toward God, the greatest of the virtues, by means of which the soul attains to immortality, while by the tree that is cognisant of good and evil things he signifies moral prudence" (*Opif.* 154). Philo has apparently no difficulty with the implication of his allegory, which is that the man should certainly be eating from these fruits![222] His concern is to depict what the soul has lost because it was "inclining to wickedness, and making light of holiness and godly fear" and so was cast forth with "no hope of a subsequent return, inasmuch as the reason given for their deception was in a high degree blameworthy" (*Opif.* 155). He will conclude his account in similar terms: "Such is the life of those who at the outset are in enjoyment of innocence and simplicity of character, but later on prefer vice to virtue" (*Opif.* 170).

Now Philo turns to the cause: the snake, who challenged the woman for "hesitating to pluck a fruit most beauteous to behold and most luscious to taste, and most useful into the bargain, since by its means she would have power to recognize things good and evil" (*Opif.* 156). He continues: "It is said that she, without looking into the suggestion, prompted by a mind devoid of steadfastness and firm foundation, gave her consent and ate of the fruit, and gave some of it to her husband; this instantly brought them out of a state of simplicity and innocence (ἀκακίας καὶ ἁπλότητος) into one of wickedness" (*Opif.* 156). This brief account embodies Philo's analysis. As a woman she had "a mind devoid of

---

[222] See, however, the discussion in M. Harl, "Adam et les deux arbres du Paradis (Gen. II-III) ou l'homme milieu de la doctrine du libre-arbitre," *RecSR* 50 (1962) 321-88, who argues that, in effect, Philo sees the two trees as presenting the man with two options, with the tree of the knowledge of good and evil representing the way of human self-sufficiency and indulgence, hence the choice: "Dieu ou lui-même, le νοῦς universel ou le νους particulier" (380).

steadfastness and firm foundation". As Runia observes, the "simplicity and innocence" here is not the childlike innocence described in *Leg.* 2, "since the ideal is the state of the first human being as described in §§137-150, and that was hardly infantile. I think Philo means here genuine virtue and goodness, not naiveté".[223] Philo dismisses the suggestion that these are "mythical fictions, such as poets and sophists delight in" (*Opif.* 157).[224] They are, instead, "modes of making ideas visible, bidding us resort to allegorical interpretation guided in our renderings by what lies beneath the surface" (*Opif.* 157).

Accordingly, Philo's explanation begins in apparent dependence on existing interpretive tradition: "Following a probable conjecture one could say that the serpent spoken of is a fit symbol of pleasure" (*Opif.* 157).[225] First he has it represent "the lover of pleasure" (φιλήδονος) similarly "weighted and dragged downwards that it is with difficulty that he lifts up his head, thrown down and tripped up by intemperance", feeding not on heavenly but on earthly food: "drunkenness, daintiness, and greediness" (*Opif.* 158).[226] And worse, "these, causing the cravings of the belly to burst out and fanning them into flame, make the man a glutton, while they also stimulate and stir up the stings of his sexual lusts (τοὺς ὑπογαστρίους οἴστρους)" (*Opif.* 158). So the snake symbolises these pleasures, including sexual pleasure, which must be understood here as indicating sexual pleasure that is inappropriate and excessive in contrast to the sexual pleasure that belongs to engaging in the act for procreation.

Philo then uses the anomaly of the speaking snake as ground for developing an allegorical explanation in which he sees it symbolising the "ten thousand champions and defenders" of pleasure, who "dare to spread the doctrine that she has assumed universal sovereignty over small and great, and that no one whatever is exempt therefrom" (*Opif.* 160), an allusion to Epicurean philosophy as commonly portrayed by its critics.[227] This could then imply that Philo is being

---

[223] Runia, *Creation*, 370.

[224] On Philo's allusion to sophists see Bruce W. Winter, *Philo and Paul among the Sophists: Alexandrian and Corinthian Responses to a Julio-Claudian Movement* (2d ed.; Grand Rapids: Eerdmans, 2002), who argues that this is not anachronistic language nor a general reference to philosophers (66, 78-79), but "denotes *contemporary*, professional orators and sophists in Alexandria" (66), portrayed as morally corrupt virtuoso performers (79), who proclaim virtue but do not display it (84), but are out for personal gain (91).

[225] Runia, *Creation*, comments: "One keeps on getting the impression that he is dependent on an anterior exegetical tradition (also partly preserved in the Allegorical Commentary), which he does not feel he has to expound at any length" (363).

[226] Runia, *Creation*, notes the explanation in Plato *Timaeus* 92A2-7 of animals' orientation to the earth (377).

[227] So Booth, "Voice of the Serpent," 168. See also Ranocchia, "Moses against the Egyptian," who argues that there are indications that Philo may well have read also the works of Epicureans or at least doxographical collections and like many of his time

dismissive of everything that follows, including the statements about the role of pleasure in procreation and in the infant's experience (*Opif.* 161). To dismiss the former would conflict, however, with his comments in *Opif.* 151 and elsewhere about pleasure's positive role.[228] It is important therefore to differentiate between what Philo can affirm and what he would deny in Epicurean doctrine here. The emphasis is on the latter. One might suppose that Philo disputes neither the role of pleasure in procreation nor in the baby's *in utero* experience, but rather what follows, where he signals distance in the words, "they tell us" (φασί):[229] "And they tell us that every living creature hastens after pleasure as its most necessary and essential end (ὡς ἐπ' ἀναγκαιότατον καὶ συνεκτικτώτατον τέλος ἡδονήν), and man above all; for while other creatures seek pleasure only through taste and the organs of reproduction, man does so through the other senses as well, pursuing with ears and eyes all such sights and sounds as can afford delight" (*Opif.* 162). For Philo that need not follow and should not. Philo certainly does not advocate for humankind: "pleasure as its most necessary and essential end", but sees this as perversion, just as he would have rejected the claim that pleasure "has assumed universal sovereignty over small and great, and that no one whatever is exempt therefrom" (*Opif.* 160). This will apply, however, also to what precedes, namely any claim that pleasure in sexual intercourse and in a baby's natural affinity[230] to

---

recognizes that they were ones who had written most about pleasure (95-96, 100-101). He concludes: "Philo remains hopelessly distant from Epicurus, from every point of view" (101), while nevertheless using sometimes his technical terms, which had probably had become part of the common heritage of philosophical schools in discussing pleasure (101).

[228] Cf. Baer, *Male and Female*, who argues that "his reference to sexual intercourse in Op. Mund. 161 is notoriously abrupt, suggesting he had this theme in mind in the preceding paragraphs as well, and that it is mainly in reference to this motif that he interprets the Genesis account of the fall", pointing also to the expression, the "wages paid by pleasure" in 167 (38 n.1). See also Sly, *Philo's Perception of Women*, (109). This is probably correct about sexual pleasure, but incorrect where Baer assumes that pleasure in sexual intercourse in *Opif.* 151 represented a fall. On the other hand he writes: "In Op. Mund 160-63a Philo demonstrates that pleasure is integral to life itself, and in Leg. All. II:8 he speaks of the important role of the passions, particularly ἡδονή, ἐπιθυμία, λύπη, and φόβος, in contributing to the permanence of the race" (91).

[229] So Runia, *Creation*, 379.

[230] Runia, *Creation*, notes that "the use of the term οἰκειοῦσθαι will have revealed to Philo's learned reader that he is making use of the famous Epicurean doctrine of *oikeiôsis*, not to be confused with the Stoic argument which uses the same concept" (379). He adds: "This is the so-called 'cradle argument,' used to prove that 'pleasure' is the *telos*. It was hotly contested by the Stoa, who affirmed that the goal was ἀρετή" (379). For detailed discussion of use of the argument see J. Brunschwig, "The Cradle Argument in Epicureanism and Stoicism," in *The Norms of Nature: Studies in Hellenistic Ethics* (ed. M.

pleasure by implication warrants making pleasure a goal. It is probably wrong, therefore, to take Philo's statements here, both about sexual intercourse and about the senses generally, as more than dismissing them as grounds for espousing pleasure as a goal, as though he denies their value altogether and thus sees no positive value at all in bodily pleasure. What he disputes is making such pleasure a, or, worse, *the* goal in life. That is the snake's lure here. From that perspective we may deem it dismissive when he writes: "A very great deal more is said in praise of pleasure, and of the great closeness of its connection and kinship with living creatures" (*Opif.* 162), since such praise elevates pleasure inappropriately. The issue with both food and sex is excess and making it one's goal.

Having explained the voice of the snake as symbolising the advocates of making pleasure one's goal, Philo continues his theme of the problematic nature of pleasure. Here he cites the reference in Lev 11:22 to the "snake-fighter" (ὀφιομάχης), to expound the importance of self-control necessary in fighting what he calls "a truceless war against intemperance and pleasure (ἀκρασίαν καὶ ἡδονήν)" (*Opif.* 164).[231] The juxtaposition of the two words is another indication that his concern is excessive and misdirected desire for pleasure. It is here that he deems intemperance as leading to the soul's death (*Opif.* 164). He then returns to the problematic nature of women: "Pleasure does not venture to bring her wiles and deceptions to bear on the man, but on the woman, and by her means on him" (*Opif.* 165). His comment here is not about women in a literal sense – though it assumes their inferiority and incompetence – but about human psychology: "For in us mind (νοῦς) corresponds to man, the senses (αἴσθησις) to woman; and pleasure (ἡδονή)) encounters and holds parley with the senses (αἰσθήσεσι) first, and through them cheats with her quackeries the sovereign mind (ἡγεμόνα νοῦν) itself" (*Opif.* 165). He then illustrates how this might work through all five senses: "for when each sense has been subjugated to her sorceries, delighting in what she proffers, ... then all of them receive the gifts and offer them like handmaids to the Reason (τῷ λογισμῷ) as to a master, bringing with them Persuasion (πειθώ) to plead that it reject nothing whatever" (*Opif.* 165). By this "Reason is forthwith ensnared and becomes a subject instead of a ruler, a slave instead of a master, an alien instead of a citizen, and a mortal instead of an immortal" (*Opif.* 165). He then depicts pleasure as a prostitute, "a courtesan and a wanton" (ἑταιρὶς καὶ

Schofield and G. Striker; Cambridge: Cambridge University Press, 1995) 69-112. On Philo's rejection of Stoic *oikeiôsis* which sees ethics generated from "an instinctive impulse common to both man and the realm of all animated beings", see Lévy, "Philo's Ethics," 146-48, of which p. 147 is cited here. He notes that both Philo's Platonism and, more importantly "his biblical theology prevents him from doing so" (148).

[231] On the "snake-fighter" as a jumping insect, see Runia, *Creation*, 380.

μαλχάς), looking for a client and employing agents (the senses) to secure a catch (*Opif.* 166). He concludes: "When she has ensnared these she easily brings the Mind under her control" (*Opif.* 166). Philo is employing the familiar figure of the seductress to typify the lure of pleasure, such as we find already in Proverbs 1 – 9 but also as a regular topos in contemporary philosophy (on which see the discussion in 1.2.3.2 below).

In the passage Runia identifies a number of strands. "It is plain that the basic attitude towards pleasure is negative. The snake is hardly a positive symbol, and the destructive effect of pleasure has already been made plain in §152."[232] He then goes on to identify "the popular platonizing theme of pleasure associated with the body, the earth, the passions of stomach and groin, and so on" ... which "goes back to Tim. 69d1 ('pleasure, the greatest lure of evil') and other texts"; "the rather verbose depictions of the 'pleasure-lover' being attracted by all manner of delicacies" as recalling "the exhortatory language of the Stoic-Cynic diatribe"; "the imagery of the prostitute in §166" recalling "the famous debate between pleasure as prostitute and virtue as modest maiden in *Sacr.* 21-23, which goes back to Prodicus as recorded in Xenophon and was greatly admired by the Stoics" and Stoic "conception of ἡδονή as a passion (πάθος) in §§163 and 166" and "the explanation in epistemological terms in §166".[233] As "the most surprising part of Philo's depiction of pleasure" Runia identifies Philo's use of "the Epicurean doctrine of pleasure as instinctive to living beings and the goal of human life" in *Opif.* 161-163, which, he notes, Philo is "very careful to place the theory in the mouth of the advocates of pleasure, to whom he himself most definitely does not belong".[234] He concludes that "in spite of the encomium of §§161-163, pleasure plays a negative role in the allegory of the events in the garden".[235] Our discussion above suggests further differentiation in assessing what precisely Philo rejects in the Epicurean material and what, not. A differentiated approach receives some support from the way Philo depicts the snake as pleasure in the *Allegorical Commentary* (see the discussion below), where both positive and negative traits exist, although the latter predominate. Runia's caution is pertinent here: "Jewish and early Christian interpretations of the snake as Satan or the devil ... are quite remote".[236]

The encounter with the snake serves here in *Opif.* as an image of what happens when people fall into sin through the lures of pleasure. It is not an inevitable fate, though it may sound that way, if we fail to appreciate Philo's rhetoric. Philo's extensive expositions assume that the right response is always an

---

[232] Runia, *Creation*, 375.
[233] Runia, *Creation*, 375.
[234] Runia, *Creation*, 375.
[235] Runia, *Creation*, 376.
[236] Runia, *Creation*, 376.

option. It is clear, however, that uncontrolled and inappropriate pleasure leads to alienation from God, from virtues, and from what God intended for the human being. While Philo includes among the lures of pleasure a range of temptations, including food, sexual pleasure is prominent and he uses the image of the seductress to represent the assault. Philo says little about the detail of the literal encounter with the snake and certainly not enough to warrant concluding that he understood the snake as engaging in sexual seduction.

1.2.3.1.2 The Snake of Pleasure in "Questions and Answers on Genesis"

In the responses to questions in *QG* we also find the equation of the snake with pleasure. Philo explains: "by passion is meant sensual pleasure, for lovers of pleasure are very clever and are skilled in arts and means …" (*QG* 1.31). Philo's assumptions about women are again apparent as he explains: "woman is more accustomed to be deceived than man" (*QG* 1.33). The fact that the woman touched the fruit before the man he deems appropriate because "it was fitting that man should rule over immortality and everything good, but woman over death and everything vile. In the allegorical sense, however, woman is a symbol of sense, and man, of mind. Now of necessity sense comes into contact with the sense-perceptible" and passes then to mind (*QG* 1.37). The fig leaves symbolically indicate "those who sew together and weave together many sense pleasures one with another. Wherefore they (the leaves) are girded round the place of the genitals, which are the instruments of greater things" (*QG* 1.41). As noted above, this reflects Philo's twofold approach to sexual pleasure: it is "great" and appropriate in marital intercourse for procreation, but inappropriate elsewhere and in excess. He explains the detail that God confronted Adam first, on the basis that man represents reason, whereas woman "was the beginning of evil and led him (man) into a life of vileness" (*QG* 1.45). This is not dissimilar to the claim that she is the beginning of a blameworthy life (*Opif.* 151). It accords with his comment that "woman is of a nature to be deceived rather than to reflect greatly" (*QG* 1.46). Philo summarises: "the serpent is a symbol of desire, as was shown; and woman is a symbol of sense, and man of mind. So that desire becomes the evil origin of sins, and this first deceives sense, while sense takes the mind captive" (*QG* 1.47), very similar to *Opif.* 165. "Since the serpent is a symbol of desire, he takes the form of lovers of pleasure" (*QG* 1.48), an equation made also in *Opif.* 158.

This account gives a similar allegorical interpretation, based on assumptions about women's inferior reasoning and vulnerability to external stimuli and applied to the irrational in the soul, but while similarly identifying the serpent with pleasure and lovers of pleasure it does not extrapolate on what these pleasures are nor use the image of the seductress as in *Opif*. Sexual themes are present, positively in acknowledging the significant role of the genitalia, but also negatively in depicting them as associated with illicit desire, but the theme is not developed.

1.2.3.1.2 *The Snake of Pleasure in "Allegorical Interpretation" and Beyond*

By contrast with the accounts in *Opif.* and *QG* 1, the discussion in *Leg.* is much more extensive. It includes a reflection on nakedness, based on Gen 3:1 (MT 2:25): "The mind that is clothed neither in vice nor in virtue, but absolutely stripped of either, is naked, just as the soul of an infant" (*Leg.* 2.53; similarly 64). Philo then writes of a nakedness where the soul "is barren of all vices, and has divested itself of all the passions and flung them away" (*Leg.* 2.54), citing images of Moses pitching his tent outside the camp (*Leg.* 2.55; Exod 33:7), the high priest entering the holy of holies without his robe (*Leg.* 2.56), Nadab and Abihu, leaving aside their garments (*Leg.* 2.57), Abraham departing country and kindred (*Leg.* 2.59), Isaac not entering Egypt (*Leg.* 2.59), and Jacob's smoothness (*Leg.* 2.59). Noah represents nakedness of virtues (*Leg.* 2.60-62). We return to these images in the next chapter. Philo then takes up the words that Adam and his wife "were not ashamed" as the basis for an excursus on shamelessness and shamefastness (*Leg.* 2.65-69). Adam and Eve had neither, but were in a neutral state, "the mind without self-exertion, the perceptive sense without perceiving, they have nothing shameful" (*Leg.* 2.70).

At this point Philo picks up the reference in Gen 3:1 to the snake. As noted above, much of this is a positive or at least neutral account of pleasure, which is made by God. It is what produces interaction between mind and the senses, hitherto both neutral, naked and without shame, which can now be positive or negative.[237] Calabi notes that "in the relationship established by love between sensation and intellect a strong Platonic influence is at work". She goes on to add: "This, however, radically changes direction when pleasure does not so much lead from love of beautiful bodies to beauty per se, but rather establishes a relationship between intellect and sensation, which cannot gain knowledge separately from one another".[238]

Philo acknowledges the variety of ways in which pleasure comes to expression, not least through food (*Leg.* 2.75-76). But, he explains, pleasures also encounter us "when the part of us that corresponds to the turbulent mob of a city, pines for the dwellings of Egypt" (*Leg.* 2.77). Then they "bring death, not the death which severs soul from body, but the death which ruins the soul by vice"

---

[237] So Baer, *Male and Female*, who writes: "pleasure in some measure is necessary for the proper interaction of mind and sense-perception", citing *Leg.* 2.71-72 (90-91).

[238] Francesca Calabi, *God's Acting, Man's Acting: Tradition and Philosophy in Philo of Alexandria* (Studies in Philo of Alexandria 4; Leiden: Brill, 2008) 130-31.

(*Leg.* 2.77).²³⁹ Here Philo brings two thoughts together: the pining of the Israelites for Egypt in the wilderness and the plague of snakes (Num 21:6), who are made to represent the dangerous pleasure which Egypt symbolises (*Leg.* 2.77). "For verily nothing so surely brings death upon a soul as immoderate indulgence in pleasures (ἀμετρία τῶν ἡδονῶν)" (*Leg.* 2.77). Again the issue is not pleasure in itself but excess and misdirection. Moses' bronze snake becomes for Philo the symbol of "self-mastery" (σωφροσύνη), described as "another serpent, opposite in kind to that of Eve ... For self-mastery (σωφροσύνη) runs counter to pleasure, a variable virtue to a variable affection, and a virtue that defends itself against pleasure its foe" (*Leg.* 2.79). Pleasure, here, depicts not all pleasure, but pleasure in its negative role of seducing to wrongdoing and excess. Philo continues, "If the mind, when bitten by pleasure, the serpent of Eve, shall have succeeded in beholding in soul the beauty of self-mastery, the serpent of Moses, and through beholding this, beholds God Himself, he shall live" (*Leg.* 2.81).

Philo extrapolates further that the biting snake of pleasure confronts us not only in the gross temptations of Egypt but also in the wilderness where we might have considered ourselves isolated from such dangers, citing his own personal experience (*Leg.* 2.84-85). The imagery enables him to take up the story of Moses' rod which becomes a snake and, grasped by the tail, reverts to a rod (*Leg.* 2.88-93; Exod 4:1-5, employed thus only here)²⁴⁰ and Jacob's crossing the Jordan with his rod (Gen 32:10, also employed thus only here), where he etymologises Jordan as going down, thus as going down to the bodily passions, and so the rod as self-restraint (*Leg.* 2.89). This, in turn, recalls for Philo the reference to Dan as a serpent on the road, biting the horse's heel and the horseman falling back in Jacob's blessing in Gen 49:16-18 (*Leg.* 2.94-102). On the road of the soul Dan (discerning) controls and destroys (bites) passion (the horse) and as the horseman

---

²³⁹ Calabi, *God's Acting, Man's Acting*, speaks of "a sudden leap, the pleasures of sight and hearing, positive, gratifying and connected to knowledge, are now replaced with the pleasures of death, the source of corruption and desolation; inordinate pleasures which lead to evil" (134-35). "The symbol, which was initially positive, now becomes decidedly negative" (144).

²⁴⁰ Calabi, *God's Acting, Man's Acting*, writes: "The snake taken by its tail represents pleasure dominated and its becoming a rod indicates that bridled pleasure becomes education. If cast away, the rod turns into a snake, just as education rejected by the soul gives way to pleasure. All this indicates that we should not flee pleasure, but govern it by means of παιδεία and, as found in other passages, σωφροσύνη. (145). "Moses is thus associated with two snakes: the bronze one that represents *sophrosyne* and counteracts excessive pleasures, and the one that turns into a rod and controls pleasure, a means of 'taking *hedone*' by the tail' and governing it" (146).

appropriately falls backward from the passions (horse).²⁴¹ This, in turn, inspires Philo to reflect on the Song of Moses about horse and rider being cast into the sea, as those belonging to Egypt and its passions (*Leg.* 2.103-104). He also notes that Leviticus forbids taking snakes (so passions) as nourishment (*Leg.* 2.105).

As Calabi notes, Philo uses the image of the snake in opposite ways: "it represents both pleasure and what combats it".²⁴²

> When ἡδονή is considered negatively, it is attacked by σωφροσύνη, ἐγκράτεια and κρίσις, symbolized by the snakes of Moses and Dan, and by the snake-fighter. The snake thus belongs to various different and contrasting semantic spheres: on the one hand, Eve's snake, a possible source of death for the soul: on the other, the snakes which lead to virtue, to life for the soul. So they are complementary symbols: moderation, self-mastery and good judgement are the right way to vanquish the poison of the other snakes, the σωφροσύνη of Moses' snake combats the ἡδονή of Eve's snake.²⁴³

The image thus functions both positively and negatively in the context of dealing with the passions. In the context of the formation of knowledge, however, "pleasure, far from representing wicked cunning, which must be subdued and if possible eliminated, constitutes the means if gaining knowledge, the *tertium* which, alone, can guarantee the union of Adam and Eve".²⁴⁴ Thus ambivalence in depicting pleasure matches the ambivalence in the image of the snake: both can lead to death but also to knowledge.

Returning to the Genesis text Philo reiterates: "all things are enthralled to pleasure (πάντα ἡδονῆς δοῦλα), and the life of bad men is under the dominion of pleasure (δεσπόζεται ὑφ' ἡδονῆς)" (*Leg.* 2.107; cf. *Opif.* 162). "Therefore set judgement (γνώμην), the serpent-fighter, against it, and contend to the end in this noble context, and strive earnestly, by defeating pleasure that conquers all others (κατὰ τῆς τοὺς ἄλλους ἅπαντας νικώσης ἡδονῆς), to win the noble and glorious crown, which no human assembly has ever bestowed" (*Leg.* 2.108). The issue is control, especially not letting pleasure rule instead of mind. He begins book 3 with the reference in Gen 3:8 to Adam and his wife hiding themselves

---

²⁴¹ Calabi, *God's Acting, Man's Acting*, writes: "the soul's facility to examine, analyse precisely, judge in such a way as to counteract the passions (the horse) which tempt the soul (the way)" (146). "The symbols shift: in both cases it is a question of fighting pleasures and passions, in the first case, however, the struggle is carried out using σωφροσύνη, in the second, the intellectualistic aspect, the use of the noetic faculty to distinguish what is advisable and what is iniquitous is supported by καρτερία, the power of the soul which counteracts ἀκρασία, intemperance" (147).

²⁴² Calabi, *God's Acting, Man's Acting*, 149, similarly 150.

²⁴³ Calabi, *God's Acting, Man's Acting*, 149-50.

²⁴⁴ Calabi, *God's Acting, Man's Acting*, 150.

(*Leg.* 3.1), which he then employs as a negative image of abandoning virtue with numerous parallels. He then interprets the place where they hid, "in the midst of the wood of the garden" (*Leg.* 3.28), which Philo takes as the mind asserting its independence of God, a form of idolatry (*Leg.* 3.28-36).

As in *QG*, he explains why God addresses Adam first not Eve, "because, being irrational, she has no capacity derived from herself to receive reproof" (*Leg.* 3.50), primarily a reference to sense-perception, but reflecting also his view of women. Philo takes the words, "the woman whom thou gavest with me (μετ' ἐμοῦ)" (Gen 3:12), not "to me" (μοι), as indicating the independence of the senses and so their danger and need for control (*Leg.* 3.56-57). On the woman's response, "The serpent beguiled (ἠπάτησέν) me and I ate" (Gen 3:13) Philo simply highlights the inevitable sequence: "For when sense-perception, meeting with the object of the sense, is filled with the presentation of it, forthwith the mind also is in contact, takes hold and in a way absorbs the sustenance which it provides" (*Leg.* 3.60). He makes nothing of the potentially sexual reference in ἠπάτησέν ("beguile/deceive/seduce"; cf. 2 Cor 11:1-3),[245] though he gives the word considerable attention. "Pleasure does not report the object to the mind such as it is, but artfully falsifies it, representing as something advantageous that which is of no benefit at all: even as it is possible to see repulsive courtesans applying pigments to their faces and painting under their eyes to conceal their ugliness" (*Leg.* 3.61-62). The focus is trickery. While Philo does not interpret Eve's fall as seduction in any literal sense, he employs the image of the seductress metaphorically to depict the lure of the passions, as he does in *Opif.* 166. "Again we may see those who are in love, often quite crazy over women most hideous to behold, while pleasure beguiles them" (*Leg.* 3.63). He continues: "Indeed they overlook those endowed with really faultless beauty (ἀμέμπτῳ κεχρημένας κάλλει) and pine for those whom I have mentioned. All kinds of consummate deception (πᾶσα ... ἀπάτη), then ... are characteristic of sense-perception: pleasure outwits and misleads the mind, showing objects not as they are, but as they are not" (*Leg.* 3.63-64). The seductress there symbolises "all kinds of consummate deception", not only the seduction of sexual pleasure. It is interesting that Philo clearly assumes it can be proper to respond sexually to "those endowed with really faultless beauty".

Conclusion

The central feature common to all three is the serpent symbolising pleasure and by extension the lover of pleasure. All three allow us to see that Philo can see pleasure as something potentially good which God has made, in *Opif.* tracing it as

---

[245] On this see Loader, *Septuagint*, 45-46.

far back as the womb, in *QG* as something "great' in the context of sexual intercourse for procreation, and in *Leg.* as made by God to bring together Mind and Sense-Perception.[246] All three reflect on the psychological processes of pleasure addressing Mind indirectly through the five senses, using this to explain why the serpent addressed the woman first, because she represents the senses.[247] Similarly *QG* and *Leg.* then explain God's addressing the man first because he represents mind. The primary focus in all three is on the danger which pleasure represents.[248] All emphasise the inferior capacity of women and correspondingly the senses to exercise appropriate discernment in dealing with the lures of pleasure and all see succumbing to pleasure as death. All three include sexual pleasure as one of the dangers, and *Opif.* and *Leg.* employ the imagery of the seductress and prostitute to depict the dangers in general. At the same time none appears to take Eve's statement about the serpent's deception in a sexual sense as seduction at the literal level, though this is developed allegorically in *Leg.*

1.2.3.2 Dangers of Sexual Pleasure Elsewhere

In the rest of the *Exposition of the Laws*, Philo has further comments about the dangers of sexual pleasure. Thus in *Abr.* while he describes the functions of the senses neutrally at first (*Abr.* 148), he turns on taste, smell, and touch as "the three most servile and animal", which, he claims, "cause particular excitation in the cattle and wild beasts most given to gluttony and sexual passion. For all day and night they fill themselves with food insatiably or are at rut" (*Abr.* 149).[249] Earlier in *Abr.* 29 he had spoken of the five senses and speech as engaging in warfare to meet their ends, only to be subdued by mind, but here sexual desire goes unmentioned.

---

[246] Calabi, *God's Acting, Man's Acting*, notes of the snake in Philo: "The snake alternatively constitutes either a means of enriching one's knowledge, an element that mediates between intellect and sensation allowing these to express themselves, or a source of transgression and excess" (127).

[247] Mattila, "Wisdom, Sense Perception, Nature," comments that "the identification of the serpent with pleasure is interesting because the Greek word for 'serpent' is masculine (ὁ ὄφις)), while the word 'pleasure' is feminine (ἡ ἡδονή). This results in Philo switching back and forth between masculine and feminine forms when speaking of this figure, and reveals how determined he is to represent the serpent, or pleasure, as 'female' (114).

[248] When Boyarin, *Carnal Israel*, writes, "In Philo, the snake stands for pleasure embodied, especially the carnal pleasure that the male has in intercourse with the female" (81), this is too undifferentiated and runs contrary to the positive aspect of sexual pleasure which Philo also acknowledges.

[249] If this implies that they are constantly at rut, Philo is ill-informed.

In his account of Joseph he hails Joseph's resistance to sexual seduction through Potiphar's wife, speaking of "the frenzy of her passion ", who "fed the fire of lawless lust till it burst into a blaze" (*Ios.* 40-41).[250] Apart from being a prime example of seduction in a literal sense she also symbolises for Philo the seduction of politicians by popular opinion: "And like a licentious woman the desire of the multitudes makes love to the statesman" (*Ios.* 63). By contrast, "When the statesman stands thus aloof from all passions, from pleasure, from fear, from pain, from desire, with the spirit of a true man, the despot-people cannot away with him, but takes him and chastises him as an enemy its friend and well-wisher" (*Ios.* 79).

In *Virt.* he recounts the tradition about the Midianites planning the seduction of Israel's young men,[251] with the explanation proffered on their leaders' lips, exhorting the women: "Now man is easily led captive by pleasure, and particularly by the pleasure of intercourse with women. You are exceedingly comely; beauty is naturally seductive, and youth easily lapses into incontinence. Do not fear the names of harlotry or adultery" (*Virt.* 36). Accordingly, the women deck themselves out to capture the youths (39) and "with meretricious glances and wheedling talk and lewd attitudes and movements, they set their bait before the weaker-minded part of the younger men" (40), leading them to idolatry. In *Mos.* 1 he portrays Balaam's strategy to counter Israel similarly: "he set himself to lead them, through wantonness and licentiousness, to impiety, through a great sin to a still greater, and put before them the bait of pleasure (*Mos.* 1.295). Accordingly, Philo has Balaam address a speech to Balak in which he begins by declaring:

"You have in your countrywomen, king, ... persons of pre-eminent beauty. And there is nothing to which a man more easily falls a captive than women's comeliness. If, then, you permit the fairest among them to prostitute themselves for hire, they will ensnare the younger of their enemies. You must instruct them not to allow their wooers to enjoy their charms at once. For coyness titillates, and thereby makes the appetites more active, and inflames the passions. And, when their lust has them in its grip, there is nothing which they will shrink from doing or suffering" (*Mos.* 1.296-297).

Both here and in *Virt.* Philo's discussion remains at the literal level. In *Virt.* he writes also of the wicked who have sold themselves to "the enjoyment of another's

---

[250] As Ellis, *Sexual Desire*, argueses over against Fredricksen, that "rather than anti-erotic, the passage is anti-licentiousness, anti-adultery, anti-madness, anti-ungovernable-desire, and so pro-self-control. It does not condemn passion or desire per se as twenty-first-century speakers of English understand passion and desire" (87); cf. David Fredrickson, "Passionless Sex in 1 Thessalonians 4:4-5," *WW* 23 (2003) 23-30, 26. Similarly Ellis disputes the latter's claim (28) that *Spec.* 3.8-10 implies the same (87-88).

[251] This appears to be an extrapolation from Num 31:15-16, which also stimulated the author of *LAB*, who similarly describes the strategy in some detail (*LAB* 18:13-14).

beauty, thus ministering to the delights of the belly and the organs below it – delights which end in the gravest injuries to body and soul" (*Virt.* 182).

Speaking of adultery as "the greatest of crimes" in *Decal.* 121, he explains that "it has its source in the love of pleasure (φιληδονίαν) which enervates the bodies of those who entertain it, relaxes the sinews of the soul and wastes away the means of subsistence, consuming like an unquenchable fire all that it touches and leaving nothing wholesome in human life" (*Decal.* 122).

While Philo is concerned with all the passions, including those associated with the chest, like anger, he gives particular attention to desire (ἐπιθυμία), especially desire for pleasure.[252] In *Spec.* 4.83 he locates it around the navel, as in Plato's *Timaeus* 70E, but, with regard to sexual desire, also in the regions below. His exposition of the final commandment in *Spec.* 4 claims: "Plunderings and robberies and repudiations of debts and false accusations and outrages, also seductions, adulteries, murders, and all wrongful actions, whether private or public …" flow from "desire" (ἐπιθυμία) as "the fountain of all evils (πηγὴ τῶν κακῶν)" (*Spec.* 4.84-85).[253] To it belongs desire "for money, reputation, government, beautiful women (εὐμορφίας) and all the innumerable objects which are held in human life to be enviable and worthy of a struggle" (*Spec.* 4.82) and it burns in the soul like fire (*Spec.* 4.83; similarly *Decal.* 150, 173). In *Decal.* he writes that "all the passions of the soul which stir and shake it out of its proper nature and do not let it continue in sound health are hard to deal with, but desire is hardest of all" (*Decal.* 142). He uses the myth of Tantalus to depict the frustration of desire, whose punishment was that "he missed everything that he wished for just when he was about to touch it, so the person who is mastered by desire, ever thirsting for what is absent remains unsatisfied, fumbling around his baffled appetite" (*Decal.* 149; similarly *Spec.* 4.81). He also draws attention to the wars which desire has unleashed: "Consider the passion whether for money or a woman or glory or anything else that produces pleasure: are the evils which it causes small or casual?" (*Decal.* 151). "Desire for money or glory or pleasure. These it is that bring disaster to the human race" (*Decal.* 153). Philo's exposition of the tenth commandment includes sexual desire, but is not restricted to sexual desire.

Frequently he links gluttony, drunkenness, and sexual wrongdoing as driven by the desires and passions of the belly and, as he puts it so often, of the region below. Thus in *Spec.* 1 he writes: "For strong drink and gross eating accompanied

---

[252] Runia, *Creation*, notes that "although Philo often refers to the theory of the four passions, it appears that for him pleasure and desire are more dangerous than fear and cowardice" (380).

[253] As Ellis, *Sexual Desire*, writes: "The statement seems an emphatic condemnation of all desire, including sexual desire, but an examination of its larger context suggests that what Philo actually condemns is not desire per se but excessive desire and lack of self-control" (85), pointing to emphases in the context on control (*Spec.* 4.79-80, 89-90) (85-87).

by wine-bibbing, while they awaken the insatiable lusts of the belly, inflame also the lusts seated below it, and as they stream along and overflow on every side they create a torrent of evils innumerable, because they have the immunity of the feast for their headquarters and refuge from retribution" (*Spec.* 1.192). This is most likely because such excesses frequently occur at banquets, which he frequently attacks.

In *QG* Philo employs the image of the seductive woman in contrast to Rebecca as an image of purity, speaking of the "symmetry of parts and beauty of form such as even harlots have", adding: "But a shameless look and an elevated neck and a continuous movement of the eyebrows and a womanish walk and not blushing at, or being ashamed of, any evil at all is the sign of a lewd soul" (*QG* 4.99). He writes of "some who through gluttony, lechery and over-indulgence are always submerged and sunken, being drowned in passion" (*QG* 4.234). In *QG* 3 he describes sense-perception as "the head and font of passion" (*QG* 3.41; cf. *Spec.* 4.84). Commenting on Gen 6:7, he treats animals allegorically as standing for sense-perception which is also destroyed when the mind is perverted (*QG* 1.94). Referring to instructions about asses in Exod 23:5 he writes that "the ass is symbolically our body, and (this) is altogether errant and roving. For the sake of bringing profit to its kindred sensual pleasure" it engages in excessive drinking and gluttony (*QE* 2.12).

In the *Allegorical Commentary* Philo also regularly focuses on the dangers of passions. Sometimes the canvass is wide and includes all passions. We shall consider in greater detail below his exposition of the curses on the snake. There we find some of Philo's most forthright condemnations of pleasure. It is the passion par excellence and is to be cursed and is bad of itself (*Leg.* 3.68, 107, 111). Philo sets it in contrast to the true pleasure of joy (*Leg.* 3.107). *Cher.* speaks of being "eternally enslaved to hard mistresses, vain fancies, lusts, pleasures, promptings to wrongdoing, follies, false opinions" (*Cher.* 71). Similarly he speaks in *Det.* of "whenever throbbing passion in the soul rages savagely, producing there itchings and ticklings arising from lust and indulgence, or again gnawing pains and scared flutterings, the result of fear and grief" (*Det.* 110).

In the thematic discourse, *Prob.*, he also speaks of such slavery: "bodies have men for their masters, souls their vices and passions" (*Prob.* 17; similarly 151; cf. also Josephus *A.J.* 1.74; 15.219; 16.198; 19.201), speaking then of "the mind at liberty from the domination of the passions" (*Prob.* 17) and of "characters which have never fallen under the yoke of desire, or fear, or pleasure, or grief" (*Prob.* 18) and of the soul "driven by desire, or enticed by pleasure, or diverted from its course by fear, or shrunken by grief, or helpless in the grip of anger" (*Prob.* 159).

Sometimes he depicts the passions as like animals, which untamed can tear the soul to pieces (*Leg.* 2.11). In *Gig.* he claims that "undisciplined pleasures are often as dogs", which can turn on us (*Gig.* 35). In *Agr.* cattle-herding inspires the comment that when our minds are not alert, the herd of our senses "gorge themselves insatiably with the lavish food brought in by the objects of sense, shake off restraint, and get unruly, going at random where they have no business to go" (*Agr.* 34). Similarly in *Sacr.* he writes:

> So then, the senses also as a kind may be either wild or tame. They are wild when, throwing off the control of their herdsman the mind, they are carried away in their unreason into the outer sphere of things perceptible by them. They are tame when they respond submissively to reflection, the ruling element in our compound nature, and accept its guidance and control. (*Sacr.* 105)

"Irrational lusts so constantly born of over-abundant appetite" are the "enemies of the soul" (*Her.* 245).

Philo can describe the assault of the passions as like warfare, "truceless and unrelenting warfare" (*Fug.* 114). "To be able to stay the fierce persistent warfare of the outward life which the multitude so eagerly pursues, and intestine battling of lust against lust in the soul, and there establish peace, is a great and glorious feat" (*Ebr.* 75). "So long as the unreasoning impulses did not stir and 'shout' within us, the mind stood firm and stedfast. But when they begin to fill the region of the soul with manifold sounds and voices, when they summon the passions and rouse them to action, they create the discord of civil war" (*Ebr.* 98). When the mind sets itself free from the body's domination, "the clamours of the passion are at once restrained" (*Ebr.* 101). Philo adds: "How shrill are the outcries of pleasure, wherewith it is wont to command what it wills! How continuous is the voice of desire, when it thunders forth its threats against those who do not minister to its wants!" (*Ebr.* 102). In other words this is a constant struggle even for one who is firmly in control. Similarly he speaks of the passions coming like waves (*Sacr.* 16). In *Conf.* he cites Psalm 79 [80]:7 on conflict with neighbours, to depict the necessity of conflict with the passions (52). In *Somn.* he also speaks of warfare with the passions: "the cruellest of wars" (*Somn.* 2.147). So he writes: "the pleasures of the body descend upon us in gathered force like a cataract deluging and obliterating one after another all the things of the mind" (*Somn.* 2.13). "Such is the cycle of unceasing warfare ever revolving round the many-sided soul" (*Somn.* 2.14).

Usually when such statements are probed we find that Philo's concerns are uncontrolled and excessive passions, and sense-perception acting in service of such passions. Thus he challenges the value of astrology with his key concerns: "How will it serve to subdue the urge of pleasure, to overthrow the power of lust, to suppress fear or grief? What surgery has it for passions which agitate and confound the soul?" (*Mut.* 72; similarly *Spec.* 1.191). By contrast he speaks of the Therapeutae as those not afflicted "by pleasures and desires and griefs and fears, by acts of covetousness, folly and injustice and the countless hosts of other passions and vices" (*Contempl.* 2).

In his concern with the passions Philo's primary focus is desire for pleasure. Thus in *Leg.* 3 he explains how he sees pleasure lying indirectly behind all the main passions: "Lust (ἐπιθυμία) comes into play through love of pleasure (ἔρωτος ἡδονῆς); pain arises as pleasure is withdrawn; fear again is engendered owing to a dread of being without pleasure. It is clear, then, that all the passions depend on pleasure (πάντα ἐφορμεῖ τὰ πάθη τῇ ἡδονῇ)" (*Leg.* 3.113). As in *Decal.* 149 and *Spec.* 4.81, he also uses the myth of Tantalus to depict the frustrated desire (*Det.* 112; *Her.* 269). In *Leg.* 3 he writes that: "passion has its lair in these parts of the body, the breast and the belly ... it haunts the belly and the parts below it" (*Leg.* 3 114). Sometimes it is identified as especially typical of the young "when appetite was a-flame" (*Post.* 71; cf. also *Contempl.* 6). In *Det.* Philo speaks of the "deadly stimulus to sexual sins which accompanies ungoverned lust" (*Det.* 174), declaring a little later: "It is better to be made a eunuch than to be mad after illicit unions" (*Det.* 176). In *Somn.* 2 he warns of those who like Joseph began well, but who then "at the very eventide of life ... have been wrecked on the rock of an unlocked tongue or insatiate greed of belly, or in uncontrolled lasciviousness of the lower-lying parts" (*Somn.* 2.147).

Here, too, Philo frequently employs the image of the seductress. Its biblical roots reach back into Proverbs 1 – 9, but he knows it as a topos of philosophy in the form preserved in Xenophon *Mem.* 2.1. This underlies the major employment of the motif in *Sacr.* 21-44. Philo introduces his exposition by quoting Deut 21:15-17, a provision protecting the right of the firstborn in the case of a man taking a second wife. Philo treats it allegorically, declaring: "For each of us is mated with two wives, who hate and loathe each other, and they fill the house of the soul with their jealous contentions. And one of these we love, because we find her winning and gentle, and we think her our nearest and dearest. Her name is pleasure. The other we hate; we think her rough, ungentle, crabbed and our bitter enemy" (*Sacr.* 20). As Sly notes, "From this introductory material he makes an awkward transition into a paraphrase of Xenophon, for when Pleasure, the first woman, makes her appearance (*Sac.* 21), she comes not as a wife but as a stranger".[254] Thus he begins:

> So pleasure come languishing in the guise of a harlot or courtesan. Her gait has the looseness which her extravagant wantonness and luxury has bred; the lascivious roll of her eyes is a bait to entice the souls of the young; her look speaks of boldness and shamelessness; her neck is held high; she assumes a stature which Nature has not given her; she grins and giggles; her hair is dressed in curious and elaborate plaits; under her eyes are pencil lines; her eyebrows are smothered in paint; she revels perpetually in the

---

[254] Sly, *Philo's Perception of Women*, 168.

warmth of the bath; her flush is artificial; her costly raiment is broidered lavishly with flowers ... a strumpet of the streets, she takes the market-place for her home; devoid of true beauty, she pursues the false. (*Sacr.* 21)

Philo elaborates the image providing her with "friends, villainy, recklessness, faithlessness, flattery, imposture, deceit, falsehood, perjury, impiety, injustice, profligacy" (*Sacr.* 22).[255] Only the last of these has probable sexual reference, so that the seductress functions here generically to represent all wickedness, not sexual wrongdoing in particular. He then outlines her pitch to the Mind, which similarly includes a wide range of "human blessings" (*Sacr.* 22). They include freedom from restraint, fear of punishment, stress and discipline (*Sacr.* 23) as well as "sweet modulations of melodious sounds, costly kinds of food and drink, abundant varieties of delicious perfumes, amours without ceasing (συνεχεῖς ἔρωτες), frolics unregulated (ἀπαιδαγώγητοι μαιδιαί), chamberings unrestricted (μίξεις ἀνεξέταστοι), language unrepressed, deeds uncensored, life without care, sleep soft and sweet, satiety ever unfilled" (*Sacr.* 23). Again, sexual wrongdoing is only a component. Her pitch runs from *Sacr.* 22 – 25. Philo then presents the second woman.

The second, "hated" woman, then makes her pitch, but, unlike in the tradition of Proverbs, her image is not sexualised. Rather "when the other heard this, standing as she was, hidden from sight, yet within earshot [like the Therapeutae women in *Contempl.* 33], she feared lest the Mind should unawares be made captive and enslaved, and carried away by this wealth of gifts and promises ... working in him the itch of desire (γαργαλισμοὺς ἐνειργάζετο)" (*Sacr.* 26). She is a picture of modesty, "without false colouring" (*Sacr.* 26), "her carriage ... unaffected, her movements quiet, her clothing plain, her adornment that of good sense and virtue" (*Sacr.* 26) and her company a long list of virtues beginning with piety (*Sacr.* 27).[256] Her extensive message (*Sacr.* 28-44!), perhaps typical of what we might expect from Philo, is primarily negative, namely a warning about the dangers of the other woman. It even offers a list of 147 adjectives or adjectival phrases to describe what a person becomes who is a lover of pleasure (*Sacr.* 32), including, as Sly notes, "womanish" (θηλυδρίας). Instead this woman commands

---

[255] On Philo's embellishment of Xenophon's image see Sly, *Philo's Perception of Women*, who notes that "Philo adds a note of judgement to his description in depicting her as "a strumpet" peddling falsehood (*Sacr.* 21) and employing trickery (*Sacr.* 26), magic (*Sacr.* 28) and snares (*Sacr.* 29) (168).

[256] Sly, *Philo's Perception of Women*, notes that "Xenophon describes this woman as modest, engaging and sober, plainly clad and moving with graceful mien (Mem.22). Her counterpart in Philo is similar, but again described more elaborately: a freeborn citizen, firm, serene, modest, honest, plainly dressed, with unaffected carriage, and a host of virtues in her train (Sac.26f)" (168).

toil, as in Xenophon,[257] and "waging war to the death against pleasure" (*Sacr.* 35). According to Philo "after hearing this the mind turns away from pleasure and cleaves to virtue, for it apprehends her loveliness, so pure, so simple, so holy to look upon" (*Sacr.* 45) and with that he returns to his favourite images of controlling the passions like a shepherd of sheep, a chariot rider, and a pilot (*Sacr.* 45). Unlike Proverbs and Sirach, Philo does not give us an image of Wisdom as a seductive lover, preserving the image of seduction only for negative use, nor does he employ here the language of wisdom and folly. His emphasis is also more strongly on the dangerous character of Pleasure than in the model topos in Xenophon.[258]

Philo's focus in employing the image of the two women is primarily *all* the dangers of pleasure, which he represents by a sexual image; it is not sexual pleasure in particular. Whereas this elaborate scene employs sexual seduction allegorically, with little reference to the literal seduction of sexual pleasure, elsewhere Philo probably has both in mind. Thus in *Gig.* he urges: "Therefore, my soul, if any of the love-lures of pleasure (τι τῶν ἡδονῆς φίλτρων) invite thee, turn thyself aside, let thine eyes look else-whither. Look rather on the genuine beauty of virtue, gaze on her continually ..." (*Gig.* 44). In *Fug.* he contrasts virtuous Tamar with "any licentious one, or a wanton, or a street-walker, or one prostituting for gain the flower of her youth, or making bright what is outside by baths and cleansings while she is foul within, or in default of natural beauty painting her face as pictures are coloured, or what is called the 'many-husband' pest, following after evil as though it were good, or a lover of polygamy, or dispersing herself upon a thousand different objects material and immaterial alike, or mocked and outraged by that multitude" (*Fug.* 153).

As in the exposition of the serpent story, so elsewhere in all three streams of commentary and beyond Philo constantly warns against the dangers of the passions and of desire for pleasure in particular, especially sexual pleasure. Many motifs repeat themselves, including warfare, slavery, fire, animals, the seductress, and many related to biblical stories such as those about Joseph, the Midianites, and many more which we shall consider in our review of Philo's treatment of Genesis and Exodus in the next major section, including spatial images of departure from

---

[257] Sly, *Philo's Perception of Women*, notes that "Each praises toil, the gift Virtue holds out for mankind. The basic difference between the two is that Philo has changed the references to Greek deities in order to comply with his belief in one God" (169).

[258] Sly, *Philo's Perception of Women*, observes: "Philo's presentation of the two women differs significantly from Xenophon's in tone. Besides giving her outward description, Philo imputes motives to Pleasure. She is presented as deceptive, using unfair tactics like magic. Whereas Xenophon's Virtue addresses Vice (Pleasure) directly in challenge, Philo's Virtue addresses the man, warning him against the traps of the other. The dangerous character of Pleasure or Vice predominates" (169).

Mesopotamia and Egypt and biological images of return to virginity. While most show clearly that the issue is excess and misdirection, some lend themselves to being read as exhortations to abandon and exterminate passions altogether, which would then include a denial of sexual passion, let alone sexual pleasure. In the following section we attempt to weigh such statements both in their contexts and in the context of Philo's works as a whole.

1.2.3.3 Eliminating Sexual Passion?

Sometimes it appears that Philo is advocating denial of the passions altogether and a cutting off from the senses.[259] Thus Baer writes:

> Philo is particularly severe in his denunciation of ἡδονή and σῶμα, which in a number of passages are described as evil by nature. Αἴσθησις is frequently referred to in highly pejorative terms, but it is never held to be inherently or absolutely evil. Pleasure, however, is bad in itself (Leg. All. III:68). It is the passion par excellence (III:107); worse than the others, for they all depend on pleasure (III: 113).[260]

---

[259] Cf. Jenny Morris, "The Jewish Philosopher Philo," in Emil Schürer, *The History of the Jewish People in the Age of Jesus Christ (175 B.C. – A.D. 135): Vol. III.2* (3 vols; ed. Geza Vermes; Fergus Millar, and Martin Goodman; Edinburgh: T&T Clark, 1987) 808–89, who writes: "Since sensuality as such is evil, sin is innate in man" (887) and "the highest principle of ethics is obviously the utmost possible renunciation of sensuality, the eradication of desire and passion ... Philo adheres primarily to Stoicism, not only in the basic idea of the extirpation of sensuality, but also in particular prescriptions such as in the doctrine of the four cardinal virtues, and the four passions" (887). Similarly, for instance, Karen L. King, "The Body and Society in Philo and the Apocryphon of John," in *The School of Moses: Studies in Philo and Hellenistic Religion: In Memory of Horst R. Moehring* (ed. John Peter Kenney; BJS 304; SPM 1; Atlanta: Scholars, 1995) 82-97, writes of Philo espousing an extirpation of passions rather than just their moderation (88-89).

[260] Baer, *Male and Female*, 92. In contrast to the positive or neutral statements Philo makes about the senses and passions "far more typical of Philo's writings as a whole are those passages where the created world is portrayed as hostile and antithetic to the good life" (91). "Man is portrayed as a sinner not because he is wrongly related to the created world but simply because he is a part of that world" (92). "This emphasis on the necessary relationship between man as created and mortal and man as a sinner, although it probably can not be reconciled with the preceding account of the nobility of the πρῶτος ἄνθρωπος (Op. Mund. 136-50), is nonetheless a common motif in Philo's writings" (92). Similarly Winston, "Philo and the Rabbis," points out that that Philo does not "think that true self-control consists of mortification of the flesh and neglect of the body, whose well-being must not be compromised in any way (*Det.* 19-21)." (207). Similarly Ellis, *Sexual Desire*: Philo "shows a strong distrust of desire and pleasure and often seems to advocate their compete avoidance or elimination. When he fleshes out this distrust, however, he focuses more on

Already Völker noted, however, that Philo's statements must not be taken in isolation or interpreted without reference to his Jewish presuppositions, not least about divine creation. He notes that while Philo uses Stoic and Platonic ideas – and this leads to considerable tension between his various statements – he does so only to express what the religion of his fathers has taught him.[261] Similarly Lévy observes: "Because Philo does not adhere to any dogma in the domain of psychology, he expresses himself sometimes in Platonic terms and sometimes in Stoic terms, depending on the biblical text he needs to discuss and on his convictions, which hardly ever coincide exactly with a specific philosophical doctrine".[262] He notes that while Philo uses Stoic categories, they did not have the same value for him. Thus while, he argues, Philo uses the language of *apatheia* and excising passions, citing the exposition of circumcision in *Migr.* 92 and *Deus* 67 as an example and Moses' cutting them out in *Leg.* 3.129, Philo rejects *apatheia*, for instance, in grief (*Abr.* 257).[263] He concludes that "in Philo there is the idea, probably Peripatetic in origin, of a unity of passion, which is given to man in order to help him, and which he can turn into the instrument of his ruin or of his perfection".[264] Similarly Dillon comments: "the actual procedures of Peripatetic pruning and Stoic uprooting would tend to come to very much the same thing, at least by the time of the Middle Stoa, where a doctrine of *eupatheia* was firmly in place, and various compromises with reality had been made—especially since the time of Panaetius—which significantly moderated the originally paradoxical nature of the Stoic position".[265] Winston draws attention to the fact

---

excess and lack of self-control than on desire per se, and, at points, he even seems to affirm sexual desire and pleasure within marriage" (83).

[261] Völker, *Fortschritt und Vollendung*, "dass er sich ihrer nur bedient, um das auszudrücken, was seine väterliche Religion ihn gelehrt hat" (88). "Philo fühlt sich als Jude, und dann fordert er keine Vernichtung der πάθη, sondern ihre Zügelung durch den λογισμός und ihre massvolle Bekämpfung durch die ἐγκράτεια" (136).

[262] Lévy, "Philo's Ethics," 155. He writes: "Philo's treatment of the passions seems to be particularly rich in contradictions and has given rise to a great diversity of interpretations" (154).

[263] Lévy, "Philo's Ethics," 159-60. He writes: "It seems, therefore, that for Philo there is a bad apathy and a good apathy. The former entails an indifference that borders on inhumanity; the latter entails the absence of excessive and bad passions and for this reason can border on what was called *metriopatheia*, 'moderation of emotion'" (160).

[264] Lévy, "Philo's Ethics," 161. On the positive role of pleasure, for instance, he draws attention to Boulluec, "Plaisir," 146.

[265] John M. Dillon, "The Pleasures and Perils of Soul-Gardening," *SPA* 9 (1997) 190-97, 193. Similarly Lévy, "Philo's Ethics," 155. Of "the three canonical *eupatheia* are *boulēsis* (willing or wishing), *eulabeia* (watchfulness or caution), and *chara* (joy)" Winston,

that "the Stoic doctrine of *apatheia* ... has been widely misunderstood both in ancient and modern scholarship".[266] It "did not signify the elimination of all emotions, but rather only of the *pathē*, defined by Stoics as diseased and irrational emotions". Accordingly "the sage, who is guided only by an *orthos logos*, experience only *eupatheiai* or rational emotions".[267] He "engenders within his own psyche only rational emotions, since they are the result of perfectly rational ideas as to what is best for the human organism".[268]

This suggests that Philo's philosophical context would have allowed the possibility that he might preserve a confined space for desire and pleasure, but never as something excessive, never as driven by itself, but always properly tamed and controlled and so serving some rational purpose. In addition we should weigh all Philo's statements not only in their immediate context and the context of his works as a whole, but also in the light of typical rhetorical excess and overstatement to make a point. Thus, writing of Philo's negative statements, Sly observes:

> Philo's Weltanschauung ... leads him to be less concerned with absolutes than with relative positions. Lower forms (designated as feminine, passive, inferior) need not be eliminated or crushed, but, rather, controlled. On the interpersonal level, woman need not be degraded or even ostentatiously put in her place. She need simply be subject to male command and male interest.[269]

"Emotions," notes that "Philo was in no way embarrassed to apply at least two of these (*boulēsis* and *chara*) to God" (203).

[266] David Winston, "Philo's Ethical Theory," ANRW II.21.1, 372-416, 402. See also his discussion in Winston, "Philo and the Rabbis," 208-11, where he cites A. Bonhöffer, *Epiktet und die Stoa* (Stuttgart: Ferdinand Enker, 1890) 34, who wrote (Winston translating) that the Stoics "did not understand the body's nothingness metaphysically as Plato did, but only ethically, and not absolutely but only relatively, insofar as the interest of the body was in competition with that of the soul" (208). Winston then points out that "Epictetus is capable of downgrading the body in the interest of moral admonition, but he never loses sight of its relative worth and is at times even carried away by transports of enthusiasm on its behalf" (209), citing *Diatr.* 2.8.12; and 3.22.67-69, 77.

[267] Winston, "Philo's Ethical Theory," 402.

[268] Winston, "Philo's Ethical Theory," 403. See also his discussion in Winston, "Emotions," where he writes: "yet in spite of Philo's fascination with the ideal of *apatheia*, he is at times content with the milder Peripatetic view" (203). "Thus it is not all that surprising to find Philo identifying *apatheia* as the highest ethical ideal, while at the same time indicating the usefulness of the passions" (204); and see his discussion in 207-11. See also Runia, *Creation*, who notes that "The distinction between pleasure (i.e. a *pathos*) and joy (i.e. a *eupatheia*) is crucial for Philo, but is not emphasized in *Opif.*" (389).

[269] Sly, *Philo's Perception of Women*, 184.

Similarly, she writes: "Philo's calls for quitting the body are rhetorical, and … the theme of his work is control of the lower elements rather than separation or elimination".[270] Winston makes the same point: "This Platonic rhetoric, in which Philo sometimes revels, does not necessarily commit him to a severe downgrading or hatred of the body as such".[271] He insists that in considering

> ancient attitudes towards the body, it is essential to decide in each case whether the author's apparent devalorization of the body is largely rhetorical, for the sake of moral emphasis, or whether it reflects an inflexibly dark view of the body unredeemed by a joyous celebration of its proper role as a part of the larger divine harmony, as is clearly the case in certain Gnostic thinkers.[272]

In what follows we encounter some of the major instances where the issues arise. Thus in *QG* 4 when Philo contrasts "the mind of the virgin, which makes use of nothing sense-perceptible, and the class of the type which receives the sense-perceptible" (*QG* 4.119), this probably means what controls the senses rather than complete absence of contact with them. This will be true also of his contrast in *QE* 2, where he writes that "such souls as love themselves honour the mind as a husband and as a father – as a husband perhaps because it sows in them the powers of the senses by which the sense-perceptible object is attained and seized" and contrasts them with

> those who are free of self-love and hasten to God to obtain from above His visitations and care as from a father, and as from a husband (they obtain) the sowing of good thoughts and intentions and words and deeds … when souls become divinely inspired, from (being) women they become virgins, throwing off the womanly corruptions which are (found) in sense-perception and passion. Moreover, they follow after and pursue the genuine and unmated virgin, the veritable wisdom of God. (*QE* 2.3)

As we shall see Philo uses both Abraham's migration and the exodus from Egypt as symbols of moving away from the passions.[273] These too might appear to imply a denial of passions altogether, but it is clear that this is not Philo's intent. Thus in *Migr.* he allegorises Abraham's departure as "removal out of three localities, namely, body, sense-perception, and speech" (*Migr.* 2), explaining,

---

[270] Sly, *Philo's Perception of Women*, 220.

[271] Winston, "Philo and the Rabbis," 206.

[272] Winston, "Philo and the Rabbis," 210.

[273] On this see also Sarah J. K. Pearce, *The Land of the Body: Studies in Philo's Representation of Egypt* (WUNT 2.208; Tübingen: Mohr Siebeck, 2007), who notes also the imagery of migration in relation to Abraham, Sodom, and Laban (100-101).

> The words, 'Depart out of these' are not equivalent to 'Sever thyself from them absolutely,' since to issue such a command as that would be to prescribe death. No, the words import 'Make thyself a stranger to them in judgement and purpose; let none of them cling to thee; rise superior to them all; they are thy subjects, never treat them as sovereign lords. (*Migr.* 7)

This is standard advice in Philo. The issue is not elimination but control. So the instruction means: depart " ... from the foul prison-house, thy body, with all thy might and main, and from the pleasures and lusts that act as its jailers" (*Migr.* 9). These are typical of Philo's extreme statements and easily misread if not qualified by comments such as those just cited above.

Similarly, in speaking of the need for the wild trees of passion (*Det.* 105) to be kept in check, he writes: "The trees of folly and licentiousness, of injustice and cowardice I will wholly cut down; I will moreover extirpate the plants of pleasure and desire, of anger and wrath and of like passions" (*Agr.* 17). The trees being uprooted are those producing "folly and licentiousness, of injustice and cowardice", not, however, the tamed and controlled passions which serve the mind. Dillon notes that in this context Philo reflects "the controversy, already of long standing by his time, between the Peripatetic doctrine of the moderation of the passions, or *metripatheia*, and the Stoic doctrine of the necessity of their extirpation (*apatheia*)".[274] Often Philo favours "*apatheia* as an ideal, and elsewhere (e.g. Leg. 3.129-132) attributes it to the perfected sage, Moses, while Aaron, who symbolizes the *prokoptôn*, or the man still making progress in virtue, can attain only to *metriopatheia*".[275] This is not however always the case, he argues, so that "at Abr. 256-7, for example, he praises Abraham, on the loss of his wife Sarah, for 'neither fretting beyond measure, nor showing a complete lack of emotion (*apatheia*), but choosing the mean rather than the extremes, and trying to moderate his passions (*metriopathein*)'".[276] Dillon concludes that "Philo is quite capable, then, of donning either a Stoic or a Peripatetic hat, according as the subject matter seems to demand it".[277] This again cautions against taking his absolute statements, for instance against passion, too literally. On *Agr.* he notes in conclusion that Philo "seems on the whole to be in a pro-Stoic frame of mind", reflected in the language of cutting down, "but, as often with Philo, the contradictions with what has preceded are more apparent than real".[278] He notes that in *Agr.* 6 Philo "is primarily concerned with cultivable bushes and trees that have gone wild, and which can be brought back to an ordered state", whereas in

---

[274] Dillon, "Pleasures," 191.
[275] Dillon, "Pleasures," 191.
[276] Dillon, "Pleasures," 191.
[277] Dillon, "Pleasures," 191.
[278] Dillon, "Pleasures," 192.

Agr. 17 "he is thinking of downright weeds and invasive wild shrubs and trees that have taken over a garden and must be rooted out".[279]

In *Leg.* 3 Philo depicts Moses as the perfect man and in that context with allusion to Lev 8:29 declares that Moses "thinks it necessary to use the knife on the seat of anger in its entirety, and to cut it clean out of the soul, for no moderation of passion can satisfy him; he is content with nothing but complete absence of passion" (*Leg.* 3.129; similarly 130, 131; similarly *Migr.* 67). He contrasts with Moses "the man who is making gradual progress, holding a lower position" of whom he writes that he "practises moderation, as I have said; for his power does not go so far as to enable him to cut out the breast and the high-spirited element, but he brings to it, as charioteer and guide, reason with the virtues attached to it" (*Leg.* 3.132). Moses, "he, being perfect, has no small or petty aims, nor any desire to moderate his passions, but goes so far as to cut off all passions everywhere; while others set out to wage war on the passions on an insignificant, not on a grand, scale" to "curb their excessive impetuosity" (*Leg.* 3.134). This could be taken to indicate that Moses obliterated all passions.[280] Thus Winston speaks of him as a "super-sage, whose perfected reason does not need to generate rational impulses, but simply computes its body's true needs and proceeds to satisfy them in the only way it knows how, which is with perfect rationality".[281] Accordingly, he argues, "since according to Philo Moses' prophetic state was virtually continuous, inasmuch as the divine spirit was ever with him, he must have had no irrational component in his soul".[282] Winston then suggests that what we are seeing here is Philo "continuing his game of 'one-upmanship' by adding to his insistence that Moses was the Father of Greek philosophy the further claim that he was also the greatest of all sages, greater even than the rare and supremely idealized species of wise person depicted by the Stoics".[283] He contrasts Isaac, who "symbolizes the wise person whose psyche generates only εὐπάθειαι or rational emotions", with Moses who goes even further, who

---

[279] Dillon, "Pleasures," 192-93.

[280] So Aune, "Mastery of the Passions," who writes: "Those who attain moral perfection will radically excise these irrational portions of the soul. Others must remain content with allowing the rational portion of the soul to rule over the irrational elements, Like a charioteer, reason has been placed over these 'high-spirited' and 'lustful' elements to bridle them (*epistomizein*) and hold them in check" (126).

[281] David Winston, "Sage and Super-Sage in Philo of Alexandria," in *The Ancestral Philosophy, Hellenistic Philosophy in Second Temple Judaism: Essays of David Winston* (ed. Gregory E. Sterling; BJS 331; SPM 4; Providence: Brown University Press, 2001) 171-80, 179. He argues that *Gig.* 55 assumes the same (180).

[282] Winston, "Sage and Super-Sage," 180. See also Winston, "Emotions," 209-10.

[283] Winston, "Sage and Super-Sage," 180.

would appear to symbolize the god-like person, 'given as a loan to earthlings' (i.e., he belongs to that category of rational souls that ordinarily never leave the supernal spheres for embodiment below), who has achieved an absolute state of ἀπάθεια or absence of passion and is no longer affected in any way by human feelings, living as it were in the disembodied realm of pure νοῦς.[284]

This is certainly different from a generalising demand on all, but still it sets up Moses as a model of the ultimate goal. There are some indications that this may, however, be a misreading. First we should note that Philo's focus is anger (an aspect of the high-spirited element), which he probably does believe should be extirpated. Thus the knife is being applied to anger in the exposition in *Leg.* 3.129-132: "to use the knife on the seat of anger" (129); "excision of the war-like part" (130); "cuts out ... anger" (131); "cut out the breast and the high-spirited element" (132). Anger then returns in the ensuing discussion: "Now that we have said this, note once more how a perfect man differs from one making progress. We have already discovered the perfect man cutting out the seat of anger entirely from the wrangling soul" (*Leg.* 3.140). The problem becomes acute, however, with regard to food where Philo writes of Moses as "the wise man, in his perfection, scouring away and shaking off pleasures, but the man of gradual improvement not so treating pleasure in its entirety, but welcoming simple and unavoidable pleasure, while declining that which is excessive and overelaborate in the way of delicacies" (*Leg.* 3.140), for he declares that Moses "rejects even necessary food and drink, being fed by the contemplation of things divine" (*Leg.* 3.141), fasting for 40 days and nights (*Leg.* 3.142). Accordingly, he concludes: "We must not fail to notice that Moses, when he refuses the entire belly, that is the filling of his stomach, practically renounces the other passions too" (*Leg.* 3.145).

Typically, however, Philo retreats from the extremities of his image to declare: "the perfect wise man can, by wholly renouncing anger, utterly avert and drive off the uprising of the spirited element in him, but to exscind the belly he is powerless.[285] Even the man of fewest needs who scorns the very necessaries of life and trains himself in abstinence from them, is forced by nature to take necessary food and drink" (*Leg.* 3.147). Again we note the return of the primary theme of anger, but also the assertion that of course Moses did not eliminate the need for food. Philo appears to make a distinction between the breast and the passion of anger associated with it, and the belly associated with food and drink and the region below the belly, the necessary generative sexual passion, though this still leaves apparent anomalies. Thus he writes: "The lover of pleasure moves on the belly; the perfect man washes out the entire belly; the man who is making gradual

---

[284] Winston, "Sage and Super-Sage," 178-79. Similarly Winston, "Emotions," 207.

[285] Against the notion that Philo is contradicting himself or being inconsistent, see Winston, "Emotions," 210.

progress washes out the contents of the belly, the man who is just beginning his training will go forth without, when he intends to curb passion by bringing reason (figuratively called a shovel) to bear upon the demands of the belly" (*Leg.* 3.159). Washing out the belly cannot, however, mean permanent abstinence from the necessities of food, nor probably from sexual intercourse for procreation, but means rather Moses is in control and will make no mess, unlike the learner who will need to take his shovel. For the latter Philo draws on Deut 23:13 about shit and the shovel to say we should "gird up our passions, not wear them flowing and loose" (*Leg.* 3.153). "Let a shovel then, that is, reason, follow the passion, preventing it from spreading abroad, for by this means we shall comply only with demands which are urgent, but from all that goes beyond this we shall abstain" (*Leg.* 3.154). Moses does achieve *apatheia*, but it still leaves room for necessities which, it seems, Moses deals with not by removing from them any pleasantness or pleasure, but by managing them all rationally, not diverted from their proper purpose.[286]

Elsewhere Philo paints Moses as a model of control: "On his belly he bestowed no more than the necessary tributes which nature has appointed, and as for the pleasures that have their seat below, save for the lawful begetting of children, they passed altogether even out of his memory" (*Mos.* 1.28). Thus he modelled "self-restraint, continence, temperance, ..." (*Mos.* 1.154). Similarly in *QG* 4 Philo corrects any possible misunderstanding about Moses' stance, writing that he was "not zealously practising apathy, for this would be ungrateful and shameless and akin to arrogance and reckless boldness, but that which is consistent with the argument given, (namely) cutting the mind off from disturbing and confusing passions" (*QG* 4.15).

It would appear then that even in relation to the super-sage it is not correct to assume that Philo envisages total extirpation of the passions, and certainly not as a general goal for all. Philo's Jewish heritage, not least, his belief in creation is too strong for that and statements which use the rhetoric of absolute denial need to be read within that broader context.

1.2.3.4 Control and Moderation of Sexual Passion

Philo's frequent comments about the need for temperance and control also imply that the senses and passions have their place when properly under the control of mind, but do not, otherwise. This theme can be followed throughout all three series of commentaries. Thus, turning to the *Exposition of the Law*, we see in the

---

[286] Cf. *Migr.* 67, where according to Winston, "Emotions," Philo again uses Lev 8:21 and 29, but here to depict Moses as dispensing "not only with the spirited element (*thymētikon*), but also with his appetitive element (*epithymētikon*), so that his reason (*logistikon*) operates in a sort of passional vacuum" (211).

interpretation of the shewbread, for instance, that he speaks of them as "emblematic of that most profitable of virtues, continence (ἐγκράτειαν), which has simplicity and contentment and frugality for its bodyguard against the baleful assaults engineered by incontinence and covetousness (ἀκολασίας καὶ πλεονεξίας)" (*Spec.* 1.173). Similarly, earlier in *Spec.* 1 he urges: "Know thyself, then (γνῶθι δὴ σεαυτόν), and do not be led away by impulses and desires beyond thy capacity (ταῖς ὑπὲρ δύναμιν ὁρμαῖς καὶ ἐπιθυμίαις), nor let yearning for the unattainable (τῶν ἀνεφίκτων ἔρως) uplift and carry thee off thy feet, for of the obtainable nothing shall be denied thee" (*Spec.* 1.44). Self-knowledge is the basis for proper control.

Thus the wise man is "armed against the pleasures and lusts (κατὰ τῶν ἡδονῶν καὶ ἐπιθυμιῶν), ever eager to take their stand superior to the passions in general (συνόλως ἐπάνω τῶν παθῶν), trained to use every effort to overthrow the formidable menace which those passions have built up against them" (*Spec.* 2.46). For "nothing is so profitable as that the laxity and free play of the appetites (τῶν ὁρμῶν) should be hampered and numbed with their vitalizing forces paralysed so that the inordinate strength of the passions may be exhausted and thus provide a breadth in which the better part of the soul may expand" (*Praem.* 48). The appetites are under control. Philo rejects philosophies which he alleges believe that senses can control passions through music and speech (*Spec.* 1.343). He also attacks authors who write "pieces of voluptuous licence" (*Mos.* 1.3). Instead he acclaims Israel because "it carries out all the rites of purification and both in body and soul obeys the injunctions of the divine laws, which restrict the pleasures of the belly and the parts below it (τάς τε γαστρὸς ἡδονὰς καὶ ὑπογαστρίους) and the horde ... setting reason to guide the irrational senses (ταῖς αἰσθήσεσιν ἡνίοχον ἀλόγοις λόγον ἐπιστήσαντες), and also check and rein in the wild and extravagant impulses of the soul (τὰς τῆς ψυχῆς ἀκρίτους καὶ πλεοναζούσας ὁρμὰς)" (*Spec.* 2.163). Of the commandments Philo notes that

> All these it seems the most holy Moses observed and therefore discarded passion in general and detesting it, as most vile in itself and in its effects, denounced especially desire as a battery of destruction to the soul, which must be done away with or brought into obedience to the governance of reason, and then all things will be permeated through and through with peace and good order, those perfect forms of the good which bring the full perfection of happy living. (*Spec.* 4.95)

The issues are obedience and control, not extirpation.

At times Philo can address the issue with some sympathy as in *Spec.* 3, where in relation to sexual passion he writes: "Now even natural pleasure (ἡ κατὰ φύσιν ἡδονή) is often greatly to blame when the craving for it is immoderate and insatiable, as for instance when it takes the form of voracious gluttony, even though none of the food taken is of the forbidden kind, or again the passionate desire for women shewn by those who in their craze for sexual intercourse behave unchastely, not with the wives of others, but with their own (καὶ οἱ φιλογύναιοι συνουσιαῖς ἐπιμεμηνότες καὶ λαγνίστερον ὁμιλοῦντες γυναιξὶν οὐκ ἀλλοτρυίαις ἀλλὰ καὶ ταῖς ἑαυτῶν)" (*Spec.* 3.9), to which he then adds: "But the blame in most of these cases rests less with the soul than with the body, which contains a great amount both of fire and of moisture; the fire as it consumes the material set before it quickly demands a second supply; the moisture is sluiced in a stream through the genital organs, and creates in them irritations, itchings and titillations without ceasing" (10), an allusion to *Timaeus* 86B-E.[287] This in no way lessens his demand, however, that mind control such urges. The much quoted statement in *Spec.* 3.9, cited above, sometimes to prove Philo's negativity about sex, places the emphasis squarely on the immoderate and excessive. While we would have no difficulty disapproving of such excess when it expresses itself in marital rape, we might find difficulty, at least, in discerning what precisely Philo has in mind beyond that. For him the bigger picture of procreation always needs to govern what is going on and sets the only context which legitimates any sexual desire and any pleasure, but the statement should not be read as an absolute negation of sexual desire and pleasure in such a context.

Moses is the model as one who "did not, as some, allow the lusts of adolescence to go unbridled" (*Mos.* 1.25), who "watched the first directions and impulses of the soul as one would a restive horse" (*Mos.* 1.26). Thus "on his belly he bestowed no more than the necessary tributes which nature has appointed, and as for the pleasures that have their seat below, save for the lawful begetting of children, they passed altogether even out of his memory" (*Mos.* 1.28). The image of the horse features in one of Philo's favourite images to depict control, that of the chariot rider reining in the passions, based on Plato's famous image in Phaedrus 253D.[288] As we noted above, it also implies that the passions are in order and proper when under mind's control. Thus he speaks of the need "to check and rein in the wild and extravagant impulses of the soul ..." (*Spec.* 2.163; similarly *Spec.* 4.79). In *Virt.* he writes that "the health of the soul is to have its faculties, reason, high spirit and desire happily tempered, with the reason in command and reining in both the other two, like restive horses" (*Virt.* 13).

Philo uses the story of Abraham's engagement with the nine cities, five prosperous cities refusing taxes to four kings, related at the literal level in *Abr.* 226-235, as an allegory of the mind's encounter with "the four passions, pleasure,

---

[287] So Winston, "Philo and the Rabbis," 217.

[288] Runia, *Creation*, observes of pilot and charioteer: "Philo habitually uses these images from ancient transport systems for the directive and providential activity of God ... They are also ubiquitous in the Platonic tradition, derived primarily from the myths in the *Phaedrus* and the *Politicus*" (191).

desire, fear and grief, ... and the five senses, sight, hearing, taste, smell and touch", reflecting his standard psychology (*Abr.* 236). The former dominate the latter, but also need the latter's supplies (*Abr.* 237). Again, as earlier in *Abr.* 148, we find touch and taste treated as especially vulnerable (*Abr.* 240-241). "Now the nine overlords, the four passions and the five senses, are corruptible and the sources of corruption, but the truly divine and holy Word, whose stronghold is in the virtues, whose place in the order of number is tenth, the supremely perfect number, comes to the contest and with the help of the mightier power of God wins an easy victory over the said overlords" (*Abr.* 244). As in the literal story, Philo does not envisage here their entire annihilation, but rather their being kept in their proper place. The exposition gives no particular attention to sexual passion.

In alluding to Exod 21:10, Philo writes of basic necessities, including sexual intercourse: "for, to say all in a word, we must not, as the Law tells us, take away from the soul these three things, 'the necessaries, the clothing, the fellowship', but afford each of them steadily" (*Migr.* 105). His use of them in this context allegorically may imply that he neglects them at a literal level, though this cannot be stated with confidence.[289] At any rate, he would doubtless read the reference to sexual relations within the parameters of his understanding that it is a legitimate desire to respond to only for the purpose of procreation. Thus "if the mind continues free from harm and sickness, it has all its tribes and powers in a healthy condition, those whose province is sight and hearing and all others concerned with sense-perception, and those again that have to do with pleasures and desires, and all that are undergoing transformation from the lower to the higher emotions" (*Migr.* 119). His instruction to the soul-traveller is to

> find out what the body is and what it must do or undergo to co-operate with the understanding; what sense-perception is and in what way it is of service to its ruler, mind; what speech is, and what thought it must express if it would contribute to nobility of character; what pleasure is, and what desire is; what pain and fear are, and what the healing art is that can counteract them, by means of which a man shall either, if he falls into their hand, without difficulty make his escape, or avoid capture altogether; what it is to play the fool, what to be licentious, what to be unjust ... (*Migr.* 219)

This recalls the challenge to self-knowledge in *Spec.* 1.44, noted above. Again, the issue is not denial but proper management.

Emphases are similar in the *Questions and Answers*. Thus in *QG* Philo speaks of the "lavish 'fatness'" of the earth (cf. Gen 27:28) as "the abundance of provisioning in accordance with the several senses when they are restrained by continence and temperance" (*QG* 4.215). Here they are positive, but as long as

---

[289] Cf. Winston, "Philo and the Rabbis," 218.

they are in control. As he puts it in *QG* 4.220, "In the same way, when continence and reason go away, which have subjugated and driven out the passions by their attack, there follows them unrestraint (which is) both the seducer and protagonist of the passions".

One of Philo's many ways of expressing proper control is through the allegory of the soul in which the female irrational is transformed into something male. Thus he writes of restoring unity within oneself

> to bring together those (elements) which have been divided and separated, not that the masculine thoughts may be made womanish and relaxed by softness, but that the female element, the senses, may be made manly by following masculine thoughts and by receiving from them seed for procreation, that it may perceive (things) with wisdom, prudence, justice, and courage, in sum, with virtue. (*QG* 2.49)

This is closely related to the idea of woman becoming virgin or even becoming man, which we discuss below. The point is not denial of the passions or the senses, but their proper alignment. This is something possible for both men and women. In *QE* 2.115 we find another allusion to the image of the charioteer moderating the passions.

The *Allegorical Commentary* has a number of passages which address control. One of the clearest is Philo's depiction of the priest of Midian and his seven daughters, who Philo takes to represent the five senses plus speech and "reproductive power" (*Mut.* 111). "Each 'draws up,' so to speak, external objects of sense until they 'fill the troughs' of the soul 'from which they water the sheep of the father,' and by these I mean the purest of flocks, the flock of reasoning which brings with it at once protection and adornment" (*Mut.* 111). This is a positive depiction, illustrating how things ought to work. "But then 'arrive' the comrades of envy and malice, the shepherds of an evil herd, and drive them from the uses prescribed by nature. For whereas the daughters take outside objects inside to the mind, which is as it were their judge and king, hoping thus under the best of rulers to perform their duty aright, the others beset and pursue them and give the opposite orders, namely that they should entice the mind outside and there deliver over phenomena into its hand" (*Mut.* 112-113). The end is then positive: "And when the maidens have escaped the onset of those who are the mind's enemies and have no aspiration but for the superfluities of life as though life were mere play-acting, they return not now to Jethro but to Raguel", whose name means "the shepherding of God" (*Mut.* 114). These senses are not infallible. They call Moses an Egyptian. "They cannot, that is, rise above their own nature. For the senses are on the border-line between the intelligible realm and the sensible" (*Mut.* 117-118).

We find a similar perspective in *Her.* where Philo writes of Abraham's departure from land, kin, and father's house as a symbol of the soul, which declares:

> "I migrated from the body," she answers, "when I had ceased to regard the flesh; from sense, when I came to view all the objects of sense as having no true existence, when I denounced its standards of judgement as spurious and corrupt and steeped in false opinion, and its judgements as equipped to ensnare and deceive and ravish truth away from its place in the heart of nature; from speech, when I sentenced it to long speechlessness, in spite of all its self-exaltation and self-pride". (*Her.* 71)

The speech then concludes: "I learnt that the better course was to quit all these three, yet dedicate and attribute the faculties of each to God, who compacts the body in its bodily form, who equips the senses to perceive, and extends to speech the power of speaking" (*Her.* 73). The faculties are not abandoned; they are put in their correct place.[290]

Similarly in *Somn.* 1 Philo can also urge people to make themselves familiar with the passions and the senses: "If therefore a man is absolutely incapable of holding intercourse with the understanding by itself, he wins in sense-perception a second-best refuge" (*Somn.* 1.44). Philo then uses Rebecca's instruction that Jacob go to Laban to illustrate the appropriateness of spending some time "in the territory of the senses", "in compliance with the necessities of the body", but not a "lifetime" (*Somn.* 1.46; similarly *Fug.* 46), just as Abraham spent some time in Haran (*Somn.* 1.47; similarly *Migr.* 195).[291] Philo sees scripture addressing the learning explorer with the advice to excavate "the openings and cavities of the body", to find out what the senses are and how they function (*Somn.* 1.55-56), that is, "Know thyself" (*Somn.* 1.57; cf. also *Spec.* 1.44 and *Abr.* 219 above), "in order that you may enjoy the happiness proper to man" (*Somn.* 1.57). While not dealing specifically with sexuality, it represents Philo's stance well, that the soul needs to know the senses, but they are not to be one's permanent dwelling or ruling purpose. That is for Mind alone. In *Her.* he employs the difference between a kiss of affection and sexual intercourse to describe the proper treatment of sense-perception: "The wise have been trained to greet her with a kiss, but not to love her, the others to love her deeply and regard her worthy of a triple measure of their affection" (*Her.* 42). In *Sacr.* he writes that "Jacob's sons, trained under an all-

---

[290] Similarly Christian Noack, *Gottesbewusstsein: Exegetische Studien zur Soteriologie und Mystik bei Philo von Alexandrien* (WUNT 2.116; Tübingen: Mohr Siebeck, 2000) 195.

[291] On this see Ellen Birnbaum, "Allegorical Interpretation and Jewish Identity Among Alexandrian Jewish Writers," in *Neotestamentica et Philonica: Studies in Honor of Peder Borgen* (ed. David E. Aune, Torrey Seland, and Jarl H. Ulrichsen; NovTSup 106; Leiden: Brill, 2003) 307-29, 318.

wise father, may go down into Egypt the passion-loving body" because they will not be dazzled by it (*Sacr.* 48). The proper response to the passions as they meet us through the senses, including sexual passion and desire, according to Philo, is to ensure they are properly controlled and responded to and not with excess. "It is best, then, that the array of women, that is of the senses, in the soul, should be propitiated, as well as that of the men, that is of our several thoughts" (*Migr.* 100).

Rejection of excess is modelled by the Therapeutae of whom Philo writes that they live simply eating only the necessary, not luxury items (*Contempl.* 25) and wear simple clothing (*Contempl.* 38). Perhaps with them in mind he writes in *Agr.* that, seen positively in the wise man, "two choirs, one from the quarters of the men, one from those of the women, with answering note and voice shall raise harmonious chant. The choir of the men shall have Moses for its leader, that is Mind in its perfection, that of the women shall be led by Miriam, that is sense-perception made pure and clean" (*Agr.* 80). Their song, the Song of Moses, celebrates the demise of the horse and rider (Exod 15:1, 21), which Philo then explains: "So it is, for vices are four in kind and passions equal to these in number. It is a victory, moreover, in which their rider has been thrown and dispatched, even virtue-hating and passion-loving mind, whose delight was in pleasures and cravings" (*Agr.* 83). Similarly in *Gig.* he declares: "There are some things which we must *admit*, as, for instance, the actual necessities of life, the use of which will enable us to live in health and free from sickness. But we must reject with scorn the superfluities which kindle the lusts that with a single flameburst consume every good thing" (*Gig.* 34). "Undisciplined pleasures are often as dogs", which can turn on us (*Gig.* 35). "If some chance occasion force us to receive more than a moderate sufficiency, let us not of our own accord go near to it. For he says. 'he shall not of himself go near to uncover shame'" (*Gig.* 35). Similarly Philo contrasts those who "desire only the bare necessities, the use of which is needed to keep life from being unhealthy and sordid", with those who indulge to excess (*Ebr.* 214). "The first of these classes who are not specialists in pleasure or voluptuousness or passion are like the ordinary public in a city who live an inoffensive and innocuous life" (*Ebr.* 215). Philo affirms basic necessities including sex: "For whereas everyone is satisfied with a certain amount of sleep and food and sexual intercourse (συνουσίας) and the like, this is rarely so with strong drink" (*Ebr.* 220). The distinction between necessities and excess is a fundamental value for Philo (see also *Sacr.* 115). He can also write sarcastically of the person bent on folly as praying "that all the promptings of his mind's purposes should fail him, so that when he attempts to commit theft or adultery, or murder or sacrilege, or any similar deed, he should not find an easy path, but rather a host of obstacles to hinder its execution" (*Conf.* 163).

Philo's favourite images to depict control, that of the chariot rider reining in the passions, also appears frequently in the *Allegorical Commentary*. We noted its appearance above in *Spec.* 2.163; *Spec.* 4.79; cf. also *Leg.* 3.118, 132, 223. It, too, carries the implication that the passions are in order and proper when under mind's control.[292] Control is "by applying bit and bridle to the irrational faculties to curb the excessive violence of their movement" (*Agr.* 94). Similarly in *Leg.* 1 Philo writes: "when the two, the high-spirited and the lustful, are guided by the reasoning faculty as horses by their driver, then justice emerges" (*Leg.* 1.72); and when not, injustice (*Leg.* 1.73) and in *Agr.*: "Desire and high spirit are horses, the one male, the other female. For this reason the one prances and wants to be free and at large and has a high neck, as you might expect of a male. The other is mean and slavish, up to sly tricks, keeps her nose in the manger and empties it in no time, for she is female. The Mind is alike mounted man and wielder of the reins" (*Agr.* 73). The two horses are thus high spirit, with which Philo associates anger in particular (e.g. *Migr.* 66; cf. also *QE* 2.115) and which he locates in the breast, and desire or lust, with which he associates in its illicit form covetousness and greed, but especially gluttony, drunkenness, and sexual lust, and which he locates in the belly and the genitals.

The charioteer image can be both positive and negative in relation to the one who would rule the passions: "like the charioteer he must sometimes give the rein to his team, sometimes pull them in and draw them back, when they rush too wildly in unreined career towards the world of external things" (*Sacr.* 49). It is not an easy task, as Philo reflects when he writes: "it is a terrible thing that the soul, so wild as it is by nature, should be suffered to go unbridled, when even under the rein and with the whip in full play it can hardly be controlled and made docile" (*Conf.* 165). Playing with the image of horse riding and control, identifying the four legs with the four passions, he writes that "the mind which rode upon the unreasoning impulses of passion, that four-footed beast which knows not the rein" (*Ebr.* 111).[293] We consider a closely related image below, namely that of the horse and rider.

---

[292] Similarly Baer, *Male and Female*, who on the basis of the image writes: "Reason is not to try to extirpate the passions but is to be master over them" (90), drawing attention to the similar notion of control rather than extirpation in 4 Macc 1:6; 2:6. "Thus it is clear that sense-perception, the body, and even passion, when under the rightful dominion of the mind, contribute to man's total well-being and are not morally blameworthy. Yet, then not fully subject to mind, they can completely thwart the higher aspirations of the soul. The parable of the charioteer aptly expresses these relationships" (91). Mattila, "Wisdom, Sense Perception, Nature," notes that in *Leg.* 3.222-224 "Plato's image of reason as charioteer and pilot over the horses of high spirit and lust, ... is applied not to Plato's tripartite division of reason, high spirit, and lust, but to a bipartite division of mind versus sense perception, in which the senses play the role of unruly horses" (116).

[293] On this see Lévy, "Philo's Ethics," 157, who writes that Philo "scrupulously retains the Stoic four-part classification of the passions, ... because it enables him to connect the Stoic theory of the passions to the Platonic description of the soul. The four passions are the

Philo also uses the image of kingship to declare: "Surely to those who can reason it is a prouder task than kingship to have the strength to rule, as a king in a city or country, over the body and the senses and the belly, and the pleasures whose seat is below the belly, and the other passions and the tongue and in general all our compound being" (*Sacr.* 49). It is a matter of control. Similarly, later in the same tractate he writes:

> So then, the senses also as a kind may be either wild or tame. They are wild when, throwing off the control of their herdsman the mind, they are carried away in their unreason into the outer sphere of things perceptible by them. They are tame when they respond submissively to reflection, the ruling element in our compound nature, and accept its guidance and control ...Whatsoever then sense sees or hears or in general perceives under the direction of the mind is male and perfect, for each perception is made under good conditions. (*Sacr.* 105)

In none of the three series nor elsewhere, therefore, do we find Philo advocating a dualism which would leave no room for the senses or the passions, perhaps with the exception of those generating violence and greed. Desire for food and for sexual union for procreation and the pleasure accompanying both, or at least accompanying the latter, belong to Philo's understanding of what it means not only to be on the way, but also to live in a state of perfection, like the first couple in the beginning. Thus Moses the perfect one marries, as does Isaac. Accordingly in relation to sexual passion he advises: "And because, with a view to the persistence of the race, you were endowed with generative organs, do not run after rapes and adulteries and other unhallowed forms of intercourse, but only those which are the lawful means of propagating the human race" (*Det.* 102). There is not only a place for the desire and pleasure of sexual intercourse to that end; it is mandated, though interestingly he never cites Gen 1:28, the command to be fruitful and multiply, nor its echo in Gen 9:1 (cited with Gen 1:28 in *QG* 2.56), as justification in this regard.[294] The fundamental issue is self-knowledge and control, often represented by the image of the charioteer, but coming in numerous other variants and images. This raises the issue of how Philo sees those who like the Therapeutae and the Essenes have separated themselves and adopted the contemplative life in celibacy.

---

four legs of the horse" (157). He suggests that in this he is "perhaps dependent on Poseidonius, who has imported into Stoicism a certain amount of metaphors from Plato" (158).

[294] David Jobling, "And Have Dominion: The Interpretation of Genesis 1:28 in Philo Judaeus," *JSJ* 8 (1977) 50-82, notes that Philo uses the reference to dominion largely to describes the way things are and not as a command nor does he link it with the command to multiply (51). See also Borgen, *Exegete for his Time*, 227.

1.2.3.5 *Sexual Asceticism and the Therapeutae/Therapeutrides*

Fraade describes asceticism as including "(1) exercise of disciplined effort toward the goal of spiritual perfection (however understood), which requires (2) abstention (whether total or partial, permanent or temporary, individualistic or communalistic) from the satisfaction of otherwise permitted earthly, creaturely desires".[295] For Philo, he suggests, "life correctly lived is a constant combat against the principal enemies of pleasure, desire, and impulse, the principal weapons in this struggle being reason, temperance (*egkrateia*) and moral effort (*ponos*)".[296] He notes that "although Philo's dualistic ideal leads him to idealize virginity as a precondition of communion with God and to claim that the wise person nourished by study has no need for even the most necessary food and drink, the reality of active life necessitates all of these, moderated, to be sure, through constant self-discipline and temporary abstinence".[297] Philo is not in favour of people simply rushing off into the wilderness to engage in contemplation before they have "developed the necessary self-discipline *within* the context of a socially and politically active life".[298] He sees in this tension between responsible community involvement and withdrawal for contemplation "a tension within Philo's own life", though also one typical of Greek philosophical and Jewish biblical traditions on which he is dependent.[299] Does Philo perhaps harbour the view that the ultimate goal is withdrawal, both socially and ascetically, including from sexual activity, after all?

Much of what Philo says about sexual passion does not fall into the category of asceticism thus defined. This is true of avoiding the lure of pleasure where it leads to sin and excess, and controlling passion and the senses so that they serve only appropriate purposes, such as procreation. Reducing vulnerability to passions to a minimum comes close, though Philo usually implies this as a way of putting passions in their place. As Horsley observes, "from his writings in general it is quite clear that Philo is not making any absolute demand for sexual continence".[300] On the other hand, he notes that "Philo mentions Moses' lengthy but temporary abstinence from food and drink, following Exod. 34,28. He especially emphasizes, however, that the sexual abstinence was long-standing and perpetual" (*Mos.*

---

[295] Steven Fraade, "Ascetical Aspects of Ancient Judaism," in *Jewish Spirituality: From the Bible through the Middle Ages* (ed. A. Green; New York: Crossroads, 1986) 1, 253-88, 257.

[296] Fraade, "Ascetical Aspects," 264.

[297] Fraade, "Ascetical Aspects," 265.

[298] Fraade, "Ascetical Aspects," citing *Det.* 19-21; *Fug.* 33-34, 36, 38 (265).

[299] Fraade, "Ascetical Aspects," 266.

[300] Richard A. Horsley, "Spiritual Marriage with Sophia," *VC* 33 (1979) 30-54, 39.

2.69).³⁰¹ He sees this as related in Philo particularly to Moses' prophetic role, citing *QE* 2.3 and *Cher.* 52, observing that "Philo does not elsewhere describe Moses or any of the other great paradigmatic Jewish figures as sexual ascetics in such explicit terms".³⁰² In *Mos.* 2.68 Philo does indeed declare that Moses

> had to be clean, as in soul so also in body, to have no dealings with any passion (μηδενὸς πάθους προσαψάμενον), purifying himself from all the calls of mortal nature, food and drink and intercourse with women (τῆς πρὸς γυναῖκας φύσεως). This last he had disdained for many a day, almost from the time when, possessed by the spirit, he entered on his work as prophet, since he held it fitting to hold himself always in readiness to receive the oracular messages. (*Mos.* 2.68-69)³⁰³

The passage goes on to acknowledge limits to his fasting, namely for forty days. His abstinence from sexual intercourse to some degree echoes Exod 19:15 and purity assumptions which require such abstinence in holy space, but Philo has translated such concerns from the discourse of purity to the discourse of his psychology. The fact that he still needed to eat and drink counts against taking at face value the statement that he had no dealings with passions. We are probably seeing here not a general rejection of the desire to eat, drink, and procreate, but a functional abstinence still based to some extent on the belief, present also in Philo's world, that oracular prophets seeking inspiration needed to be sexually abstinent (cf. also Luke 12:36; Acts 21:9; and possibly as background to the celibacy of John the Baptist and Jesus).³⁰⁴ In that sense Moses is not a model for all, about which Philo might secretly carry guilt that he does not follow, but rather that Moses is taking on an exceptional role. There are other special exceptions to whom Philo draws attention.

---

[301] Horsley, "Spiritual Marriage," 40.

[302] Horsley, "Spiritual Marriage," 40.

[303] On this see also Geza Vermes, *Jesus the Jew: A Historian's Reading of the Gospels* (London: Collins, 1973), who also draws attention to *Sifre Num* 12.1 on Philo's abstention from intercourse in association with his prophetic calling (99-102). See also Pieter W. van der Horst, "Celibacy in Early Judaism," *RB* 109 (2002) 390-402, 396-98; Harvey McArthur, "Celibacy in Judaism at the time of Christian Beginnings," *AUSS* 25 (1987) 163-81, 171-72; William Loader, *Sexuality and the Jesus Tradition* (Grand Rapids: Eerdmans, 2005) 216.

[304] Cf. Karen Strand Winslow, *Early Jewish and Christian Memories of Moses' Wives: Exogamist Marriage and Ethnic Identity* (Lewiston: Edwin Mellen, 2005), who writes: "Philo's view that Moses renounced sex seems to be less the result of exegesis prompted by speculation on specific scriptural texts than a product of Philo's fundamental assumptions about the incompatibility of the 'female' with the attainment to knowledge of the divine". Philo's Moses reasoned that women, like meat and drink, would obstruct his attention to the commands of God" (272).

One clear exception is to be found in the Therapeutae and Therapeutrides.[305] Philo claims that they were a group of male and female contemplatives living close by Alexandria. This makes it doubtful that what he claims about them is to be relegated to the sphere of philosopher's dreaming.[306] In her comprehensive account, which encompasses also findings of her earlier publications, Joan Taylor addresses a wide range of issues concerning the "Mareotic community", her preferred description, since, as she demonstrates, "Therapeutae" and "Therapeutrides" are not to be understood as names but reflect use of these words to describe religious devotees.[307] She notes that in *Contempl.* Philo appears to be writing for highly educated people beyond Alexandria, probably in Rome, and so must explain both biblical and local Egyptian detail.[308] Philo may well be countering the claims of the Stoic Chaeremon, one of the ambassadors of the Alexandrian Greeks to Claudius.[309] Chaeremon appears to draw on the fanciful account of Iambulus, a late third century or early second century B.C.E. author, who described a wondrous community on a faraway island among whom marriage was unknown and who held all in common, presumably also women, and lived a simple lifestyle (Diodorus Siculus 2.55-60).[310] Chaeremon wrote about Egyptian priests as philosophers devoted to contemplation and who practised sexual abstinence before performing their priestly duties. There is much else both in the

---

[305] So Horsley, "Spiritual Marriage," 40.

[306] Cf. Troels Engberg-Pedersen, "Philo's De Vita Contemplativa as a Philosopher's Dream," *JSJ* 30 (1999) 40-64, who does not deny the possibility of their existence but sees them as so idealized as to be little different from fiction (48), "utopian fantasy done for a serious purpose" (43). See the critical discussion in Mary Ann Beavis, "Philo's Therapeutai: Philosopher's Dream or Utopian Construction?" *JSP* 14 (2004) 30-42.

[307] Joan E. Taylor, *Jewish Women Philosophers of First Century Alexandria: Philo's 'Therapeutae' Reconsidered* (London: Oxford University Press, 2004) 72-73; see also the discussion in pp. 54-68.

[308] Taylor, *Jewish Women Philosophers*, 43. See also David M. Hay, "Foils for the Therapeutae: References to Other Texts and Persons in Philo's 'De vita contemplativa'," in *Neotestamentica et Philonica: Studies in Honor of Peder Borgen* (ed. David E. Aune, Torrey Seland, and Jarl H. Ulrichsen; NovTSup 106; Leiden: Brill, 2003) 330-48, who speaks of cultured Hellenistic Jews or cultured Gentiles attracted to Judaism (347).

[309] Taylor, *Jewish Women Philosophers*, 44. See also Hay, "Foils for the Therapeutae," 340-41.

[310] Doron Mendels, "Hellenistic Utopia and the Essenes," *HTR* 72 (1979) 207-22, draws attention to the account in relation to the Essenes. "The people of the island of the sun do not marry but have women in common in order not to break the communal brotherhood (Diod. Sic. 2.58.1)" (215). For its relevance to Philo's depiction of the Mareotic community, see Beavis, "Philo's Therapeutai," 33-40. Among the significant differences she notes proximity to civilization, size, and absence in Philo's account of miraculous animals and plants, and self-euthanising (41).

fantasy of Iambulus and the report of Chaeremon that echoes what Philo reports of the Mareotic group, but which lies beyond the scope of the present discussion. The matters pertaining to sexuality, considered on their own, do not really count as strong parallels. Taylor may be right that Philo may have been trying to better Chaeremon or Chaeremon, Philo.[311] On the possible Roman context Niehoff suggests that "Roman discourse provides a meaningful background to Philo's discussion of the Classical Greeks and their flaws. ... Avoiding luxurious indulgence and pederasty, the Therapeutae have been cast precisely into the role which the Roman elite had assumed for itself in relation to 'the Greeks'".[312]

Taylor describes the "Mareotic community" as "comprised of people who came from the affluent and rather refined circle *Philo himself* came from",[313] being "not particularly large, and composed of certain people from an affluent, educated circle in Alexandria".[314] She suggests that they may well have belonged to the extreme sector of the allegorical school.[315] This suggests, at least, that "some of Jewish women of Alexandria were in fact studying a sophisticated allegorical form of biblical interpretation, the highest type of philosophy, as Philo defined it".[316] Like Szesnat,[317] she sees Philo confronted by a problem in having such women present in the community. The Essenes, who were male only, better suited his

---

[311] Taylor, *Jewish Women Philosophers*, 45. Hay, "Foils for the Therapeutae," writes: "It seems quite likely that Philo's treatise is partly modeled on such a description of non-Jewish contemplatives—if not on Chaeremon's treatise itself" (341).

[312] Niehoff, *Philo on Jewish Identity*, 150.

[313] Taylor, *Jewish Women Philosophers*, 98. Ross S. Kraemer, "Monastic Jewish Women in Greco-Roman Egypt: Philo Judaeos on the Therapeutrides," *Signs: Journal of Women in Culture and Society* 14 (1989) 342-59, notes that reference to leaving families and estates assumes wealth (349). "Clearly, becoming a Therapeutic was an alternative available only to a very few Jewish women in the first century C.E.–those who already had the requisite education, which not only included literacy but also favored the allegorical school of interpretation associated especially with Alexandria" (359).

[314] Taylor, *Jewish Women Philosophers*, 103.

[315] Taylor, *Jewish Women Philosophers*, 153, 170. She notes their use of a solar calendar like that of the *Temple Scroll* and *Jubilees* (169).

[316] Taylor, *Jewish Women Philosophers*, 237-38. Similarly Kraemer, "Monastic Jewish Women," 350; Martina Böhm, *Rezeption und Funktion der Vätererzählungen bei Philo von Alexandria: Zum Zusammenhang von Kontext, Hermeneutik und Exegese in frühen Judentum* (BZNW 128; Berlin: de Gruyter, 2005): "Daraus lässt sich folgern, dass für Philo Frauen unter wirtschaflichem Aspekt zwar ins Haus gehörten, dass ihm zumindest aber freie, vornehme und darum wohl auch gebildete Frauen in religiöser Hinsicht als genauso erkenntnisfähig wie Männer galten" (198).

[317] Holger Szesnat, "'Mostly Aged Virgins': Philo and the Presence of the Therapeutrides at Lake Mareotis," *Neot* 32 (1998) 191-201, 197.

values.³¹⁸ "In fact," she adds, "Philo tends to forget, conveniently, that women are there in the Mareotic group at all in several places".³¹⁹

Philo had to pick his way through a minefield of difficulties. These include that fact which he could not deny, namely, that women were present in the community and that both men and women were celibate. The authority which their young women apparently had to decide not to marry probably reflected the values of the movement from which they were drawn.³²⁰ Behind the choice for celibacy may well have been notions linking celibacy to cultic service, as in the cult of Isis.³²¹ For these extreme allegorists "sexual differences inscribed in the body are also devalued. Both males and females could be circumcised in the soul, or serve as 'priests' and 'attendants' in the 'Temple', because ultimately cultic service was dependent on the soul rather than the body".³²² It may reflect an association between celibacy and the prophetic state (cf. *Mos.* 2.68-69), as noted above.³²³ It may also reflect the growing popularity of sexual abstinence as an ideal among some Stoic and Cynic philosophers. Philo may have wanted to show that Jews

---

³¹⁸ Taylor, *Jewish Women Philosophers*, 228. So also Szesnat, "Mostly Aged Virgins," 198.

³¹⁹ Taylor, *Jewish Women Philosophers*, 228. Similarly Szesnat, "Mostly Aged Virgins," who notes that the first mention of the women is about gathering with the wall separating them from the men (32-33); then again at (68) and then at the choir (80, 83) (pp. 194-95). See also Shari Golberg, "The Two Choruses Become One: The Absence/Presence of Women in Philo's *On the Contemplative Life*," *JSJ* (2008) 459-70, 461-62.

³²⁰ Taylor, *Jewish Women Philosophers*, 260, 262-63. She also notes the evidence of high class women choosing to delay or avoid marriage and the Augustan laws promulgated to counter this (260). Otherwise women could marry at 12 or 13, usually not bear children till 15, marry usually in their late teens, by 20 3/5 were married and by their late 20s nearly all at least once, 80% still married at 30, 40% by late 40s, so that there would be a sizeable group of widows or divorcees (261). She notes that lifelong celibacy would be rare though possible (261).

³²¹ Taylor, *Jewish Women Philosophers*, 258.

³²² Taylor, *Jewish Women Philosophers*, 307-308. "The Sanctuary is not then material space, in this sacred symposium, and the suppliants and attendants of God Philo describes in Contempl. are no longer entirely configuring themselves in terms of bodily materiality. the modest separations between male and female begin to break down" (310). See also Celia Deutsch, "The Therapeutae, Text Work, Ritual, and Mystical Experience," in *Paradise Now: Essays on Early Jewish and Christian Mysticism* (SBLSym 11; ed. April D. DeConick; Atlanta: SBL, 2006) 287-311, who argues that the white robes recall those of the high priest (*Contempl.* 66), the bread of the feat, the bread of the presence (*Contempl.* 73, 81), and the prohibition of the high priest drinking wine before entering the tent of meeting "is extended to include the whole of the members' lives—they drink only water, whether in the sanctuary of their individual dwellings or in the assembly's celebrations (37, 74)" (291). The espousal of celibacy would be consistent with this.

³²³ Taylor, *Jewish Women Philosophers*, 256-57.

could go one better,[324] but for him procreation was of paramount importance. If he described the women as virgins, his readers may well have questioned the reality of all those males living in isolation with virgins, who might be seen as typically as philosophers' sexual partners,[325] or if pictured as cultic virgins, this might evoke images of the castrated *galli*.[326] If he described the women as like the men in having abandoned their families, this, too, would not fit well the notions of proper womanhood.[327] "His solution to the problem of how to make the apparently non-domestic masculinized *therapeutrides* safe is to make them conceptually domestic: virgin matrons in the household of perfect philosophy".[328] Accordingly Philo describes them as "mostly aged virgins" (*Contempl.* 68), which Taylor sees as "a smoke screen to avoid the direct discussion of the tricky issues of celibacy".[329] This shifts ground to the allegorical, portraying them as bearing spiritual fruit and as espoused to Sophia/Wisdom.[330] Taylor argues: "Philo has in fact side-tracked

---

[324] Joan E. Taylor, "Philo of Alexandria on the Essenes: A Case Study on the Use of Classical Sources in Discussions of the Qumran-Essene Hypothesis," *SPA* 19 (2007) 1-28, 24. She goes on to add: "Philo himself believed strongly that it was important for men to fulfil the commandment of God to multiply (Det. 147-148, cf. Gen 1.28)". "He states outright in Praem. 108-109 that 'all genuine attendants (θεραπευταί) of God will fulfil the law of Nature for the procreation of children'" (24).

[325] On this see Taylor, *Jewish Women Philosophers*, 213-15, 228. Szesnat, "Mostly Aged Virgins," suggests "this would have invited the kind of 'knowing laughter' which accompanied the frequent re-telling of the story of Socrates spending a night alone with the beautiful (and willing) Alcibiades without having sexual intercourse with him (Plato Symp 216c-219e)" (187).

[326] Taylor, *Jewish Women Philosophers*, 259.

[327] Taylor, *Jewish Women Philosophers*, 260. Cf. Kraemer, "Monastic Jewish Women," who sees failure to mention leaving husbands as indicative that they were unmarried (352-53). She suggests, in addition, that most of them were probably post-menopausal (353-54). This would not make them any less capable of sexual expression. Szesnat, "Mostly Aged Virgins," disputes that Philo employs the postmenopausal motif here, arguing that Philo restricts it to allegorical use (197).

[328] Taylor, *Jewish Women Philosophers*, 246. "The identification of the senior women as mothers is important not only because it enables these women to fulfil the role of a good woman in formatively gendered society, but because in much of the ancient world, as in the world today, a woman's *status* in a given social group was connected to her being a mother" (247).

[329] Taylor, *Jewish Women Philosophers*, 253. She notes also the potential ambiguity. Does "mostly" refer to "virgins" or to "elderly"? It appears, in any case, to indicate that there were others, probably meaning those who were younger.

[330] Taylor, *Jewish Women Philosophers*, 252. Kraemer, "Monastic Jewish Women," takes this as "one more indication that Philo conceptualizes the Therapeutrides as no longer female" (354). She notes that Philo does speak of the men as having spiritual offspring (355). Baer, *Male and Female*, comments: "Philo is able to accept a kind of equality among

the reader from seeing the real women of the group. 'Woman' leads to 'virgin', which leads to virgin soul, which leads to 'children of the virgin soul', and we are led out of the door. Suddenly the actual women are almost living incarnations of the pure and ever-virginal number 7".[331] When Philo espouses virginity allegorically, this does not convert into espousing it literally.[332]

According to Taylor, then, in describing the Mareotic community Philo confronts difficulty with the espousal of celibacy. "Philo makes this group acceptable by indicating that the men already had wives and children, thereby fulfilling the divine command to multiply. He cannot or does not indicate that the women left husbands or children".[333] He does not resolve the issue by masculinizing the women: "The women of the community have not become male,

---

the men and women of the Therapeutae precisely because these women either are virgins or live as virgins and thus in one sense are women in name only. In a sense they have progressed beyond the sphere of sexual polarity, and thus their femininity is not a barrier to participation in the worship and other rites of the community. Both men and women have left behind their sexuality and have attained to a higher unity of the spirit" (100). Golberg, "Two Choruses," sees the Therapeutrides as "Philo's own stand-in for Diotima at his own literary symposium" (464), noting the similar motifs of their being prophetesses/priestesses linked to mystery cults, and connected to pregnancy of the soul, a motif Philo employs elsewhere in relation to men, but not here to avoid the same-sex associations of Plato's *Symposium* (465-66). She contemplates the possibility that they are symbols like the matriarchs of virtues, but concludes that they are best seen as representing sense perception made pure and clean, like Miriam, who frequently features in the work, beside Moses (467-69). Ultimately she questions whether "Philo's text is actually meant to depict any real women at all" (470). The specificity of location and Philo's treatment of the matriarchs suggest that the account is likely to be more than just allegory and that, in turn, it seems to me, makes the psychological model less likely than one which affirms their prophetic role.

[331] Taylor, *Jewish Women Philosophers*, 252-53.

[332] Taylor, *Jewish Women Philosophers*, 251. She notes that "Philo's imagery is therefore inconsistent and at times contradictory on purpose" 251. "The virgin soul really indicates a kind of masculinised soul, whether this soul is in a male or female body" (251). "In order to satisfy society's expectation of the maternal role of women, and also in order to justify their celibate lifestyle, Philo uses the image of the fruitful soul (which does not in fact require celibacy, in his opinion)" (264).

[333] Taylor, *Jewish Women Philosophers*, 264. Taylor also notes that Philo must deal with the problem of women's participation in worship with men. He was uncomfortable with women attending synagogues and assumes that in the ideal upper class, men would report goings on to their wives at home (276), citing *Hypoth.* 7.14. Philo apparently envisages the meeting space of the Mareotic community not as a public place, but as a private civil one, which made women's presence and joint meals acceptable (277-79, 283-86). Their becoming one choir ceases to be a problem, Philo having so strongly emphasised modesty (312-14).

but retain the identification of being women, displaying modesty (*Contempl.* 33, 69) and maternity".[334] Despite needing to deal with some problematic features Philo clearly affirms this community.[335] As Hay argues, it "gives us a picture of lived-out spirituality that Philo honored, even though we cannot assume that he himself lived by all the norms of the Therapeutae or regarded them as universally valid".[336] Among the elements he valued were their "striving to transcend their bodies as far as possible", their inclusion of women, based on Gen 1:27, within defined parameters which guarded against sexual temptation, and their understanding of "pleasure (ἡδονή) as likely to prompt sin (*Contempl.* 2, 58, 68-69)".[337] Hay goes on to observe: "The life of the soul that the Therapeutae maintain is a kind of 'nearly realized eschatology.' They are not completely free from their bodies at present, but they give them minimal attention".[338] Philo affirms them while he "nowhere says that woman as such is the source of evil, nor does he denounce sexual activity within marriage".[339]

---

[334] Taylor, *Jewish Women Philosophers*, 264, similarly 237. She writes: "Philo can clearly play the card of the 'One of the guys' woman if it suits him. He accounts for the historical virtue of Sarah—as well as providing a rationale for his symbolism of the matriarch as virtue—by masculinizing her" (233).

[335] So Hay, "Foils for the Therapeutae," 344. "They are, as it were, living proofs of the value of the Jewish religion" (345). See also James M. Scott, "Dionysus in Philo of Alexandria: A Study of *De Vita Contemplativa*," *SPA* 20 (2008) 33-54, who argues that "*De Vita Contemplativa* portrays the Therapeutae as an ideal group that practices a rarified form of Judaism comparable to the highest form of the Dionysiac mysteries" (54).

[336] David M. Hay, "Philo's Anthropology, the Spiritual Regimen of the Therapeutae, and a Possible Connection with Corinth," in *Philo und das Neue Testament: Wechselseitige Wahrnehmungen: I, Internationales Symposium zum Corpus Judaeo-Hellenisticum 1.-4. Mai 2003* (ed. Roland Deines and Karl Wilhelm Niebuhr,; Tübingen: Mohr Siebeck, 2004) 127-42, 135. Deutsch, "Therapeutae," comments: "Perhaps Philo is holding out—first of all, to himself—the hope that, even if the idea is possible only for the very few, the philosophical life is possible, at least in some measure, for every Jew who studies the sacred writings" (310).

[337] Hay, "Philo's Anthropology," 139. Kraemer, "Monastic Jewish Women," concludes: "All this suggests that the Therapeutrides were able to participate in the contemplative life on a more or less equal basis with men only when they renounced the distinctive (though not definitional) aspects of being women–sexuality and childbearing. It is difficult to assess how much they might have internalized the perception of themselves as male, or at least as no longer female" (360).

[338] Hay, "Philo's Anthropology," 140; similarly Hay, "Foils for the Therapeutae": "living at the summit of human experience" (347).

[339] Hay, "Philo's Anthropology," 140; similarly Szesnat, "Mostly Aged Virgins," 193. Kraemer, "Monastic Jewish Women," argues that "overall, Philo's depictions of Jewish women in Alexandrian life and his personal attitudes toward women do not conflict with his portrayal of the Therapeutrides. For example, to the extent that Philo thought women ought

To some extent Philo's depiction of the Essenes confirms his own stance, including towards sexual abstinence. Though we lack his treatise which immediately preceded *Contempl.*, we do have references to the Essenes elsewhere. The account in *Prob.* 75-91 of Essenes in Palestinian Syria makes no reference to sexual matters. In *Hypoth.*, however, Philo notes that "no Essene is a mere child nor even a stripling or newly bearded, since the characteristics of such are unstable with a waywardness corresponding to the immaturity of the age, but full grown men and already verging on old age, no longer carried under the tide of the body nor led by the passions, but enjoying the veritable, the only real freedom" (*Hypoth.* 11.3). Being "no longer carried under the tide of the body nor led by the passions" will doubtless include allusion to sexual desires, but here they are depicted as simply outgrown by age.[340]

At a later point Philo reports: "Furthermore they eschew marriage because they clearly discern it to be the sole or principal danger to the maintenance of the communal life, as well as because they particularly practise continence. For no Essene takes a wife, because a wife is a selfish creature, excessively jealous and an adept at beguiling the morals of her husband and seducing him by her continued impostures" (*Hypoth.* 11.14). Here Philo grounds their decision in two main concerns: maintaining community life and avoiding danger. On the first this may well have limited application. It assumes the special situation of living as a group in community. In that context Philo believes that having wives, whether one's own or in common,[341] would presumably create problems by causing dispute. The second concern helps reinforce this and both should probably be read closely together. Thus Philo declares: "a wife is a selfish creature, excessively jealous", which makes sense on Philo's terms of being a root cause of division within such a community and "an adept at beguiling the morals of her husband and seducing him by her continued impostures" might also address related dangers. Further on, Philo declares: "For he who is either fast bound in the love lures of his wife or under the

---

to be removed from public spheres of activity and confined to private areas, the Therapeutrides would have conformed to his values" (356). Maren Niehoff, "Mother and Maiden, Sister and Spouse: Sarah in Philonic Midrash," *HTR* 97 (2004) 413-44, comments that "While Philo considered these Jewish women to be exceptional figures whose example could not be recommended for the whole community, he was nevertheless proud of them" (438).

[340] As Taylor, "Philo of Alexandria on the Essenes," observes, "The Essenes do not have wives, but it is not stated by Philo that these older men who have acquired property have never had wives" (21; similarly 24).

[341] Taylor, "Philo of Alexandria on the Essenes," suggests that in *A.J.* 18.21 Josephus is rejecting Plato's notion of a community of wives when he reports that the Essenes "do not bring them into their shared possessions" (23).

stress of nature makes his children his first care ceases to be the same to others and unconsciously has become a different man and has passed from freedom into slavery" (*Hypoth.* 11.17). The focus on community is clear in the words, "ceases to be the same to others". Philo depicts this as a form of slavery, which carries the implication that it applies in any situation of a married man with children anywhere, but then this, too, is qualified. It concerns the man in whom "the love lures of his wife" and "the stress of nature" rule, rather than the mind.

None of this has to do with asceticism. Philo is not making celibacy an ideal for all, but explaining what works for such a community and why it makes sense. While it is true generally that in Philo "the Essenes are not shown as some peculiar sect that is unrepresentative of what most Jews think, but as a kind of apogee of excellence within the Jewish philosophia",[342] we should not conclude that it is to be taken as a paradigm for how Jews should live in the wider community.[343] In addition, as Taylor notes, absence of reference in Philo to the married Essenes of whom Josephus speaks, need not mean that Philo knows of none. "Given the education of newcomers and the agedness of Philo's actual Essenes, his discussions presuppose there were at least Essene-friendly others in the wider context of Judaean society from which the new commune-dwellers were drawn."[344] In this way Philo accounts for Essene celibacy as making good sense in their particular communal lifestyle, while not compromising his overall stance which affirms sexual relations, including appropriate sexual passion, as having its place when geared towards procreation. This probably is also how we should see the Mareotic community though there Philo gives even less information about the basis for their celibacy so that we are left speculating that it may have reflected similar concerns to those which inform Philo's depiction of the exceptional role of Moses.

---

[342] Taylor, "Philo of Alexandria on the Essenes," 8. She notes on the other hand, that "from the perspective of rhetoric, it is also clear that Philo, in creating the Essenes as an example of 'the good' would have been highly unlikely to state at the outside that this pinnacle of goodness within Judaism spurned the entire sacrificial system of the Jerusalem Temple, if not the Temple itself' (13).

[343] See also the discussion in Loader, *Dead Sea Scrolls on Sexuality*, 368-76.

[344] Taylor, "Philo of Alexandria on the Essenes," 27.

1.2.4 Life Beyond the Garden (Gen 3:14 – 4:1)

1.2.4.1 The Consequences of Failure

1.2.4.1.1 The Consequences of Failure in "On Creation"

In *Opif.* Philo deals rather briefly with the consequences of failure: "The woman incurred the violent woes of travail-pangs, and the griefs which come one after another all through the remainder of life. Chief among them are all those that have to do with children at birth and in their bringing up, in sickness and in health, in good fortune and evil fortune" (*Opif.* 167). He then adds: "In the next place she tasted deprivation of liberty, and the authority of the husband at her side, whose commands she must perforce obey" (*Opif.* 167). Neither is allegorised. He makes no reference to her "return" to her husband (Gen 3:16).

Then "the man, in his turn, incurred labours and distress in the unceasing sweat of his brow to gain the necessaries of life. He was without those good things which the earth had been taught to bear of itself independently of all skill in the husbandman" (*Opif.* 167), again remaining at the literal level and consistent with his earlier expressed detail of the man at home with God and the world around him, which provided him and the woman with all they needed. Now, by God's generosity, he is not totally bereft of such provision, but still must toil (*Opif.* 169). And so Philo concludes: "Such is the life of those who at the outset are in enjoyment of innocence and simplicity of character, but later on prefer vice to virtue" (*Opif.* 170). Earlier, however, he notes the consequences for the man in generalised form: "Men have flung themselves unrestrainedly into the indulgence of their passions and left uncontrolled their guilty cravings, cravings which it were sinful even to name (τῶν ἀνθρώπων ἀνέδην ἐκκεχυμένων εἴς τε τὰ πάθη καὶ τὰς ἀκράτορας καὶ ὑπαιτίους ἃς οὐδ' εἰπεῖν θέμις ὀρέξεις), a fitting penalty is incurred, due punishment of impious courses. That penalty is difficulty in obtaining the necessaries of life" (*Opif.* 80). Failure to control passions has not only corrupted the individual; it has brought with it the punishment that nature no longer provides sustenance without toil, Philo's interpretation of God's judgement on Adam in Gen 3:17-19. As Runia notes, "Surprisingly, after the heavy emphasis that the subject received in §§151-156, Philo does not dwell on the aspect of mortality and death".[345]

---

[345] Runia, *Creation*, 387.

Man and Woman: Beginning from Genesis 1 – 3 111

1.2.4.1.2 The Consequences of Failure in "Questions and Answers on Genesis"

In *QG* Philo is similarly brief. Here he alludes also to the judgement on the snake in 3:15, which Philo explains as meaning: "desire has a natural enmity toward sense, which (Scripture) symbolically calls woman" (*QG* 1.48). His reference to the consequences for women, "increase in sorrow and lamentation and in giving birth and in turning (ἐπιστροφῇ) to her husband and being under his rule" (*QG* 1.49), is limited and terse: "This experience comes to every woman who lives together with a man. It is (meant) not as a curse but as a necessity" (*QG* 1.49). He then relates it symbolically to the mind and the senses, arguing that the senses of the worthless man suffer, but "according to the deeper meaning, there takes place a turning of sense to the man, not as to a helper, for it is a subject of no worth, but as to a master, since it prizes force more than righteousness" (*QG* 1.49) and Philo sees such submission as appropriate. Similarly the judgement on man addresses the man "zealous for pleasure, through which spiritual death is brought about" (*QG* 1.51).

1.2.4.1.3 The Consequences of Failure in "Allegorical Commentary" and Beyond

By contrast, in *Leg.* Philo attends to minute detail. First he notes that the snake receives no right of reply and explains that this is because "the serpent, pleasure, is bad of itself" (ἐξ ἑαυτῆς ἐστι μοχθήρα) (*Leg.* 3.68). "She has in her no seed from which virtue might spring, but is always and everywhere guilty and foul" (*Leg.* 3.68). This stands somewhat in tension with earlier statements and statements elsewhere that pleasure can also be something positive. We must conclude that he means here only that pleasure as represented in the story by the snake and its intent, which was clearly bad. Of the woman's being given a right of reply he explains "We have to say, then, that sense-perception comes under the head neither of bad nor of good things, but is an intermediate thing common to a wise man and a fool, and when it finds itself in a fool it proves bad, when in a sensible man, good" (*Leg.* 3.67). "It is not pronounced guilty till it has owned that it followed evil" (*Leg.* 3.67). Philo concludes that "What a serpent does to a man, that pleasure does to the soul, and therefore the serpent was taken to represent pleasure" (*Leg.* 3.76).

After a lengthy discourse illustrating the wise and the foolish, Philo returns to the cursing of the serpent (*Leg.* 3.107; Gen 3:14) and explains: "Pleasure, the passion *par excellence* (ἡδονή, τὸ πάθος), deserves cursing; it shifts the standards of the soul and renders it a lover of passion, instead of a lover of virtue" (*Leg.* 3.107), and is as cursed as removing the landmarks (cf. Deut 27:17), leading the blind astray (Deut 27:18) (*Leg.* 3.108). "Pleasure, then, has cheated poor maimed sense of the power of apprehending matters ... giving it a craving for that which produces pleasure" (*Leg.* 3.109; cf. Deut 27:19). "Accursed on these grounds is pleasure" (*Leg.* 3.111). Philo speaks of "when we have glutted ourselves with immoderate pleasure" (*Leg.* 3.111), so that "when we are in the very midst of the enjoyments it affords, we find ourselves utterly deprived of the support that we obtain through the co-operation of the senses" (*Leg.* 3.112). "Lust comes into play through love of pleasure; pain arises as pleasure is withdrawn; fear again is engendered owing to the dread of being without pleasure. It is clear, then, that all the passions depend on pleasure" (*Leg.* 3.113). This makes pleasure a central concern. It is important however to see that the declaration of pleasure as "the passion *par excellence*" in *Leg.* 3.107 follows the statement: "Just as joy, being a good condition of soul (ὥσπερ ἡ χαρὰ εὐπάθεια οὖσα), deserves prayer". In using the Stoic term, εὐπάθεια, Philo creates room for appropriate emotion, including the pleasure of joy.

Taking up the curse that the snake is to go henceforth on its breast and belly (Gen 3:14), Philo predictably observes: "For passion has its lair in these parts of the body, the breast and the belly ... it haunts the belly and the parts below it (τὴν γαστέρα καὶ τὰ μετ' αὐτήν)" (*Leg.* 3.114). In this context he identifies the three parts of the soul: reasoning, high spirit and desire, located respectively in the head, breast, and the abdomen (*Leg.* 3.115). Accordingly, he writes: "To the lustful portion (τῷ δὲ ἐπιθυμητικῷ) of the soul they assign the quarter about the abdomen and the belly, for there it is that lust, irrational craving (ἐπιθυμία ὄρεξις ἄλογος), has its abode" (*Leg.* 3.115). The advantage of the analysis is that it suits the image of the charioteer of reason set over high spirit and lust (*Leg.* 3.118). This prompts his lengthy contrast between Aaron and Moses on the basis of Lev 8:29, "Moses took the breast and removed it as a crowning offering before the Lord" (*Leg.* 3.129), noted above in our discussion of excising passions (1.2.2.3).

Remaining with the curse on the snake, Philo notes its reference to movement: "Thou shalt go ...", which he uses to paint pleasure not as stationary but "as the flame is in movement, so, not unlike a blazing thing, passion moving in the soul does not suffer it to be calm" (*Leg.* 3.160), the familiar image of passion as fire (similarly *Opif.* 158). That the serpent is to eat dirt enables Philo to contrast earthly and heavenly food, exploiting the image of the manna (*Leg.* 3.162-178), also an image suited to counselling avoidance of excess and taking only what is necessary (*Leg.* 3.166).

The exposition of the snake's curse continues as Philo reflects on the enmity put between the snake and the woman. He declares: "In reality pleasure is foe to sense, albeit thought by some to be a close friend" (*Leg.* 3.182). The word "between" he sees as indicating the arena of warfare, namely "drinkables, eatables, [and] what is adapted to all such purposes" (*Leg.* 3.184). "What pleasure, then, is to sense, and passion is to mind. Since, therefore, the former pair are mutually hostile, the latter must also be at war with each other" (*Leg.* 3.185). He continues: "Through passion all the war of the soul is fanned into flame" (*Leg.* 3.187). The prediction, "he shall watch thy head, and thou shalt watch his heel" (Gen 3:15; *Leg.* 3.188), Philo takes to refer to the mind and the snake: "The foolish mind will show itself a guardian and steward of pleasure, seeing that its delight is in pleasure; but the good mind will prove its enemy" (*Leg.* 3.189). The image enables Philo to refer to Jacob who "shall not let go the heel of his adversary, passion, till it has given in" (*Leg.* 3.190), just as he sees his wrestling as the struggle "with passions and wickedness" (*Leg.* 3.190).

In turning to the prediction of the woman's greatly multiplied sorrows and groanings (Gen 3:16), Philo offers reflections on grief and gladness as occupying the same quarter of our being (*Leg.* 3.200). On the words, "'And to thy husband,' He says, 'shall be thy resort [return] (ἀποστροφή)'" he declares that sense "has two husbands, the one lawful, the other a seducer" (*Leg.* 3.220). To respond to the seducer is for sense to act on sight or sound – nothing necessarily sexual here – whereas "to sense that has been turned (ἀποστραφείση) from all else to Mind (νοῦν), her lawful husband, vast benefit befalls" (*Leg.* 3.221). "Most profitless is that the Mind (νοῦν) should listen to Sense-perception (αἰσθήσεως), and not Sense-perception (αἴσθησιν) to Mind (νοῦ); for it is always right that the superior should rule and the inferior be ruled; and Mind (νοῦς) is superior to Sense-perception (αἰσθήσεως)" (*Leg.* 3.222), providing another occasion for employing the metaphor of the charioteer and the pilot (*Leg.* 3.223-224). While the focus is the dangers of following sense-perception, rather than any one passion, Philo uses female imagery because he believes women are dangerous, citing the women of Moab, and Potiphar's wife.

Turning to God's judgement on the man, Philo notes that "the serpent, we saw was pleasure (ἡδονή), an irrational elation of soul (ἔπαρσις ἄλογος ψυχῆς)" and "that she attaches herself only to a worthless man" (*Leg.* 3.246). "For in so far as he is mind, his nature is neither bad nor good, but under the influence of virtue and vice it is his wont to shift towards good and bad" (*Leg.* 3.246). The "thorns" (Gen 3:18) Philo interprets as the passions (*Leg.* 3.248, 250). The foolish man is then condemned to eat grass, "food of an irrational creature; and such is a bad man with the right principle cut out of him; irrational also are the senses, being a part of the soul" (*Leg.* 3.251). Such a life is "exceeding painful and burdensome ... as he pursues with greedy desire all things that are productive of pleasures and of all things that wickedness loves to bring about" (*Leg.* 3.251). His returning to the earth is returning to his origin, which like the rest of the judgement Philo takes not as a description of all men but only of the foolish and wicked.

The sequel *Cher.* notes the expulsion from the garden of pleasure, likening it allegorically to forsaking the symbol of virtue, Sarah, for lower learning, Hagar. Isaac's birth, representing true happiness, comes after Sarah has "ceased from the manner of women and died to the passions" (*Cher.* 8), but Philo gives no attention to sexual themes. They are probably included, but only incidentally where Philo contrasts the delight of Eden to "the weak and wanton sort, which the brute passion pleasure brings" (*Cher.* 12). In *Cher.* 10 he expounds the expulsion as representing the rejection of false options: "Since then the sophist, who is ever sophist, and his mother, the instruction in the preliminary learning, are expelled and banished by God from the presence of wisdom and the wise, on whom he confers the titles of Sarah and Abraham, can we wonder that he has cast forth Adam, that is the mind, which is sick with the incurable sickness of folly, from the dwelling-place of virtue for ever and permits him not to return?" Reaching Gen 4:1, 2, that Adam knew his wife and she conceived and bore Cain, Philo declares that "the persons to whose virtue the lawgiver has testified, such as Abraham, Isaac, Jacob and Moses, and others of the same spirit, are not represented by him as knowing women" (*Cher.* 40). This is allegorical, not literal; for he continues: "For since we hold that woman signifies in a figure sense-perception, and that knowledge comes into being through estrangement from sense and body, it will follow that the lovers of wisdom reject rather than choose sense". Sexual intercourse becomes a major symbol in Philo's argumentation.

We noted above that Philo had already exploited the image of the snake in his exposition of the temptation in *Leg.*, bringing it into connection with Dan as a serpent in Gen 49:17, the plague of snakes in the wilderness and Moses' bronze serpent, Moses' and Jacob's rods, and the Song of Moses (*Leg.* 2.77-105). Since he also develops the image in relation to the snake's curse, we consider the related complex of imagery here. In *Migr.* he cites Gen 3:14 in support of his observation: "Some, exceeding all bounds, in their determination to kindle into activity all the irrational portion of the soul, and to destroy the mind, have not only indulged all that comes under the head of desire, but taken to them also its brother passion, fierce spirit" (*Migr.* 66). Earlier he wrote: "For it says, 'If thou go out to war against thine enemies and see horse and rider,' that is passion, the insolent, the restive, the unruly, and the passion-loving mind mounted on it" (*Migr.* 62, citing Gen 49:17). Alluding to the Song of Moses about horse and rider being thrown into sea he writes in *Ebr.* of "the mind which rode upon the unreasoning impulses of passion, that four-footed beast which knows not the rein" (*Ebr.* 111). In *Somn.* 2 Philo repeats the image of horse and rider cast into the sea from Exod 15:1 to celebrate victory over passion (*Somn.* 2.269). The wicked "betake themselves to pleading the cause of pleasure and lust and of every superabundant appetite and raise up unreasoning passion to menace the ruling reason" (*Somn.* 2.276). They are to be confronted, as by the prophet: "It is as characteristic of him, that he should ever go out to the spreading tide of unreasoning passion, as it is of the wise to meet its strong current, whose waters are the advocacy of pleasure and lust" (*Somn.* 2.278), thus "to overthrow and lay low the plausibilities which plead the cause of passion" (*Somn.* 2.278). This depiction of victory over "the passions of Egypt" (*Somn.* 2.281) remains general with no specifically sexual references.

We find this also elaborated in *Agr.* Beginning similarly from the Song of Moses it declares: "So it is, for vices are four in kind and passions equal to these in number. It is a victory, moreover, in which their rider has been thrown and dispatched, even virtue-hating and passion-loving mind, whose delight was in pleasures and cravings" (*Agr.* 83). Philo then makes a connection with the royal code in Deut 17:15-16 about not appointing a foreigner and not multiplying horses. They were "not to appoint a horse-rearer to be a ruler, regarding as unsuited for such high authority any man who resembles an unbridled and unruly horse, and, in his wild excitement over pleasures, lusty, and amours, knows no restraint" (*Agr.* 84). Typically Philo explains: "He is speaking about that irrational and unmeasured and unruly movement in the soul to check which is in her interest, lest some day it turn back all her people to Egypt, the country of the body, and forcibly render it a lover of pleasure and passion rather than of God and virtue" (*Agr.* 88).

He then introduces a change to the imagery, following the more familiar notion, noted in the previous section in relation to the image of the charioteer, that the mind is the horseman who is to control the horses, the passions: "For these are able by applying bit and bridle to the irrational faculties to curb the excessive violence of their movement" (*Agr.* 94). The same thought occurs in *Spec.* 4: "So if a man does not set bounds to his impulses and bridle them like horses which defy the reins he is the victim of a well-nigh fatal passion" (*Spec.* 4.79). From here in *Agr.* Philo makes the connection to Dan in Genesis 49 and so to the image of the serpent in the garden and Moses' serpent in the wilderness, as in *Leg.* (*Agr.* 94-96). "Told in this way, these things are like prodigies and marvels, one serpent emitting a human voice and using quibbling arguments to an utterly guileless character, and cheating a woman with seductive plausibilities; and another proving the author of complete deliverance to those who beheld it" (*Agr.* 96). "Her serpent is pleasure, a crawling thing with many a twist, powerless to raise itself upright, always prone" (*Agr.*97; similarly on proneness: *Opif.* 158); "the serpent of Moses is the disposition quite contrary to pleasure, even stedfast endurance" (*Agr.* 97). Accordingly, "self-mastery, that averter of ills, is an antidote to licentiousness" (*Agr.* 98). "For lack of self-control, and gluttony, and all else that issues from the womb of those immoderate and insatiable pleasures that ever conceive by the abundance of external comforts, never allow the soul to go along the straight course" (*Agr.*101). "Most fitly therefore did he say that temperance keeps to the right road, since the opposite condition, that of licentiousness, finds no road at all" (*Agr.*101). "For there is no single thing that does not yield to the enticement of pleasure, and get caught and dragged along in her entangling nets, through which it is difficult to slip and make your escape" (*Agr.* 103). "Eve's serpent is represented by the lawgiver as thirsting for man's blood" (*Agr.*107), "whereas Dan's serpent, of which we are now speaking, is represented as biting, not a man's, but a horse's heel. For Eve's serpent, being as was shewn before, a symbol of pleasure, attacks a man, namely, the reasoning faculty in each of us; for the delightful experiences of abounding pleasure is the ruin of the understanding; whereas the serpent of Dan, being a figure of endurance, a most sturdy virtue, will be found to bite a horse, the symbol of passion and wickedness, inasmuch as temperance makes the overthrow and destruction of these its aim" (*Agr.*108-109). The particular detail in Gen 49:17 that the horseman fell backwards is as in *Leg.* a symbol of falling back away from passions (*Agr.* 122). These elaborations remain at a general level without specifically sexual themes, though sexual wrong will be included under the references to "licentiousness".

Within this extensive exposition, especially if we read it in the light of what Philo had already written about the serpent earlier, we can see that the primary themes remain the same. God has made pleasure which produces engagement between mind and sense-perception, meant to be something good, but it has the opposite potential. This receives the major emphasis, producing the dramatic declarations that pleasure is something accursed and evil producing slavery of the mind to sense-perception and the passions.

1.2.4.1.4 Conclusion

Common to all three accounts is some mention of the judgement on the woman and the man, but this differs among them. In *Opif.* Philo remains at the literal level, supplementing the account of women's woes by including the challenges of upbringing. In *QG* we find reference to enmity towards sense, symbolised by woman, but apart from that primarily a literal interpretation depicting women's pain and submission as necessary rather than a curse. Here the man is represented as "zealous for pleasure" resulting in spiritual death. This is closer to what we find in *Leg.* where Philo seems not to speak of all but only of "the foolish man", who is condemned to eat grass, the irrational, and encounter thorns, the passions, and return to the origin of the wicked, the earth. This appears to cohere with his exposition earlier of some made to be bad and some, good. He does not attribute universal physical death to God's judgement here.[346] His treatment of the curse on the woman in *Leg.* exploits the motif of enmity, only briefly noted in *QG*, to the extent of declaring ongoing warfare between all three: snake – woman – man; pleasure – sense-perception – mind. The reference to woman's pain in childbirth receives no attention at a literal level, serving instead as a trigger for discussing

---

[346] So Termini, "Philo's Thought," who notes that "for Philo physical death is not part of the divine punishment" (105).

grief and gladness as occupying the same quarter of our being, and the pain of repentance. Only in *Leg.* do we find exposition of the snake's curse and there we find a number of typically absolute statements about pleasure as evil, which are too easily misread in an unqualified way. They are about the lure of illicit and excessive pleasure in contrast to the pleasure of joy that belongs to soul properly ordered by the mind. We also find extensive development of the imagery of the snake with multiple biblical allusions, serving the common theme of controlling the passions and not succumbing to the illegitimate lures of pleasure which bring death.

1.2.4.2 Conception, Childbirth, and Human Biology

While in *Opif.* Philo notes that "the woman incurred the violent woes of travail-pangs, and the griefs which come one after another all through the remainder of life" and that "chief among them are all those that have to do with children at birth and in their bringing up, in sickness and in health, in good fortune and evil fortune" (*Opif.* 167), in *QG* he notes of pain in childbirth that "this experience comes to every woman who lives together with a man. It is (meant) not as a curse but as a necessity" (*QG* 1.49). Philo makes frequent references elsewhere to conception and childbirth. They belong within the broader context of Philo's human biology of sexuality and sexual reproduction. Sometimes Philo provides such information directly at a literal level, sometimes indirectly at a symbolic level. In what follows we consider first what he tells us about human biology. We discuss his extensive symbolic use of this material below in 1.4.5.

In *Opif.*, while expounding the significance of seven, Philo notes that human beings pass developmental phases each period of seven years, beginning with the first in which "the growth of the teeth begins"; then describing the second, to 14, characterised by developing "the capacity for emitting seed"; the third to 21, by "growing of the beard"; the fourth to 28 by "increase of strength"; the fifth, to 35 by "ripeness for marriage"; the sixth, to 42, when "understanding reaches its bloom"; the seventh to 49 by "progressive improvement of mind and reason"; the eighth to 56, by "the perfecting of both these"; the ninth to 63, when "forbearance and gentleness emerge, owing to the more complete taming of the passions"; and the tenth to 70, "the desirable end of life" (*Opif.* 103). He then cites a lengthy citation from Solon as source for the ideas (*Opif.* 104), though it makes no mention of seed at stage two.[347] He also notes that Hippocrates (Hippocrates of Cos ca 460 – 370 B.C.E.) writes of only seven stages (*Opif.* 105), also without specifically sexual references.

---

[347] Runia, *Creation*, notes that it does feature "in other arithmological accounts, e.g. at Theon 104.6" (278).

In *Congr.* Philo describes the first stage as being one when "the soul is reared with none but passions to be its comrades, griefs, pains, excitements, desires, pleasures, all of which come to it through the senses" (*Congr.* 81). On this developmental view stage one is not bad in itself, but by implication remaining at that stage would be. In adolescence "there springs from the single root the twofold stalk, virtue and vice" (*Congr.* 82). He then expounds Egypt as the first stage, symbolising sense, and Canaan as the second, symbolising vice (*Congr.* 83-87). Both must be left behind: "They are the practices of passion and vices, from which spring the many multitudes of the impious and the workers of unholiness" (*Congr.* 87) pointing to Lev 18:1-5 (*Congr.* 86), the source of the dual reference to Egypt and Canaan, but not going on to address anything specific in the chapter. To remain at the first stage or the second is to make no progress on the journey of life. Philo does not express this interesting developmental view elsewhere in his writings.

On a few occasions he notes sexual development in the second stage. In the speech with which he wards off Potiphar's wife, Joseph speaks of young men in pagan communities reaching fourteen, allowed from then on to engage with prostitutes (*Ios.* 42). By contrast, Philo has Joseph declare what he claims as the Jewish norm: "Before the lawful union we know no mating with other women, but come as virgin men to virgin maidens" (*Ios.* 43). Of Ishmael's circumcision at age thirteen, Philo comments that it was close to fourteen "when the generative movements are brought to their seed" (*QG* 3.61). In *Leg.*1 he writes: "during his second period of seven years he reaches complete consummation; consummation meaning the power of reproducing his like; for at about the age of fourteen we are able to beget offspring like ourselves" (*Leg.* 1.10; similarly *QG* 2.5); and similarly in *Her.* he speaks of the second stage as most aflame "when the smouldering passions are being fanned into a flame" (*Her.* 296), though otherwise his extended discussion there of human development in four stages (*Her.* 293-299), including propensities to sin, says nothing more pertaining to sexuality.

Philo follows Solon in depicting the years, 29-35, as the time for a man to enter marriage (*Opif.* 103, 104). In *QG* 4.88 he speaks of Isaac being of mature and marriageable age without being specific, but later in the same work he writes that Isaac was forty: "The fortieth year is the right time for the marriage of the wise man, for it is good (for him) to be trained and directed and abound in the right forms of discipline in youth and to have regard for nothing else whatever and not to wander in any other direction toward things which are not to be liked but thoroughly to enjoy the thoughts and company of those (studies) and be more happy in them" (*QG* 4.154). Philo supports the suitability of this age by drawing attention to what he reports physicians of his day claim, namely that the seed injected in the womb becomes a formed creature after 40 days (*QG* 4.154), though he offers no explanation why the two should correlate. It is more as an extreme when Philo quotes the comment of Heracleitus that 30 can be called a generation because "From a man of thirty years old there can come a grandfather, for he attains manhood in his fourteenth year, when he is able to sow seed, and the (child) sown within a year comes into being and similarly after fifteen years begets one like himself" (*QG* 2.5). We find no reference to the age of women at marriage, but may assume it would have between 12 and 20.

In *Spec.* 3.72 Philo makes reference to pre-nuptial agreements. Satlow comments that "Philo clearly knows the practice of couples 'betrothing' (*hyperēnguēsōsi*) by means of written 'agreements' (*homologiai*) that contain the names of the husband and wife and other details relating to the marriage", but argues that such agreements have more moral than legal force".[348] They are not indicative of the practice in Alexandria of inchoate marriage, otherwise attested in the period only in Matt 1:18-19.[349] He notes that such documents "were almost certainly not constitutive of marriage: the marriage existed with or without the document. All marriage contracts in antiquity, whether Jewish or not, focused primarily on economic relations, occasionally giving some attention to the way that spouses should treat each other. The purpose of Jewish marriage documents was not to create the marriage, but to clarify and codify economic obligations within it".[350] He notes also that Philo mentions "bridal sacrifices and feasts" (*Spec.* 3.80), which probably took place on the wedding day and before the consummation, a contemporary practice perhaps under the influence of Greek and Roman custom.[351]

Philo says very little about women's sexual engagement. He is of the view that women are less interested in sex than men. In the context of describing the Egyptian practice to "circumcise marriageable youth and maid in the fourteenth (year) of their age, when the male begins to get seed, and the female to have a menstrual flow" (*QG* 3.47), he explains why "the divine legislator" required only male circumcision, offering as his first reason: "that the male has more pleasure in, and desire for, mating than does the female, and he is more ready for it" (*QG* 3.47), but offers no evidence for the claim. He asserts it as uncontroversial fact and it probably reflects a widespread (and mistaken) view of his day which survived to our own time, and which has been taken by men as justifying their seeing intercourse primarily from their own perspective and not women's.

---

[348] Michael L. Satlow, *Jewish Marriage in Antiquity* (Princeton: Princeton University Press, 2001) 71. He sees Philo trying to interpret "these customary Greek documents" in relation to "three discrete [] pieces of data: (1) the customary Greek premarital agreement; (2) popular disapproval of women who have intercourse with another man after having been engaged by such an agreement; and (3) the biblical institution of inchoate marriage" (72).

[349] Satlow, *Jewish Marriage*, 72.

[350] Satlow, *Jewish Marriage*, 84.

[351] Satlow, *Jewish Marriage*, 174-75.

On the other hand, he makes a number of references to menstruation. In *Opif.* in listing significant sets of seven he observes that "for women the duration of the monthly cleansing is at the most seven days" (*Opif.* 124; similarly *Leg.* 1.13),[352] though makes nothing more of it in the context. Twice he shows that he understands that there is a link between menstrual blood and the foetus: "From this it is clear that the wet substance we have mentioned must be part of the earth which gives birth to all things, just as with women the running of the monthly cleansings; for these too are, so physical scientists tell us, the bodily substance of the *fetus*" (*Opif.* 132; similarly *QG* 3.3). This reflects his espousal of a particular understanding of conception to which we return shortly. In *QG* 4 he cites "There ceased to be to Sarah the ways of women", explaining "The literal meaning is clear. For (Scripture) by a euphemism calls the monthly purification of women 'the ways of women'" (*QG* 4.15; similarly *Post.* 134) before going on to allegorical application which we will consider in discussing use of her image in the next chapter. Rachel's feigned menstruation to prevent Laban from finding his idols, claiming "the custom of woman" was upon her (Gen 31:35), Philo treats as an allegory of women's propensity to surrender to custom (*Ebr.* 54). In the context of expounding Gen 16:7, which speaks of the angel of the Lord finding Hagar "at the water-spring", Philo offers a number of different readings of "spring" (*Fug.* 177-210), including one in which he relates it to menstruation (*Fug.* 188-89). He cites the prohibition of sexual intercourse with a menstruating woman (Lev 20:18) and immediately allegorises it. Accordingly, "the Lawgiver ... gives to sense-perception the name woman, suggesting Mind as her husband" (*Fug.* 188). Sense-perception becomes a spring of folly when the mind goes to sleep instead of staying awake. In the final chapter we discuss laws relating to intercourse during menstruation, but here Philo uses menstruation to symbolise the "spring of folly", probably playing with the notion of its sometimes unpredictable onset which serves the image of catching mind unawares. Philo connects it to imagery of the flood in Gen 7:11 to speak of the deluge of sense-perception, which burst upon the mind "as in a cataract; and from sense-perception below, as it were from the earth, passions come welling up" (*Fug.* 192). It is part of Philo's negative use of female imagery and probably reflects notions of taboo in relation to menstrual blood, as

---

[352] Runia, *Creation*, observes that menstruation "is not so common in other arithmological authors", citing Ps.-Iamblicus 61.2-4 and Macrobius 1.6.62 (292). See also Moehring, "Arithmology," who notes that Philo will have taken over the list in *Opif.* 89-128 "from some neopythagorean work either on arithmology in general, or on the number seven" (159), and that it forms the basis for the list in *Leg.*, but that he frequently includes material to which no further attention is drawn (159). The allusions to menstruation belong to these.

Sly suggests,[353] a stance widely reflected, also within Philo's biblical heritage, but should not be read as necessarily negative at a literal level.

We have noted above Philo's firm view that engagement in sexual intercourse is legitimate only when it serves procreation and is within marriage and that in this the pleasure of sexual intercourse is appropriate. In *Opif.* he notes that "the first approaches of the male to the female have pleasure to guide and conduct them, and it is through pleasure that begetting and the coming of life is brought about" (*Opif.* 161; similarly *Abr.* 102 which speaks of union "brought about by pleasure"). This may simply address attraction through the prospect of sexual pleasure. It might reflect the view that pleasure in intercourse enhances fertility. Philo expresses the view that parents' engagement in intercourse generates affection for the resultant offspring (*QG* 3.48; similarly 4 Macc 15:5). He also comments that parents "dote on their late-born children" as their long hoped for or last (*Abr.* 195).

Philo understands the reproductive process on the model espoused by Aristotle, *Gen. An.* 2.3-4.[354] Accordingly in *Opif.* he writes that "seed is the original starting-point of living creatures. That this is a substance of a very low order, resembling foam, is evident to the eye. But when it has been deposited in the womb and become solid, it acquires movement, and at once enters upon natural growth" (*Opif.* 67). We noted above that he saw the capacity to emit seed as developing around 14. He lists "the natural normal emission of seed through the genital organs" as one of the natural seven discharges of the body (*Opif.* 123). In his daring image of divine impregnation in *Migr.* 33 Philo may allude to semen as snow: "For the offspring of the soul's own travail are for the most part poor abortions, things untimely born; but those which God waters with the snows of heaven (ὅσα δὲ ἂν ἐπινίθων ὁ θεὸς ἄρδῃ) come to the birth perfect, complete and peerless" (*Migr.* 33).

Philo is consistent: "The man sows the seeds into a womb as into a field (σπείροντος μὲν εἰς μήτραν ἀνδρὸς ὡς εἰς ἄρουραν), the woman receives the seed for safe-keeping (γυναικὸς δ' ὑποδεχομένης τὰ σπέρματα σωτηρίως); nature invisibly moulds and shapes each part of the body and soul (τῆς δὲ φύσεως ἀοράτως ἕκαστα καὶ τῶν τοῦ σώματος καὶ τῶν τῆς ψυχῆς διαπλαττούσης μερῶν) and bestows upon the race as a whole what individually we were not able to receive, namely immortality" (*Aet.* 69; similarly *Abr.* 101; *Spec.* 2.29; *QG* 3.47; *QE* 2.3; *Ebr.* 211; *Sacr.* 101). He notes also the importance of sustenance from the mother: "The double sustenance from the earth, moist and dry is a very great factor in its growth and the embryos moulded in the womb cannot be brought to life merely from the seed, but need also the fostering sustenance from outside which the pregnant mother administers" (*Aet.* 98). In

---

[353] Sly, *Philo's Perception of Women*, 88.
[354] Runia, *Creation*, 218-19.

Prov. he writes of animals: "But all kinds which are created out of their proper substance by a seminal and primary process of nature (ὅσα δ' ἐξ οἰκείας ὕλης κατὰ φύσιν σπερματικὴν καὶ προηγουμένην ἔχει γένεσιν) are reasonably ascribed to providence" (*Prov.* 2.59). In *Legat.* he notes that "the seminal forces (ἐν τοῖς σπερματικοῖς ... λόγοις) preserve similarities of the body in form and carriage and gait, and of the soul in projects and actions" (*Legat.* 55), having just referred to seed as carrying potential for rule (*Legat.* 54).

Philo's most direct calls to sexual engagement occur in symbolic contexts, such as *Somn.* 1: "Mount then, all ye right thoughts and reasonings of wisdom, impregnate, impart seed, and whenever you catch sight of a soul of deep rich virgin soil, pass it not by, but inviting it to union and intercourse with yourselves, render it pregnant and so effect its consummation; for all that it brings forth shall be goodly, male offspring 'consisting of pure white, speckled and ashly-sprinkled'" (*Somn.* 1.200). In his allegorical explanations, which we discuss in 1.2.4.5 below, he frequently notes that sexual engagement of the soul with God changes it from a woman to a virgin, reversing the effects of literal intercourse (*QE* 2.3; *Cher.* 50; *Post.* 134; *Somn.* 2.185), never, however, disparagingly.

As for the processes of conception and the development of the foetus, he cites authorities: "Hippocrates, that expert in the processes of nature, says that in seven days both the solidifying of the seed and the formation of the embryo take place" (*Opif.* 124), paraphrasing "part of the opening words of the Ps.Hippocratean treatise *On the sevens*".[355] Runia notes that "questions of conception, gynaecology and embryology ... were commonly associated with the hebdomad in the arithmological tradition", citing Macrobius 1.6.62-70; Theon 104.1-5; and Nicomachus at Ps.-Iamblichus 61.2-63.5.[356] In *QG* 4 he cites physicians to the effect that "the generation of living beings (is accomplished) in forty (days), during which, physicians say, the seed injected into the womb is formed and, especially when it is a male, becomes a formed creature." (*QG* 4.154). Earlier in a discourse on numbers he adds that a human embryo is formed in 45 days, "rarely in forty, and less (often) in more, for it is productive. And again, in the same number of days is the embryo formed in the womb, in the case of almost (all) nine-month (infants), for in the case of seven-month (infants) it takes thirty-five days, as they say similarly" (*QG* 4.27). In *Congr.* he speaks of indistinct and ill-defined visions as "like the embryo not yet fully formed" (*Congr.* 136).

We noted above that Philo plays with the etymology of woman, γυνή, in the acclamation of Gen 2:23 to declare that "The woman is called the power of giving

---

[355] Runia, *Creation*, 292.

[356] Runia, *Creation*, 291-92. He writes: "Both Macrobius and Nicomachus refer to a passage in Hippocrates in which empirical evidence is given for the formation of the embryo at seven days" (292).

birth with fecundity, and truly so; either because after receiving the seed, she conceives and gives birth (*QG* 1.28). "Nature has given the womb to women as the proper part for generation of living offspring" (*Sacr.* 103). Writing of Hagar he notes that "it is not in the power of man to know that the embryo is a male, nor to know the principle that is to govern the life of one who is not yet born" (*Fug.* 204). He frequently writes of the womb as the "workshop of nature" (φύσεως ... ἐργαστήριον) (*Mos.* 2.84; *Spec.* 3.33, 109; *Legat.* 56), a borrowed phrase as he indicates in *Aet.* 66: "For the place which generates life of the womb, the 'workshop of nature' (φύσεως ... ἐργαστήριον), as someone calls it, where alone the living are moulded into shape, and this is not a part of the earth but of a female creature framed for generation of other creatures".

In comments already cited above we have references to length of pregnancies: nine months and seven months (*QG* 4.27). In *Leg.* he apparently appeals to common knowledge: "Who does not know that seven months' infants come to the birth, while those that have taken a longer time, remaining in the womb eight months, are as a rule still-born?" (*Leg.* 1.9). He says the same in *Opif.*: "The fruit of the womb is brought by nature to full ripeness in seven months, with a most strange result, namely that seven months' children come to the birth, whereas eight months' children as a rule fail to do so alive" (*Opif.* 124). In *Aet.* he writes of "women who in pregnancy labour with very grievous burdens for some ten months and when they are on the point of child-birth often actually die in the pains of travail (*Aet.* 65). Runia observes that "the conviction that at seven months the fetus is fully formed and able to survive when born is extremely common in the arithmological literature", including that 8 months old babies do not.[357] He notes that "a treatise in the Hippocratic corpus entitled 'On the eight-month-olds' explains why these do not survive", identifying the eighth month as a difficult period of growth making it also difficult for birth, whereas "the double problem does not occur for seven-, nine- and ten-month-olds, and so they can survive".[358]

Philo frequently mentions the pain of giving birth (*Aet.* 66; *Migr.* 33; *Ebr.* 59-60; *Sacr.* 103; *Deus* 137), including, negatively, of Lot's daughters: "guilt in their travailing, and a curse upon their offspring" (*Post.* 176) and "of the soul that is one" which "departs from the one and is in travail with many" (*Deus* 14; similarly negative; *Post.* 74; *Leg.* 1.76), but also of creation as born by Knowledge (*Ebr.* 30-31; similarly *Opif.* 36), citing Prov 8:22, of the earth in travail (*Opif.* 43), and of the mind giving birth to thoughts (*Det.* 127). In line with *QG* 4.59, mostly Philo treats the pains of childbirth as part of life rather than as something negative or punitive.

---

[357] Runia, *Creation*, 292, then citing Nicomachus at Ps. Iamblichus 63.1-5.
[358] Runia, *Creation*, 293. He goes on to note that according to Aristotle this applies to Greek women but not Egyptian women (*Hist. an.* 9.4, 584a36-b14) (293).

In *Aet.* he makes the obvious comment that "during the time following closely on the birth the things generated are smaller but afterwards increase in size till they reach their full consummation" (*Aet.* 100). He cites as an explanation for human seeking after pleasure the so-called "cradle argument," of the baby "leaving a place of fiery warmth in the womb" (*Opif.* 161).[359] He often refers to breast-feeding. "Nature has bestowed on every mother as a most essential endowment teeming breasts (πηγάζοντας ... μαστούς), thus preparing in advance food for the child that is to be born" (*Opif.* 133), then going on to employ the image of earth as mother, like Demeter (*Opif.* 133), and citing Plato to the effect that earth does not imitate women but women, earth (*Opif.* 133); and continues: "on earth also, most ancient and most fertile of mothers, did Nature bestow, by way of breasts, streams of rivers and springs, to the end that both the plants might be watered and all animals have abundance to drink" (*Opif.* 133). Similarly in *Plant.*: "For He willed her to be at once mother and nurse. For, even as in woman and all female kind there well up springs of milk when the time of delivery draws near, that they may furnish necessary drink of a suitable kind to their offspring ..." (*Plant.* 15; cf. also *Opif.* 38, 43). This stands in contrast to *Aet.* where, in arguing against the myth that earth once gave birth to humans, he declares that earth did not produce such milk nor did it act as midwives and mothers wrapping children in swaddling cloths (*Aet.* 67). In *Somn.* 2 he uses the image negatively: "Babes who want to be fed, when they are going to suck the milk, squeeze and press the nurse's breast, so the maker of incontinence presses hard on the fountain from which the curse of wine-bibbing pours like rain, to find in the squeezed droppings a nourishment of delicious sweetness" (*Somn.* 2.204).

Usually to serve his allegorical purposes he differentiates negatively between male and female offspring, depicting the latter as inferior products of less worthy men or even as vices. Thus in *Sacr.* he writes: "nature has given the womb to women as the proper part for generation of living offspring, so she has set in the soul for the generation of things a power by which the understanding conceives and travails and is the mother of many children. Of the thoughts thus brought to the birth some are male and some female, just as in the case of living beings" (*Sacr.*103). We then read: "The female offspring of the soul is vice and passion, that emasculating influence which affects us in each of our pursuits. The male offspring is health of soul and virtue, by which we are stimulated and strengthened" (*Sacr.*103). Similarly of Sarah he writes: "Virtue then shall bear thee a true-born, male child, one free from all womanish feelings, and thou shalt call his name by the feeling which he raises in thee, which feeling is most surely joy" (*Mut.* 261). Philo appears to apply the principle literally to Lot, who produced daughters, but otherwise gives no evidence of using it as a rule in a literal sense.

---

[359] See the discussion above.

On the other hand, for Philo daughters were in fact inferior and of lesser worth, but, like the senses which they can symbolise, they are not in themselves bad, and, appropriately married off and submissive, are useful, indeed, essential.

While procreation comes about through sexual intercourse, Philo insists that ultimately God makes the begetting possible. Thus in *Her.* he writes of "Him who causes all things to be sown and come into being, through whom it is that the father and mother appear to generate, though they do not really do so, but are the instruments of generation" (*Her.* 171). Humans copy the creative activity of God and "the immortal powers": "They in virtue of their nature generate all things, but have permitted mortality also at the final stage to copy their creative art and to beget. For God is the primary cause of generation, but the nethermost and least honoured kind, the mortal-kind, is the ultimate" (*Her.* 172). Similarly in *QG* 3 Philo writes: "When a barren woman gives birth, it is not by way of generation but the work of the divine power" (*QG* 3.18). To claim self-sufficiency in propagation is a grave sin comparable to idolatry and atheism.

1.2.4.3 Household Management

The words spoken to the woman about her husband in Gen 3:16 that "your ἀποστροφή (which Philo reads as "return" rather than "refuge") shall be to your husband and he shall rule over you" cohere with Philo's view of how relations in the household should be, but are hardly for him the main argument for his view, which lies instead in the nature of created woman. He does not relate ἀποστροφή "return" to sexual desire. Rather it is subordinated to the thought of what is appropriate, namely putting oneself under his control, which suits Philo's symbolic interpretation that the senses should be ruled by the mind, as in *Leg.* 3.220. Thus, as we have seen above, in *Opif.* he remains at the literal level in noting that the woman "tasted deprivation of liberty, and the authority of the husband at her side, whose commands she must perforce obey" (*Opif.* 167), making no reference to the returning, and in *QG* he portrays the experience depicted in Gen 3:16 of birth pangs and living together with a man (summarising returning and being ruled) not as a curse but as a necessity (*QG* 1.49). Just as Philo does not treat the ἀποστροφή "return" as an aetiology of sexual desire, he also scarcely treats the words about submission as an aetiology of household order. The latter occurs in the context of his exposition of Gen 2:21-24, where he also emphasises the important role of women as partners in sexual intercourse making procreation possible, so vital for the household and its survival. On the other hand, his comments on Gen 3:16 certainly reflect his understanding of good household order.

We have already noted above in discussing women in Philo how he sees their place as necessarily subordinate and can therefore use this allegorically for his psychology, where health means having the senses and passions under control. At best, as we saw, this values women – in their place. We will not repeat the previous discussion about women and households, but simply note the salient references. Sarah models the true wife, always at her husband's side, "his true partner in life and life's events" (*Abr.* 246). The husband is to rule and teach his household (*Hypoth.* 7.3, 14) and the ideal household is one where "no one is slow in showing kindness; but women and men, slaves and free, are full of zeal to do service to their guests" (*Abr.* 109), a "household, like a well ordered crew" serving the guiding pilot (*Abr.* 116). The man's sphere of action is primarily beyond the home in the "market-places and council-halls and law-courts", the woman's, "indoor life which never strays from the house, within which the middle door is taken by the maidens as their boundary, and the outer door by those who have reached full womanhood" (*Spec.* 3.169; similarly 171-172; *QG* 1.27). The woman is essential for running a household – "lack of her is ruin" (*QG* 1.26). As she moves from her father's house to her husband's, she is to serve him, and he, like her father before him, is to care for her (*QG* 1.27).

Sometimes Philo gives us details of household life indirectly while developing allegory. Thus in *QG* 4 he refers to a dwelling as having "partly men's quarters, partly women's quarters" (*QG* 4.15) and in *Leg.* 3 he writes: "In our houses the women's apartments have the men's quarters outside them and the passage inside them, and the courtyard door is outside the court but inside the gateway" (*Leg.* 3.40; cf. also *Sacr.* 103). Philo is presumably writing of the wealthier households of those with whom he keeps company.[360] In *Flacc.*, in describing Jewish households directly, he speaks of "their women kept in seclusion, never even approaching the outer doors, and their maidens confined to the inner chambers, who for modesty's sake avoided the sight of men, even of their closest relations" (*Flacc.* 89; similarly *Ps.-Phoc.* 215-216; 2 Macc 3:19; 3 Macc 1:18; 4 Macc 18:7).[361] Similarly, in describing "household management" as assigned to women, he writes that "a woman then, should not be a busybody, meddling with matters outside her household concerns, but should seek a life of seclusion. She should not shew herself off like a vagrant in the streets before the eyes of other men" (*Spec.* 3.171). Modesty is fundamental, modelled by the Therapeutae who gather in a meeting room divided with a wall 3-4 cubits high "This arrangement serves two purposes: the modesty becoming to the female sex is preserved, while the women sitting within ear-shot can easily follow what is said since there is nothing to obstruct the voice of the speaker" (*Contempl.* 33).

---

[360] Similarly Tal Ilan, *Jewish Women in Greco-Roman Palestine* (Tübingen: Mohr Siebeck, 1995; Peabody: Hendricksen, 1996) 132-34.

[361] Pieter W. van der Horst, *Philo's* Flaccus: *The First Pogrom: Introduction, Translation and Commentary* (Leiden: Brill, 2003) observes that Philo's sentiments were shared by later rabbis, referring to *b. Yebam.* 77a; *Meg.* 14b; and by Seneca, *Helv.* 19.6 (180), but notes that this was atypical of Alexandrian culture of the time.

Philo's concern for households is particularly evident in his rationale for the prohibition of adultery (*Decal.* 126-131), discussed below (3.1.1), where core concerns include not only breach of faith, but also for offspring, their paternity, their rights, and the dishonour brought on all three families affected. Viability was measured not only in substance but also in the currency of honour and shame. Similarly, ensuring the future of the household and new households needed great care according to Philo. Thus he reports Abraham's instruction to Isaac and placing his hand under his thigh: "Being about to bind him by an oath concerning the betrothal, he bids him place his hand close to the place of generation, including a pure association and an unpolluted marriage, not having sensual pleasure as its end but the procreation of legitimate children" (*QG* 4.86). In *Fug.* he addresses the generous man: "You will contribute freely to needy friends, will make bountiful gifts to serve your country's wants, you will help parents without means to marry their daughters, and provide them with an ample dowry" (*Fug.* 29). The latter task was essential for those without support. Similarly in relation to Isaac's sponsor seeking Rebecca's hand Philo reports in *QG* 4: "In the first place, it is to be said that this law is written by the holy father concerning a virgin who is to be betrothed when she has no guardian, that they may not be led by force like maidservants or captives but may go willingly and accept marriage of their own accord and enter into an harmonious union" (*QG* 4.132). Links among households come up in *Legat.* where he explains: "Intermarriage is a lien between unconnected households bringing the status of stranger into one of affinity, and if this be broken the community of interests is broken also" (*Legat.* 72).

In relation to marriages, he has Lysimachus report about Philo himself in *De Animalibus*: "he is *my* uncle, and *my* father-in-law as well. As you are not unaware, his daughter is engaged to be my wife" (*Anim.* 2).[362] In Joseph's response to Potiphar's wife Philo tells of us that "before the lawful union we know no mating with other women, but come as virgin men to virgin maidens. The end we seek in wedlock is not pleasure but the begetting of lawful children" (*Ios.* 43). Later we learn that the king "betrothed him to the most distinguished of the ladies of Egypt, the daughter of the priest of the Sun" (*Ios.* 121) and that the wedding followed with guests arranged according to age (*Ios.* 201-203), but not reclining, because Philo informs us that was not the practice at that time. Toasts and best wishes followed (*Ios.* 206). Otherwise he tells us nothing of wedding practices.

There are few references to slaves of relevance to sexual issues. Philo does make much of the story of Hagar and also gives attention in his allegories to the handmaids of Leah and Rachel. The assumption appears to be that the household

---

[362] On this see Terian, *De Animalibus*, who also notes that Philo speaks of such betrothal agreements (ὁμολογίαι) in *Spec.* 3.71 (112-13). "It is reasonable to assume that Alexander's daughter, who was betrothed to her cousin, Lysimachus, was a minor in *patria potestas*" (113).

head has sexual access to slaves, in these instances, with their mistresses' consent. Philo contrasts the intemperance of those who "because of their concubines, whom they madly love, look down upon their wise wives" with Abraham: "For with the concubine the embrace was a bodily one for the sake of begetting children. But with the wife the union was one of the soul harmonized to heavenly love" (*QG* 3.21). We turn to these images in greater detail in 1.2.4.5 below. Philo has Potiphar's wife falsely accuse Joseph of sexually exploiting fellow slaves: "not content with taking merely the women who were his fellow-servants, so utterly lewd and lascivious has he shown himself, he has attempted to violate me by force, me his mistress" (*Ios.* 51). Of slave purchase Philo writes: "Indeed, some of those thus bought and sold reverse the situations to such an extreme extent that they become the masters of their purchasers instead of their slaves. I have often myself seen pretty little slave girls with a natural gift for wheedling words, who with these two sources of strength, beauty of face and charm of speech, stormed the hearts of their owners" (*Prob.* 38). On another occasion he uses detail of the slave market to attack same-sex relations: "It is said, for instance, that looking at one of the purchasers, an addict of effeminacy, whose face showed that he had nothing of the male about him, he went up to him and said, 'You should buy me, for you seem to me to need a husband'" (*Prob.* 124). These are incidental reflections of the world of his day where slaves were sexually exploited. Philo does not address the injustice involved.

In his discussion of laws Philo deals with the captive wife, divorce, and inheritance, including allegorical meanings. Inheritance issues include the priority of sons over daughters, when they can inherit, and why the rights of the firstborn must be protected in case of a second marriage. This includes the status of the offspring of concubines. We discuss these issues further in 2.2.5 below. In *Congr.* he compares sojourners to adopted children "in so far as they inherit from their adopters, rank with the family; in so far as they are not their actual children, with outsiders" (*Congr.* 23). In *Fug.* he reports: "I know fathers whose effeminacy has made them unwilling to face the strict and philosophic life of their sons, and who out of shame have chosen to live in the country instead of in the city" (*Fug.* 3). The reverse is true of the Therapeutae/Therapeutrides: "they flee without a backward glance and leave their brothers, their children, their wives, their parents, the wide circle of their kinsfolk, the groups of friends around them, the fatherlands ..." (*Contempl.* 18). Theirs is a model which Philo admires for its focus and its symbolism, but by no means as a norm.

1.2.4.4 Death and Hope

As noted above, in *Opif.* Philo depicts the judgement on the man as entailing his need now to toil hard for what the earth produced before freely of its own accord

(*Opif.* 167, similarly 80), and even that is God's generosity (*Opif.* 169), but the exposition does not discuss the declaration that he must die and return to the earth. In *QG* Philo's focus is allegorical, depicting the man as "zealous for pleasure, through which spiritual death is brought about" (*QG* 1.51). In *Leg.* Philo appears to apply the judgement only to the worthless and foolish man (*Leg.* 3.246) and again, allegorically, whose life is therefore "exceeding painful and burdensome ... as he pursues with greedy desire all things that are productive of pleasures and of all things that wickedness loves to bring about" (*Leg.* 3.251). "Thorns" represent passions (*Leg.* 3.248, 250). The foolish man is to eat grass, "food of an irrational creature" (*Leg.* 3.251). Returning to the earth then symbolises his abandoning the heavenly and returning back to earth whence he came. In *Cher.* he allegorises expulsion from the garden similarly as representing abandonment of virtue (*Cher.* 8) and of the mind "sick with the incurable sickness of folly" (*Cher.* 10). As with women's submission to men, so with man's death; Philo does not use the judgement of Gen 3:19 as a major source for reflections on death.

The idea of spiritual death finds expression in *Opif.* where Philo says of intemperance that it "gives a like welcome to superfluity and extravagance, which induce softness and voluptuousness in soul and body, and these result in the culpable life, the life that in the view of right-minded people is worse than death" (*Opif.* 164). Later, in *Praem.* he speaks of the soul full of "passions and vices with her children, pleasures, desires, folly, incontinence, injustice, gathered around her" as "feeble and sick and dangerously near to death" (*Praem.* 159).

In *QG* he writes: "If we resort to drunkenness and fine cooking and chasing after women and to altogether lewd and loose behaviour, we shall be corpse-bearers in our body" (*QG* 2.12). Philo can speak of the undoing of spiritual death. Thus in *QE* 2 he writes: "For the sanctuary is the place of piety and holiness and every virtue, and when the mind reaches this, it altogether acquires perfect reason, which controls and directs and seizes the reins so as to restrain the passions, especially anger, which is wont to be refractory toward it" (*QE* 2.115).

In the *Allegorical Commentary* Philo employs etymology to expound the notion of spiritual death. Thus in *Leg.* 3 he allegorises his etymology of Er as "leathern" to depict him as spiritually dead, a corpse (*Leg.* 3.69). In *Post.* he allegorises Methuselah's name as "a dispatch of death" and speaks of "soul-death, which is the change of soul under the impetus of irrational passion" (*Post.* 73) and then goes on to portray this in the language of conception and pregnancy: "When the soul has conceived this passion, it brings forth with sore travail-pangs incurable sicknesses and debilities, and by the contortion brought on by these it is bowed down and brought low" (*Post.* 74), a thought which finds a parallel in Jas 1:15 (cf. also *Det.* 127). In *Her.* Philo interprets his text of Gen 3:20, Adam's naming his wife, Ζωή ("Life"), to speak of "each one among us who honours and admires the nurse and foster-mother of our mortal race, that is Sense, on whose just-fashioned form the earthly mind, called Adam, looked and gave the name of what was his own death to her life" (*Her.* 52). In discussing Gen 2:17, the threat of death to those who eat from the tree, Philo acknowledges the problem that Adam and Eve do not in fact die, proffering them the explanation that "death is of two kinds, one that of the man in general, the other that of the soul in particular. The death of the man is the separation of the soul from the body, but the death of the soul is the decay of virtue and the bringing in of wickedness" (*Leg.* 1.105) and accordingly goes on to speak of "the soul becoming entombed in passions and wickedness of all kinds" (*Leg.* 1.106).[363]

It is a constant presupposition of Philo's writings that change is possible, the journey can be undertaken, and progress can be made. He can speak of a threefold division in humankind, equating to the perfect, the gradual, and those who do not make the journey at all (*Gig.* 60-61). In *Leg.* 3 he depicts Moses as the perfect and Aaron as the gradual (*Leg.* 3.129-159). There he claims that Moses

> goes so far as to cut off all passions everywhere; while those others set out to wage war on the passions on an insignificant, not on a grand, scale" to "curb their excessive impetuosity. (*Leg.* 3.134)

> Now that we have said this, note once more how a perfect man differs from one making gradual progress. We have already discovered the perfect man cutting out the seat of anger entirely from the wrangling soul ... while the man of gradual improvement was found powerless to cut away the passion, for the breast is Aaron's portion, but schooling it by well-tested speech, attended by two virtues, clearness and truth. (*Leg.* 3.140)

> In a corresponding manner we shall now find Moses, the wise man, in his perfection, scouring away and shaking off pleasures, but the man of gradual improvement not so treating pleasure in its entirety, but welcoming simple and unavoidable pleasure, while declining that which is excessive and overelaborate in the way of delicacies. (*Leg.* 3.140)

We noted this passage in addressing whether Philo advocates doing away with the passions altogether. The broader context shows that this is not the case. Accordingly he explains:

> The perfect wise man can, by wholly renouncing anger, utterly avert and drive off the uprising of the spirited element in him, but to exscind the belly he is powerless. Even the man of fewest needs who scorns the very necessaries of life and trains himself in

---

[363] On Philo's use of the traditional Platonic motif of the body as tomb of the soul, see Pearce, *Land of the Body*, who notes that despite such language Philo does not condemn the body, since it is God's creation and has its place when put to the right purpose (87).

abstinence from them, is forced by nature to take necessary food and drink. (*Leg.* 3.147)

to which he then adds also the need to procreate. He concludes:

> The lover of pleasure moves on the belly; the perfect man washes out the entire belly; the man who is making gradual progress washes out the contents of the belly, the man who is just beginning his training will go forth without, when he intends to curb passion by bringing reason (figuratively called a shovel) to bear upon the demands of the belly. (*Leg.* 3.159)

In *Fug.* he advises:

> Begin, then, by getting some exercise and practice in the business of life both private and public; and when by means of the sister virtues, household-management and statesmanship, you have become masters in each domain, enter now, as more than qualified to do so, on your migration to a different and more excellent way of life. For the practical comes before the contemplative life. (*Fug.* 36)

The contemplative life is the goal.

Hope in Philo relates, however, not only to overcoming the passions and contemplating God. It also has a corporate future and this can have implications for the place of sexuality in Philo's thought. Apart from noting that "heaven is an eternal day, wherein there is no night or any shadow" (*Ios.* 146), possibly reflecting traditional eschatology but now transferred to heaven, Philo says little about traditional future hope. His depiction in *Opif.* of the man's judgement, that he now must toil for what previously was available in abundance, might imply that any hope should entail a return to such abundance, but this is not developed at this point. When in *Praem.* we reach the end of the *Exposition of the Laws*, it is not surprising to find such notions making an appearance. There having spoken of rewards to individuals (*Praem.* 14-51) and houses (*Praem.* 52-65) and of punishments (*Praem.* 66-78)[364] during this life, Philo addresses himself to future blessings, focused on the nation as a whole. The first promise is "victory over enemies" (*Praem.* 79) if they keep the commandments, which, he argues, is not an impossible demand (*Praem.* 79-84). First, he discusses enmity, expressing the hope that the enmity of wild beasts would one day cease (*Praem.* 85-90) and then that enmity amongst human beings would cease. On this he begins by suggesting that people would be shamed into giving up enmity when they see animals becoming peaceful (*Praem.* 91-92). He then links this to the hope of the nation, citing Lev 26:6 to declare that "war will not pass through the land of the godly at

---

[364] There has been loss of material after 78.

all" (*Praem.* 93), but then faces the prospect that enemies may attack with the assurance that they will be beaten back, again drawing on biblical promises (Lev 26:8; Deut 28:7) (*Praem.* 94).

In this context Philo also cites the opening words of Num 24:7 LXX (ἐξελεύσεται ἄνθρωπος ἐκ τοῦ σπέρματος αὐτοῦ καὶ κυριεύσει ἐθνῶν πολλῶν καὶ ὑψωθήσεται ἡ Γωγ βασιλεία αὐτοῦ καὶ αὐξηθήσεται ἡ βασιλεία αὐτοῦ), namely ἐξελεύσεται ἄνθρωπος, ("there shall come forth a man"), of whom he then says, that "leading his host to war he will subdue great and populous nations, because God has sent to his aid the reinforcement which befits the godly, and that is dauntless courage of soul and all-powerful strength of body" (*Praem.* 95). This may well reflect Philo's espousal of messianic expectation, or at least, of the notion embedded in the rest of the citation of a victorious ruler who would rule over many nations.[365] As with most Jews of his time, however, and unlike in the Christian movement, agency was not the focus, so that it appears here incidentally and receives no mention elsewhere. While Philo envisages bloodshed (*Praem.* 94-95), he also opines that some victories will be bloodless, won by wasps (as Exod 23:28 and Deut 7:20; cf. also Wis 12:8) or by imposing "dignity, strictness, benevolence" (*Praem.* 97). As Tobin notes, "the pattern that emerges is one which maximizes the importance of the practice of virtue and the observance of God's commandments and minimizes the role played by violence. In fact, the appearance of the intermediate figure of Num 24:7 [LXX] as the leader of an army is not even necessary".[366]

More important for our theme, is Philo's description of the blessings which ensue. They include not only peace (*Praem.* 97-98), but also wealth and abundance (*Praem.* 98-105). "Sometimes so vast will be the fertility that no one will take any thought for the harvest that is past but will leave it unhusbanded and unhoarded for all who wish to use it without fear or scruple" (*Praem.* 103). Philo connects wealth in heaven and wealth on earth: "For those who possess stored up in Heaven the true wealth whose adornment is wisdom and godliness have also

---

[365] Peder Borgen, "'There Shall Come Forth a Man': Reflections on Messianic Ideas in Philo," in *The Messiah: Developments in Earliest Judaism and Christianity* (First Princeton Symposium on Judaism and Christian Origins; ed. James H. Charlesworth; Minneapolis: Augsburg Fortress, 1992) 341-61, looks for traces of such messianism elsewhere in Philo. He points to the citation of Num 24:3-9 in *Mos.* 1.289-291 (346), but there Philo makes nothing of 24:7 in the context. On this see Thomas H. Tobin, "Philo and the Sibyl: Interpreting Philo's Eschatology," *SPA* 9 (1997) 84-103, 95; Burton L. Mack, "Wisdom and Apocalyptic in Philo," *SPA* 3 (1991) 21-39, 34; Lester Grabbe, "Eschatology in Philo and Josephus," in *Judaism in Late Antiquity; Volume 3.4: Death, Life-after-Death, Resurrection and the World-to-Come in the Judaisms of Antiquity* (ed. A. J. Avery-Peck and J. Neusner; Leiden: Brill, 2001) 163-85, 171.

[366] Tobin, "Philo and the Sibyl," 101.

wealth of earthly riches in abundance" (*Praem.* 104). For Philo both matter. Heightened fertility will produce abundance "both of the necessaries, corn, wine and oil, the means of enjoyable life, that is the numberless kinds of tree fruits, and also by the fruitful multiplying of oxen and goats and other cattle" (*Praem.* 107). More significantly and as the zenith of hope, Philo then declares: "And therefore he crowns his boons by saying that no man shall be childless and no woman barren" (οὐδεὶς ἄγονος οὐδὲ στεῖρα γενήσεται), citing Exod 23:26 (οὐκ ἔσται ἄγονος οὐδὲ στεῖρα ἐπὶ τῆς γῆς "No one shall miscarry or be barren in your land"), and continues:

> but all the true servants of God will fulfil the law of nature for the procreation of children (πάντες δὲ οἱ θεραπευταὶ θεοῦ γνήσιοι νόμον ἐκπληρώσουσι φύσεως τὸν ἐπὶ παιδοποιίᾳ). For men will be fathers and women mothers both happy in those they beget or bear (ἔσονται πατέρες καὶ πατέρες εὔπαιδες καὶ γυναῖκες ἔσονται μητέρες καὶ μητέρες εὔτεκνοι), so that each family will be a plenitude with a long list of kinsfolk, with no part nor any of the names which signify relationship missing. (*Praem.* 108-109)

Thus Philo's vision of the future envisages a proper place for sexual desire, expressing itself in the pleasure of sexual intercourse in marriage for procreation, a reflection of what he insists should be the norm in the present. People will still die but none prematurely and will "leave a great house of goodly children to fill his place" (*Praem.* 110). Recapping, he writes: "So much for the external blessings promised, victories over enemies, successes in wars, establishments of peace and abundant supplies of the good things of peace, honours and offices and the eulogies accompanying the successful ..." (*Praem.* 118) and also complete freedom from disease (*Praem.* 119).

He then speaks of the land: "when she looks around and sees none of the destroyers of her former pride and high name, sees her market places void of turmoil and war and wrongdoing, but full of tranquillity and peace and justice, she will renew her youth and bloom and take her rest calm and serene during the festal seasons of the sacred Seven, rallying her strength like a wrestler after his first bout" (*Praem.* 157). He then continues: "Young once more she will be fruitful and bear a blameless generation (πάλιν δὲ νεάσασα εὐφορήσει καὶ τέξεται γενεὰν ἀνεπίληπτον) to redress the one that went before. For she that is desolate (ἡ γὰρ ἔρημος), says the prophet, will have children many and fine (εὔτεκνός τε καὶ πολύπαις), a saying which is also an allegory of the soul" (*Praem.* 158), an allusion to Isa 54:1 (εὐφράνθητι στεῖρα ἡ οὐ τίκτουσα ῥῆξον καὶ βόησον ἡ οὐκ ὠδίνουσα ὅτι πολλὰ τὰ τέκνα τῆς ἐρήμου μᾶλλον ἢ τῆς ἐχούσης τὸν ἄνδρα εἶπεν γὰρ κύριος "Sing, O barren one who did not bear; burst into song and shout, you who have not been in labor! For the children of the desolate woman will be more than the children of her that is married, says the LORD"). The allegory then states: "For when the soul is 'many', full that is of passions and vices with her children, pleasures, desires, folly, incontinence, injustice, gathered around her, she is feeble and sick and dangerously near to death" (*Praem.* 159). But, by contrast, "when she has become barren and ceases to produce these children or indeed has cast them out bodily she is transformed into a pure virgin. Then receiving the divine seed she moulds it into shape and beings forth new life in forms of precious quality and marvellous loveliness, wisdom, courage, temperance, justice, holiness, piety and the other virtues and good emotions" (*Praem.* 159-160).

Philo can then combine his future hope with his ethical and spiritual concerns when he writes of the ingathering of the diaspora:

> One signal, as it were, one day will bring liberty to all. This conversion in a body to virtue will strike awe into their masters, who will set them free, ashamed to rule over men better than themselves. When they have gained this unexpected liberty, those who but now were scattered in Greece and the outside world over islands and continents will arise and post from every side with one impulse to the one appointed place, guided in their pilgrimage by a vision divine and superhuman unseen by others but manifest to them as they pass from exile to their home. (*Praem.* 164)

As Tobin notes, "like many Jews of his time, he expects that in the future Jews scattered around the world will return to their land and experience there unimagined prosperity".[367] Then Philo returns to the image of abundance: "When they have arrived the cities which but now lay in ruins will be cities once more; the barren will change into fruitfulness (ἡ στειρωθεῖσα γῆ μεταβαλεῖ πρὸς εὐγονίαν); all the prosperity of their fathers and ancestors will seem a tiny fragment, so lavish will be the abundant riches in their possession .." (*Praem.* 168) and "reversed to the prosperity of their ancestral past" (*Praem.* 170).

Noting Philo's use in *Praem.* of many common eschatological motifs, Tobin argues that Philo may well be deliberately reacting to the kind of eschatology espoused by the author of the *Sibylline Oracles*. "The eschatological views seem to have been so prevalent among Egyptian Jews that Philo himself could not avoid being influenced by them. On the other hand, in using these biblical passages as the only basis for his description of the eschatological state of the Jewish people, he in effect also undercuts the authority of the oracles".[368] By contrast, Mack emphasises missing elements: apocalyptic scenarios of mass devastation are replaced by natural events; there is no emphasis on vindication and condemnation and mention of a future temple and reversal is based on images from "wisdom

---

[367] Tobin, "Philo and the Sibyl," 102.
[368] Tobin, "Philo and the Sibyl," 97.

mythologies of creation and (re) generation".[369] "For Philo," he argues, "belonging to Israel was the same as being in the school of Moses. And being in the school of Moses meant living in the world in accord with wisdom. One could do that without the benefit of the temple state in Judaea".[370] Similarly Grabbe concludes: "in the end Philo has no cosmic eschatology—or, rather his cosmic eschatology is not distinguished from his individual eschatology. All emphasis is placed on the goal and fate of the individual souls. He says nothing about a cosmic cataclysm, the intervention of God at the end of history, a universal resurrection, or an endtime judgment of all human beings".[371]

Clearly, Philo frequently slips into allegory in *Praem.* and focuses on the individual, but as Tobin, notes, "these allegorical interpretations do not undo the corporate character of Praem. 79-172, but they do emphasize the importance within the corporate concerns of the treatise of the practice of virtue by the individual".[372] Pointing to *Mos.* 2.44, Hay notes that Philo envisages "a future when the Jewish people will prosper as they have not prospered for a long time; 'if they should do so,' all the gentile nations will be converted to honoring only the Jewish laws".[373]

The evidence suggests that Philo does affirm a form of traditional Jewish eschatology which envisions the future as one where what once was lost is restored and how life should be now is established, including proper sexual relations. He does not, however, speak of the future as a re-entry to the garden of Eden,[374] but rather, apparently, a proper settlement of the land, though it will share many of the elements characteristic of Eden: like the virtuous life, senses and passions in order, pleasure in sex for procreation, tame and tamed animals, and abundant resources. Philo appears to be able to embrace such corporate hope despite mostly laying his emphasis elsewhere, namely on the life of contemplation and the rewards of well-being which it promises.[375]

---

[369] Mack, "Wisdom and Apocalyptic," 37.

[370] Mack, "Wisdom and Apocalyptic," 38.

[371] Grabbe, "Eschatology," 173.

[372] Tobin, "Philo and the Sibyl," 99.

[373] David M. Hay, "Philo of Alexandria," in *Justification and Variegated Nomism: I: The Complexities of Second Temple Judaism* (ed. D. A. Carson, P. T. O'Brien and M. A. Seifrid; Tübingen: Mohr Siebeck; Grand Rapids: Baker, 2001) 357-79, 372.

[374] Borgen, *An Exegete for his Time*, notes: "In Praem. 98-125 the direct reference back to the ideal condition of the first human beings is less direct, however. Philo rather draws on various scriptural texts such as Lev 26:23-4" (264).

[375] On Philo's espousal of the goal of well-being see David T. Runia, "Eudaimonism in Hellenistic-Jewish Literature," in *Shem in the Tents of Japhet: Essays on the Encounter of Judaism and Hellenism* (ed. James L. Kugel; JSJSup 7; Leiden: Brill, 2002) 131-57, who notes that "Philo argues that devotion to God and his Law results in the excellences of piety (*eusebeia*) and justice (*dikaiosunē*), which in turn are rewarded by the life of well-being

1.2.4.5 Sexual Intercourse as Symbol of the Soul's Relationships

The immediate sequel to the story of the expulsion from the garden is the story of the birth of Cain: Αδαμ δὲ ἔγνω Ευαν τὴν γυναῖκα αὐτοῦ καὶ συλλαβοῦσα ἔτεκεν τὸν Καιν "Now Adam knew is wife Heua, and after she had conceived, she bore Kain" (Gen 4:1 NETS). While it begins a new chapter, it sparks Philo's imagination in *Cher.* 40 for an extensive discourse in which he employs sexual intercourse as a symbol of the soul's possible relationships. It is so closely related to our review of these in a literal sense within this subsection of our discussion, that I include it here. It is, like most of the theme considered thus far, foundational for all that follows.

Philo applies the image of sexual intercourse in different ways. In this section we group these thematically. In *Opif.* he can speak of the earth in the beginning as pregnant to God and giving birth (*Opif.* 36, 43).[376] In *Deo* he writes of "the male nature of Being, by which it spreads seed in the universe and out of compassion begets the mortal nature by its own living nature", going on later to add: "For the female is passive matter, while the male is the Creator of the world" (*Deo* 3).[377] In *Ebr.* Philo employs Prov 8:22 to depict God as engaging in sexual intercourse with Knowledge (ἐπιστήμην) and begetting created being (*Ebr.* 31). In *Fug.* Philo employs the complicated image of the high priest forever betrothed to a maiden who is simultaneously wisdom, who "had adopted, as her one Husband and Father, God the All-sovereign" (*Fug.* 114).

But God also impregnates people and begets virtues through them, often symbolised by the names of their offspring. So God visits Sarah, opens the womb of Leah, engages Rebecca, Zipporah (*Cher.* 46-47; *Post.* 135; *QG* 3.54), and Hannah (*Gig.* 5). Similarly in *Mut.* Philo speaks of God's intercourse with women, symbols of virtue (*Mut.* 255), and also with virtue (*Leg.* 3.181). On the same basis Philo claims that people of virtue, "such as Abraham, Isaac, Jacob, and Moses and others of the same spirit, are not represented ... as knowing women (γνωρίζοντας γυναῖκας οὐκ εἰσάγει)", that is, did not engage in sex with women (*Cher.* 40). The former, the women, gave birth to, and these men begat, righteousness offspring. Philo appeals to Jer 3:4 which similarly portrays God as a husband of

---

(*eudaimonia*), as exemplified in the blessings and promises accorded the Patriarchs and the people of Israel" (140). Philo illustrates this achievement throughout the *Exposition of the Law* through depictions of the patriarchs, explanation of the law, and in Praem. (141-43) and does so similarly in the *Allegorical Commentary* (143). Rather than being simply a Greek description for the Jewish idea of shalom, Runia argues that its Greek origins are evident in Philo's depiction of God as *eudaimōn* and so as model (150-51).

[376] Cf. also Mattila, "Wisdom, Sense Perception, Nature," 121.

[377] Cf. also Mattila, "Wisdom, Sense Perception, Nature," 123.

Israel's virginity (*Cher.* 50) and describes his insight as a mystery by which God sows the seeds of immortality and the virtues (*Cher.* 48-49).[378] He plays further with the notion, contrasting male-female intercourse as making a virgin a woman (*Cher.* 50) with the soul through intercourse with God being made a virgin, and then modifying the anthropomorphism somewhat by suggesting God's relation is not with virgins but virginity (*Cher.* 51-52; similarly *QE* 2.3).[379]

The word, μυστήριον ("mystery") occurs also in Eph 5:32, where the author similarly employs sexual imagery allegorically, to describe the relation of Christ to the church.[380] Niehoff notes that "Philo's insistence that his teaching is only meant for the initiate suggests that he wished to keep from sounding any mythological overtones when speaking of the deity's intercourse with real human women".[381] She comments that the imagery is reminiscent of the depiction of the wise with Wisdom in Wis 8:2, though that author exhibits less anxiety about the imagery than Philo.[382] Such imagery abounds also in Sirach (Sir 4:11-19; 6:18-31; 14:20 – 15:10; 24; 51:13-30).[383] Cohen observes that while Philo uses the metaphor of God fathering elsewhere, "he never again expresses it in terms of such overtly sexual imagery, and this perhaps explains why, after having toned it down, he no longer termed it a 'mystery'".[384]

---

[378] On this see Niehoff, "Mother and Maiden," 435-36; Christof Riedweg, *Mysterienterminologie bei Platon, Philon und Klemens von Alexandrien* (Berlin: de Gruyter, 1987) 76. He notes the connections between the practice of allegorical interpretation and mystery cults and Philo's use of such imagery based on profane usage (88-90).

[379] Baer, *Male and Female*, notes that where the focus is on God's action Philo speaks of the human being as being made a virgin, whereas when the focus is on mind controlling the passions, the focus is on becoming male (54-55). On the notion of divine impregnation of the soul see his discussion on pp. 55-64 and on man's intercourse with God, pp. 58-61. "In all these texts, God is shown to be the source of all goodness and virtue" (61).

[380] On this see Sly, *Philo's Perception of Women*, 134.

[381] Niehoff, "Mother and Maiden," 436. On Philo's use of the language of the mysteries to express key notions, see Sly, *Philo's Perception of Women*, 133. While noting use of mystery terminology among the Stoics, she argues that it is to be traced back, "perhaps through Stoic convention, to Plato: specifically, to his use of mystery language to frame important doctrine, and to his figure of the impregnation of the soul" (135-36).

[382] Niehoff, "Mother and Maiden," 436.

[383] On this see Ibolya Balla, "Ben Sira / Sirach," in William Loader, *The Pseudepigrapha on Sexuality: Attitudes Towards Sexuality in Apocalypses, Testaments, Legends, Wisdom, and Related Literature* (Grand Rapids: Eerdmans, forthcoming) 362-98, 392-96.

[384] Naomi G. Cohen, "The Mystery Terminology in Philo," in *Philo und das Neue Testament: Wechselseitige Wahrnehmungen: 1. Internationales Symposium zum Corpus Judaeo-Hellenisticum 1.-4. Mai 2003* (ed. Roland Deines and Karl Wilhelm Niebuhr,; Tübingen: Mohr Siebeck, 2004) 173-87, 184.

The image of the soul's relation to God in sexual or marital terms generates other metaphors. Philo uses it depict the soul's separation or divorce from God, the "husband and father of the universe" (*Det.* 147) and to reflect on whether that is permanent or reconciliation is possible. He also applies it to inspiration. Thus, having just spoken of God watering the soul with divine snow to bring forth perfect offspring (*Migr.* 33), Philo interprets his own moments of inspiration as a kind of female orgasm (*Migr.* 35): after finding his "understanding incapable of giving birth to a single idea" and being amazed "at the might of Him that is to Whom is due the opening and closing of the soul-wombs", on other occasions he has "suddenly become full, the ideas falling in a shower from above and being sown invisibly, so that under the influence of the Divine possession" he has "been filled with corybantic frenzy" (*Migr.* 34-35). He then associates this with the rod which made waters sweet and the tree of life itself of Eden amid its garden of virtues (*Migr.* 35-36).

Philo can also use the image to describe the mind's intercourse with virtue (*QG* 4.11), sometimes dramatically so: "Mount then, all ye right thoughts and reasonings of wisdom, impregnate, impart seed, and whenever you catch sight of a soul of deep rich virgin soil, pass it not by" (*Somn.* 1.200). In *Her.* he speaks of "zeal to sow and beget the children of the soul" (*Her.* 38) and of such children having innocence as their "nurse and fostermother" and their souls being "virgin and tender and rich in nature's gifts", an allusion to Plato's *Phaedrus* 245A (LCL). Similarly, using Tamar as an image of virtue he writes: "Thou shalt win the rewards if Judah's daughter-in-law become thy wife, even Tamar, which means a palm-tree, the sign of victory" (*Leg.* 3.74).

He can also reverse the image effectively having the virtues make mind pregnant (*Abr.* 101-102; *Spec.* 2.29-30; 3.104). In addition we find the notion of Wisdom as a partner, including as male (*Fug.* 52; similarly 114; cf. also *QE* 2.3). Similarly in *Fug.* 50 Philo must explain how Rebecca's father, Bethuel, whose name he explains means "daughter of God", can symbolise Wisdom, the daughter of God, and yet be spoken of as father. He explains: "That which comes after God, even though it were chiefest of all things, occupies a second place, and therefore was termed feminine to express its contrast with the Maker of the Universe who is masculine, and its affinity to everything else" (*Fug.* 51), but then urges: "Let us, then, pay no heed to the discrepancy in the gender of the words, and say that the daughter of God, even Wisdom, is not only masculine but father, sowing and begetting in souls aptness to learn, discipline, knowledge, sound sense, good and laudable actions" (*Fug.* 52).[385] His sexual metaphors require such flexibility.[386] He

---

[385] Leslie Baynes, "Philo, Personification and the Transformation of Grammatical Gender," *SPA* 14 (2002) 31-47, writes: "Philo, however, treats grammatical gender with characteristic gravity, but at the same time he juggles it audaciously ... with few exceptions to elevate the male and to denigrate the female" (33). She notes similar juggling on the

makes much of the image of Sarah as virtue, speaking of the Mind's intercourse with her (*Congr* 12; *Mut.* 261), producing male offspring, also emphasising that she is motherless, begotten by God alone (*QG* 4.68), and expanding the imagery to include also the Mind's preliminary intercourse with Hagar representing schooling (*Mut.* 255; Congr 7, 9, 12, 14; *Ebr.* 33). This is the major theme of the book which appropriately bears the title, "Sexual Intercourse" (*Congr.*). The high priest's wife is said to become male (*Somn.* 2.185), in much the same way in which Philo's frequent allusion to Sarah's leaving the ways of women behind symbolises her allegiance to the male (*Cher.* 50; *Det.* 28; *Post.* 134; *Ebr.* 59-60).

Sexual intercourse also serves to explain the relations of the mind to the senses, understood as male and female. This can describe the proper processes of the senses receiving the input of the mind (*QG* 2.49). In *Fug.* he explains that Moses "gives to sense-perception the name woman, suggesting Mind as her husband" (*Fug.* 188). Playing with the idea of separation during menstruation and merging it with the prohibition of intercourse during menstruation he then adds:

> Sense-perception is 'in separation,' which is 'sitting a long way off,' when, having forsaken Mind, her lawful husband, she plants herself on the objects of sense that ensnare and corrupt, and passionately embraces them one after another. At such a time, then, if Mind goes to sleep, when he ought to be awake, 'he has unclosed the spring' of sense-perception, himself to wit – for, as I have already said, he himself is the spring of sense-perception – that is, he has exposed himself, without covering or wall of defence, to the plots of his enemies. (*Fug.*189)

---

grammar of joy in *QG* 4.18 and virtue and mind in *Abr.* 101-102 (39). She shows Philo's familiarity with discussion among Stoics who often resorted to etymology to deal with distortions (45). Of *Fug.* 51-53 she writes: "Grammatical gender, instead of clarifying, often obstructs meaning. Hence Philo without compunction may maintain the etymological meaning of Bathouel, daughter of God, and at the same time correct the misleading terminology of grammatical gender, thus uncovering the essential truth behind imperfect language" (45). She notes that in the contrast between the two women in *Sacr.* 20-34 Philo leaves the gender intact, probably because it was a common topos (45). It is also not in a hierarchical setting.

[386] Baer, *Male and Female*, writes of the imagery relating to Wisdom and Virtue: "It is most likely this active-passive polarity and not the influence of some mythological androgynous figure that is chiefly responsible for the alternation between male and female that we find in Sophia and Areté. Sophia and Areté are never portrayed as bisexual, i.e. both male and female at the same time. They are represented as female-passive in relationship to God and male-active in relationship to man." "The maleness or femaleness of Sophia and Areté is not to be understood in terms of actual sexuality at all but rather in terms of the more or less ad hoc demands of each individual passage. Like God, the Logos, and the rational soul of man, Sophia and Areté are asexual" (62). Accordingly Philo offers no biography of Areté (63).

Alternatively Philo can speak of the mind becoming pregnant and being in travail with its thoughts which speech brings to expression like a midwife (*Det.* 127). Similarly he writes in *Spec.* 2 that reasoning "deposits seed of virtue in the soul as in a fertile field" (*Spec.* 2.29). More often the image functions negatively. Sense-perception paradoxically impregnates mind producing vain and evil thoughts (*Cher.* 57), then claiming them as its own, an arrogance Philo sees in the name "Cain ("Possession"), but also in Laban's claiming his daughters as his own and Joseph claiming the wisdom of his dreams (*Cher.* 67, 124, 128). This even "unmans" the mind (*Cher.* 52). In *Congr.* he writes: "the wicked man begets vice by his legitimate wife and passion by his concubine ... The bodily nature is the concubine, and we see that through it passion is generated, for the body is the region of pleasures and lusts" (*Congr.* 59). To let the passions rule is to engage in an illicit sexual liaison which can be seen as both dethroning the mind's control and also, as in the prophetic biblical image, engaging in infidelity over against God. Philo describes the offspring of such pursuits as either a multitude of clinging children weighing one down or as abortions (*Post.* 73-74; *Deus* 14-15; *Mut.* 144; *Migr.* 33; *Leg.* 1.76). Similarly he speaks of "the king of Egypt, under which figure is symbolized the mind which loves the body, acts a part as in a theatre and assumes a counterfeited fellowship, he, the licentious with chastity, the profligate with self-control" (*Abr.* 103). The allegory moves beyond concern with sexual wrongdoing as such to express concern with passions in general, the choice between "two hostile natures, vice and virtue" (*Abr.* 105).

Philo can press the allegory further arguing that the manly mind begets only males, the wicked and unmanly beget females (*Gig.* 4-5; *Somn.* 1.200) and also that male should join only with male, not advocating same-sex relations, but on the basis that the female is made male by following the manly thoughts of mind and receiving its seed (*QG* 2.49). The angels' sex with women symbolises the mind's mating with the passions (*Deus* 3), the woman of Zarephath's widowhood, the opposite (*Deus* 136).

In all of these instances the focus is not licit or illicit intercourse, but proper behaviour defined by the mind controlling the senses and passions in accordance with divine law, written in the Law and embedded in nature. That includes as an element the affirmation of sexual intercourse, including its pleasure as divinely purposed, namely for procreation, and the rejection of sexual passion in excess, wrongly directed, and not serving that purpose. The extent of Philo's employment of the image is surely to be taken as an indicator that it is for him a matter of significant interest and something to be valued. His positive statements at a literal level indicate that his allegorical employment of the motif of sexual intercourse is not indicative of some kind of psychological compensation and denial of sex in real life. Rather sex in real life comes clearly within the sphere of the larger agenda of living according to the law of nature as enshrined in divine law and that means not its extirpation but its control and dethronement from any claim to rule.

1.3   Sexual Allusions and Images Beyond Genesis 1 – 3

In 1.2 we used the framework of Gen 1:2 – 4:1 to discuss Philo's major presuppositions in relation to sexuality and sexual issues. This matched Philo's emphasis in dealing with these chapters. In this section we survey images and motifs which occur in the rest of Genesis and beyond and which Philo relates to sexual issues in some way, including sexual images which he uses in ways that have nothing to do with sex. Many of the images below occur with regularity through Philo's writings. I have chosen to order them according to the sequence in the biblical material. In doing so I also take into account especially the three sets of "commentaries" on this material.

1.3.1   Significant Motifs Generated by Genesis 4 - 11

The span of Genesis from Cain to Babel provides Philo with a rich quarry for expounding his themes. Those which feature significantly include references to conception and birth, the deviant angels, Noah's ark and the flood, Noah's agriculture, his drunkenness and nakedness, and the tower of Babel. A number of minor details also play a role, including Cain's place of exile, his buildings and laws, the two Enochs, and Nimrod. In this section we encounter writings from three main directions: the few paragraphs at the beginning of *Abr.* (1-47) in the *Exposition of the Law*; the relatively concise *Questions and Answers on Genesis* 1.57 – 2.82, covering Gen 3:24 – 10:8-9, and the rather extensive expositions found in the *Allegorical Commentary*: *Cher.* 1-39 (Gen 3:24); 40-130 (Gen 4:1); *Sacr.* (Gen 4:2-4); *Det.* (Gen 4:8); *Post.* (Gen 4:16); *Gig.* (Gen 6:1-4); *Deus* (Gen 6:4-12); *Agr.* (Gen 9:20-27); *Plant.* (Gen 9:20-27); *Ebr.* (Gen 9:20-27); *Sobr.* (Gen 9:20-27); and *Conf.* (Gen 11:1-9).

1.3.1.1   Cain

Little in Philo's treatment of Cain touches sexual issues, beyond his conception and birth which we noted in the previous chapter. There are a number of minor allusions in the *Allegorical Commentary*. Philo notes the conundrum presented by Gen 4:17 that Cain had a wife, but typically uses allegory to explain it away (*Post.* 33). He designates Cain's buildings "plausible inventions contrary to the truth" and his laws as "various forms of lawlessness", where he doubtless intends a sexual reference in the words, "licentiousness" and "immoderate indulgence in pleasures, unnatural lusts that may not be named" (*Post.* 52), the latter probably same-sex relations, because he refers to them in those terms elsewhere (see 1.4.1.3.6 below). Cain's place of exile, Naid, is aptly named "Tossing" since the foolish man is tossed about as on a sea, likely to face shipwreck (*Post.* 22; similarly *Cher.* 12). He uses maritime metaphor again in *Agr.* 89, speaking of the soul "swaying and tossing like a vessel, now to the side of the mind now to the body, owing to the violence of the passions and misdeeds that rage against her".

1.3.1.2 The Enochs

In the *Exposition of the Laws* Philo treats Enoch's being taken and not being found as indicating withdrawal and turning away from vice to virtue, "from voluptuousness to self-control" (*Abr.* 24), an image of repentance.[387] Later in the same work, however, where Philo looks back on the triad, Enos, Enoch, and Noah, and looks forward to the triad, Abraham, Isaac, and Jacob, he treats the former as symbolising the studies of children, and the latter, "the exercises of athletes" for sacred games and "victory over their antagonists, the passions" (*Abr.* 48), which will include sexual passions.[388]

In the *Allegorical Commentary* Philo notes the two Enochs of Gen 4:17 and 5:18, and contrasts them, highlighting the second as one leaving the passions behind (*Post.* 40-43). We find another positive treatment in *Mut.*, where Philo depicts him as the "type of character which was well-pleasing to God, meaning doubtless that though actually existing he was hidden from us and shunned our company ... and journeyed as an emigrant from the mortal life to the immortal" (*Mut.* 38), going on to place him in the special company of "men inspired with heaven-sent madness, men who have gone out into the wild", a category to whom his Therapeutae will also belong, in comparison with "others who have followed a tame and gentle wisdom, and such are both eminent in the practice of piety and do not despise human things" (*Mut.* 39). This elevates Enoch significantly, but Philo appears to derive this primarily from the biblical text. He shows no sign of knowing early Enoch literature.[389] The relevance of his treatment of Enoch to

---

[387] Robert A. Kraft, "Philo (Josephus, Sirach and Wisdom of Solomon) on Enoch," *SBLSP* (1978) 253-57 notes that the Greek of Sir 44:16 also treats him as an example of repentance, so that Philo may depend on tradition here (255).

[388] On this see Kraft, "Philo on Enoch," who writes: "To a large extent the pre-diluvian generations are symbolic lessons (not literal 'historical' persons) to Philo" (255).

[389] Loren Stuckenbruck, "To What Extent did Philo's Treatment of Enoch and the Giants Presuppose a Knowledge of the Enochic and Other Sources Preserved in the Dead Sea Scrolls?" *SPA* 19 (2007) 131-42, observes: "Philo's view of the prediluvian figure

sexual issues is very indirect, namely, abandoning uncontrolled passions including the negation of illicit sexual desire.

1.3.1.3 The Angels' Sex with Women

Philo makes very little of the angels' sex with women. In *QG* he lays blame on both the angels and the women for producing the giants (*QG* 1.92; cf. *1 Enoch* 8:1), but makes nothing more of it. He has no question related to Gen 6:1-2 in *QG*. In *QG* 2.82 he treats Nimrod as one with the Titans who defy the heavens, an Ethiopian and hunter, so at home with the bestial passions. We find no traces of elaborations of the Watcher myth found in Enoch literature, unless blaming the women belongs here, although Philo was likely to do that anyway.

In *Gig.* the "literal" story receives no attention. Instead Philo allegorises the ἄγγελοι ("angels")[390] as evil ones, in effect, evil minds engaging the senses (women) and setting no limit to the range and extent of their desires (17-18; similarly *Deus* 3).[391] The giant, Nimrod ("Desertion"), founder of Babylon, is depicted in *Gig.* 65 as doing the same, deserting the path of reason.[392] The original act of sexual wrongdoing is noted but receives little emphasis and is not treated

---

seems highly different from the Enoch we meet in the 1 Enoch literature and related traditions that refer to him" (131), but see his comments on Nimrod below.

[390] On Philo's reading ἄγγελοι in Gen 6:2, attested only in a revision in Codex A, and not υἱοί, see John M. Dillon and David Winston, *Two Treatises of Philo of Alexandria: A Commentary on De Gigantibus and Quod Deus Sit Immutabilis* (BJS 25; Chico: Scholars, 1983), who suggest that Philo is using a text which reflects someone having taken offence at the latter and replacing it by the less offensive ἄγγελοι which the Hebrew also warrants (236-37).

[391] On this see Valentin Nikiprowetzky, "Sur une lecture démonologique de Philon d'Alexandrie, De Gigantibus 6–18," in Hommage à Georges Vajda. Études d'histoire et de pensé juives (ed. G. Nahon et C. Touati; Louvain: Peeters, 1980) 43-71; John M. Dillon, "Philo's Doctrine of Angels," in *Two Treatises of Philo of Alexandria: A Commentary on De Gigantibus and Quod Deus Sit Immutabilis* (ed. David Winston and John Dillon; BJS 25; Chico: Scholars, 1983) 197-205, 205. On *Deus* 3 Dillon and Winston, *Two Treatises*, write: The ἄγγελοι are plainly here not evil spirits of any sort, but represent the irrational impulses, which 'mate' with the passions to produce evil actions" (274). Archie T. Wright, "Some Observations of Philo's *De Gigantibus* and Evil Spirits in Second Temple Judaism," *JSJ* 36 (2005) 471-88, suggests that Philo's attack on superstition and fear reflects familiarity with the Watcher tradition (479, 488).

[392] Stuckenbruck, "Philo's Treatment of Enoch", suggests that Philo's depiction of Nimrod may reflect "an awareness on his part of a tradition that was likewise associating this figure with the 'giants' mentioned in Gen 6:4" (138) and points to Pseudo-Eupolemos, from whom, however, he differs in not portraying Abraham as a giant (138).

aetiologically. It serves instead as symbolic depiction f mishandling the passions in general, which, of course, still include sexual desire.

1.3.1.4 Noah

1.3.1.4.1 Noah's Ark

On *the story of Noah's ark* we have commentary only in *QG*, where Philo sees the ark as symbolising the human body, which he addresses in detail, but, in doing so, passes over the genitals without mention. The ark's windows are the senses (*QG* 2.34) and the raven links them to passions and desires (*QG* 2.39), but when Philo asserts of the body that "by pleasure it is truly preserved and sustained in measure and in accordance with nature" (*QG* 2.46), we are probably hearing a positive assessment of pleasure, certainly in relation to food and possibly in relation also to the pleasure of procreative sex. Predictably, Philo depicts the flood as the passions which drown the wicked (*QG* 2.9). Entering and leaving the ark symbolises withholding from and then going out to engage in sexual intercourse, deemed only appropriate when life can begin again, not for sexual enjoyment in the interim (*QG* 2.49). This reflects not any special status of the ark, but solely Philo's stance that only procreative sex is licit pleasure. Philo sees the link between the command to multiply in Gen 9:1-2 and 1:28, from which he deduces that the text depicts a second genesis (*QG* 2.56). Outside of *QG* there is little. In *Plant.* Philo works with a different focus, but still depicting the ark as a body: wild animals, the passions, enter it, in contrast to Eden, the garden of virtues, where all are tame (*Plant.* 43). In *Fug.* while interpreting the "spring of folly", Philo employs the imagery of the flood also to depict the passions and their assault through the senses (*Fug.* 192).

1.3.1.4.2 Noah's Name

Noah's name, understood as "rest", brings Philo to speak of rest from the warfare of the soul for "the faculties within us, for six of them wage ceaseless and continuous war on land and sea, namely the five senses and speech" over which mind as the seventh is to rule and bring rest (*Abr.* 29). In *Leg.* 3 he cites Noah, in whose name he sees "rest" and "righteous", as one "who rests from sinful and unrighteous acts" (*Leg.* 3.77).

1.3.1.4.3 Noah and Agricultural Imagery

By contrast we have extensive expositions of the few details in Gen 9:20-27. Philo exploits the agricultural imagery to the full. Trees of licentiousness are to be cut down and plants of passions pulled up (*Agr.* 17). These will include unruly sexual passions, but, as noted above in 1.2.3.3), despite the language, Philo is not espousing denial of sexual desire entirely. Good trees of virtue are to be cultivated (*Agr.* 97-98). As outgrowths to be pruned away, Philo appears to make direct reference to courtesans and prostitutes, who mostly function symbolically as the seductress representing passions as a whole (*Agr.* 104-105). Similarly the senses which run riot are to be controlled (*Agr.* 109). Images of fishing suggest the nets of pleasures (*Agr.* 24); cattle-herding, the wild insatiable and uncontrolled senses (*Agr.* 34). Despite the language of denial the issue is control not extirpation.

1.3.1.4.4 Noah and Drunkenness

Noah's drunkenness inspired three books in the *Allegorical Exposition*. The two which survive, plus the considerable discussion already in *Plant.* advocate, as with the passions in general, not abstinence but moderation (*Plant.* 145, 162). In *Fug.* he enunciates the principle: "never debase pleasure to the displeasure of others, but, if we may so speak, get soberly drunken" (*Fug.* 32). Philo can even entertain the wise man becoming drunk on the basis that it will render him "more kindly and well-disposed" (*Plant.* 171-172). Similarly in *Somn.* 2 he notes that it need not affect all the same way.

> With some it relaxes pensiveness and gloom, lightens the stress of cares, softens wrath and fears, tutors the temperament to reasonableness and makes the soul contented with itself. With others it lubricates anger, screws up grief, excites amorousness and rouses discourtesy. It unlocks the mouth and unbridles the tongue, unbars the senses, maddens the passions, and makes the mind savage and wild and flustered with everything it meets. (*Somn.* 2.165).

The connection with sexual wrongdoing is clear. In *QE* he likens the person who drinks too much to an ass (*QE* 2.12), and in 2.18 declares: "For wine-drinking and cookery which are done with insatiability and gluttony, because of their being artificial produce illness and the causes of greater illnesses".

Mainly he emphasises the connection between drunkenness and vulnerability to sexual passion, as in *Somn.* 2.165 above. It became the basis for Lot's incest with his daughters, though Philo gives little attention to the illicit nature of the act (*Post.* 175-176). In *Opif.* Philo links both drunkenness and gluttony to enflaming sexual lusts (*Opif.* 158; similarly *Mos.* 2.185; *QG* 2.12). In *Mos.* 2 he speaks of "a scene of drunkenness and gluttony and lewdness and the other insatiable lusts, the parents of that grossness of flesh which is the enemy of quickness of mind" (*Mos.* 2.185). We also find reference to feasts as likely settings for such behaviour (*Leg.* 2.29, 33), typical of city clubs "with a large membership, whose fellowship is founded on no sound principle but on strong liquor and drunkenness and sottish carousing and their offspring, wantonness" (*Flacc.* 136; cf. *Legat.* 312).[393] Similarly in *Cher.* 92; *Agr.* 160 Philo depicts drunkenness at feasts, promoting loose sexual behaviour. In these drunkenness and gluttony combine (*Agr.* 37-38; similarly *Spec.* 1.148, 150). Thus in *Spec.* he explains: "For strong drink and gross eating accompanied by wine-bibbing, while they awaken the insatiable lusts of the belly, inflame also the lusts seated below it, and as they stream along and overflow on every side they create a torrent of evils, innumerable, because they have the immunity of the feast for their headquarters and refuge from retribution" (*Spec.* 1.192). In this context Philo also inculcates "flute-players and harpers and the whole range of unmanly and effeminate music the kind of music" characteristic of the theatre (*Agr.* 35; *Cher.* 92; *Post.* 155; cf. Josephus *A.J.* 1.64; *LAB* 2:8). Not all music is bad. He affirms the Song of Moses and even notes positively the myth of the birth of the Muses from Mnemosyne (*Plant.* 129). Elsewhere Philo mentions theatres in the context of the disapproved life which Enoch abandons, but offers no detail (*Abr.* 20). In contrast Philo can speak of hope as drinking of the wine of God's beneficent power as a holy people "which but now lay under the yoke of many pleasures and many lusts and the innumerable distresses which its vices and lusts entail, but has been redeemed into freedom by God" (*Praem.* 124).

1.3.1.4.5 Noah and Nakedness

Noah's nakedness prompts the reflection in *QG* 2.69 that this is of the category of involuntary transgression, noting a second category as that of becoming naked of the passions' hold, that is free from it.[394] In *Sobr.* Philo argues that Ham made his sin more grave by speaking of it (*Sobr.* 6). We noted in 1.2.3.1.2 the extensive discussion of nakedness prompted by Gen 2:25 (3:1) in *Leg.*, where Philo outlines not two but three kinds of nakedness (*Leg.* 2.55-56, 58-60). He illustrates positive nakedness, nakedness of the passions (that is, being free from their control), by pointing to Moses, who fixes his tent outside the camp (2.55; (Exod 33:7); to the high priest, who enters the Holiest place without his robe (*Leg.* 2.56); to Nadab and Abihu, who remove their garments (*Leg.* 2.57); to Abraham, who leaves his kin; to Isaac. who never enters Egypt, the place of passions (*Leg.* 2.59); and to Jacob, whose smooth nakedness contrasts with Esau's roughness (*Leg.* 2.59).

---

[393] On this see Torrey Seland, "Philo and the Clubs and Associations of Alexandria," in *Voluntary Associations in the Graeco-Roman World* (ed. John S. Kloppenborg and Stephen G. Wilson; London: Routledge, 1996) 110-27, who notes also the relevance of Philo's description of the symposia in *Contempl.* for understanding behaviour at clubs (116-17). See also van der Horst, *Philo's* Flaccus, 95-96.

[394] On this see also Louis H. Feldman, "Questions about the Great Flood, as Viewed by Philo, Pseudo-Philo, Josephus, and the Rabbis," *ZAW* 115 (2003) 401-22, who notes that Philo treats it as "within the modesty of his home" (417).

Here, too, as in *QG* 2.69, Noah's nakedness is in the negative category (*Leg.* 2.60). The third category beyond those also in *QG* 2.69 is the innocence of childhood before the advent of pleasure (*Leg.* 2.53, 64). Philo does not, however, set this up as an ideal state to be recovered. His models are the men who have passions and manage them.

As in *QG*, here in *Leg.* we find Philo differentiating between Noah's sin and Ham's, which he attributes to Canaan, of reporting in public what was seen. Noah's sin is foolish but not so grave since "he was made naked in his house" and not for all to see (*Leg.* 2.60-61). He acknowledges the problem that Canaan, not Ham is cursed, but solves it by allegory, Ham a symbol of quiescent, Canaan, of active vice (*Sobr.* 44), just as Shem's name, meaning "good", points to his worthy descendants who show their goodness by conquering passions (*Sobr.* 65). Philo briefly addresses nakedness also in *Spec.* 3 in relation to women seeing naked sports and men seeing women naked (*Spec.* 3.176). Philo makes no reference to the story of David and naked Bathsheba or Susanna and only indirectly to Reuben and Bilhah.

1.3.1.5 Babel

In the building of the tower Philo sees a consonance of evil (*Conf.* 15) which must be shattered (cf. *Conf.* 198). He illustrates that wickedness by pointing to Sodom, but understood only allegorically, namely as passions assaulting thoughts (*Conf.* 27). Among the names for the tower are some with sexual connotations, "seductions with adulteries", "unbridled lust with unmeasured pleasures" and he depicts the polytheist builders, typically, as sons of prostitutes whose polytheism reflects that they do not know who their real father is (*Conf.* 144) and belong to those deemed in Deut 23:1-2 ineligible to belong to the congregation. Otherwise no sexual themes appear.

1.3.2 Significant Motifs Generated by Genesis 12 – 50

Most of the motifs which Philo develops from these chapters centre on the patriarchs, their wives, concubines, and children and those with whom they are set in contrast. In each instance we find some material pertaining to sexuality. For Philo, the patriarchs attest to the Law since they embody it.[395] Circumcision, which

---

[395] Thus David T. Runia, "The Place of *De Abrahamo* in Philo's *Oeuvre*," *SPA* 20 (2008) 133-50, comments on *Abr.*: "The lives of the ancestors, both of the first and of the second triad, are set before the reader in order to show that the ordinances of the law are not inconsistent with nature ... and that the injunction to obey the law is not a heavy task, as

at one level belongs here, will be discussed below in the section on law (3.2.1). In this section we encounter writings from four main directions, from the *Exposition of the Law*: *Abr.*, *Ios.*, (*On Isaac* and *On Jacob* unfortunately have not survived); the relatively concise *Questions and Answers on Genesis* 3.1 – 4.245, covering Gen 15:7 – 28:8-9; from the *Allegorical Commentary*: *Migr.* (Gen 12:1-4, 6); *Her.* (Gen 15:2-18); *Congr.* (Gen 16:1-6); *Fug.* (Gen 16:6-12); *Mut.* (Gen 17:1-5, 15-22); and the second and third books on *Dreams*, the first of which has not survived, which include material mainly pertaining to Jacob and Joseph.

1.3.2.1 Abraham

1.3.2.1.1 Abraham's Migration

Abraham is a major figure in Philo's allegorical expositions. He normally symbolises Mind. Philo employs his migration from Mesopotamia in different but related ways: "removal out of three localities, namely, the body, sense-perception, and speech" (*Migr.* 2; similarly *Her.* 71, 73; *Leg.* 2.59; *Leg.* 3.44). Exodus from Egypt can function similarly. It does not mean their denial altogether, to "sever thyself from them absolutely," as he puts it (*Migr.* 7), but departure from where they rule to where they are now ruled, or, again, in his words: "Make thyself a stranger to them in judgement and purpose; let none of them cling to thee; rise superior to them all; they are thy subjects, never treat them as sovereign lords" (*Migr.* 7). For then "pleasures and lusts" act as jailers of the body (*Migr.* 9).

Philo can also use the image differently, citing the first stage, the short sojourn in Haran, as representing that it is desirable that Mind make itself familiar with the senses and the passions (*Migr.* 195; *Somn.* 1.47). He does the same in interpreting the sojourn of Jacob's sons in Egypt and Jacob's with Laban (*Somn.* 1.46). This is best understood not as a phase of development, though elsewhere Philo can depict the first seven years of life as one dominated by passions (*Congr.* 81), but as an aspect of continuing awareness. To excavate "the openings and cavities of the body", to find out what the senses are and how they function (*Somn.* 1.55-56), is to fulfil the ancient injunction, "Know thyself" (*Somn.* 1.57), "in order that you may enjoy the happiness proper to man" (*Somn.* 1.57).

In another sense Philo does see Abraham's migration as representing a journey whose goal is having Mind fully in control of sense and passions, but more than that. For the positive goal is to have the Mind become wise and contemplate the incorporeal and God. So he depicts some as never starting, others

---

shown by the fact that these men were able to carry it out when the laws were not even written down (*Abr.* 5)" (145).

as making progress, and some as reaching the goal (*Gig.* 62-64). The latter is expressed mostly not as reaching a location, but as engaging intimately with Sarah. When speaking in this context of the dangers of the passions, which sense-perception mediates to mind, Philo sometimes makes specific reference to sexual passion, though more often he writes symbolically of the sexual seduction of all errant passions. The sexual comes especially to the fore in describing the mind's relationships, and here Abraham's relationship with Sarah provides Philo with rich imagery.

1.3.2.1.2 Abraham and Sarah

We noted above (1.4.6) the broad range of applications Philo has for the image of sexual intercourse. In relation to Abraham and Sarah there are variations. He can describe "Abraham, Isaac, Jacob and Moses, and others of the same spirit" as not "knowing women" (*Cher.* 41), but mean thereby that they do not share intimacy with sense-perception that allows it to dominate. More frequently Philo takes marriage to Sarah as a symbol of the soul's espousal of Virtue or Wisdom which Sarah symbolises (*Abr.* 99-101; *QG* 4.68; *Congr.* 12; *Cher.* 10), so that "the righteous man is a consort of righteousness" (*QG* 4.68). Philo exploits a number of motifs in association with Sarah. Her barrenness can mean barrenness with regard to all that is bad (*Congr.* 4; *Mut.* 133-134; *Praem.* 159-160) – in her, passions are calmed (*Spec.* 2.54) – but also proof that ultimately God begets (*Migr.* 142). While in one sense barren, "she bears ceaselessly, successively, from moment to moment, and her offspring are no infants" (*Congr.* 4).

He regularly uses the reference that "there ceased to be to Sarah the ways of women" (Gen 18:11). While the Hebrew refers to the menstrual cycle, the word, γυναικεῖα, used for this in Gen 18:11 LXX, also has a broader range of meaning and can refer to "matters pertaining to women", from biology to garments and household quarters.[396] As Niehoff notes, Philo also took the verb transitively, to produce the meaning, in effect, that "Sarah 'stopped turning to womanly things'".[397] In *Cher.* 50; *Ebr.* 60, Philo adds "all" before τὰ γυναικεῖα thus removing the reference to menstruation,[398] enabling him to shift the focus from the literal to allegory and to portray Sarah as choosing rational thought (male) above irrational (female) (see also *QG* 4.15; *Det.* 28; *Post.* 134). Accordingly, "the female sex is irrational and akin to bestial passions, fear, sorrow, pleasure and desire, from which ensue incurable weaknesses and indescribable diseases. He

---

[396] On this see Niehoff, "Mother and Maiden," 413-44.

[397] Niehoff, "Mother and Maiden," 434. She notes that in *Fug.* 128 Philo even omits the "grammatically superfluous" γίνεσθαι (434).

[398] Niehoff, "Mother and Maiden," 434.

who is conquered by these is unhappy, while he who controls them is happy" (*QG* 4.15). That transition he also explains paradoxically as her becoming a virgin (*Congr.* 7; *Somn.* 2.185; *Cher.* 50; *Post.* 134; *Praem.* 159-160). He can complicate the matters even further by playing with the contrast between literal marriage in which a virgin becomes a woman and the allegorical where the woman becomes a virgin (*Abr.* 99-101; *Somn.* 2.185).

Philo also exploits Abraham's defence over against Abimelech that Sarah is truly his sister, the daughter of his father, not his mother (οὐκ ἐκ μητρός Gen 20:12, originally alluding to her as step-sister) to claim that Sarah has no female parenthood (*QG* 4.60, 68; *Her.* 62). In effect Sarah can serve as a symbol not only of virtue and wisdom but also of the wise rational mind, which on Philo's understanding must necessarily be male.[399] He notes the paradox in *Abr.* where he depicts virtue's natural function as sowing seed (*Abr.* 100-101). Similarly, he can interpret Sarah's name as "sovereignty in me" (*Congr.* 2; cf. also *Cher.* 41), symbolising mind in control, "the virtue-loving mind" (*Ebr.* 59). Thus ceasing from the ways of woman "clearly belongs to minds full of Law, which resemble the male sex and overcome passions and rise above all sense-pleasure and desire and are without sorrow and fear and, if one must speak the truth, without passion" (*QG* 4.15). He qualifies the latter: "not zealously practising apathy, for this would be ungrateful and shameless and akin to arrogance and reckless boldness, but that which is consistent with the argument given, (namely) cutting the mind off from disturbing and confusing passions" (*QG* 4.15).

While the latter allegorical development virtually makes Sarah male,[400] Philo can nevertheless still affirm Sarah the wife at the literal level, not least in expressing "wifely love" (*QG* 3.20) as model wife in the household supporting her husband (*Abr.* 245-246), and concerned with producing offspring for him as a key

---

[399] Niehoff, "Mother and Maiden," suggests that the figure of Athena, "described in antiquity as a motherless virgin and Zeus's daughter, who sprang directly from his head and not from a motherly womb" has influenced Philo's image of Sarah here, citing Hesiod *Theogn.* 924 (440). She notes that he draws on Pythagorean tradition in associating seven and the virgin Nike, with whom Athena was assimilated, also in depicting the seventh day and the seven-branched menorah (440-42). She notes that "Philo's choice is all the more remarkable as Athena was in Egypt identified with Isis, a goddess of wisdom described, like Sarah, as both wife and sister to her husband", though Philo's choice is not to take over her feminine characteristics but to employ the more masculine traits characteristic of Athena in tradition (443).

[400] Sly, *Philo's Perception of Women*, writes: "When she is allegorized, Sarah is absorbed into Abraham as a quality of his character. He is the wise man; she is his wisdom. ... He is the virtuous man; she is his virtue" (152). "The effect of the allegory thus is both to elevate and to dissolve her" (152). She speaks of Philo seeking "to minimize Sarah's womanhood" (152).

role (*QG* 3.20),⁴⁰¹ and also as physically/sexually attractive (*Abr.* 93).⁴⁰² Sly writes: "When he treats her on the human level, he alters the Biblical account to make her into the ideal, but subservient, wife. When he accepts the vigorously independent Sarah of Scripture, he robs her of both her womanhood and her humanity, through allegory. The person Sarah whom Philo allows to emerge is thus only a shadow of the Biblical Sarah".⁴⁰³ However, this appears to me to confuse categories by transferring the allegorical image onto the literal, producing an overly negative assessment. Sly then seeks to explain this on the basis of Hellenistic influence.⁴⁰⁴

Niehoff similarly challenges this assessment noting that the biblical stories already assume patriarchy and that in *Jubilees* Sarah has marginal significance.⁴⁰⁵ Pointing to the obituary in *Abr.* 245-246, which she notes is "unique in ancient exegesis",⁴⁰⁶ she observes that "within this patriarchal structure ... Philo stresses her significance and idealizes her as an exemplary wife".⁴⁰⁷ On the migration, Philo gives Sarah much greater significance than Gen 12:10, portraying her as κοινωνός, a term which "normally refers in Philo's work to the partnership between priests who perform sacrifices or rulers who share power", and is used of Moses as partner of God (*Mos.* 1.155).⁴⁰⁸. Thus "Philo's Sarah enjoys much more equality than her biblical original. Philo suggests that Sarah perfectly fulfilled her role as wife because she was indeed a true partner of her husband".⁴⁰⁹ She, too, exercises control over her passions, and endures the difficulties of migration without complaint. Niehoff notes that "in his obituary [*Abr.* 248-250], Philo claims that the clearest proof of Sarah's character is to be found in her offer of Hagar to Abraham" (whose symbolic significance we discuss in the next section), where beyond the biblical text she gives full explanation of her motives, which are a summary of Philo's principles of marriage and makes her a mouthpiece for what is usually deemed the male quality of self-control.⁴¹⁰ Rather than more self-effacing

---

⁴⁰¹ Niehoff, "Mother and Maiden," 413-44, 420-21.

⁴⁰² Satlow, *Jewish Marriage*, notes that Philo shifts the focus to her beauty of soul (244). Generally, commenting on Philo's use of the biblical material, he notes that "Philo is the first, and foremost, biblical exegete to turn these biblical shreds into an example of a marriage worthy of emulation" (243).

⁴⁰³ Sly, *Philo's Perception of Women*, 154.

⁴⁰⁴ Sly, *Philo's Perception of Women*, 127-28.

⁴⁰⁵ Niehoff, "Mother and Maiden," 415.

⁴⁰⁶ Niehoff, "Mother and Maiden," 419.

⁴⁰⁷ Niehoff, "Mother and Maiden," 420.

⁴⁰⁸ Niehoff, "Mother and Maiden," 420.

⁴⁰⁹ Niehoff, "Mother and Maiden," 420.

⁴¹⁰ Niehoff, "Mother and Maiden," 421, 422. She writes: "Her commitment to the Mosaic ideal of procreation thus proves far stronger than her personal attachment to Abraham. Her mind controls her emotions, setting a perfect example for her husband as

than in the biblical text, as Sly suggests,[411] Philo does not know the Hebrew text of Gen 16:2 which reports Sarah's own desire to have children ("it may be that I shall obtain children by her" אולי אבנה ממנה), but only the LXX which speaks only of Abraham's desire for children ("that you may obtain children by her" ἵνα τεκνοποιήσῃς ἐξ αὐτῆς).[412] Niehoff also notes that Philo sanitises Sarah's image by omitting reference to her maltreatment of Hagar.[413] In relation to Philo's account of Abraham and Sarah at Pharaoh's court, she notes that Philo gives more attention to Sarah than the biblical account, emphasising her beauty and then, unlike the biblical accounts and its parallels and retellings, addresses Sarah's plight, describing her thoughts and feelings, defending Abraham against potential accusations that he abandoned her and depicting the two in harmonious prayer.[414] Niehoff concludes: "his sympathetic reading of Sarah's story is by no means subversive, but remains firmly anchored in a patriarchal framework" and speaks of Philo "inserting some gynocentric snapshots into a generally androcentric album".[415]

On the angels' announcement of Sarah's progeny in Gen 18:1-15, Niehoff notes that Philo, by contrast with the biblical account, does not confine Sarah to her tent, has the couple receive the promise together and both doubt, but then mollify Sarah's laughter by having her recall her early training which could help her believes that nothing is impossible for God. Her "fear" (ἐφοβήθη) (Gen 18:15 LXX) thus becomes an indicator of her piety.[416] Niehoff goes on to note that while Philo passes over negative aspects of Sarah's image in literal interpretation, he takes them up into his allegorical interpretations.[417] She observes that in employing Sarah to depict spiritual processes of the soul "she herself has been allegorized out of existence".[418] In contrast, therefore, with his "exceptionally

---

well" (422). Similarly Böhm, *Vätererzählungen*: "In der Darstellung der Ehe Abrahams und Saras kann Philo auch seine – ganz jüdisch geprägte – Sexualmoral transportieren: Die Ehe dient allein dem Zweck des Zeugens legitimer Nachkommen" (166).

[411] Sly, *Philo's Perception of Women*, 150.

[412] Niehoff, "Mother and Maiden," 421 n. 26. She notes also that Sarah's motherhood is crucial for Philo because he assumes that "the child's status is determined by the mother as well as by the father" (423).

[413] Niehoff, "Mother and Maiden," 422.

[414] Niehoff, "Mother and Maiden," 423-26. She notes the similar motif of Abraham's prayer in Genesis Apocryphon (1QapGen ar/1Q20 12-16), though sees Philo's creative exegesis as more likely than dependence on a common tradition (425).

[415] Niehoff, "Mother and Maiden," 426.

[416] Niehoff, "Mother and Maiden," 427.

[417] Niehoff, "Mother and Maiden," 429.

[418] Niehoff, "Mother and Maiden," 431. She discusses Philo's allegorical interpretations of Gen 17:16 (430-33); 18:11 (433-38); and 20:12 (438-43).

sympathetic" portrait of Sarah as a woman at the literal level, in allegory he goes out of his way to remove the feminine: "Sarah is thus appreciated precisely because she lacks female genealogy and feminine characteristics: she is the masculine daughter of a masculine God".[419] She sees a parallel contrast between the literal and allegorical portraits of Joseph, who at one level is a model and at another represents a current danger of assimilation to Egypt. She suggests that the allegorical portrait of Sarah similarly seeks to counter a danger, namely the influence of the feminine and is represented by his choice of the Pythagorean model of Athena rather than the more feminine Isis image popular in his context.[420]

That, in turn, underlies the values enshrined in his allegorical extrapolations, where within the soul the feminine irrational is to serve the rational male mind. Where this is achieved we have what Philo describes by using the language of sexual intimacy with Sarah. In Philo sexual intercourse including its pleasurableness has a sole purpose: procreation of offspring. Isaac, the self-taught, symbolises virtue's offspring (*Fug.* 167; *QG* 4.122).

1.3.2.1.3 Abraham, Sarah, and Hagar

Philo develops the image of sex with Sarah also differently to describe not the move to the mind's ruling the dangerous passions and sense-perception, but levels of education. For this he exploits the image of Hagar. According to Borgen, Philo is here importing into Jewish discourse a model based on Homer's image of Penelope. "Ps.-Plutarch says that those who, being unable to attain philosophy, wear themselves out in the encyclical disciplines, like the suitors of Penelope, who when they could not win the mistress, contended themselves with her maids (Ps.-Plutarch, *De liberis educandis* 7D)."[421] Philo exploits this. "This transformation of Penelope and her maids into Sarah and Hagar meant that Philo produced a parallel interpretation within a Jewish context, to express a Jewish point of view regarding encyclical education: the encyclical education is the school which the Jews have in common with their pagan surroundings".[422]

---

[419] Niehoff, "Mother and Maiden," 443. Similarly Böhm, *Vätererzählungen*: "In der Konsequenz dieser ganz am Einzelterminus und Wort orientierten, entpersonalisierten und dehistorisierten Deutung liegt auch eine völlige Entschlackung der symbolisch als Tugenden gedeuteten Erstfrauen von jedweder Sinnlichkeit und Weiblichkeit" (260).

[420] Niehoff, "Mother and Maiden," 444.

[421] Borgen, *Exegete for his Time*, 163.

[422] Borgen, *Exegete for his Time*, 163. See also Sly, *Philo's Perception of Women*, who suggests that Philo's treatment of Hagar in this context reflects debate in Plato's time with Isocrates about the latter's emphasis on rhetoric in *Resp.* 6.509C5-D6 (127). She notes that Philo "does retain the essential features of a) the progressive nature of learning, that is, the

Philo praises Sarah's generosity in offering Abraham her maidservant to provide offspring for him (*Abr.* 248, 250, 253; cf. Gen 16:1-6). In the *Allegorical Commentary* however he exploits it as a symbol of Sarah/Wisdom's generosity to provide children for Abraham/mind through her maidservant, who stands for school learning (*Leg.* 3.244-245; *Congr.* 5, 9, 12, 14, 71; *Ebr.* 64; *Cher.* 3). This image rightly serves as the title for the book focused most on this theme: *On Mating [Intercourse] with Preliminary Studies*. One should have intercourse with both, first Hagar, then Sarah. Unlike the sex with Sarah noted above, where abandoning passions might include sexual concerns, these are absent here. Discussing the literal story, Philo ensures we note that once Hagar became pregnant Abraham ceased having intercourse with her and that the intercourse was purely functional, that is, without focus on pleasure (*Abr.* 253). The focus in the allegory is not passions, but learning. The ultimate goal remains "a mating of the mind with virtue. Mind desires to have children by virtue, and, if it cannot do so at once, is instructed to espouse virtue's handmaid, the lower instruction" (*Congr.* 12; similarly *Somn.* 1.44). The contrast of the two levels of education recalls the distinction Philo makes between the triad, Enos, Enoch, and Noah, and the triad Abraham, Isaac, and Jacob, the former symbolising the studies of children, the latter, "the exercises of athletes" for sacred games and "victory over their antagonists, the passions" (*Abr.* 48).

The literal event of Hagar's expulsion (Gen 16:6-9) provides for further development of the image. Symbolically, Hagar must be expelled, if the Mind becomes engrossed at that level and does not move on (*Congr.* 77, 152). Elsewhere Philo depicts remaining with Hagar as being too much under the influence of customs (*Ebr.* 64) and or bearing the fruit of sophistry and deserving like Adam to be expelled from the garden (*Cher.* 10). Accordingly, Philo assures us at the end of *Congr.* that we should not see Sarah's actions as reflecting the jealousy which he sees as typical of women, but as meant only to carry symbolic meaning (*Congr.* 180). In fact he ignores Sarah's violence, despite citing it from Gen 16:6a at the beginning of the following book, which focuses on her flight (*Fug.* 1). It is important rather that he depict Hagar as inferior, unable to draw the waters of Wisdom (*Fug.* 204) or to pour water as can Rebecca (*Post.* 137-139). At the same time he does not want to deny that she bears useful fruit, "noble practices and deeds" (*Mut.* 255),[423] even though incomparable to the self-contained wisdom, the joyous offspring of Virtue, which Isaac represents (*Mut.* 261).

---

need for the encyclia to precede philosophical studies, b) the dependence of the encyclia on sense-perception, and c) the eventual freeing of the mind from the senses" (127).

[423] Borgen, *An Exegete for his Time*, notes that "in his *Ad Lucilium Epistulae Morales* 88 Seneca defends a position which shows many similarities to that of Philo in Mut. 253-63. Like Philo, Seneca also closely associates the terms, 'virtue (*virtus*) and 'wisdom'

Philo can turn the marital imagery to a different purpose again when commenting on Abraham's marriage to Keturah. Here he urges marriage to three wives, understood as the three senses sight, hearing, and smell, contrasted with the other two, touch and taste which he associates with negative influence (*QG* 4.147). Abraham's household also provides Philo with another image, that of Masek, "from a kiss" (*Her.* 40). It enables him to argue that the Mind should treat sense-perception with affection, but not with love, thus a kiss not sexual intercourse, another variation of ensuring that it and the passions it purveys do not dominate (*Her.* 42, 52-53).

1.3.2.1.4 Abraham and Sarah, Pharaoh and Abimelech

The account of Abraham also provides negative foils. The description at a literal level of Pharaoh's abduction of Sarah affirms her sexual attractiveness (*Abr.* 94), highlights his licentiousness beside the breach of hospitality, which is given equal weight (*Abr.* 94, 95, 107), and underlines that Sarah's chastity was untouched (*Abr.* 98), without which, Philo assumes, the marriage would have had to end and the promise of a people dearest to God with priest and prophet, would have come to naught (*Abr.* 98). He suppresses here Abraham's ploy of claiming Sarah as his "sister", but develops it in the account of Abimelech's abduction of Sarah in *QG*. Here he wards off allegations of incest (*QG* 4.60-61), partly by explaining "sister" as a sign of marital affection "sweet, tender, fitting", something Philo values (*QG* 4.66), but also by allegory, expounding the view noted above of Sarah as virtue, born solely from God (*QG* 4.68). Literal concerns surface as he notes, as in *Abr.* 98 above, that Sarah was not defiled (*QG* 4.63, 66-67). In both, Sarah's death, understood literally, becomes occasion for wider reflection. Thus Abraham models restrained grief, moderate and controlled engagement of passion, the way of the wise (*Abr.* 257-258; *QG* 4.73). One may be struck by such impulses but should then turn away, here extending this to apply to other impulses as well, including the impulse to adultery (*QG* 4.73).

The place of the double cave of Sarah's burial, "Hebron", Philo interprets, as elsewhere, as "union", "coupling", or "the companionship of women" (*QG* 4.83; *Det.* 15; *Post.* 60-61) and writes: "it is possible to join and fit together companionship and sincere liking, and to make the body genuinely (devoted) to the soul, the one as the ruler, and the other as the minister", in this way acting as a "queen" ruling over "external things" and "sense-perceptible objects" (*QG* 4.83).

(*sapientia*), with philosophy in contrast to encyclical education (*artes liberales*)" (164), though Seneca does so more sharply than Philo (165).

In *Post.* 60-61 he shows that the image of Hebron may be used positively or negatively, depending on whether the soul rules or is ruled by the body.

1.3.2.2 Sodom and Lot

1.3.2.2.1 Sodom's Sins

Most striking of the negative foils is the story of Lot and Sodom. Here we find both the allegorical and the literal, and, not least, concern with sexual wrongdoing. Philo brings a literal account in *Abr.* 133-141. He sees the sexual wrongdoing within the context of a broad spectrum of sins of passion, including "gluttony and lewdness" and "every other possible pleasure" (*Abr.* 133), as well as greed (*Abr.* 134). He depicts them as engaging in "deep drinking of strong liquor and dainty feeding and forbidden forms of intercourse (ὀχείας ἐκθέσμους)" (*Abr.* 135). The sexual wrongdoing included adultery and sex with other males: "Not only in their mad lust for women did they violate the marriages of their neighbours (οὐ γὰρ μόνον θηλυμανοῦντες ἀλλοτρίους γάμους διέφθειραν), but also men mounted males without respect for the sex nature which the active partner shares with the passive (ἀλλὰ καὶ ἄνδρες ὄντες ἄρρεσιν ἐπιβαίνοντες, τὴν κοινὴν πρὸς τοὺς πάσχοντας οἱ δρῶντες φύσιν οὐκ αἰδούμενοι)" (*Abr.* 135). Philo's concern is with acts contrary to nature, males assuming the passive, female, role, resulting in feminisation of men, which he calls the "female disease" (θηλείαν ... νόσον) (*Abr.* 136), and with what Philo believes is the result: male impotence, which still did not stop them from continuing; and the fear of depopulation because procreation of offspring, the only valid ground in Philo's view for sexual intercourse, was not happening (*Abr.* 137). In this account nothing is said of pederasty.

The account in *QG* 4 deals with the story at both levels, literal and allegorical. While Philo notes that the literal meaning of "Bring them out that we may know them" (Gen 19:5) "indicates servile, lawless and unseemly pederasty (lit. unseemly and male pederasty)" (*QG* 4.37), perhaps played on in the reference to boys in 39, and "denotes an excess of licentiousness" (*QG* 4.41), his primary interest is allegorical. Here the story depicts the assaults of the lure of pleasure upon the soul, a battle which the man on the journey to wisdom must face, and where he must be prepared to let go the feminine (the daughters) in the interest of maintaining the mind's (male) integrity. In these allegorical expositions nothing more is said about sexual wrongdoing in itself, let alone same-sex relations. The concern is eradication of desire and anger and their dwelling place (*QG* 4.42). We return to both these accounts in more detail below (1.4.1.3.6).

In other brief references we hear concrete echoes of Sodom's distinctive sexual wrongdoing: they committed "strange and monstrous practices of iniquity and all their heinous acts of impiety aimed at subversion of the statutes of nature" (*Spec.* 2.170); they performed "deeds of licence and followed eagerly still more grievous practices" (*Mos.* 2.55); indulged in "licentious living and fed every pleasure and every lust with lavish supplies of fuel like a flame when the brushwood is piled upon it" (*Mos.* 2.58); preferred "lower passions to higher emotions" (*Her.* 77); "left no stone unturned to carry out their unnatural and unholy lust" (*Fug.* 144); and engaged in "immoderate indulgence in pleasures, unnatural lusts that may not be named" (*Post.* 52).

On a number of occasions Philo explains the name Sodom as meaning "blindness" and "sterility" (*QG* 4.23, 31; *Congr.* 109; *Fug.* 142; *Somn.* 2.192; *Ebr.* 222). "Sterility" is not for Philo a cause for sympathy; rather it marks failure to propagate the species and so grievous sin. He similarly condemns eunuchs for failing that obligation. Intratextually within the corpus such sterility is probably evoking Philo's understanding of the story according to which men chose ways of engaging in sex which had no prospect of procreation. We discuss the issue of same-sex relations in general in 1.4.1.3.6 below.

The allegorical may inform some allusions to the Sodomites elsewhere (*QG* 4:23; *Conf.* 27-28; perhaps *Congr.* 109). Philo cites Deut 32:32, "'Their vine,' he says, 'is of the vine of Sodom and their tendrils of Gomorrah, their grapes are grapes of gall, a cluster of bitterness to them'" to depict folly (*Somn.* 2.191) and "those who are under the thrall of wine-bibbing and gluttony and the basest of pleasures" (*Ebr.* 222), and sees Sodom as indicating that "folly is blind and unproductive of excellence" (*Somn.* 2.192) and illustrating "the violence of the malady's impetuous course" (*Sacr.* 121-122). Philo exhorts us to flee "without a backward glance from the unions which are unions of sin" (*Conf.* 40).

1.3.2.2.2 Lot's Wife and Daughters

Other aspects of the story of Sodom which receive Philo's attention are the responses of Lot and his wife to Sodom and the action of Lot's daughters. Lot "alone did not fall in with the multitude, when they turned aside to licentious living and fed every pleasure and every lust with lavish supplies of fuel like a flame when the brushwood is piled upon it" (*Mos.* 2.58). Typically Philo depicts leaving Sodom as leaving behind "all sense-perceptible, corporeal and subject to passion" to be seen as "exhalation, furnace and smoke" (*QG* 4.53; similarly *Migr.* 13). Accordingly, his wife's looking back symbolises sense-perception inclining back to the world of the passions (*QG* 4.53; *Somn.* 1.247; *Conf.* 40): "being enamoured of Sodom and reverting to the characters that had been overthrown by God" (*Leg.* 3.213) and reflecting typical feminine addiction to custom (*Ebr.* 164). Philo alludes to this in having the Therapeutae do the opposite: "they flee without a backward glance and leave their brothers, their children, their wives, their parents, the wide circle of their kinsfolk, the groups of friends around them, the fatherlands ..." (*Contempl.* 18).

Philo's depiction of Lot's daughters, who make him drunk and have sex with him in order to enable the race to survive, varies. In *Questions and Answers* he can depict their plight, which led them to incest, with sympathy: "This undertaking against the present custom of marriage is somewhat unlawful and an innovation, but it has an excuse. For these virgins, because of their ignorance of external matters ... supposed that the whole human race ..." had been destroyed (*QG* 4.56; cf. Josephus *A.J.* 1.205). This extends to his depiction of their offspring: Moab, "from my father", son of the daughter called "Counsel" (*QG* 4.56, 58) is treated positively in contrast to Ammon "from my people" by the daughter called "Consent", typifying concession to sense-perception, a "feminine thing" (*QG* 4.58).

By contrast, in *Allegorical Commentary* Philo depicts Lot unsympathetically. He is "the man who, after having been impelled upwards, wavered and went downwards through weakness of soul" (*Post.* 175), and as "the parent of daughters only and could rear no male or perfect growth within his soul" (*Ebr.* 164). The daughters fail to trust God, desiring "to have children by Mind their father" and "so they advocate the doctrine of a drunken and frenzied soul" (*Post.* 175; similarly *Ebr.* 165-169). "We see then that the mind is fitly represented as labouring under absence of knowledge, when its two daughters, Deliberation and Assent, are in contact with it and become its bed fellows" (*Ebr.* 203). That lack of knowledge reflects "people that suppose that sense-perception and mind, a male and a female, act as father and mother for the procreation of all things, and take this process to be in very truth the cause of creation" (*Post.* 177). Similarly he condemns "those energies of the soul that have been unstrung by lewd and licentious intercourse with Mind's daughters, the senses, as though they were common strumpets" (*Somn.* 1.88). He then makes the link with Shittim where Israel confronted Moab and declares: "For he says 'and the people abode in Shittim' – the meaning of this name is 'thorns,' a symbol of passions pricking and wounding the soul – 'and was defiled to commit whoredom with the daughters of Moab' – these are the senses, entitled daughters of Mind; for the translation of 'Moab' is 'from a father'" (*Somn.* 1.88-89). Their exclusion from the people of God (Philo assumes permanently) in Deut 23:1-2 (*Post.* 177; *Leg.* 3.81) serves thus Philo's common theme of asserting the importance of mind ruling senses and not the other way round, for they had nothing to offer Israel when it "came out from the passions of Egypt" (*Leg.* 3.81).

1.3.2.2.3 Lot, Abraham, and the Kings

A third connection with Sodom is found in Philo's exposition of the earlier story in Genesis, namely Abraham's defeat of the four kings threatening the five cities of the plain. The numbers are ideal for Philo to mount an exposition of the five senses and four passions (*Abr.* 149; 236; similarly *Ebr.* 105). Among the five senses he asserts a hierarchy, linking taste, smell, and touch, as relating to gluttony and sexual passion in animals, cattle and wild beasts (*Abr.* 149; similarly 241), claiming that "all day and night they fill themselves with food insatiably" and adding erroneously: "or are at rut" (*Abr.* 149). Accordingly God "destroyed the four, because they were in slavery to flesh and the passions of flesh" (*Abr.* 164), though he makes no reference to Sodom's particular sexual sins. He concludes: "Now the nine overlords, the four passions and the five senses, are corruptible and the sources of corruption, but the truly divine and holy Word, whose stronghold is in the virtues, whose place in the order of number is tenth, the supremely perfect number, comes to the contest and with the help of the mightier power of God wins an easy victory over the said overlords" (*Abr.* 244). Philo also interprets Abraham's refusal to accept the king of Sodom's horses, predictably, as rejection of the dangerous passions (*Leg.* 3.24, 197). In *Leg.* 3 he also mentions Melchizedek, meaning "king of peace" and "righteous king", like Isaac, created as such, a king who rules the passions (*Leg.* 3.79-80).

1.3.2.3 Isaac and Rebecca

Most of Philo's comments about Isaac are at the level of allegory. Many of these expositions begin with or assume the literal level, including the promise of his birth, the birth itself, swearing an oath with hand under Abraham's thigh about marriage, the servant's travel to find a suitable wife, marriage to Rebecca at forty, entering his mother's house, Abimelech's abduction of Rebecca, his seeing the couple at play, and Isaac's advice not to go down to Egypt. Thus Isaac features as the promised offspring of Sarah, who is Virtue and Wisdom, as such, one who is self-taught, that is, has inborn wisdom (*Abr.* 52; *QG* 4.122, 148; *Mut.* 261; *Deus* 4; *Leg.* 3.85-87) and is predictably male, since female offspring are inferior and reflect the inferior state of their parents (*QG* 4.148). Sarah's barrenness in old age becomes the basis for the claim that Isaac is begotten by God (*Migr.* 142; *Mut.* 132). Philo even merges conception and birth in one event on the basis of the biblical statement "she conceived and gave birth" (*Fug.* 167) and has him born not needing weaning but able to take solid food (*Somn.* 2.10), perhaps reflecting legends of babies born already mature, such as we find of Noah and Melchizedek (*1 Enoch* 106:2-3; *2 Enoch* 71:17-18). Isaac's name helps Philo to depict his birth as a moment of true joy (*Mut.* 261; *QG* 4.128). It also accounts for the joy he sees reflected in Isaac's sexual play with Rebecca, observed by Abimelech (*QG* 4.185-188; *Plant.* 166), though Philo treats the marriage to Rebecca ("Constancy" *QG* 4.97, 200; *Congr.* 36; cf. *Cher.* 41, "steadfastness in excellence") and especially as his sole wife, primarily as a symbol of his permanent connection with "the queen and mistress virtue" (*Congr.* 36; similarly *QG* 4.200) and treats his entering his mother's house as connecting to motherless wisdom (*QG* 4.145). It belongs thus to the ideal image of self-taught wisdom. Philo even explains the fact that Abraham instructs his servant, not Isaac, about not seeking a wife from among the Canaanites, to illustrate both that Isaac by nature needs no instruction and that he would never have engaged in what a Canaanite symbolises, the school of "those out of their mind" (*QG* 4.88). Under the image of nakedness he describes Isaac as having always been naked in this sense, shown by his following the injunction not to go down to Egypt, which Philo depicts as the place of the passions (*Leg.* 2.59).

Despite the heavy overlay of allegory, sometimes Philo's comments reflect on aspects of sexuality in a literal sense. He commends Isaac's marriage at forty as a worthy model to follow, which he seems to mean literally, even though he supports it with rather abstruse argument by appealing to the formation of an embryo in the womb usually in forty days (*QG* 4.154). Literal sexual references comes also, though indirectly, in his exposition of Abraham's request that in making an oath about Isaac's betrothal his servant place his hand under his thigh (Gen 24:2), as he explains, adjacent to his genitals, "indicating a pure association and an unpolluted marriage, not having sensual pleasure as its end but the procreation of legitimate children" (*QG* 4.86). Procreation is paramount but the references to joy/pleasure in this context show that Philo envisages joy and pleasure in sex as proper where procreation is the goal. Thus in *QG* 4.154 he explains: "It is necessary to receive enjoyment of love and affection from a wife and to fulfil the law concerning the rearing of children", which surely also includes sexual love. The sexual play which Abimelech sees, "lawful commerce[424] with one's wife", belongs here (*QG* 4.188; similarly *Plant.* 169), which Philo, having identified the literal meaning, hastens to allegorise as "the game and delight of the soul", noting that the wicked man "has no marriage with wonderful pleasure" (*QG* 4.188). Nevertheless it seems that the literal sense is not being denied here.

Elsewhere Philo can list Isaac among those whom Moses does not represent "as knowing women" (*Cher.* 41), but clearly addressing the mind's domination by the senses and not meant literally. Philo cites God's instruction to Isaac not to go down to Egypt (Gen 26:2), predictably as a call to shun the passions (*Leg.* 2.59; *Conf.* 81). Philo speaks of him in this context as "the only example of freedom

---

[424] Marcus, *Philo Supplement I*, notes that behind the Armenian, *hawasarout'ium*, which usually translates κοινωνία is probably the word, συνουσία, the Old Latin reading *coitus*, and the paraphrase of Procopius (471).

from passion beneath the sun" when deploring Esau's initiative to persuade his father to ignore this advice (*Det.* 46). Philo can also set Isaac's level of wisdom, along with the others of his triad, Abraham and Jacob, in contrast to the former triad of Enos, Enoch, and Noah, who represent lower learning (*Abr.* 48).

As Sly notes, Philo deliberately bypasses "the familiar stories of Rebecca's helping Jacob to trick Isaac. Instead he presents the married Rebecca as a person whose thoughts and actions completely harmonize with her husband's".[425] In addition, referring to *QG* 4.142, she notes: "The motives of modesty and veneration on which the literal Rebecca acted are characteristic of Philo's model wife, and are his own addition to Scripture".[426] Accordingly, "Once Rebecca and Isaac are married, Philo is at pains to emphasize their complete harmony, even at the expense of the natural sense of Scripture", referring to Gen 25:28 (*QG* 4.166), where Philo argues that the aorist and imperfect tenses on the parents' love for Esau (ἠγάπησεν) and Jacob (ἠγάπα) indicates harmony, since both love both, but only the love for Jacob is ongoing.[427]

In depicting Rebecca, aside from as Isaac's wife, Philo portrays her as like Sarah, Leah, and Zipporah a recipient of divine seed (*Cher.* 45-47). He focuses primarily on her (symbolic) virginity, uncorrupted by passion (*QG* 4.95, 97; *Post.* 133). As noted above, Philo exploits the name of her father, Bethuel, read as "daughter of God", to speak of him as wisdom (*Fug.* 50; *QG* 4.97) and depict her as wisdom's child, despite the complications he must face through having a male referred to as a female. He takes pains to address this in *Fug.* 51-52, urging the hearer to ignore the gender of words and recognise that in its superior position Wisdom is be seen as male.

The twins' struggle in her womb reflects for Philo that "every virtue (is related) to every vice, and conversely", for "wisdom gives place to folly, and temperance to unbridled lasciviousness, and injustice to justice, and cowardice to courage, and the other contraries similarly" (*QG* 4.159), thus including a possible indirect reference to sexual wrongdoing. Rebecca's concern with Esau's Canaanite wives receives both allegorical treatment when he depicts them as symbols of senselessness and "unrestrained impulses" (*QG* 4.241), and comment at a literal level about intermarriage. Thus he notes that "the father orders his son to make a journey to a foreign (land) (and) to seek in marriage a wife of his (own) race" (*QG* 4.243) and that Moses disapproves even of Esau's taking additional wives,

---

[425] Sly, *Philo's Perception of Women*, 157. "Philo downplays the questionable morality of Rebecca's action; he emphasizes rather that she enriches her husband's soul with her astuteness. The part of the story Philo uses most frequently to illustrate this quality is Rebecca's advice to Jacob to go away and visit Laban until Esau's anger (at her deceitful action) has abated" (159).

[426] Sly, *Philo's Perception of Women*, 155.

[427] Sly, *Philo's Perception of Women*, 156.

because he did not discard the existing ones (*QG* 4.245). In addition one of the new ones had the name "'Mahalath,' which is to be interpreted 'from the beginning'" (*QG* 4.245). She then embodies for Philo a reference to sensual pleasure "congenital to every living creature from the beginning and from the first creation" and "the cause of many evils" (*QG* 4.245). Thus Philo uses such intermarriage again symbolically to address the mind's craving after pleasure. He can also use Rebecca for his contrast between higher and lower levels of learning, contrasting Rebecca and Hagar, and the levels from which they pour water (*Post.* 137-139, 146).

1.3.2.4 Jacob and Esau

As indicated in the symbolism of the twins in the womb, Philo contrasts Jacob and Esau, removing negative traits from the former. "The elder was disobedient, indulging without restraint the pleasures of the belly and the lower lying parts" (*Virt.* 208), a specifically sexual reference. In a rare glimmer of positivity he interprets Isaac's initial preference for Esau as based on the fact that he is a hunter, hunting down the passions (*QG* 4.167), but then the negative returns and is dominant. He is a "slave to the pleasures of the belly" (*QG* 4.168), the redness of his pottage, reflecting both passion and the blushing shame it produces (*QG* 4.170). He represents "licentiousness, the disturber of the passions of the soul" that wants to kill its brother (*QG* 4.238). Esau sold his birthright "for a little sensual pleasure" (*QG* 4.224).

In *Allegorical Commentary* Philo depicts him as one who "hunts after the passions" (*Leg.* 3.1-2). Accordingly, Jacob and Esau typify opposite choices (*Sacr.* 17-18). Esau represents "the bad man ... based on vice and passion" (*Sacr.* 81), who wants his father to ignore the warning about going down to Egypt, that is, the passions (*Det.* 46). His hairiness contrasts with Jacob's smoothness, a symbol for Philo of the nakedness which depicts separation from the passions (*Leg.* 2.59).

Both Isaac's fallibility in making the wrong choice among his offspring, in contrast to Rebecca, and the shortcomings of Jacob's character find no mention in Philo's sanitised accounts (on this see the discussion of Gen 25:28 above). Thus he insists that Jacob did not, in fact, rob Esau of his birthright or blessing (*QG* 4.229). His name, "Supplanter", refers rather to "the task of a supplanter in the practice of virtue to disturb and shake and upset the supports on which passion rests, and all the firmness and stability which they have" (*Mut.* 81).

Philo depicts Jacob as one who quits "the dwelling-place of the senses" in contrast to Joseph (*Migr.* 214). He understands Rebecca's advice that he visit Laban as illustrating the appropriateness of spending some time "in the territory of the senses", "in compliance with the necessities of the body", like Abraham did in Haran (*Somn.* 1.46; *Fug.* 46), but not a "lifetime" (*Somn.* 1.47). It belonged to knowing oneself and being able to "enjoy the happiness proper to man" (*Somn.* 1.57). His need to flee from Laban serves then to depict fleeing the domination of sense-perception which Laban represents (*Migr.* 28; *Leg.* 3.16; *Fug.* 18), who shows his lower level of learning by asserting the value of customs about the order of marrying daughters (*Fug.* 46-47; *Ebr.* 47), by thinking he owned them (*Cher.* 67), and by owning idols, thoughts to be destroyed or put out of sight (*Leg.* 3.23). Jacob's entering Egypt and allowing his sons to do the same symbolises not failure but the value of reconnaissance, much like Rebecca's advice to him, namely, to get to know the senses and passions. Thus "Jacob's sons, trained under an all-wise father, may go down into Egypt the passion-loving body" and there will not be dazzled (*Sacr.* 48; similarly *Post.* 31).

The only remotely sexual themes in Philo's account of Jacob relate to finding his wives, but that receives scant attention. At the allegorical level sexual issues are at most implied in concern about the passions. Philo exploits the allusion to Jacob's falling asleep before his dream at Bethel (Gen 28:11) as occasion for an excursus on the effects of profligacy, including gluttony, drunkenness, and sexual wrongdoing, probably including same-sex relations (*Somn.* 1.122-125), but this has only superficial connection with Jacob's story.

1.3.2.5 Leah and Rachel

Another important element in Philo's portrayal of Jacob's story is the depiction of his wives, Leah and Rachel. In *Virt.* he seems concerned at a literal level to elevate the status of Zilpah and Bilhah, "women born beyond the Euphrates, in the extreme parts of Babylonia, who were handmaids and were given as dowry to the ladies of the house at their marriage" who then "passed on from mere concubinage to the name and position of wedded wives, and were treated no longer as handmaids, but as almost equal in rank to their mistresses, who, indeed, incredible as it seems, promoted them to the same dignity as themselves" (*Virt.* 223). The focus of the context is on discrimination against outsiders, these, then, being spoken of in a literal sense. It was also about ensuring that the offspring could be seen in Roman law to be legitimate.[428]

In *Allegorical Commentary* Philo sometimes employs Jacob's relations with his two wives and his two concubines in the context of his discourse about levels of education. Accordingly, Leah represents reasoning, and Rachel, unreasoning,

---

[428] On this see Satlow, *Jewish Marriage*, who notes that Philo's "understanding of concubinage is a standard Greek one. Greek 'concubines' were 'kept women' who — like their biblical counterparts — were expected to remain faithful to their husbands with no expectation of reciprocity" (193). Their children were considered illegitimate. In Roman law such women had a status which existed probably because there was a legal impediment to marriage. See also 3.1.3.2 below.

"acting through the senses and the other parts of our unreasoning nature" (*Congr.* 26-27). Though at a lower level, such learning has its value and can even be termed a "virtue". Having said that "each has its own virtue or excellence (ἀρετὴν ἑκατέρῳ), the reasoning Leah, the unreasoning Rachel" (*Congr.* 26), he goes on to say that the latter: "trains us to despise all that should be held of little account, reputation and wealth and pleasure, ..." (*Congr.* 27), whereas "Leah teaches us to avoid the rough and uneven path, impassable to virtue-loving souls, and to walk smoothly along the level highway where there are no stumbling-blocks or aught that can make the foot to slip" (*Congr.* 28). Zilpah ("walking mouth") then symbolises speech and Bilhah ("swallowing") physical needs (*Congr.* 30). Thus Jacob, "the Man of Practice", engages in intercourse with all four, symbols of faculties (*Congr.* 31). "He desires the smooth, the Leah movement, which will produce health in the body, noble living and justice in the soul. He loves Rachel when he wrestles with the passions and when he goes into training to gain self-control" (*Congr.* 31). He also needs the other two (*Congr.* 33). The symbolism is interesting, given his negative treatment of Rachel elsewhere.[429]

Elsewhere we find affirmation of Leah as the symbol of virtue, like Sarah (*Migr.* 95, 99; *Mut.* 255; *Somn.* 1.37; *Post.* 135) and, in contrast, negative treatments of Rachel. Leah's fertility and Rachel's infertility and her response to it in Gen 29:31 – 30:24 provides Philo with a rich quarry for allegorical contrasts. Thus in *Post.* he picks up the detail that Leah was hated (Gen 29:31) and Rachel's use of pomegranates (Gen 30:14-15) disapprovingly (cf. *T. Iss.* 2:5): "Leah who is above the passions, cannot tolerate those who are attracted by the spells of the pleasures (φίλτρα ... ἡδονῶν) that accord with Rachel, who is sense-perception; wherefore, finding themselves treated with contempt by her they hate her" (*Post.* 135). He then emphasises Leah's fertility: "For Leah, estrangement on the human side brings about fellowship (οἰκείωσιν) with God, and from Him she receives the seed of wisdom, and is in birth-throes, and brings forth beautiful ideas worthy of the Father Who begat them" (*Post.* 135; similarly also *Leg.* 3.181). Sexual intercourse with God produces virtues as offspring. In *Her.* he even employs the contrast between the hated and beloved woman in Deut 21:15-17, to depict Rachel as the beloved and Leah as the hated (*Her.* 47-49; similarly *Leg.* 2.47-48). Accordingly, God opened the womb of Virtue (Leah), but made Sense (Rachel) barren (*Her.* 51). In *Leg.* 3.180-181 he similarly noted Leah as the hated (Gen 29:31) and her fruitfulness, but also picks up Rachel's complaint in Gen 30:1 that Jacob should give her children, which he takes as denial that God is the true source. In *Post.* 179, Philo returns to this, reporting that Rachel accepted her rebuke, "made a recantation breathing true holiness", and as a result conceived.

---

[429] On Philo's diverse treatment of Rachel see Sly, *Philo's Perception of Women*, 161-66.

Philo does not appear to read this as complete rehabilitation or permanent repentance. For instance, in *Ebr.* he portrays Rachel as an example of the person "who looks with admiration only on that which is perceived by the senses", citing her response to her father that "the custom of women" was upon her (Gen 31:35), which Philo takes as typical of women's propensity to surrender to custom (*Ebr.* 54).[430] Philo still distinguishes between two levels of offspring among the twelve sons: "half of them belonging to Leah or Virtue the mother of six patriarchs, and half to the children of Rachel and the base-born sons of the concubines" (*Her.* 175; cf. the contrast in *Fug.* 73 between those set over blessing, Symeon, Levi, Judah, Issachar, Joseph and Benjamin, and those set over cursing). Indeed Philo accounts for Joseph's deficiencies by noting Rachel's (*Somn.* 2.16) and has her death at Benjamin's birth symbolise the "birth of vainglory" and "the death of the soul" (*Mut.* 96). Jacob is then buried not with her, but with Leah (*Post.* 62).[431]

Whereas Philo sometimes speaks of the sisters together without differentiating them, such as in his description of Jacob's departure from Laban in *Fug.* 16-18, Leah emerges much more strongly in Philo's account than in the biblical record (similar to *Jubilees*)[432] and Rachel much more negatively. Philo declares: "I admire ... all-virtuous Leah" (*Migr.* 95) and goes on to depict her as a model who is appreciated by both male and female elements, worthy "to have a good reputation in the men's quarters, but to receive the praises of the women's as well" (*Migr.* 95-96), enough to prompt Philo to a brief discourse on valuing women's contribution, illustrated by what they brought to the construction of the tabernacle (*Migr.* 97). He then slips into allegory to speak of praise from "citizen women and worthy of their citizenship" (*Migr.* 99): "It is best, then, that the array of women, that is of the senses, in the soul, should be propitiated, as well as that of the men, that is of our several thoughts" (*Migr.* 100). Thus Philo makes Leah an ideal of the properly adjusted soul where senses and passions have their place in harmony with the rule of mind. This is an important aspect in considering Philo's attitude towards sexual desire, but that is not directly in focus in his depiction of Leah except at an allegorical level as love of God giving birth to his offspring.

---

[430] On this see Sly, *Philo's Perception of Women*, 165-66. She sees Philo's portrait as sufficiently uneven to conclude: "Philo does not appear to have thought through his position on Rachel" (174).

[431] Sly, *Philo's Perception of Women*, 174.

[432] On this see William Loader, *Enoch, Levi, and Jubilees on Sexuality: Attitudes towards Sexuality in the Early Enoch Literature, the Aramaic Levi Document, and the Book of Jubilees* (Grand Rapids: Eerdmans, 2007) 268-69.

1.3.2.6 Joseph

1.3.2.6.1 Joseph in the Positive

One might have expected to see Philo hailing Joseph as another model of the wise mind, not least because of his resistance to sexual wrongdoing. His work, *On Joseph*, in the *Exposition of the Law*, gives such a positive picture. There Philo tells the familiar story:

> While he was winning a high reputation in household affairs, his master's wife made him the object of her designs, which were prompted by licentious love; for wrought up to madness by the beauty of the youth, and putting no restraint upon the frenzy of her passion, she made proposals of intercourse to him which he stoutly resisted and utterly refused to accept, so strong was the sense of decency and temperance which nature and the exercise of control had implanted in him (διὰ τὴν ἐκ φύσεως καὶ μελέτης ἐνυπάρξασαν κοσμιότητα καὶ σωφροσύνην). And, since, as she fed the fire of lawless lust till it burst into a blaze, her constant efforts to gain as constantly failed, at last in an accession of passion she was fain to employ violence. (*Ios.* 40-41)

Joseph's refusal includes the important statement:

> We children of the Hebrews follow laws and customs which are especially our own. Other nations are permitted after the fourteenth year to deal without interference with harlots and strumpets and all those who make a traffic of their bodies (πόρναις καὶ χαμαιτύπαις καὶ ταις ὅσαι μισθαρνοῦσιν ἐπὶ τοῖς σώμασι μετὰ πολλῆς ἀδείας χρῆσθαι), but with us a courtesan is not even permitted to live (παρ' ἡμῖν δὲ οὐδ' ἑταίρα ζῆν ἔξεστιν), and death is the penalty appointed for women who ply this trade. Before the lawful union we know no mating with other women (πρὸ δὴ συνόδων νομίμων ὁμιλίαν ἑτέρας γυναικὸς οὐκ ἴσμεν), but come as virgin men to virgin maidens (ἀλλ' ἁγνοὶ γάμων ἁγναῖς παρθένοις προσερχόμεθα). The end we seek in wedlock is not pleasure but the begetting of lawful children (τέλος οὐχ ἡδονὴν ἀλλὰ γνησίων παίδων σποράν). To this day I have remained pure, and I will not take the first step in transgression by committing adultery, the greatest of crimes (ἀπὸ μοιχείας, τοῦ μεγίστου τῶν ἀδικημάτων). (*Ios.* 42-44)

Potiphar's wife, then, is the model of uncontrolled passion, typically depicted as a burning fire. Joseph's response broadens the issues from the case of a "lovesick woman" (τῆς ἐρωμένης γυναικός) (cf. *Ios.* 80) to the professional seductress. It also provides interesting information about the role of prostitutes and male behaviour outside Jewish communities – as Philo portrays it, and about the claim of premarital chastity in the Jewish community.[433] Its declaration of adultery as "the greatest of crimes", matches Philo's claims elsewhere that the decalogue (as he knows it) has it first in the second table of the commandments (*Decal.* 131; similarly 168, *Spec.* 3.8). Joseph's speech of refusal also alludes to the dangers of the cuckolded husband, claiming that all men "count the culprits worthy of a multitude of deaths" (*Ios.* 44). His concern not to, as he puts it "defile my mistress and my master's wife (δέσποιναν καὶ δεσπότου γυναῖκα διαφθείρειν) ...debasing his bed, his household, and his kin (νοθεύων αὐτοῦ γάμον, οἰκίαν, συγγένειαν)" (*Ios.* 45) reflects both the view that he would thereby render her impure for her husband and that the act would be ultimately an act against him. He also expresses the fear of a bad conscience showing in his demeanour (*Ios.* 48).

The literal focus continues as Philo portrays the false allegation which she makes against him: "not content with taking merely the women who were his fellow-servants (ταῖς γὰρ ὁμοδούλοις οὐκ ἐξήρκεσεν αὐτῷ χρῆσθαι μόναις), so utterly lewd and lascivious has he shown himself, he has attempted to violate me by force, me his mistress (πειρᾶν δὲ καὶ τὴν δέσποιναν ἐπεχείρησεν ἐμὲ καὶ βιάζεσθαι)" (*Ios.* 51). This may assume some normalcy had he engaged in sex with fellow slaves. Philo uses Joseph's self-control in this instance to draw attention to the "misfortunes which licentiousness (ἐξ ἀκρασίας) brings to nations" (*Ios.* 56), adding that "the majority of wars, and those the greatest, have arisen through amours and adulteries and the deceits of women, which have consumed the greatest and choicest part of the Greek race and the barbarian also, and destroyed the youth of their cities" (*Ios.* 56). Philo notes Joseph's jailing because of "false charges of a love-sick woman" (*Ios.* 80). He then notes the corrupting influence there on jailers of "thieves, burglars, men of violence, and outrage, who commit rape, murder, adultery and sacrilege" (*Ios.* 84). When Joseph effectively assumes the role of prisoner, he exemplifies temperance and virtue (*Ios.* 87). Having related the story of the dreams, including Pharaoh's, Philo notes Joseph's betrothal "to the most distinguished of the ladies of Egypt, the daughter of the priest of the Sun" (*Ios.* 121) with no indication of disapproval. In *Ios.* 148 he notes with triumph that Joseph mounts the king's second chariot.

He then approves of allegorical exposition which sees the king of Egypt as mind capable of becoming enamoured of the body, by bread, meat and drink, represented by the roles of the eunuchs (*Ios.* 151-152). As eunuchs, he argues, they are therefore barren of the chief necessities, "temperance, modesty, self-restraint,

---

[433] In this Maren Niehoff, *The Figure of Joseph in Post-Biblical Literature* (AGJU 16; Leiden: Brill, 1992) sees evidence that Philo "turns confrontation into an encounter between Egyptian and Jewish culture" (79), and suggests that Philo may well have in mind the danger of foreign men falling for Egyptian women, typified by Mark Antony and Cleopatra (80-81).

justice and every virtue; for no two things can be more hostile to each other than virtue is to pleasure, which makes the many disregard what alone deserves their care, satisfy their unbridled lusts and submit to whatever those lusts command" (*Ios.* 153). The associations here are with gluttony not sexual themes. Returning to the literal level he reports the brothers' visits to Egypt, with incidental reference to disapproving feasts "where the pleasures outnumber the disagreeables (ἔνθα τῶν ἀηδιῶν αἱ ἡδοναὶ πλείους)" (*Ios.* 202), and has them praise Joseph's virtues (*Ios.* 246). Joseph's story thus symbolises that "no good man is dead, but will live for ever, proof against old age, with a soul immortal in its nature no longer fettered by the restraints of the body" (*Ios.* 264). Beyond the encounter with the temptress, sexual themes appear at most indirectly present in the criticism of banquets.

1.3.2.6.2 Joseph in Question

In the *Allegorical Commentary* Philo also notes Joseph's response to Potiphar's wife as right and representative. Thus in *Migr.* Philo writes: "What, then, are the uncorrupted parts? His having nothing to do with Pleasure when she says, 'Let us lie together' and enjoy the good things of mankind: the shrewdness coupled with the resoluteness which enabled him to recognize the products of empty fancies ..." (*Migr.* 19). The positive citing of Joseph continues: "he was proclaimed not the subject, but the ruler of all Egypt, the domain of the body" (*Migr.* 20). "He derided lusts and all passions and their gross excesses (τὸ ἐμπαίζειν ἐπιθυμιῶν καὶ πάντων παθῶν ἀμετρίαις): he feared God even though he was not yet ready to love Him" (*Migr.* 21). Here, however, we note some qualification: "even though he was not yet ready to love Him (εἰ καὶ μηδέπω γέγονεν ἀγαπᾶν ἱκανος)" (*Migr.* 21), signalling Philo's negative view of Joseph's other exploits.

He reports similarly positively in *Somn.* 2: "when he rises from his deep slumbering to abiding wakefulness and welcomes clearness before uncertainty, truth before false supposition, day before night, light before darkness; when moved by a yearning for continence (ἐγκρατείας) and a vast zeal for piety he rejects bodily pleasure, the wife of the Egyptian, as she bids him come in to her and enjoy her embraces" (*Somn.* 2.106) and a little later in the same work: "For he deemed it a grievous shame to suffer any fair blossom of the soul to be withered or flooded and drowned by the streams which the Egyptian river of passion, the body, pours forth unceasingly through the channel of all the senses" (*Somn.* 2.109). This, however, follows his claim that there is hope that Joseph may change (*Somn.* 2.105), "from his deep slumbering" (*Somn.* 2.106).

In *Leg.* 3 he mentions Joseph and the wife of Potiphar (*Leg.* 3.236), initially addressing the problem "how, being eunuch (εὐνοῦχος [Gen 39:1]), he comes to have a wife", especially for those seeking its literal meaning. He finds some resolution in the figurative meaning that someone serving Pharaoh is incapable of begetting wisdom, though concedes it could be a good thing "to escape wickedness and unlearn passion" (*Leg.* 3.237). His primary focus is Joseph: "So, Joseph too, the self-controlling character (ὁ ἐγκρατὴς τρόπος), when pleasure says to him, 'Sleep with me and being human indulge human passions and enjoy the delights that come in life's course,' refuses to comply with her saying, 'I shall be sinning against God the Lover of virtue, were I to show myself a lover of pleasure (φιλήδονος); for this is a wicked deed'" (*Leg.* 3.237). Philo concedes that in this instance Joseph did the right thing and went on doing so since "meanwhile pleasure does not desist from struggling" (*Leg.* 3.239). He then portrays Joseph as reasoning: "'If,' he says, 'I am going to be a slave to passion for the sake of the matter that is productive of it (εἰ μέλλω, φησί, δουλεύειν πάθει διὰ τὴν ποιητικὴν ὕλην), I will even leave passion behind and go forth outside (ἐξελεύσομαι ἀπὸ τοῦ πάθους ἔξω)'; for 'leaving his garments in her hands he fled and went forth outside'" (*Leg.* 3.240). He concludes that Joseph "being but a youth and lacking strength to contend with the Egyptian body and vanquish pleasure, runs away" (*Leg.* 3.242). The words, "'If,' he says, 'I am going to be a slave to passion for the sake of the matter that is productive of it" may be pointing to Joseph's ambitions to serve other passions, namely those of Egypt as a whole.

This negative assessment comes to expression particularly in Philo's depiction of "the politician's frame of mind" (*Migr.* 159) as wanting to be "in touch with both the real and the reputed virtues" (*Migr.* 158), which he portrays as typical of Joseph, who wants "to be equally in touch with the concerns of the body, which is Egypt, and those of the soul which are kept as in a treasury in his father's house" (*Migr.* 160). He scolds Joseph for mounting Pharaoh's second chariot (*Migr.* 160; cf. *Ios.* 148) and swearing an oath of loyalty to two conflicting sides: "The oath containing the negative is one that his father's house would prescribe, being always a mortal foe to passion and wishing it dead; the other oath is one that Egypt might prescribe, for passion's welfare is dear to it" (*Migr.* 162). Similarly he writes of him as one "who hails as friends the body and the things outside the body, him who is usually called 'Joseph'. So great is his devotion to these ...". "He sets up laws moreover for all Egypt that honour may be paid to the senses" (*Migr.* 203).

In *Mut.* he contrasts Abraham Isaac, and Jacob with "the controller of bodily necessaries (ὁ τῶν τοῦ σώματος ἐπιτηδείων προστάτης), Joseph" (*Mut.* 89). "The provider and superintendent of these, Joseph, is found to have the appropriate name of 'Addition,' since he is invested with the direction of the imported adventitious wealth which is an addition to the natural" (*Mut.* 90). Noting that Joseph's Egyptian name means "right answer", he writes: "Every fool thinks that the man of wealth ... must of necessity be able to reason aright, be capable of answering questions ..." (*Mut.* 91). Here too he depicts Rachel accordingly as "the mother of vainglory" (*Mut.* 96; cf. *Somn.* 2.15-16). Joseph led "away the mind to desert its foster-brethren the goods of the soul for the numberless lusts of the body, and to debase the ancestral coinage, the coinage of virtue its birth-fellow" (*Mut.* 171). "With such hopes the pleasure-loving mind is not content merely to angle with the baits of every lust for the younger sort, the novices in the training-schools of temperance, but revolts from the idea that it should be unable to subjugate the older thinking, in which the frenzy of passion had passed its prime" (*Mut.* 172). One wonders here if Philo has for a moment forgotten Joseph's resistance at least against sexual lust. He continues: "And also, says the Pleasure-lover, 'I will give you of all the good things of Egypt, and ye shall eat the marrow of the land'" (*Mut.* 174), to which Philo would have us respond: "We do not accept the body's good, for we have seen the things of the soul. For so deeply has our strong yearning for these sunk into us that it can make us forget all that is dear to the flesh" (*Mut.* 174). He then has Jacob wondering how he could "stem the tide of pleasure's ceaseless urge" (*Mut.* 214) and addressing his son (and Philo adds: also every man), using the image of a boat and warning against prosperity: it can "swell our canvas speed on to the enjoyments of the passions, and never do we draw in the loose and slack licence of our lusts until we strike the rocks and wreck the whole bark of the soul" (*Mut.* 215). Sexual wrongdoing doubtless belongs here, despite Joseph's success in that regard. Then we hear Philo's sarcastic irony: "If you do not behave well to your wife, you must not honour your parents either … If you delight in pleasure, you must not refrain from covetousness" (*Mut.* 226).

Such negativity towards Joseph leaves its traces elsewhere in the *Allegorical Commentary*. In *Agr.* Philo scolds Joseph for calling his family cattle rearers, not shepherds (*Agr.* 59), and writes: "Joseph, always having as the object of his thought and aim the rule of life based on the body and on the surmises of vain imagination, does not know how to govern and direct irrational natures" (*Agr.* 56). Similarly in *Sobr.*, citing Joseph as younger than his brothers, he explains:

> Now Joseph is the champion of bodily ability of every kind, and the staunch and sincere henchman of abundance in external things, but the treasure which ranks in value and seniority above these, the seniority of the soul, he has never yet gained in its fullness. For if he had gained it, he would have fled quite away from the length and breadth of Egypt, and never turned to look back. But as it is, he finds his chief glory in cherishing and fostering it – this Egypt over which the Man of Vision sings his hymn of triumph to God when he sees its fighters and its leaders sunk in the sea and sent to perdition. (*Sobr.* 13)

He "still consorts with the base-born" of his brothers (*Sobr.* 14). In *Conf.* he indicts Joseph of "the many-sided pride of worldly life" (*Conf.* 71), in *Leg.* 3 of "being occupied in toiling at these things" (the body and the senses) in contrast "to Judah who openly acknowledges God" (*Leg.* 3.26), and as offering food which does not nourish the soul (*Leg.* 3.179).

In the two books, *On Dreams*, which have survived, Philo's primary emphasis is on Joseph as a compromised figure. Initially the focus is on the conflicted values of statecraft, which Philo sees represented in multicoloured coat (*Somn.* 1.215-227). He then depicts Joseph as typical of men pursuing the honours of high office, commenting: "when they turn away and stray out of the course which leads to virtue, sense-perception, the woman inherent in their nature, makes them stray still more, and forces them to run aground" (*Somn.* 1.246), a psychological description reflecting his typical notion of sense-perception as female and so dangerous, though here without particular sexual reference.

In *Somn.* 2, which deals with dreams associated with Joseph and those who play a role in his career, Philo's introductory exposition distinguishes between those who see the good as unmixed and related to mind and those who associate it also with "the body and things external to us" (*Somn.* 2.9). He then identifies the latter as belonging "to the softer and luxurious way of life, having been reared up for the greater part of the time from their very cradle in the women's quarter and in the effeminate habits of the women's quarter", typical of Philo's disapproval of what he calls elsewhere the disease of effeminacy (*Somn.* 2.9). Of the former he writes:

> The noble company is led by Isaac who learns from no teacher but himself, for Moses represents him as weaned, absolutely disdaining to make any use of soft and milky food suited to infants and little children, and using only strong nourishment fit for grown men, seeing that from a babe he was naturally stalwart, and was ever attaining fresh vigour and renewing his youth. (*Somn.* 2.10)

Of the latter he writes:

> The company which yields and is ready to give in is led by Joseph, for he is one who does not indeed take no account of the excellences of the soul, but is thoughtful for the well-being of the body also, and has a keen desire to be well off in outward things; and he is naturally drawn in different directions since he has set before him many ends in life. (*Somn.* 2.10-11)

He depicts Joseph thus as drawn in different directions:

> For there is manifest in him, on the one hand, the rational strain of self-control, which is of the masculine family, fashioned after his father Jacob: manifest, again, is the irrational strain of sense-perception, assimilated to what he derives from his mother, the part of him that is of the Rachel type: manifest also is the breed of bodily pleasure, impressed on him by association with chief butlers and chief bakers and chief cooks: manifest too is the element of vainglory, on to which as on a chariot his empty-headedness makes him mount up, when puffed with pride he lifts himself aloft to overthrow equality from its seat. (*Somn.* 2.15-16).

In this "rough sketch of Joseph's character" (ὁ μὲν δὴ τοῦ 'Ιωσὴφ χαρακτήρ) (*Somn.* 2.17), as he puts it, no sexual themes appear, not surprisingly since resistance to sexual pleasure is the one element for which he elsewhere celebrates Joseph. Rachel and the eunuchs represent domination by the senses and by pleasure. Philo even picks up "Methought" (ᾤμην) from his dream interpretation (Gen 37:7) to argue that Joseph seems at a loss (*Somn.* 2.17) and lacks understanding of the mysteries of his own dream about reaping, which Philo then expounds (*Somn.* 2.30). Philo speaks negatively of Joseph's elevation in Egypt, dismissing its honour as "more insignificant and absurd in wisdom's judgement than the infliction of indignity and defeat" (*Somn.* 2.43), his golden collar contrasted with Tamar's necklace, his ring, with Judah's given to Tamar (*Somn.* 2.44) and his mounting the second chariot beside Pharaoh, "elated by mental dizziness and empty conceit" as "keeper of the body's treasuries" thus threatening "serious danger to the soul" (*Somn.* 2.46).

His name, meaning "Addition" typifies adding "to what is sufficient what is excessive, to vitality debauchery (θρύψιν), to life's maintenance vanity" (*Somn.* 2.47). Philo then assures us that there is nothing wrong with food. The issue is excess (*Somn.* 2.48). He elaborates that theme in relation to food and drink (48-51), clothing (52-53), houses (54-55), beds (56-57), unguents (58-59), cups (60-61), and garlands (62), concluding "And therefore the Holy Word did well in giving the name of Addition to one who was the enemy of simplicity and the friend of vanity" (*Somn.* 2.63) and commenting: "And so the practisers of sound sense, perceiving that Joseph first with his senses, and afterwards with his understanding, pursues this way of artificiality, cry outright, 'An evil beast has seized and devoured him'" (*Somn.* 2.65). Despite the mention of "debauchery" above, he does not relate it to sexual excesses. Thus Philo affirms the brothers' rejection of Joseph's dream: "Praise therefore is due to those also who are here under consideration, because they did not give way to the champion of vainglory but resisted him and said: 'Shalt thou indeed reign over us? Not so'" (*Somn.* 2.93). Only after all this does Philo contemplate the glimmer of hope that Joseph might wake up and change (105), based on his earlier resistance against the temptress.

Joseph's descendants receive brief mention, including in the older-younger contrast Ephraim's priority over Manasseh (*Sobr.* 28) and the five daughters of Zelophehad (Num 27:3), of the tribe of Manasseh (*Mos.* 2.233-245), taken in *Migr.* as representing the five senses (*Migr.* 205), "daughters of the irrational portion of the soul" (*Migr.* 206).[434]

---

[434] On the broader issues of Philo's hybrid portrait of Joseph see the discussion in Nikiprowetzky, *Commentaire*, 218-19; Earle Hilgert, "A Survey of Previous Scholarship on Philo's *De Josepho*," *SBLSP* (1986) 262-70; Thomas H. Tobin, "Tradition and Interpretation in Philo's Portrait of the Patriarch Joseph," *SBLSP* (1986) 271-77; Niehoff,

1.3.2.6.3 Joseph and the Eunuchs

The story of Joseph is the main context in which Philo makes comments about eunuchs. Given Philo's major emphasis on procreation, the eunuch is a serious problem for him. Thus he has Abraham pray concerning Sarah's sterility: "I know that thou, who givest being to what is not and generatest all things, hast hated the childless and barren soul, since Thou has given as a special grace to the race of them that see that they should never be without children or sterile" (*Her.* 36) and goes on to speak of his "zeal to sow and beget the children of the soul" (*Her.* 38).

In his most sympathetic account of Joseph, in the *Exposition of the Law*, he describes eunuchs as "possessing to all appearance the organs of generation but deprived of the power of using them" (*Ios.* 58), so, allegorically, like the multitude, "unproductive of wisdom" (*Ios.* 59). The cook then symbolises one "solely occupied in endlessly providing superfluous pleasures for the belly" (*Ios.* 61), concerned only to address the "pleasure for the moment. And like a licentious woman the desire of the multitude makes love to the statesman" (*Ios.* 63). Obsession with excessive pleasure which eunuchs serve characterises the general public and seduces politicians, the sexual functioning here solely as metaphor.

This concern is also evident in the *Allegorical Commentary*, where Philo similarly sees eunuchs engaged in pursuits designed to heighten enjoyment of pleasure and so suspect also on that count. The eunuch "has scant store of excellence and has lost by mutilation the soul's organs of generation, unable further to sow and beget anything that tends to discipline ... and with his elaborately seasoned dishes arouses and excites the appetites of fruitless passions, appetites which should rather be tamed and calmed" (*Mut.* 173). In *Somn.* 2 he has the chief butler speak as eunuch: "Thus I, the servant of that Pharaoh who keeps his stubborn incontinent thinking in an intensity of looseness, am an eunuch, gelded of the soul's generating organs, a vagrant from the men's quarters, an exile from the women's, a thing neither male nor female, unable either to shed or receive seed, twofold yet neuter, base counterfeit of the human coin" (*Somn.* 2.184). Here we see Philo's view of eunuchs serving indulgence to excess, but also their state of impotence. Accordingly he has the speech continue, asserting that they are: "cut off from the immortality which, through the succession of children and children's children, is kept alight for ever, roped off from the holy assembly and congregation, 'For he that hath lost the organs of generation is absolutely

---

Figure of Joseph; Jacques Cazeaux, "'Nul n'est prophète en son pays' – contribution à l'étude de Joseph d'après Philon," in *The School of Moses: Studies in Philo and Hellenistic Religion: In Memory of Horst R. Moehring* (ed. John Peter Kenney; BJS 304; SPM 1; Atlanta: Scholars, 1995) 41-81; Françoise Frazier, "Les visages de Joseph dans le De Josepho," *SPA* 14 (2002) 1-30.

forbidden to enter therein'" (*Somn.* 2.184). This is typical of Philo's negative stance, focused on failure to procreate, service to incontinence, and citing Deut 23:1, which bans their entry into the assembly of God's people. A little later Philo asks: "Were it not a better course, instead of confessing that he was the teacher of incontinence, to ascribe the incentives to passion to the incontinent one himself as inventor and author of his own base, unmanly, invertebrate life?" (*Somn.* 2.202). Again the themes of excess and shameful impotence appear. Such "cup-bearers" stand in contrast to the "devotees of virtue" (*Det.* 26). In *Hypoth.* we read the explicit prohibition that a man: "must not make abortive the generative power of men by gelding nor that of women by sterilising drugs and other devices" (7.7).

In *Ebr.* Philo elaborates:

> Why is it that not a single one of these offices is entrusted to a real man or woman? Is it not because nature has trained men to sow the germs of life and women to receive them, and the mating of these two is the cause of generation and of the permanence of the All, while on the other hand it is the nature of the soul which is impotent and barren, or rather has been made so by emasculation, to delight in costly bakemeats and drinks and dishes elaborately prepared? For such a soul is neither able to drop the truly masculine seeds of virtue nor yet to receive and foster what is so dropped, but like a sorry field is only capable of blighting the successive growths, which were meant to live. (*Ebr.* 211)

Again he alludes to the exclusion of the eunuch, "neither male nor female" (*Ebr.* 212), from the congregation (Deut 23:1), but at the level of allegory: "For what use can he find in listening to holy words, who can beget no offspring to wisdom, when the knife has cut away the power of faith, and the store of truths which might best profit human life he cannot keep in his charge?" (*Ebr.* 213). Similarly in *Deus*, he speaks of the eunuch as having a "mind which loves the body and the passions and has been sold in slavery to that chief cateress of our compound nature, Pleasure. Eunuch-like it has been deprived of all the male and productive organs of the soul, and lives in indigence of noble practices, unable to receive the divine message, debarred from the holy congregation in which the talk and study is always of virtue" (*Deus* 111) and being "cast into the prison of the passions".

1.3.2.7 Dinah

Philo alludes to the abduction of Dinah in the *Allegorical Commentary* in both *Migr.* and *Mut.* In the former Philo launches immediately into an allegorical reading in speaking of the toil of education: "It is a vital matter that he who would be perfect should ply this toil, to the end that the soul's court of justice called 'Dinah,' which means 'judgement,' may not be ravished by him who sinks under the opposite kind of toil, which is the insidious foe of sound sense" (*Migr.* 223).

Here Dinah serves allegory. Philo continues: "For the man who bears the name of this place, Shechem, being son of Hamor, that is of an irrational being – for 'Hamor' means 'ass' – practising folly and nursed in shamelessness and effrontery, essayed – foul wretch that he was – to corrupt and defile the judgement faculties of the understanding" (*Migr.* 224).[435] The focus is the corrupting of the soul's judgement. Philo sustains the allegory:

> But the hearers and pupils of sound sense, Symeon and Levi, were too quick for him. They made secure their own quarters and went forth against them in safety, and overthrew them when they were still occupied in the pleasure-loving, passion-loving, toil of the uncircumcised; for albeit there was a Divine decree that 'of the daughters of Israel, the seeing one, none might ever become a harlot', these men hoped to carry off unobserved the virgin soul. (*Migr.* 224).

Much of this runs quite contrary to the biblical story which depicts them not as uncircumcised men engaging in pleasure but as still in distress recovering from circumcision. The detail about abduction also reflects Philo's judgement of the act in a literal sense, but his focus is elsewhere. Interestingly he makes no mention of the circumcision ploy, even has them in an uncircumcised state, nor of any disapproval of Simeon and Levi (cf. Gen 34:30; 49:5-7).[436] The allegory continues "Justice … the befriender of those who are wronged, bringing failure upon the aims of those who shame virtue, upon whose fall the soul, that had seemed to have been shamed, becomes again a virgin. Seemed, I said, because it never was defiled" (*Migr.* 225). This, too, reflects an interesting take on the story, since it assumes that like Sarah she was abducted but not sexually violated, but it is more likely that Philo's meaning here is only at the allegorical level. The original account is still reflected in his speaking of her becoming a virgin again, when he writes of justice as befriender of the wronged, so that "the soul, that seemed to have been shamed, becomes again a virgin (εἰς παρθένον πάλιν ἡ δόξασα αἰσχυνθῆναι μεταβάλλει ψυχή)". He then, however, adds: "Seemed, I said, because it never was defiled (δόξασα δ' εἶπον, ὅτι οὐδέποτε ἐφθείρετο)". Enigmatically Philo concludes: "It is with sufferings which we have not willed, as

---

[435] Louis H. Feldman, "Philo, Pseudo-Philo, Josephus, and Theodotus on the Rape of Dinah," *JQR* 94 (2004) 253-77, notes that Shechem can symbolise the virtue of "the toil of the lover of learning" as in *Migr.* 221 and the opposite (*Migr.* 223) (256).

[436] Mary Anna Bader, *Tracing the Evidence: Dinah in Post-Hebrew Bible Literature* (Studies in Biblical Literature 102; New York: Peter Lang, 2008) speculates that this may reflect Philo's belonging to the tribe of Levi (147). Feldman, "Rape of Dinah," notes in addition failure to mention Shechem's status as "highly respected son of the leader of his people; that after having relations with Dinah he became deeply attached to her; that he and his father carried on negotiations in good faith with Jacob and Jacob's sons" (256). Philo also generalises: the act is not just Shechem's but that of "these men" (*Migr.* 224) (256).

it is with wrongdoings which we have not intended. As there is no real doing in the second case, so there is no real suffering in the first" (*Migr.* 225). Here, too, Philo appears to want to play down the actual suffering, again, probably for the sake of his allegory, but possibly also from a Stoic perspective of denying suffering. Philo shows no interest here in Dinah's suffering sexual violation.[437]

In *Mut.* 193-200 Philo returns to the story, this time with some attention to the literal as an illustration: "The wicked man sometimes gives admirable expression to noble thoughts, but his actions are most vile and their method equally so. Such a one is Shechem, the son of folly, for his father is Hamor whose name is translated by 'ass,' while his own is interpreted as 'shoulder,' the symbol of toil" (*Mut.* 193). He explains: "Thus the oracles say that Shechem spake 'according to the mind of the virgin' after first humiliating her. Are not these words 'according to the mind of the virgin' added with exact thought so as almost to shew that his actions were the opposite of his words?" (*Mut.* 194). This subverts the Genesis account which has him speak sincerely to her Gen 34:3.[438] He then again reflects his view that Dinah was not violated as he shifts to allegory:

> For Dinah is incorruptible judgement, and justice which is the assessor of God, the ever virgin, for the word 'Dinah' by interpretation is either judgement or justice. The fools who attempt to seduce her by their plottings and their practices repeated day by day seek by means of specious talking to escape from conviction. Now they should either make their actions conform to their words or if they persist in iniquity keep still. (*Mut.* 194-195)

The allegory then hails Simeon and Levi as heroes: "The vindicators will come strong and doughty, inspired with zeal for virtue. They will strip off all this complication of wraps and bandages which the perverted art of the talkers has put together, and beholding the soul naked in her very self they will know the secrets hidden from sight in the recesses of her nature" (*Mut.* 199). There is some hint of the circumcision ploy in the reference to bandages, but otherwise Philo has suppressed it. The allegory contrasts the inviolate Dinah with the perjured soul: "Exposing to every eye in clear sunlight her shame and all her disgraces they will point the contrast between her real character, so hideous, so despicable, and the spurious comeliness which disguised in her wrappings she counterfeited. And the champions who stand ready to repel such profane and impure ways of thinking are two in number, Simeon and Levi, but they are one in will" (*Mut.* 199-200). Thus not Dinah but the soul as female is shamed. Philo notes the blending of the two

---

[437] As Bader, *Tracing the Evidence*, notes that "for today's reader one realizes that the virginity of a rape victim is not restored or returned. The allegorizing and spiritualizing of this incident is problematic" (148).

[438] See Feldman, "Rape of Dinah," 257-58.

brothers, Simeon into Levi, in Deut 33:8, but as in *Migr.* suppresses Jacob's disapproval of their actions.[439] There is little interest in the act of abduction at the literal level. As Sly notes, "Dinah does not appear in Philo as a person, and there is no outrage addressed to the fact of being the victim of rape".[440]

1.3.2.8 Tamar and Judah

We begin with the presupposition for the main story, namely Onan's refusal to engage in procreative sex with Tamar (cf. also *Leg.* 3.69). Philo takes Onan as a symbol of self-love. In *Post.* he brings the brief report in the context of attacking the philosophy of human self-sufficiency: "The chief representative of this doctrine is Onan, kinsman of the leathern Er. For it says 'this man knowing that the seed should not be for him, when he went in to his brother's wife, spilled it on the ground', going beyond all bounds in love of self and love of pleasure" (*Post.* 180-181). This allusion to love of self and love of pleasure may target masturbation, although, given the context of concern with philosophy, it more likely has Epicureanism in its sights. Philo then comments: "I should therefore address him thus: 'Will you not' – so I would say to him – 'by providing only your individual profit, by doing away with all the best things in the world, unless you are to get some advantage from them, honour paid to parents, loving care of a wife, bringing up of children, happy and blameless relations with domestic servants, management of a house ... ?" (*Post.* 180-181). In this appeal to move beyond self-interest it is interesting to note the value put on "loving care of a wife, bringing up of children" and life in the household. In *Deus* Philo returns to Onan: "Some there are who through self-love have brought upon themselves not only defeat but death. Thus Onan 'perceiving that the seed will not be his', ceased not to destroy the reasoning principle, which in kind is the best of all existing things, till he himself underwent utter destruction" (*Deus* 16). Here, too, the reference to self-love (also *Deus* 18) could target masturbation, but the focus is more likely to be Epicureanism since Philo writes of the "evil suggestion of an unnatural creed, called Onan" (*Deus* 18). "We must indeed reject all those who 'beget for themselves,' that is all those who pursue only their own profit and think not of others" (*Deus* 19) and see themselves as "born for themselves only and not for the innumerable others, for father, for mother, for wife, for children, for country, for the human race" (*Deus* 19), echoing Philo's challenge cited above (*Post.* 181).

---

[439] On Philo's omitting the brothers' deceitful ploy, Feldman, "Rape of Dinah," notes that Philo similarly suppresses deceit on the part of Abraham and Jacob (260). "Philo would surely have found it impolitic to recall the details of an incident in which Jews demanded conversion and then were guilty of perfidy once it had been agreed to" (261).

[440] Sly, *Philo's Perception of Women*, 175.

For Philo, Tamar, like Sarah, Rebecca, and Leah, is a symbol of virtue. He often refers to her. In *Virt.* he speaks of her deserting to piety and keeping her life stainless (*Virt.* 222), a model proselyte like Bilhah and Zilpah. As Sly notes, "Philo may be serving an apologetic aim here, justifying Tamar's place in the royal lineage of Israel, or he may be making allowances for the intermarriage he sees around him, but establishing certain limits to it".[441] In *Congr.* he depicts virtue as being like Tamar: "Sometimes she makes trial of her scholars, to test their zeal and earnestness; and then she does not meet them, but veils her face and sits like Tamar at the cross-roads, presenting the appearance of a harlot to the passers-by. Her wish is that inquiring minds may unveil and reveal her and gaze upon the glorious beauty, inviolate, undefiled and truly virginal, of her modesty and chastity" (*Congr.* 124). While allegory, it implies a positive view of Tamar's action (cf. Gen 38:13-14). It also assumes a positive image of Judah: "Who then is he, the investigator, the lover of learning, who refuses to leave aught of the things that are veiled, unexamined and unexplored? He can only be the chief captain, the king, whose name is Judah, who persists and rejoices in confessing and praising God" (*Congr.* 125). Then, in a manner which the allegory does not require, but rather the literal story, he explains: "'He turned aside his path to her' it says, and said, 'Suffer me to come in unto thee.' 'Suffer me,' he means (for he would not use force to her [ἀλλ' οὐκ ἔμελλε παραβιάζεσθαι]), 'suffer me to see what is the virtue which veils its face from me, and what purpose it is prepared to serve'" (*Congr.* 126). Philo then goes on, "And so then after he went in to her, we read of a conceiving or taking (γέγραπται 'καὶ συνέλαβε')", and discusses what "take" or "conceive" might mean, indicating: "Who it is who conceives or takes we are not told in so many words", though the literal meaning is blatantly obvious. Exploiting sexual metaphor he then adds: "the art or science that is studied does seize and take hold of the learner and persuades him to be her lover", as the "the learner takes his instructress" (*Congr.* 126). The theme of education and learning remains, but ultimately it is about the life of virtue. Thus Philo writes: "The souls then whose pregnancy is accompanied with wisdom, though they labour, do bring their children to the birth, for they distinguish and separate what is in confusion within them ... but where its pregnancy is without wisdom, the soul either miscarries or the offspring is the quarrelsome sophist" (*Congr.* 129). Similarly in *Fug.* Tamar represents Virtue (*Fug.* 149-156), in contrast to the image of a

> licentious one, or a wanton, or a street-walker, or one prostituting for gain the flower of her youth, or making bright what is outside by baths and cleansings while she is foul within, or in default of natural beauty painting her face as pictures are coloured, or what is called the 'many-husband pest, following after evil as though it were good, or a

---

[441] So Sly, *Philo's Perception of Women*, 176.

lover of polygamy, of dispersing herself upon a thousand different objects material and immaterial alike, or mocked and outraged by that multitude. (*Fug.* 153)

She becomes an allegory of Judah's true mind: "Is it not my heart-felt prayer that my understanding should be a true and high-born lady, eminent for chastity and modesty and all other virtues, devoted to one husband and keeping watch with delight over the home of one, and exulting in a sole ruler?" (*Fug.* 154). As Sly notes, "Philo does not discuss the morality of Tamar's or Judah's actions. he stresses that she is not what she appears; that is, although she appears to be a harlot, and therefore representative of Judah's body, she is actually a high-born lady, his mind (Fug.153f)".[442]

The imagery is even more daring in *Mut.*, where, having spoken of God as husband of Leah (virtue), he goes on to speak of Tamar: "And Tamar too; she bore within her womb the divine seed, but had not seen the sower. For we are told that at that hour she veiled her face" (*Mut.* 134). Judah thus symbolises God. Accordingly, Philo writes: "Whose is the ring, the pledge of faith, the seal of the universe, the archetypal idea by which all things without form or quality before were stamped and shaped? ... ", going to detail the pledges (*Mut.* 135), and answers: "Are they not God's alone? And therefore the temper which makes confession of thankfulness, that is Judah, pleased at the divine inspiration which masters her, says with all boldness, 'She is justified since I gave her to no mortal', for he holds it impiety to defile the divine with things profane" (*Mut.* 136). This is an extraordinary turn of interpretation, which alludes to the assertion that both sinned, Judah more than Tamar, but suppresses all negative connotations. Similarly in *Deus* Philo speaks of Tamar, who for her father's sake "left for ever the intercourse and society of mortals, and remained desolate and widowed of human pleasures" (*Deus* 137) and "thus she receives the divine impregnation, and, being filled with the seeds of virtue, bears them in her womb and is in travail with noble actions" (*Deus* 137), her name meaning a palm, "the symbol of her victory" (*Deus* 137). Similarly in *Leg.* 3 he speaks of reward: "if Judah's daughter-in-law become thy wife, even Tamar, which means a palm-tree, the sign of victory" (*Leg.* 3.74; cf. also *LAB* 9:5 which portrays her as a model, indeed as "our mother").

1.3.2.9. Reuben

Contrasted with Joseph, "Reuben ... is the symbol of natural excellence" (*Mut.* 98). Here Philo seems to ignore the rape and incest with Bilhah (Gen 35:22) and Jacob's rebuke (Gen 49:3-4). The allusion to Reuben in *Somn.* 2 as the "seeing

---

[442] Sly, *Philo's Perception of Women*, 175.

son", "in so far as he is a son not perfect, but in so far as he is a man with power to see" (*Somn*. 2.33), may reflect it, but Philo makes nothing of it.

1.3.3 Significant Motifs Generated by the Story of Moses and Exodus

1.3.3.1 Moses

1.3.3.1.1 Moses in Mos. 1

The primary account of Moses' life, including the exodus, is to be found in *Mos*. 1, which consists to a large degree in retelling Moses' story in a way that highlights *his exemplary character* and rarely ventures into allegorical exposition. There is more of the latter in *Mos*. 2, which elaborates on Moses' legislative, high priestly and prophetic roles. In addition we have *QE*, which covers Exod 12:2-23; 20:25 – 28:34, little of which relates to actual story and most of which concerns laws.

Mos. 1 remains largely at a literal level in depicting Moses as exemplary. He models "self-restraint, continence, temperance" especially as ruler (*Mos*. 1.154). Among the positive elements of his story are a number related to issues of sexuality. Thus Philo highlights that *Moses' father and mother* were "the best of their contemporaries, members of the same tribe (φυλέτας ὄντας), though with them mutual affection was a stronger tie than family connexions (ἡ ὁμοφροσύνη μᾶλλον ᾠκείωσεν ἢ τὸ γένος)" (*Mos*. 1.7), reflecting both Philo's valuing of marital affection and the probable assumption that marriage within one's own tribe was to be highly regarded. He retells the plight of the Hebrews whose male children the Pharaoh ordered killed, allowing only the female to survive "since her natural weakness makes a woman inactive in war" (*Mos*. 1.8), and the subversion that "unknown to all but few, he was kept at home and fed from his mother's breast for three successive months" (*Mos*. 1.9). Philo tells the story of Moses meeting Jethro's daughters (*Mos*. 1.52-59), but without the allegorical overlay present elsewhere, and reports simply that he "gave him the fairest of his daughters in marriage, and, by that one action, attested all his noble qualities" (*Mos*. 1.59). Here Philo makes no mention of this being a marriage with a foreigner, which elsewhere he defends against what he calls the shamelessness of Miriam's criticism of Moses for marrying an Ethiopian (*Leg*. 2.66-67).[443]

---

[443] Winslow, *Moses' Wives*, argues that Philo "never decries intermarriage any more than he disapproves of any sort of physical intercourse. In Philo, women are denigrated generally, with no particular focus on their insider/outsider status" (230-31). Our discussion of intermarriage below indicates that this is too broad a claim.

His account here of Moses' youth paints him as exemplary in relation to what Philo considers paramount. Thus "he did not, as some, allow the lusts of adolescence to go unbridled (οὐχ ὡς ἔνιοι τὰς μειρακιώδεις ἐπιθυμίας ἀχαλινώτους ἐῶν)" (*Mos.* 1.25), but kept the reins tight. "And each of the other passions which rage so furiously if left to themselves, he tamed and assuaged and reduced to mildness ... and in general he watched the first directions and impulses of the soul as one would a restive horse" (*Mos.* 1.26). Philo doubtless had sexual passion in mind especially. Thus he writes: "For on his belly he bestowed no more than the necessary tributes which nature has appointed, and as for the pleasures that have their seat below (τῶν τε ὑπογαστρίων ἡδονῶν), save for the lawful begetting of children (εἰ μὴ μέχρι σπορᾶς), they passed altogether even out of his memory" (*Mos.* 1.28). Pleasure in sexual intercourse belongs solely in the context of procreation.

1.3.3.1.2 Moses Beyond Mos. 1

When Philo elsewhere expounds "the deeper meaning" of this story, as he often puts it, he picks up many of the details of the story mentioned above and sometimes also at the literal level. Thus he speaks of Moses' father as a "man of the tribe of Levi who took one of the daughters of Levi and had her to wife, and she received in her womb and bore a male child" (*Congr.* 131), similarly reflecting a valuing of inner-tribal marriage. In relation to the Hebrew children, Philo alludes to Exod 1:19, according to which Hebrew women sometimes gave birth before the midwives came, in order to speak of barren Sarah's giving birth, a symbol of virtue (*Congr.* 3; *Migr.* 142; *Fug.* 168). Elsewhere he praises the Hebrew midwives as symbols of those who made houses of virtues for themselves (*Migr.* 215; similarly *Leg.* 3.3) or as models of courage (*Leg.* 3.243).

Fundamental to Philo's exposition of Moses and the exodus at an allegorical level is his designation of *Egypt as body and as the place of the passions*. The predicted 400 years of sojourn in Egypt thus convey the soul's captivity to passion (*QG* 3.10; *Her.* 269). "It must needs be that mortal man shall be oppressed by the nation of the passions and receive the calamities which are proper to created being, but it is God's will to lighten the evils which are inherent in our race" (*Her.* 272). Egypt represents "those who love the body" (*Conf.* 70, 88), "the refuge of a dissolute and licentious life" (*Post.* 156). Interpreting God's word to Isaac not to go down to Egypt he writes of Egypt as passion (*Conf.* 81). Egyptian building construction is "naturally depraved" for "they first mix the unreasoning and exuberant impulses of passion with the gravest vices" (*Conf.* 90), and then divide it, including "passion into pleasure and lust" (*Conf.* 90). "They wished in this way to shew that good is the slave of evil and passion stronger than the higher emotions" (*Conf.* 91). Thus he depicts Moses as an "alien" in the body (*Conf.* 82) and as slaying the "Egyptian character, which was assailing the soul from the vantage-ground of pleasure" (*Fug.* 148; similarly *Leg.* 3.37-39), here making a connection between "the doctrine that pleasure is the prime and greatest good, and the doctrine that atoms are the elementary principles of the universe" (*Fug.* 148). Similarly Moses fights shy of the sophists of Egypt seen as the body (*Det.* 38) and "withdraws from the godless opinion of Pharaoh, which the passions follow as their leader, and withdraws into Midian" (*Leg.* 3.13). To pine to return to Egypt like the wilderness generation is to pine to return to the passions (*Leg.* 2.77), "a downward course into the bodily passions" virtue must never take (*Her.* 316).

Moses' encounter with Jethro and his daughters becomes a major source for exposition of Philo's psychology in *Mut.* He employs the two names of Moses' father-in-law symbolically to contrast the opposing ways. "Jethro values the human above the divine, custom above laws, profane above sacred, mortal above immortal, ... seeming above being" (*Mut.*104). In *Agr.* he interprets his name as meaning "uneven" and representing "self-conceit" (*Agr.* 43). Elsewhere he uses Jethro as a symbol of the "promiscuous horde, who swing to and fro as their idle opinions carry them" (*Ebr.* 36). As Philo develops the image in *Mut.*, he moves from the priest of Midian to his favourite priest, Phinehas, who confronted the Midianites, who were "initiated in the unholy rites of Baal Peor, and widening all the orifices of the body to receive the streams which pour in from the outside ... flood the ruling mind and sink it to the lowest depths" (*Mut.* 107), and took his lance to "pierce passion through the womb" (*Mut.* 108). He then returns to seven daughters of the priest of Midian, who represents "the judicial (κριτικόν), justice-dispensing (δικαστικόν) type" (*Mut.* 110)[444] and whose daughters who serve as images of his psychology, five senses plus speech and "reproductive power" (γονή) (*Mut.* 110). "Each 'draws up,' so to speak, external objects of sense until they 'fill the troughs' of the soul 'from which they water the sheep of the father,' and by these I mean the purest of flocks, the flock of reasoning which brings with it at once protection and adornment" (*Mut.* 111). This is a positive depiction, illustrating how things ought to work, including a positive appreciation of sexual passion, "reproductive power". He then portrays the negative, represented by the evil shepherds, and how things can go wrong, from whom the daughters escape to Raguel, the name of their father in a positive role. We discuss the allegory in 1.3.4 above. Mind's questioning brings all under control and the outcome is Moses' marrying Zipporah, "the winged, inspired and prophetic nature" (*Mut.* 120). He is the ideal who has not driven all senses away but harnessed them, so to speak, in

---

[444] Louis H. Feldman, "Philo's Interpretation of Jethro," *ABR* 51 (2003) 37-46, notes: "he is saying, in effect, that Moses, who, as we have seen, represents justice, found a proper match for himself in marrying the daughter of one who represents justice" (41).

marriage. On Philo's depiction of Moses' celibacy in relation to his prophetic role, see 1.2.3.5 above.

1.3.3.2 The Exodus

1.3.3.2.1 The Departure from Egypt

The *departure from Egypt* symbolises abandoning the life ruled by passion (*Leg.* 3.44, 81, 175; *Decal.* 2), just as Abraham's migration from Mesopotamia, Jacob's flight from Laban, and Lot's from Sodom.[445] The plagues represent "when the most dominant elements of blind passion are destroyed" (*Sacr.* 134). Reluctance to leave, such as depicted in Exod 21:5 of the slave reluctant to leave his master, wife, and children, is to choose bondage to sense-perception (*Leg.* 3.198-199; *Cher.* 72; *Her.* 186).

Philo attributes problems during the wandering in the wilderness to *the mixed crowd* who departed. In *Mos.* 1 he claims departing crowd

> were accompanied by a promiscuous, nondescript and menial crowd, a bastard host, so to speak, associated with the true-born. These were the children of Egyptian women by Hebrew fathers into whose families they had been adopted, also those who, reverencing the divine favour shewn to the people, had come over to them, and such as were converted and brought to a wiser mind by the magnitude and the number of the successive punishments. (*Mos.* 1.147).

In *Mos.* 2 he cites the blasphemer of Lev 24:10-16 as an instance, "A certain baseborn man, the child of an unequal marriage, his father an Egyptian, his mother a Jewess", who embraced Egyptian atheism (*Mos.* 2.193-208), probably reflecting an underlying concern with mixed marriages. Similarly in *Migr.* Philo explains problems which arose in the wilderness on the basis that those who left, a "mixed and rough multitude, a conglomeration of promiscuous and diverse opinions" (*Migr.* 154), included offspring of mixed marriages: "It is this mixed multitude which takes delight not in a few species of lusting only (ὁ μὴ μόνον ὀλίγοις εἴδεσιν ἐπιθυμίας χαίρων), but claims to leave out nothing at all, that it may follow after lust's entire genus (ἵνα ὅλον δι' ὅλων τον γένος), including all its species. For we read 'the mixed people that was among them "craved after lust,"

---

[445] On this see Pearce, *Land of the Body*, who notes a range of motifs in relation to departure from Egypt employed by Philo, including not only the exodus, itself, but also the transfer of Joseph's bones, Jacob's return, and the Passover (103). She observes that Philo appears to assume exegetical tradition which derived the etymology of "Egypt" from צרר, to "oppress" (83) and which appears to have interpreted Egypt in a Platonic sense as the body (103). She notes that for Philo neither the body nor Egypt is seen as wholly evil (106).

after the genus itself (ἐπεθύμησεν ἐπιθυμίαν αὐτοῦ τοῦ γένους), not some single species, 'and sat down and wept'" (*Migr.* 155; cf. Num 11:4).[446] This appears to include both sexual excess and sexual deviation, as Philo sees it, though no further explanation follows. The motif of the mixed multitude continues in *Migr.* 158: "they aim at being in touch with both the real and the reputed virtues".

1.3.3.2.2 Marah, Manna, and the Golden Bull

The *bitter waters at Marah* serve Philo as a symbol of the bitterness which must come in the "unlearning of passion" (*Congr.* 162-163; similarly *Post.* 155). In *Migr.* however he depicts his own moments of inspiration as a kind of orgasm (*Migr.* 35), associating this with the image of the rod which made waters sweet and the tree of life itself of Eden amid its garden of virtues (*Migr.* 35-36).[447] In *Mos.* 2 he sees the fruit of Aaron's rod, which he takes to be nuts, as a "parable of the practising soul" (*Mos.* 2.183) prepared to toil and be tough like a nut, for "in voluptuous livers, whose souls are emasculated and whose bodies run to waste with ceaseless luxury, ... virtue cannot make its lodging; but it will first procure its divorce for misusage in the court of right reason, and then seek another home" (*Mos.* 2.184). Philo exploits the image of the manna to contrast earthly and heavenly food (*Leg.* 3.162-178), also to counsel avoidance of excess and taking only what one needs (*Leg.* 3.166).

In *Decal.* he notes the requirement of purity before Sinai: "They had kept pure from intercourse with women and abstained from all pleasures save those which are necessary for the sustenance of life. They had cleansed themselves with ablutions and lustrations for three days past, and moreover had washed their clothes" (*Decal.* 45), typically not denying the necessities of life, but for these days, that did not include sexual intercourse as it did elsewhere.[448]

In a brief reference to Aaron's sons, Nadab and Abihu, citing them as examples of positive nakedness, Philo ignores the negative account in Lev 10:1-2, describing them as carried in their coats, as men "naked of vain and mortal glory ... by bursting every bond of passion and of bodily constraint, in order that their nakedness and freedom from the body should not be debased by the irruption of impious thoughts" (*Leg.* 2.57).

Philo takes up the incident of *the golden bull* at Sinai, treating it both literally as an instance where "revelling and carousing the livelong night, and unwary of

---

[446] As Colson and Whitaker, *Philo IV*, note, "Philo takes ἐπιθυμίαν, which in the LXX. is a cognate accusative representing the familiar Hebrew way of intensifying the verb ... as if it was the direct object of ἐπεθύμησεν" (220).

[447] On this see the discussion on pp. 122, 148 above.

[448] On purity in relation to worship in Philo, see Jutta Leonhardt-Balzer, *Jewish Worship in Philo of Alexandria* (TSAJ 84; Tübingen: Mohr Siebeck, 2001) 261.

the future, they lived wedded to their pleasant vices" (*Mos.* 2.162), and symbolically, the bull, a symbol of Egypt and the passions (*Ebr.* 95),[449] depicting the soul as sometimes needing to deal with outcries (*Ebr.* 97). He goes on to note "when they begin to fill the region of the soul with manifold sounds and voices, when they summon the passions and rouse them to action, they create the discord of civil war" (*Ebr.* 98; similarly 104), but that they can be contained with divine help "so that the clamours of the passions are at once restrained" (*Ebr.* 101). He then exclaims: "How shrill are the outcries of pleasure, wherewith it is wont to command what it wills! How continuous is the voice of desire, when it thunders forth its threats against those who do not minister to its wants!" (*Ebr.* 101-102). In *Spec.* 3 Philo refers to the slaughter of the 24000 who worshiped the golden bull and engaged in "feasts which were no feasts and danced dances of death" (*Spec.* 3 125), but makes no sexual references. Chopping up the burnt remains of the golden bull then symbolises the way to life and sweetness (*Post.* 158). "For the lover of virtue, set on fire by the brilliant appearance of the beautiful, burns up the pleasures of the body, and then chops and grinds them up" (*Post.* 159). He writes disparagingly of the making of the bull as "the work of an effeminate and sinew-less soul", symbolised in the use of women's ear-rings (*Post.* 166).

The warnings remain generic without specific reference to sexual sin and Philo makes no link to the Sotah rite of the suspected adulteress (cf. *LAB* 12:7). In *Leg.* 2.54 he depicts Moses as one who "fixes his tent outside the camp, a long way from the camp, and it was called the tent of testimony", alluding to Exod 33:7, miscuing the meaning to imply that Moses' abode outside was the tent of testimony, but making the point that Moses representing "the soul that loves God, having disrobed itself of the body ... and fled abroad far away from these, gains a fixed and assured settlement in the perfect ordinances of virtue" (*Leg.* 2.55).

1.3.3.3 Midianites, Moabites, and Phinehas

The *conflict with the Midianites* contains sexual themes which Philo elaborates. In recounting the literal story in *Mos.* Philo portrays Balaam's strategy to counter Israel: "he set himself to lead them, through wantonness and licentiousness, to impiety, through a great sin to a still greater, and put before them the bait of pleasure" (*Mos.* 1.295). Accordingly Philo gives Balaam a speech to Balak in which he begins by declaring:

> You have in your countrywomen, king, ... persons of pre-eminent beauty. And there is nothing to which a man more easily falls a captive than women's comeliness. If, then, you permit the fairest among them to prostitute themselves for hire, they will ensnare

---

[449] Pearce, *Land of the Body*, notes that the identification of the calf with Egyptian religion is first attested in Philo (292).

the younger of their enemies. But you must instruct them not to allow their wooers to enjoy their charms at once. For coyness titillates, and thereby makes the appetites more active, and inflames the passions. And, when their lust has them in its grip, there is nothing which they will shrink from doing or suffering. (*Mos.* 1.296-297).

Philo is dealing directly with sexual seduction through the lure of prostitutes and exploiting his understanding of its effects in men. From what follows it is clear that he does not consider men helpless victims, but still holds them responsible for their actions. The speech continues a little later: "Then the lover, caught in the meshes of her multiform lures, her beauty and enticements of her wheedling talk, will not gainsay her, but, with his reason trussed and pinioned, will subserve her orders to his sorrow, and be enrolled as a slave of passion" (*Mos.* 1.299). Accordingly, Philo reports, "the king, thinking that the proposal was good, ignoring the law against adultery, and annulling those which prohibited seduction and fornication as though they had never been enacted at all, permitted the women, without restriction, to have intercourse with whom they would" (*Mos.* 1.300). We note the emphasis on the law, forbidding adultery and, less clearly, seduction. Philo continues: "Having thus received immunity, so greatly did they mislead the minds of most of the young men, and pervert them by their arts to impiety, that they soon made a conquest of them" (*Mos.* 1.301). He then brings in Phinehas: "Phinehas, the son of the high priest, greatly angered at what he saw, and horrified at the thought that his people had at the same moment surrendered their bodies to pleasure and their souls to lawlessness and unholiness, shewed the young, gallant spirit which befitted a man of excellence" (*Mos.* 1.301), reporting the incident in Numbers 25.

> For, seeing one of his race offering sacrifice and visiting a harlot, not with his head bowed down towards the ground, nor trying in the usual way to make a stealthy entrance unobserved by the public, but flaunting his licentiousness boldly and shamelessly, and pluming himself as though his conduct called for honour instead of scorn, he was filled with bitterness and righteous anger, and attacking the pair whilst they still lay together he slew both the lover and his concubine, ripping up also her parts of generation because they had served to receive the illicit seed. (*Mos.* 1.302)

He notes the massacre of 24000 by "those who were zealous for continence and godliness" (*Mos.* 1.303). Later he returns to speak of Balak's action "in the execution by the licentiousness and wantonness of the women, who had caused the ruin of their paramours, of their bodies through lust, of their souls through impiety" (*Mos.* 1.305) and the justification for the slaughter of "the women because they had bewitched the younger Hebrews and thus led them into licentiousness and impiety and finally to death" (*Mos.* 1.311). All of this remains at a literal level and serves as a warning against sexual seduction. We meet a similar retelling of the story in *Virt*. The Midianites "sent for the most exquisitely beautiful among their women and said to them, ..." and proposed they seduce them (*Virt*. 35), with a similar rationale: "Now man is easily led captive by pleasure, and particularly by the pleasure of intercourse with women. You are exceedingly comely; beauty is naturally seductive, and youth easily lapses into incontinence. Do not fear the names of harlotry and adultery" (*Virt*. 36). So the women lured them to participate in sacrifices: "with meretricious glances and wheedling talk and lewd attitudes and movements, they set their bait before the weaker-minded part of the younger men" (*Virt*. 40) and lured them to participate in sacrifices.

The Midianites' alleged strategy of seduction has slim footing in the biblical record. Num 25:6-9 reports one incident to which Phinehas responds, but then 25:16-18 reports that the Lord urged the defeat of the Midianites not only on the basis of that incident but also of an earlier one, attributed in 25:1-5 to the people of Moab, with whose women the people began to have sexual relations, and with whom they then went on to offer sacrifices to their gods, depicted as a plague. The narrative in Numbers appears to connect both incidents by reporting the slaughter of the 24000 (25:9) immediately after Phinehas' action (25:6-8). Then in Num 31:15-16 after victory over the Midianites and capture of their wives alive, Moses declares: "Have you allowed all the women to live? These women here, on Balaam's advice, made the Israelites act treacherously against the LORD in the affair of Peor, so that the plague came among the congregation of the LORD". This is then how Philo understands it. The idea of a seduction strategy has this slim footing. It was enough to stir storytellers's imagination as the elaborations in *LAB* 18:13-14 and Josephus (*A.J.* 4.129-144) show. Philo knows the tradition.

In *Leg*. 3 Philo exploits the words, "The women kindled yet further a fire in Moab" (*Leg*. 3.225) and its context (Num 21:27-30; only here thus interpreted) to depict the mind controlled by Sense-Perception (*Leg*. 3.225-233). This is similar to disasters subverting a doctor's healing or a farmer's crops (*Leg*. 3.226-227; cf. also *Sacr*. 121). "It was not, however, enough for Mind to have the troubles that are peculiar to it and belong to its own sphere, but over and above these the women, the senses, that is, lit a fire, a huge conflagration, to add to its disasters" (*Leg*. 3.234).

Phinehas is a hero. We noted that Philo mentions him in the context of telling the story of the Midianite Jethro and his daughters (*Mut*. 107-108), where, as in *Mos*. 1.301-302, *Leg*. 3.242; *Ebr*. 73; *Spec*. 1.56-57; and *Conf*. 42, Philo notes that he not only killed the couple; he ripped open the woman's womb. He interprets this appaling detail symbolically as putting an end to an evil and what it might reproduce. In *Virt*. 40 and *Spec*. 1.56-57 the concern includes seduction to idolatry beside sexual wrongdoing, but generally Philo's focus is both sexual wrongdoing in a literal sense, including response to the lures of seductive prostitutes and with non-Israelites, and, more abstractly, falling to the temptations of the passions.

Thus Phinehas belongs to the special category of priests and prophets like Moses (*Ebr.* 65). "It was in abhorrence of pleasure that there arose the priest and minister of Him Who alone is Beautiful, Phinehas the controller of the inlets and outlets of the body, who takes care that none of them act amiss and break out in insolence, his very name meaning, 'Mouth-muzzle'" (*Post.* 182). In *Leg.* he emphasises the symbolic meaning: "Phinehas, the priest, who was zealous with the zeal of God, has secured his own safety, not by flight, but grasping the 'spear,' i.e. the spirit of zeal, he will not desist before he has 'pierced the Midianitish woman,' the nature that has been sifted out of the sacred company, 'through her womb,' that she may never be able to cause plant or seed of wickedness to shoot up" (*Leg.* 3.242). He then explains: "To such a woman, therefore, we must not hearken, wicked sense I mean" (*Leg.* 3.243).[450]

1.4 Sexual Issues in Philo's Exposition of Law

In this chapter we turn to Philo's treatment, literal and allegorical, of the laws. We begin with the major theme of adultery, examining his treatment first in *Decal.* and *Spec.* and beyond. We then return to *Decal.* which comments on each of the ten commandments and to *Spec.*, which uses each commandment as a heading under which to gather other related laws, and parallels elsewhere in the corpus, before considering other provisions which he does not deal with here.

1.4.1 Adultery and Associated Issues

1.4.1.1 Adultery in "On the Decalogue"

One of the primary manifestations, in Philo's view, of excessive sexual desire, is adultery which he highlights above all within his discussion of the Decalogue in the book devoted to it, but also in the broader discussion of *Spec.* and on many other occasions in his writings. In *Decal.* Philo gives an extensive exposition of the prohibition. He deems it "the greatest of crimes" (μέγιστον ἀδικημάτων) (*Decal.* 123), repeated in Joseph's rejection of Potiphar's wife (*Ios.* 44a), and buttressed later (*Decal.* 131; similarly 168, *Spec.* 3.8) with the observation that it therefore comes first in the second table of the commandments, as in Philo's LXX

---

[450] On the significance of Phinehas within priestly circles which resisted Rome and that Philo's adulation of Phinehas reflects use of such tradition, see David Goodblatt, *Elements of Ancient Jewish Nationalism* (Cambridge: Cambridge University Press, 2006) 104.

it doubtless did.[451] In *Decal.* he goes on to substantiate the claim with detailed argument. "For in the first place it has its source in the love of pleasure (φιληδονίαν) which enervates the bodies of those who entertain it, relaxes the sinews of the soul and wastes away the means of subsistence, consuming like an unquenchable fire all that it touches and leaving nothing wholesome in human life" (*Decal.* 122). In other words, the powerful and self-destructive desire for pleasure drives it. In the parallel discussion in *Spec.* 3 he speaks of pleasure as "a mighty force felt throughout the whole inhabited world" (πανταχοῦ τῆς οἰκουμένης μέγα πνεῖ), citing also the animal world (*Spec.* 3.8). "Secondly, it persuades the adulterer not merely to do the wrong but to teach another to share the wrong by setting up a partnership in a situation where no true partnership is possible" (*Decal.* 123). In other words, it involves someone else in the wrong as well. "For when the frenzy has got the mastery, the appetites cannot possibly gain their end through one agent only, but there must necessarily be two acting in common, one taking the position of the teacher, the other of the pupil, whose aim is to put on a firm footing the vilest of sins, licentiousness and lewdness" (*Decal.* 123). He then notes that this affects both body and soul of the female partner in the act: "We cannot even say that it is only the body of the adulteress which is corrupted, but the real truth is that her soul rather than her body is habituated to estrangement from the husband, taught as it is to feel complete aversion and hatred for him" (*Decal.* 124). Philo's perceptive observation is that such adultery not only wrongs the woman's husband but also produces inner alienation of her from him and similarly he notes the secrecy and deceit commonly entailed in such liaisons (*Decal.* 125).

He then extends his argument to take into account all three families affected:

> Indeed it makes havoc of three families: of that of the husband who suffers from the breach of faith, stripped of the promise of his marriage-vows and his hopes of legitimate offspring, and of two others, those of the adulterer and of the woman, for the infection of the outrage and dishonour and disgrace of the deepest kind extends to the family of both. And if their connexions include a large number of persons through intermarriages and widespread associations, the wrong will travel all round and affect the whole State. (*Decal.* 126-127)

The three families are those of the wronged husband, the perpetrator and the woman, meaning here her parents, since normally her family and that of the perpetrator are the same. Interestingly, Philo notes the harm to the cuckolded husband as breach of faith, failure of what marriage vows promised, and loss of progeny. The promise of marriage vows, identified as an item in itself, probably means that Philo is thinking of more than fidelity and progeny, always a major

---

[451] On this see Loader, *Septuagint,* 5-8, 12-14.

concern, but also what he values elsewhere, namely the happiness of marital partnership. Shame and dishonour – for all three families and their extended families – was typically a major concern. Philo is not finished. He notes, too, the harm inflicted on the children and the danger to the household: "very painful, too, is the uncertain status of the children, for if the wife is not chaste there will be doubt and dispute as to the real paternity of the offspring. Then if the fact is undetected, the fruit of the adultery usurp the position of the legitimate and form an alien and bastard brood and will ultimately succeed to the heritage of their putative father to which they have no right" (*Decal.* 128). Concern with household security is typical in society where it played such a central role in people's lives. Thus "the adulterer having in insolent triumph vented his passions and sown the seed of shame, his lust now sated, will leave the scene and go on his way mocking at the ignorance of the victim of his crime, who like a blind man knowing nothing of the covert intrigues of the past will be forced to cherish the children of his deadliest foe as his own flesh and blood" (*Decal.* 129). He adds the sin of arrogance. Returning to the children's plight he notes: "If the wrong becomes known, the poor children who have done no wrong will be most unfortunate, unable to be classed with either family, either the husband's or the adulterer's. Such being the disasters wrought by illicit intercourse, naturally the abominable and God-detested sin of adultery was placed first in the list of wrongdoing" (*Decal.* 130-131). This is a surprisingly perceptive exposé of what adultery meant in Philo's time – seen from a male perspective. We would want to hear more of the plight of the woman and perhaps also of her potential responsibility. His conclusion notes that on the second table "the first head is that against adultery, under which come many enactments against seducers and pederasty, against dissolute living and indulgence in lawless and licentious forms of intercourse" (*Decal.* 168), which he then deals with in the longer discussion in *Spec.*

1.4.1.2 Adultery in "Special Laws" and Elsewhere

When Philo returns to the theme in *Spec.*, we find many of the same emphases. Thus he repeats the importance signalled by the prohibition receiving prime position on the second table, "because pleasure is a mighty force felt through the whole inhabited world" (*Spec.* 3.8), but here there appears to be an element of sympathy. For he writes:

> Now even natural pleasure is often greatly to blame when the craving for it is immoderate and insatiable, as for instance when it takes the form of voracious gluttony, even though none of the food taken is of the forbidden kind, or again the passionate desire for women shewn by those who in their craze for sexual intercourse behave unchastely, not with the wives of others, but with their own. (*Spec.* 3.9)

The focus is broader than adultery; it includes marital sex; and broader than that: gluttony. The explanation which follows, however, is specifically sexual:

> But the blame in most of these cases rests less with the soul than with the body, which contains a great amount both of fire and of moisture; the fire as it consumes the material set before it quickly demands a second supply; the moisture is sluiced in a stream through the genital organs, and creates in them irritations, itchings and titillations without ceasing. (*Spec.* 3.10)

Such biological pressures of the body are no excuse for the soul which deliberately chooses adultery: "It is not so with men who are mad to possess the wives of others, sometimes those of their relations and friends, who live to work havoc among their neighbours, who go about to bastardize wholesale widespread family connexions, to turn their prayers for married happiness into a curse (τὰς μὲν ἐπὶ γάμοις εὐχὰς παλιμφήμους) and render their hopes of offspring fruitless" (*Spec.* 3.11). Again we note Philo's positive valuing of marriage. Philo appears to consider that people bent on carving such a swathe of promiscuity in society are incurable and sees in that the warrant for the biblical death penalty: "Here it is the soul which is incurably diseased. Such persons must be punished with death as the common enemies of the whole human race, that they may not live to ruin more houses with impunity and be tutors of others who make it their business to emulate the wickedness of their ways" (*Spec.* 3.11; similarly *Hypoth.* 7:1; based on Lev 20:10; Deut 22:22). Tutoring here probably goes beyond simply involving second persons as in *Decal.* 123 and probably including the influence which such modelling has. Later in *Spec.* 4 he recalls his exposition, in arguing that the forbidding of mating between different kinds also reinforces the prohibition of adultery:

> The first of these prohibitions has been mentioned in our denunciation of adulterers to suggest still more clearly the wickedness of conspiring against the wedlock of other people, thereby ruining the morals of the wives as well as any honest hopes of begetting a legitimate family. For by prohibiting the crossing of irrational animals with different species he [Moses] appears to be indirectly working towards the prevention of adultery. (*Spec.* 4.203)

The primary model elsewhere for resisting adultery is Joseph, who refuses to surrender the purity he has upheld throughout his youth, not engaging with prostitutes from age fourteen on like other nations, and determined to remain pure till marriage, and so defies her request that he "take the first step in transgression by committing adultery, the greatest of crimes" (*Ios.* 44). He also notes the dangers such an act creates with an offended husband (*Ios.* 44), in his case a sense of disloyalty (*Ios.* 45) and defiling her in his eyes and bringing much shame (*Ios.* 45) and his potential exposure resulting from a bad conscience (*Ios.* 48).

Philo regularly cites adultery in depictions of sins (*Ios.* 84; *Spec.* 4.84; *QG* 4.73; *Conf.* 117, 163; *Hypoth.* 7:1). He would surely affirm what he depicts as his nephew's comment: "They infringe on the marital rights of others and do not even blush during trial before the magistrates. They fear neither the present laws concerning adultery nor the raging and inexorable wrath of husbands threatening with death, having the freedom to kill, unhindered by inexperience in evil" (*Anim.* 49).[452] Philo notes that Balaam's seductive strategy defies the prohibition (*Mos.* 1.300; similarly *Virt.* 36), tells of the threats of adultery entailed in the abductions of Sarah and Rebecca by Pharaoh and Abimelech (*Abr.* 90-98) and wards off the implication of his allegories that Sarah's sexual intimacy with the divine be understood as adultery (*Mut.* 132). Adultery was an element in the men of Sodom's excess, whose behaviour, which we would label bisexual, included also same-sex intercourse, a typical combination (*Abr.* 135); similarly *Spec.*, where he speaks of the one who uses the organs of generation "for abominable lusts and forms of intercourse forbidden by all laws. He not only attacks in his fury the marriage-beds of others, but even plays the pederast and forces the male type of nature to debase and convert itself into the feminine form, just to indulge a polluted and accursed passion" (*Spec.* 2.50). He notes, too, the "amours and adulteries and the deceits of women, which have consumed the greatest and choicest part of the Greek race and the barbarian also, and destroyed the youth of their cities" (*Ios.* 56).

Likewise in *Det.* he exhorts: "and because, with a view to the persistence of the race, you were endowed with generative organs, do not run after rapes and adulteries and other unhallowed forms of intercourse, but only those which are the lawful means of propagating the human race" (*Det.* 102). In *Somn.* 2.147 he notes that some men who begin well make such shipwreck of the lives late in life, "because they have never known even in their dreams the intestine war kindled by passion, the cruellest of wars – and then at the very eventide of life they have been wrecked on the rock of an unlocked tongue or insatiate greed of belly, or in uncontrolled lasciviousness of the lower-lying parts".

We shall see below that he reinterprets Deut 24:1-4 to mean that remarriage to one's former wife who has in the interim been married to another constitutes adultery (*Spec.* 3.31). Adultery also becomes for Philo a means for measuring the severity of other transgressions, so that he can declare "if anyone dishonours by violence a woman widowed by the death of her husband or through any other form

---

[452] Terian, *De Animalibus*, notes that this statement reflects Roman law in requiring trial before magistrates and in allowing only the husband to kill the offender when caught in the act in revenge, whereas Jewish law allowed others to do so who witnessed the act (162).

of separation, the crime he commits is less serious than in adultery" (*Spec.* 3.64) and "The corruption of a maiden is a criminal offence closely akin to adultery" (*Spec.* 3.65).

1.4.1.3 Laws treated under the Heading of the Prohibition of Adultery

In *Spec.* 3 Philo uses the heading of adultery's prohibition to assemble other prohibitions: "Excellent also are the other injunctions laid down by the law on the relation of the sexes" (*Spec.* 3.12), introducing a number of themes that reach to *Spec.* 3.82, before he turns to the next Decalogue prohibition, murder. These include incest (12-28), expounding Leviticus 18:6-18; intermarriage (29), based on Exod 34:16; Deut 7:3; remarriage of a divorced wife (30-31), based on Deut 24:1-4; intercourse during menstruation (32-33), returning to Leviticus 18 (18:19); intercourse with sterile women (34-36); pederasty (37-42), based on Lev 18:22 (cf. also 20:13); bestiality (43-50), based on Lev 18:23 (cf. also 20:15-16; Exod 22:19); prostitution (51), based on Deut 23:17; accusations of adultery (52-63) based on Num 5:12-31; rape of a widow or divorcee (64); seduction (65-68) or rape of an unmarried, unbetrothed woman (69-71), based on Exod 22:16-17 and Deut 22:28-29; intercourse with a woman espoused to be married to another, by consent (72-73), by force within or beyond the city (73-78), based on Deut 22:23-27; and accusations that one's wife was not a virgin (79-82), based on Deut 22:13-21. Our discussion follows Philo's sequence.

1.4.1.3.1 Incest

Philo moves directly from the prohibition of adultery in *Spec.* 3.7-11 to Leviticus 18, which will be the basis for his exposition of incest, menstrual sex, same-sex relations, and bestiality. He devotes considerable attention to incest. His opening statement, that the Law "commands abstinence not only from the wives of others but also from widows [means women without husbands] in cases where the union is forbidden by the moral law" (*Spec.* 3.12), might apply broadly to intercourse with all widows and divorcees, but appears in the light of what follows to be targeting incest, and so envisage intercourse with one's father's widow or divorced wife. He begins accordingly with the first Leviticus prohibition (18:7-8), launching immediately into what he calls a Persian custom, to which he claims the Law "at once shows its aversion and abhorrence and forbids it as a very grave offence against holy living. For the Persian magnates marry their mothers and regard the children of the marriage as nobles of the highest birth" (*Spec.* 3.13). He abhors that "a father's bed, which should be kept untouched as something sacred, should be brought to shame" (*Spec.* 3.14) elaborating its implications that the man is simultaneously son and husband, the mother simultaneously wife; the children, "brothers to their father and grandsons to their mother" and she, mother and grandmother, and he, father and half-brother (*Spec.* 3.14). He then cites the unwitting incest of Oedipus and what he describes as its disastrous consequences (*Spec.* 3.15-16),[453] returning to similar consequences to be seen among the Persians (*Spec.* 3.17-18), concluding: "All these things appear to me to be the result of the ill-matched matings of sons with mothers" (*Spec.* 3.19). He then notes that the Law has "not even permitted the son of a first marriage to marry his stepmother after the death of his father, both on account of the honour due to his father and because the names of mother and stepmother are closely akin, however different are the feelings called up by the two words" (*Spec.* 3.20) (Lev 18:8). He adds: "For he who has been taught to abstain from another's wife because she is called his stepmother, will *a fortiori* abstain from taking his natural mother" (*Spec.* 3.21), reinforcing this comment with the claim that "the honour which he pays to both his parents will certainly keep him from entertaining the idea of violating his mother in any way" (*Spec.* 3.21). It may seem strange that such an issue warranted so much attention, but in a society where the age differential between husbands and wives often well exceeded 10 years, the chances that a son might be enamoured especially of a stepmother were probably quite high.

Following the order in Leviticus, Philo next addresses incest with one's sister (*Spec.* 3.22-25; Lev 18:9, 11). Again he points to instances beyond his own culture, citing Solon's law allowing marriage to half-sisters and Spartans allowing it with sisters but not half-sisters, but worse, the Egyptian lawgiver who allowed both: "With a lavish hand he bestowed on bodies and souls the poisonous bane of incontinence and gave full liberty to marry sisters of every degree whether they belonged to one of their brother's parents or to both", including even between twins (*Spec.* 3.23). In contrast Moses "stoutly forbade the union of a brother with a sister whether both her parents were the same as his or only one" (*Spec.* 3.24). Philo then points to the positive advantages which marriage outside one's family brings: "For intermarriages with outsiders create new kinships not a wit inferior to blood-relationships" (*Spec.* 3.25). Next Philo expounds Lev 18:10, 12 expressed as "not allowing marriage with a son's daughter or a daughter's daughter, nor with an aunt whether paternal or maternal, nor with one who had been the wife to an uncle or son or brother, nor again with a stepdaughter whether widow or unmarried" (*Spec.* 3.26). Here Philo goes beyond the biblical provision by including the maternal aunt, widows of uncles or sons or brothers, and stepdaughters, as widows or unmarried, adding that a stepfather has the same responsibilities as a father (*Spec.* 3.26). He then brings the prohibition of Lev 18:18, "Again, he does not

---

[453] As Niehoff, *Philo on Jewish Identity*, notes, Philo could have employed the Oedipus myth more sympathetically, but appears to be "relying on a Roman stereotype of Greek licentiousness" (97). He might also have mentioned Plato's censure of incest in *Leg.* 8.838A-B (98).

allow the same man to marry two sisters either at the same time or at different times, even if the person in question has repudiated the one he married first" (*Spec.* 3.27). Philo makes no connection to the marriage of Jacob to Leah and Rachel. He grounds Moses' prohibition as follows: "For while she is still alive either as his consort or divorced, whether she is remaining in widowhood or has married another, he considered that the law of holiness required that the sister should not take the position which the wife has lost by her misfortune" since it breached "the rights of kinship" and wronged the sister (*Spec.* 3.27). He then claims "From this source grow grace jealousies and bitter feuds bringing with them train upon train of evils without number" (*Spec.* 3.28), something he compares with tensions within one's own body (*Spec.* 3.28).

Elsewhere in the corpus Philo shows sensitivity to the issue of incest which his daring allegory of God's sexual intercourse with Sarah, also described as God's daughter, raises, only to reject it as monstrously absurd (*QG* 4.60; *Mut.* 132). In expounding Egypt as the first stage, symbolising sense, and Canaan as the second, symbolising vice, in the journey of the soul (*Congr.* 83-87), both of which are to be left behind, Philo writes that "they are the practices of passion and vices, from which spring the many multitudes of the impious and the workers of unholiness" (*Congr.* 87) pointing to Lev 18:1-5 (86), but without going on to address anything specific in the chapter. In *Gig.* he cites Lev 18:6, "For the same cause the lawgiver, when he is minded to do away with all lawless and disorderly intercourse and union, prefaces his command thus, 'a man, a man shall not go near to any that is akin to his flesh to uncover their shame'" (*Gig.* 32), but immediately allegorises: "pleasures which are the friends and kin of the body" (*Gig.* 33). Similarly the allusion to Lev 18:7 in *Fug.* in the context of concern about passions serves allegory: "That is why Moses prohibits the 'disclosing of the shame of father and mother', well knowing how great an evil it is not to keep back and conceal the sins of the mind and of sense-perception, but to make them public as though they were achievements of righteousness" (*Fug.* 193).

1.4.1.3.2 Intermarriage

At this point Philo continues the theme of marriage by alluding to the prohibition of intermarriage: "Do not enter into the partnership of marriage with a member of a foreign nation, lest some day conquered by the forces of opposing customs you surrender and stray unawares from the path that leads to piety and turn aside into a pathless wild" (*Spec.* 3.29). He offers the rationale that "there is much to be feared for your sons and daughters. It may well be that they, enticed by spurious customs which they prefer to the genuine, are likely to unlearn the honour due to the one God, and that is the first and the last stage of supreme misery" (*Spec.* 3.29). The implied link with idolatry probably derives from Exod 34:16 and Deut 7:3, which emphasise that link. Such dangers posed by intermarriage underlie the account of the Midianites' attempted seduction and Phinehas' zealous intervention (*Spec.* 1.56), discussed above. Philo accounts for Israel's rebelliousness in the wilderness by attributing it to the offspring of mixed marriages between Hebrews and Egyptians (*Mos.* 1.147; *Mos.* 2.193; *Migr.* 144-145).

The issue is reflected in Philo's exposition of Abraham's instruction to his servant to find "a virgin of their family" (*QG* 4.90; similarly 4.88), Rebecca's advice and Isaac's instruction to Jacob similarly (*QG* 4.243), in Esau's wrong choices and then refusal to dismiss his Canaanite wives (*QG* 241, 245), but also in the objection from Miriam to Moses' marrying an Ethiopian, countered with the assertion that this was God's doing (*Leg.* 2.67) and elsewhere reported without any sign of a problem (*Mos.* 1.59). Moses' parents offer what Philo normally sees as the preferred model, his "father and mother the best of their contemporaries, members of the same tribe, though with them mutual affection was a stronger tie than family connexions" (*Mos.* 1.7). Accordingly, he writes of finding preferred husbands for daughters: "And these should be, if possible, of the same family as the girls, or if that cannot be, at any rate of the same ward and tribe, in order that the portions assigned as dowry should not be alienated by inter-marriage with other tribes, but should retain the place given to them in the allotment originally made on the basis of tribes" (*Spec.* 2.126). The same rationale informs the Book of Tobit's strictures (4:12). Thus Philo favours endogamy in the narrow sense, and certainly excludes intermarriage with foreigners – unless the divine override the prohibition or they become proselytes like Tamar, Zilpah, and Bilhah! When in *Spec.* 3 he writes, "Intermarriages with outsiders create new kinships not a wit inferior to blood-relationships" (*Spec.* 3.25), his argument is not against endogamy, but against incest.

Niehoff notes that "Philo defined a Jew by birth as someone born to two Jewish parents, who had legally been married at the time of his or her birth. He required the mother of a Jew not only to be Jewish but also free. He made the latter mandatory, because according to Roman law only a free woman had *conubium* and could enter a formal marriage".[454] This had various implications, including that Philo had difficulty in accepting foreigners "within the pedigree of Israel's heroes", with the consequence that "he converted the foreign mothers and raised the social status of those who were handmaids as well".[455] On this basis Niehoff

---

[454] Niehoff, *Philo on Jewish Identity*, 23, citing *Spec.* 3.67. Similarly Böhm, *Vätererzählungen*, "Nach römischem Zivilrecht war der ethnische Status der Mutter für den Sozialstatus der legitikmien Nachkommen ausschlaggebend" (167). See also the discussion in D'Angelo, "Gender and Geopolitics," who writes of Philo's "apologetic response, which represents the moral demands of Judaism as meeting, and indeed exceeding, those of the imperial order" (64-65).

[455] Niehoff, *Philo on Jewish Identity*, 24.

can explain why Philo omitted mention of Hagar's expulsion with Ishmael: "because he had already dismissed him on new legal grounds".[456] Hagar becomes a Jew by adopting her master's lifestyle, attested by Sarah in *Abr.* 250-251, and following an assumption already developed in the time of the Maccabees.[457] Similarly Philo packs the mention of Isaac's birth with legal terminology to underline its legitimacy: "to the sage was born from his wedded wife a lawful son, beloved and only" (υἱὸς ἐκ τῆς γαμετῆς γίνεται τῷ σοφῷ γνήσιος, ἀγαπητὸς καὶ μόνος, τό τε σῶμα κάλλιστος καὶ τὴν ψυχὴν ἄριστος) (*Abr.* 168). Conversely, "the application of Roman provincial law to Scripture enabled him to interpret Ishmael as a bastard who had no claims on his father's status".[458]

On the handmaids, Zilpah and Bilhah, Niehoff suggests that Philo is at first at a loss how to treat them (so *Leg.* 2.94), but then according to *Virt.*, "while giving birth as handmaids, Bilhah and Zilpah subsequently improved their status and 'passed from mere concubinage to the name and role of wedded wives'" (*Virt.* 223).[459] This applied to the handmaids what will have occurred with Jewish soldiers in Egypt who married locals, which made it possible for the offspring to be adopted. In both Hagar's and Tamar's case Philo assumes a process of conversion,[460] so that Tamar is treated "as the female equivalent of Abraham" who also abandoned idolatry.[461] Thus "applying the contemporary Roman concerns to the Biblical stories, Philo began to pay attention to the maternal pedigree of important heroes. He was the first Jewish exegete who retroactively improved the status of foreign mothers in order to protect their offspring".[462] Interestingly, Philo left the problem of Aseneth unaddressed, though presumably he would have approved the version of *Joseph and Aseneth* which depicted her acceptability only after she renounced her idols. Niehoff notes that Philo's views were so upper class and Roman-influenced that he would have left most Jews out of account. His depiction of Joseph is deliberately framed to counter assimilation, both as positive model in relation to Potiphar's wife and negatively in becoming too closely

---

[456] Niehoff, *Philo on Jewish Identity*, 24.

[457] Niehoff, *Philo on Jewish Identity*, 25-26. She notes: "On the basis of Gen.17:12-3 Philo would in any case have preferred her to become Jewish in order to guarantee the observation of Jewish ritual in her master's house" (26).

[458] Niehoff, *Philo on Jewish Identity*, 27. She argues that "Rome's impact on Philo's definition of Jewish descent can especially be appreciated by considering the fact that his matrilineal legislation contradicted his medical doctrine", which saw male seed as the source of new being (27).

[459] Niehoff, *Philo on Jewish Identity*, 28.

[460] Niehoff, *Philo on Jewish Identity*, 29.

[461] Niehoff, *Philo on Jewish Identity*, 29-31.

[462] Niehoff, *Philo on Jewish Identity*, 31.

embroiled in Egyptian society and its values.[463] Niehoff suggests that "Philo's interpretation of Joseph seems to have been revolutionary"[464] She also sees Philo having to deal with rumours about Moses' marriage and alleged Egyptian origins. Accordingly he rewrites his early history to remove all trace of an Egyptian education and replace it with Jewish influence.[465]

On priests and high priests Philo outlines the marriage provisions in *Spec.* 1. Accordingly, expounding Lev 21:7 he writes: "Since a priest is a man well before he is a priest and must and should feel the instinct for mating, Moses arranges for his marriage with a pure virgin whose parents and grandparents and ancestors are equally pure, highly distinguished for the excellence of their conduct and lineage" (*Spec.* 1.101). Even a reformed prostitute is out of the question (*Spec.* 1.101). Then based on Lev 21:13-14 he reports that "so strict are the regulations laid down for the marriage of the high priest that he is not even permitted to marry a widow [= no longer married woman, as the following context makes clear], whether her isolation is due to the death of her husband or divorce from him while still alive" (*Spec.* 1.105), explaining: "This is laid down first in order that the holy seed may pass into pure and untrodden soil and the issue receive no admixture with another family" (*Spec.* 1.105) and "Secondly, that by mating with souls entirely innocent and unperverted they may find it easy to mould the characters and dispositions of their wives, for the minds of virgins are easily influenced and attracted to virtue and very ready to be taught. But she who has had experience of another husband is naturally less amenable to instruction" (*Spec.* 1.105-106). Thus "let the high priest then take a virgin who is innocent of marriage" (*Spec.* 1.107). Again Philo clarifies: "When I say 'virgin' I exclude not only one with whom another man has had intercourse but also one with whom any other has been declared to have an agreement of betrothal, even though her body is that of a maid intact" (*Spec.* 1.107). "As for the subordinate priests, while the other marriage regulations are the same for them as for those who hold the highest priesthood, they are permitted to wed with immunity not only virgins but widows, though only such as have lost their husbands by death", to avoid potential quarrels (*Spec.* 1.108).

With regard to range of marriage partners within such restrictions Philo reports that "the high priest must not propose marriage save to one who is not only a virgin but a priestess descended from priests, so that bride and bridegroom may be of one house and in a sense of the same blood and do, harmoniously united, shew a lifelong blending of temperament firmly established" (*Spec.* 1.110). In this he reads ἐκ τοῦ γένους αὐτοῦ (Lev 21:14) in the narrow sense of "from the extended family", not in the broader sense of "from his own people" (cf. מעמיו),

---

[463] Niehoff, *Philo on Jewish Identity*, 64-67.

[464] Niehoff, *Philo on Jewish Identity*, 67.

[465] Niehoff, *Philo on Jewish Identity*, 69-70.

i.e. not a foreigner. As one might expect, Philo concludes: "These and similar regulations as to marriage are intended to promote the generation of children (χάριν παίδων γενέσεως)" (*Spec.* 1.112). Of other priests he writes: "the rest are permitted to marry the daughters of others than priests, partly because the restrictions required to maintain their purity are slight, partly because the law did not wish that the nation should be denied altogether a share in the priestly clanship or be entirely excluded from it" (*Spec.* 1.111). He explains: "This was the reason why he did not forbid the other priests to intermarry with the laity of the nation, for intermarriage is kinship in the second degree" (*Spec.* 1.111). Thus Philo does not restrict priests to marrying the daughters of other priests, a position some, I believe mistakenly, see espoused in 4QMMT and *1 Enoch* 6 – 16. He imposes this only on the high priest.[466]

In *Fug.* Philo applies the strictures on the high priest allegorically:

> To him there is betrothed moreover a maiden of the hallowed people, pure and undefiled and of ever inviolate intention; for never is he wedded to a widow or one divorced or to a profane woman or to a harlot, but against them he ever wages a truceless and unrelenting warfare. For hateful to him is widowhood (lit. being unmarried) from virtue, and the plight of one cast out and driven from her doors, and any conviction that is profane and unholy. But the promiscuous polyandrous cause of polytheism, or rather atheism, the harlot, he deigns not even to took at, having learned to love her who had adopted, as her one Husband and Father, God the All-sovereign. (*Fug.* 114)

1.4.1.3.3 Remarriage of a Divorced Wife

Next Philo addresses remarriage to an original wife, expounding the prohibition found in Deut 24:1-4. "Another commandment is that if a woman after parting from her husband for any cause whatever (καθ' ἥν ἄν τύχῃ πρόφασιν) marries another and then again becomes a widow [=woman no longer married, as the following context requires. i.e., widow or divorcee], whether this second husband is alive or dead, she must not return to her first husband but ally herself with any other rather than him" (*Spec.* 3.30). This initial statement differs from the biblical text in not depicting the issuing of a certificate of divorce. The words "for any cause" (καθ' ἥν ἄν τύχῃ πρόφασιν) leave wide open the possibilities, from divorce, in which case she is sent away, to her deserting the marriage.[467] The fact

---

[466] Jacob Milgrom, "Philo the Biblical Exegete," *SPA* 9 (1997) 79-83, notes that this extreme interpretation of Lev 21:14 was later espoused by the Karaites, but rejected by the rabbis (81).

[467] Against the view that it reflects a view comparable to that of Hillel (*m. Git.* 9:10), see Belkin, *Philo and Oral Law*, 231, who notes that *Spec.* 3.8 shows that divorce was by no means easy in Alexandria (230-31). He sees Philo as closer to the Shammaite view

that she marries another suggests proper divorce which implied consent to marry another. Philo complicates matters by continuing: "because she has broken with the rules that bound her in the past (θεσμοὺς παραβᾶσα τοὺς ἀρχαίους) and cast them into oblivion when she chose new love-ties in preference to the old (ὧν ἐξελάθετο φίλτρα καινὰ πρὸ τῶν παλαιῶν ἑλομένη)" (*Spec.* 3.30). This suggests the divorce took place on grounds that she chose another lover (and had perhaps committed adultery, though that is perhaps not envisaged since then both would according to biblical law have faced execution) (Lev 20:10). Philo adds: "and if a man is willing to contract himself with such a woman, he must be saddled with a character for degeneracy and loss of manhood (μαλακίας καὶ ἀνανδρίας ἐκφερέσθω δόξαν)" (*Spec.* 3.31). Unlike in Deut 24:1-4, the grounds for the prohibition here are that it is wrong to accept someone who has been immoral. Thus Philo explains:

> He has eliminated from his soul the hatred of evil, that emotion by which our life is so well served and the affairs of houses and cities are conducted as they should be, and has lightly taken upon him the stamp of two heinous crimes, adultery and pandering (δύο τὰ μέγιστα τῶν ἀδικημάτων εὐφόρως ἀπομαξάμενος, μοιχείαν τε καὶ προαγωγείαν). For such subsequent reconciliations are proofs of both. The proper punishment for him is death and for the woman also. (*Spec.* 3.31)

The accusation that he takes on himself the guilt of pandering and adultery is difficult. Had the grounds for her divorce been adultery, one should have expected the penalty of execution of both then and there. She can hardly be accused of adultery on any other count, however, nor can he. Pandering, that is, soliciting illicit intercourse, could be laid against both; hence Philo's citing their subsequent reconciliation as proof.[468] The text appears to demand that that reconciliation also be read as proof of adultery, but if so, then it must mean acceptance (forgiveness) of what Philo assumes is her adultery in the first place, though that still leaves unanswered the question why no penalty was demanded to begin with. Alternatively we can take Philo's depiction of the initial act more seriously and see her departure not as divorce, about which Philo is silent, but abandonment, in which case we may still have a case of adultery, but subsequent to her departure, and perhaps therefore not so easily prosecuted. Perhaps by not prosecuting, the

---

which accepted only serious grounds of sexual misdemeanour, which was not however restricted to adultery. See also Loader, *Septuagint*, 76. Cf. David Instone-Brewer, *Divorce and Remarriage in the Bible: The Social and Literary Context* (Grand Rapids: Eerdmans, 2002) 115.

[468] The charge of pandering could be laid against a husband who does not dismiss his wife for adultery according to Augustan law, *Lex Julia*.

first husband lays himself open to the charge of pandering: allowing the wife to go off with someone else without prosecution. Philo's interpretation may also reflect the likely reality that in his day the death penalty was not applied for adultery, though that stands in tension with what he is claiming that the Law in fact demands in this instance.

Elsewhere Philo refers to divorcees in the context of marriage partners forbidden to high priests and priests (*Spec.* 3.105, 108; *Fug.* 114); of priests' daughters who are divorced, who may return home to their families and participate in the family (*Spec.* 1.129-130); and of slanderers seeking grounds for divorcing wives out of favour, but "finding no pretext for divorce (μηδεμίαν ἀπαλλαγῆς πρόφασιν ἀνευρίσκοντες)" (*Spec.* 3.80). To avoid potential conflict with former husbands, priests should not marry divorcees (*Spec.* 1.108). His treatment of vows includes the special case of widows and divorcees (*Spec.* 2.25, 31; *Leg.* 2.63; cf. Num 30:9). On rape or seduction of a betrothed woman he notes prevention of divorce in such cases which result in marriage (*Spec.* 3.70; cf. Deut 22:17) and on rape of a widow or divorcee, that the crime is less serious, probably because no male rights are infringed. In *Spec.* 3.27 he notes that the incest prohibition against marrying a sister includes when the original wife has been divorced.

Beyond that Philo uses divorce allegorically to describe virtue procuring "its divorce for misusage in the court of right reason" from the soul obsessed with indulgence (*Mos.* 2.184); a person's learning "in effect to divorce from what is mortal, you will go on to receive an education in your conceptions regarding the Uncreate" (*Migr.* 192); the soul divorcing itself from God (*Det.* 127); and finally death as the time when the soul "will claim its divorce in court and depart, leaving our home desolate of life's body (*Cher.* 115).

Philo nowhere addresses laws on divorce directly, at one level not surprisingly given its incidental occurrence in biblical law, yet surprisingly, given that it must have been an issue in his day as much as it is in any other. We may assume that following both Deut 24:1-4 and Augustan law he would have seen divorce as at least mandatory in the case of adultery.

1.4.1.3.4 Intercourse during Menstruation

Philo continues in *Spec.* 3 by returning to Leviticus 18 and the subject of intercourse during menstruation (Lev 18:19; cf. also 15:24; 20:18). Accordingly he reports: "Whenever the menstrual issue occurs, a man must not touch a woman, but must during the period refrain from intercourse and respect the law of nature" (*Spec.* 3.32). Philo makes no mention of uncovering nakedness, as in Lev 18:19 and 20:18, nor of contracting impurity as in Lev 15:24, but instead argues from wasted semen: "He must also remember the lesson that the generative seeds should not be wasted fruitlessly for the sake of a gross and untimely pleasure" (*Spec.*

3.32). What makes the "pleasure" "gross and untimely" is accordingly that it has been separated as a goal from where it belongs: the processes of procreation. Thus it is like a drunken farmer scattering seeds in ponds or in mountain streams (*Spec.* 3.32). The agricultural metaphor continues: "Now nature also each month purges the womb as if it were a cornfield – a field with mysterious properties, over which, like a good husbandman, he must watch for the right time to arrive" (*Spec.* 3.33).

> So while the field is still inundated he will keep back the seed, which otherwise will be silently swept away by the stream, as the humidity not only relaxes, but utterly paralyses the seminal nerve-forces, which in nature's laboratory, the womb, mould the living creature and with consummate craftsmanship perfect each part both of body and soul. But if the menstruation ceases, he may boldly sow the generative seeds, no longer fearing that what he lays will perish. (*Spec.* 3.33)

Philo cites the prohibition in Lev 20:18 in *Fug.* 188 in service of his depiction of the "spring of folly". "'Whosoever shall have slept with a woman in her separation hath unclosed her spring, and she hath unclosed the flow of her blood; let them both be put to death'". Here, he explains, Moses "gives to sense-perception the name woman, suggesting Mind as her husband. Sense-perception is 'in separation,' which is 'sitting a long way off,' when, having forsaken Mind, her lawful husband, she plants herself on the objects of sense that ensnare and corrupt, and passionately embraces them one after another" (*Fug.* 189). The allegorical exposition continues: "At such a time, then, if Mind goes to sleep, when he ought to be awake, 'he has unclosed the spring' of sense-perception, himself to wit – for, as I have already said, he himself is the spring of sense-perception – that is, he has exposed himself, without covering or wall of defence, to the plots of his enemies" (*Fug.* 189). He then elaborates: "Moreover she too 'unclosed the flow of her blood'; for every sense, in its flow towards the external object of sense, is covered over and drawn in when controlled by reason, but is left destitute when widowed of an upright ruler, and as it is the most grievous evil for a city to be without walls, so it is for a soul to be without a protector" (*Fug.* 190).

1.4.1.3.5 Intercourse with Sterile Women

On the same grounds Philo goes on in *Spec.* 3 to condemn intercourse with sterile women, though without biblical warrant: "They too must be branded with reproach, who plough the hard and stony land" (*Spec.* 3.34). "For in the quest of mere licentious pleasure like the most lecherous of men they destroy the procreative germs with deliberate purpose" (*Spec.* 3.34). Their purpose cannot be procreation, but "can only be inordinate frenzy, and incontinence past all cure" (*Spec.* 3.34). Then Philo shows some flexibility towards those who have unwittingly married wives who turn out to be infertile. "Those who marry maidens in ignorance at the time of their capacity or incapacity for successful motherhood, and later refuse to dismiss them, when prolonged childlessness shews them to be barren, deserve our pardon" (*Spec.* 3.35). He continues somewhat sympathetically: "Familiarity, that most constraining influence, is too strong for them, and they are unable to rid themselves of the charm of old affection imprinted on their souls by long companionship" (*Spec.* 3.35). He accedes to their remaining married, but surprisingly does not then state that they should remain celibate, as his previous argument about menstruants would have to imply. In this he clearly attributes value to marital friendship.

He is unambiguous, however, about those knowingly marrying such women: "But those who sue for marriage with women whose sterility has already been proved with other husbands, do but copulate like pigs and goats, and their names should be inscribed in the lists of the impious as adversaries of God" (*Spec.* 3.36). Philo depicts intercourse purely for pleasure as behaving like animals elsewhere, depicting the passions as like animals. Again the grounds for Philo's objections are clear: "For while God in His love both for mankind and all that lives spares no care to effect the preservation and permanence of every race, those persons who make an art of quenching the life of the seed as it drops, stand confessed as the enemies of nature" (*Spec.* 3.36). In *QG* he similarly refers to those who take wives who have passed their prime, asserting that they are to be criticized for destroying the laws of nature (*QG* 1.27).

For Philo, infertility like impotence, is a curse, as he explains in expounding the exclusions in Deut 23:1 in *QE* 2:

> he places infertility and barrenness among the curses (and) says that they shall not be (found) among those who act with justice and lawfulness. For (as) a prize to those who keep the divine writing of the Law He offers the more ancient law of immortal nature, which was laid down for procreation and the begetting of sons for the perpetuity of the race. (*QE* 2.19).

Philo's stances towards sterile women and to eunuchs is similar, although he attributes to the latter a greater tendency to engage in indulgent and unnecessary passions and further them, including sexual passions, in others. While Philo never explicitly warns women about infertile men,[469] this should not be taken as approval of such marriages.

Logically one would expect Philo also to oppose intercourse during pregnancy, a prohibition we detect elsewhere on other grounds, such as harming the embryo. There may be a trace of this in Philo's comment that immediately Hagar became pregnant he ceased engaging in intercourse with her (*Abr.* 253),

---

[469] So Adele Reinhartz, "Parents and Children: A Philonic Perspective," in *The Jewish Family in Antiquity* (ed. Shaye J. D. Cohen; Atlanta: Scholars, 1993) 61-88, 70.

though that is reported primarily to underline her function as surrogate. In our discussion above of Philo's limitations on sexual intercourse we noted Niehoff's observation that it is unlikely that Philo expected people to police every act of intercourse within marriage.[470] It probably sufficed, given their less defined awareness of the menstrual cycle which remains a challenge at times even for us, to ensure that couples saw their coming together in the pleasure of intercourse as always belonging to their procreative role. Clearly marital affection also weighed strongly in Philo's considerations, but where limits could be defined, such as during menstruation and probably during pregnancy he insisted on abstinence. Otherwise, including where the wife was no longer fertile, he did not.

1.4.1.3.6 Pederasty and Same-Sex Intercourse

Philo next moves to the theme of same-sex relations (*Spec.* 3.37-42); he skips Lev 18:20, the prohibition of adultery, dealt with earlier, and offering offspring to Molech (Lev 18:21), as outside the theme. So he comes to Lev 18:22 (with its parallel 20:13). It is another instance of wasted seed,[471] but even more serious, though not as much as bestiality which is "even worse" (ἐτὶ λαγνιστέρων) (*Spec.* 3.43). Thus he begins: "Much graver than the above (πολὺ τοῦ λεχθέντος μεῖζον κακόν) is another evil, which has ramped its way into the cities, namely pederasty (παιδεραστεῖν)" (*Spec.* 3.37). He writes: "In former days the very mention of it was a great disgrace" (λεχθῆναι μέγα ὄνειδος) (*Spec.* 3.37). We find a number of references in Philo to sin which is unmentionable, and in many instances it most probably refers to same-sex intercourse (see the discussion below). He continues: "but now it is a matter of boasting not only to the active but to the passive partners who habituate themselves to endure the disease of effemination (οὐ τοῖς δρῶσι μόνον, ἀλλὰ καὶ τοῖς πάσχουσιν, οἳ νόσον θήλειαν νοσεῖν ἐθιζόμενοι), let both body and soul run to waste, and leave no ember of their male sex-nature to smoulder (μηδὲν ἐμπύρευμα τῆς ἄρρενος γενεᾶς ἐῶντες ὑποτύφεσθαι)" (*Spec.* 3.37). Beyond wasting semen, therefore, this activity, Philo alleges, feminises the passive males and undermines their male nature. Elsewhere he explains this as also rendering them impotent (*Abr.* 135). This may be included in their soul and body going to waste and will be implied in their loss of their male sex drive. He then expands the focus on femininity: "Mark how conspicuously they braid and adorn the hair of their heads, and how they scrub and paint their faces with cosmetics and pigments and the like, and smother themselves with fragrant unguents" (*Spec.* 3.37). This implies that Philo is

---

[470] Niehoff, *Philo on Jewish Identity*, 100-102 and see the discussion in 1.2.5.2 above.

[471] As Szesnat, "Pretty Boys," notes, the concern is not the sperm itself but its wastage (96-97).

envisaging consensual intercourse, though that may be meaningless where the young had been trapped into such service and had little choice other than to submit and play along.[472] *Pseudo-Phocylides* similarly warns against braiding the hair of young men, lest they become prey of male predators (210-214). Of fragrance Philo declares: "Of all such embellishments, used by all who deck themselves out to wear a comely appearance, fragrance is the most seductive" (*Spec.* 3.37) – Philo's assessment. He continues: "In fact the transformation of the male nature to the female is practised by them as an art and does not raise a blush (καὶ τὴν ἄρρενα φύσιν ἐπιτηδεύσει τεχνάζοντες εἰς θήλειαν μεταβάλλειν οὐκ ἐρυθριῶσι)" (*Spec.* 3.37), whereas Philo sees it as deeply shameful not only because it changes what was meant to be but also because female is inferior.

Then Philo applies Lev 20:13, which alone mentions the death penalty, but Philo takes it much further, claiming such activity warrants immediate execution: "These persons are rightly judged worthy of death by those who obey the law, which ordains that the man-woman who debases the sterling coin of nature (τὸν ἀνδρόγυνον τὸ φύσεως νόμισμα παρακόπτοντα) should perish unavenged, suffered not to live for a day or even an hour, as a disgrace to himself, his house, his native land and the whole human race" (*Spec.* 3.38). He then turns to the active male partner: "And the lover of such (ὁ παιδεραστής) may be assured that he is the subject of the same penalty. He pursues an unnatural pleasure (τὴν παρὰ φύσιν ἡδονήν) and does his best to render cities desolate and uninhabited by destroying the means of procreation (διαφθείρων τὰς γονάς)" (*Spec.* 3.39). The παρὰ φύσιν ("unnatural" or "contrary to nature") could be focusing on failure to procreate, but more likely its main focus is on what precedes, namely men behaving contrary to their nature as men and having others do so. Philo's typical concern with procreation rests on an apparently genuine fear that the spread of such activity will lead to depopulation of cities. As with his attack on adultery, he also names the effect such behaviour has on others, teaching them the vice: "Furthermore he sees no harm in becoming a tutor and instructor in the grievous vices of unmanliness and effeminacy (ἀνανδρίας καὶ μαλακίας) by prolonging the bloom of the young and emasculating the flower of their prime (τοὺς νέους ὡραΐζων καὶ τὸ τῆς ἀκμῆς ἄνθος ἐκθηλύνων), which should rightly be trained to strength and robustness" (*Spec.* 3.39). Again we see his concern about feminisation which for Philo implies weakening of the male. He then repeats the concern with procreation using his favourite agricultural imagery: "Finally, like a bad husbandman he lets the deep-soiled and fruitful fields lie sterile, by taking steps to keep them from bearing, while he spends his labour night and day on soil from which no growth at all can be expected" (*Spec.* 3.39). Taking steps to keep

---

[472] J. Edward Ellis, "Philo's View of Homosexual Activity," *PRSt* 30 (2003) 313-23, notes that Philo does not address the issue of slaves being pressed into such service (314).

them from bearing is unlikely to refer to contraception here and more likely simply to refer to neglecting of engaging in intercourse with women. The assumption is that the man engaging in such acts should be engaging in intercourse with his wife, which probably means that here as elsewhere, where Philo attacks such people for both same-sex acts and adultery, he understands such men to be what we might call bisexual, or perhaps even heterosexual, since he assumes that they are acting contrary to their nature.

Philo proffers an explanation for the flourishing of this kind of behaviour: "The reason is, I think, to be found in the prizes awarded in many nations to licentiousness and effeminacy (ἀκρασίας καὶ μαλακίας). Certainly you may see these hybrids of man and woman (ἀνδρογύνους) continually strutting about through the thick of the market, heading the processions at the feasts, appointed to serve as unholy ministers of holy things, leading the mysteries and initiations and celebrating the rites of Demeter" (*Spec.* 3.40). The focus here is again the effeminised passive partners, their prominence, an advertisement for their lifestyle. He sees this then as going to extremes: "Those of them who by way of heightening still further their youthful beauty (τὴν καλὴν νεανιείαν προσεπιτείνοντες) have desired to be completely changed into women (εἰς ἄπαν ὠρέχθησαν μεταβολῆς τῆς εἰς γυναῖκας) and gone on to mutilate their genital organs (τὰ γεννητικὰ προσαπέκοψαν), are clad in purple like signal benefactors of their native lands, and march in front escorted by a bodyguard, attracting the attention of those who meet them" (*Spec.* 3.41). We are now clearly dealing with more than just exploited slaves. Perhaps Philo's reference to mutilation of the genital organs deliberately evokes Deut 23:1 where anyone with such mutilation (ἀποκεκομμένος) is excluded from the assembly.

This is a surprisingly comprehensive description and assessment. Same-sex intercourse surfaces as a theme for extended discussion in two other books, *Contempl.* and *Abr.* We noted in 1.3.2.2.1 the discussion of same-sex intercourse in relation to Sodom in *Abr.* 133-141. There it belongs in the context of excess. "The land of the Sodomites ... was brimful of innumerable iniquities (ἀδικημάτων μυρίωμ ὅσων γεμισθεῖσα), particularly such as arise from gluttony and lewdness (μάλιστα τῶν ἐκ γαστριμαργίας καὶ λαγνείας), and multiplied and enlarged every other possible pleasure (μεγέθη καὶ πλήθη τῶν ἄλλων ἡδονῶν) with so formidable a menace that it had at last been consumed by the Judge of All" (*Abr.* 133). He speaks of the inhabitants' "extreme licence" (τῆς περὶ τὸ ἀκολασταίνειν ἀμετρίας) (*Abr.* 134). Here Philo cites Menander with approval: "the chief beginning of evils (μεγίστη δ' ἀρχὴ κακῶν), as one has aptly said, is goods in excess (τὰ λίαν ἀγαθά)" (*Abr.* 134). Then we read: "incapable of bearing such satiety, plunging like cattle, they threw off from their necks the law of nature (ἀπαυχενίζουσι τὸν της φύσεως νόμον) and applied themselves to deep drinking of strong liquor and dainty feeding and forbidden forms of intercourse (ἄκρατον πολὺν καὶ ὀψοφαγίας καὶ ὀχείας ἐκθέσμους μεταδιώκοντες)" (*Abr.* 135). Excess greed, excess liquor, excess sex go together for Philo. He then elaborates the latter: "Not only in their mad lust for women did they violate the marriages of their neighbours (οὐ μόνον θηλυμανοῦντες ἀλλοτρίους γάμους διέφθειρον), but also men mounted males (ἀλλὰ καὶ ἄνδρες ὄντες ἄρρεσιν ἐπιβαίνοντες) without respect for the sex nature which the active partner shares with the passive (τὴν κοινὴν πρὸς τοὺς πάσχοντας οἱ δρῶντες φύσιν οὐκ αἰδούμενοι)" (*Abr.* 135). This is typical of accounts of same-sex behaviour as excessive and ill-directed behaviour in depicting same-sex relations not as an alternative practised by men who were somehow different in their orientation, such as we might speak of homosexuals and some of their time spoke of people with such an orientation from birth, but as an extension of excess committed by males who also engaged in illicit relations with women.

Philo then expresses his belief that "when they tried to beget children they were discovered to be incapable of any but a sterile seed (παιδοσποροῦντες ἠλέγχοντο μὲν ἀτελῆ γονὴν σπείροντες). Yet the discovery availed them not, so much stronger was the force of the lust which mastered them (ὑπὸ βιαιοτέρας νικωμένων ἐπιθυμίας)" (*Abr.* 135). In other words such behaviour rendered them impotent. This, as we saw, is the likely meaning of the image of leaving "no ember (ἐμπύρευμα) of their male sex-nature to smoulder" in *Spec.* 3.37. As there Philo connects it to effeminisation:

> Then, as little by little they accustomed those who were by nature men to submit to play the part of women (εἶτ᾽ ἐκ τοῦ κατ᾽ ὀλίγον ἐθίζοντες τὰ γυναικῶν ὑπομένειν τοὺς ἄνδρας γεννηθέντας), they saddled them with the formidable curse of a female disease (θήλειαν κατεσκεύασαν αὐτοῖς νόσον, κακὸν δύσμαχον). For not only did they emasculate their bodies by luxury and voluptuousness (οὐ μόνον τὰ σώματα μαλακότητι καὶ θρύψει γυναικοῦντες) but they worked a further degeneration in their souls and, as far as in them lay, were corrupting the whole of mankind (τὸ σύμπαν ἀνθρώπων γένος διέφθειρον). (*Abr.* 136)

According to Philo men playing the female role, being penetrated, presumably anally, took on female (therefore inferior and less honourable) characteristics, seen as a "disease" for males.[473] Here he is depicting both the active and the passive

---

[473] On this see Szesnat, "Pretty Boys," 97-106. He observes: "Philo's basically Aristotelian conviction that a woman is a lesser man also has something to do with the term θήλεια νόσος", noting that "the connection between a man's passive role in sexual intercourse and 'disease' is fairly widespread in contemporary sources" (104). Women are not, however, depicted as diseased, for to be associated with passion and desire is their

partner as taking initiatives. He adds: "Certainly, had Greeks and barbarians joined together in affecting such unions, city after city would have become a desert, as though depopulated by a pestilential sickness" (*Abr.* 136). The assumption is twofold: both impotence and wasted semen would prevent propagation and so desolate population, the concern expressed also in *Spec.* 3.39. This is a divine concern. For

> God, moved by pity for mankind whose Saviour and Lover He was, gave increase in the greatest possible degree to the unions which men and women naturally make for begetting children (τὰς μὲν κατὰ φύσιν ἀνδρῶν καὶ γυναικῶν συνόδους γινομένας ἕνεκα παίδων σπορᾶς ηὔξησεν ὡς ἔνι μάλιστα), but abominated and extinguished this unnatural and forbidden intercourse (τὰς δ' ἐκφύλους καὶ ἐκθέσμους διαμισήσας ἔσβεσε), and those who lusted for such He cast forth (καὶ τοὺς ὀργῶντας ἐπὶ ταύτας) and chastised with punishments not of the usual kind but startling and extraordinary, newly created for this purpose. (*Abr.* 137)

In *Abr.* therefore Philo almost certainly assumes that men who do such things are also likely to engage in illicit heterosexual sex. Nothing indicates that he is operating with a notion of some as naturally homosexual, either condemning them or excluding them from condemnation. He assumes that these are normal males engaging in excessive and perverse behaviour, contrary to nature and their nature, which destroys their potency, renders the passive partners effeminate, and threatens the survival of the human race. Unlike in *Spec.* 3.37-42, he makes no reference here to the young and to pederasty. This is surely not excluded, but the primary focus is on adult-adult male sex. The story of the attempted male rape at Sodom also assumes adults.

We noted in discussing Sodom above (1.3.2.2.1) that in the places where Philo speaks of its blindness and sterility (*QG* 4.23, 31; *Congr.* 109; *Fug.* 142; *Somn.* 2.192; *Ebr.* 222) he in all probability refers to its same-sex intercourse which wastes semen and produces impotent men. Sodom is associated with

---

natural state (102, 104-105). See also William R. Schoedel, "Same-Sex Eros: Paul and the Greco-Roman Tradition," in *Homosexuality, Science, and the "Plain Sense" of Scripture* (ed. David L. Balch; Grand Rapids: Eerdmans, 2000) 43-72, who draws attention to the theories about different sexual responses in Pseudo-Aristotle *Problemata* 4.26 (879a36-880a5), including that semen in the anus incites desire for friction (52-53). He suggests that "a shift of emphasis from physical abnormality to psychological disorder aided the tendency in Jewish and Christian sources of the period to go still further and to deal with all forms of homosexuality as species of the same abnormality" (57), and that "in the world of Philo the models for male and female same-sex eros were converging so that the blanket condemnation normally reserved for same-sex eros among females was being stretched to include forms of same-sex eros among males" (56).

unnatural and strange sexual behaviour also in *Her.* 77; *Fug.* 144; *Post.* 52; *Spec.* 2.170; *Mos.* 2.55; and *Conf.* 40. The account in *QG* 4 is both literal and allegorical. It takes "Bring them out that we may know them" (Gen 19:5) as an allusion to pederasty (*QG* 4.37), as is the reference to boys in *QG* 4.39, and emphasises excess (*QG* 4.41). Otherwise Philo treats the story of Sodom as an allegory of pleasure's assaults on the soul, which should then surrender the feminine (the daughters) to survive (*QG* 4.42). Above in 1.3.2.2.1 we noted also the allegorical use of Sodom elsewhere (*QG* 4.23; *Conf.* 27-28; perhaps *Congr.* 109) and in the imagery of Gomorrah's tendrils from Deut 32:32 to depict folly and those captive to the passions (*Somn.* 2.33, 192; *Ebr.* 222), as a disease (*Sacr.* 121-122).

In *Contempl.* Philo addresses the issue in the context of contrasting meals of the Therapeutae with banquets in his world: "For waiting there are slaves of the utmost comeliness and beauty (διακονικὰ ἀνδάποδα εὐμορφότατα καὶ περικαλέστατα), giving the idea that they have come not so much to render service as to give pleasure to the eyes of the beholders by appearing on the scene (μᾶλλον ἢ τοῦ φανέντα τὴν τῶν θεωμένων ὄψιν ἡδῦναι)" (*Contempl.* 50). He then describes some "who are still boys" (παῖδες ἔτι ὄντες) and others "full-grown lads fresh from the bath and smooth shaven, with their faces smeared with cosmetics and paint under the eyelids and the hair of the head prettily plaited and tightly bound" (*Contempl.* 50). He provides a graphic description of their hairstyle and attire (*Contempl.* 51). His account then moves to another category: "In the background are others, grown lads newly bearded with the down just blooming on their cheeks (μειράκια πρωτογένεια,[474] τοὺς ἰούλους ἄρτι ἀνθοῦντες, ἀθύρματα), recently pets of the pederasts (πρὸ μικροῦ παιδεραστῶν γεγονότες), elaborately dressed up for the heavier services, a proof of the opulence of the hosts as those who employ them know, but in reality of their bad taste" (*Contempl.* 52). As Szesnat notes, "like his 'pagan' contemporaries, Philo does not seem to think that there is anything particularly odd about the object choice of the active partners; yes, they are to be condemned, *inter alia* for not controlling ἡδονή, but Philo tacitly acknowledges that the beauty of boys attracts male sexual desire (cf. 50); that is why the slave boys have been dressed up, for it enhances their beauty—albeit, in Philo's view, unnaturally so".[475] The focus here, unlike in *Abr.* 133-141, is clearly pederasty. The elaborate description continues in Philo's depiction of the sumptuous fare, the response of guests to entertainment, and their gluttony and drunkenness (*Contempl.* 53-56). He notes that many have condemned such excesses and doubtless expects his readers' assent (*Contempl.* 56). For him they serve as a foil to the frugality of the Therapeutae.

---

[474] I follow Colson's reading here (*Philo IX*, 142).
[475] Szesnat, "Pretty Boys," 95.

It is at this point that he turns to two famous banquets held in Greece in which Socrates participated and, as he notes, deemed worthy to be described by Xenophon and Plato (*Contempl.* 57). He makes his intent clear: "Even these if compared with those of our people who embrace the contemplative life will appear as matters for derision" (*Contempl.* 58). Philo then cites Xenophon's account of the banquet "as more concerned with ordinary humanity (ἀνθρωπικώτερον). There are flute girls, dancers, jugglers, fun-makers, proud of their gift of jesting and facetiousness, and other accompaniments of more unrestrained merry-making" (*Contempl.* 58; cf. Xenophon, *Symp.* 2). As Colson notes, this is a "very superficial" account which "does no justice to the mixture of banter and seriousness (ἀναμὶξ ἔσκωψ ἐάν τε καὶ ἐσπούδασαν) which characterizes most of the talk, nor to the real seriousness in Socrates' longer speech" and ignores the prominence of the love theme which he attacks in portraying Plato's symposium.[476]

Turning to Plato's *Symposium*, Philo declares that "the talk is almost entirely concerned with love (περὶ ἔρωτος), not merely with love-sickness of men for women, or women for men (οὐκ ἀνδρῶν γυναιξὶν ἐπιμανέντων ἢ γυναικῶν ἀνδράσιν αὐτὸ μόνον), passions recognized by the laws of nature (ὑποτελοῦσι γὰρ αἱ ἐπιθυμίαι αὗται νόμοις φύσεως), but of men for other males differing from them only in age (ἀλλὰ ἀνδρῶν ἄρρεσιν ἡλικίᾳ μόνον διαφέρουσι)" (*Contempl.* 59), a clear allusion to pederasty, as are the allusions to the young men earlier. Again the argument about nature relates to what Philo assumes as given, namely that sexual passions are naturally directed towards the opposite sex not one's own. He acknowledges some subtle humour in the way the account deals with "heavenly Love and Aphrodite" (*Contempl.* 59). His primary concern is with what he terms "the common vulgar love (ὁ κοινὸς καὶ πάνδημος ἔρως) which robs men of the courage (ἀνδρείαν) which is the virtue most valuable for the life both of peace and war, sets up the disease of effeminacy in their souls (θήλειαν δὲ νόσον ταῖς ψυχαῖς ἐναπεργαζόμενος) and turns into a hybrid of man and woman (ἀνδρογύνους κατασκευάζων) those who should have been disciplined in all the practices which make for valour" (*Contempl.* 60), reflecting perversion of the male. The word ἀνδρείαν here is about maleness, which Philo following the values of his time, enshrined in the language, equates with courage. Here, too, then, as in the two other accounts above, Philo sees feminisation as the effect of such practices.

Philo then addresses the issue in relation to pederasty directly: "And having wrought havoc with the years of boyhood (λυμηνάμενος δὲ τὴν παιδικὴν ἡλικίαν) and reduced the boy to the grade and condition of a girl besieged by a lover (εἰς ἐρωμένης τάξιν καὶ διάθεσιν ἀγαγών) it inflicts damage on the

---

[476] Colson, *Philo IX*, 521.

lovers also in three most essential respects, their bodies, their souls, and their property" (*Contempl.* 61). He then explains: it blinds the lover "to all other interest, private and public; his body wastes away through desire, particularly if his suit is unsuccessful, while his property is diminished by two causes, neglect and expenditure on his beloved" (*Contempl.* 61). As Szesnat notes, these are standard arguments.[477] Then Philo draws attention to the dire consequences of failure to produce offspring: "Cities are desolated, the best kind of men who become scarce, sterility and childlessness ensue through the devices of these who imitate men who have no knowledge of husbandry by sowing not in the deep soil of the lowland but in briny fields and stony and stubborn places, which not only give no possibility for anything to grow but even destroy the seed deposited within them" (*Contempl.* 62). The fear of depopulation and the agricultural imagery met us in the accounts above (*Spec.* 3.32-33, 39; *Abr.* 135-36).[478] Procreation is a primary concern. He then cites Aristophanes' myth of "double-bodied men who were originally brought by unifying forces into cohesion with each other and afterwards came asunder, as an assemblage of separate parts might do when the bond of union which brought them together was loosened" as "seductive enough, calculated by the novelty of the notion to beguile the ear", but to be treated by "the disciples of Moses trained from their earliest years to love the truth ... with supreme contempt" (*Contempl.* 63).

Many have noted the strikingly unsympathetic approach to Plato, here, compared with the respect and deference Philo shows elsewhere. If *Contempl.* has a Roman audience in mind, we may see this as an appeal which matches typical Roman sentiment against what they described as the Greek way of life, *perigraecari*.[479] Seduction of a young male citizen was *stuprum* in Roman law.[480]

This account clearly focuses on pederasty. It is distinctive in addressing the issue in the specific context of profligate banquets, in depicting such acts as the outcome of excessive indulgence there, in its detailed description of the young men involved, and in associating the attack with what was a typically Roman disapproval of what they saw as a Greek practice. Otherwise it repeats the key elements of Philo's diagnosis. Such practice is contrary to nature because it directs passion to other males instead of to women; it damages boys and young men, feminising them to the extent that they lose their maleness, including their ability to procreate, and rendering them, therefore sick with "the female disease"; and, as a consequence, threatens to depopulate cities by undermining propagation. Here, too, nothing in the account suggests that Philo assumes that these are anything

---

[477] On this as a classical argument in relation to the lover, see Szesnat, "Pretty Boys," 95.

[478] On the common agricultural topos see Szesnat, "Pretty Boys," 96.

[479] Niehoff, *Philo on Jewish Identity*, 149.

[480] Niehoff, *Philo on Jewish Identity*, 149.

other than ordinary men in his terms whose natural sexual orientation is and should be towards the opposite sex.

We may assume that Philo would have no argument with his nephew when he portrays him as observing: "Some resolve to wickedness and fall into such violent passion for unlawful sexual indulgence that they commit sodomy. They disturb not only communities but also the very order of nature. However truth herself convicts them for transgressing unalterable law, for committing immoral acts, for giving the seed to the immature, and for wasting and destroying the seed" (*Anim.* 49). The focus is failure to procreate by wasting the limited supply of semen in the young, another allusion to pederasty.[481]

In *Prob.* he refers to purchases for pederastic purposes: "It is said, for instance, that looking at one of the purchasers, an addict of effeminacy (ὅν θήλεια νόσος εἶχεν), whose face showed that he had nothing of the male about him, he went up to him and said, 'You should buy me, for you seem to me to need a husband" (*Prob.* 124). This reflects exploitation of slaves. In his digression prompted by reference to Jacob's falling asleep before his dream at Bethel, Philo deplores profligate people who live in ways that harm their own body: "into it they convey an unlimited supply of eatables one after another, until the reasoning faculty is drowned, and the sensual passions born of excess are aroused and raging with a fury that brooks no check, after falling upon and entangling themselves with all whom they meet, have disgorged their great frenzy and have abated" (*Somn.* 1.122). This echoes the emphasis on the role of excess in the accounts above. He then continues: "At night, when it is time to retire to bed, they recline exceedingly delicately on costly couches and gaily-coloured bedding with which they have provided themselves, aping the luxury of women to whom nature allows an easier mode of life, agreeable to the body of softer stamp which the Creator Artificer has wrought for them" (*Somn.* 1.122-123). As elsewhere Philo connects gluttony with the arousal of the sensual, which here means sexual, and then depicts abuse as men becoming effeminate, probably including engagement in same-sex relations, about which this concern is most expressed. In contrast to such men are those who exercise moderation, without denying the necessities of life such as food, but living in all things modestly (*Somn.* 1.124-125), though here Philo makes no mention of the sexual aspect.

Philo frequently expresses disdain of effeminacy in men. Thus the making of the bull was "the work of an effeminate (ἐκτεθηλυμμένης) and sinew-less soul", symbolised in the use of women's ear-rings (*Post.* 166). In *Her.* he speaks of the liberated, living in the restraints of the body as those "not lured by any of them to embrace like some hybrid, man-woman or woman-man (οἷα ἀνδρόγυνος ἢ γύνανδρος), the pleasant-seeming evils, but holding to its own nature of true

---

[481] On this see Terian, *De Animalibus*, 163.

manhood (ἐπὶ τῆς ἑαυτοῦ φύσεως ἀνήρ) has the strength to be victor instead of victim in the wrestling-bout" (*Her.* 274) and *Fug.* of knowing of "fathers whose effeminacy (ἀβροδίαιτον) has made them unwilling to face the strict and philosophic life of their sons, and who out of shame have chosen to live in the country instead of in the city" (*Fug.* 3). Of the effeminate he writes: "actions, meriting praise and calling out enthusiasm, and, if the expression may be permitted, masculine, they have rendered effeminate (ἐξεθήλυναν), and in performing them made them base instead of noble" (*Plant.* 158). He attacks effeminacy as among the vices of riotous feasting (*Ebr.* 21) and alleges that eunuchs, the impotent who are "neither male nor female" (*Ebr.* 212), tend to delight in the dishonourable, or, as he puts it in *Somn.* 2, in "the softer and luxurious way of life, having been reared up for the greater part of the time from their very cradle in the women's quarter and in the effeminate habits of the women's quarter (τοῖς γυναικωνίτιδος ἐκτεθηλυμμένοις ἔθεσεν)" (*Somn.* 2.9). Philo sees Deut 23:1 banning "men who belie their sex and are affected with effemination, who debase the currency of nature and violate it by assuming the passions and the outward form of licentious women. For it expels those whose generative organs are fractured or mutilated, who husband the flower of their youthful bloom, lest it should quickly wither, and restamp the masculine cast into a feminine form" (*Spec.* 1.325).

In *Spec.* 2.50 Philo condemns the man who employs the organs of generation

> for abominable lusts and forms of intercourse forbidden by all laws (πρὸς ἐνομωτάτος οἴστρους καὶ μίξεις ἀθέσμους). He not only attacks in his fury the marriage-bed of others (ἀλλοτρίοις γάμοις), but even plays the pederast and forces the male type of nature to debase and convert itself into the feminine form (ἀλλὰ καὶ παιδεραστῶν καὶ βιαζόμενος τὸν ἄρρενα τῆς φύσεως χαρακτῆρα παρακόπτειν καὶ μεταβάλλειν εἰς γυναικόμορφον ἰδέαν), just to indulge a polluted and accursed passion. (*Spec.* 2.50)[482]

Here we see not only the concern with effeminacy, but also the dual concern with adultery and same-sex relations, such as in Philo's account of Sodom in *Abr.*, where we noted this appears to assume what we would call bi-sexual behaviour.

---

[482] Ellis, "Philo's View of Homosexual Activity," reads this as rape, which may be so (315), though it could refer more to the process of feminisation. Rape is certainly mentioned in *Hypoth.* 7.1, as he notes and attempted rape is to be assumed in the Sodom story. He writes that Philo speaks of two kinds of male homosexual activity, pederasty and adult to adult, with the possibility of allusions to both involuntary and voluntary participation in each case (316). He notes three levels of objection on Philo's part: that such acts contravene nature by having one partner play a female role (317, 321-23); they reflect the excesses of over-indulgence in pleasure (318-20); and they do not serve procreation (320).

The primary focus here is pederasty, but it is interesting to see how often Philo links the two. In *Spec*. 4 he lists pederasty beside adultery among other acts of wickedness: "If the object is bodily beauty they are seducers, adulterers, pederasts (παιδεραστάς), cultivators of incontinence and lewdness, as though these worst of evils were the best of blessings" (*Spec*. 4.89), though, on the other hand, his exposition of the prohibition of adultery which lists much else (*Spec*. 4.203) fails to mention it. The two appear together also in *Hypoth*: "If you are guilty of pederasty (παιδεραστρῆς) or adultery or rape of a young person, even of a female, for I need not mention the case of a male, similarly if you prostitute yourself or allow or purpose or intend any action which your age makes indecent the penalty is death" (*Hypoth*.7.1). In contrasting Jewish morality with behaviour of his day in *Legat*. Philo singles out the two, speaking of "lasciviousness venting itself on boys and women (λαγνεῖαι διὰ παίδων καὶ γυναικῶν), and everything else that can destroy soul and body and the bonds in both which keep them together ... Self-restraint is rewarded by strength and health, incontinence by infirmity and sickness bordering on death" (*Legat*. 14). The juxtaposition of boys and women probably reflects Philo's assumption that these are not two different groups of men and their activities, but that men often engaged in both.

In other instances, allusion to same-sex relations may be present, especially when Philo speaks of the unspeakable desires or generalises. Thus the exposition of Cain's laws as promoting "unnatural lusts that may not be named (τῶν παρὰ φύσιν ἄλεκτοι ἐπιθυμίαι)" (*Post*. 52) may allude to same-sex behaviour. The same may be true of similar allusions such as "cravings which it were sinful even to name (ἅς οὐδ᾽ εἰπεῖν θέμις ὀρέξεις)" (*Opif*. 80). Same-sex intercourse may well be envisioned in the claim in *Migr*. concerning the mixed multitude of those who escaped Egypt: "It is this mixed multitude which takes delight not in a few species of lusting only (ὁ μὴ μόνον ὀλίγοις εἴδεσιν ἐπιθυμίας χαίρων), but claims to leave out nothing at all, that it may follow after lust's entire genus, including all its species. For we read 'the mixed people that was among them 'craved after lust,' (ἐπεθύμησεν ἐπιθυμίαν) after the genus itself, not some single species, 'and sat down and wept'" (Num 11:4) (*Migr*. 155).

The concern about males not losing their masculinity for inferior femininity finds expression also in Philo's exposition of the prohibition of cross-dressing: "It lays down rules even about the kind of garment which should be worn. It strictly forbids a man to assume a woman's garb, in order that no trace, no merest shadow of the female, should attach to him to spoil his masculinity (ἕνεκα τοῦ μηδὲν ἴχνος ἢ σκιὰν αὐτὸ μόνον τοῦ θήλεος ἐπὶ λύμῃ τῆς ἄρσενος γενεᾶς προσάψασθαι)" (*Virt*. 18). Philo then explains: "For since it saw as clearly, as if they were outlines on a flat surface, how unlike the bodily shapes of man and woman are, and each of the two has a different life assigned to it, to the one a domestic, to the other a civic life, it judged it well in other matters too to prescribe rules all of which though not directly made by nature were the outcome of wise reflection and in accordance with nature" (*Virt.* 19). Accordingly, he argues, "It considered that in such matters the true man should maintain his masculinity, particularly in his clothes, which as he always wears them day and night ought to have nothing to suggest unmanliness (ἀνανδρίας). In the same way he trained the women to decency of adornment and forbade her to assume the dress of a man, with the further object of guarding against the mannish-woman as much as the womanish-man (πόρρωθεν ὡς ἀνδρογύνους οὕτως καὶ γυνάνδρους φυλαξάμενος)" (*Virt.* 20-21).[483]

While Philo mostly addresses same-sex intercourse between males, he also indicates disapproval of the same between woman.[484] Thus in *QG* 2 he writes: "But after (the flood) had ceased and come to an end and they had been saved from the evil, He again instructed them through the order (of their leaving the ark) to hasten to procreate, by specifying not that men (should go out) with men nor women with women but females with males" (*QG* 2.49). Similarly in *Virt.* as just noted above, he warns of "the mannish-woman as much as the womanish-man (ὡς ἀνδρογύνους οὕτως καὶ γυνάνδρους)" (*Virt.* 20-21) and in *Her.* he reflects disdain for the "hybrid, man-woman or woman-man (ἀνδρόγυνος ἢ γύνανδρος)" (*Her.* 274).[485] Szesnat notes that Philo always uses γύνανδρος ("woman-man/mannish-woman") with ἀνδρόγυνος (man-woman/womanish-man"), the latter used 8 times to depict the feminised man carrying the same sense

---

[483] On the offensiveness of women behaving as men, especially as argued by Philo in *Virt.* 1-50 see Walter T. Wilson, "Pious Soldiers, Gender Deviants, and the Ideology of Actium: Courage and Warfare in Philo's *De Fortitudine*," *SPA* 17 (2005) 1-32. Where "women are relegated to the domestic sphere, men to the political, ... the masculine woman (ἀνδρόγυνος) is as much a threat to the law's version of courage as its corollary, the feminine man (γύνανδρος)" (21). He notes that the Midianite women function "not only as an effective enemy but also as a perverse antitype, a moral inversion of the Mosaic paradigm of virtue. This is evident in the Midianite women's contraposition both to qualities attributed to the Israelite army (especially in 24-25, 32-33, 42-45) and to the rules regarding gender differentiation laid out in 18-21" (21). He goes on to argue that Philo alludes to the battle of Actium: "By subordinating himself to a woman, Antony personified the emasculated male who abandons ancestral customs and succumbs to his desire for sex and exotic luxuries" (24). This reflected a widespread anxiety about "the need to restrict the role of women in society and control female sexuality" (24). Accordingly, "the ideology of Actium projected male ambivalence toward female otherness onto the culture of the vanquished enemy, mapping gender dominance onto the structure of Eastern conquest" (25).

[484] On this see Holger Szesnat, "Philo and Female Homoeroticism: Philo's Use of γύνανδρος and Recent Work on *Tribades*," *JSJ* 30 (1999) 140-47.

[485] So Szesnat, "Philo and Female Homoeroticism," 143.

as the verb ἐκθηλύνω (*Cher.* 52; *Spec.* 3.39) or θηλυδρίας (*Gig.* 4; *Sacr.* 32).[486] While γύνανδρος can be a synonym for ἀνδρόγυνος, its use in *Virt.* 18-21 about cross-dressing, in *Sacr.* 100 about men and women not contesting each other's roles, and in *Her.* 274, where it would otherwise be redundant, shows that "in Philo, γύνανδρος is a reference to a woman who takes on male gender characteristics".[487] The rejection of Aristophanes' mythical aetiology of same-sex desire in *Contempl.* also implies rejection of lesbian relations, though Philo does not make that explicit.

It is clear that espousing, expounding and applying the biblical prohibition of same-sex relations in Lev 18:20 and 20:13, Philo assumes that men who engage in such acts are denying what he sees as nature's proper direction and purpose for sexual desire and sexual intercourse, namely, directed to the opposite sex and for the purpose of procreation. Nothing indicates that he believes that some men are by nature otherwise oriented; indeed he lampoons Aristophanes' aetiology of sex. He frequently depicts the same men as equally profligate with women, but, again, would be unlikely to espouse the view that they were naturally bi-sexual. Most, but not all, of his statements envisage same-sex relations occurring between an older man and a youth, pederasty, sometimes voluntarily, sometimes by force, especially in exploitation of slaves, and frequently associated with excess, typified by wild parties characteristic of banquets. His exposition of the Sodom story indicates that he also viewed adult to adult male sex acts similarly. Beside noting the standard complaints of lovers suffering loss of money, time, and composure when unfulfilled, he sees same-sex acts by men as collusion by both partners in seriously undermining and perverting the masculinity of the passive partner, making him soft, feminine, and infertile, and so rendering him victim to the "female disease', a disease distinctive to men. He also cites dangers of depopulation when semen is so wrongly sown and such men become impotent. For Philo same-sex relations are one of the most serious manifestations of failure to control and rightly direct passion. While most of Philo's statements are concerned with males and reflect the settings where male same-sex relations occurred, namely, banquets, there is also sufficient evidence to assume that he condemned same-sex relations among women equally.

---

[486] Szesnat, "Philo and Female Homoeroticism," 143.

[487] Szesnat, "Philo and Female Homoeroticism," 144, and see the discussion of texts (144-46). See already Baer, *Male and Female*, 83. In Prov 18:8; 19:15 LXX the term may well also refer to the passive partners in same-sex relations.

1.4.1.3.7 Bestiality

Following his fairly extensive discussion of pederasty Philo turns to bestiality, the next in sequence in Leviticus 18 (18:23; cf. also 20:15-16; Exod 22:19), declaring: "Even worse that this is the conduct of some who have emulated the lusts of the Sybarites and those of others even more lascivious than they" (*Spec.* 3.43). Again he does not isolate bestiality but sees it belonging to the context of excess. Thus he writes: "These persons begin with making themselves experts in dainty feeding, wine-bibbing and the other pleasures of the belly and the parts below it (ταῖς ἄλλαις ταῖς γαστρὸς καὶ τῶν μετὰ γαστέρα ἡδοναῖς)" (*Spec.* 3.43). Their excess then goes beyond these: "Then sated with these they reach such a pitch of wantonness, the natural offspring of satiety, that losing their senses they conceive a frantic passion, no longer for human beings male or female, but even for brute beasts" (*Spec.* 3.43). Then, as with incest and same-sex relations, he turns for illustration to other cultures, here recalling the myth of Pasiphaë wife of King Minos of Crete who mated with a bull via the creative construction of Daedalus who had he crouch in the body of a wooden cow, as a result of which the half-beast Minotaur was born (*Spec.* 3.44). Philo comments: "Probably, if passions are suffered to go unbridled, there will be other Pasiphaës, and not only women but also men will be frantically in love with wild beasts, which will produce unnatural monsters to serve as monuments of the disgusting excesses of mankind" (*Spec.* 3.45). He also mentions "Hippocentaurs and Chimeras and the like, forms of life hitherto unknown and with no existence outside mythology" (*Spec.* 3.45). Such allusions may suggest that despite describing it as terribly grave he may not have much knowledge of the practice nor of its frequency in his time. He gives no contemporary instances. He rather goes on to forbidden cross-breeding among animals and their offspring such as mules, and then observes: "In making this provision he considered what was in accord with decency and conformity to nature, but beyond this he gave us as from some far-off commanding height a warning to men and women alike that they should learn from these examples to abstain from unlawful forms of intercourse (ὁμιλιῶν ἐκνόμων)" (*Spec.* 3.48). He then concludes: "Whether, then, it is the man who uses a quadruped for this purpose, or the woman who allows herself to be used, the human offenders must die and the beasts also; the first because they have passed beyond the limits of licentiousness itself by evolving abnormal lusts, and because they have invented strange pleasures than which nothing could be more unpleasing, shameful even to describe (ὧν καὶ ἡ διήγησις αἰσχίστη)" (*Spec.* 3.49). He adds also "the beasts because they have ministered to such infamies, and to ensure that they do not bear or beget any monstrosity of the kind that may be expected to spring from such abominations" (*Spec.* 3.49). The death penalty derives from Lev 20:15-16 (briefly also Exod 22:16), so that Philo in following Leviticus 18 is also consulting

Leviticus 20, as shown also in his citing the death penalty for same-sex intercourse.

Philo's belief that such monstrosities do occur is reflected in the speech he gives to his nephew in *Anim.* and with which he doubtless concurs. There he writes of human excesses:

> When their prostitutes are engaged by others, they pursue new passions and are incited to do unusual things. It is said that Pasiphae, daughter of Minos of Crete, was enamoured of a bull and gave birth to a monster, the Minotaur. Some men have similar insidious lusts, like that ram which lusted after Glauce the harpist. Otherwise how would a different, odd looking, and monstrous creature come into being if not through promiscuous intercourse of unlike species?" (*Anim.* 66; cf. also *Spec.* 3.43-44).

Again we find no contemporary examples. In *QG* 2 Philo says of Nimrod the hunter: "He who is among beasts seeks to equal the bestial habits of animals through evil passions" (*QG* 2.82), but these need not imply bestiality. It is interesting that while Philo acknowledges that both men and women may engage in such acts, his illustrations are all about women, whereas bestiality is probably more commonly practised by men.

1.4.1.3.8 Prostitution

Philo then moves beyond Leviticus 18 to address prostitution, though quite briefly (*Spec.* 3.51). The biblical basis appears to be Deut 23:17, which originally concerned prostitution in relation to the temple, as the following verse suggests, forbidding bringing a prostitute's earnings into the temple, but the LXX prefixes the statement about temple prostitution in 23:17 with a reference to prostitution in general:

> לא תהיה קדשה מבנות ישראל ולא יהיה קדש מבני ישראל
> None of the daughters of Israel shall be a temple prostitute; none of the sons of Israel shall be a temple prostitute.
> οὐκ ἔσται πόρνη ἀπὸ θυγατέρων Ισραηλ καὶ οὐκ ἔσται πορνεύων ἀπὸ υἱῶν Ισραηλ οὐκ ἔσται τελεσφόρος ἀπὸ θυγατέρων Ισραηλ καὶ οὐκ ἔσται τελισκόμενος ἀπὸ υἱῶν Ισραηλ.
> There shall not be a prostitute among the daughters of Israel; there shall not be one that practices prostitution among the sons of Israel.
> There shall not be an initiate among the daughters of Israel, and there shall not be anyone initiated among the sons of Israel. (NETS) Deut 23:17

Philo understands the prohibition of prostitution in a broad sense, but focuses only on the female prostitute:[488] "Again, the commonwealth of Moses' institution does not admit a harlot (πόρνην), that stranger to decency and modesty and temperance and the other virtues" (*Spec.* 3.51). He then explains: "She infects the souls both of men and women with licentiousness (ἀκολασίας). She casts shame upon the undying beauty of the mind and prefers in honour the short-lived comeliness of the body (τὴν δὲ τοῦ σώματος ὀλιγοχρόνιον εὐμορφίαν)" (*Spec.* 3.51). The women infected with licentiousness will be the prostitutes, themselves, the men, their clients. Typically Philo contrasts external beauty and beauty of the mind, attributing to prostitutes a preference for the former. This suggests he sees them not just acting as professionals, but actually having specific interest in external beauty, something which need not follow, since external appearance may simply serve to lure clients. He goes on: "She flings herself at the disposal of chance comers, and sells her bloom like some ware to be purchased in the market. In her every word and deed she aims at capturing the young (τῶν νέων), while she incites her lovers each against the other by offering the vile prize of herself to the highest bidder" (*Spec.* 3.51). The emphasis on the young reflects the situation where men usually did not marry until around thirty and so were a ready market for prostitutes till then. Philo also informs us here that prostitutes played the market selling themselves to the highest bidder. He then concludes: "A pest, a scourge, a plague-spot (ὡς λύμη καὶ ζημία καὶ κοινὸν μίασμα)–she who has corrupted the graces bestowed by nature (τὰς της φύσεως διαφθείρασα χάριτας), instead of making them, as she should, the ornament of noble conduct" (*Spec.* 3.51). This is interesting on two counts. "The graces bestowed by nature" must refer to proper sexual behaviour, understood by Philo as always combining procreation and pleasure, as "the ornament of noble conduct", as positive comment about sex in the right context. The other is that he cites the death penalty "let her be stoned to death", without biblical foundation.[489]

Prostitution features frequently in Philo, as one might expect since it is one of the main channels through which he sees illicit sexual pleasure plaguing men. For that reason it also features representatively of all assaults of the passions and

---

[488] John William Wevers, *Notes on the Greek Text of Deuteronomy* (SBLSCS 39; Atlanta: Scholars, 1995) interprets the expanded translation thus: "A πόρνη as τελισφόρος is a female cult prostitute, whereas a πορνευών/τελισκόμενος was a male who made use of such a prostitute" (372). "The translator was obviously not satisfied with a ban on prostitution; it was therefore connected with religion by means of the second rendering" (372).

[489] On the death penalty Belkin, *Philo and the Oral Law*, comments: "I believe that all the passages in Philo which speak about harlotry as a capital offense are merely apologetic in character" (256); otherwise, he argues, it makes little sense that Philo can speak of allowing marriage to former prostitutes (257).

allegorically of all illicit relations. In Joseph's rejection of Potiphar's wife's seduction he declares: "Other nations are permitted after the fourteenth year to deal without interference with harlots and strumpets (πόρναις καὶ χαμαιτύπαις) and all those who make a traffic of their bodies, but with us a courtesan is not even permitted to live (παρ' ἡμῖν δὲ οὐδ' ἑταίρᾳ ζῆν ἔξεστιν), and death is the penalty appointed for women who ply this trade" (Ios. 43). Philo's allegation about other nations probably contains some grain of truth. It makes sense given the age disparity at time of marriage between men and women. We note another reference to the death penalty (also in Hypoth. 7.1) and also the three words for prostitutes, courtesans belonging more at the level of the elite.

In Mos. 1 Philo deplores those going to prostitutes without shame, with head held high (Mos. 1.302). He also has his nephew deplore men "who are not satisfied with their wives alone but look elsewhere and stray to prostitutes" (Anim. 49) or who "when their prostitutes are engaged by others, they pursue new passions and are incited to do unusual things" (Anim. 66).

Philo acknowledges the commercial interest of the prostitute more strongly in Plant., where he writes that "in the tree of friendship there are outgrowths, such as I shall describe, to be pruned and cut off for the sake of preserving the better part. Such outgrowths are practices of courtesans (ἑταιρῶν) for taking in their lovers, ways parasites have of deceiving their dupes" (Plant. 104). His focus here is on deceit: "You may see women, who earn money by the prostitution of their bodily charms, clinging to those enamoured of them as though they intensely loved them. It is not these that they love; they love themselves and are greedy for their daily takings" (Plant. 105). Philo refers to the range of prostitutes' accomplices when speaking of the worthless man of wealth "living in a whirl of prodigality, ever ready to fling away money and to guzzle—an ever-active patron of courtesans, pimps, panders, and every licentious crew (ἑταιρῶν καὶ πορνοτρόφων καὶ μαστροπῶν καὶ παντὸς ἀκολάστου θιάσου χορηγὸς φιλοτιμότατος)" (Fug. 28).

Philo also allows us some insight into abuse of prostitutes when he describes one of the curses of the future as when men shall see "the women whom they took in lawful wedlock for the procreation of true-born children, chaste domestic loving wives, outraged as though they were harlots" (Praem. 139) and targets of rape (Praem. 140). In Virt. he warns against exploiting a captive wife, having noted the 30 day waiting period: "After this, live with her as your lawful wife, because holiness requires that she who is to enter a husband's bed, not as a hired harlot (μὴ κατὰ μισθαρνίαν ὡς ἑταίραν), trafficking her youthful bloom, but either for love of her mate or for the birth of children (δι' ἔρωτα τοῦ συνιόντος ἢ διὰ τέκνων γένεσιν), should be admitted to the rights of full wedlock as her due" (Virt. 112). In expounding the law on false accusations against wives, Philo speaks of those who "retain no conjugal affection for their wives (μηδὲν οἰκεῖον ἐπὶ ταῖς γαμεταῖς πάθος σῴζοντες), and insult and treat the gentlewomen as if they were harlots (ἀλλ' ὑβρίσαντες καὶ ὡς ἑταίραις ταῖς ἀσταῖς προσενεχθέντες)" (*Spec.* 3.80), implying abuse of prostitutes was somehow normal. His allegorical use of the image in *Her.* also reflects abuse, when it depicts the soul as "a chaos of unreasoning passions, held down by a multitude of vices; sometimes mauled by greed and lust, like a strumpet in the stews (ὥσπερ ἐν χαμαιτυπείῳ περιυβριζομένην), sometimes fast bound as in a prison by a multitude of ill deeds, ..." (*Her.* 109).

In depicting the abduction of Dinah, Philo echoes the brothers' objection in Gen 34:31 ("Should our sister be treated like a whore?") in the words, "for albeit there was a Divine decree that 'of the daughters of Israel, the seeing one, none might ever become a harlot' (οὐκ ἂν γένοιτό ποτε πόρνη τῶν τοῦ βλέποντος, Ἰσραήλ, θυγατέρων), these men hoped to carry off unobserved the virgin soul" (*Migr.* 224), an allusion to Deut 23:17 LXX. Then in the story of Judah and Tamar, in which Philo nowhere condemns Tamar's act, who for him symbolises virtue (*Congr.* 125-126; *Fug.* 153), he slips in and out of allegory to emphasise that in "Suffer me to come in unto thee" by "'Suffer me,' he means (for he would not use force to her), 'suffer me to see that is the virtue which veils its face from me, and what purpose it is prepared to serve.'" (*Congr.* 126). He did not rape her. His efforts to sanitise reflect that Philo knows that in reality it often turned out otherwise for such women. Depicting her as veiled (*Congr.* 125) reflects another detail of practice.

On the other hand, Philo makes a case for men (though not priests) marrying a former prostitute: "Nor let anyone else be prevented from taking her in marriage, but let her not come near to the priest" (*Spec.* 1.102). Philo grounds the prohibition against priests marrying prostitutes (Lev 21:7) as follows: "a harlot is profane in body and soul, even if she has discarded her trade and assumed a decent and chaste demeanour, and he is forbidden even to approach her, since her old way of living was unholy" (*Spec.* 1.102), adding: "For in the souls of the repentant there remain, in spite of all, the scars and prints of their old misdeeds" (*Spec.* 1.103). It would also, he argues, result in some of her money coming into the temple, expressly forbidden in Deut 23:18 (*Spec.* 1.104).

Philo frequently depicts what he sees as the prostitute's demeanour. Thus in *QG* 4 he asserts that "beauty of form, which consists of symmetry of parts and beauty of form such as even harlots have ... a shameless look and an elevated neck and a continuous movement of the eyebrows and a womanish walk and not blushing at, or being ashamed of, any evil at all is the sign of a lewd soul" (*QG* 4.99). The Midianites' strategy of seduction of young men by beautiful women acting as prostitutes probably reflects the usual focus of the trade, though here it serves another purpose. In this context Philo has the strategists reflect typical values. They "sent for the most exquisitely beautiful among their women and said to them, ..." (*Virt.* 35). They explained: "Now man is easily led captive by pleasure (ἡδονῇ δ' ἁλωτὸν ἄνθρωπος), and particularly by the pleasure of intercourse with women (μάλιστα συνουσίᾳ τῇ πρὸς γυναῖκα). You are exceedingly comely; beauty is naturally seductive, and youth easily lapses into incontinence (ἡ δὲ νεότης εἰς ἀκρασίαν εὐόλισθον). Do not fear the names of harlotry and adultery (ἑταιρήσεως ἢ μοιχείας)" (*Virt.* 36). Accordingly, the women deck themselves out to capture the youths (*Virt.* 39) and "with meretricious glances and wheedling talk and lewd attitudes and movements, they set their bait before the weaker-minded part of the younger men" (*Virt.* 40), leading them to idolatry. Similarly in *Mos.* 1 he reports Balaam's advice: "'You have in your countrywomen, king,' he said, 'persons of pre-eminent beauty. And there is nothing to which a man more easily halls a captive than women's comeliness. If, then, you permit the fairest among them to prostitute themselves for hire, they will ensnare the younger of their enemies'", even proffering the subtlety: "You must instruct them not to allow their wooers to enjoy their charms at once. For coyness titillates, and thereby makes the appetites more active, and inflames the passions (ὁ γὰρ ἀκκισμὸς ὑποκνίζων τὰς ὁρμὰς ἐπεγείρε μᾶλλον καὶ τοὺς ἔρωτας ἀναφλέγει). And, when their lust has them in its grip (τραχηλιζόμενοι δὲ ταῖς ἐπιθυμίαις), there is nothing which they will shrink from doing or suffering'" (*Mos.* 1.296-297).

Often Philo's depiction of the prostitute serves a symbolic end, as she represents the seductress, the lure of illicit pleasure, quite often with no particular focus on sexual wrongdoing itself. So Philo depicts her as Pleasure, who "being a courtesan and a wanton (ἑταιρὶς καί μαλχάς), eagerly desires to meet with a lover (γλίχεται τυχεῖν ἐραστοῦ), and searches for panders (μαστροποὺς ἀναζητεῖ), by whose means she shall get one on her hook" (*Opif.* 166). Similarly in *Sacr.* he introduces his extensive depiction of the seductress, as the loved wife of Deut 21:15-17, with the words:

> So pleasure come languishing in the guise of a harlot or courtesan. Her gait has the looseness which her extravagant wantonness and luxury had bred; the lascivious roll of her eyes is a bait to entice the souls of the young; her look speaks of boldness and shamelessness; her neck is held high; she assumes a stature which Nature has not given her; she grins and giggles; her hair is dressed in curious and elaborate plaits; under her eyes are pencil lines; her eyebrows are smothered in paint; she revels perpetually in the warmth of the bath; her flush is artificial; her costly raiment is broidered lavishly with flowers ... a strumpet of the streets, she takes the market-place for her home; devoid of true beauty, she pursues the false. (*Sacr.* 21).

Philo also treats the prohibition of bringing a prostitute's earnings into the temple (Deut 23:18) symbolically of banning spiritual prostitution: "There is a very excellent ordinance inscribed in the sacred tables of the law, that the hire of a harlot should not be brought into the temple; the hire, that is, of one who has sold her personal charms and chosen a scandalous life for the sake of the wages of shame" (*Spec.* 1.280). He continues: "But if the gifts of one who has played the harlot are unholy, surely more still are the gifts of the soul which has committed whoredom, which has thrown itself away into ignominy and the lowest depths of outrageous conduct, into wine-bibbing and gluttony, into the love of money, of reputation, of pleasure, and numberless other forms of passion and soul-sickness and vice" (*Spec.* 1.281). Here he goes on to note that "the harlot's traffic indeed is often brought to a close by old age", when the bloom fades, in contrast to the soul (*Spec.* 1.282).

In Deut 23:1-2, which stipulates who may not enter the congregation, Philo found another reference to a prostitute, where LXX renders ממזר by ἐκ πόρνης: "he that is born of a harlot shall not enter the congregation of the Lord" (οὐκ εἰσελεύσεται ἐκ πόρνης εἰς ἐκκλησίαν κυρίου). He frequently gives this an allegorical meaning as indicating polytheists, who are like persons born of prostitutes and not knowing the true father and so honouring all (*Decal.* 8-9; *Spec.* 1.326, 331-332; *Migr.* 69; *Conf.* 144; *Mut.* 205). He can then transfer that symbolism so that in allegorising the high priest he writes: "But the promiscuous polyandrous cause of polytheism, or rather atheism, the harlot, he deigns not even to look at, having learned to love her who had adopted, as her one Husband and Father, God the All-sovereign" (*Fug.* 114). As noted above, he also uses this text both literally and metaphorically in relation to eunuchs, the sterile, and the effeminate who castrate themselves and in *Ebr.* to apply to the builders of Babel and even Joseph, when he symbolises engagement with pleasure, people unable to generate offspring to wisdom (*Ebr.* 213). As noted above, Philo can also use the image of the prostitute to depict the plight of the soul which denies dependence on God and claims its own self-sufficiency in relation to soul, senses, and speech, as trapped and imprisoned like a vulnerable prostitute, "held down by a multitude of vices; sometimes mauled by greed and lust, like a strumpet in the stews (ὥσπερ ἐν χαμαιτυπείῳ περιυβριζομένην), sometimes fast bound as in a prison by a multitude of ill deeds, ..." (*Her.* 109).

Philo's Bible leaves him in no doubt that prostitution is outlawed, though he goes beyond it in requiring the death penalty. Both his literal and allegorical references reflect a setting where prostitution was familiar and widely used. It will have been a significant issue for single young men through their twenties. We may assume that represented one of the major ways in which Philo would see them failing to control their passions. His descriptions provide us an image of various kinds of prostitution, from the basic to the sophisticated courtesan, as well detail of their attire and techniques, such as using agents and pimps. His accounts also allow us to see the wretched plight which prostitutes could face. By allegory he escapes facing up to Tamar's act of prostitution, turning it on its head, so that Judah can even symbolise God. Much of the time the image does not address sexual wrongdoing in particular but stands for the dangers of seduction to wrongdoing and surrender of the mind to the senses in general.

1.4.1.3.9 Accusations of Adultery

Next Philo also alludes to the law dealing with accusation of adultery by a wife (*Spec.* 3.52-63; cf. Num 5:12-31). Perhaps the association with what precedes is that some wives might engage in prostitution, which would also be adultery. Here Philo adds a preliminary hearing (*Spec.* 3.53-55). He then adds: "So careful is the law to provide against the introduction of violent changes in the institution of marriage that a husband and wife, who have intercourse in accordance with the legitimate usages of married life, are not allowed, when they leave their bed, to touch anything until they have made their ablutions and purged themselves with water" (3.63). Philo is referring to the purity law in Lev 15:18, "If a man lies with a woman and has an emission of semen, both of them shall bathe in water, and be unclean until the evening". Philo ignores the issues of timing (though he notes it in *Spec.* 1.119)[490] and treats the bathing as signifying the level of care which the Law demands, which then, by extension, belongs to anything else relevant to keeping the marriage in order, not least avoiding adultery: "This ordinance extends by implication to a prohibition of adultery, or anything which entails an accusation of adultery" (*Spec.* 3.63). This still leaves open the question whether Philo would have observed the literal requirement or espoused it. In all probability he did, rather than taking the stance of the radical allegorisers attacked in *Migr.* 89-93, who probably would not have.

In *Cher.* he writes about uncovering the woman's head (cited also in *Spec.* 3.56), treating it as a symbol of her exposure to divine knowing: "Now we see the cause why Reason, the priest and prophet, is bidden to set the soul 'over against the Lord' with her head uncovered, that is with the dominant principles, which constitute her head, laid bare, and the motives which she has cherished, stripped of their trappings, so that, being judged by the all-penetrating eye of God the incorruptible, she may either like counterfeit coinage have her lurking dissimulation revealed, or being innocent of all evil may, by appealing to the testimony of Him who alone can see the soul naked, wash away the charges brought against her" (*Cher.* 17). When Philo alludes to the case of suspected adultery in Num 5:27 allegorically in *Leg.* 3.148, he does so to speak of the soul's

---

[490] On *Spec.* 3.63 see Belkin, *Philo and the Oral Law*, who notes that *Spec.* 1.119 records waiting till sunset, but applied only to the priest (224).

breaching its relation to its lawful husband by having "intercourse with soul-defiling passion (προσκεχωρηκυῖα τῷ μιαίνοντι τὴν ψυχὴν πάθει)".

1.4.1.3.10 Rape of a Widow or Divorcee and Seduction or Rape of an Unmarried, Unbetrothed Woman

Philo then goes on in *Spec.* 3 to address the rape of a widow or divorced woman: "if anyone dishonours by violence (βιασάμενος αἰσχύνῃ) a woman widowed by the death of her husband or through any other form of separation, the crime he commits is less serious than in adultery" (*Spec.* 3.64), probably because he considers fewer people affected, not least another man's interests. While this is unaddressed in biblical law,[491] it is closely related to the case of sex with an unmarried, unbetrothed, woman, which immediately follows (*Spec.* 3.65-71), which is addressed as seduction in Exod 22:16-17 and rape in Deut 22:28-29. On this he writes: "The corruption (φθορά) of a maiden is a criminal offence closely akin to adultery (μοιχείας), its brother in fact, for both spring as it were from one mother, licentiousness (ἀκολασίας), which some whose way is to bedizen ugly things with specious terms, ashamed to admit its true nature, give the name of love (ἔρωτα)" (*Spec.* 3.65). This is a perceptive observation about the processes of rationalisation to avoid responsibility. Philo then modifies the comparison with adultery: "Still the kinship does not amount to complete similarity, because the wrong caused by the corruption is not passed on to several families as it is with adultery, but is concentrated in one, that of the maiden herself" (*Spec.* 3.65). It also dishonours her family in Philo's frame of thinking. He then addresses the perpetrator with the advice: "If you have, heart and soul, centred your affections on the girl, go to her parents, if they are still alive, or, if not, to her brothers or guardians or others who have charge of her, lay bare before them the state of your affections, as a free man should, ask her hand in marriage and plead that you may not be thought unworthy of her" (*Spec.* 3.67). His advice reflects the patriarchal system of guardianship of daughters by the father, then next the brothers, and next other appointed guardians in that order of right.

Philo then addresses the situation where such advice is refused: "But if anyone in furious frenzy will have nothing to say to the suggestions of reason, but regarding wild passion and lust as sovereign powers (δυναστείαν τὸν οἶστρον καὶ τὴν ἐπιθυμίαν ὑπολαβών) and giving the place of honour to violence above law (νόμου βίαν), as the saying goes, turns to rapine and ravishment and treats free women as though they were servant-maids (ἁρπάζῃ καὶ φθείρῃ ταῖς

---

[491] Belkin, *Philo and the Oral Law*, suggests it probably reflects jurisprudence in Alexandrian courts (257-58). That much of Philo's exposition in *Spec.* reflects such practice see Böhm, *Vätererzählungen*, 179.

ἐλευθέραις ὡς θεραπαίναις χρώμενος), acting in peace as he might in wartime, he must be brought before the judges" (*Spec.* 3.69). This reflects his psychology: passions rule instead of being ruled. His comment about treating free women "as though they were servant-maids" and "acting in peace as he might in war" assumes sexual exploitation of household slaves and victims of war, but it is not clear if in citing these, Philo approves or disapproves, though nothing elsewhere suggests anything other than the former.

Here Philo addresses the issues of payment: "And if the victim of the violation has a father he must consider the question of espousing her to the author of her ruin. If he refuses, the seducer must give a dowry to the girl, his punishment being thus limited to a monetary fine, but if the father consents to the union, he must marry her without any delay and agree to give the same dowry as in the former case, and he must not be at liberty to draw back, or to make difficulties" (*Spec.* 3.70). Here Philo has merged the two biblical accounts, Exod 22:16-17 and Deut 22:29, choosing the Exodus text as his base, which speaks of assent or refusal by the father,[492] but Philo has changed the penalty from a bride-price or its equivalent as a fine paid to the father to a dowry or its equivalent paid to the woman. This probably reflects the standard practices of his day, where bride prices did not feature and Philo's reading of the Greek φερνή as dowry.[493] The comment, "he must not be at liberty to draw back, or to make difficulties", is probably Philo's interpretation of the words in Deut 22:17: "Because he violated her he shall not be permitted to divorce her as long as he lives". Thus Philo goes on to explain that "This is in the interest both of himself, to make the rape appear due to legitimate love rather than to lasciviousness, and of the girl, to give her for the misfortune, which she has suffered at their first association, the consolation of a wedlock so firmly established that nothing but death will undo it" (*Spec.* 3.70). Nothing in this suggests that Philo might consider that the daughter, herself, should have a say, even though he notes her wronging, so she remains a victim of men's interests. He does suggest she be given a say where her father is no longer alive: "If she has lost her father, she must be asked by the judges whether she wishes to consort with the man or not" (*Spec.* 3.71). This is interesting since Philo makes no mention here of brothers or other guardians, but rather assumes a court hearing, perhaps reflecting practice in his community. He then adds: "And whether she agrees or refuses, the terms agreed upon must be the same as they would have been if her father were alive" (*Spec.* 3.71).

---

[492] Cf. the merging of these texts also in the *Temple Scroll* (11QT^a/11Q19 66.1-8a). On this see Loader, *Dead Sea Scrolls on Sexuality*, 31-32.

[493] See Satlow, *Jewish Marriage*, 69-72. He notes that the LXX uses φερνή to translate מֹהַר (*mohar*) ("bride price"), e.g., Exod 22:16.

1.4.1.3.11 Intercourse with a Woman Espoused to be Married to Another

Philo then turns to what precedes the account of the unbetrothed woman in Deut 22:28-29, namely intercourse with a woman betrothed to another man (Deut 22:23-27; *Spec.* 3.72). Again he relates it to adultery: "Some consider that midway between the corruption of a maiden and adultery (φθορᾶς καὶ μοιχείας) stands the crime committed on the eve of marriage (ὑπογάμιον), when mutual agreements (ὁμολογίαι) have affianced the parties beyond all doubt, but before the marriage was celebrated, another man, either by seduction or violence, has intercourse with the bride (ἕτερος ἀπατήσας τις ἢ καὶ βιασάμενος εἰς ὁμιλίαν ἔλθῃ)" (*Spec.* 3.72). He considers this "a form of adultery" (μοιχείας ... εἶδος) (*Spec.* 3.72). The detail reflects the probable situation that Philo does not know of a longer period of betrothal, but only of final agreements just before the marriage.[494] Of these he writes: "For the agreements (ὁμολογίαι), being documents containing the names of the man and the woman, and the other particulars needed for wedlock, are equivalent to marriage. And therefore the law ordains that both should be stoned to death, if, that is, they set about their misdeeds by mutual agreement with one and the same purpose" (*Spec.* 3.72-73). The penalty accords with Deut 22:23-24a. He cites the death penalty for rape also in *Hypoth.* 7.1.

Philo then proceeds to expound the qualifications brought in the biblical text relating to non-consensual sex. "Naturally it is greater if the act is committed in the city and less if it is committed outside the walls and in a solitude" (*Spec.* 3.74). The focus is the woman's guilt on the assumption that she should have cried out and could have been heard, had she done so, in the city, where according to Philo there is always "a champion ready to do battle for anyone who to all appearance has been wronged" (*Spec.* 3.75). Thus for the girl outside the city "pity and forgiveness attend her" (*Spec* 3.76), but for the other there is "inexorable punishment". Philo then notes the fallibility of the biblical provision based on place: "Indeed her position demands careful inquiry from the judge who must not make everything turn upon the scene of the act. For she may have been forced against her will in the heart of the city, and she may have surrendered voluntarily to unlawful embraces outside the city" (*Spec.* 3.77). This cuts both ways: against a woman making location outside the city an excuse (*Spec.* 3.77) and in favour of a woman who might have been bound and gagged in the city (*Spec.* 3.78).

---

[494] So Satlow, *Jewish Marriage*, 71-72.

1.4.1.3.12 Accusations that One's Wife was not a Virgin at Marriage

Philo then generalises his concern about abuse of women: "There are some persons who show fickleness in their relations to women (περὶ τὰς ὁμιλίας ἀψίκοροι), mad for them and loathing them at the same time (γυναικομανεῖς ἐν ταὐτῷ καὶ μισογύναιοι), each of them a mass of chaotic and promiscuous characteristics (συγκλύδων καὶ μιγάδων ἠθῶν ἀνάπλεῳ)" (*Spec.* 3.79). Again Philo reaches a significant level of discernment in noting that anger against women can masquerade as love and lead to sexual abuse. His psychology sees such men surrendering immediately "to their first impulses (ὁρμαῖς) of any and every kind and let them go unbridled instead of reining them in as they should" (*Spec.* 3.79). Philo then uses this to introduce his exposition of the man who falsely accuses his wife of not having been a virgin at their marriage, working backwards through Deuteronomy 22 to take up 22:13-21.

> In the case of persons who take maidens in lawful matrimony and have celebrated the bridal sacrifices and feasts (κόρας οἱ ἀγόμενοι νόμῳ καὶ γάμους θύσαντές τε καὶ ἑστιαθέντες), but retain no conjugal affection for their wives (μηδὲν οἰκεῖον ἐπὶ ταῖς γαμεταῖς πάθος σῴζοντες), and insult and treat these gentlewomen as if they were harlots (ἀλλ' ὑβρίσαντες καὶ ὡς ἑταίραις ταῖς ἀσταῖς προσενεχθέντες)— if such persons scheme to effect a separation (διάζευξιν τεχνάζωσι), but finding no pretext for divorce (μηδεμίαν ἀπαλλαγῆς πρόφασιν ἀνευρίσκοντες) resort to false accusation and through lack of matters of open daylight shift the charges to secret intimacies and bring forward an incriminating statement that the virgins whom they supposed they had married were discovered by them, when they first came together, to have lost their virginity already—then the whole body of elders will assemble to try the matter and the parents will appear to plead the cause in which all are endangered. (*Spec.* 3.80)

The passage is rich in its incidental references: to "bridal sacrifices and feasts"; proper passion for wives (οἰκεῖον ἐπὶ ταῖς γαμεταῖς πάθος), abuse of prostitutes, and procedures for divorce, namely finding a cause (cf. Deut 24:1). Philo goes on to note that "the danger affects not only the daughters whose bodily chastity is impugned, but also their guardians, against whom the charge is brought not only that they failed to watch over them at the most critical period of adolescence, but that the brides they had given as virgins had been dishonoured by other men, and thereby the bridegrooms were cheated and deceived" (*Spec.* 3.81), reflecting especially the arena of male concerns and male honour. In this context he makes no mention of showing sheets (cf. Deut 22:16-17), possibly because he perceives its flawed character – it would be easy to produce blood stains, nor of inspections before or after to confirm virginity (cf. 4Q159/4QOrd^a 2-4+8 8-10),[495] but deals only with punishments, and then, with focus only on the male accuser (*Spec.* 3.81-82).[496] Thus he mentions the fines stipulated in Deut 22:19, but not the amount of 100 shekels, but then adds: "bodily degradation in the form of stripes, and what is most distasteful of all to the culprits, confirmation of the marriage, if, that is, the women can bring themselves to consort with such persons" (*Spec.* 3.82). He then elaborates: "For the law permits wives to stay or separate as they wish, but deprives the husbands of any choice either way, as a punishment for their slanderous accusations" (*Spec.* 3.82). The restriction on husbands reflects Deut 22:19, which does not mention the wife's freedom, though Philo probably adduces it on the basis of the limitation being applied only to the husband.

1.4.2 Beyond the Prohibition of Adultery and Associated Laws

Thus far we have considered the prohibition of adultery and what Philo associates with it, especially following *Decal.* and *Spec.* 3. In what follows we consider other laws in *Decal.* and *Spec.* 1-4 which have some relevance to sexual issues, following the sequence, therefore of the commandments of the decalogue, but dealing only with matters not already addressed above and which pertain to the theme.

1.4.2.1 *Circumcision*

We follow Philo's own lead in *Spec.* of first addressing circumcision before taking up the decalogue as a set of headings.[497] Philo has no doubt about the requirement of circumcision, firmly rejecting "some who, regarding laws in their literal sense in the light of symbols of matters belonging to the intellect, are over

---

[495] On this see Loader, *Dead Sea Scrolls on Sexuality*, 217-21.

[496] So Belkin, *Philo and the Oral Law*, who notes also that punishment by stripes reflects not the language of Deut 32:13 LXX, but probably reflects court practice in Alexandria. "It is to be noted that though Philo allows the double penalty for the husband who falsely reproaches his wife, he has no basis for it in the Bible. This conclusively shows that he is not interpreting the biblical text, but is referring to the procedure of the Alexandrian courts" (268).

[497] Reinhard Weber, *Das "Gesetz" bei Philon von Alexandrien und Flavius Josephus: Studien zum Verständnis und zur Funktion der Thora bei den beiden Hauptzeugen des hellenistischen Judentums* (ARGU 11; Frankfurt: Peter Lang, 2001) suggests that Philo places it first because it was especially attacked and ridiculed by Jewish opponents (147), but notes that Philo treats it not only as a sign of the covenant but as something commendable to all humanity (149).

overpunctilious about the latter, while treating the former with easy-going neglect" (*Migr.* 89), including the Sabbath, the festivals and circumcision (*Migr.* 91-92). Much of his discussion in *Spec.* 1 is paralleled but in greater detail in *QG* 3, so that we consider both together. He compares Israel's practice of circumcising males on the eighth day with that of Egypt of circumcising both males and females and then only at the age of 14 (*QG* 3.47; cf. also *Spec.* 1.2), dismissing the need for circumcising females on the grounds that in his view "the male has more pleasure in, and desire for, mating" (*QG* 3.47), an extraordinary claim, but a widely held male myth until even recent times. He also justifies the practice of circumcision of males on grounds of preventing infection and that it ensures the semen does not become lost in the foreskin's folds (*QG* 3.48; *Spec.* 1.4, 7), reflecting the widespread view that semen can be wasted and is in danger of therefore running out. Accordingly, he claims that "such nations as practise circumcision increase greatly in population" (*QG* 3.48). He notes Ishmael's circumcision at age thirteen, appropriate, he argues, since it was close to fourteen "when the generative movements are brought to their seed" (*QG* 3.61) since it is right for "him who is about to undertake marriage by all means to circumcise his sense-pleasures and amorous desires, rebuking those who are lascivious and lustful, in order that they may restrain their excessive embraces, which usually come about not for the sake of begetting children but for the sake of unrestrained pleasure" (*QG* 3.61). Here we see Philo's symbolic interpretation. Similarly in *Spec.* 1 he speaks of

> excision of pleasures which bewitch the mind (ἡδονῶν ἐκτομῆς, αἳ καταγοητεύουσι διάνοιαν). For since among the love-lures of pleasure the palm is held by the mating of a man and woman (ἐπειδὴ γὰρ τὰ νικητήρια φέρεται τῶν ἐν ἡδοναῖς φίλτρων ἡ ἀνδρὸς πρὸς γυναῖκα συνουσία), the legislators thought good to dock the organ which ministers to such intercourse, thus making circumcision the figure of the excision of excessive and superfluous pleasure (αἰνιττομένοις περιτομὴν περιττῆς ἐκτομὴν καὶ πλεοναζούσης ἡδονῆς), not only of one pleasure, but of all the other pleasures signified by one, and that the most imperious (οὐ μιᾶς, ἀλλὰ διὰ μιᾶς τῆς βιαστικωτάτης καὶ τῶν ἄλλων ἁπασῶν). (*Spec.* 1.9)

This is a good example of where a superficial reading of Philo's rhetoric might seize on ἡδονῶν ἐκτομῆς, ("excision of pleasures") to conclude that Philo advocates denial of pleasure, including, therefore, sexual pleasure, whereas the concluding comments make very clear that the issue is excess. Similarly in *QG* 3 he writes: "the greatest desire is that of intercourse between man and woman, since it forms the beginning of a great thing, procreation, and brings about in the progenitors a great desire toward their progeny, for it is rather natural to be very fond of, and tender toward, them. And it indicates the cutting off not only of excessive desires but also of arrogance and great evil and such habits" (*QG* 3.48).

The note of affection, while here related to attitudes to offspring, is probably also implied as belonging also to the relation of husband and wife, expressed in their sexual intimacy. The act of circumcision says something about curbing both excessive sexual pleasure, and excess in relation to all pleasure. Thus in *Spec.* 1 he uses agricultural metaphor to say the same: "'Circumcise the hardness of your hearts!' make speed, that is, to prune away from the ruling mind the superfluous overgrowths sown and raised by the immoderate appetites of the passions and planted by folly, the evil husbandman of the soul" (*Spec.* 1.305). In *QE* 2 he so emphasises the symbolic meaning that it almost calls the literal into question: "the sojourner is one who circumcises not his uncircumcision but his desires and sensual pleasures and the other passions of the soul. For in Egypt the Hebrew nation was not circumcised" (*QE* 2.2). Philo's approach here is consistent with his stance elsewhere. Sexual desire and pleasure have their place and that is in the context of intercourse for procreation. Anything beyond that is excess. Circumcision is a physical reminder for the male of this danger, but not a rejection of sexual desire in itself.

1.4.2.2 Laws treated under the Headings of the First Five Commandments

1.4.2.2.1 The First Two Commandments: Worship and Idolatry

In *Spec.* 1 Philo takes the first two commandments as a stepping off point to discuss a range of matters related to worship. He depicts God's response to Moses' prayer, that God show himself, as including the words: "*Know thyself* (γνῶθι δὴ σαυτόν), then, and do not be led away by impulses and desires beyond thy capacity (ταῖς ὑπὲρ δύναμιν ὁρμαῖς καὶ ἐπιθυμίαις), nor let yearning for the unattainable uplift and carry thee off thy feet, for of the obtainable nothing shall be denied thee" (*Spec.* 1.44), a central plank of Philo's preaching, reflecting his understanding of the Delphic oracle as pointing to the need to know about one's urges and control them, including one's sexual urges. He affirms *proselytes* (*Spec.* 1.51-53) underlining their right to special friendship and "more than ordinary goodwill" (*Spec.* 1.52), presumably then also affirming marriage to proselytes. The theme of idolatry evokes the story of Phinehas, which we discussed above (*Spec.* 1.56-57) (1.3.3.3). These commandments are also the context for discussing the temple. We find nothing here about intercourse in relation to the temple and its precincts. Here he mentions the annual offering of the first fruits, "ransom money" (*Spec.* 1.77) (Exod 30:12-16).

In *Her.* he gives the *didrachmon* a symbolic interpretation: one drachma paid to the God who "releases with a mighty hand from the cruel and bitter tyranny of passions and wrongdoings (ὠμῆς καὶ πικρᾶς παθῶν καὶ ἀδικημάτων δεσποτείας)" (*Her.*186); "the other half we are to leave to the unfree and slavish kind of which he is a member who says, 'I have come to love my master,' that is, 'the mind which rules within me,' and my wife, that is 'sense' the friend and keeper of the passion's household, 'and the children,' that is the evil offspring of the passions, 'I will not go out free'" (Exod 21:5) (*Her.*186). This a very negative slant on family life, which Philo does not always assume, but employs for allegory.

In this context in *Spec.* 1 he discusses the *priesthood*. Among the provisions are those concerning *marriage*, which Philo introduces with the words: "Since a priest is a man well before he is a priest and must and should feel the instinct for mating (καὶ ταῖς πρὸς συνουσίαν ὁρμαῖς ἐξ ἀνάγκης ὀφείλει χρῆσθαι), Moses arranges for his marriage with a pure virgin whose parents and grandparents and ancestors are equally pure, highly distinguished for the excellence of their conduct and lineage" (*Spec.* 1.101) (based on Lev 21:7), going on to exclude a prostitute and give reasons why, as noted above, including an allusion to a prostitutes' earnings not coming to the temple (Deut 23:18). Philo is affirming that to be a man means naturally to want to marry and to engage in sexual relations. This instinct and passion is affirmed. He then summarises Lev 21:13-14 concerning the high priest, for whom only a virgin will do, ruling out not only prostitutes but divorcees, widows, and even virgins once betrothed, thus keeping the seed pure and having the advantage that young virgins, as Philo claims, are more teachable (*Spec.* 1.105-107). Priests have fewer restrictions, but should not marry divorcees unless widowed, to avoid potential conflict with former husbands (*Spec.* 1.108). Mingling the two sets of rules he notes that unlike ordinary priests, high priests should marry only women from priestly families (*Spec.* 1.110-111), as noted above. As one might expect, Philo concludes: "These and similar regulations as to marriage are intended to promote the generation of children (χάριν παίδων γενέσεως)" (*Spec.* 1.112).

Elsewhere the *high priest* is the frequent focus of Philo's reflection, sometimes with pertinence to sexual issues. Thus in *Fug.* he allegorises the marriage provision: "To him there is betrothed moreover a maiden of the hallowed people (παρθένος ἐκ τοῦ ἱεροῦ γένους ἁρμόζεται), pure and undefiled and of ever inviolate intention; for never is he wedded to a widow or one divorced or to a profane woman or to a harlot, but against them he ever wages a truceless and unrelenting warfare" (*Fug.* 114). So far the literal, which again confirms the reading of ἐκ τοῦ γένους αὐτοῦ (Lev 21:14). Then we read: "For hateful to him is widowhood from virtue, and the plight of one cast out and driven from her doors, and any conviction that is profane and unholy. But the promiscuous polyandrous cause of polytheism, or rather atheism, the harlot, he deigns not even to look at, having learned to love her who had adopted, as her Husband and Father, God the All-sovereign" (*Fug.* 114). Similarly in *Somn.* 2 he writes: "The high priest is blameless, perfect, the husband of a virgin, who, strange paradox, never becomes a woman, but rather has forsaken that womanhood through the company of her husband. And not only is he a husband, able to sow the seed of undefiled and virgin thoughts, but a father also of holy intelligences" (*Somn.* 2.185). This has left the literal behind altogether and through allegory and gender hierarchy transformed the marriage into an image of the perfect soul who has the senses made masculine, though paradoxically virgin, by having no life of their own except under full control of male mind.

In the context of discussing *priestly impurity* he notes that a priest may have "leprous eruptions" or suffer "from a seminal issue", presumably gonorrhoea, precluding him from touching the holy table or food associated with it (*Spec.* 1.118) (Lev 22:4a), then that "if a priest touches any impure object or, as often happens, has an emission during the night, he must not during that day partake of consecrated food but bathe himself, and after sundown he should not be debarred from its use" (*Spec.* 1.119) (Lev 22:4b-7). Presumably what "often happens" in the night refers to more than seminal emission during sleep. He also notes the provision about the return of a priest's daughter to his family if divorced and her qualifying then to eat priestly food, but not if there are children in which case she must go with them to the husband's family (*Spec.* 1.129-130) (Lev 22:13). Philo does not allegorise these provisions away.

In expounding the law of *offering the first born* (Exod 13:2; 22:29), Philo speaks of children as "separable parts of their parents, or rather to speak more truly, inseparable parts, joined to them by kinship of blood, by the thoughts and memories of ancestors, invisible presences still alive among their descendants, by the love-ties of the affection which unites them, by the indissoluble bonds of nature" (*Spec.* 1.137). Elsewhere Philo expands this understanding. Here he stresses the point to underline that nevertheless the first born are to be offered to God in thanksgiving "for the blessings of parenthood realized in the present and the hopes of fruitful increase in the future" (*Spec.* 1.138), reflecting Philo's constant concern with procreation of offspring. In this context he then emphasises marriage. "At the same time he shews his wish that marriages, the first produce of which is a fruit sacred to His service, should be not only blameless but worthy of the highest praise" (*Spec.* 1.138). Accordingly he argues: "reflection on this should lead both husbands and wives to cherish temperance and domesticity and unanimity (σωφροσύνης καὶ οἰκουρίας καὶ ὁμονοίας), and by mutual sympathy shewn in word and deed to make the name of partnership (κοινωνίαν) a reality securely founded on truth" (*Spec.* 1.138). This is high praise for marriage as he understands it, namely, a harmonious, hierarchical unity. Only then does he note that, of course, the law does not require the offering of firstborn, but in its place money (*Spec.* 1.139), but without specifying the amount (given as five shekels in Num 18:15-16).

In dealing with *sacrificial law* Philo accounts for some practices on the basis of his allegorical psychology. Thus in *Spec.* 1.148 he writes of the belly as the "manger of that irrational animal, desire, which drenched by wine-bibbing and gluttony, is perpetually flooded with relays of food and drink administered to it, and like a sow rejoices to make its home in the mire". He continues: "And therefore the place of dregs and leavings has been assigned as by far the fittest for a licentious and most unseemly animal" (*Spec.* 1.148). A little later he writes: "So then desire, profane, impure and unholy (ἐπιθυμία μὲν οὖν βέβηλος καὶ ἀκάθαρτος καὶ ἀνίερος), has been expelled outside the confines of virtue and well deserved is its banishment" (*Spec.* 1.150). By contrast, he argues, "Let continence (ἐγκράτεια), that pure and stainless virtue which disregards all concerns of food and drink and claims to stand superior to the pleasures of the stomach, touch the holy altars and bring with it the appendage of the belly as a reminder that it holds in contempt gluttony and greediness and all that inflames the tendencies to lust (πάντων ὅσα τὰ εἰς τὰς ἐπιθυμίας ἀναφλέγει)" (*Spec.* 1.150). Were it not for the final words, one might see the concern as primarily with gluttony and greed, but typically Philo associates these also with what they can enflame, namely illicit sexual desire.

In *Spec.* 1.172 he turns to the *showbread* (cf. Lev 24:5-8), which he sees as "emblematic of that most profitable of virtues, continence (ἐγκράτειαν), which has simplicity and contentment and frugality for its bodyguard against the baleful assaults engineered by incontinence and covetousness (ἀκολασίας καὶ πλεονεξίας). For bread to a lover of wisdom is sufficient sustenance" (*Spec.* 1.173), whereas dainty food, he argues, appeals to the low sense of taste which serves "lusts of the wretched belly" (*Spec.* 1.174). Sexual lust is not in focus. "Those who are minded to live with God" and men "trained to disregard the pleasures of the flesh and practised in the study of nature's verities, pursue the joys and sweet comforts of the intellect" (*Spec.* 1.176). Later, in *Spec.* 2 he notes that the loaves "are all unleavened, the clearest possible example of a food free from admixture, in the preparation of which art for the sake of pleasure has no place, but only nature, providing nothing save what is indispensable for its use" (*Spec.* 2.161).

His comments on the festivals contain little of relevance to our theme. Elsewhere, however, they receive more symbolic treatment: thus the *Atonement Day*, described as the fast (*Spec.* 1.186-188). In *Spec.* 2, contrasting it with the usual kind of feasting of his day, he notes that it does not include "the merriment and revelry with frolic and drollery, nor dancing to the sound of flute and harp and timbrels and cymbals, and the other instruments of the debilitated and invertebrate kind if music which through the channel of the ears awaken the unruly lusts (τὰς ἀκαθέκτους ἐπιθυμίας)" (*Spec.* 2.193). The Fast is about self-restraint "controlling the tongue and the belly and the organs below the belly (τῶν μετὰ γαστέρα)" (*Spec.* 2.195). Self-restraint exercised in relation to food and drink which Philo describes "absolutely necessary" (*Spec.* 2.195) prepares one for such restraint over against "the superfluities of life" (*Spec.* 2.195). Similarly in *Spec.* 2.201 he notes that the point of the Fast is not starvation of necessities. It also makes one grateful (*Spec.* 2.203). He makes a similar contrast in *Mos.* 2 with the celebrations of the Greeks where "the untempered wine flows freely, and the board is spread sumptuously, and all manner of food and drink are lavishly provided, whereby the insatiable pleasures of the belly are enhanced, and further cause the outburst of the lusts that lie below it (προσαναρρηγνῦσαι καὶ τὰς ὑπογαστρίους ἐπιθυμίας)" (*Mos.* 2.23). By contrast, he writes, "in our fast men may not put food and drink to their lips, in order that with pure hearts, untroubled and untrammelled by any bodily passion (μηδ' ἐμποδίζοντος σωματικοῦ πάθους)" (*Mos.* 2.24). In both there is a clear allusion to sexual wrongdoing.

After describing the daily sin-offering as "applying medicine to the sin and surgery to the passions (θεραπείας ἁμαρτημάτων καὶ παθῶν ἐκτομῆς)", the basis for a truly joyful feast (*Spec.* 1.191), Philo returns to the contrast: "These festal occasions of relaxation and cessation from work have often ere now opened up countless avenues of transgressions" (*Spec.* 1.192). He then explains: "For strong drink and gross eating accompanied by wine-bibbing, while they awaken the insatiable lusts of the belly, inflame also the lusts seated below it, and as they stream along and overflow on every side they create a torrent of evils, innumerable, because they have the immunity of the feast for their headquarters and refuge from retribution" (*Spec.* 1.192). Accordingly, he writes, "all this the lawgiver observed and therefore did not permit his people to conduct their festivities like other nations, but first he bade them in the very hour of their joy make themselves pure by curbing the appetites for pleasure" (*Spec.* 1.193). In Philo's day banquets were a typical location for excessive indulgence of the passions, including gluttony, drunkenness, and sexual promiscuity. This setting occurs frequently in his accounts.

In discussing *sacrificial animals* Philo reflects his assessment of female as inferior to male. Thus he explains that the "whole burnt-offering is male because the male is more compete, more dominant than the female, closer akin to causal activity, for the female is incomplete and in subjection and belongs to the category of the passive rather than the active" (*Spec.* 1.200), going on to explain: "So too with the two ingredients which constitute our life-principle, the rational and the irrational; the rational which belongs to the mind and reason is of the masculine gender, the irrational, the province of sense, is of the feminine. Mind belongs to a genus wholly superior to sense as man is to woman" (*Spec.* 1.201). He makes the same distinction again in *Spec.* 1.228 and 233. Describing the preparation of the sacrifice he again employs symbolism. Thus commenting on the direction to wash the belly and feet he writes: "Under the figure of the belly he signifies the lust which it is well to clean away, saturated as it is with stains and pollutions, with wine-bibbing and sottishness, a mighty force for ill, trained and drilled to work havoc in the life of men" (*Spec.* 1.206), here, without a focus on sexual wrongdoing.

Similarly in *Leg.* 3 he writes: "The lover of pleasure moves on the belly; the perfect man washes out the entire belly; the man who is making gradual progress washes out the contents of the belly, the man who is just beginning his training will go forth without, when he intends to curb passion by bringing reason (figuratively called a shovel) to bear upon the demands of the belly" (*Leg.* 3.159), shovel making a connection with Deut 23:13 about burying excrement to which we turn below. This comes at the end of a long discussion which began in *Leg.* 3.129 with Philo's allusion to Lev 8:29 which describes how Moses removed the breast of the ram in the preparation of Aaron's ordination and then his use of it allegorically to depict Moses as the perfect man, who "thinks it necessary to use the knife on the seat of anger in its entirety, and to cut it clean out of the soul, for no moderation of passion can satisfy him; he is content with nothing but compete absence of passion" (*Leg.* 3.129; similarly 130, 131). He contrasts with Moses "the man who is making gradual progress, holding a lower position" (*Leg.* 3.132), represented by Aaron. We discussed its implications for understanding Philo's approach to passion in the first chapter.

Of *the one offering sacrifices* he writes: "The law would have such a person pure in body and soul, the soul purged of its passions and distempers and infirmities and every viciousness of word and deed (ἀπό τε τῶν παθῶν καὶ νοσημάτων καὶ ἀρρωστημάτων καὶ κακιῶν τῶν ἔν τε λόγοις καὶ πράξεσι), the body of the defilements which commonly beset it (τὸ δὲ σῶμα ἀφ' ὧν ἔθος αὐτῷ μιαίνεσθαι)" (*Spec.* 1.257), reflecting Philo's sense of purity as having mind in control and not passions, but also his respect for bodily purity laws. Disqualified from entry into the temple is "anyone whose heart is the seat of lurking covetousness and wrongful cravings (αἱ πλεονεξίαι καὶ ἐπιθυμίαι τῶν ἀδικιῶν)" (*Spec.* 1.270). Similarly in *QE* 1 Philo writes: "he who was about to offer the sacrifice should first prepare his soul and body—the latter by abstaining from uncleanness in holiness and purity, and the former by quietly giving himself up to God in order that it might be released, even though not altogether, from the passions that disturbed it, for, according to the saying, one should not enter with unwashed feet on the pavement of the temple of God" (*QE* 1.2). As Leonhardt-Balzer observes, "For Philo true purity cannot be internal or external, it must be both".[498]

---

[498] Leonhardt-Balzer, *Jewish Worship*, 267. "The principle which governs all the ritual passages is that purification is required before any contact with the divine takes place (*V. Mos.* I 216; *Decal.* 45)" (268). For Philo, she argues, "the rituals are a vehicle for spiritual

The remaining discussions in *Spec.* 1 include reference to the earnings of a prostitute with related themes and to circumcising the heart, both treated above. Philo continues his exposition of Laws in *Spec.* 2. Again, much of the discussion has little to do with sexuality.

1.4.2.2.2 The Third Commandment: Vows

In discussing the third commandment Philo notes the *laws about vows* in Num 30:3-15, that the vows of daughters and wives may be overridden, arguing that this is "surely reasonable, for the former, owing to their youth, do not know the value of oaths, so that they need others to judge for them, and the latter often, through want of sense, swear what would not be to their husband's advantage" (*Spec.* 2.24). The latter reflects Philo's view of women's deficient sense and therefore the need for the husband to be in control. He then notes the exception, namely, widows and divorcees (Num 30:9): "Widows (and divorcees) who have none to intervene on their behalf, neither husbands from whom they have been parted, nor fathers whom they left behind them when they set out to find a new home in marriage, should be slow to swear, for their oaths stand beyond repeal" (*Spec.* 2.25). Philo then goes on to allegorise father and husband as depicting "nature's right reasoning (ὁ τῆς φύσεως ὀρθὸς λόγος)" (*Spec.* 2.29). "It acts as a husband because it deposits seed of virtue in the soul as in a fertile field" (*Spec.* 2.29), one of Philo's favourite images of impregnation and as father in begetting. Thus "the mind is likened on the one hand to a virgin, on the other to a woman either in widowhood, or still united to a husband. As a virgin it keeps itself pure and uncorrupted from the malignant passions, pleasures and desires and griefs and fears" (*Spec.* 2.30). Then Philo turns to the image of wife: "But when, like a wife, it dwells with virtuous reasoning as its worthy mate, that same reasoning promises to take charge of it and impregnates it husband-like with thoughts of highest excellence" (*Spec.* 2.30). The widow and divorcee then represent loss of connection with sound sense and right reasoning, the mind bereft of wisdom and left to its own resources (*Spec.* 2.31). This is yet one more version of Philo's constant theme of urging the mind's adherence to virtue.

Noting the laws of votive offerings, Philo simply repeats the differential between men and women, but without his usual comment on women's inferiority (*Spec.* 2.32-34) (cf. Lev 27:2-8). The numbers must have said enough. In *Leg.* he alludes briefly to vows made by women in the house of father or husband, as able to be annulled, and of widows and divorcees, as not to be annulled, to symbolise

---

improvement, but spirituality does not replace them" (271). In this Philo is also sharing assumptions common to both Jews and Greeks (270, 272).

the difference between sins forgivable and those not (*Leg.* 2.63). Using the same analogy, the vows of widows and divorcees symbolise irrecoverable action. In *Hypoth.* Philo reports that "If a man has devoted his wife's sustenance to a sacred purpose he must refrain from giving her that sustenance" (*Hypoth.* 7.5), a practice under attack in Mark 7:8-13.

1.4.2.2.3 The Fourth Commandment: Sabbath

At this point in *Spec.* 2 we reach the commandment to keep *the Sabbath* (*Spec.* 2.39). Back in *Decal.* 102, Philo employs numerology, noting that seven "is the virgin among the numbers, the essentially motherless, the closest bound to the initial Unit" (*Decal.* 102). In *Spec.* 2 he sets the Sabbath in the context of the feasts and then argues that in fact for "all who practice wisdom" (*Spec.* 2.44) every day is like a feast. He describes them as "filled with high worthiness, inured to disregard ills of the body or of external things, schooled to hold things indifferent as indeed indifferent" (*Spec.* 2.46). To this point the focus is typically Stoic self-sufficiency and *apatheia*, and then Philo continues: "armed against the pleasures and lusts (κατὰ τῶν ἡδονῶν καὶ ἐπιθυμιῶν), ever eager to take their stand superior to the passions in general, trained to use every effort to overthrow the formidable menace which those passions have built up against them" (*Spec.* 2.46). By contrast the wicked man finds no joy, "whose every plan is for evil, whose lifemate is folly (συζῶν ἀφροσύνῃ), with whom everything, tongue, belly and organs of generation (τὰ γεννητικά), is against what is seasonable (ἀκαιρευόμενος)" (*Spec.* 2.49). Philo then takes up each element, speech, excessive drinking and then, in a text we discussed above in relation to same-sex acts, the genitals: "he misuses them for abominable lusts and forms of intercourse forbidden by all laws (πρὸς ἐκνομωτάτους οἴστρους καὶ μίξεις ἀθέσμους). He not only attacks in his fury the marriage-bed of others, but even plays the pederast and forces the male type of nature to debase and convert itself into the feminine form, just to indulge a polluted and accursed passion" (*Spec.* 2.50). In contrast he cites the model of Sarah, "a certain mind of rich intelligence, her passions now calmed within her, smiled because joy lay within her and filled womb", an allusion to Isaac, whose name means laughter (*Spec.* 2.54).

Only after that extended discourse on who finds the really joyful feast, does Philo pick up the imagery of the Sabbath which he had used in *Decal.*, similarly describing it here as "virgin" and "motherless": "begotten by the father of the universe alone, the ideal form of the male sex with nothing of the female. It is the manliest and doughtiest of numbers, well gifted by nature for sovereignty and leadership" (*Spec.* 2.56).[499] Both here and there the description reflects Philo's

---

[499] On this see the discussion of numerology above (p. 36).

view of the female as inferior. The same kind of thinking is present also when Philo writes in *Mos.* 2 that the seventh day is "motherless, exempt from female parentage, begotten by the Father alone, without begetting, brought to the birth, yet not carried in the womb" and "ever virgin, neither born of a mother nor a mother herself, neither bred from corruption nor doomed to suffer corruption" (*Mos.* 2.210; similarly *Opif.* 79, 100). The female contaminates.

Philo rejects that any of this should imply non observance in a literal sense: "There are some who, regarding laws in their literal sense in the light of symbols of matters belonging to the intellect, are over overpunctilious about the latter, while treating the former with easy-going neglect" (*Migr.* 89), including of the Sabbath (*Migr.* 91-92). In *Spec.* 2 Philo nevertheless affirms both male and female, again via numerology, arguing that the universe has been brought into being by the number six of which the odd (male) and even (female) parts are essential components (*Spec.* 2.58), an explanation he also proffers in *Opif.* 13).

Here, too, we find reference to the *seventh year, the year of release*, referring to the benefits it brings to widows and orphans (*Spec.* 2.108). In *Migr.* he uses it as a symbol of abundance in the liberated soul: "For the offspring of the soul's own travail are for the most part poor abortions, things untimely born; but those which God waters with the snows of heaven come to the birth perfect, complete and peerless" (*Migr.* 33), noted above as perhaps an erotic image if snow here evokes semen.

In *Spec.* 2.124 he notes the law of Num 27:8-11 (cf. also 36:1-12) about *sons inheriting before daughters*, which is only loosely connected to the context in which he had been expounding the sabbatical year, though connected with issues of justice and fairness. Philo proffers the rationale: "For just as in nature men take precedence of women, so too in the scale of relationships they should take the first place in succeeding to the property and filling the position of the departed", reflecting typically his assessment of women's inferiority. He then adds: "But if virgins are left without a dower (ἀνέκδοται), nothing of the kind having been settled on them by the parents while still alive, they should share equally with the males" (*Spec.* 2.125). The head magistrate is then to have charge of ensuring their development, support, and education, and also "when the time comes, the duty of arranging a suitable marriage and choosing husbands who are selected on their merits and approved in all respects". This reflects the typical practice of arranged marriages. Philo then adds: "And these should be, if possible, of the same family as the girls, or if that cannot be, at any rate of the same ward and tribe, in order that the portions assigned as dowry should not be alienated by inter-marriage with other tribes, but should retain the place given to them in the allotments originally made on the basis of tribes" (*Spec.* 2.126). As noted above in relation to intermarriage the focus here as in Tobit is on preserving inheritance. Philo treats the same provision in detail in *Mos.* 2, making specific mention of Zelophehad's five daughters of the tribe of Manasseh (*Mos.* 2.234-245). In *Migr.* they are taken as representing the five senses, "daughters of the irrational portion of the soul" (*Migr.* 205-206).

Philo then turns to *the inheritance rights of the firstborn*, expounding Deut 21:15-17. Unlike the biblical text which speaks simply of a loved second wife and a hated first one who produced the firstborn, Philo greatly embellishes the image of the husband: "There are some who after marrying and begetting children unlearn in their later days what they knew of self-restraint and are wrecked on the reef of incontinence (ἐξώκειλαν εἰς ἀκρασίαν)" (*Spec.* 2.135). He uses the imagery of moral shipwreck in a sexual context elsewhere. He continues: "Seized with a mad passion for other women (ἐπιμανέντες γυναιξὶν ἑτέραις), they maltreat those who hitherto belonged to them and behave to the children they have begotten by them as though they were uncles rather than fathers, copy the unrighteousness shewn by stepmothers to the first family and altogether devote themselves and all they have to the second wives and their children, overcome by the vilest of passions, voluptuousness (ἡδονῆς, αἰσχίστου πάθους, ἥττους γενόμενοι)" (*Spec.* 2.135). This reflects Philo's psychology, namely, that such behaviour in shifting one's affections to a new wife reflects abandonment to the passions. Accordingly he adds: "Such lusts the law would not have hesitated to bridle if it were possible, and prevent them from frisking and plunging still more" (*Spec.* 2.135). Philo likens the man to "one in the grip of an incurable disease (ἀθεραπεύτῳ νόσῳ)" (*Spec.* 2.136). The situation assumes polygyny, but Philo's focus is elsewhere. He does not address polygyny as such, here or elsewhere (cf. *Virt.* 110-115 on Deut 21:10-13), but attacks the man for following passions for another. Similarly while the original focused only on the rights of the firstborn, which Philo also emphasises and justifies (*Spec.* 2.137-139), he is concerned with a range of injustices, including towards the women and the children.

This law provides Philo with fruitful ground for allegory. Its citation in *Sacr.* 19 is the starting point for the lengthy contrast between the seductress, pleasure, and virtue (*Sacr.* 20-44), employing the well-known topos from Xenophon. Philo cites the law also in *Leg.* 2 to serve the same contrast (*Leg.* 2.48), and in *Her.* uses it allegorically to contrast what Leah and Rachel symbolise (*Her.* 47-49). In *Sobr.* 21, where he cites it yet again, interestingly he misreads the text, as though it implies that the son of the hated woman is not literally the firstborn, but it achieves his allegorical purpose.

Still within his expositions under the heading of Sabbath, Philo turns to the *Passover* (*Spec.* 2.145-149). It, too, lends itself to allegory. Thus he writes: "To those who are accustomed to turn literal facts into allegory, the Crossing-festival suggests purification of the soul" (*Spec.* 2.147). Clearly alluding to a tradition of interpretation in which he stands and which he affirms, he continues: "They say that the lover of wisdom (τὸν σοφίας ἐραστήν) is occupied solely in crossing from the body and the passions (ἀπὸ τοῦ σώματος καὶ τῶν παθῶν διάβασιν), each of which overwhelms him like a torrent, unless the rushing current be dammed and held back by the principle of virtue" (*Spec.* 2.147). The same interpretation occurs frequently. In *Migr.* he speaks of Passover as passing over from the passions (*Migr.* 25) and goes on similarly to speak of the danger of being "swept down by the violence of that passion's current" (*Migr.* 26) in the context of highlighting Moses as a model. Similarly, in *Sacr.* he writes of Passover, as "the passage from the life of the passions to the practice of virtue (τὴν ἐκ παθῶν εἰς ἄσκησιν ἀρετῆς διάβασιν)" (*Sacr.* 63; similarly *Leg.* 3.165, 172) and in *Her.* of the soul studying "to unlearn irrational passion (ἄλογον πάθος ἀπομαθεῖν)" (*Her.* 192) and of "crossing from passion 'with haste'" (*Her.* 255). In *QE* the various comments touch on various motifs, so that beside meaning "to give up the pursuits of youth and their terrible disorder" (*QE* 1.4) and "to purify his entire soul with his inner desires," (*QE* 1.17), its accompaniments also address the issue. Thus "bitter herbs are a manifestation of a psychic migration, through which one removes from passion to impassivity and from wickedness to virtue. For those who naturally and genuinely repent become bitter toward their former way of life" having been deceived by desire in "the prime of their youth" (*QE* 1.15). Then of eating with girdles and staff he writes: "The girdles represent drawing together and the coming together of the sensual pleasures and other passions, which, being, as it were, released and let go, overtake all souls ... a girdle about the middle, for this place is considered as the manger of the many-headed beast of desire within us" (*QE* 1.19). None of this specifically sexual, though almost certainly the passions of youth would include this.

In the context of expounding the *feast of unleavened bread* in *Spec.* 2 Philo comments that the "man of worth may be regarded as equivalent to a feast held by one who has expelled grief and fear and desire and the other passions and distempers of the soul" (*Spec.* 2.157). In explaining the frugality represented by unleavened bread he alludes to the spring festival which he describes as a "reminder of the creation of the world" when "its earliest inhabitants, children of earth in the first and second generation, must have used the gifts of the universe in their unperverted state before pleasure had got the mastery (μήπω τῆς ἡδονῆς παρευημερούσης)" (*Spec.* 2.160), arguing that accordingly to live frugally is "as far as possible to assimilate our present-day life to that of the distant past (τὸν ἡμῶν καθ' ὅσον οἷόν τε ἦν ἐξομοιῶσαι τῷ παλαιῷ)" (*Spec.* 2.160). The focus here is more likely to be excess in food than sexual excesses. Still expounding the seven days of unleavened bread, he explains the *offering of the Sheaf* on the first day as firstfruits representing an offering related to the whole earth and all of humanity in which he then sees the Jewish people as being like a priesthood. In this context he writes that "it carries out all the rites of purification and both in body and soul obeys the injunctions of the divine laws, which restrict the pleasures of the belly and the parts below it (ὑπογαστρίους) and the horde ... setting reason to guide the irrational senses, and also check and rein in the wild and extravagant impulses of the soul ..." (*Spec.* 2.163), here including specific reference to the dangers of sexual pleasures. Nothing in his exposition of Pentecost or the feat of trumpets pertains to sexuality. He comes then in *Spec.* 2.193 to speak of the Day of Atonement, which he calls "the Fast". We discussed it above where it first appears, namely in *Spec.* 1.186-188.

1.4.2.2.4 The Fifth Commandment: Honouring Parents

The fifth commandment about *honouring parents* prompts Philo to reflect in *Decal.* that it is on the borderline of the two sets of five (*Decal.* 106) and to explain: "The reason I consider is this: we see that parents by their nature stand on the border-line between the mortal and the immortal side of existence, the mortal because of their kinship with men and other animals through the perishable-ness of the body; the immortal because the act of generation assimilates them to God, the generator of the All (διὰ τὴν τοῦ γεννᾶν πρὸς θεὸν τὸν γεννητὴν τῶν ὅλων ἐξομοίωσιν)" (*Decal.* 107), a probable echo of καθ' ὁμοίωσιν ("according to our likeness") in Gen 1:26. The connection to both and the role of generation he sees as important. He then goes on to explain that some focus only on the one side, whom he is happy to call "lovers of God" (φιλοθέους), and others only on the human side, called "lovers of men" (φιλανθρώπους), but it is clear that Philo himself wants to affirm connectedness in both directions. By implication he is unsympathetic to those opting for celibacy, even though he can acknowledge them to be lovers of God. "Both come but halfway in virtue; they only have it whole who win honour in both departments" (*Decal.* 110). In fact he argues that both are like animals (*Decal.* 110). He asks: "how could the begotten beget in his turn those whose seed he is, since nature has bestowed on parents in relation to their children an estate of a special kind which cannot be subject to the law of 'exchange'"? (*Decal.* 112).[500] He then challenges the situation where "children, because they are unable to make a complete return, refuse to make even the slightest" (*Decal.* 112), noting that even animals like watch-dogs and sheep-dogs display gratitude. So he declares: "Parents are the servants of God for the task of begetting children (θεοῦ γὰρ ὑπηρέται πρὸς τέκνων σπορὰν οἱ γονεῖς), and he who dishonours the servant dishonours also the Lord" (*Decal.* 119), another reflection of the priority he gives to procreation. In *Spec.* 2 he recapitulates what he has said in *Decal.*: "Parents are midway between the natures of God and man, and partake of both; the

---

[500] Colson notes here an allusion to Attic law where "a citizen nominated to perform a "leiturgia" might call upon a person not so nominated whom he considered to be wealthier than himself to exchange properties with him" (*Philo VII*, 64).

human obviously because they have been born and will perish, the divine because they have brought others to the birth, and have raised not-being into being. Parents, in my opinion, are to their children what God is to the world" (*Spec.* 2.225).

This theme is apparent also in *Her.* where he writes of the fifth commandment: "This is of the sacred kind, since its reference is not to men, but to Him who causes all things to be sown and come into being, through whom it is that the father and mother appear to generate, though they do not really do so, but are the instruments of generation" (*Her.* 171), going on to underline the procreative role: The "immortal powers ... in virtue of their nature generate all things, but have permitted mortality also at the final stage to copy their creative art and to beget. For God is the primary cause of generation, but the nethermost and least honoured kind, the mortal-kind, is the ultimate" (*Her.* 172).

1.4.2.3 Laws treated under the Headings of the Last Four Commandments

Following Philo's account through *Decal.* and *Spec.* we pass over his treatment of adultery and related issues, discussed above, and turn to the exposition of the final four commandments. Nothing in his exposition of murder, theft and false witness in *Decal.* pertains to sexual issues.

1.4.2.3.1 The Seventh Commandment: Killing

Within his exposition in *Spec.* 3, however, Philo notes the provision in Exod 21:22 about two men fighting who in the process *strike a pregnant woman* resulting in a miscarriage. "If a man comes to blows with a pregnant woman and strikes her on the belly and she miscarries, then, if the result of the miscarriage is unshaped and undeveloped, he must be fined both for the outrage and for obstructing the artist Nature in her creative work of bringing into life the fairest of living creatures, man" (*Spec.* 3.108). This goes beyond the biblical provision in two respects: it makes no mention of two men fighting but only of a man striking a woman and it differentiates the crime on the basis of the stage of development of the foetus. Thus Philo continues: "But, if the offspring is already shaped and all the limbs have their proper qualities and places in the system, he must die, for that which answers to this description is a human being, which he has destroyed in the laboratory of Nature (ἐν τῷ τῆς φύσεως ἐργαστηρίῳ) who judges that the hour has not yet come for bringing it out into the light" (*Spec.* 3.108-109). Here Philo reflects halakhic tradition. We note also Philo's personification of Nature and the image of the womb as a laboratory (similarly *Spec.* 3.33). He goes on to speak of birth as like bringing a statue to light from its place of sculpting. In *Congr.*, on the other hand, he treats the law symbolically, to compare destroying what is complete in the mind from destroying what is incomplete, what is real from what is just hope (*Congr.* 136-138).

Philo goes on from here to *infanticide* which he sees implied in the previous ordinance: "This ordinance carries with it the prohibition of something else more important, the exposure of infants (βρέφων ἔκθεσις), a sacrilegious practice which among many other nations, through their ingrained inhumanity, has come to be regarded with complacence" (*Spec.* 3.110), not expressly addressed in biblical law. One of the charges which Philo levels against parents who do this is that "they are breaking the laws of Nature and stand self-condemned on the gravest charges, love of pleasure, hatred of men, murder (φιληδονίαν, μισανθρωπίαν, ἀνδροφονίαν) and, the worst abomination of all, murder of their own children (τεκνοκτονίαν)" (*Spec.* 3.112). "Love of pleasure" implies engaging in sexual intercourse for reasons other than procreation. Accordingly Philo continues: "For they are pleasure-lovers when they mate with their wives, not to procreate children and perpetuate the race, but like pigs and goats in quest of the enjoyment which such intercourse gives" (*Spec.* 3.113). Philo reflects on the difference between this and the previous provision, apparently accepting the view of "natural philosophers" and "physicians" of his day that "the child while still adhering to the womb below the belly is part of its future mother (τὰ μὲν ἔτι κατὰ γαστρὸς προσεχόμενα τῇ μήτρᾳ τῶν κυουσῶν εἶναι μέρη)" (*Spec.* 3.117) and so differentiating that state from exposure: "When the child has been brought to the birth it is separated from the organism with which it was identified .. and therefore infanticide undoubtedly is murder" (*Spec.* 3.118). This leaves uncertain how Philo would view abortion, which is surprisingly absent from his extrapolations of the commandment not to murder, though his insistence on procreation makes it almost certain that he would have opposed it, and he mentions its prohibition in *Hypoth.* 7.7. Philo is sharply critical of exposing infants in *Virt.*, calling such parents to hide their faces in shame (*Virt.* 131-133).[501]

In the context of explaining cities of refuge, Philo makes reference to the slaughter of the 24000 who worshiped the golden bull and engaged in "feasts which were no feasts and danced dances of death" (*Spec.* 3.125), but makes no sexual references. As an example of brutality he mentions a tax collector who in response to his poor debtors taking flight "carried off by force their womenfolk and children and parents and their other relatives and beat and subjected them to every kind of outrage" (*Spec.* 3.159), doubtless including sexual abuse, though

---

[501] Adele Reinhartz, "Philo on Infanticide," *SPA* 4 (1992) 42-58, suggested that Philo was not just targeting the practice in the pagan world but also among Jews (52-56). But see the review of research and the evidence in Daniel R. Schwartz, "Did the Jews Practice Infanticide in Antiquity?" *SPA* 16 (2004) 61-95, who concludes that the evidence is not secure (82-87).

Philo does not mention that specifically. In the broader context of abuse Philo then turns to proper order and the *proper place of men and women*: men in "Marketplaces and council-halls and law-courts and gatherings and meetings where a large number of people are assembled, and open-air life with full scope for discussion and action" and women in "indoor life which never strays from the house, within which the middle door is taken by the maidens as their boundary, and the outer door by those who have reached full womanhood" (*Spec.* 3.169), contrasting statesmanship with household management (*Spec.* 3.170). We discussed this above in our comments on his understanding of men and women in society (1.2.4.3). Women's modesty by implication keeps them safe, their audacity exposes them to danger and is shameful, especially in men's fights (*Spec.* 3.172). To join in would be to "unsex herself" and to "outrage herself by befouling her own life with the disgrace and heavy reproaches which boldness carried to an extreme entails" (*Spec.* 3.173).

Philo then goes on to the prohibition of a woman in such a context *grabbing the genitals* of her husband's opponent (Deut 25:11-12): "it is a shocking thing, if a woman is so lost to a sense of modesty, as to catch hold of the genital parts of her opponent" (*Spec.* 3.175), the penalty being that her hand be cut off (*Spec.* 3.175). Modesty also requires debarring women from *naked sports* and men from seeing *women naked* (*Spec.* 3.176). Philo goes on to give this an allegorical meaning, apparently known to him from tradition, "from highly gifted men", that the male in the soul clings to God and the female in the soul "to all that is born and perishes" (*Spec.* 3.178). "It stretches out its faculties like a hand to catch blindly at what comes in its way" (*Spec.* 3.178). "Naturally therefore we are commanded in a symbol to cut off the hand which has taken hold of the 'pair,' not meaning that the body should be mutilated by the loss of a most essential member, but to bid us exscind from the soul the godless thoughts which take for their basis all that comes into being through birth; for the 'pair' are a symbol of seed-sowing and birth" (*Spec.* 3.179). He goes on to speak of honouring the dyad, the image "of matter passive and divisible" above the monad "the image of the first cause" is to hold matter in higher esteem than God, for "there is no greater impiety than to ascribe to the passive element the power of the active principle" (*Spec.* 3.180). Employing sexual imagery he has moved beyond the sexual, though, of course, illicit sexual desire belongs to that "female" world and what it grasps for. This also fits Philo's notion of female as both inferior and potentially dangerous.

The prohibition of grasping a man's genitals receives similar treatment in *Somn.* 2 where Philo writes: "So then, O soul, that art loyal to thy teacher, thou must cut off thy hand, thy faculty, when it begins to lay hold of the genitals, whether they be the created world or the cares and aims of humanity" (*Somn.* 2.68). He continues: "For he often bids us cut away the hand that has taken hold of the 'pair', first because it has thereby given a welcome to the pleasure which it should hate, secondly because it has judged that to beget rests with ourselves, and thirdly because it has ascribed to the created the power of its maker" (*Somn.* 2.69). While one might see this as literal, suggestive of an attack on masturbation (though this hardly fits grasping the testicles!) and of arrogance of human self-sufficiency in relation to procreation, the focus, as the introductory words indicate, lies on laying hold of "the created world or the cares and aims of humanity", typical in the context of Joseph's concerns with the body. The broader concern is reflected in his link to Adam's sin: "Observe that Adam, that mass of earth, is doomed to die when he touches the twofold tree" (*Somn.* 2.70). The issue is not touching one's genitals but engaging in forbidden pleasure mediated by the body.

1.4.2.3.2 The Tenth Commandment: Coveting

In both *Decal.* and *Spec.* 4 Philo's treatment of theft, where one might perhaps have expected adultery to feature had he seen it that way, and false testimony yield nothing pertaining to sexuality. That changes with the final commandment, not to covet. This is an essential aspect of Philo's understanding of human psychology, which we discussed earlier, so will not be revisited here. Instead we shall note here relevant aspects in Philo's treatment of laws under this heading. His discussion of food laws which he brings here is as to be expected, primarily concerned with gluttony and at an allegorical level with gentle, domestic animals. Gaca claims that according to Philo "Moses established the dietary prohibitions in Leviticus because he knew that the prohibited types of animal flesh, such as pork, are particularly laced with an aphrodisiac surplus (*Spec* 4.100-18)" and accordingly "So long as they keep the forbidden food off their plates, sexual restraint will follow". [502] The passage cited does not, however, make such a connection. She rightly notes, however, that in expounding the tenth commandment, Philo's emphasis is on excess, noting that in *Spec.* 4.87 he cites Plato's list of vices resulting from excess in *Resp.* 575B6-9. She notes that Philo does not advocate not having desire at all, but "concurs with Plato that persons neither can nor should try to extinguish the appetites altogether".[503]

In his exposition of the *prohibition of eating blood* (Lev 17:10-16), Philo emphasises "that it is the essence of the soul, not of the intelligent and reasonable soul, but of that which operates through the senses, the soul that gives life which we and irrational animals possess in common" (*Spec.* 4.123). This is in contrast to the essence of "that other soul" which is "divine spirit" for which Philo appeals to Gen 2:7. Philo makes a similar point in *Her.* when he links "life from a kiss" (Masek) with Damascus (*Her.* 61), meaning "the blood of a sackcloth robe",

---

[502] Gaca, *Making of Fornication*, 196.
[503] Gaca, *Making of Fornication*, 196-97.

which enables him via Lev 17:11 (the soul of every flesh is the blood) to contrast two souls, one living by the flesh and its desires and the other by reason and divine inbreathing, alluding to Gen 2:7 (*Her.* 54-57). He returns to the image in 63 asking: "Can he who desires the life of the blood and still claims for his own the things of the senses become the heir of divine and incorporeal things?" (*Her.* 63), clearly answering "No", for such a one is among other things "aflame with seething passions and burning lusts" (*Her.* 64). Philo's exposition of people grabbing more quails for food than they needed prompts him to cite the location as meaning "Monuments of Lusts" (*Spec.* 4.130), clearly concerned with gluttony not sex. Generally Philo rarely makes links between food laws and sexual issues. An exception is his allegorical note in *Leg.* 2 that Leviticus forbids taking serpents (so passions) as nourishment (*Leg.* 2.105).

Having, as he puts it, "discussed the matters relating to desire or lust as adequately as our abilities allow, and thus completed our survey of the ten oracles, and the laws which are dependent on them" (*Spec.* 4.132), Philo goes on to other laws. Among them we find the *prohibitions of mixing*: "injunctions all on the same lines by forbidding them to mate their cattle with those of a different species, or to sow the vineyards for two kinds of fruit, or to wear a garment adulterated by weaving it from two materials" (*Spec.* 4.203), based on Lev 19:19 (cf. also Deut 22:9-11, which addresses not the mating but the yoking of different species). He then recalls that "the first of these prohibitions has been mentioned in our denunciation of adulterers to suggest still more clearly the wickedness of conspiring against the wedlock of other people, thereby ruining the morals of the wives as well as any honest hopes of begetting a legitimate family. For by prohibiting the crossing of irrational animals with different species he appears to be indirectly working towards the prevention of adultery" (*Spec.* 4.203).

In the context of discussing suppression of revolt, Philo addresses the issue of *protecting women*: "They must spare the women, married and unmarried, since these do not expect to experience at their hands any of the shocks of war as in virtue of their natural weakness they have the privilege of exemption from war service" (*Spec.* 4.223; cf. Deut 20:14). Women's plight in war is reflected in *Praem.* which holds in prospect the curse that "they will see too the women whom they took in lawful wedlock for the procreation of true-born children, chaste domestic loving wives, outraged as though they were harlots" (*Praem.* 139), victims of rape (*Praem.* 140).

In *Virt.* Philo picks up from the rules of engagement in war the humaneness of *exempting the man from war* who is about to be married (*Virt.* 28-30) (Deut 20:5-7), but then at an allegorical level declares that those ready for war are "persons into whom no passion has found an entry and there made its home" (*Virt.* 31), for "a robust body will be ruined if the soul is afflicted with a passion which does not accord with the task before it" (*Virt.* 31). Similarly in *Agr.* he cites it only to dismiss literal reference to the consummation of marriage (which he still notes positively) and to treat it as an allegory denoting the priority of life toward God and warfare against the senses (*Agr.* 148, 153). He goes on to explain: "What the Law means is that man's main consideration is not house or vineyard or the wife already betrothed to him; how he is to take to wife her whom he has wooed and won; how the planter of the vineyard is to cull and crush its fruit ... but that the faculties of a man's soul are a man's main consideration" (*Agr.* 157). Then employing the imagery of wooing he writes: "Beginnings are seen in a wooer, for, just as he who is wooing a woman has wedlock still in futurity not already being a husband, in the same way the well-constituted man looks forward to one day marrying Discipline, a high-born and pure maiden, but for the present he is her wooer" (*Agr.* 158; cf. also 166).

Elsewhere Philo has more to say about women in war, especially *women captive in war*. Thus in *Virt.* he summarises the law in Deut 21:10-13 about the captive woman: "if you find among the booty a comely woman for whom you feel a desire, do not treat her as a captive, and vent your passion on her, but in a gentler spirit pity her for her change of lot and alleviate her misfortunes by changing her condition for the better in every way" (*Virt.* 110). Typically he adds the reference to passion. Accordingly, he writes, after shaving her head and leaving her alone for 30 days "live with her as your lawful wife, because holiness requires that she who is to enter a husband's bed, not as a hired harlot, trafficking her youthful bloom, but either for love of her mate or for the birth of children, should be admitted to the rights of full wedlock as her due" (*Virt.* 112). His additions introduce the reference to treating her like a prostitute and continue typically: "he did not allow rebellious desire to go unbridled, but curbed its violence by the thirty days grant of liberty" (*Virt.* 113) and "tests whether the man's love is wild and giddy and wholly inspired by passion (πότερον ἐπιμανὴς καὶ ἀψίκορος καὶ ὅλος τοῦ πάθους), or contains an element of reason and so has something of the purer kind" (*Virt.* 113). He then elaborates the rest of the provision:

> And if anyone, having satisfied his desire to the full and surfeited therewith (ἐὰν δέ τις τῆς ἐπιθυμίας ἀποπληρωθεὶς καὶ διακορὴς γενόμενος), is no longer minded to continue his association with the captive, the law imposes what is not so much a loss of property as an admonition and correction leading him to improve his ways. For it bids him not sell her, nor yet keep her as a slave, but grant her freedom, and grant her, too, the right to depart in security from the house, lest if another wife comes in to supersede her, and quarrels ensue as they often do, this jealousy, with the master too under the sway of the charms of a new love and neglectful of the old, may bring her some fatal disaster. (*Virt.* 115)

It is important to note that Philo does not write disapprovingly of the initial fulfilment of desire. It is also clear that he envisages polygyny here and one of its typical side-effects, which is then the focus of what immediately follows the biblical provision, namely Deut 21:15-17. In *Hypoth.* Philo reports that the law requires that "children must not be parted from their parents even if you hold them as captive, nor a wife from her husband even if you are her owner by lawful purchase" (*Hypoth.* 7.8).[504]

1.4.3 Legal Provisions Beyond "On the Decalogue" and "Special Laws"

I turn now to legal provisions of potential relevance for our theme not addressed in *Decal.* or *Spec.* but found elsewhere. In many cases the relevant material is brief and in most cases Philo's interest is allegorical.

In alluding to Exod 21:10 he writes of basic necessities, including sexual intercourse: "for, to say all in a word, we must not, as the Law tells us, take away from the soul these three things, 'the necessaries, the clothing, the fellowship (τὴν ὁμιλίαν)', but afford each of them steadily" (*Migr.* 105). Philo regularly uses ὁμιλία to refer to sexual intercourse and that is surely its meaning here. Philo's interest is not the literal, for he then goes on to apply this symbolically: "Now the 'necessaries' are the good things of the mind, which are necessary, being demanded by the law of nature; the 'clothing', all that belongs to the phenomenal world of human life; and the 'fellowship,' persistent study directed to each of these kinds" (*Migr.* 105), thus sexual intercourse functions as an image for engaging in learning.

On the requirement to help the fallen donkey of an enemy (Exod 23:5) he writes: "the ass is symbolically our body, and (this) is altogether errant and roving. For the sake of bringing profit to its kindred sensual pleasure" it engages in excessive drinking and gluttony (*QE* 2.12).

Philo cites the difference in length of days for purification after birth of a male child compared with a female (Lev 12:2-5) in support of view that Gen 2:21-22 implies that "woman is a half of a man's body" and so requires 80 rather than 40 days (*QG* 1.25).

He uses the obligation on males (but not females) to present themselves to God three times a year (Deut 16:16) to declare: "Through three seasons, then, O soul, that is throughout the whole of time with its threefold divisions, make thyself ever manifest to God, not dragging after thee the weak feminine passion of sense-perception" (*Leg.* 3.11).

In *Agr.* he cites the *royal code in Deut 17:15-16* about not appointing a foreigner and not multiplying horses, to serve his imagery of controlling the

---

[504] On the extensive parallels among *Hypoth.* 6.10 – 7.20, Josephus *Ap.* 2.190-219; and *Pseudo-Phocylides*, see pp. 358-59 below.

passions, noting that the directions forbid the appointment of a "a horse-rearer to be a ruler, regarding as unsuited for such high authority any man who resembles an unbridled and unruly horse, and, in his wild excitement over pleasures, lust, and amours, knows no restraint" (*Agr.* 84).

Deut 21:18-21 about the wayward son forms the basis of an extensive discourse about the four failings of the wayward son and then of four different kinds of sons (*Ebr.* 13-98).

Philo frequently appeals to Deut 23:1-2, forbidding from the congregation those with crushed or cut genitals and those born of prostitution, including in a number of instances discussed above. He applies it both literally and metaphorically. Thus he uses it of eunuchs who are "cut off from the immortality which, through the succession of children and children's children, is kept alight for ever, roped off from the holy assembly and congregation 'For he that hath lost the organs of generation is absolutely forbidden to enter therein'" (*Somn.* 2.184). "None such does Moses permit to enter the congregation of God, for he says, 'He who has lost the organs of generation shall not come into the congregation of the Lord' ... For what use can he find in listening to holy words, who can beget no offspring of wisdom, when the knife has cut away the power of faith, and the store of truths which might best profit human life he cannot keep in his charge?" (*Ebr.* 213). Here he slips into allegory. The reading is clearly so in *Deus*, where describes the eunuch as having a "mind which loves the body and the passions and has been sold in slavery to that chief cateress ... of our compound nature, Pleasure. Eunuch-like it has been deprived of all the male and productive organs of the soul, and lives in indigence of noble practices, unable to receive the divine message, debarred from the holy congregation ... in which the talk and study is always of virtue", being "cast into the prison of the passions" (*Deus* 111), an allusion to Joseph who symbolises this lifestyle. He uses it also of the children of prostitutes, primarily as a symbol of atheism. The builders of the tower of Babel belong to those whom he describes as no different from "the harlot's offspring, whom the law has banished from God's congregation with the words, 'he that is born of a harlot shall not enter the congregation of the Lord'" (*Conf.* 144), a common charge against polytheists. Similarly, in *Migr.* 69 he lodges an attack on atheism and polytheism, using his argument about prostitutes' children not knowing their father and so claiming them all: "the Law has expelled both of these doctrines from the sacred assembly, atheism, by debarring a eunuch from membership of it; polytheism, by likewise forbidding the son of a harlot to be a listener or speaker in it. ... For the sterile man is godless; and the son of a whore is a polytheist, being in the dark about his real father, and for this reason ascribing his begetting to many, instead of to one" (*Migr.* 69; similarly *Decal.* 8-9; *Spec.* 1.326, 331-332; *Mut.* 205).

Philo frequently uses *the law in Deut 23:13 about carrying a shovel to bury one's excreta* as a way of talking about dealing with the effects of illicit passion. Thus in *Leg.* 3 he takes it to mean that we should "gird up our passions, not wear them flowing and loose" (*Leg.* 3.153), the shovel interpreted as reason, which should "follow the passion, preventing it from spreading abroad, for by this means we shall comply only with demands which are urgent, but from all that goes beyond this we shall abstain" (*Leg.* 3.154) and "curb and bridle the impetuous rush of the passion (τὴν ῥύμην καὶ φορὰν τοῦ πάθους)" (*Leg.* 3.155). It even unpacks the words "you shall dig" to mean: "thou shalt lay bare and distinguish by means of reason, the nature which each passion possesses, eating, drinking, sexual indulgence, that thou mayest discern them and learn the truth about them. For then shalt thou know that in none of these is there the thing which is good, but that which is useful only and necessary" (*Leg.* 3.157), so that "all unseemliness of flesh and passion is covered, and hidden, and put out of sight" (*Leg.* 3.158). Again this shows that Philo is not concerned to deny the passions, including sexual desire, altogether but to control them and put them to proper use. Earlier in *Leg.* 2 he wrote: "Whenever the mind forgets itself amid the luxuries of a festive gathering and is mastered by all that conduces to pleasure, we are in bondage and we leave our 'unseemliness' uncovered" (*Leg.* 2.29).

In *Leg.* 3 he employs the references in the curses to removing the landmarks (cf. Deut 27:17), leading the blind astray (Deut 27:18) for similarly symbolic ends: "Pleasure, then, has cheated poor maimed sense of the power of apprehending matters ... giving it a craving for that which produces pleasure" (*Leg.* 3.108-109; cf. also Deut 27:19).

1.4.4 Conclusion

The interpretation of biblical law forms a central part of Philo's series, the *Exposition of the Law*. In it he seeks to show the good sense, as he perceives it, in Mosaic law. His discussion is not impartial, but engaged positively and perhaps even apologetically in demonstrating that these laws both make sense and belong to the divine law, properly recognised as the law of nature and retrospectively recognised as embodied in the lives of the patriarchs. Given that the first part of the series, namely the tractates on Abraham, Joseph and the lost tractates on Isaac and Jacob – and one might include here the related tractates on Moses – demonstrated such embodiment, it is perhaps surprising that Philo did not relate his exposition of particular laws more strongly than he has, to these works. Our discussion of the laws has found even less connection with the *Allegorical Commentary* and *Questions and Answers*, though underlying these is the fundamental system of values on the basis of which Philo approaches each provision.

1.5 Conclusion

Matters sexual are scarcely peripheral to Philo's concerns. They regularly feature throughout his extensive corpus, both in allegory and literally. For Philo, sexual relations properly come to expression between a man and a woman in marriage. This is the order of divine creation and so also, therefore, what is according to nature. Excessive passion can result in men engaging in adulterous acts and in engaging in sex with other men, usually, though not exclusively, younger men and boys, but Philo sees this as contrary to nature and to divine ordering. The same applies to sexual relations between women, though this rarely receives his attention.

Philo's understanding of what is natural and according to divine order derives in part from his understanding of creation. Both creation of man and woman, on the one hand, and their coming together in sexual union through sexual attraction and pleasure, on the other, belong to God's creation. Sexual union serves procreation. While Philo can envisage this purely functionally as in his depiction of Abraham's intercourse with Hagar, usually it properly belongs within a more complex interaction which includes marital love, sexual desire, and pleasure. Such sexual pleasure and desire is not the result of divine punishment for sin, producing in women a compulsion ever to return to their husbands to fall pregnant and suffer the consequences nor the juice of plucking a forbidden fruit, but part of the divine order.

That experience of sexual pleasure, which Philo hails as the greatest among all pleasures, both serves the propagation of the race and creates a potential problem which can become the downfall of humanity. That downfall is central among Philo's concerns and as a result he gives major emphasis to the dangers which pleasures, not least sexual pleasures, pose. In this he makes rich use of Stoic rhetoric and psychology to demand denial of the passions, at times graphically depicting the need for surgery to excise them. It is relatively easy to cite such statements and draw from them what appears to be the obvious conclusion that Philo espoused the passionless life and must therefore have disapproved of sexual passion and indeed seen it as sin and even as sin's origin. Our discussion confirms what others too have observed, namely that one must weigh Philo's rhetoric both in the immediate context of his discourse and in the context of his work as a whole. There not only to do we find passages which affirm a place for proper sexual passion towards one's wife and hence which contradict the negative rhetoric, but often Philo himself moderates his extreme claims with caveats within the immediate context, not infrequently conceding that, of course, he does not mean denial of responding to life's necessities, including for food, drink, and sex for procreation.

While one solution is to see Philo expressing himself inconsistently and contradicting himself, a common enough human trait which we should not deny him if it fits, a more likely solution is that we recognise that he employs extreme rhetoric at times for emphasis. Any absolute dualism which would declare the body or any of its parts evil would have been difficult for Philo given his unambiguous belief in divine creation. That belief enables him to portray the human person in its entirety, rational and irrational, mind and senses and associated passions, as essentially good. Nowhere does he indicate that any act of sin, such as a fall, changed that constitutional reality. Human sexuality is not a flaw, let alone an evil.

The closest Philo comes to a created dualism is in his claim that "let us make" in Gen 1:26 implies a partnership of God with helpers and that their involvement rendered the outcome less than perfect in the case of human beings (and only them). Nowhere, however, does he specify particular parts that they made which are faulty. Indeed he describes the physical body as made of the very best materials available. Unlike Plato's demiurge in the *Timaeus* Philo's God did not delegate the act, but simply teamed up with his lesser powers for the task. Similarly, unlike in the *Timaeus*, women were not the result of failed men on a scale of devolution which would lead to even lesser beings that cling to the earth, but God's creation. They are, however, in Philo's assessment, inferior in both physical and mental ability, a view he shared with many of his time. Just as animals are even more inferior, this is not because God abdicated the creative act. On the contrary God made all such without helpers. His use of helpers relates only to creation of humankind, and initially the man, not specifically to the woman. Thus it was God, and so divine ordering, who made woman inferior to man. This is not misogyny, but reality as far as Philo is concerned, and matched by many other features of his world where the male is seen as superior to the female, including within the structure of the universe itself and its numbers as Pythagorean learning had established.

On the positive side, Philo values women as he understands them: less able intellectually and physically, less sexually engaged, but also less capable of controlling their passions, including their sexuality, and so best seen as partners with men in marriage and household, who can then control them. In Philo's day a wife would usually be around ten years younger than her husband, and exercise responsibility for managing the household (not insubstantial), while he dealt with the more important issues of community affairs, to put it in terms of the wealthy elite household which Philo presupposes. Philo can admit to some equality between the two in the processes of procreation, but there, too, he espouses the

Aristotelian view that the man produces the seed, the woman only the field in which it is sown. In sex as in other areas he also sees the male as active and the woman as passive, which coheres with his view that women, he believes, have less sexual drive.

Within this framework, nevertheless, Philo finds a place for sexual relations between men and women and understands such coming together as designed for purposes of procreation. While he very clearly espouses the biblical prohibition of intercourse during menstruation, which he sees warranted because it cannot lead to procreation, and would probably have seen intercourse during pregnancy similarly, he nowhere proceeds down the path of further definition to determine the matter, so that we are probably right to assume that apart from those exceptions he saw marital intercourse, including as an expression of love and an enjoyment of pleasure, as a total package and always likely to result in procreation and so always appropriate. This probably explains how he can countenance continuing intercourse between a couple who find themselves having become infertile and does not feel he must insist they separate or become celibate.

Philo's concern with excess does also impinge on marriage when he condemns men for engaging in intercourse just for lust and treating their wives like prostitutes. Part of his meaning, as we have seen, would relate to what is frequently abusive marital sex which disregards the rights and integrity of the partner, as in various forms of what is effectively marital rape. It is possible to read Philo as insisting that intercourse in marriage is not to be enjoyed or that its ecstasy should be toned down. Where Philo addresses excessive lust in marriage, however, he is usually comparing it with the behaviour of animals, so that it is not at all clear that he is wanting to dampen down the intensity of the pleasure which he sees as proper to marriage. His employment of the metaphor of intercourse, including, it seems, its ecstasy, in allegory may indicate otherwise.

Philo's warnings about the dangers of pleasure, and desire for sexual pleasure in particular, are widespread throughout his writings. The transition from acknowledging the legitimate pleasure of man and woman coming together in intercourse to seeing experience of such pleasure as raising all kinds of aberrant behaviours is reasonable, given his presuppositions. When seeking pleasure becomes a goal in itself, then the likelihood that other interests, including the best interests both of others and oneself, might take second place, be ignored or even damaged, is high. In that respect, it makes sense to declare pleasure the root of all evil, even if that needs significant qualification, which Philo, it seems, always assumes. The treatment of the snake illustrates this well. Primarily a negative symbol of the danger of pleasure and its lure, it also serves Philo, albeit briefly, as representing pleasure as something positive which makes communication between mind and senses, not to speak of bringing together man and woman for procreation, possible.

Conclusion

Philo never equates the snake and the devil, but he certainly portrays the encounter with pleasure as a battle which must be won. His hearers would surely have affirmed his attacks on the excesses of gluttony, drunkenness, and sexual profligacy characteristic of the feasts and banquets of his day. Neither food, nor drink, nor sex, is evil, but excess and ill direction are ruinous. At most, Philo can tolerate drunkenness where it is safe and has positive outcomes and might well have seen proper enjoyment of sex similarly. Mostly, however, he is concerned both to warn against the excesses and their lure, frequently symbolised with the sexual image of the seductress, even where sexual seduction itself may not have been in mind, and to urge development of ethical maturity to enable people to manage and control their passions.

It is easiest for him to speak of eliminating the passion of anger altogether, which, following Platonic psychology, he locates in the breast. He speaks of Moses doing so. Such elimination hardly makes sense in relation to those of the abdomen, hunger, thirst, and sexual desire. Nevertheless Philo espouses a model of human maturity which goes far beyond obedience to commandments. It includes developing self-knowledge, understanding oneself, one's senses and passions, but moving beyond them to a level where one's mind is fully in control and they fall into their proper place. For Philo, such maturity means embracing life with all its senses and passions in a way that conforms to the divine ordering of nature, which includes, in relation to sexuality, marrying, engaging in sexual intercourse, and bearing children.

This is the norm, though he can also recognise exceptions in relation to distinctive callings, such as Moses' call to be a prophet, for which Philo sees sexual abstinence as a requirement, probably reflecting cultic presuppositions derived both from his biblical heritage concerning Sinai and contemporary assumptions. The Therapeutae and Essenes are also exceptions in espousing celibacy, which Philo partly explains on pragmatic grounds of age (the women are post-menopausal) and its suitability to the style of communal life which, in Philo's view, marriage and women's jealousies would disrupt.

Most of Philo's exhortations concerning the control of passions, however, occur through his allegories. A fundamental allegory derives from the creation stories, in particular, the creation of woman. Accordingly, Philo takes woman to symbolise the senses, the irrational, in the human person, and man to symbolise the mind, the rational. This produces complications because women, too, have a psychology; they, too, have minds. Mostly what he writes of how men should be, namely in control of their senses and the related passions, can be equally true of women, except that, on Philo's presuppositions, they will find that more difficult because of their inferior abilities. In fact, it is on the basis of these presuppositions, that Philo obviously found it suitable to designate the parts of the soul the way he does: the superior and more able part – the mind – as male, and the inferior, less able parts – the senses – as female.

As with men and women, so with the mind and the senses, both are elements of divine ordering and divine creation. Both need to remain in their proper place: women under control, senses and related passions under control. This basic allegory of the soul becomes then the framework for a wide range of further allegorical developments which describe the processes which Philo sees as essential. Spatial movement from worse to better can symbolise movement from the state where passions and senses dominate (which at one point Philo identifies with a stage in developmental psychology where one should not remain stuck): Abraham's journey from Mesopotamia; Lot's departure from Sodom; Jacob's from Laban; Israel's from Egypt. Leaving behind the passions means not suppressing them but getting them under control.

Sexual metaphors abound because Philo focuses on relations both within and beyond a person. Mostly these are very positive and incidentally show that Philo can see sexual relations in a very positive light. Thus we reviewed the wide range of ways in which Philo applied the image: to God and the soul; wisdom or virtue and the soul; the mind and the senses; and even God and the earth. Gender floats around at times in ambiguity because Philo operates with a hierarchy where male is always superior and female inferior, so that whoever is on top, so to speak, is always male, which is not a problem in describing God as the active partner, but becomes difficult where Wisdom and Virtue, traditionally and as nouns feminine, have to become male and where mind has to become female. Philo shows himself fully aware of these complexities, but always asserts that the meaning should be clear, chiding the inflexibility of objectors.

Some of these metaphors are quite daring, which, again, at times he acknowledges, so dubbing them "mysteries", like the author of Ephesians, or clarifying that, of course, he should not be misheard as speaking in a literal sense of incest. At times he can depict bringing everything under control as making even the senses male or, alternatively, plays with the notion of women becoming if not male, then virgins. It is important to appreciate these images in their contexts and not to derive from them, for instance, that in any literal sense Philo wants all women to become virgins, that is, celibate, or that he is thereby demeaning sex and sexual relations. At the same time, we can see in Philo's many allegories which use male female imagery the consistent presupposition shining through, that woman is, of course, inferior, and male, superior, as God made them to be.

When Philo addresses specific instances of law, as in the *Exposition of the Law*, it is important to see that he understands them within the broader perspective of his concerns and not just as rules. This includes the fact that, as the sequence of his tractates in that *Exposition* indicates, he sees the written laws as manifestation of the divine law which is both the law of nature as God made it and the law lived out by the patriarchs. His approach, however, is not, then to handle the Decalogue and its extrapolations in the discussion of specific laws selectively, as if to pick and choose among them. For in his view such laws are authoritative, in what they demand literally and are not to be explained away with the extreme allegorists by allegory, as he himself is wont to do elsewhere, for instance where the literal in narrative seems to make no sense. But they are also autjhoritative in their broader allegorical meaning. Nevertheless, while standing on the biblical text, so to speak, he has an eye on a range of other concerns both arising out of his allegory of the soul and of his environment, including political and social factors such as what the elite of his community deemed right and proper, not least in accord with Augustan reforms relating to sex and marriage. This probably explains both his reshaping patriarchal stories to ensure offspring have legitimacy by elevating the status of maids to wives, his emphasis on women's seclusion, a developing Roman ideal, and his apparent sensitivity about celibates to affirm they have done their procreational duty in the past.

His exposition of adultery, given due prominence befitting its place in his LXX as the first of the second table, goes beyond simply reinforcing the demand to providing astute social analysis of its impact. Similarly, in dealing with abusive husbands, he provides shrewd and insightful observations about men who both love and hate women. These and other comments suggest that either he himself has been engaged in administering Jewish law in his communities on such matters or has observed it closely. It is likely that in those instances where he depicts as Jewish law what is unaddressed in Mosaic law he is reflecting local practice. Despite his many asseverations, also going beyond biblical law, about execution for transgression (for instance, of prostitutes), in his setting it is highly unlikely that such penalties were carried out. This probably explains his rather unusual exposition of Deut 24:1-4 which appears to assume that the woman has in fact committed adultery, but has not been executed. Its banning of reconciliation with the first husband is another instance where Philo can show biblical law conforms to Augustan law.

Philo's expositions reflect a setting where young men marry at around thirty and young women in their late teens, thus creating a ready market for prostitution to thrive on the frustrations of young men. Prostitutes feature regularly, both in the depictions of instances of sexual wrongdoing – though surprisingly active rather than passive, but for that reason also to be condemned – and as symbols for the lures of all passions. Philo's incidental comments allow us to see that they frequently suffered abuse. His comments also allow us to see that slaves faced abuse, not only through pederasty but also simply through being deemed accessible to their masters, something Philo assumes and never questions. He appears also to be familiar with polygynous marriage and its associated problems of rivalry between wives and over inheritance. He may imply disapproval of fertility devices in general, when he cites Rachel's use of pomegranates to that end, but otherwise does not address it. Nor does he address contraception or abortion, though he is vehement in condemning those who cause abortion by violence and especially those who expose infants.

Philo seldom writes of the future, including life after death, though he affirms the gift of immortality. Clearly he grounds hope in his faith that to contemplate God is to enter an ongoing relation of love and oneness. He does, however speak of Israel's hope as a people in describing rewards and punishment and in this context hails the future for his people as one of being gathered in its land and enjoying both the earth's abundance and abundance of offspring, clearly assuming that the future will be what the present should ideally be, including, therefore, proper engagement in the pleasure of sexual relations in marital bliss for the propagation of the species. His future hope in this way mirrors what he most values in the present when it occurs according to divine order and so according to nature. While abundance will restore the abundance forfeited through Adam's failure and his being cast out to a life of toil, Philo does not develop an eschatology or a restored Eden or a re-entry to the garden, let alone to anything like a pre-sexual state of naked innocence.

PART TWO

Attitudes towards Sexuality in the Writings of Josephus

2.1 Introduction: Issues in Reading Josephus on Sexuality

The works of Josephus form the most extensive corpus of a single Jewish writer from the period under review.[1] They include an account of the *Jewish War*, first composed in Aramaic not long after the completion of the war, 66 – 74 C.E., for the eastern Jewish diaspora and then translated into Greek, and reaching its final form in which it has survived, probably in the early 80's C.E. It appears to have been given official imperial recognition by the Flavian emperors. It portrays the events leading up to the war, beginning in the early 2nd century B.C.E., and depicting the war as the result of extremists on the Jewish side and perverse leadership among some on the Roman side, in contrast to the overall goodwill which existed and allegedly should exist between the Jewish people and Rome.

Over the following decade and a half Josephus appears to have worked on his twenty volume *Antiquities of the Jews*, emulating the twenty volume history of the Roman people by Dionysus of Halicarnassus a century earlier. The *Antiquities*, published in the mid to late 90's C.E., appears more strongly apologetic, making

---

[1] For a general introduction in overview see Nickelsburg, *Jewish Literature*, 288-96; Louis H. Feldman, "Josephus (CE 37—c. 100)," *CHJ* 3 (1999) 901-21; Louis H. Feldman, "Flavius Josephus Revisited: The Man, His Writings, and his Significance," *ANRW* 2.21, 2 (Berlin: de Gruyter, 1984) 763-805; Tessa Rajak, *Josephus: The Historian and His Society* (London: Duckworth, 2002); Per Bilde, *Flavius Josephus between Jerusalem and Rome: His Life, His Works, and Their Importance* (JSPSup 2; Sheffield: JSOT Press, 1988).

the case for the antiquity of the Jewish nation, the eminence of its ancestors, not least, Abraham and Moses, and the excellence of its constitution and laws.[2] The concern with making the case for his nation's respectability is inseparable from his concern with his own image, expressed in particular in his autobiography, *The Life*, in which to a large degree he defends himself against disparaging accounts of his role in Galilee by his rival, Justus of Tiberias.[3] Defence also marks his two-volume work, known as *Against Apion* where he addresses critics of his people, including, but by no means pre-eminently, Apion, and mounts the case that the Jewish constitution and law surpasses that of others, not least, the Greeks.[4] All of his works are highly political in the sense of seeking to position the Jewish people and himself within the context of the Roman world.

Josephus' personal agenda reflects his own involvement, first as a military commander in Galilee, then as a prisoner of Vespasian. He curried favour with his captors, accompanied them through the siege of Jerusalem, and was rewarded with status and a pension in Rome. There he could write his quasi-official account of the war and at the same time engage in the delicate process of seeking to rehabilitate the reputation of his people and himself. His resolve not only to report the war, but also to give an account of his people produced an extensive body of

---

[2] Steve Mason, "'Should Any Wish to Enquire Further' (Ant. 1.25): The Aim and Audience of Josephus's *Judean Antiquities/Life*," in *Understanding Josephus: Seven Perspectives* (ed. Steve Mason; Sheffield: Sheffield Academic Press, 1998) 64-103, depicts its aim as providing "a handbook of Judean law, history and culture for a Gentile audience that is keenly interested in Jewish matters" (101), so that it answers the question: what if I were to adopt Judaism? (95). Mason sees this as in continuity with *Against Apion* in which Josephus seeks conversion. See Steve Mason, "The *Contra Apionem* in Social and Literary Context: An Invitation to Judean Philosophy," in *Josephus'* Contra Apionem: *Studies in Its Character and Context with a Latin Concordance to the Portion Missing in Greek* (ed. Louis H. Feldman and John R. Levison; AGJU 34; Leiden: Brill, 1996) 187-228, 213-14, but see the critical discussion in Christine Gerber, *Ein Bild des Judentums für Nichtjuden von Flavius Josephus: Untersuchungen zu seiner Schrift* Contra Apionem (AGJU 40; Leiden: Brill, 1997) 374-75 and the discussion in Gunnar Haaland, "Jewish Laws for a Roman Audience: Toward an Understanding of Contra Apionem," in *Internationales Josephus-Kolloquium, Brüssel 1998* (Münster: Lit, 1999) 282-304.

[3] Mason, "Should Any Wish," argues that the aim is less to defend himself against Justus and more to portray his own status (102-103).

[4] On the various views of its function see Haaland, "Jewish Laws for a Roman Audience", who argues that "Where *Antiquitates* tends to picture plurality, flexibility, rationality, vices and virtues, *Contra Apionem* maintains uniformity, strictness, authority and absolute law-abidance", the latter matching Roman ideals (301), so that the purpose in *Against Apion* is the quest not to identify with Hellenistic culture, nor to depict Judaism as a philosophy (such language is rare in it), but to outbid it. Thus "by placing Jewish culture outside Greek culture, Josephus implicitly attempts to make space for Judaism within the Roman mind" (301).

writing which included both a retelling of biblical narratives, and also an account of post-biblical history of the Jewish people up to his own time, which is a rich source of information, albeit cast within the framework of his special concerns. Such a broad sweep of history necessarily includes many matters pertaining to sexuality, both in narrative and law, but, beyond that, Josephus' writings frequently show a special interest, at least in the erotic, and more generally in the depiction of love, hate, jealousy, and romance,[5] not to speak of marriage and divorce, as part of the mix of intrigue which characterised much of the history he reports.

Assessing his attitude to sexual matters within such complexities faces a range of difficulties. On the one hand, it is at times unclear to what extent Josephus is reproducing attitudes embedded in his sources, which he has rewritten to the point that they are irrecoverable by reconstruction, or conveying his own.[6] We can at best compare biblical accounts with his versions to see additions, omissions, reorderings, and particular slants. That is easier to do where we know the sources independently, such as biblical material, where he knows both Hebrew and Greek versions and 1 Maccabees, which he uses as a source for the early Hasmoneans. It is much more complicated for Herod's reign where he tells us of Nicolas of Damascus as his source, but appears then and later to have used also various other sources – none of which we can recover and compare. Thus one might with Ilan reckon nearly all the erotic allusions in Herod's reign to Nicolas and argue that these are not to be taken as indicative of Josephus's attitudes at all.[7] Similarly

---

[5] On this see Louis H. Feldman, *Josephus's Interpretation of the Bible* (Berkeley: University of California Press, 1998), who writes of Josephus' "preference towards emphasizing and strengthening the dramatic, pathetic, erotic and short story features in the sources so as to make them more attractive in the eyes of his Greco-Roman readers" (186).

[6] On the issue of sources, see the discussion of Daniel R. Schwartz, "Composition and Sources in Antiquities 18; The Case of Pontius Pilate," in *Making History: Josephus and Historical Method* (ed. Zuleika Rodgers; JSJSup 110; Leiden: Brill, 2007) 125-46, who argues against a retreat from looking at sources to focusing mainly on composition and makes the case that certain phenomena in the text are best explained by use of sources rather than stylistic variation or authorial latitude or lapses. Reconstruction of sources is often fraught with difficulty, but not for that reason to be abandoned. As far as the current investigation is concerned, the received text has to be our starting point, but all the while retaining awareness of possible sources and, not least, possible historical allusions to actual events.

[7] Tal Ilan, "Josephus and Nicolaus on Women," in *Geschichte-Tradition-Reflexion: Festschrift für Martin Hengel zum 70. Geburtstag: Bd 1: Judentum* (ed. Hubert Cancik, Hermann Lichtenberger, and Peter Schafer; Tübingen: Mohr Siebeck, 1996) 221-62, concluding, for instance, that "all powerful women of the Hasmonean and Herodian dynasties who dominate Josephus' writings are the literary creations of Nicolaus of

there are indications that in the later books of the *Antiquities* Josephus employed others to produce the material. While acknowledging the potential problems posed by the issue of Josephus' use of sources, I shall proceed in this discussion on the assumption that it is possible to evaluate the attitudes reflected in the writings, whether or not they always reflect those of the author, whose actual views may be irrecoverable. At the same time, this treatment will not ignore the potential problems and, where appropriate, will weigh their significance in reconstruction.

The discussion which follows is based on consideration of the text of Josephus' works as currently available, assuming the edition of Niese,[8] which is by and large the text reproduced in the Loeb Classical Library edition.[9] Unless otherwise indicated, English translations derive from the Loeb edition. Secondary resources for research on Josephus have been greatly enriched in recent years by the major commentary series, *Flavius Josephus: Translation and Commentary* (ed. Steve Mason; Leiden: Brill, 2000-). It embodies the extensive research of leading specialists in the field, some of which had already appeared in articles, not least, that of Louis H. Feldman,[10] but also Christopher Begg,[11] and Steve Mason.[12] The

---

Damascus, who wrote drama and firmly believed that women were the root of all evil" (262).

[8] Benedictus Niese, *Flavii Iosephi Opera* (7 vols.; Berlin: Weidmann, 1885–95).

[9] H. St John Thackeray, Ralph Marcus, Allen Wikgren, and Louis H. Feldman, *Josephus* (LCL 10 vols.; London: Heinemann; Cambridge, MA: Harvard University Press, 1926–1965). On the text see the recent detailed overview in Tommaso Leoni, "The Text of Josephus's Works: An Overview," *JSJ* 40 (2009) 149-84; and earlier: Heinz Schreckenberg, "Text, Überlieferung und Textkritik von Contra Apionem," in *Josephus' Contra Apionem: Studies in Its Character and Context with a Latin Concordance to the Portion Missing in Greek* (ed. Louis H. Feldman and John R. Levison; AGJU 34; Leiden: Brill, 1996) 49-82.

[10] Louis H. Feldman, *Judean Antiquities Books 1-4* (Flavius Josephus: Translation and Commentary 3; Leiden: Brill, 2000). See the collections of his earlier essays: Louis H. Feldman, *Studies in Josephus' Rewritten Bible* (JSJSup 58; Leiden: Brill, 1998) and Louis H. Feldman, *Josephus's Interpretation of the Bible* (Berkeley: University of California Press, 1998). We will also take into account more recent articles.

[11] Christopher T. Begg, *Judean Antiquities Books 5-7* (Flavius Josephus: Translation and Commentary 4; Leiden: Brill, 2005); Christopher T. Begg, and Paul Spilsbury, *Judean Antiquities Books 8-10* (Flavius Josephus: Translation and Commentary 5; Leiden: Brill, 2005), which were preceded and have been followed by numerous short articles.

[12] Steve Mason, *Life of Josephus* (Flavius Josephus: Translation and Commentary 9; Leiden: Brill, 2001); Steve Mason, *Judean War 2* (Flavius Josephus: Translation and Commentary 1b; Leiden: Brill, 2008), preceded by the major works: Steve Mason, *Flavius Josephus on the Pharisees: A Composition-Critical Study* (SPB 39; Leiden: Brill, 1991) and Steve Mason, *Josephus and the New Testament* (2d ed.; Peabody: Hendrickson, 2003). To this point the other published commentary in the series is that of John M. G. Barclay, *Against Apion* (Flavius Josephus: Translation and Commentary 10; Leiden: Brill, 2007).

range of issues in research on Josephus is very broad and has produced an immense body of secondary literature.¹³ Mostly, matters related to sexuality scarcely feature. The exceptions are in discussions of Josephus' depiction of the Essenes in relation to celibacy and Qumran,¹⁴ his depiction of women, usually seen as misogynist, and his erotic and romantic embellishments of narrative.

The area pertaining to some extent to sexuality which has received most extensive attention is Josephus' depiction of women. This is, of course, of far wider significance than interest in sexuality and conversely, issues of sexuality are necessarily not to be limited to female sexuality. The major treatments of women include Bailey's discussion of the matriarchs, who noted that Josephus treated women as a separate category from men and compared women nearly always only with other women and has reshaped the image of the matriarchs to conform to the roles he saw as appropriate for women in his day.¹⁵ Halpern-Amaru then provided a detailed discussion of both the positive and negative models in Josephus' portrayal of women, identifying three models, represented by Sarah, "most notable for her submissiveness and her chastity",¹⁶ Rebecca, depicted as assertive, strategic, and generous of heart, and Rachel as "Josephus' female lead in a romance".¹⁷ She then went on to show that the villainesses are counterpoints to these roles. Much of her discussion of individual figures has relevance to our discussion of attitudes towards sexuality below. Schuller examined Josephus'

---

¹³ See the earlier bibliographies in Louis H. Feldman, *Josephus and Modern Scholarship (1937-1980)* (Berlin: de Gruyter, 1984); Louis H. Feldman, *Josephus: A Supplementary Bibliography* (New York: Garland, 1986).

¹⁴ Todd S. Beall, *Josephus' Description of the Essenes Illustrated by the Dead Sea Scrolls* (SNTSMon 58; Cambridge: Cambridge University Press, 1988); Roland Bergmeier, *Die Essener-Bericht des Flavius Josephus: Quellenstudien zu den Essenertexten im Werk des Jüdischen Historiographen* (Kampen: Kok Pharos, 1993); Per Bilde, "The Essenes in Philo and Josephus," in *Qumran between the Old and New Testaments* (ed. Frederick H. Cryer and Thomas L. Thompson; JSOTSup 290; Sheffield: Sheffield Academic Press, 1998) 32-68; James S. McLaren, "Josephus' Summary Statements regarding the Essenes, Pharisees and Sadducees," *ABR* 48 (2000) 31-46; Steve Mason, "What Josephus Says About the Essenes in his Judean War," in *Text and Artifact in the Religions of Mediterranean Antiquity: Essays in Honour of Peter Richardson* (ed. S. Wilson and M. Desjardins; Waterloo: Wilfrid Laurier University Press, 2000) 423-55.

¹⁵ James L. Bailey, "Josephus' Portrayal of the Matriarchs," in *Josephus, Judaism and Christianity* (ed. Louis H. Feldman and Gohei Hata; Leiden: Brill, 1987) 154-79.

¹⁶ Betsy Halpern-Amaru, "Portraits of Biblical Women in Josephus's Antiquities," *JJS* 39 (1988) 143-70, 145.

¹⁷ Halpern-Amaru, "Portraits of Biblical Women," 151.

portrait of women of the Exodus period,[18] and Brown, the figures of Deborah, Jephthah's daughter and Hannah.[19] Mayer-Schärtel presented a comprehensive survey which goes beyond the biblical parallels to consider the whole range of Josephus' portraits down to his own time, concluding that Josephus consistently depicts women within the framework of men's priorities and interests, not least through marriages which cement convenient alliances and ensure status.[20] On the erotic, which features especially strongly in the Herodian period, Ilan argued that we are for the most part dealing not with Josephus' interests, but those of his sources, and that Josephus in fact has little interest in women as such.[21] Much of this research, but by no means all of it, has relevance for addressing at least half the story of sexuality in Josephus' works and so has informed the discussion below.

Within the extensive corpus of Josephus' writings we find a wide range of elements pertinent to sexual issues, some of them quite incidental, though frequent, such as the many references to women captives in war, and others within extensive tales of love and intrigue. There are also passages where Josephus deals directly with related issues of law. We shall begin with a review of passages where Josephus retells stories which he found in his sources, biblical and post-biblical, and note also any significant omissions. Our aim will not be to rehearse the details of each, but rather to identify anything relevant to discerning Josephus' attitude to sexual issues. In this section we follow the order of *Antiquities* for convenience, but this should not be misunderstood as implying that *Antiquities* is especially representative of Josephus' views, which sometimes vary significantly among his works, so that we shall use the sequence only as a framework in which to discuss the range of his works. We will then discuss sexual issues in his major treatments of law, before drawing together thematically the numerous other brief references within the context of a summary review which also takes into account the preceding discussions of narrative and law.

While much of what Josephus says about sexual matters is incidental, at one point we are reminded that they were directly existential. He goes out of his way to explain that his first wife, forced on him by Vespasian, though a prisoner, was a virgin (*Vit.* 414-415). Thereby he appears to exonerate himself in the light of the provision that a priest not marry a captive woman (cf. *A.J.* 3.276).

---

[18] Eileen M. Schuller, "Women of the Exodus in Biblical Retellings of the Second Temple Period," in *Gender and Difference in Ancient Israel* (ed. Peggy Day; Minneapolis: Fortress, 1989) 178-94.

[19] Cheryl A. Brown, *No Longer Be Silent: First Century Jewish Portraits of Biblical Women* (Louisville: Westminster John Knox, 1992).

[20] Bärbel Mayer-Schärtel, *Das Frauenbild des Josephus: Eine sozialgeschichtliche und kulturanthropologische Untersuchung* (Stuttgart: Kohlhammer, 1995).

[21] Ilan, "Josephus and Nicolaus on Women," 233.

Her departure (or divorce) at their release, his remarriage, subsequent divorce, and remarriage, have spawned speculation that these experiences generated in him a negative stance towards women.[22] Our measure cannot, however, be what might have gone on in his mind and feelings, to which we have no access, but what stands before us of what he wrote.

In what follows I have adopted the convention of using common anglicised names for biblical and historical figures (and for simplicity use Abraham and Sarah throughout, not Abram and Sarai), but at each first occurrence I note in parenthesis Josephus' distinctive form of the name – which sometimes varies considerably – as transliterated in the Loeb translation.

2.2. Narratives Pertinent to Issues of Sexuality

2.2.1 The Creation Account

Josephus' account of creation *A.J.* 1.27-51 reflects modifications over against Genesis. He reports the sixth day in a way that emphasises not that God made humankind male and female, which he omits, but that "He created (δημιουργεῖ)[23] the race of four-footed creatures, making them male and female", then adding: "on this day also He formed man" (*A.J.* 1.32). As Franxmann notes, he "pares the Sixth Day to the bone".[24] There is no mention of God making man in his image and likeness, possibly because images had been a sensitive issue, not least in the war;[25] nor of the hortative, "let us make", probably to avoid the suggestion of polytheism;[26] nor of the command to rule creation and to be fruitful and multiply. The latter is surprising given his emphasis on marriage for procreation. The latter

---

[22] Feldman, *Interpretation*, writes: "One guesses that Josephus must have been difficult to live with, to judge from the fact that he was, it appears, married three times" (188), rightly dismissed by Ilan, "Josephus and Nicolaus on Women," as sheer speculation (221-22).

[23] Feldman, *Judean Antiquities Books 1-4*, notes that for some the verb would recall Plato's prediction of the δημιουργός in *Timaeus* 40C (12).

[24] Thomas W. Franxman, *Genesis and the "Jewish Antiquities" of Flavius Josephus.* (BibOr 35; Rome: BIP, 1979) 45.

[25] So Jacob Jervell, "Imagines und Imago Dei: Aus der Genesis-Exegese des Josephus," in *Josephus – Studien: Untersuchungen zu Josephus, dem antiken Judentum und dem Neuen Testament: Otto Michel zum 70. Geburtstag gewidmet* (ed. Otto Betz, Klaus Haacker, and Martin Hengel; Göttingen: Vandenhoeck und Ruprecht, 1974) 197-204, 204. He also notes that Josephus omits it in dealing with Gen 5:1-3 and 9:6 (198).

[26] On Josephus' avoidance of the attendant problems of plurality of creators and anthropomorphism see Feldman, *Judean Antiquities Books 1-4*, 12.

is present in his description of the fifth day when God "let loose in the deep and in the air the creatures that swim or fly, linking them in partnership and union to generate and to increase and multiply their kind (συνδησάμενος αὐτὰ κοινωνίᾳ καὶ μίξει γονῆς ἕνεκα καὶ τοῦ συναύξεσθαι καὶ πλεονάζειν αὐτῶν τὴν φύσιν)" (A.J. 1.32).[27] One might compare *Jubilees*, which includes reference to making humankind male and female and to the command to rule (2:14), but similarly omits reference to being made in God's image and the command to be fruitful and multiply.[28] Its presence, however, already in the description of the fifth day, suggests that it is assumed for all other creatures mentioned subsequently, thus including humankind, but at least we can conclude that by doing it this way Josephus gives no special emphasis to multiplying in relation to human beings.

The implied connection with the animal world in relation to sexual intercourse for procreation also comes to expression in Josephus' account of the creation of woman. Possibly his etymology of Adam as "red" (πυρρόν) with the explanation: "because he was made from the red earth kneaded together; for such is the colour of the true virgin soil" (ἐπειδήπερ ἀπὸ τῆς πυρρᾶς γῆς φυραθείσης ἐγεγόνει· τοιαύτη γάρ ἐστιν ἡ παρθένος γῆ καὶ ἀληθινή) (A.J. 1.34) also has sexual connotations.[29] Then he picks up the association of male and female with animals as he writes that "God brought before Adam the living creatures after their kinds, exhibiting both male and female" (A.J. 1.35). He then has God, not Adam, name them (cf. Gen 2:20), so that now all the focus falls on Adam's response to the animals, especially their being male and female. As in *Jubilees*, God does not create the animals to be partners (Gen 2:18-19a; cf. *Jub.* 3:1), but rather Josephus has God see "Adam to be without female partner and consort [lit. not having sexual relations/intercourse with a female] (for indeed there was none) (οὐκ ἔχοντα κοινωνίαν πρὸς τὸ θῆλυ καὶ συνδιαίτησιν, οὐδὲ γὰρ ἦν)" and observe him "looking with astonishment at the other creatures who had their mates (ξενιζόμενον δ' ἐπὶ τοῖς ἄλλοις ζώοις οὕτως ἔχουσι)" (A.J. 1.35). Similarly *Jubilees* reads: "Adam was looking at all of these – male and female among every kind that was on the earth. But he himself was alone" (3:3).

---

[27] Noted by Jervell, "Imagines und Imago Dei," 198.

[28] The observations made here and in what follows go to some extent beyond the significant analysis of Betsy Halpern-Amaru, "Flavius Josephus and The Book of Jubilees: A Question of Source," *HUCA* 72 (2001) 15-44, who, in addition to the 19 significant parallels noted previously between Josephus and Jubilees, adds a further 29. Her list includes: having God respond to Adam's solitude not with the animals but only with the woman; Eve as well as Adam instructed about the forbidden fruit; and the creation of both occurring before the entry into the garden (34, 39).

[29] Without making this connection, Franxman, *Genesis*, suggests that Josephus has made the connection between red and virgin soil on the basis of Gen 2:4-6, which he omits, where virgin soil produces plants (48).

The focus in both is on companionship, including sexual companionship such as the animals exhibited.³⁰ *Jubilees* has God take the initiative to address the situation (3:4), and only then cites Gen 2:18. Similarly, according to Josephus it was in response to this perceived need that God extracted a rib from Adam while he slept and formed woman (*A.J.* 1.35), bringing her to him (cf. *Jub.* 3:6), who recognised her as made from himself (*A.J.* 1.36). This is as in Genesis but without the direct speech (cf. Gen 2:22-23). Josephus says nothing more except to note that she is called *essa* in Hebrew, but not explaining the original play on words, אשה איש (Gen 2:23), which underlines the common substance. From Gen 3:20 he then notes her name, Eve, as meaning the mother of all living (*A.J.* 1.36). He says nothing of men leaving parents to become joined to their wives and so become one flesh (cf. Gen 2:24), although the focus on sexual differentiation and partnership in the context allows one to conclude that he saw such sexual union as positive and at the heart of creation of the partnership between man and woman. He may have avoided Gen 2:24 as a text which could be read as giving too much recognition to the woman, including because of its unusual statement about a man leaving his family rather than, as was common practice, a woman leaving hers.

Mentioning the park after the creation of woman, the order also followed by Philo in *Opif.*, unlike there, leads to Josephus' describing God's bringing both into it (*A.J.* 1.37-38; cf. Gen 2:8-17). As in *Jubilees*, therefore, the creation of woman takes place outside the park/garden (*Jub.* 3:3-8), to which they were then subsequently introduced (*Jub.* 3:9) and as *Jub.* 3:18 presupposes, God instructs both, not just Adam (cf. Gen 2:16), "to abstain from the tree of wisdom" (*A.J.* 1.40). Unlike *Jubilees*, however, Josephus says nothing of the park being a sanctuary (cf. *Jub.* 3:12). He also omits reference to the couple being naked and not ashamed (cf. Gen 2:25), perhaps, as Feldman suggests, "because the juxtaposition of the serpent with Eve's nakedness would lead the reader to the grotesque thought that he has sexual designs upon her",³¹ but possibly also because of disapproval of nakedness in sports and sculptures of his time.

We then hear that the serpent "grew jealous of the blessings which he supposed were destined for them" (*A.J.* 1.41). The motif of envy, absent from the Genesis account, appears in Wisdom (2:24),³² and, as a reference to what the serpent once enjoyed, in the *Apocalypse of Moses* 16:1-3.³³ Here in Josephus the focus is potential future blessing rather than existing advantage which had supplanted benefits enjoyed by the serpent. The lure is the life of bliss and being

---

³⁰ Feldman, *Judean Antiquities Books 1-4*, contemplates a similar possibility: "the reason why God brings the animals, male and female, before Adam might be to arouse in him the instinct for a female mate" (14).

³¹ Feldman, *Judean Antiquities Books 1-4*, 16.

³² On this see Loader, *Pseudepigrapha on Sexuality*, 406.

³³ On this see Loader, *Pseudepigrapha on Sexuality*, 337.

like God. Certainly a "life of bliss" (βίον εὐδαίμονα) is what God intended, as Josephus explains in *A.J.* 1.46, but not by this means. There is nothing in the description of the serpent's deceit which suggests the verb is understood as seduction in a sexual sense[34] nor is their awareness of nakedness depicted as something evil in itself (*A.J.* 1.44), or as sexual awareness, understood as something evil. Josephus even sees the tree as giving them intelligence to know what to do when they become ashamed of being exposed to the light of day: cover themselves (*A.J.* 1.44). Accordingly they "believed themselves the happier for having found what they lacked before" (*A.J.* 1.44). As Franxman notes, therewith Josephus makes no further mention of nudity - problem solved—omitting it from God's speech and from the account of the final verses of Genesis 3.[35] The account of dealing appropriately with nudity nowhere suggests that sexual awareness was the result of sin, let alone that it is sin. The importance Josephus has given to sexual union remains therefore undiminished by the account of subsequent sin.

In depicting God's entering the garden Josephus innovates by supplying God with a speech in which he has God explain the plans he had for them:

> I had decreed for you to live a life of bliss (βίον εὐδαίμονα), unmolested by all ill, with no care (ἀπαθῆ) to fret your souls; all things that contribute to enjoyment and pleasure (πρὸς ἀπόλαυσιν καὶ ἡδονήν) were, through my providence, to spring up for you spontaneously, without toil or distress of yours; blessed with these gifts, old age would not soon have overtaken you and your life would have been long. (*A.J.* 1.46).

This is not only Josephus' innovative insertion, but also God's first reported speech in Josephus' entire account, so to be taken as an important statement of his viewpoint. As Feldman notes, the notion of an original life of bliss derives from "a tradition found particularly in Hesiod (*Op.* 90-93)".[36] It was also reasonable to expect that people would read the Genesis narrative in this way and we see this reflected, for instance, in Philo (*Opif.* 167). Within the statement Josephus expresses his own ideal for humanity. The "life of bliss" (βίον εὐδαίμονα) is "without care" (ἀπαθῆ), all needs supplied, but not without "enjoyment and pleasure" (ἀπόλαυσιν καὶ ἡδονήν). The following context relates these to abundant provisions, primarily of food, but the affirmation of "enjoyment and pleasure" is indicative that for Josephus pleasure is not something negative, unless sought in the wrong ways and places. Thus while God's speech says nothing about sexuality, it would cohere with the preceding narrative context to conclude that

---

[34] On this see Loader, *Septuagint*, 45-46.
[35] Franxman, *Genesis*, 51, 58-59.
[36] Feldman, *Judean Antiquities Books 1-4*, 17.

Josephus would view the pleasure of sexual engagement (in the right place and right manner) as something positive.

The report of blaming, by Adam of the woman, and then by the woman of the snake, includes reference to "her deception" [lit. "having been deceived by her"] (ὑπ' αὐτῆς ἐξαπατηθείς) (A.J. 1.48), but without any apparent sexual connotation. Halpern-Amaru notes that, with the deletion of Eve's dialogue here with God and earlier with the snake, "we are left with a strikingly flat portrait of Eve, who now serves as an uninteresting link in the chain of events leading to Adam's fall".[37] Josephus reverses the order of God's judgements on Adam, Eve, and the snake, accusing Adam of "yielding to a woman's counsel" (lit. "for becoming subject/an inferior to womanly/female counsel/advice" [ἥττονα γυναικείας συμβουλίας αὐτὸν γενόμενον]) (A.J. 1.49). Feldman notes that Homer similarly has Odysseus reflect on Agamemnon's death as resulting from "womanish counsels" (γυνναικείας ... βουλάς) (Od. 11.436-439).[38] The emphasis is not so much that he disobeyed God's command, nor even that he subjected himself to his wife, but that in doing so he subjected himself to his wife as a woman.[39] The issue is not sexual seduction, but gender, as the adjective γυναικείας indicates. This assumes that to do so is in principle an error on the basis that women are inferior and lack intelligence and wisdom. Josephus declares this directly in Ap. 2.201 when he writes of woman as "in all things inferior to the man".[40]

Following the Hebrew account he reports Eve's punishment as related to childbirth and pain in giving birth.[41] He makes no mention, however, of her תשוקתך "desire" or ἀποστροφή "return/refuge" in relation to her husband nor that he is to rule over her (cf. Gen 3:16). Thus the potentially sexual implications of such desire or constant returning are absent, including any notion that women's sexual passion is imposed by God's judgement. Sexual desire, as affirmed in human creation, is exempt from any negative implications which might flow from the failures that follow and this appears to apply not only to Adam, whose needs prompted God's creation of woman, but also to Eve and women. Similarly, the absence of reference to the husband's ruling over the wife needs to be read within the wider context, where it is quite clearly assumed as necessary, given the inferior nature of women's wisdom, including that this would have pertained already before Eve's sin. Josephus may have sensed the discrepancy between this fact and

---

[37] Halpern-Amaru, "Portraits of Biblical Women," 168.
[38] Feldman, *Judean Antiquities Books 1-4*, 17-18.
[39] So rightly Franxman, *Genesis*, 61.
[40] See the discussion of Josephus' attitude to women in 2.4.12 below.
[41] As Mayer-Schärtel, *Frauenbild*, notes, the fact that he later portrays Moses as having had an easy birth (A.J. 2.218) was one of Josephus' ways of indicating his mother's state of virtue (288).

the report that submission came as punishment, since he assumes it is a natural consequence of women's inferiority in the first place.

Overall Josephus' account of creation, which deserves particular attention as interpreting the first and foundational narrative of the biblical tradition, clearly affirms sexual union between man and woman as belonging within the divine order also characteristic of the animal world and as initiated directly by God, leading to the creation of woman. While the command to procreate is omitted in relation to the creation of humankind, it is certainly implied as belonging to the maleness and femaleness of all creatures. In the accounts of nakedness, sin, awareness of nakedness, excuses and blaming, and God's punishments, the positive status of sexual union remains undiminished. His account of God's first speech affirms appropriate pleasure and we may assume that Josephus would have included sexual union in God's ideal for humanity. Any suggestion that sex played a role in leading to the first sin, emerging from it, or as punishment for it is absent. At the same time Josephus allows us to see that he considers women as inferior to men already from creation, as Eve illustrated, and by implication that women should be ruled by men.

2.2.2 From Cain to Noah

Josephus describes Cain as settling with his wife in Nod (Nais) and descending into vice: "He indulged in every bodily pleasure (ἡδονὴν μὲν πᾶσαν ἐκπορίζων αὑτοῦ τῷ σώματι), even if it entailed outraging his companions (κἂν μεθ' ὕβρεως τῶν συνόντων δέῃ ταύτην ἔχειν) ... and became their instructor in wicked practices" (*A.J.* 1.60-61).[42] These will most likely be meant to include sexual wrongdoing and perhaps same-sex relations. In describing Cain's descendant Lamech, Josephus speaks of his having had seventy-seven children by his two wives (*A.J.* 1.63), scarcely credible, but which must relate in some way to Gen 4:24 which has him cursed seventy-sevenfold (*LAB* 2:6-10). Perhaps Josephus implies excessive behaviour or it could rest on a reading of יקום ("will set up") for יקם ("will be avenged").[43] Another descendant, Jubal, invented harps and lutes, which Josephus appears to treat negatively. His stepbrother, Tubal-cain (Jubêl), among other things, procured by the arts of war "the means for satisfying the pleasures of the body (τὰ πρὸς ἡδονὴν τοῦ σώματος), and first invented the forging of metal" (*A.J.* 1.64). This recalls *LAB* 2:8 which sees music as evil[44] and

---

[42] Feldman, *Judean Antiquities Books 1-4*, notes that Philo similarly depicts Cain as occupied with pleasure (cf. Philo *Det.* 119) (21).

[43] Feldman, *Judean Antiquities Books 1-4*, 22.

[44] On this see Loader, *Pseudepigrapha on Sexuality*, 260-61.

also *1 Enoch* which connects metal forging to ornaments and female seduction (8:1),[45] though these links are not explicit here and *1 Enoch* attributes this to the sinful angels.

By contrast, Josephus speaks positively of Adam's being "seized with a passionate desire to beget a family (δεινὸς εἶχεν αὐτὸν γενέσεως ἔρως)" (*A.J.* 1.67), something Josephus affirms, and so Adam begets Seth, to whom the discovery of astronomy is attributed (*A.J.* 1.69). The reference to passionate desire here doubtless intends something more than family planning in a neutral sense, but rather reflects Josephus' affirmation of sexual passion in what he sees as its proper context: procreation.

Josephus mentions the consorting of angels of God with women and compares their offspring with the giants[46] of Greek traditions (*A.J.* 1.73). He does not dwell on the angels' sin as sexual; nor does he depict the giants' deeds as sexual, though he describes them as "completely enslaved to the pleasure of sin (ἰσχυρῶς ὑπὸ τῆς ἡδονῆς τῶν κακῶν κεκρατημένους)" (*A.J.* 1.74), but then describes the resultant danger as murderous. Thus the focus appears to be violence (as Gen 6:13). Josephus follows a tradition according to which the giants are destroyed in the flood (Wis 14:6; cf. *1 Enoch* 10:9-10; *Jub.* 5:7). Josephus makes no mention of the command to multiply after the flood and of humankind as made in God's image (cf. Gen 9:6-7). This matches the omission in his retelling of Gen 1:27-28. Interestingly, he attributes the building of the tower of Babel to an attempt to thwart any future punishment by flood (*A.J.* 1.114). Unlike in *Jubilees*, Canaan's (Chananaeus) settlement in Palestine is not portrayed as illegitimate (*A.J.* 1.134; cf. *Jub.* 10:29-34).[47]

Josephus recounts the story of Noah's drunkenness and being seen naked by Ham. He apparently attaches no guilt to Noah for being drunk. He rewrites the story so that Ham's sin was not so much the seeing but his mockery of his father and showing him to his brothers (*A.J.* 1.141; cf. Gen 9:22).

2.2.3   Abraham

2.2.3.1 Abraham and Sarah in Egypt

According to Josephus Sarah (Sarra) was Abraham's niece (*A.J.* 1.151), identified with Iscah (Gen 11:29; cf. *Jub.* 12:9, which seeks to expunge niece marriages from

---

[45] On this see Loader, *Enoch, Levi, and Jubilees*, 19.

[46] Halpern-Amaru, "Josephus and Jubilees," notes that Josephus and *Jubilees* share the designation of the offspring as giants (37).

[47] On the other hand, see Halpern-Amaru, "Josephus and Jubilees," on the convergences of detail in describing the allocations (25).

the tradition and follows Gen 20:12 in depicting her as Abraham's half-sister). He differentiates legitimate from illegitimate children, i.e. those born of a concubine (*A.J.* 1.153), probably reflecting the concerns of Roman law.[48] Josephus narrates Abraham and Sarah's visit to Egypt, mentioning Abraham's instruction to Sarah that she declare him her brother (*A.J.* 1.161-165). He embellishes the story with the note that Abraham was "fearing the Egyptians' frenzy for women (τὸ πρὸς τὰς γυναῖκας τῶν Αἰγυπτίων ἐπιμανές)" (*A.J.* 1.162). This is both an attempt to explain why Abraham had to resort to deceit[49] and a typical, erotic embellishment. In the same vein he twice mentions her beauty (*A.J.* 1.162, 163) and that "Pharaothes, the king of the Egyptians, ... was fired with a desire to see her (θεάσασθαι σπουδάσας)" (*A.J.* 1.163), but, as Halpern-Amaru observes, in a way that does not allow her beauty to be misconstrued as seductive or erotic, and so justifies the deception "not so much by the fact of her beauty as by the Egyptian 'frenzy for women'".[50] Feldman observes that, as elsewhere, Josephus introduces "erotic elements reminiscent of Hellenistic novels" to cater for "the romantic interest that his Hellenistic readers craved".[51] This includes Pharaoh's asking who the man was who accompanied her and the direct meeting and conversation between Pharaoh and Sarah.[52]

Josephus does not mention her abduction but only that the Pharaoh was "on the point of laying hands on her" (οἷός τ' ἦν ἅψασθαι) (*A.J.* 1.163), which could also be translated, "was about to have sexual intercourse with her",[53] when God intervened: "God thwarted his criminal passion (τὴν ἄδικον ἐπιθυμίαν) by an outbreak of disease and political disturbance" (*A.J.* 1.164). Omitting the abduction and the reference to Pharaoh's providing benefits to Abraham removes any suspicion that she would have been for some significant time in Pharaoh's hands and so, as most would have assumed, have been sexually assaulted. To the traditional motif of disease (Gen 12:17) Josephus adds "political disturbance", matching his belief that all such things are to be seen as God's providence,[54] and that Pharaoh sought advice of priests through sacrifices, as a result of which God reveals the truth through Egyptian priests (similarly *Ps. Eupolemus* 9.17.7; 1QapGen ar/1Q20 20.19). God's wrath, his priests declare, is directed against him

---

[48] On this see Satlow, *Jewish Marriage*, 192-93; D'Angelo, "Gender and Geopolitics," 64-65.

[49] So Feldman, *Interpretation*, 259, 287.

[50] Halpern-Amaru, "Portraits of Biblical Women," 145.

[51] Feldman, *Judean Antiquities Books 1-4*, 61. See also Feldman, *Interpretation*, 258.

[52] Feldman, *Judean Antiquities Books 1-4*, 62; Feldman, *Interpretation*, 186, 259.

[53] So Feldman, *Interpretation*, 259, citing the use of the verb in 4.257.

[54] Feldman, *Interpretation*, notes that mention of plague and political disturbance might recall the opening of Sophocles' *Oedipus Rex* (260).

for wanting "to outrage the stranger's wife (ὑβρίσαι τοῦ ξένου τὴν γυναῖκα)" (*A.J.* 1.164), a serious breach of widely held hospitality rules.⁵⁵

Josephus then has Pharaoh excuse himself on the basis of misunderstanding, and assure Abraham that he intended marriage (Josephus' addition), and "not to outrage her in a transport of passion (οὐκ ἐνυβρίσαι κατ' ἐπιθυμίαν ὡρμημένος)" (*A.J.* 1.165), with Josephus leaving the hearer in no doubt in the light of his description of his passion in *A.J.* 1.164 as criminal and as prompting God's action, and of the priests' correct perception pertaining to God's wrath, that this is false. It is therefore, difficult to support the conclusion of Feldman that Josephus means us to believe Pharaoh.⁵⁶ Within the narrative Abraham appears to have believed it and this then accounts for the sequel in which, unlike Gen 12:16 but like *Jubilees*, Pharaoh does not bestow riches on him during Sarah's stay, but unlike both does not expel him, for Abraham must remain and give instruction to the Egyptians (*A.J.* 1.165; similarly *Ps. Eupolemus* 9.17.8; cf. *Jub.*).

Josephus returns to the story in the account of his speech to the inhabitants of Jerusalem enduring the Roman siege (*B.J.* 5.380-381). There he speaks of Sarah, whom he calls "a princess (βασιλίδα) and the mother of our race" being carried off by Pharaoh Necho (Nechaos), described as a ravisher (τὸν ὑβριστήν), a figure of much later times, not in Egypt but in Judah which he invaded (2 Kgs 23:18-30; 2 Chr 35:20-27).⁵⁷ He recounts the story to hail Abraham's restraint in praying and not fighting, and so trusting divine providence, as a result of which "the queen (ἡ βασίλισσα), after one night's absence, [was] sent back immaculate (ἄχραντος) to her lord (lit. husband) (ἄνδρα)". Beyond Josephus' playfulness in the move from "princess" to "queen", he is keen to emphasise that the ravisher did not in fact ravish her. Again, what Genesis assumes is an extended period becomes a single night.

2.2.3.2 Sodom, Lot, and his Daughters

Josephus mentions Sodom, including its subsequent destruction to become the Dead Sea, and the battle with the Assyrians, who also subdued the descendants of the giants (*A.J.* 1.174; cf. Gen 14:5 LXX). In *A.J.* 1.183 he mentions Abraham's

---

⁵⁵ Niehoff, "Mother and Maiden," suggests that Josephus has it seem like God is more angry about Pharaoh's transgressing norms than about Sarah (417).

⁵⁶ Feldman, *Judean Antiquities Books 1-4*, 62.

⁵⁷ See Feldman, *Judean Antiquities Books 1-4*, for the differences, including also that Abraham there controlled many armies, but chose not go to war, that there are no diseases or political disturbances, but only a vision on the one single night when Sarah was away (60).

request for an heir and again in *A.J.* 1.186,[58] where he mentions Sarah's sterility and God's command (Josephus' innovation) to Sarah to bring Hagar (Agar) to Abraham, removing therefore any suggestion that she, herself, might have instructed her husband to do what might have seemed immoral.[59] He also mentions her becoming pregnant and then the conflict with Sarah, but in a way that makes Hagar the guilty party for showing insolence (*A.J.* 1.188).[60] Circumcision serves to keep his posterity "from mixing with others" (*A.J.* 1.192), a theme not unrelated to intermarriage to which we return in 2.4.3 below.

Returning to the Sodomites, he notes that they are "insolent" (ὑβρισταί) (*A.J.* 1.194),[61] especially because they "hated foreigners and declined all intercourse with others (πρὸς ἄλλους ὁμιλίας)" (*A.J.* 1.194) – the very accusation with which Jews were being charged in Josephus' time![62] ὁμιλίας here could refer to sexual intercourse, but given the events to be described this would seem an unlikely irony. These are grounds for God's deciding to destroy the city. Following the order of Genesis, Josephus recounts the visit by the angels who announce Sarah's pregnancy, at which she only smiles (cf. Gen 18:12),[63] but also Sodom's destruction (*A.J.* 1.197-198). His account of the behaviour of the Sodomites assumes sexual wrongdoing:

> The Sodomites, on seeing these young men of remarkably fair appearance (εὐπρεπείᾳ τῆς ὄψεως διαφέρεντας) whom Lot had taken under his roof, were bent only on violence and outrage to their youthful beauty (ἐπὶ βίαν καὶ ὕβριν αὐτῶν τῆς ὥρας ἐτράπησαν). Lot adjured them to restrain their passions (σωφρονεῖν) and not to proceed to dishonour his guests, but to respect their having lodged with him, offering

---

[58] Feldman, *Judean Antiquities Books 1-4*, notes that here Abraham is depicted as distressed at not having children, not Sarah, as Genesis 16 (71).

[59] Bailey, "Josephus' Portrayal," 159. Niehoff, "Mother and Maiden," 416; Feldman, *Judean Antiquities Books 1-4*, 71; Halpern-Amaru, "Portraits of Biblical Women," 147, who similarly notes that before the visit to Egypt Abraham does not seek Sarah's help in calling him her brother but rather instructs her to do so (145).

[60] Bailey, "Josephus' Portrayal," 159; Feldman, *Interpretation*, 244-45; Halpern-Amaru, "Portraits of Biblical Women," 147.

[61] Feldman, *Judean Antiquities Books 1-4*, notes the argument of Levine that Josephus links wealth with insolence (73), referring to Daniel B. Levine, "*Hubris* in Josephus' *Jewish Antiquities* 1-4," *HUCA* 64 (1993) 51-87, 64. He points also the motif of their prosperity in Ezek 16:49. See also Judith H. Newman, "Lot in Sodom: The Post-Mortem of a City and the Afterlife of a Biblical Text," in *The Function of Scripture in Early Jewish and Christian Tradition*, (JSNTSup 154; ed. Craig A. Evans and James A. Sanders; Sheffield: Sheffield Academic Press, 1998) 34-44, 38.

[62] So Feldman, *Interpretation*, referring to the parallel accusation in Wis 19:13-14 (245).

[63] Halpern-Amaru, "Portraits of Biblical Women," 147.

in their stead, if his neighbours were so licentious (ἀκρατῶς), his own daughters to gratify their lust (ταῖς ἐπιθυμίαις αὐτῶν). (A.J. 1.200-201)

Josephus offers no comment beyond the narrative, but clearly condemns their actions as wanting to do sexual violence to guests and thereby breaching hospitality rules, like Pharaoh and Abimelech (A.J. 1.164, 208). Josephus also understands Lot's willingness to offer his daughters as giving higher priority to the obligation to hospitality than to the welfare of his daughters.[64] Unlike Philo, he does not use the occasion to reflect on same-sex relations in general and pederasty, which he addresses elsewhere (see 2.4.9 below). He also avoids the contradiction of having Lot describe his daughters as virgins (Gen 19:8) and then shortly after having him address sons-in-law who had married his daughters (τοὺς γαμβροὺς αὐτοῦ τοὺς εἰληφότας τὰς θυγατέρας αὐτοῦ) (Gen 19:14), by depicting the sons-in-law only as suitors (μνηστῆρες) (A.J. 1.202). Josephus is not reluctant to describe the young men as "of remarkably fair appearance (εὐπρεπείᾳ τῆς ὄψεως διαφέρεντας)" and to write of "beauty" (αὐτῶν τῆς ὥρας), implying that he recognises also that they were sexually attractive. That does not alter the fact that he sees any same-sex relations with them by force or otherwise as unacceptable.

His brief description of Lot's daughters' initiative to sleep with their father passes without moral comment, except perhaps to excuse what would have been seen as outrageous, on the basis of their mistaken belief (A.J. 1.205; similarly Philo QG 4.56, 58) and his being isolated from the rest of humanity (A.J. 1.204).[65] Josephus offers no moral evaluation and trims away the potentially offensive detail of the biblical story about their very explicit discussions and their getting him drunk on successive nights.[66]

2.2.3.3 Abraham, Sarah, and Abimelech

When Josephus comes in A.J. 1.207-212 to the incident of Abimelech's abduction of Sarah in Gen 20:1-18, he notes the connection with the previous incident (A.J. 1.207). His erotically touched up version[67] says of Abimelech that he too "being enamoured of Sarra was prepared to seduce her (ἐρασθεὶς τῆς Σάρρας φθείρειν οἷος τε ἦν)" and speaks of his "lustful intent (τῆς ἐπιθυμίας)" (A.J.

---

[64] On this see Michael Avioz, "Josephus's Portrayal of Lot and His Family," *JSP* 16 (2006) 3-13, 8.

[65] On this see Avioz, "Josephus's Portrayal of Lot," 8, who also concludes: "I believe that Josephus does not condemn the actions of Lot and his daughters because of their relation to King David" (11). See also 1.3.2.2.2 above in Philo's treatment of the story.

[66] On this see Feldman, *Judean Antiquities Books 1-4*, 78.

[67] So Feldman, *Judean Antiquities Books 1-4*, 78-79; Feldman, *Interpretation*, 186.

1.207-208), also a much more negative picture in contrast to Genesis where God in a dream accepts that he acted with integrity (Gen 20:6) and had therefore stopped him from sinning, that is, having intercourse with a married woman (Gen 20:3, 6). Josephus imports from the previous story the motif of God afflicting Abimelech with disease, absent from the Genesis account, though perhaps suggested by the threat of death in 20:3, 7, but reports from 20:3-7 the motif of the dream, though not its dialogue. Josephus focuses on the sin as outrage to a stranger's wife. God instructing him "to do no outrage to the stranger's wife (μηδὲν ὑβρίζειν τὴν τοῦ ξένου γυναῖκα)" (*A.J.* 1.208), as before, emphasising the hospitality issue (cf. "to outrage the stranger's wife [ὑβρίσαι τοῦ ξένου τὴν γυναῖκα])" (*A.J.* 1.164), and has Abimelech emphasise that God's providence prevailed and that "he would receive her back inviolate (ἀνύβριστον), as God and the woman's conscience would testify" (*A.J.* 1.209). Again we see the concern to avert any notion that she could have been defiled. Having Abimelech fall ill gave greater credibility to that claim. Josephus revises Abraham's defence of his calling Sarah his sister, namely that she was his step-sister (the daughter of his father but not his mother; Gen 20:12) by depicting her as the daughter of his brother, and so his niece, probably to avert the accusation of incest (*A.J.* 1.211).

Both episodes contribute to the image of Sarah in Josephus. In his retelling of both incidents he seeks to ensure that no one could believe that Sarah was violated, both because of the humiliation and because it would presumably have rendered her unclean for Abraham. In both stories he emphasises the strength and misdirection of sexual passion on the part of Pharaoh and Abimelech and in no way allows the impression that Sarah, herself, was to blame. At the same time he does this not by robbing her of her beauty, which must include sexual attractiveness. She is made the model, submissive, chaste wife *par excellence*, as Halpern-Amaru emphasises,[68] but not at the expense of her sexuality. It belongs within her marriage and to her husband, so that the threats of violation against her are depicted as flouting the rules of hospitality towards him.

2.2.4 Isaac and Rebecca

Josephus reports the birth and circumcision of Isaac, the flight of Hagar and Ishmael, and his marriage, without significant variation for our theme, though

---

[68] Halpern-Amaru, "Portraits of Biblical Women," writes: "Josephus models Sarah along the lines of the Hellenistic ideal of the traditional wife. Her chaste beauty, her public silence, her submissiveness and her maternal concern are the traditional virtues which define her femininity and bring honour to her spouse" (148). She is the "ideal spouse for a dominant, strong founding father" (145).

diminishing Sarah's importance. Perhaps his suggestion that Abraham concealed his intent to sacrifice Isaac from Sarah[69] is part of his positive depiction of her character (otherwise she should have objected). He reports the initiative to find a wife for Isaac without the warning against marrying a Canaanite (cf. Gen 24:3), instead having Abraham identify Rebecca as the intended from the beginning (*A.J.* 1.242), thus also removing the element of apparent chance from the arrangement, as in *Jubilees*.[70] The story otherwise follows the detail of Genesis, but elaborated in novelistic style by depicting a journey through difficult territory, winter mud, summer drought, beset by brigands (*A.J.* 1.244) and by an initially inhospitable reception, reminiscent of the story of Odysseus and Nausicaa (Homer *Od.* 6.198-210).[71] Josephus has Rebecca refer to Laban as "guardian of [her] maidenhood (τῆς ἐμῆς παρθενίας ἐπιμελόμενος)" (*A.J.* 1.248), reflecting that her father, Bethuel (Bathuel), was dead (*A.J.* 1.248; cf. Gen 24:50), and that he had taken over that responsibility from him. The servant makes the point that Isaac could have married a rich local, but "in honour of his own kin now plans this marriage" (*A.J.* 1.253), an echo of the intermarriage prohibition omitted earlier, yet ambiguously open.[72]

In recounting Isaac's sojourn in Gerar with Abimelech Josephus makes no mention of the abduction of Rebecca (cf. Gen 26:6-11). This may well cohere with Josephus' recasting of Rebecca's image which removes references to her virginity and physical beauty (cf. Gen 24:16), as Bailey suggests, and so removes the main trigger for the story.[73] Instead, Josephus depicts her as focussed on hospitality and moral goodness and acting on God's behalf to bring blessing to her people.[74] Similarly, Halpern-Amaru speaks of Josephus' deleting the "physical characteristics which could be associated with seductive wiles" and casting her as an assertive woman, who takes initiatives, though still diminished by having key roles taken from her and given to men.[75] Rebecca's sexuality is not, therefore, in

---

[69] Bailey, "Josephus' Portrayal," 160.

[70] On this see Betsy Halpern-Amaru, *The Empowerment of Women in the Book of Jubilees* (JSJSup 60; Leiden: Brill, 1999) 38, 41-42.

[71] So Feldman, *Interpretation*, 186, 261.

[72] Feldman, *Judean Antiquities Books 1-4*, suggests the omission of reference to Canaanites as wives both from Gen 24:37 and 24:3 may indicate that Josephus wants to portray Abraham as "not close-minded" (99); similarly Bailey, "Josephus' Portrayal," 162.

[73] Bailey, "Josephus' Portrayal," 162, 164.

[74] Bailey, "Josephus' Portrayal," 162, 164-65.

[75] Halpern-Amaru, "Portraits of Biblical Women," 148. She notes Rebecca's assertiveness in relation to both the servant and Jacob and organising his journey (149-50), but also the changes, so that Isaac, not Rebecca, receives the promise about Jacob and Esau, and Jacob, not Rebecca, prepares the meal and puts on the skins in the strategy to receive the blessing, so that she remains behind the scenes with wisdom and foreknowledge (also omitting her eaves-dropping and deceit) and to that extent is also less exposed to criticism

focus. In addition, like *Jubilees*, Josephus omits reference to her sterility (cf. Gen 25:21).[76]

2.2.5 Esau, Jacob and Rachel

Josephus mentions Esau's marriages to two daughters of Canaanite chieftains (cf. Gen 26:34, but preferring the names given in 36:2)[77] as "contracted on his own responsibility without consulting his father, for Isaac would never have permitted them, had his advice been sought, having no desire to form ties of affinity with the indigenous population" (*A.J.* 1.265), indicated thus as preference rather than law as later. As Feldman observes, this is part of Josephus' seeking to ward off the charge of misanthropy against Jews, which too strong an emphasis on prohibition of intermarriage might arouse.[78] In the same vein, Josephus notes that Isaac did not demand that they be divorced, as would Ezra later, but "resolved to hold his peace (σιγᾶν ἔκρινε)" (*A.J.* 1.266), depicted as a model response,[79] and omits the bitterness engendered for Isaac and Rebecca (cf. Gen 26:35). The latter does, however, make an appearance, as in Gen 27:46, in the reason for sending Jacob to find his wife in Mesopotamia, but in "restrained language" [80] (*A.J.* 1.276-278). As with Isaac, so, here, Josephus, like *Jubilees*, does not tolerate the chance element in the Genesis account, but has Rebecca specify that he was to marry the daughter of her brother, Laban (*A.J.* 1.278).

Reporting the story of the encounter with Rachel and Laban, Josephus transfers the mention of Jacob's love for Rachel and of her beauty to before the meeting with Laban, with the result that he depicts the encounter with Rachel in greater detail and as the occasion of his falling in love, "overcome with love for the maid (ἔρωτι τῆς παιδὸς ἡττηθείς)" and "amazed at the sight of beauty such as few women of those days could show" (*A.J.* 1.288). Feldman notes Josephus'

---

(150). She concludes that "she might well appear no different from the women in Herodotus' *Histories* who manipulate their situations for the highest interests of the family" (151).

[76] Samuel S. Kottek, *Medicine and Hygiene in the Works of Flavius Josephus* (Leiden: Brill, 1994), notes that in addition to Gen 25:22 Josephus has Isaac observe that Rebecca was "inordinately big with child" so anxiously consulting God (1.257) (46).

[77] Gen 26:34 lists Basemath as one of them, but Josephus treats her as daughter of Ishmael taken to placate his family's discontent with his Canaanite wives (1.277), referred to in Gen 28:9 as Mahalath, but in some LXX MSS as Μασεμάθ. See the discussion in Feldman, *Judean Antiquities Books 1-4*, 108-109.

[78] Feldman, *Judean Antiquities Books 1-4*, 164.

[79] Feldman, *Interpretation*, 300.

[80] So Feldman, *Judean Antiquities Books 1-4*, 109.

enhancement of the encounter with elements typical of Hellenistic romances, such as suspense, love at first sight, Rachel's all surpassing beauty, and also her "childish delight ... highly reminiscent of the reaction of Nausicaa (Hom., *Od.*, Book 6), when the stranger, Odysseus, tells her whence he has come and she offers to supply him with his wants". [81] The setting is now in the suburbs with both young men and girls, not just three flocks of sheep (Gen 29:2).[82] Josephus clearly views these responses positively, enhancing them further in depicting her response: "she, as young people are wont to do ... from filial affection burst into tears and flung her arms around Jacob, and after tenderly embracing him said that he had brought the most cherished and keenest "pleasure" to her father and to all their household" (*A.J.* 1.291-292), clearly a joy both at the family connection and at her own pleasure. This greatly enhances the meagre detail of Gen 29:11 which has Jacob kiss Rachel and weep aloud and reverses it so that here, as more commonly in the romances of the time, the woman bursts into tears.[83] Josephus shows himself here affirming sexual love. Halpern-Amaru notes that, in contrast to playing down the romantic in his depictions of Sarah and Rebecca, Josephus makes Rachel "an impetuous, affectionate 'young thing'" and the "female lead in a romance".[84]

Laban's response includes reference to his dissatisfaction that Rebecca's marriage had been contracted over in the land of the Canaanites, an element added by Josephus (*A.J.* 1.299), though not a reflection on intermarriage issues. In the tale of Laban's deceit over Rachel, Josephus adds that Jacob was "deluded by wine and the dark" to explain how he did not see that he was sleeping with Leah (*A.J.* 1.301; cf. Gen 29:23).[85] He omits Laban's appeal to the customs of his country (Gen 29:26), though alludes to a constraint without naming it (*A.J.* 1.302). Perhaps Josephus rejected the principle, though, like Genesis, he does not address the breach of the prohibition of marrying two sisters (cf. Lev 18:18). He then enhances the emphasis on Jacob's love for Rachel as motivating his working another seven

---

[81] Feldman, *Judean Antiquities Books 1-4*, 111-12. On the enhanced erotic emphasis see also Feldman, *Interpretation*, 186.

[82] Bailey, "Josephus' Portrayal," 165; Feldman, *Interpretation*, 330.

[83] Halpern-Amaru, "Portraits of Biblical Women," 152.

[84] Halpern-Amaru, "Portraits of Biblical Women," 151.

[85] Feldman, *Judean Antiquities Books 1-4*, notes the parallel "from Greek mythology, the relations between Theias (Cinyras), who is drunk, and his daughter Myrrha, which resulted in the birth of Adonis (Ovid, Met. 10.298-518)" (114). See also Feldman, *Interpretation*, 332. One may also compare the account of Reuben and Bilhah in *T. Reub.* 3:13, which has Bilhah drunk (see p. 412 below).

years (*A.J.* 1.302; cf. Gen 29:27 according to which he must wait only a week for Rachel, and thereafter serve his seven years).[86]

The account of the polygynous rivalry follows Gen 29:31 – 30:24, but makes the point that Zilpah (Zelpha) and Bilhah (Balla) were not slaves but subordinates, concubines (*A.J.* 1.305-306, 308), omits Rachel's desperate confrontation of Jacob, and reports the negotiation over the mandrake apples (μανδραγόρου μῆλα) (*A.J.* 1.307)[87] without any evaluation over the propriety of such means. The focus moves from rivalry over fertility to concern over losing love.[88] Overall Leah's acceptability is enhanced.[89] The depiction of Laban's confrontation of Jacob over his surreptitious flight is with enhanced pathos,[90] raising the marriage issue (*A.J.* 1.315), as is Jacob's response, also returning to the issue of the marriages and then arguing that "affection which wedded wives are wont to have for their husbands" had them go away with him (*A.J.* 1.318). Josephus mentions Rachel's feigned menstruation without evaluation, on the assumption that she would not therefore be desecrating objects she had been taught to reverence (*A.J.* 1.322-323; Gen 31:35).[91] Rachel's story is important in enabling us to recognise that Josephus can have a positive view of sexual love.

2.2.6   Dinah

Josephus' version of the abduction of Dinah adds that her going into the city was on the occasion of a festival, mentioned also in the version of Theodotus (4 7-9), to whom Josephus refers in *Ap.* 1.216, and because she wanted to see "the finery of the women of the country" (*A.J.* 1.337-341).[92] His description of Shechem's (Sychem) abduction follows Genesis except for omitting his speaking tenderly to her and then Hamor's (Emmor) report of his love (cf. Gen 34:3).[93] He adds that

---

[86] Halpern-Amaru, "Portraits of Biblical Women," 390; Feldman, *Interpretation*, 186, 331.

[87] Feldman, *Judean Antiquities Books 1-4*, suggests that Josephus may have equated them with the love apples of Aphrodite who was known according to Hesychius by the epithet Μανδραγορῖτις (116).

[88] Halpern-Amaru, "Portraits of Biblical Women," 152; Feldman, *Interpretation*, 332.

[89] Feldman, *Interpretation*, 304.

[90] So Feldman, *Judean Antiquities Books 1-4*, 118.

[91] So Feldman, *Judean Antiquities Books 1-4*, 119.

[92] As Bader, *Tracing the Evidence*, notes, Josephus offers no value judgement on Dinah's acts (158). On the version of Theodotus see Loader, *Pseudepigrapha on Sexuality*, 476-84.

[93] Feldman, "Rape of Dinah," notes that Josephus "makes no mention of Hamor's statement that Shechem longed deeply (חשקה) for Dinah and asked 'please' (נא) to give her

because of the latter's higher rank, Jacob could not refuse his request that Shechem have his daughter, an element not present in the original. The same is true of the explanation that this was despite Jacob's deeming it "unlawful to marry his daughter to a foreigner" (*A.J.* 1.338), a principle Josephus emphasises elsewhere (see 2.4.3 below). As Feldman notes, he also omits the offer by the Shechemites (Sikimites) of opening their land to Jacob and his people and of intermarrying "since this would presumably have aroused the readers' sympathies for the Shechemites".[94] Josephus speaks of the act as ravishing, and seduction (αὐτὴν ... φθείρει δι' ἁρπαγῆς καὶ ... ἐρωτικῶς), but not as outrage (cf. "he had committed an outrage [ἄσχημον] in Israel by lying with his daughter for such a thing ought not to be done" Gen 34:7) or defilement (cf. Gen 34:5, 13, 27).[95] While Spilsbury argues that for Josephus the Dinah episode has more to do with intermarriage than with disgrace of what they did to Dinah,[96] Feldman notes that he has enhanced sympathy for Dinah both by adding that she was Jacob's daughter and in reporting that she was visiting a festival, "since it was presumably a religious festival; and to be raped, especially at such a time, would appear to be sacrilege".[97]

Instead of Hamor consulting both Jacob and his sons, as in Gen 34:8, Josephus' account has a consultation only with Jacob, after which Hamor departs, and Jacob then consults with his sons. This removes the deceitful response by the sons to Hamor. More significantly, like *Jubilees*, Josephus makes no mention of the circumcision ploy, instead portraying the plan of Dinah's brothers, Simeon and Levi, who made a night attack during the festival and slew all the men and recovered Dinah. Josephus mentions that Jacob was aghast and angry at their action, a stronger emphasis on disapproval, probably designed to dampen potential criticism, just as omitting reference to the circumcision ploy removed what could

---

to Shechem as a wife, since such apparently genuine feeling and politeness would have reflected badly on the Israelites if they had refused" (263). On the omissions and variations see Christopher T. Begg, "Josephus' Retelling of Genesis 34," in *Studies in the Book of Genesis* (ed. A. Wénin; Leuven: Peeters, 2001) 599-605, 603.

[94] Feldman, *Judean Antiquities Books 1-4*, 123; Feldman, "Rape of Dinah," 264.

[95] Feldman, "Rape of Dinah," writes that "non-Jews might have objected to the reason for this indignation, namely that Shechem had committed an outrage in Israel by lying with a daughter of Jacob" (263). He also notes the parallel to the abduction of the Sabine women (264).

[96] Paul Spilsbury, *The Image of the Jew in Flavius Josephus' Paraphrase of the Bible* (Tübingen: Mohr Siebeck, 1998) 78. See also Begg, "Josephus' Retelling of Genesis 34," 603.

[97] Feldman, "Rape of Dinah," 262.

easily have fuelled anti-Jewish sentiment.[98] Feldman compares this with Josephus' account of Phinehas' spontaneous act and suggests that there Josephus has less hesitation because the act is committed against fellow Jews.[99] Thus Josephus has imported into the narrative the tone of disapproval apparent in Gen 49:5-7, which he otherwise passes over.[100] He apparently considered his hearers could accept some validity in the brothers' revenge, even though it was excessive, but would have found the circumcision ploy unpalatable. Thus, as Begg notes, for his Gentile readers Josephus writes to reassure and counteract prejudices, and for Jews has the twofold message on the one hand of not engaging in intermarriage and on the other hand of not engaging in Zealot-like behaviour.[101]

As Feldman notes, "Josephus might well have omitted the whole episode as embarrassing to the Jewish people, as he omits the incident of Reuben's intercourse with his father's concubine (Gn 35:22), the story of Judah and Tamar (Gn 38), and the first account of the Golden Calf (Ex 32:1–20)."[102] That he has not done so is probably best explained by its usefulness in showing Jacob's disapproval of violent extremism while nevertheless expressing disapproval of intermarriage. The stories of Reuben's rape of Bilhah and of Judah's incest with Tamar had no such redeeming features for someone wanting to depict the noble ancestry of his people.

2.2.7 Joseph

More promising was the encounter of Joseph's encounter with Potiphar's (Pentephres) wife (*A.J.* 2.41-60),[103] not least because the notion that Egyptian women were seductive and dangerous had been well learned through the escapades of Antony. Josephus has significantly elaborated the account, more than any other biblical account, and "given the episode the style and psychology of a Greek novel".[104] She "became enamoured of him" (ἐρωτικῶς διατεθείσης) not

---

[98] Feldman, *Interpretation*, 313; Feldman, "Rape of Dinah," notes accusations in Horace and Tacitus that Jews proselytise (265).

[99] Feldman, "Rape of Dinah," 271.

[100] Feldman, "Rape of Dinah," 271.

[101] Begg, "Josephus' Retelling of Genesis 34," 604.

[102] Feldman, "Rape of Dinah," 262.

[103] Feldman, *Judean Antiquities Books 1-4*, notes that Josephus omits to mention that he is a eunuch, either because he recognised that this meant an official or perhaps also because he is depicted as having a wife (142).

[104] Feldman, *Judean Antiquities Books 1-4*, 144. He calculates that the account has grown from 22 lines in Hebrew, 32 in LXX, to 120, and notes "a striking similarity between Josephus' account of Potiphar's wife's initiative in approaching Joseph and Phaedra's

just because he was attractive, but also, Josephus adds, because of "his dexterity in affairs" (of management) (*A.J.* 2.41). He adds that she assumed he would see advantage in being solicited by his mistress, when she declared her passion (*A.J.* 2.41). To his rejection Josephus adds that he proffered the advice that she "govern her passions (κρατεῖν τε τοῦ πάθους)", since they would dissipate if no fulfilment was in prospect (*A.J.* 2.43). He then psychologises that the rejection instead spurred the intensity of her passion (*A.J.* 2.44). He makes the occasion of the final assault a festival, which would account for her husband's absence and her feigning illness to stay home (*A.J.* 2.45; similarly *T. Jos.* 7:1-2, though not as a ploy to be alone with Joseph). Elaborating her appeal, he has her blame Joseph for not responding earlier, which would have relieved her plight of having excess passion and so acting beneath her dignity, a backhanded gloss by Josephus on what was at stake: excess passion (*A.J.* 2.46). He has her promise present and future benefits and threaten consequences if he set great store on his reputation for chastity (similarly *T. Jos.* 3:2), since she would falsely accuse him to her husband (*A.J.* 2.48-49).

Josephus then has his hero reflect on the consequences of taking advantage of the indulgence of a moment, namely deserving death (*A.J.* 2.51), and appeal to her to place greater store on her marriage where "union with her husband afforded enjoyment without danger (τῆς δὲ προς τὸν ἄνδρα κοινωνίας ἀπόλαυσιν ἐχούσης ἀκίνδυνον)" than on "the transient pleasure of lust (προσκαίρῳ τῆς ἐπιθυμίας ἡδονῇ)" (*A.J.* 2.51-52) (cf. Gen 39:9 appealing to prohibition of adultery) and in that way also to sustain her authority as mistress and live without guilt and fear of being found out (*A.J.* 2.52). Thus he sought to "curb the woman's impulse and to turn her passion into the path of reason (τὴν τῆς γυναικὸς ὁρμὴν ἐπέχειν ἐπειρᾶτο καὶ τὸ πάθος αὐτῆς εἰς λογισμὸν ἐπιστρέφειν) " (*A.J.* 2.53). This focus on reason echoes Josephus' depiction of Joseph in *A.J.* 2.40 as having φρόνημα (good sense) to be able to cope with life's trials. Similarly elaborated is the sequel, namely Joseph's escape and her slandering him to her husband (*A.J.* 2.54-59), which Josephus describes as something that "seemed to her alike wise and womanly (σοφὸν ἅμα καὶ γυναικεῖον)" (*A.J.* 2.54). Here Josephus embellishes with typically psychologising observations about her fear, hurt, confusion, and disappointment about her "lust" (τῆς ἐπιθυμίας) and

---

initiative in the earlier version of Euripides' *Hippolytus* in soliciting Hippolytus" (144; similarly 146). See the earlier discussion in Martin Braun, *History and Romance in Greco-Oriental Literature* (Oxford: Blackwell, 1938), focusing primarily on the parallels with the *Testament of Joseph* (44-95). On this see also Halpern-Amaru, "Portraits of Biblical Women," who notes that unlike Phaedra, Potiphar's wife "is not a sympathetic character ... not a victim of the goddess, of social convention, or of a tragic flaw ... to the contrary, she is the temptress" (155); and Niehoff, *Figure of Joseph*, 102.

"attempt at violation" (πείρᾳ διαφθορᾶς) (*A.J.* 2.54-55). He also depicts Potiphar as falling uncritically for his wife's desperate story, "unduly influenced by his love for her (τῷ τε πρὸς αὐτὴν ἔρωτι πλέον νέμων)" (*A.J.* 2.58).

The incident served well the cause of moral instruction and we see in Josephus' account what will have been some of its key elements: warnings about sexual abuse of power in relation to inferiors, instruction to govern (but not extirpate) passions, their likely waning when prospect of fulfilment diminishes, the danger of excessive passion, the lure of the moment of passion, the plight of fearing being found out and living with a bad conscience.[105] Halpern-Amaru notes the three key concepts employed in the narrative, ἐπιθυμία; ἔρως; πάθος, and writes that, driven by these three, Potiphar's wife is the "polar opposite of Moses who, according to Josephus, had so much control of his passions (*pathos*) that he 'only knew their names through seeing in others rather than himself'" (*A.J.* 4.328).[106] By contrast, Joseph is not passionless, but is the model for showing how young men should respond.[107] "Virtue and villainy in female characters are measured by the extent to which women use or do not use their powers of enticement over against male vulnerability", whereas men are more or less heroic depending on their ability to overcome it.[108] It is important also to see the positive side: namely the positive valuing of the enjoyment of sex within marriage.

Reference to the prohibition of intermarriage either in Joseph's words or Josephus' commentary is notably absent, but this makes sense because Joseph will marry the Egyptian woman, Aseneth,[109] whom Joseph depicts as a most noble and worthy virgin and even has Pharaoh initiate the match.[110]

---

[105] Halpern-Amaru, "Portraits of Biblical Women," argues that in portraying Potiphar's wife, Josephus shifts focus from female ability to seduce to "the vice of sexual passion in a female" (155). This suggests that Josephus sees sexual passion as such as a vice. The evidence does not support this.

[106] Halpern-Amaru, "Portraits of Biblical Women," 156.

[107] Niehoff, *Figure of Joseph*, observes that Josephus' typical sensual interests also come to expression in his describing Joseph's beauty in relation to Rachel as an inherited comeliness, which helps account for Jacob's favouring him (85), noting that the *Testament of Joseph* similarly emphasises the beauty of Jacob and Joseph though without erotic connotations (86).

[108] Halpern-Amaru, "Portraits of Biblical Women," 156.

[109] Spilsbury, *Image of the Jew*, 87.

[110] On this see Niehoff, *Figure of Joseph*, 106.

2.2.8 Moses and the Exodus

2.2.8.1 Moses and his Marriages

As part of his account of Moses' military successes against the Ethiopians, not derived from biblical sources,[111] Josephus mentions a marriage to the daughter of their king, who "fell madly in love with him (εἰς ἔρωτα δεινὸν ὤλισθεν αὐτοῦ); and under the mastery of this passion (καὶ περιόντας τοῦ πάθους) she sent to him the most trusty of her menials to make him an offer of marriage" (*A.J.* 2.252), which Moses accepted on condition that the town surrender (*A.J.* 2.253). At one level this is typical of political marriages of allegiance, but in Josephus' account it clearly had an emotional base, at least on her side. Josephus indicates neither approval nor disapproval, though the latter is unlikely given his idealised image of Moses elsewhere. He does not speak of any passion or love on Moses' part. Such a marriage is the butt of Aaron and Miriam's criticism in Num 12:1, but Josephus does not engage the intermarriage theme here. He then returns to the biblical material in reporting Moses' flight to Midian (Madian), but on grounds of general disaffection among the Egyptians, not because he killed one (cf. Exod 2:11-12). The report then follows of the encounter with Raguel's daughters with typical elaboration. Josephus enhances the depiction of Moses' reactions: emphasising his disapproval of the injustice to the girls and, by contrast, his kindness towards them (*A.J.* 2.260, 262), who themselves, rather than Jethro as in Exod 2:20, take the initiative to reward him (*A.J.* 2.261). He then reports Raguel's adoption of Moses[112] and giving him one of his daughters in marriage (*A.J.* 2.263), but she is unnamed and the detail is minimal. Raguel's frequent references to God

---

[111] On this see the discussion in Feldman, *Judean Antiquities Books 1-4*, who notes that "the sole biblical basis for the lengthy episode of Moses' Ethiopian campaign is a single verse", Num 12:1 (200). Demetrius and Ezekiel the Tragedian identify Midian and Ethiopia which would support the identification of the woman as Zipporah, as in *Exod Rab* 1:27. Feldman suggests that Josephus develops the episode to expose the causes of hatred against Jews, to show Jews are not cowards and inept in war, to round out the image of Moses as a leader, to put divine ibises in their place, and to exploit the romantic associations his Greek and Roman hearers will have connected with Ethiopia (200-201). See also his discussion of its possible sources (midrash; Artapanus, who has similar material but not the romance; or popular Hellenistic legend) (201-202).

[112] Cf. Abraham's adopting Lot in *A.J.* 1.154 and Pharaoh's adopting Moses (*A.J.* 2.232), probably reflecting Roman adoption practice. So Feldman, *Judean Antiquities Books 1-4*, who notes that the positive relation with a barbarian serves Josephus' interest in countering the slander that Jews were intolerant of any but their own (208).

effectively render him the equivalent of a proselyte and so remove the potential problem that this was intermarriage.[113]

2.2.8.2 *The Midianite Women*

Josephus, like Philo (*Mos.* 1.295-298) and *LAB* 18:13-14, greatly elaborates the brief reference in Num 25:6 to the seduction of Israelite men by Midianite women (*A.J.* 4.129-144).[114] It now forms part of Balaam's advice to Balak and the princes of Midian. Accordingly they are to select the most beautiful and seductive of their daughters, deck them out as attractively as possible and send them to the Hebrews' camp to entice the young men but not yield till they turned from their own laws and God to follow those of the seducers. Thus Josephus, with embellishments typical of romantic tales,[115] depicts the young men as enticed into slavery to their sexual passions and so to the women, who successfully mounted their case that they abandon their traditional ways, so that the men accepted foreign gods and practices, including foods, and "became insatiably intoxicated with them" (*A.J.* 4.140).[116] Josephus here introduces the instance of Zimri (Zambrias), who rejected Moses' appeal to dissuade the young men (*A.J.* 4.141-144) as attempted tyranny and affirmed his right to have married a foreign wife (*A.J.* 4.145-149).[117] He then reports Phinehas' (Phinees) killing of Zimri and all like offenders (*A.J.* 4.154-155), but without mention of his zealotry.[118]

---

[113] Louis H. Feldman, "Josephus's Biblical Paraphrase as a Commentary on Contemporary Issues," in *Interpretation of Scripture in Early Judaism and Christianity: Studies in Language and Tradition* (ed. Craig A. Evans; JSPSup 33; Sheffield: Sheffield Academic Press, 2000) 124-201, 193.

[114] On this see Feldman, *Judean Antiquities Books 1-4*, 377. He notes that the reference in Num 25:6 will have led to his changing them from Moabites to Midianites (cf. Num 25:1) (378).

[115] On this see Feldman, *Judean Antiquities Books 1-4*, 378. Harold W. Attridge, *The Interpretation of Biblical History in the* Antiquitates Judaicae *of Flavius Josephus* (HDR 7; Missoula: Scholars, 1976) draws attention to the parallels (and significant differences) in the story to Herodotus' account of the Sauromatians (129-30).

[116] Feldman, *Judean Antiquities Books 1-4*, notes that this incident along with those of Samson are "directed, apparently, to those Jews who sought assimilation with gentiles" (378). The issue, he observes, would be one of sensitivity and might expose him to the charge against Jews of "misanthropy and illiberalism", citing Tacitus' comment that Jews do not engage in intercourse with foreign women (*Hist.* 5.5.2), which he deems rhetorical exaggeration (378).

[117] Halpern-Amaru, "Portraits of Biblical Women," speaks of his giving Zimri an encomium on Hellenization (155).

[118] So Willem Cornelis. van Unnik, "Josephus' Account of the Story of Israel's Sin with Alien Women in the Country of Midian (Num 25:1ff)," in *Travels in the World of the*

The extensive treatment afforded this story in all likelihood reflects Josephus' strong concern with intermarriage, including the arguments and counterarguments which he saw playing themselves out around the issue.[119] Interestingly, the resultant defeat of the Midianites resulted in "unmarried women, numbering about 32,000" being taken captive (*A.J.* 4.163), presumably many of them to become captives wives of men of Israel! The difference is that they would have been converted or submitted to Israelite religion, the reverse of their ploy.

2.2.9 The Period of the Judges

2.2.9.1 Rahab

In the story of the conquest Josephus describes Rahab of Jericho as having an inn (καταγωγίῳ), rather than being a prostitute (*A.J.* 5.8). Thackeray and Marcus point to the tradition also found in *Tg. Josh* 2:1 which uses the word *pundekita* (πανδοκεύτρια or πανδόκισσα "inn-keeper").[120] Perhaps women who kept inns were often also prostitutes. Thus in *A.J.* 3.276 Josephus has Moses forbid priests marrying innkeepers.[121] This is then more likely than that Josephus is deliberately suppressing the connection with prostitution here, though his change renders it slightly less visible.

2.2.9.2 The Rape at Gibeah

Josephus brings the account of the rape of the Levite's concubine at Gibeah (Gaba) and its consequences (*A.J.* 5.136-155; Judges 19 – 21) at an earlier stage

---

Old Testament: Studies Presented to Prof. Mabveek on the Occasion of his 65th Birthday (ed. M. S. H. G. Heerma van Voss et al.; Assen. Van Gorcum, 1974) 241-61, 259. Louis H. Feldman, "The Portrayal of Phinehas by Philo, Pseudo-Philo, and Josephus," *JQR* 92 (2002) 315-45, notes that Phinehas would have posed a problem for Josephus, not least because Zealots probably appealed to him as their model, though he never says so explicitly, while Josephus saw in him a positive priestly forebear (326-27). He argues that Josephus tones down Phinehas' zealotry, has the assembly dissolved (4.151) and only then mentions Phinehas' entry into to Zimri's tent, reporting the slaying but without the gory details and mention of rewarding such an act outside the law (4.153) (331). See also Spilsbury, *The Image of the Jew*, 79.

[119] Similarly Feldman, *Judean Antiquities Books 1-4*, 382; Feldman, "Portrayal of Phinehas," 328. He notes that, as in the story of Samson, Josephus' interest is in castigating intermarriage rather than illicit passion (329).

[120] Thackeray and Marcus, *Josephus V*, 5.

[121] See Begg, *Judean Antiquities Books 5-7*, 4.

than in Judges, namely as a manifestation of the evils recounted in Judg 2:11-15.[122] Variations in his account include adding that the woman was not a concubine but a wife, perhaps to enhance the severity of the offence, which some might have seen as less serious if it had been against a concubine,[123] and that the Levite was "deeply enamoured of his wife and captivated by her beauty (ἐρῶν δὲ σφόδρα τῆς γυναικὸς καὶ τοῦ κάλλους αὐτῆς ἡττημένος)" (*A.J.* 5.136), typical of Josephus' romanticising additions, obviously seen as something positive in itself, and the more she withdrew from him, "he thereby only became the more ardent in his passion" (καὶ διὰ τοῦτο μᾶλλον ἐκκαιομένου τῷ πάθει) (*A.J.* 5.137), typical, again, of Josephus' psychologising additions.[124] The daily wrangling about staying or going after he went to fetch her from her parents' place where she had fled (Judg 19:4-8) is replaced by a general statement of reluctance and then by the report that on the fifth evening the two set out to return home (*A.J.* 5.138). Whereas in the biblical account the men of Gibeah want to have sex with the Levite who lodged there the night as guest of an old man (Judg 19:22), Josephus portrays them as having seen the attractive woman and as wanting to have sex with her (*A.J.* 5.143). Josephus has the host speak of their wanting to violate the laws "at the beck of pleasure (δεινὰ ὑφ' ἡδονῆς)" and of "their lusts" (ταῖς ἐπιθυμίαις αὐτῶν), then offer his daughter (cf. "virgin daughter and his concubine"; Judg 19:24), whereupon the men instead seized the Levite's wife and carried her off and raped her; she returned the next morning, collapsed and died. The sequence is then much as in Judges, including, ultimately, the need to find wives for the Benjaminites "to beget children" (παιδοποιῶνται) from 400 virgins left alive after the massacre (*A.J.* 5.168; cf. 165) and through allowing them to abduct girls from a festival (*A.J.* 5.171), for which Josephus adds an apology to the townspeople (*A.J.* 5.171).[125]

The major change is to have switched the desire from male to female rape. Perhaps Josephus wanted to suppress evidence that Israelites engaged in such

---

[122] On this see Begg, *Judean Antiquities Books 5-7*, 33.

[123] Halpern-Amaru, "Portraits of Biblical Women," suggests that the change reflects Josephus' discomfort that a Levite would marry a faithless concubine, pointing to *A.J.* 3.276; 4.244, and so rehabilitates her (158). Similarly Louis H. Feldman, "Josephus' Portrayal (Antiquities 5.136-174) of the Benjaminite affair of the Concubine and its Repercussions (Judges 19-21)," *JQR* 90 (2000) 255-92, 270.

[124] Halpern-Amaru, "Portraits of Biblical Women," notes that the problem is no longer her unfaithfulness to him (assuming the Hebrew of 19:2), but her response to him (158). She argues that Josephus uses the story "to demonstrate danger of excessive passion (even directed toward one's spouse)" (158). It is not clear to me that this is at any point in question here.

[125] Feldman, *Interpretation*, 187.

practices, which he severely condemns elsewhere,[126] such as when practised by the men of Sodom in the parallel episode, who were Gentiles.[127] At the same time the story in his hands depicts two opposite responses to sexual passion: abuse, but also positive engagement, and enables us to see another example of Josephus' psychologising interest in the erotic and perhaps another instance of finding common ground with his Roman audience in the parallel with the rape of the Sabine women by the Romans as recounted by Livy 1.9. [128]

2.2.9.3 Deborah and Jephthah

In his retelling of the story of Deborah (Dabora) he adds that she rebukes Barak for resigning to a woman the rank bestowed on him (*A.J.* 5.203) and omits her prediction about Sisera (Sisares) falling into the hands of a woman and so bringing glory to a woman (Judg 4:9), though he later alludes to it in the account of Jael's (Iale) deed (*A.J.* 5.209). At least by his addition he gives his own expression to his presupposition that women are inferior. The erotic suggestivity has gone from the narrative of Jael's slaying of Sisera.[129] Altogether, while retaining accounts of their achievements, Josephus has redrafted both women into more traditional roles.[130] Brown draws attention to Josephus' etymology of Deborah's name as meaning "bee" (*A.J.* 5.201), which in Greek, as Melissa, was used of priestesses at Delphi who lived segregated lives and had no contact with men.[131] If Josephus is aware of the connection, it may indicate that he espouses the view that celibacy is in some way related to the prophetic role, though it does not function as the basis for his depiction of Essene celibacy, as we shall see (2.4.13). He does not however develop this in the text, though it may be significant that he omits mention of her husband.

---

[126] On this see Feldman, "Benjaminite Affair," 274-75 and our discussion in 2.4.9 below.

[127] Begg, *Judean Antiquities Books 5-7*, notes that he retains the motif in the account of Sodom because they were not Jews (35).

[128] On this see the detailed comparison in Feldman, "Benjaminite Affair," 284-87.

[129] Brown, *No Longer Be Silent*, 80; Feldman, *Rewritten Bible*, 160.

[130] See especially the discussion in Brown, *No Longer Be Silent*, 71-81. She notes that Josephus omits Deborah's roles as military leader, judge, and by not including her song, as poetess, retaining only her role as prophetess (71). See also the cautions expressed by Mark Roncace, "Josephus' (Real) Portraits of Deborah and Gideon: A Reading of *Antiquities* 5.198-232," *JSJ* 31 (2000) 247-74, who argues that Josephus still attributes considerable authority to Deborah, both religious (251) and in playing the role of a general (254), and that Barak's elevation is not to the status of judge, but general (258) and that omission of the poem need not imply something negative because Josephus frequently omits them (258).

[131] Brown, *No Longer Be Silent*, 73-74.

The tale of Jephthah and his daughter has also undergone numerous revisions and been greatly reduced.[132] Of relevance to sexual matters is Josephus' attributing Jephthah's rejection by his brothers through reference to the fact that "he was not their full brother but unconnected on his mother's side, who had been inflicted upon them by their father through his amorous desire (ἐρωτικὴν ἐπιθυμίαν)" (*A.J.* 5.259), an eroticising revision of Judg 11:2, which describes his mother as a prostitute (γυναικὸς ... ἑταίρας)[133] and that in Josephus the daughter and fellow citizens bewail her youth, whereas Judg 11:37-40 emphasises the bewailing of her virginity and that she died never having slept with a man,[134] which then becomes an occasion for an annual four day lament. Perhaps Josephus wanted to avoid mentioning such a festival which might sound too much like fertility cults.[135]

2.2.9.4 Manoah and his Wife

The Samson saga receives considerable attention (*A.J.* 5.276-313), beginning with Manoah (Manoch) and his wife (*A.J.* 5.276-285). Josephus adds, typically, that she was "remarkable for her beauty and pre-eminent among the women of her time", that Manoah constantly prayed for offspring of his wife and "was moreover madly enamoured of his wife (ἦν δὲ καὶ μανιώδης ὑπ' ἔρωτος ἐπὶ τῇ γυναικί) and hence inordinately jealous (καὶ διὰ τοῦτο ζηλότυπος)" and that the angel was "in the likeness of a comely and tall youth" (*A.J.* 5.276-277). The jealousy motif, absent from the biblical story, continues in the depiction of Manoah's response to his wife's report about the angel, "extolling the young man's comeliness and stature", so that "he in his jealousy was driven by these praises to distraction and

---

[132] Brown, *No Longer Be Silent*, notes Josephus' embellishment of Jephthah's return home: "The language here evokes the image of shipwreck, which, in turn, recalls the similar vow made by Idomeneus, a heroic figure in Greek literature", thus setting the scene for the Greco-Roman audience who would then expect a returning home to a child whose destiny is determined by the father's words, of which the child is unaware (119). Similarly Christopher T. Begg, "The Josephan Judge Jephthah," *SJOT* 20 (2006) 161-88, 185.

[133] Begg, "Josephan Judge Jephthah," 167.

[134] Josephus mentions her virginity in the context of his return (5.264).

[135] Feldman, *Rewritten Bible*, suggests the omission might be to avoid a range of associations, including with the Vestal Virgins, Artemis who resided on mountains, rites of lament as for Persephone at Eleusis or Osiris in Egypt or Tammuz in Babylonia or Attis in Asia Minor or Adonis in Syria (184-85). On the close parallels to the story of Iphigenia devoted to Artemis in exchange for her father's victory in the Trojan war, see Brown, *No Longer Be Silent*, 120-22, though there the daughter is rescued. She notes that Josephus directly alludes to Artemis to dissociate God from such beliefs and practices (123). Begg "Josephan Judge Jephthah," notes that Josephus "sets the biblical Deity in sharp contrast with Artemis to whom the same verb is applied by the chorus of Euripides' *Iphigeneia in Aulis* when it sings of the goddess' 'pleasure' in human blood" (185).

to conceive the suspicions that such passion arouses (ὑπόνοιαν τὴν ἐκ τοιούτου πάθους)" (*A.J.* 5.279). Josephus' psychologising observation points to a fatal flaw: when passion is out of control, which he describes as "mad" (similarly *A.J.* 8.190-191; 13.417; 15.240; 16.194). Those who had heard his account of Herod and Mariamme might recall Herod's jealousy. Manoah's wife (not he, as in the biblical account) asked God to have the angel reappear, which he did, initially again to her alone as in Judges, and she summoned her husband, who, Josephus adds, at first still harboured jealousy. The rest of the story follows without significant variation. Josephus may have simply deduced the jealousy to enhance its storytelling quality.[136] It was both a popular theme and one of relevance for stories still to be told in his grand narrative.

2.2.9.5 Samson

Josephus reports Samson's first marriage to a Philistine woman and his parents' initial disapproval that he should contemplate marrying a woman from the "uncircumcised Philistines" (Judg 14:3). In his version he omits the potentially insensitive reference to Philistines as "uncircumcised".[137] He would have shared the parents' view except that he adds that this marriage was divinely sanctioned (*A.J.* 5.286). He also locates the initial encounter during a festival (as in the Dinah episode)[138] and adds that Samson "became enamoured (ἐρᾷ)" of her (*A.J.* 5.286) and constantly visited her household (*A.J.* 5.287).[139] Describing the wedding feast, Josephus notes the occasion of Samson's posing his riddle as "when the drinking was far gone and joviality prevailed, as is customary on such occasions" (*A.J.* 5.289), although it is not clear whether these words about what is customary are in disapproval. Josephus omits Samson's apparent allegation in Judg 14:18 that his opponents had slept with his bride ("If you had not plowed with my heifer"), but ends similarly with the girl being given to his best man (νυμφοστόλῳ) (*A.J.* 5.294). He then truncates the biblical account which has Samson wanting to go back to his wife and instead proceeds directly to Samson's revenge as a result of

---

[136] On the subtle changes in the portrayal of both Manoah and his wife see Halpern-Amaru, "Portraits of Biblical Women," 157-58 who notes that Josephus has made her more supportive and less heroic and put the focus less on her interests in having a child and more on his problems with jealousy.

[137] Feldman, *Interpretation*, 138.

[138] Feldman, *Interpretation*, notes also that the brides of Shiloh were also captured during a festival (479).

[139] Christopher T. Begg, "Samson's Final Erotic Escapades According to Josephus," *Hermenêutica* 6 (2006) 39-63, 51, 60. Begg, *Judean Antiquities Books 5-7*, notes also that his account has Samson bring all the honey to the girl (288; cf. Judg 14:9) (72-73). See also Feldman, *Interpretation*, 479.

which the Philistines burned both her and her kinsfolk (as LXX; cf. her and her father: Judg 15:6) alive. Josephus then omits reference to Samson's visit to a prostitute (Judg 16:1-3), instead, like *LAB* 43:5, merging it with the account of Delilah (Dalala) and so depicting her, unlike in Judg 16:4, as a prostitute ("being enamoured of a woman who was a harlot" γυναικὸς ἑταιριζομένης ... ἐρασθείς), indeed, a courtesan (*A.J.* 5.306).[140] He introduces the account with the judgement: "He was already transgressing the laws of his forefathers and debasing his own rule of life by the imitation of foreign usages; and this proved to be the beginning of his disaster" (*A.J.* 5.306).

The focus in particular is upon foreign marriages, the first notwithstanding, because his liaison with Delilah contravened the prohibition of intermarriage and would be his undoing, as Josephus goes on to report as he enhances the image of Delilah's wiles.[141] The story thus carries a double message: the prohibition of intermarriage and the disastrous consequences of not resisting the seductive wiles of women who seek to undermine men's self-control. Josephus might gain some sympathy for his account in noting Samson's failure to respect ancestral law, which every good Roman knew to cherish.

2.2.9.6 Ruth

Next Josephus recounts the story of Ruth (*A.J.* 5.318-340), where he both abbreviates[142] and introduces subtle variations. Thus Elimelech (Abimelech) arranges for his two sons to marry Moabite wives; it does not occur after his death (cf. Ruth 1:3-4). Male initiative mattered[143] and here a positive relation with neighbouring peoples is being claimed.[144] Similarly he then has Boaz provide the needy Naomi (Naamis) and Ruth with hospitality when they return to Bethlehem (*A.J.* 5.323), rather than portraying them as courageously fending for themselves

---

[140] Begg, *Judean Antiquities Books 5-7*, notes that ἑταιρίζω occurs in Josephus only here and in *A.J* 8.417 in relation to Ahab's death (77). Feldman, *Interpretation*, notes that Greece was famous for its courtesans (481).

[141] Halpern-Amaru, "Portraits of Biblical Women," 167.

[142] Feldman, *Rewritten Bible*, 193.

[143] Gregory E. Sterling, "The Invisible Presence: Josephus's Retelling of Ruth," in *Understanding Josephus: Seven Perspectives* (ed. Steve Mason; Sheffield: Sheffield Academic Press, 1998) 104-71, suggests Josephus may have in mind the role of the *paterfamilias* in Roman society (119).

[144] Feldman, *Rewritten Bible*, 197. John R. Levison, "Josephus' Version of Ruth," *JSP* 8 (1991) 31-44 suggests that Boaz's hospitality may serve a similar end, indicating generosity of Jews to outsiders (36).

(Ruth 1:22).[145] Of particular relevance for our theme is rewriting of the episode on the threshing floor, where he reports Naomi's initiative which had Ruth sleep at Boaz's feet, with the explanation that she deemed "that he would be gracious to them after consorting with the child (ὁμιλήσαντα τῇ παιδί)", that is, having sexual intercourse with her (*A.J.* 5.328). This takes any ambiguity out of the original story and frees Ruth's image from the taint she might have conspired in illicit sex (Ruth 3:4). Rather she was acting on instruction and in obedience.[146] Josephus then rewrites what happens, omitting the potentially euphemistic detail of her uncovering his feet (instead having her sleep at his feet) and her request that he spread his cloak/wing over her (cf. Ruth 3:7, 9)[147] and adding that (contrary to Naomi's instruction and Ruth's willing compliance) "nothing had passed (μὴ γεγονόσι)" (*A.J.* 5.330).[148] Boaz was not drunk but fast asleep;[149] his conversation with Ruth at midnight becomes early morning resolutions and suggests nothing untoward. The midnight exchange is reduced to identification but he responds with silence.[150] and he has her return home at first light unnoticed to preserve good reputation,[151] though traces of the original story remain in his intimation that he wanted to marry her (*A.J.* 5.329-331; cf. Ruth 3:8-15).[152] As Sterling notes, "one of the most heavily edited scenes in Josephus's secondary version is the threshing floor scene that the historian has painstakingly reworked to preserve the moral purity of the major actors".[153] There follows the account, as in Ruth, of the nearest of kin renouncing his right to inherit and Boaz then assuming the inheritance including marrying Ruth (*A.J.* 5.332-336; cf. Ruth 4:1-13). In this Josephus unscrambles the complication of the original story which mixes Levirate law Deut 25:5-10 and redemption of property Lev 25:23-55, Josephus resolving this by mentioning property in his interpretation of Deut 25:5-10 and rewriting the detail about taking off sandals so that it matches the law's provision.[154]

---

[145] Sterling, "Invisible Presence," 124; Halpern-Amaru, "Portraits of Biblical Women," 163.

[146] Feldman, *Rewritten Bible*, 200; Sterling, "Invisible Presence," 126.

[147] Sterling, "Invisible Presence," 114, 121-22; Halpern-Amaru, "Portraits of Biblical Women," 163-64.

[148] Feldman, *Rewritten Bible*, 193; 201.

[149] Sterling, "Invisible Presence," 112, who notes that some MSS delete "and he drank" (112).

[150] Sterling, "Invisible Presence," 119.

[151] Sterling, "Invisible Presence,"126-27.

[152] Sterling, "Invisible Presence," 127; Halpern-Amaru, "Portraits of Biblical Women," 164.

[153] Sterling, "Invisible Presence," 119.

[154] Sterling, "Invisible Presence," 120-21; Levison, "Josephus' Version of Ruth," 39-40.

Beyond the sanitising of the account of any suggestion of illicit sex, Josephus recasts the story in the light of other concerns. He reduces to a single instance the five references to Ruth as a Moabitess.[155] Feldman notes the omission also in relation to Solomon's wives (8.191 cf. 1 Kgs 11:1) and its omission from Josephus version of the list of prohibited marriages (*A.J.* 3.274-275; 4.244-245; *Ap.* 2.199-203, cf. Deut 23:4), thus setting Boaz in a good light.[156] He deletes the well-known acclamation by Ruth: "Your people shall be my people; and your God my God", probably because it might suggest Josephus and other Jews harboured an agenda of conversion.[157]

In contrast to many of Josephus' accounts where he heightens and eroticises, here he eliminates most references to strong emotions, including, being surprised, kissing, and weeping.[158] Rather Josephus portrays "ordinary women who unknowingly serve God's purposes"[159] benefitting from divine providence because of their piety and generosity.[160] Accordingly Ruth is a fitting forebear of David, a model of sexual propriety, which Josephus emphasises by de-eroticising, to ensure no other conclusion can be drawn.

2.2.10 The Period of the Kings

2.2.10.1 David

Josephus brings the account of Hannah (Anna) and her sterility without the constant taunts from Peninnah (Phenanna) (cf. 1 Sam 1:6-7), but still noting her as the one loved by Elkanah (Alkanes). He portrays her as bursting into tears when she sees Peninnah and her children and enhances the image of her distress, before retelling the story of her answered prayer and the birth of Samuel (*A.J.* 5.341-

---

[155] Feldman, *Rewritten Bible*, 197.

[156] Feldman, *Interpretation*, 138; Feldman, *Rewritten Bible*, 198.

[157] Feldman, *Interpretation*, 159; Feldman, *Rewritten Bible*, 198.

[158] Sterling, "Invisible Presence," 111. This includes the potentially ambiguous instruction of Boaz to his men that they are not to touch her (*A.J.* 5.324-325; cf. Ruth 2:8-9) (111).

[159] Halpern-Amaru, "Portraits of Biblical Women," 164. See also Levison, "Josephus' Version of Ruth," 33.

[160] Ruth's piety is evident in her generosity towards Naomi, her avoidance of illicit sex, and her honouring the memory of her husband (rather than just Naomi), all of which Josephus emphasises. So Levison, "Josephus' Version of Ruth," 36; Sterling, "Invisible Presence," 121-122, 126. Levison notes that Ruth has a child one year later (*A.J.* 5.335), thus ruling out anything from this encounter (37). See also his comments on the role of divine providence in the story (43).

347).¹⁶¹ The next major saga of relevance is that of David. Already in reporting the women's responses to David which angered Saul, he adds that they included both older and younger women (γυναῖκες ... παρθένοι) (*A.J.* 6.193; cf. 1 Sam 18:6). Perhaps Josephus already had in mind Saul's daughter,¹⁶² of whom he goes on to relate that she "was still a virgin; and so overmastering was her passion (τοῦ πάθους ὑπερκρατοῦντος) that it betrayed her and was reported to her father" (*A.J.* 6.196), typically expanding 1 Sam 18:20 with emotional detail¹⁶³ and providing clearer grounds for its coming to Saul's attention.¹⁶⁴ Here the issue is not passion but her failure to control it.¹⁶⁵ He had omitted Saul's offer of his daughter, Merab (1 Sam 18:17-19; also absent in LXX B). Josephus has David agree to provide to Saul 600 heads of decapitated Philistines (6.198), rather than 100 foreskins (cf. 1 Sam 18:25), suggesting forced circumcision which he would doubtless have deemed offensive to his hearers.

Interwoven in the saga is the account of David's friendship with Jonathan who is described as "loving the lad and reverencing him for his virtue (τὸν νεανίσκον ἀγαπῶν καὶ τὴν ἀρετὴν αὐτοῦ καταιδούμενος)" (*A.J.* 6.206), the emphasis on virtue helping obviate any impression that something erotic is intended.¹⁶⁶ Later he depicts them when David was forced to flee as "putting their arms about each other" and taking "a long and tearful farewell, bewailing their youth, the companionship which was begrudged them and their coming separation, which seemed to them nothing less than death" (*A.J.* 6.241). Again Josephus reports their embracing and renewing oaths of life-long, mutual affection and fidelity (*A.J.* 6.275), and on Jonathan's death that he had been "his most faithful friend" (*A.J.* 7.5) and again later his remembering his "friendship and devotion" (*A.J.* 7.111). Josephus refers to, but does not cite David's lament over Jonathan (*A.J.* 7.5; 2 Sam 1:19-27), which contains the words, "I am distressed for you, my brother Jonathan; greatly beloved were you to me; your love to me was wonderful, passing the love

---

¹⁶¹ On the image of Hannah in Josephus see Brown, *No Longer Be Silent*, who notes that Josephus reduces her role and enhances that of Elkanah, transforming a woman's story into a man's story (163-64). See also Halpern-Amaru, "Portraits of Biblical Women," 168-69.

¹⁶² Christopher T. Begg, "David, Object of Hate and Love According to Josephus," *REJ* 166 (2007) 395-410, notes that the link if already made in LXX B text of 1 Sam 18:16 (401).

¹⁶³ Feldman, *Interpretation*, 187.

¹⁶⁴ Begg, *Judean Antiquities Books 5-7*, 154.

¹⁶⁵ Halpern-Amaru, "Portraits of Biblical Women," notes that while this reflects negatively in Michal, Josephus also portrays her as a woman who will seek blessing on David and probably wants to cast the daughter of Israel's first king in a positive light (167-68).

¹⁶⁶ Feldman, *Interpretation*, 566.

of women" (2 Sam 1:26), which have caused some to speculate whether this was also a sexual relationship. Indeed, Feldman suggests that the omission indicates that Josephus was "careful to avoid the implication that the friendship of Jonathan and David was a homosexual affair",[167] though Josephus commonly omitted poetic material anyway. Nothing, however, suggests that Josephus saw it this way.[168]

Much of the story of David is retold without producing anything of special relevance to sexuality beyond what is in the sources. This includes his marriage to Nabal's wife, Abigail (Abigaia), honoured for her "modest and upright character and also because of her beauty" (6.308; "clever and beautiful"; so 1 Sam 25:3) (*A.J.* 6.296-308), the capture of his two wives and their release (*A.J.* 6.357, 364-365), the return of Michal (Melcha), whom Saul had given to Palti (Pheltias) (*A.J.* 6.309; 7.25-26), her confronting David about dancing naked before the ark in front of the servants (*A.J.* 7.87); and the employment of Abishag (Abisake) with whom he did not have sexual intercourse, as 1 Kgs 1:4 noted, but to which Josephus adds that "at his age he was too feeble to have sexual pleasure or intercourse with her" (*A.J.* 7.343-344). Josephus gives no indication that Michal's return might in some way contravene Deut 24:1-4, possibly because her separation from him was not through his divorcing her. He greatly elaborates the account of Saul's visit to the witch of Endor, who is depicted as an exemplary woman (*A.J.* 6.330-340).

The affair with Bathsheba (Beethsabe) assumes great importance (*A.J.* 7.130-158), since of David, he assures us, that he "never sinned in his life except in the matter of Uriah's wife" (*A.J.* 7.153) and, again later: "never once did he do wrong, except in the matter of Uriah's wife" (*A.J.* 7.391). To the biblical account Josephus adds that she was bathing "with cold water", but omits that "she was purifying herself after her period",[169] in typically novelistic style of the time adds that her beauty "surpassed all other women", and then, typically psychologising, comments that "he was captivated by the beauty of the woman and ... was unable to restrain his desire". It is clear that Josephus does not thereby excuse David,[170] but rather portrays him as facing overwhelming passion and failing to control it. Of Bathsheba he adds that she was concerned on becoming pregnant, on the grounds that "according to the laws of the fathers, she was deserving of death as an

---

[167] Feldman, *Interpretation*, 566.

[168] So Feldman, *Interpretation*, 565-567.

[169] As Begg, *Judean Antiquities Books 5-7*, notes that thereby Josephus avoids making "David a violator also of the prohibition of having sexual relations with a menstruating woman of Lev 18:19" (245).

[170] Cf. Mayer-Schärtel, *Frauenbild*, 115. On the other hand Halpern-Amaru, "Portraits of Biblical Women," notes that Josephus does shift some of the responsibility onto Bathsheba for Uriah's death by having her press David to find a way to hide their relationship (166).

adulteress" (*A.J.* 7.130-131), a law Josephus thereby underlines. In recounting the ploy to get Uriah to sleep with her, he has David add that "this was the natural thing for men to do when they return from abroad" (*A.J.* 7.133), another instance of Josephus' psychologising wisdom in matters erotic. Nathan's judgement of David is then made more explicit, identifying that one of David's sons would violate (βιασθήσεσθαι) his wives (*A.J.* 7.152; cf. "I will take your wives before your eyes, and give them to your neighbor, and he shall lie with your wives in the sight of this very sun" 2 Sam 12:11).

2.2.10.2 The Rape of Tamar

Josephus reports the rape of Tamar (Thamara) by Amnon (*A.J.* 7.162-180; cf. 2 Sam 13:1-22), again typically adding about her beauty that "she surpassed all the fairest of women" (*A.J.* 7.162) and that "she was closely guarded" (*A.J.* 7.163), as, in Josephus' view, should be the case with virgin daughters. He repeats Tamar's proposal that he ask David to allow him to marry her without any comment on the conflict with Lev 18:11 (*A.J.* 7.169; 2 Sam 13:13),[171] and the detail about clothing of the time (*A.J.* 7.171; 2 Sam 13:18). He adds reference to emotions to the description of the act: he was "burning with desire and goaded by the spur of passion (τῷ δὲ ἔρωτι καιόμενος καὶ τοῖς τοῦ πάθους κέντροις μυωπιζόμενος) when he "violated his sister (βιάζεται τὴν ἀδελφήν)" (*A.J.* 7.169).[172] Passion, unrestrained, produces violence and disaster. Josephus then retells the story of Absalom, including his following Ahithophel's (Achitophel) advice (2 Sam 16:20-22), to lie with his father's concubines (*A.J.* 7.213-214), to which Josephus sees no need to add comment about its obvious contravention of biblical law.

2.2.10.3 Solomon

To David's advice to Solomon to uphold the commandments, Josephus typically adds: not to neglect them "by yielding either to favour or flattery or lust or any other passion (μήτ' ἐπιθυμίᾳ μήτε ἄλλῳ πάθει)" (*A.J.* 7.384; cf. 1 Kgs 2:3). In reporting Adonijah's (Adonias) initiative to marry Abishag, Josephus makes

---

[171] Begg, *Judean Antiquities Books 5-7*, reads Tamar's appeal that Amnon not transgress the law as an allusion to the prohibition of incest between siblings (Lev 18:9, 11; 20:17), and so reads her proposal here as "playing for time" and not genuine (253). Alternatively the first appeal to the law is about rape and her proposal here is in conflict with the prohibition.

[172] Begg, *Judean Antiquities Books 5-7*, notes that "words of the βια-stem ... permeate Josephus' version of 2 Samuel 13, occurring a total of 6 times" (253). Josephus goes on in *A.J.* 7.170 to speak of "rape" (διακόρησιν).

explicit that she remained a virgin since David "by reason of his age had not had intercourse with her" (A.J. 8.5). He repeats the detail of 1 Kgs 3:1 that Solomon married Pharaoh's daughter, but without evaluative comment (A.J. 8.21). His account of the prostitutes' (ἑταῖραι)[173] dispute over the baby is told more elaborately (A.J. 8.26-34; 1 Kgs 3:16-28), but without significant change.[174] The account of the visit of the queen of Sheba, depicted as queen of Ethiopia and Egypt (A.J. 8.165-78; noted already in 8.159; cf. 1 Kings 10), serves primarily to highlight Solomon's wisdom and achievements.

Then Josephus turns to his failures, following the biblical account (1 Kgs 11:1-13). Josephus prefixes the account with the assessment that he "abandoned the observance of his fathers' customs ... for he became madly enamoured of women and indulged in excesses of passion (εἰς δὲ γυναῖκας ἐκμανεὶς καὶ τὴν τῶν ἀφροδισίων ἀκρασίαν)" (A.J. 8.190-191). Again the appeal to ancestral law would appeal to Roman hearers. This is clearly negative and condemns not passion or sexual desire itself, but Solomon's failure to control it. As Feldman notes, Josephus uses similar language of Herod in B.J. 1.443.[175] He then follows 1 Kgs 11:2, but generalises the prohibition of foreign marriages which it cites from Deut 7:3-4, and the dangers they bring of idolatry, but retains its import, adding that Solomon espoused idolatry "to gratify his wives and his passion for them (ταῖς γυναιξὶ καὶ τῷ πρὸς αὐτὰς ἔρωτι χαριζόμενος)" (A.J. 8.192). Again there is greater emphasis on sexual passion in itself and inappropriate response to it. Along the same lines he elaborates further, adding that Solomon was "carried away by thoughtless pleasure (ὑπενεχθεὶς εἰς ἡδονὴν ἀλόγιστον)" (A.J. 8.193; cf. also Sir 47:20). The detail of the number of wives (700)[176] and concubines (300), in addition to the daughter of Egypt, stands under that negative evaluation. He introduces a prophet into his account to voice God's judgement (A.J. 8.197; cf. 1 Kgs 11:11) and then recounts the fulfilment of the predictions in what follows.

In the way that he portrays Solomon's openness towards relations with other nations in the first part of his presentation, Josephus somewhat counteracts the otherwise very negative impression that his account of Solomon's failures might evince, not least as confirming the allegation that Jews are hostile to foreigners.[177] As Feldman notes, by speaking of his failures in terms of disregard for ancestral

---

[173] Begg/Spilsbury, *Judean Antiquities Books 8-10*, note that the noun occurs only here in Josephus' works apart from a variant reading in *B.J.* 7.399 (9).

[174] On the minor variations see Feldman, *Interpretation*, 581. He notes that having the two live in the same room (A.J. 8.27) enhances the dramatic interest of the story (624).

[175] Feldman, *Interpretation*, 626.

[176] Begg/Spilsbury, *Judean Antiquities Books 8-10*, note that he adds that some were daughters of nobles probably because he sensed that the claim that they were all princesses strained credibility (51).

[177] Feldman, *Interpretation*, 615.

tradition, Josephus is implicitly appealing for sympathy for his portrait among Romans, by whom ancestral traditions were highly revered,[178] while still not surrendering his commitment to the prohibition of intermarriage. For the rest of the period of the kings and the divided kingdom sexual references are largely minor and will be picked up in later discussion.

2.2.11 Exile and the Return

2.2.11.1 Darius' Bodyguards

The next passage of substance relevant to the theme comes in Josephus' version of the speeches of Darius' three bodyguards from 1 Esdras 3 – 4 (*A.J.* 11.34-58). His version of the speech on women stays close to the original, though he omits the words "clings to his wife" after mention of leaving one's father and mother (*A.J.* 11.52; cf. 1 Esdr 4:20), making the allusion to Gen 2:24 less apparent, and then omits the references to having no thought for father and mother and country (1 Esdr 4:21), loving one's wife more than one's father or mother and men's losing their mind because of women (1 Esdr 4:25-26), perhaps out of respect for Roman sensitivities about family.[179]

2.2.11.2 Ezra and Intermarriage

Josephus makes much of the issue of illicit marriages. Thus he reports the expulsion from among the returnees, of priests' "wives whose descent they themselves could not tell and who could not be found in the genealogies of Levites and priests", of which there were 525 (*A.J.* 11.71), for which neither Ezra nor 1 Esdras provides evidence. Then he returns to these in reporting Ezra's response to the accusations against "some of the common people as well as Levites and priests of having violated the constitution and broken the laws of the country by marrying foreign wives and mixing the strain of priestly families" (*A.J.* 11.140; cf. Ezra 9:1).[180] Josephus omits the specific reference to particular peoples with whom

---

[178] Feldman, *Interpretation*, 617.

[179] On the importance of family in Roman values see Eva Marie Lassen, "The Roman Family: Ideal and Metaphor," in *Constructing Early Christian Families: Family as Social Reality and Metaphor* (ed. Halvor Moxnes; London: Routledge, 1997) 103-20, 104-105.

[180] Feldman, *Interpretation*, seeks to make the case that Josephus lessens Ezra's involvement by emphasising that he did not take the lead in breaking up the marriages but needed persuading by Jeconiah, who "tried to persuade" (ἔπειθε) Ezra (11.145) (138). This may give too much weight to the imperfect. Certainly Josephus shows Ezra complying without hesitation and having been appalled in the first place.

these marriages had taken place (cf. Ezra 9:1), probably to help reinforce it as a general rule. He then goes beyond the biblical account in reporting that Ezra feared he might not be listened to (perhaps also Josephus' experience) (*A.J.* 11.142) and therefore was reluctant to act immediately (Ezra 9:3-4). He reports Ezra's prayer, the advice of Shecaniah (Achonios), and the resultant expulsion of the foreign wives and their children as in Ezra 10; 1 Esdr 8:91 – 9:36, adding that the ruling "remained fixed for the future" (*A.J.* 11.153) and clearly still matters for him. That he omits the list of names of those involved need not reflect, as Feldman suggests, a diminished emphasis on the prohibition.[181] Describing it, however, as entailing respect for the nation's constitution (*A.J.* 11.140) and as "having more regard for the observance of the laws than for the objects of their affection (τῆς τῶν νόμων φυλακῆς ἢ τῶν πρὸς αὐτὰ φίλτρων ποιούμενοι πλείονα λόγον)" (*A.J.* 11.152) would likely win sympathy from his audience, including that it might recall Pericles' restriction on citizens in 451/450 B.C.E.[182] Josephus makes no mention of the attention to intermarriage in Neh 10:1-30 and 13:23-29.

Schwartz argues that Josephus does not present Ezra as concerned with intermarriage generally but only in relation to priests.[183] To support this he notes that 1 Esdr 8:67 speaks of "the holy seed" (τὸ ἱερατικὸν γένος) mixing with foreign nations and that Josephus uses the same term in *A.J.* 11.140. To narrow it in this way would require that we ignore the preceding statement in each case where the concern is very clearly with the nation as a whole: "The people of Israel and the rulers and the priests and the Levites have not put away from themselves" (τὸ ἔθνος τοῦ Ισραηλ καὶ οἱ ἄρχοντες καὶ οἱ ἱερεῖς καὶ οἱ Λευῖται) (1 Esdr 8:69); "some of the common people as well as Levites and priests" (τινες τοῦ πλήθους καὶ τῶν ἱερέων καὶ Λευιτῶν) (*A.J.* 11.140); cf. "The people of Israel, the priests, and the Levites have not separated themselves" (οὐκ ἐχωρίσθη ὁ λαὸς Ισραηλ καὶ οἱ ἱερεῖς καὶ οἱ Λευῖται) (Ezra 9:1). Similarly Josephus reports of those instructed to swear to put away their foreign wives, that they included "the chiefs of the priests, Levites and Israelites" (*A.J.* 11.146, 151), and has Ezra address a mixed crowd of the tribe of Judah and Benjamin with the accusation (*A.J.* 11.148-149).

---

[181] Feldman, *Interpretation,* 139.

[182] So Feldman, *Interpretation,* 139.

[183] Daniel R. Schwartz, "Doing Like Jews or Becoming a Jew? Josephus on Women Converts to Judaism," in *Jewish Identity in the Greco-Roman World / Jüdische Identität in der griechisch-römischen Welt* (ed. Jörg Frey, Daniel R. Schwartz, and Stephanie Gripentrog; AGJU 71; Leiden: Brill, 2007) 93-109, 103.

2.2.11.3 Manasseh and Intermarriage

The issue recurs in Josephus' account of the marriage of the high priest's brother, Manasseh (Manasses), to the daughter of Sanballat (Sanaballetes) of Samaria (*A.J.* 11.302-303; cf. Neh 13:28). The historical details appear confused possibly by Josephus identifying the wrong Sanballat,[184] but Josephus' message is not. He applauds the action taken against Manasseh, whose deed the elders of Jerusalem feared might become "a stepping-stone for those who might wish to transgress the laws about taking wives and that this would be the beginning of intercourse with foreigners", and saw as the kind of thing which had warranted their nation's former captivity (*A.J.* 11.306-307). Sanballat persuaded Manasseh not to divorce his daughter but to stay with him and that he would erect a temple where he could serve (*A.J.* 11.311). According to Josephus not only Manasseh but "many priests and Israelites were involved in such marriages" and "all these deserted to Manasses" (*A.J.* 11.312). Accordingly Sanballat constructed the Samaritan temple with Alexander's consent and with Manasseh as high priest (*A.J.* 11.322-324). Thus Josephus makes the Samaritans a prime example of what can go wrong when people intermarry with foreigners.

2.2.11.4 Esther

In this book Josephus also recounts the tale of Esther (*A.J.* 11.184-296), strangely, without making any connection to the seemingly obvious issue of marriage to a foreigner. He depicts Esther as "a Jewish woman of royal family" (*A.J.* 11.185), apparently deriving this from the genealogy given in Esther 2:5. He supplements the detail of Queen Vashti's (Aste) refusal to come to the parallel male feast hosted by the king by adding the grounds for her refusal: "observance of the laws of the Persians, which forbid their women to be seen by strangers" (*A.J.* 11.191).[185] Another addition is his comment that "the king was in love with her" (διακείμενος δὲ πρὸς αὐτὴν ἐρωτικῶς) and so was aggrieved that having enforced the law that she be sent away for disobedience he could not reconcile with her (*A.J.* 11.195). The rewriting also couches the quest for virgins from throughout the realm as designed to enable him to let go of his love for Vashti, so that "his affection for her would gradually be diverted to the woman living with

---

[184] On this see Lester L. Grabbe, *A History of the Jews and Judaism in the Second Temple Period: Volume 1: Yehud: A History of the Persian Province of Judah* (London: T&T Clark, 2004) 157-58; James C. VanderKam, *From Joshua to Caiaphas: High Priests after the Exile* (Minneapolis: Fortress; Assen: Gorcum, 2004) 75-76.

[185] As Halpern-Amaru, "Portraits of Biblical Women," observes Josephus has rehabilitated Vashti "from a headstrong, defiant creature into a beautiful woman tragically torn between the laws of the Persians and the authority of her husband" (164).

him" (*A.J.* 11.196), somewhat typical of Josephus' psychological observations about the processes of love elsewhere. He depicts Esther as Mordecai's niece (*A.J.* 11.198, 207), not his cousin as Esther 2:7. Josephus reports her being prepared and then coming to Ahasuerus (Artaxerxes), who "had fallen in love with her" (πεσὼν τῆς κόρης εἰς ἔρωτα) (*A.J.* 11.202; similarly Esther 2:17 OG: καὶ ἠράσθη), "made her his lawful wife" (νομίμως αὐτὴν ἄγεται γυναῖκα), Josephus' addition, holding the wedding "in the twelfth month, called Adar" (as Esther 2:16 OG; cf. MT), celebrating the occasion with a month long feast (cf. Esther 2:18 OG, 7 days). Josephus' addition appears to rule out that Ahasuerus first tried out having sexual intercourse with Esther,[186] in contrast to the other concubines where he is more explicit than his source in speaking of sexual intercourse (*A.J.* 11.201), instead implying love at first sight and then proper lawful marriage.[187] In fact both Esther and Ahasuerus emerge from Josephus' retelling as admirable characters. He portrays Ahasuerus as a tragic victim of his own imposition of the law on Vashti[188] and as a person later able to respond compassionately to Esther (*A.J.* 11.236-237).[189] The initial half of the story has a romantic quality with elements typical of the storyteller's art, such as Ahasuerus' searching the whole world for beautiful women and the specific reference to the number of women: 400! (*A.J.* 11.200).[190]

Josephus notes Mordecai's supplication and Esther's prayer in face of the impending disaster facing her people, known to us as Addition C (*A.J.* 11.229-33).[191] He includes reference to her putting on clothes of mourning, but makes no mention of her declaration there that she abhors the bed of the uncircumcised and the alien, as well as her regal position, and her diadem which she deems like a filthy rag, and nor of her having had no joy since her abduction (C 26-29).[192] Josephus' version of the addition may have lacked these verses or perhaps he simply ignored them, since he also does not take up the detail in the Old Greek B text that Mordecai wanted Esther as his wife (2:7), implying a very unwilling abduction.[193] Such negative details might have served Josephus' emphasis on deploring intermarriage with foreigners, but that is not in focus in using the story. His interest is in exposing hatred against the Jews. Haman becomes a lesson for others (*A.J.* 11.268). He has left the tale largely intact with regard to its sexual

---

[186] So Mayer-Schärtel, *Frauenbild*, 116, 256.

[187] Feldman, *Interpretation*, 136.

[188] Halpern-Amaru, "Portraits of Biblical Women," 165.

[189] Feldman, *Interpretation*, writes: "What is most striking about Josephus's version of Ahasuerus is that there is not even a single hint in it that is negative" (136).

[190] Feldman, *Interpretation*, 187.

[191] On Josephus' knowledge of Additions C and D in *A.J.* 11.234-242 see Feldman, *Interpretation*, 51.

[192] On this see Loader, *Pseudepigrapha on Sexuality*, 236-43, esp. pp. 240-41.

[193] Loader, *Pseudepigrapha on Sexuality*, 242.

dimension, thereby remaining closer to the spirit of the Hebrew, than to that of the Greek, which he must have known, which depicts Esther's enlistment as forced (and so her marriage excusable) and her response to it as very negative.[194]

2.2.12. The Early Hasmonean Period

2.2.12.1 The Tobiad Romance

The next relevant passage of substance comes within the account of Joseph son of Tobias and his family. Much of the story is taken up with tax farming and the tensions with the high priesthood. Within it Josephus recounts the tale of Joseph's marriage to his niece (*A.J.* 12.186-189). Already married, but falling in love with a foreign dancing girl in Alexandria, Joseph solicited his brother, Solymius' help to make it possible for him to satisfy his desire to have sex with the girl undetected, "since the Jews were prevented by law from having intercourse with a foreign woman (ἐπεὶ καὶ νόμῳ κεκώλυται παρὰ τοῖς ᾽Ιουδαίοις ἀλλοφύλῳ πλησιάζειν γυναικί)" (*A.J.* 12.187). Solymius had come to Alexandria with his daughter to marry her to one of the Jews of high rank. So he sent Joseph his beautiful daughter instead and the drunken Joseph slept with her "and when this had happened several times, he fell still more violently in love with her", and finally, with Joseph now also anxious because the king may disapprove of his using one of his women in this way (*A.J.* 12.188), Solymius revealed his ploy to save his brother from disgrace, whereupon Joseph married her.

As often Josephus leaves any moral commentary, though he would clearly have affirmed both the assumption that sex with foreigners, was illicit and that marriage to nieces was acceptable. We may surmise also that he would have also disapproved of Joseph's giving way to his sexual passions. The story, which recalls to some degree Laban's sending Leah to Jacob who was also drunk according to Josephus (*A.J.* 1.301),[195] assumes that these Tobiads saw themselves as Jews. It takes the form of entertainment with some unreality (would Joseph really have had sex night after night with the wrong woman without knowing it?), but with embodied but expressed values on mishandled sexual passion, forbidden sexual intercourse with a Gentile, and proper marriage. It also exposes the vulnerability of the daughter[196] and all daughters of the time to decisions of their masters, a matter which nowhere appears among Josephus' concerns.

---

[194] So Loader, *Pseudepigrapha on Sexuality*, 241-42.
[195] On this see Mayer-Schärtel, *Frauenbild*, 255.
[196] So Mayer-Schärtel, *Frauenbild*, 255.

2.2.12.2 John Hyrcanus, Alexander Janneus, and Salome Alexandra

As Josephus employs 1 Maccabees as his source, we find, as there, little pertinent to sexual matters. What could be allusions to the intermarriage issue in its opening chapter (1 Macc 1:11-15)[197] are not read that way by him. Most details of relevance are minor and will be treated under the thematic section below. At most we note here what Josephus describes as the false accusation against John Hyrcanus that his mother had been a captive woman (*A.J.* 13.292) and therefore the similar slander against his son, Alexander Janneus (*A.J.* 13.373), forbidden as wives of priests and high priests according to Josephus (*A.J.* 3.276-277) almost certainly on the grounds that they will have been raped while in captivity.

When he summarises Salome Alexandra's significance, we again see his assumptions about gender.[198] Thus he depicts her as "a woman who showed none of the weakness of her sex (γυνὴ τῷ ἀσθενεῖ τοῦ φύλου κατ' οὐδὲν χρησαμένη)" (*A.J.* 13.430), but as one who brought negative consequences upon her successors among other things "because of her desire for things unbecoming a woman (ἐπιθυμίᾳ τῶν μὴ προσηκόντων γυναικί)" (*A.J.* 13.431). Earlier he reports that her son Aristobulus denounced his mother and blamed the people "for their misfortunes, in allowing a woman to reign who madly desired it in her unreasonable love of power (κατὰ φιλαρχίαν ἐλελυσσηκυίᾳ γυναικί), and when her sons were in the prime of life" (*A.J.* 13.417), an assessment clearly informed by self-interest. In the *Jewish War* he praises her observance of Jewish laws (*B.J.* 1.108), but claims that she showed too much deference to the Pharisees (*B.J.* 1.111; cf. in *A.J.* 13.401 on the advice of her husband, Janneus), whom he describes as "taking advantage of an ingenuous woman (τὴν ἁπλότητα τῆς ἀνθρώπου)" (*B.J.* 1.111). He also depicts her acting "from superstitious motives" (*B.J.* 1.113). Sexual issues play no significant role in the account.

---

[197] See Loader, *Pseudepigrapha on Sexuality*, 247-49.

[198] On Josephus' image of Salome, including complications relating to the possibility that she was a widow before marrying Janneus, whether that was a levirate marriage, should she have been childless, and further complications that Janneus was high priest marrying a widow (cf. Lev 21:14; Ezek 44:22), as well as the conflicting images between *Antiquities* and the *Jewish War*, see Joseph Sievers, "The Role of Women in the Hasmonean Dynasty," in *Josephus, the Bible, and History* (Leiden: Brill, 1989) 132-46, 135-39.

2.2.13 Herod

2.2.13.1 The Marriage of Herod and Mariamme

In the material pertaining to Salome Alexandra's sons, and the subsequent history up to and including the time of Herod, there are many details about marriages, for love or for convenience or both, and tensions which result. Most will be gathered in the thematic treatment, but of special significance is Herod's marriage to Mariamme, granddaughter of Salome Alexandra's son, the former high priest, Hyrcanus. Much of the detail is not pertinent to our theme, but some elements are central.[199] Josephus first mentions the marriage in *Antiquities* in the context of Herod's expulsion from Judea of Antigonus, son of Aristobulus, brother and rival of Hyrcanus, and Herod's feted entry into Jerusalem (*A.J.* 14.297-299). There Josephus informs us: "As Herod had already become connected by an agreement of marriage with the family of Hyrcanus, he was for that reason the more protective of him; he was, in fact, about to marry the daughter of Aristobulus' son Alexander and granddaughter of Hyrcanus" (*A.J.* 14.300). He adds: "He had previously married a plebeian woman of his own nation, named Doris, by whom he had his eldest son Antipater" (*A.J.* 14.300). In *Jewish War* he notes that on ascending to the throne he dismissed Doris (*B.J.* 1.432) and in the context of his feted entry, that the marriage to Mariamme also helped reconcile to him those who had stood aloof from him (*B.J.* 1.240). In the account of Herod and his accusers facing off before Antony, we again find mention of the connection with Hyrcanus, "who had by then become Herod's kinsman by marriage" (*A.J.* 14.325; similarly *B.J.* 1.243). The marriage had still not taken place by then, but the agreement was enough to affirm kinship. We have another allusion to the connection in the reference to Hyrcanus' daughter, Alexandra, Mariamme's mother, helping Herod with information in relation to the Parthians (*A.J.* 14.351; in *B.J.* 1.262 it was Mariamme, herself), so that he could escape with the women who were under threat from them, another reference to Mariamme, "whom he was to marry" (*A.J.* 14.353; similarly *B.J.* 1.264). Finally we read of the marriage taking place at the point where Herod is about to wrest control of Jerusalem. He put others temporarily in charge while he "went off to Samaria to marry the daughter of Alexander, son of Aristobulus, to whom he was betrothed, as I have said before" (*A.J.* 14.467; similarly *B.J.* 1.344, though there he fetches her from Samaria for the wedding). Josephus has much to say about the relationship, but shows himself aware of what was in actual fact probably its main significance, namely, an

---

[199] We noted above in 2.1 the caution in Ilan, "Josephus and Nicolaus on Women," about the extent to which one can take much of this material as indicative of Josephus' own attitudes. They are at least indicative of the attitudes embodied in the material he was happy to publish in his name.

2.2.13.2 Herod, Antony, and Cleopatra

2.2.13.2.1 Antony's Sexual Predation

Herod's relationship with Mariamme plays a key role in Josephus's account and is inextricably linked to intrigues and tensions within and beyond his household. Our focus is on sexual aspects which often appear incidentally. Thus Herod's appointment of "a rather undistinguished priest from Babylon" as high priest (*A.J.* 15.22), and not Hyrcanus' "extraordinarily handsome (τὸν μὲν ὥρᾳ κάλλιστον)" 16 year old grandson, Aristobulus, born to his daughter, Alexandra, and son-in-law, Alexander, and so Mariamme's brother, had Alexandra writing to Cleopatra to ask her to persuade Antony to change this (*A.J.* 15.24). Antony's agent had paintings made by Alexandra of both Aristobulus and Mariamme because of their beauty (*A.J.* 15.25) to take to impress Antony.[200] The real intent was to display them to Antony as desirable sexual objects. He, however, restrained himself in relation to Mariamme to avoid offending Herod, but sent off to Herod for the boy. In *Jewish War* Josephus mentions the allegation concocted by Herod's sister and mother that Mariamme herself had her portrait sent to Antony (*B.J.* 1.439).

Josephus tells us that Herod was aware in relation to Aristobulus that Antony "was ready to use him for erotic purposes and was able to indulge in undisguised pleasures because of his power (ἕτοιμον δὲ τοῖς ἐρωτικοῖς αὐτὸν ὑποθεῖναι καὶ τὰς ἡδονὰς ἀπαρακαλύπτως ἐκ τοῦ δύνασθαι ποριζόμενον)" (*A.J.* 15.29). It would have gone down well with Josephus' Roman hearers to denigrate Antony, who had become a model of failure through not controlling his sexual urges. It is typical that the homoerotic and the heteroerotic are seen as belonging together in such excesses. Herod accordingly reversed his decision and acceded to having Aristobulus become high priest, in part to prevent his being able to leave the country and in part in response to the lobbying by both Alexandra (whom he publicly chided for subversion but then forgave) and her daughter and his wife, Mariamme (*A.J.* 15.31-35). Historico-politically, however, this concession would have run counter to his interests of controlling Hasmonean influence. Accordingly, when in the following years the young man's popularity grew, Herod had him drowned, purporting it was an accident.

In response, Alexandra again approached Cleopatra, who had Antony summon Herod (*A.J.* 15.63-64; *B.J.* 1.437). In this context we hear that Herod duly

---

[200] On the issue of plausibility that such images would have been made contrary to Jewish law, see Sievers, "Role of Women," 142.

complied, but left his uncle Joseph to guard Mariamme with the instruction to kill her if things turned out for the worst for him (*A.J.* 15.65; *B.J.* 1.441). While this reflected fairly obvious political concerns (so, later *A.J.* 15.73) – she, a surviving descendant of Hyrcanus – Josephus returns to Antony's sexual predation, explaining that Herod "was very much in love with his wife and feared the outrage (it would be to his memory) if even after his death she were pursued by another man because of her beauty" (*A.J.* 15.65-66). He continues: "All this was a way of indicating Antony's desire for the woman, of whose beauty, as it happened, he had long before casually heard" (*A.J.* 15.67; not so casually according to *A.J.* 15.26!).

2.2.13.2.2 Herod's Love and Fear of Mariamme: First Story

The mention of Herod's strong love for Mariamme plays a major role in much of what follows. Joseph had been so intent on impressing it on Mariamme that he had revealed Herod's plot to her and at the initial rumours that things had gone awry for Herod they had fled and hoped for a connection with Antony as a way back to power (*A.J.* 15.73). Herod, however, acquitted himself successfully and Antony even trimmed Cleopatra's ambitions, and, returning to be informed by his sister, Salome, Joseph's husband, about the women's flight (cf. *A.J.* 15.72), Herod was enraged, particularly because of her allegation that Joseph had "frequently had intercourse with Mariamme" (*A.J.* 15.81). Again Josephus returns to Herod's love, who "had always felt a burning love for Mariamme (θερμῶς ἀεὶ καὶ λίαν ἐρωτικῶς πρὸς Μαριάμμην)" (*A.J.* 15.82), noting that "he was at once violently disturbed (ἐξετετάρακτο) and was scarcely able to bear his jealousy (τὴν ζηλοτυπίαν), but he had enough control of himself all this time (ἐπικρατούμενος δ' ἀεί) not to do anything rash because of his love" (*A.J.* 15.82). The issue is control of sexual passion and what it generates, namely jealousy and fear. After questioning Mariamme he believed her denials, and "let himself be persuaded" and "being overcome by his fondness for his wife (ἡττώμενος τῆς περὶ τὴν γυναῖκα φιλοστοργίας), he actually apologized for seeming to believe what he had heard" (*A.J.* 15.83). Again, the issue is control of passion, in this instance whether one lets it blind reason. He also "acknowledged how fond of her and how devoted to her he was. Finally, as is usual with lovers, they fell to weeping and to embracing one another with great intensity" (*A.J.* 15.83-84). Thus Josephus takes us off into popular psychologising about *eros* and provides an entertaining drama.

Josephus then reports her complaint to Herod that his contemplating killing her was not the act of a lover, at which Herod swung back to rage, believing now that she must have lied in denying sexual intimacy with Joseph, which would explain why she disclosed Herod's plan. Accordingly he had Joseph executed and Alexandra put under guard (*A.J.* 15.86-87). Earlier in *Jewish War* he put it differently: "When Herod, on his return, in familiar intercourse was protesting with many oaths his affection for her and that he had never loved any other woman, 'A fine exhibition you gave,' she replied, 'of your love for me by your orders to Joseph to put me to death!'" (*B.J.* 1.442) and he concluded adultery with Joseph (*B.J.* 1.443), but, unlike in *Antiquities*, has them both instantly put to death (*B.J.* 1.443). Josephus' accounts, perhaps strongly shaped by his source material, effectively distracts the hearer from the more serious political dangers which were at stake here and which could easily have aroused Roman concern about the ambitions also of the descendants of the players involved.

2.2.13.2.3 *Herod and Cleopatra*

The account of Herod intersects with that of Cleopatra, whom Josephus depicts as greedy for territory, including Judea,[201] and holding sway over Antony "not only because of his intimacy with her but also because of being under the influence of drugs" (*A.J.* 15.93). As van Henten notes, Josephus shares with his contemporaries the view that Antony became enslaved to Cleopatra, already noting this in *B.J.* 1.243 and locating the commencement of the romance earlier than in other sources.[202] He also shares the view that had developed by his time that Cleopatra was also greedy for sex in itself and not just for political ends, so that in *Antiquities* and *Against Apion* she takes on for him the character of the strange woman of Proverbs 7 and according to van Henten becomes "a key example of Josephus' distrust of woman in general".[203]

Accordingly, Josephus writes that during her visit to Judea and "having Herod's company very often, Cleopatra attempted to have sexual relations with the king (διεπείραζεν εἰς συνουσίαν ἐλθεῖν τῷ βασιλεῖ), for she was by nature used to enjoying this kind of pleasure without disguise (φύσει μὲν ἀπαρακαλύπτως ταῖς ἐντεῦθεν ἡδοναῖς χρωμένη)" (*A.J.* 15.97). Josephus adds: "Perhaps, too, she really felt some measure of passion for him (τάχα δέ τι καὶ παθοῦσα πρὸς αὐτὸν ἐρωτικόν), or, what is more probable, she was secretly arranging that any violence which might be done her should be the beginning of a trap for him" so that "she gave the appearance of being overcome by desire (ἐξ ἐπιθυμίας ἡττῆσθαι)" (*A.J.* 15.97). Josephus notes (with approval) Herod's holding her in contempt for "if it was through lust that she went so far (εἰ

---

[201] On her territorial ambitions see Jan W. van Henten, "Cleopatra in Josephus: From Herod's Rival to the Wise Ruler's Opposite," in *Wisdom of Egypt* (Leiden: Brill, 2005) 115-34, 125-27.

[202] Van Henten, "Cleopatra in Josephus," 116

[203] Van Henten, "Cleopatra in Josephus," 129. He notes that in *Against Apion* she has become the arch enemy of Rome and of her own people, condemned also because she refused to aid the Jews of Alexandria (134).

δι' ἀσέλγειαν εἰς τοῦτο πρόεισιν)" and his awareness of the potential trap (*A.J.* 15.98), and so on advice found a way "to avoid the sin to which she was inviting him (ἀποκρουσάμενον τὴν ἁμαρτίαν εἰς ἥν ἐκείνη παρακαλεῖ)" by plying her with gifts and escorting her to Egypt (*A.J.* 15.103).

The danger posed by Cleopatra as Josephus indicates it is not that she was a sexually attractive woman, but that she both used her sexual attractiveness to seduce men to meet her political ambitions and also sought to meet her own sexual ambitions at their expense. Men were not her victims, as though we should have pity for Antony, but are fools for failing to discern what was happening. In this scene Herod comes off relatively well, because he did not allow himself to succumb to Cleopatra's apparently ambiguous wiles. In his own relationship with Mariamme Herod showed much less wisdom and control.

2.2.13.3 Herod, Caesar, and Mariamme

2.2.13.3.1 Herod's Love and Fear of Mariamme: Second Story

The tensions with Alexandra, who "had an aggressive and very womanly nature (γυναικεῖον αὐτῆς)", by which Josephus means here both persistence and the negative traits he associates with being woman, such as allowing emotion to override reason, reignite when she succeeds in persuading her father Hyrcanus, to get military help from Malchus, the Arab king (*A.J.* 15.167) only for Hyrcanus to be found out and executed (*A.J.* 15.169-178). On Octavian's accession, Herod, who had supported Antony, travelled to Rome to re-align himself, and, again, Josephus reports that in view of the uncertain outcome Mariamme and Alexandra were to be guarded, this time by Soemus, and to be executed if things went awry (*A.J.* 15.185-186). The account reads like a duplicate of Herod's being summoned by Antony when he did the same under the charge of Joseph and as a result of which, according to *Jewish War* Mariamme was executed. Both women in this second account were angry at his return "and Mariamme considered the king's love to be a pretence and a sham especially meant for his own advantage" (*A.J.* 15.203), not least because their guard, Soemus, was persuaded to expose Herod's instructions (*A.J.* 15.207). Again Josephus notes the king's love: "Soemus knew that the king's love for Mariamme was beyond all reason (ἠπίστατο γὰρ τὸν πρὸς τὴν Μαριάμμην ἔρωτα μείζονα λόγου τῷ βασιλεῖ)" (*A.J.* 15.207). It is interesting that Josephus does not apparently see it as Mariamme did, but rather depicts Herod not as being unloving, but as failing to keep his passion under proper control. This love features in his depiction of Herod's return: "Now when Herod returned ... he naturally brought the good news to his wife first of all and because of his love for her and the intimacy between them (διὰ τὸν ἔρωτα καὶ τὴν οὖσαν αὐτῷ συνήθειαν) he singled her out from all others to embrace her"

(*A.J.* 15.209). Her groaning response to his embrace upset Herod not least because it was public (*A.J.* 15.210-211). According to Josephus, mutual hostility grew, though Herod refused to believe the slanders against her made by Herod's sister and mother (*A.J.* 15.213-215). Later he reports that the historian Nicolas alleges that Marianne was licentious, but this Josephus disputes as deriving from his sympathies for Herod (*A.J.* 16.183-186). His own judgement of Herod is for allowing his love to blind his reason, so that he did not take adequate account of danger.

The love theme returns when Josephus notes that "the love which he felt for Mariamme was no less intense than those justly celebrated in story (ἔρωτα γὰρ οὐδενὸς ἐλάττω τῶν ἱστορουμένων ἐπεπόνθει μετὰ τοῦ δικαίου τῆς Μαριάμμης)" (*A.J.* 15.218), Josephus perhaps at this point revealing that such popular stories might have been models for his development of this aspect of his account. He notes of Mariamme that "she was in most respects prudent and faithful to him but she had in her nature something that was at once womanly and cruel (καὶ γυναικεῖον ὁμοῦ καὶ χαλεπὸν ἐκ φύσεως), and she took fulladvantage of his enslavement to passion" (*A.J.* 15.219). Here is clear disapproval not of Herod's love, but his enslavement to it, matching his disapproval of Antony's. Josephus juxtaposes γυναικεῖον ("womanly") and χαλεπόν ("cruel"), not to contrast the two as though womanly is the opposite of cruel and something positive, but, as usual, depicting womanly as weak, vulnerable, and fallible because of emotions. The double criticism finds an echo later where Josephus writes of her; τὸ δ᾽ ἐπιεικὲς ἔλειπεν αὐτῇ καὶ πλεῖον ἦν ἐν τῇ φύσει τὸ φιλόνεικον ("lacking in reasonableness and of too quarrelsome a nature") (*A.J.* 15.237). Josephus notes that her hostility was less about threat and danger, than about politics and rivalry, not least on the basis of her high birth and his low birth (*A.J.* 15.220).

2.2.13.3.2 Herod and Mariamme's Execution

Josephus tells us that hostility came to a head when she refused to lie down with him at midday, for he "out of the great fondness which he always had for her (ὑπὸ φιλοστοργίας ἧς ἀεὶ περὶ αὐτὴν εἶχεν) called for Mariamme" (*A.J.* 15.222), and instead she reproached him for killing her grandfather and brother (cf. *B.J.* 1.437). The implication is that Herod is tragically out of control of his reasoning because he has allowed such love to dominate his thoughts. Salome then concocted a story about Mariamme preparing a love-potion for Herod and had his butler report his caution to Herod (*A.J.* 15.223-227), presumably that it might be poison, who, in turn, tortured Mariamme's eunuch to no avail, though he revealed that Soemus had made known Herod's plot to Mariamme. This had Herod suspect that Soemus had "gone too far in his intimacy with Mariamme (περαιτέρω προεληλύθει τῆς πρὸς τὴν Μαριάμμην κοινωνίας)" (A.J. 15.228), paralleling his conclusion earlier about Joseph, with the result that he had him executed and Mariamme brought to trial on the trumped up charge about the love-potion and also sentenced to death (A.J. 15.229). Josephus then contrasts the outrageous behaviour of her mother, Alexandra, at her trial, who slandered her daughter to save her own skin, with Mariamme, whom he describes going "to her death with a wholly calm demeanour and without change of colour, and so even in her last moments she made her nobility of descent very clear to those who were looking on" (A.J. 15.236), a very clear exposure of Josephus' own values, and as

> γυνὴ καὶ πρός ἐγκράτειαν καὶ πρὸς μεγαλοψυχίαν ἄριστα γεγενημένη, τὸ δ' ἐπιεικὲς ἔλειπεν αὐτῇ καὶ πλεῖον ἦν ἐν τῇ φύσει τὸ φιλόνεικον. κάλλει δὲ σώματος καὶ τῷ περὶ τὰς ἐντεύξεις ἀξιώματι μειζόνως ἢ φράσαι τὰς κατ' αὐτὴν ὑπερῇρεν.
> a woman unexcelled in continence and in greatness of soul, though lacking in reasonableness and of too quarrelsome a nature. But in beauty of body and in dignity of bearing in the presence of others she surpassed her contemporaries more greatly than one can say. (A.J. 15.237)

Josephus affirms beauty, which includes sexual attractiveness. He attributes her "excessive freedom of speech" to her "being constantly courted by him because of his love (θεραπευομένη γὰρ ἀεὶ διὰ τὸν ἔρωτα)" (A.J. 15.238; similarly B.J. 1.437). The love theme continues even after her death as Josephus reports that "the king's desire for her burned still more strongly (μᾶλλον ἐξήφθη τὰ περὶ τὴν ἐπιθυμνίαν τοῦ βασιλέως), for such had been his feeling even earlier" (A.J. 15.240). He adds:

> οὐ γὰρ ἀπαθὴς οὐδ' οἷος ἄν ἐκ συνηθείας ἦν ὁ πρὸς αὐτὴν ἔρως, ἀλλὰ καὶ πρότερον ἦρξεν ἐνθουσιαστικῶς, καὶ τῇ παρρησίᾳ της συμβιώσεως οὐκ ἀπενικήθη μὴ πλείων ἀεὶ γίνεσθαι.
> For his love for her was not passionless nor such as arises from familiarity, but in its very earliest beginnings had been a divine madness, and even with freedom of cohabitation it was not restrained from growing greater. (A.J. 15.240)

Again we see Josephus' psychologising "expertise" about love: it allegedly abates where it is not forbidden. The word, ἐνθουσιαστικῶς, translated "divine madness", echoes a common theme in popular narrative about love, like the stories of Cupid's arrows, and recalls Josephus' description of mad love elsewhere (cf. Manoah, A.J. 5.276-277; Solomon, 8.190-191; Pheroras, 16.194). One could take ἀπαθὴς οὐδ' οἷος ἄν ἐκ συνηθείας ("passionless [n]or such as arises from familiarity") as Josephus' ideal for love, but this puts too much weight on his rhetorical contrast and conflicts with his affirmation of sexual desire elsewhere.

This madness now afflicted Herod after his death so that "he seemed to be a prey to it as if by a kind of divine punishment ... and he would frequently call out for her and frequently utter unseemly laments ... and was so far overcome by his passion (τοσοῦτον ἥττητο τοῦ πάθους) that he would actually order his servants to summon Mariamme as if she were still alive" (*A.J.* 15.241-242; similarly *B.J.* 1.444). Herod is both tragic and pathetic because he has failed to control his emotions.

In *Jewish War* Josephus similarly emphasises Herod's love for Mariamme. Thus he speaks of

ὁ Μαριάμμης ἔρως ... καθ' ἡμέραν ἐκκαίων Ἡρώδην λαβρότερος, ὡς μηδενὸς τῶν διὰ τὴν στεργομένην λυπηρῶν αἰσθάνεσθαι. τοσοῦτον γὰρ ἦν μῖσος εἰς αὐτὸν τῆς Μαριάμμης, ὅσος ἐκείνου πρὸς αὐτὴν ἔρως.
Herod's passion for Mariamme, the continuing ardour of which increased from day to day, so that he was insensible to the troubles of which his beloved one was the cause; for Mariamme's hatred of him was as great as was his love for her (*B.J.* 1.436).

In both accounts, therefore, the hearer might be distracted from the more obvious political dimensions of the execution by the well-embroidered love story.[204]

2.2.13.4 Herod and Further Sexual Adventures

2.2.13.4.1 Herod and Mariamme 2, Daughter of Simon

Josephus next addresses Herod's sexual behaviour when he reports that "at the prompting of his amorous desire (κινηθεὶς ἐξ ἐρωτικῆς ἐπιθυμίας) he married again, for he had no qualms about living solely for his own pleasure (μηδένα τοῦ κατὰ τὴν οἰκείαν ἡδονὴν ζῆν ὑπολογισμὸν ποιούμενος)" (*A.J.* 15.319). Clearly Josephus disapproves. The objection is that Herod allows his response to sexual desire of getting its fulfilment in pleasure govern his life and this makes Herod now more reminiscent of Antony. He then reports that Herod heard about another Mariamme, "considered to be the most beautiful woman of her time (καλλίστην τῶν τότε νομιζομένην)", daughter of a priest, Simon, but, though "smitten by the girl's loveliness (ἡ τῆς παιδὸς ἐξέπληξεν ὥρα)", appropriately restrained himself from "abusing his power in order to achieve his full desire", sought to marry her (*A.J.* 15.321), elevating her status to be closer to his own by deposing the current high priest and appointing Simon in his place, an action of which Josephus shows elsewhere he strongly disapproves (*A.J.* 15.40). There is more shade than light in this account, the only positive being Herod's restraint

---

[204] On the political significance see Mayer-Schärtel, *Frauenbild*, 259.

from violence. Thus he exercises some control of his sexual passion, but his pursuit of its fulfilment Josephus clearly depicts here as self-indulgent and exploitative.

The first Mariamme's execution produced major new conflicts as her two sons, Aristobulus and Alexander, sought to avenge their mother and were in conflict with Herod's sister, Salome and her associates. This prompted Herod to bring the son of his first marriage, Antipater, and his mother, Doris, back into the household (*A.J.* 16.85). Josephus makes no comment on the appropriateness of this in relation to Deut 24:1-4.

2.2.13.4.2 Pheroras and the Female Slave

The account of the conflicts which followed bear little on our theme beyond the various marriages and allegiances and Pheroras' falling in love with his slave girl, much to Herod's (and Josephus') disgust (*A.J.* 16.194). Josephus describes Pheroras as "the victim of his mad passion for this creature (lit. "person") and so possessed by it (ἥττητο δὲ τῆς ἀνθρώπου μεμηνότως ἐπὶ τοσοῦτον κρατούμενος) that he scorned the king's daughter [his niece], who had been betrothed to him, and gave his thought only to his slave girl" (*A.J.* 16.194). The Loeb translation imports "creature" and "it" into the text, doubtless to give expression to the disgust, but the Greek does not depersonalise her. With one of his typical psychologising comments Josephus reports that "in the belief that his brother's passion had passed its peak (οἰόμενος ἤδη παρηκμακέναι τὴν ἐπιθυμίαν), Herod took him to task for his amorousness and asked him to take his second daughter, whose name was Cypros" (*A.J.* 16.196). He was accordingly persuaded "to suppress his love (καταβαλεῖν τὸν ἔρωτα)" and that it was "disgraceful for him to lose his head over a slave girl (αἰσχρὸν εἶναι δούλης ἡττώμενον)" (*A.J.* 16.197). The assumption appears to be that he could have sex with a slave but it should not be more than that. Thus "he put away the woman although he had already had a child by her" and "took an oath that he would no longer consort with the woman who had been put away", the equivalent of what Josephus describes elsewhere as belonging in the divorce certificate (*A.J.* 4.253), and promised to marry Herod's daughter in 30 days (*A.J.* 16.198).

When the time came, "he was so enslaved to his love (τοσοῦτον ἦν ἥττων τοῦ ἔρωτος) that he was unable to do any of the things that he had promised (ὥστε μηδὲν μὲν ἔτι ποιῆσαι τῶν ὡμολογημένων) but resumed relations with the first woman" (*A.J.* 16.199). The translation suggests he was "unable", something not represented in the Greek, which rather speaks of his being so in love that he was not willing to keep his promises. Josephus assumes that he could have, but did not, and was therefore blameworthy, not that he was unable to do so and had that as an excuse. Pheroras then found himself embroiled in a plot falsely alleging that Herod had sexual designs on one of his daughters-in-law, and was sent away by Herod along with Salome, his sister, the plot's instigator (*A.J.* 16.201-219). Pheroras' wife reappears in the context of Herod's fining 6000 Pharisees for refusing to take an oath of allegiance to him, where, Josephus reports, that she, "Pheroroas' wife" (ἡ Φερώρου γυνή), paid the fine (*A.J.* 17.42). The assumption is that she is his wife, probably on the basis of cohabitation. Herod found out and charged her, including for abusive behaviour towards his virgin daughters, and requested Pheroras to give her up, who responded that "he would prefer death rather than endure to live without a wife so dear to him" (*A.J.* 17.49). Such touching love fits well the storyteller's art. Josephus reports that "a rumour was current that Pheroras' wife was actually intimate with Antipater and that Antipater's mother helped to bring them together" (*A.J.* 17.52). For his persistence in loyalty to her, Herod sent Pheroras off to his own territory (*A.J.* 17.58), but despite the conflict cared for him in his last days. Pheroras' death, however, brought out an allegation by his freedmen that he had been poisoned by what was "ostensibly to stimulate his erotic feeling (προσποιήσεσιν ἐρώτων) ... a love-potion (φίλτρον)", it turned out, at the instigation of Antipater's mother, Doris, and also designed for use against Herod (*A.J.* 17.62-64). Accordingly Herod banished Doris (*A.J.* 17.68), but also Mariamme 2 who had been implicated in the plot (*A.J.* 17.78). At the hearing against Antipater, Nicolas of Damascus, speaking for Herod, included reference to Antipater's mother speaking "in the frivolous ways of a woman (κουφολογία γυναικείῳ)" and to "Antipater's licentious affairs with the women of Pheroras in the form of drinking bouts and erotic excesses" (*A.J.* 17.121). Thus beside the shameful marriage of Pheroras to one far below his status, another act of folly by a man failing to control his passions, the complex court intrigues included a number of allegations of illicit sexual relations.

2.2.13.4.3 Salome and Syllaeus

Salome, Herod's sister, also features within the sexual aspects of the larger story. Josephus had noted with disapproval that she had divorced her (second) husband, Costobarus: she "sent him a document dissolving their marriage, which was not in accordance with Jewish law. For it is (only) the man who is permitted by us to do this, and not even a divorced woman may marry again on her own initiative unless her former husband consents" (*A.J.* 15.259). We return to this below in our discussion of divorce (2.4.7). She "repudiated her marriage" on grounds that her husband had plotted against Herod.[205] In *Jewish War* Josephus mentions her first husband who had been executed for adultery (*B.J.* 1.486).

---

[205] As Mayer-Schärtel, *Frauenbild*, notes, she showed greater loyalty to Herod her brother than to her husband (194).

Her marital endeavours come up again in the account of Syllaeus who managed Arabia, who, while dining with Herod, "saw Salome and set his heart on having her. And as he knew that she was a widow, he spoke to her about his feeling" (*A.J.* 16.220-221). Salome, Josephus tells, "was eager for marriage with him" and during the ensuing days "there appeared numerous and unmistakable signs of an understanding between these two" (*A.J.* 16.222). Pheroras reported to Herod on his request that "both made their passion clear by their gestures and looks" (*A.J.* 16.223; cf. also *B.J.* 1.487). Syllaeus approached Herod about marrying Salome and she confirmed agreement, but nothing eventuated because he refused to be circumcised, without which "marriage would be impossible", and she was left facing accusations of illicit sex with the man (*A.J.* 16.225-226). He was later accused of adultery with women both in Arabia and Rome (*A.J.* 16.340). That failed attempt at marriage also featured in fraudulent correspondence instigated by Antipater from a certain Acme alleging that Salome had written to her mistress, Julia, wife of Caesar, about Herod because of her desire to marry Syllaeus, and done so subversively (*A.J.* 17.134-145). In the intrigues of Antipater and Salome against Mariamme's sons, Josephus reports that Antipater was "perpetually coaxing and working upon his aunt's feelings, as though she had been his wife (ὡσ ἂν γαμετὴν οὖσαν)" (*B.J.* 1.475), which may suggest illicit sexual relations, though this is not explicit.[206] In *Antiquities* he reports that Alexander provoked Herod with the report that Salome had forced him to have sex with her (*A.J.* 16.257). Josephus reports the intervention of Alexander's father-in-law, which succeeded in deceiving Herod by castigating his son-in-law and by seeming to threaten to dissolve the marriage with his daughter (*A.J.* 16.263; cf. *B.J.* 1.500). The outcome of this deception was temporary relief for both Alexander and Pheroras.

2.2.13.4.4 Herod, Aristobulus, and the Eunuchs

Another element in the wider story Josephus describes as "disgraceful" (οὐκ εὐπρεποῦς) (*A.J.* 16.229). He reports that "the king had some eunuchs of whom he was immoderately fond because of their beauty (διὰ κάλλος οὐ μετρίως ἐσπουδασμένοι)" (*A.J.* 16.230). This presumably refers to some kind of erotic same-sex behaviour, probably in relation to the one who was entrusted "with putting the king to bed" (κατακοιμίζειν βασιλέα) (*A.J.* 16.230) . Allegations reached Herod that his son Alexander had corrupted them with money. Herod's inquiry indicates that sexual relations are in view: "When Herod asked whether they had had intimate relations with Alexander, they confessed to this (ἀνακρίνοντι δὲ περὶ μὲν τῆς γεγενημένης πρὸς αὐτὸν κοινωνίας καὶ

---

[206] On this see Mayer-Schärtel, *Frauenbild*, 272.

μίξεως ὡμολόγουν)" (*A.J.* 16.231; cf. also *B.J.* 1.488-492 εἰς τὰ παιδικά), though what concerned Herod more was subversion. The only hint of Josephus's undoubted disapproval of such same sex behaviour[207] is in his comment about Herod's immoderate response to their beauty (*A.J.* 16.229). What might a moderate response have looked like? His chief interest appears to lie elsewhere, including an implied parallel with the behaviour of Absalom who challenged David's power by engaging in sex with those meant only for David (*A.J.* 7.213-214).[208]

2.2.14 Tales from Parthia and Rome

2.2.14.1 Phraates and the Italian Female Slave

Josephus reports the story of Phraates, king of the Parthians, who, though already married with "legitimate children, was in love with a young Italian slave girl named Thesmusa, who had been sent to him along with other gifts by Julius Caesar" (*A.J.* 18.40). The story assumes sexual access to one's slaves. Josephus add: "At first he treated her as a concubine, but he was so smitten by her abundant charm of face and figure that with time, after she had borne a son Phraataces, he declared this wench to be his wedded wife and held her in honour" (*A.J.* 18.40), a contravention of Josephus' values about status, and which he later describes as "upstart degradation" (*A.J.* 18.44). He then notes her plot to do away with the legitimate children so that her son would be heir, of whom Josephus reports allegations that "he also had sexual relations" with his mother (*A.J.* 18.43). The story recalls the account of Pheroras, where Josephus expresses similar disapproval, and for such disapproval would assume a good hearing from his Roman audience for whom marriage to slaves was forbidden.

2.2.14.2 Mundus, Paulina, and the Priests of Isis

In the course of describing the procuratorship of Pilate, Josephus reports an incident in Rome (*A.J.* 18.65-80) concerning Mundus, a high ranking Roman official. He was "was in love with (ταύτης ἐρᾷ)" (18.67) Paulina, wife of Saturninus, and having unsuccessfully plied her with gifts, "his passion was inflamed all the more (ἐξῆπτο μᾶλλον)" (18.67), so he offered her 200,000 Attic drachma if she would sleep with him. His freedwoman, Ida, lifted him from

---

[207] Missed by Mayer-Schärtel, *Frauenbild*, who suggests Josephus has remained quite neutral (268).

[208] On this see Mayer-Schärtel, *Frauenbild*, 268.

despair at again being rejected. Securing 50,000 from him, with 25,000 she enlisted the priests to send for Paulina, indicating that the god Anubis had fallen in love with her and wanted to sleep with her, to which she and even her husband agreed with no qualms. They then exposed her to this Mundus as the god, who the next day revealed to her that he was the one who had slept with her. Emperor Tiberius crucified both the priests and Ida, razed the temple, and banished Mundus. It is not clear why Josephus tells the story except for its entertainment value and because it maligns Isis worship. At another level it aligns Jewish and Roman disapproval of adultery, and so serves the case for compatibility of Jews and Jewish values with the best of Rome's.

2.2.14.3 Anilaeus and Asinaeus

Josephus brings another Parthian story involving sex and intrigue in *Antiquities* 18, entailing the Jewish bandits Anilaeus and Asinaeus. Hearing of the beauty of the Parthian commander's wife, so Josephus tells us, Anilaeus "became at once her lover and her enemy" (*A.J.* 18.342). He would have to capture her and "considered his lust hard to gainsay (τὸ δὲ ὑπὸ τοῦ δυσαντίλεκτον κρίνειν τὴν ἐπιθυμίαν)" (*A.J.* 18.342), never a valid excuse from Josephus' perspective. So, somewhat recalling the story of David and Bathsheba, he had her husband killed as an enemy and "his widow was captured and became the wife of her passionate wooer", but brought with her her ancestral idols (*A.J.* 18.344). Then "those who ranked highest at the court of the brothers merely told Anilaeus that his actions were quite contrary to Hebraic custom (οὐδαμῶς πράσσοι Ἑβραϊκά), and not consonant with their laws, in that he had taken a gentile wife (γυναῖκα ἠγμένος ἀλλόφυλον)–one who transgressed the strict rules of their accustomed sacrifices and rituals" (18.345). They warned him of "too great indulgence of fleshly lust (τὰ πολλὰ τῇ ἡδονῇ τοῦ σώματος συγχωρῶν)" (*A.J.* 18.345). Dissatisfaction escalated, but his brother "excused his brother as mastered by his passion, a vice that he could not resist (συγγνώμην νέμων ὡς ὑπὸ κρείσσονος κακοῦ τῆς ἐπιθυμίας νικωμένου)" (*A.J.* 18.350). He finally relented and demanded his brother send her away, but he refused and she poisoned the complaining brother (*A.J.* 18.352). Subsequently Anilaeus captured and humiliated Mithridates, a Parthian leader, married to the king's daughter (*A.J.* 18.353-356). On his release Mithridates' wife threatened divorce if he did not seek revenge (*A.J.* 18.361-362) and with a large army he then routed Anilaeus, who escaped with some of his men only to be discovered drunk and slain (*A.J.* 18.363-370), a fate which Josephus will have seen as divine retribution for his flouting of marriage law.

For Josephus this is another example of unrestrained sexual passion. Its strength for him is no excuse. It also provides him an opportunity to reinforce the law forbidding intermarriage, linking it here both to failure to control sexual passion and to the traditional consequence of idolatry. Probably the fact that it involved the far away Parthia made Josephus less reluctant to spell out the prohibition. Perhaps he assumed that his audience would also view such rebels negatively in the first place.

2.2.15 Herodian Marriages

2.2.15.1 Antipas and Herodias

Josephus reports tensions between Antipas and Aretas of Petra over Antipas' dissolution of his longstanding marriage to Aretas' daughter, to marry his half-brother, Herod's wife, Herodias. She was the daughter of their mutual brother, Aristobulus, thus their niece, and sister of Agrippa 1 (*A.J.* 18.109-110, 136). In a summary Josephus writes of "taking it into her head to flout the way of our fathers" in that "she parted from a living husband" (*A.J.* 18.136). Josephus reports that Antipas had broached marriage with her and agreed to divorce Aretas' daughter (*A.J.* 18.110). The latter, informed in advance, had Antipas send her unwittingly to Machaerus, from where she made her way to her father to report the plot. He subsequently defeated Antipas in battle (*A.J.* 18.111-116). Josephus then notes that some saw this defeat as divine vengeance for his killing John the Baptist on grounds of the impact of his sermons and the possibility of sedition (*A.J.* 18.117-119).[209] He says nothing of John's criticising the marriage as breaching incest laws (cf. Mark 6:17-18) nor of the tale of Antipas' birthday feast, the dancing of Herodias' daughter, and John's decapitation (Mark 6:21-29). Later Josephus reports Herodias' incitement of Antipas to jealousy of Agrippa 1 and the disastrous consequences of his following her initiative (*A.J.* 18.240-256).

2.2.15.2 Later Herodian Marriages

Josephus reports the marriages of Agrippa 1's three daughters, Berenice, Mariamme, and Drusilla (*A.J.* 19:354). At his death Berenice, 16 years old and

---

[209] On the complexities posed by the issues of dating, especially if one assumes that Antipas' defeat by Aretas in 36 C.E. followed shortly after his marriage and then tries to place John the Baptist's criticism and execution within that time frame, see Ross S. Kraemer, "Implicating Herodias and her Daughter in the Death of John the Baptizer: A (Christian) Theological Strategy?" *JBL* (2006) 321-49, who proposes the abandonment of the attempt to find an historical synthesis and that one treat both accounts separately, arguing that Mark's story derives from Christian invention to put John the Baptist in his place. On the problems of dating and identity, especially of the dancing girl in Mark, see Nikos Kokkinos, "Which Salome did Aristobulus Marry?" *PEQ* 118 (1986) 33-50.

already once widowed, was married to Herod of Chalcis, her uncle, another niece marriage, and the other two unmarried, but betrothed by him to Julius Archelaus, son of Helcias, and Epiphanes, son of Antiochus, king of Commagene respectively (*A.J.* 19.355; 20.140). After his death, his son Agrippa 2 gave his sister, Drusilla, in marriage to "Azizus king of Emesa, who had consented to be circumcised" to marry her (*A.J.* 20.139), because the marriage to Epiphanes had not come to stand because "he was not willing to convert to the Jewish religion (μὴ βουληθεὶς τὰ Ἰουδαίων ἔθη μεταλαβεῖν), although he had previously contracted with her father to do so" (*A.J.* 20.139). Clearly Josephus assumes that such conversion represented by circumcision means the marriage does not breach the prohibition of intermarriage with foreigners.

Of Drusilla he tells us that the Procurator Felix on seeing her "inasmuch as she surpassed all other women in beauty, ... conceived a passion for the lady" (*A.J.* 20.142) and she, to escape her sister Berenice's malice related to her beauty, "was persuaded to transgress the ancestral laws to marry Felix" (*A.J.* 20.143). This clearly was a breach of prohibition of intermarriage, as usual, couched in language palatable to the Roman audience who revered ancestral law. The demise of her son, Agrippa, with his wife in the context of the eruption of Vesuvius is probably deemed by Josephus to be divine judgement (*A.J.* 20.144).

Josephus also knows to tell of Berenice,[210] whose husband, Herod, had died, and who then stayed with her brother Agrippa 2 and wielded significant influence (see also Acts 25:13, 23; 27:30).[211] She was already a young widow when she married Herod, her first husband, Philo's nephew, Marcus, having died after a very short time.[212] To protect herself against the allegation that she had sexual relations with Agrippa 2, her brother, she then entered a marriage with Polemo, king of Cilicia, who agreed to be circumcised to make it possible (*A.J.* 20.145). In noting that the marriage did not last, Josephus speaks of his being relieved of "adherence to the Jewish way of life", but also of her licentiousness (ἀκολασία) (*A.J.* 20.147).[213] The underlying assumption here, and perhaps in the story of Ruth,

---

[210] On Berenice see Mayer-Schärtel, *Frauenbild*, 243-44; Ilan, "Josephus and Nicolaus on Women," 229-30.

[211] Klaus-Stefan Krieger, "Berenike, die Schwester König Agrippas II, bei Flavius Josephus," *JSJ* 28 (1997) 1-11, who notes that Josephus praises her in *B.J.* 2.310-314 (3) and records her intercession on behalf of the Jews 2.333 (4, 5). See also Ross S. Kraemer, "Typical and Atypical Jewish Family Dynamics: The Cases of Babatha and Berenice," in *Early Christian Families in Context: An Interdisciplinary Dialogue* (ed. David L. Balch and Carolyn Osiek; Grand Rapids: Eerdmans, 2003) 130-56.

[212] Ilan, "Josephus and Nicolaus on Women," 229.

[213] Ilan, "Josephus and Nicolaus on Women," observes that this is a stock charge (232), that the negative picture is surprising given that Agrippa 2 was his sponsor (233), but suggests that this may reflect his sources. Krieger, "Berenike," notes Josephus' trend in

though not enunciated in his version, is that marriage to those who effectively become what are later called proselytes is acceptable.[214] Josephus fails to mention that Berenice then became the lover of Titus (Tacitus *Hist.* 2.2.1), which might have been sensitive at the time of writing *Jewish War*,[215] but was not likely to have been so at the time of the later writings. She would have become a non-practising Jew like her brother-in-law from her first marriage, Tiberius Alexander, and her sister Drusilla with Felix in Rome.[216] Mariamme's marriage also did not last, but she subsequently married an Alexandrian Jew, Demetrius, a man, Josephus assures us, of noble birth (*A.J.* 20.147).

Through the accounts of these marriages we see Josephus' emphasis on the importance of upholding the prohibition against intermarriage with Gentiles, who can only be made acceptable partners by adopting Jewish customs, including circumcision. Underlying the accounts is also disapproval of women abandoning their husbands and disapproval of any form of adultery or illicit sexual intercourse. The accounts also illustrate the extent of male control, by father, then brother, but also the extent of independence of more experienced women to make their own choices.

Antiquities to attack the Jewish elite and have them carry more responsibility for the disaster of the war because of their disregard of ancestral law (7, 9), so probably also gives some credence to the accusation of incest (6-7). He also points out that she intervened on behalf of Justus, Josephus' critic (*Vit.* 345, 355) (8). On Josephus' disapproval of her and other women acting independently, see Kraemer, "Family Dynamics," 136, 144, 153.

[214] On Gentile women and the issue of their becoming proselytes, see the discussion in Schwartz, "Doing Like Jews or Becoming a Jew?", who argues that while Josephus suppresses the traditional markers of Ruth becoming a proselyte, he assumes that Gentile women marrying Jews adopted Jewish ways (99) and where they would not, intermarriage was forbidden (100).

[215] Ilan, "Josephus and Nicolaus on Women," 230.

[216] Krieger, "Berenike," 11.

2.3 Laws and Related Issues

In this section we consider the three main accounts in which Josephus deals with laws pertaining to sexuality, and a fourth as a special case: the Essenes.

2.3.1 The Law Given at Sinai

The first main treatment is part of his account of the Law given at Sinai (*A.J.* 3.83-286). Having described instructions about the temple and temple service, he proceeds to report Moses' instruction relating to purity. He applies the legislation banning lepers (Lev 13:46; 14:3) and those with gonorrhoea from the camp (cf. Lev 15:1-5) to banning them from the city (*A.J.* 3.261).[217] Within this he reports that women "beset by their natural secretions, he secluded until the seventh day" (as Lev 15:19), the same requirement, he notes, as for "those who have paid the last rites to the dead" (as Num 19:11; 31:19) (*A.J.* 3.261-262). Within the same context of purity he notes that women after childbirth are forbidden to enter the temple or touch sacrifices for 40 days after birth of a male and 80, after a female, and then to do so only after offering sacrifices (*A.J.* 3.269; as Lev 12:20). He goes on to note the law about a woman suspected of adultery (*A.J.* 3.270-273; Numb 5:11-31). Josephus' account includes minor differences: he specifies that most of the grain offering goes to the priests, that they position the woman at the gates which face the temple, that the oath she swears includes that her *right* leg will be put out of joint (cf. Num 5:27), and otherwise if innocent she would give birth in the tenth month to a male child, and the priest gathers bits of temple soil and sprinkles it in the water before she drinks.[218]

Thereafter he reports the prohibition of adultery with the comment that Moses "deemed it blessed that men should be sane-minded concerning wedlock and that it was to the interest alike of the state and the family that children should be legitimate" (*A.J.* 3.274). The concern with the state would resonate especially with his Roman audience and the concern with legitimacy reflects the fundamental issue of inheritance which was crucial for the survival of future generations of a family. From there he moves to the prohibition of incest with one's mother, which, he writes, "is condemned by the law as grossest of sins", his own addition (*A.J.* 3.274; Lev 18:7), noting that the prohibition also applies to "a stepmother, an aunt, a sister, or the wife of one's child" (*A.J.* 3.274; Lev 18:8, 12, 9, 15). The sequence from adultery to incest indicates that he is following the order in Lev 20:10-12. He continues: "he moreover forbade cohabitation with a menstruous woman, mating

---

[217] On this see Feldman, *Judean Antiquities Books 1-4*, 308.

[218] See the discussion in Feldman, *Judean Antiquities Books 1-4*, 311-12.

with a beast, or the toleration of the practice of sodomy in the pursuit of lawless pleasure (μηδὲ τὴν πρὸς τὰ ἄρρενα μῖξιν τιμᾶν διὰ τὴν ἐπ' αὐτοῖς ὥραν ἡδονὴν θηρωμένους παράνομον)" (*A.J.* 3.275; better translated more literally: "in trying to procure lawless pleasure, valuing intercourse with a male because of the beauty of them"[219] (cf. Lev 20:18, 15, 13; 18:19, 23, 22). This appears to acknowledge sexual attractiveness but demands denying response to it. He goes on to note that "for those guilty of such outrages (κατὰ δὲ τῶν εἰς ταῦτ' ἐξυβρισάντων) he decreed the penalty of death" (similarly *Ap.* 2.215), the "outrages" going back to and including adultery.[220] Compared with Leviticus 20 he makes no mention of the prohibition of intercourse with a woman and her mother (Lev 20:14). The prohibition of incest with stepmother, sister, and aunt derives from Lev 18:6-18, but Josephus has omitted the prohibition of incest with grandchildren (18:10), stepsisters (18:11), sisters-in-law (18:16), a woman and her children and grandchildren (18:17) or two sisters (18:18). The addition of "in the pursuit of lawless pleasure (ἡδονὴν θηρωμένους παράνομον)" to sodomy, lit. "sexual intercourse with a male (τὴν πρὸς τὰ ἄρρενα μῖξιν)" (*A.J.* 3.275), suggests that Josephus understands sodomy as an expression of excessive and misdirected desire for pleasure.

Josephus then notes the restrictions imposed on priests, that they are not to marry prostitutes (τὰς ἑταιρηκυίας lit. "those who have prostituted themselves", thus including former prostitutes), a prohibition applied to all, not just priests, in *A.J.* 4.245, slaves, applied to all in *A.J.* 4.244, prisoners of war, "or such women as gain their livelihood by hawking or innkeeping or who have for whatever reasons been separated from their former husbands" (*A.J.* 3.276). Here Josephus is expounding Lev 21:7, which forbids prostitutes, defiled women and divorcees, by expanding the second category on the assumption that women who engage in hawking or innkeeping (like Rahab of Jericho; *A.J.* 5.8) or are separated from their husbands, even if not divorced, are likely to have had illicit sex and that this is also likely to be the case with slaves and captives in war. His histories provide ample illustration of the latter. He then reports the stricter provisions for the high priest who in addition may not marry a widow, but only a virgin from his own tribe (*A.J.* 3.277; as Lev 21:13-14).

---

[219] Feldman, *Judean Antiquities Books 1-4*, 313.

[220] Feldman, *Judean Antiquities Books 1-4*, notes that Leviticus does not demand the death penalty for sex with a menstruating woman (313).

2.3.2 The Law Reviewed before Moses' Farewell

Josephus returns to his depiction of the law in describing Moses' farewell instruction, as suggested by Deuteronomy (*A.J.* 4.176-319). In *A.J.* 4.206 he alludes to the prohibition in Deut 23:18 about using the proceeds of prostitution, female and male (dog), to pay for sacrifices, but expands it. To the reference to proceeds from female prostitution he adds "for the Deity has pleasure in naught that proceeds from outrage (ἀφ' ὕβρεως), and no shame could be worse than the degradation of the body (τῆς ἐπὶ τοῖς σώμασιν αἰσχύνης)". This clearly implies Josephus' disapproval of prostitution. He does not, however, relate "dog" to male prostitution, but, as his reference to the matings of different kinds of dogs shows, takes the statement literally as referring to proceeds, presumably from breeding.

Within this instruction he returns to laws pertaining to sexual relations. Thus he has Moses declare: "Let your young men, on reaching the age of wedlock marry virgins, freeborn and of honest parents" (γαμείτωναν δὲ ἐν ὥρᾳ γάμου γενόμενοι παρθένους ἐλευθέρας γονέων ἀγαθῶν) (*A.J.* 4.244). This is not explicitly derived from pentateuchal law and is not demanding that everyone marry a virgin, as the next statements show. For he continues: "he that will not espouse a virgin must not unite himself to a woman living with another man, corrupting her or wronging her former husband" (*A.J.* 4.244). This is based on the prohibition of adultery, but he applies it to the unmarried young man seeking a wife. He goes on to declare that "female slaves must not be taken in marriage by free men, however strongly some may be constrained thereto by love: such passion must be mastered by regard for decorum and the proprieties of rank" (*A.J.* 4.244).[221] This appears to reflect Roman law and values.[222] It also reflects Josephus' hierarchical assumptions. It need not imply that he disapproved of having sex with household slaves; one should just not marry them. This was already implied in the reference to marrying "virgins, freeborn" (παρθένους ἐλευθέρας) (*A.J.* 4.244).

There follows what in biblical law (Lev 21:7 and *A.J.* 3.276) applies only to priests: "Again, there must be no marriage with a prostitute (μηδὲ ἡταιρημένης εἶναι γάμον), since by reason of the abuse of her body God could not accept her nuptial sacrifices" (*A.J.* 4.245), echoing the prohibition of bringing the proceeds from prostitution into the temple (*A.J.* 4.206). Again, we appear to have imposition

---

[221] Feldman, *Judean Antiquities Books 1-4*, notes that this is not forbidden in biblical law, but that a sacrifice must be brought if he has sex with a slave betrothed to someone else (Lev 19:20-22) (423).

[222] On this see Marilyn B. Skinner, *Sexuality in Greek and Roman Culture* (Oxford: Blackwell, 2005) 206; Lassen, "Roman Family," 108.

of Roman law which forbad marriage to prostitutes.[223] We may contrast Philo's defence of such marriages on the grounds that this would do reformed prostitutes an injustice (*Spec.* 1.102). "Nuptial sacrifices" (cf. also Philo *Spec.* 3.80) do not feature in biblical law, though Tobias' incense offering may indicate some apotropaic rite was practised in Jewish circles (8:2).[224] Next Josephus adds a rationale that applies to these instructions as a whole: "For so only can your children have spirits that are liberal and uprightly set towards virtue, if they are not the issue of dishonourable marriages or of a union resulting from ignoble passion (ἐκ γάμων φύντες αἰσχρῶν μηδ' ἐξ ἐπιθυμίας οὐκ ἐλευθερίας)" (*A.J.* 4.245). Marriages beneath one's station or resulting from unrestrained passion such as with slaves and prostitutes fall into this category.

At this point Josephus returns directly to the biblical law to report the procedures to follow where a husband accuses his bride of not having been a virgin (*A.J.* 4.246-248; Deut 22:13-21). The biblical account begins with the case of a husband making fraudulent charges. Josephus begins with genuine accusation and refers to the man "relying upon what evidence he may have to prove it". This is vague and differs from the biblical account which proposes evidence of the presence or absence of blood on the bedding. Josephus, not without precedent, drops this as evidence, probably because it was too easily concocted (similarly dropped in 4QD^f/4Q271 3 12b-15; 4QOrd^a/4Q159 2-4+8 8-10).[225] To the biblical law, which mentions the father in defence, he adds "brother or whosoever, failing these, be considered her next of kin", reflecting usual assumptions about guardianship of women. The biblical law prescribes punishment, and 100 shekels payable to the father of the woman falsely accused, and forbids the husband ever to divorce his wife. Josephus specifies 39 stripes (cf. Deut 25:3), 50 shekels, and the forbidding of divorce, but then allows an exception: "save only if she furnish him with grave and undeniable reasons for so doing" (*A.J.* 4.247). If guilty, she is to be stoned (*A.J.* 4.248, as Deut 22:21), but, adds Josephus, burned if she is of priestly parentage. This probably derives from Lev 21:9 where it is the penalty for a priest's daughter who engages in prostitution, but has been given broader application, as in *Jub.* 30:7.

Josephus then presents the law concerning the rights of the firstborn in a polygynous marriage (*A.J.* 4.249-250; Deut 21:15-17). His main additions are in expanding the reference to the man loving his second wife to read: "of whom the one is held in special honour and affection, be it for love and beauty, or for other cause", typical of Josephus' tendency to describe such love.

---

[223] Skinner, *Sexuality*, 206.
[224] Satlow, *Jewish Marriage*, 174-75.
[225] On this see Loader, *Dead Sea Scrolls on Sexuality*, 217-18.

He next turns to the law about intercourse with someone betrothed to another (cf. Deut 22:23-24), but depicts it as consensual, not necessarily implied in the biblical law, and so makes no mention of her failure to cry for help. Instead he speaks of her acceding "for pleasure or for lucre" (δι' ἡδονὴν ἢ διὰ κέρδος), implying sexual immorality or prostitution (A.J. 4.251). He then cites the case of a man forcing a betrothed woman to have sex; the man must be executed (A.J. 4.252; cf. Deut 22:25-27), but omits the biblical specification about place, "in the open country" compared with "in the city", writing simply "somewhere" (που), because he has also omitted from both accounts the role of the cry for help and made the first instance consensual. He then brings a version of the provision about a man's having sex with an unbetrothed virgin, changing the biblical provision that he must marry her, pay the father 50 shekels, and never divorce her (Deut 22:28-29), by requiring the payment only if the father does not agree to the marriage (A.J. 4.253), thus treating it as a fine, not a bride price.[226]

In treating divorce Josephus speaks of a man "who desires to be divorced from the wife who is living with him for whatsoever cause (καθ' ἀσδηποτοῦν αἰτίας) – and with mortals many such may arise (πολλαὶ δ' ἂν τοῖς ἀνθρώποις τοιαῦται γίγνοιντο) – must certify in writing that he will have no further intercourse with her (γράμμασι μὲν περὶ τοῦ μηδέποτε συνελθεῖν ἰσχυριζέσθω); for thus will the woman obtain the right to consort with another (συνοικεῖν ἑτέρῳ), which thing ere then must not be permitted" (A.J. 4.253; Deut 24:1). Josephus assumes that only the man divorces, clearly interprets ערות דבר very liberally, as the school of Hillel (m. Git. 9:10) and describes the substance of the certificate in terms of his ceasing to have sex with her, which, only by implication, therefore frees her to marry another.[227] This is interesting in reflecting the view that engaging in sexual intercourse apparently constitutes a marriage and its deliberate cessation effectively terminates it. He reiterates the prohibition of remarriage to the first husband, also forbidden in Roman law, but unlike Deut 24:1-4 adds to the second husband's death also his maltreatment of her (A.J. 4.253).[228] As Feldman notes, he makes no mention of abomination or of bringing guilt on the land.[229]

The provision of Levirate marriage follows (A.J. 4.254-256; Deut 25:5-10). Josephus expands the account of its value: it "will at once be profitable to the public welfare, houses not dying out and property remaining with the relatives, and it will moreover bring the women an alleviation of their misfortune to live with the

---

[226] On this see Mayer-Schärtel, *Frauenbild*, 218.

[227] Feldman, *Judean Antiquities Books 1-4*, contrasts *m. Git.*, which reads "lo, you are permitted to another man" (9.3) (427).

[228] On this see Skinner, *Sexuality*, 205-206.

[229] Feldman, *Judean Antiquities Books 1-4*, 428.

nearest kinsman of their former husbands". The link with property helps make sense of the application of Levirate marriage in the story of Ruth (see 2.2.9.6 above). He also adds that refusal to marry insults the memory of his brother and that the council asks him the reasons for his refusal.[230] Josephus is putting the case for the reasonableness of the practice to his hearers who might have found it strange. His account retains the detail about the rite of reproach should the brother refuse.

He then brings the provision about the captive wife (*A.J.* 4.257-259; Deut 21:10-14). Josephus specifies that she may be a virgin or already married, but this makes apparently no difference,[231] and adds to the requirement that she be allowed 30 days for mourning, the words: "before turning to the festivities and ceremonies of marriage" and then that "it is honourable and just that, in taking her to bear him children, he should respect her wishes (θεραπεύειν αὐτῆς τὸ βουλητόν), and that he should not, intent solely on his own pleasure (τὴν ἰδίαν ἡδονὴν διώκοντα μόνον), neglect what might be agreeable to her (τοῦ κατ' αὐτὴν ἀμελεῖν κεχαρισμένου)" (*A.J.* 4.258). Here we see some attempt on Josephus' part to ameliorate the captive woman's vulnerability by emphasising the need for respect, possibly to assuage the concerns of his hearers[232] and perhaps reflecting his own – though the situation still appears to sanction what is effectively rape. We also see his emphasis on marriage and sexual intercourse for procreation ("taking her to bear him children") and not just for pleasure. Instead of "if you are not satisfied with her" (Deut 21:14), Josephus writes: "should he, however, sated with his passion (ἐμπλησθεὶς τῆς ἐπιθυμίας), disdain to keep her as his spouse" (*A.J.* 4.259), again emphasising disapproval of sexual intercourse primarily to satisfy passion. He has omitted references to the shaved head, pared nails, removal of captive garb (Deut 21:12-13) and replaced bewailing her father and mother (Deut 21:13) with bewailing kinsmen and friends who have fallen in battle, adding reference to tears.[233]

The emphasis on intercourse for procreation returns in his extensively elaborated version of the provision about rebellious sons, which follows (*A.J.* 4.260-265; Deut 21:18-21). There he has the parents declare "that they came together in matrimony not for pleasure's sake (συνελθεῖν μὲν ἀλλήλοις οὐχ ἡδονῆς ἕνεκα), nor to increase their fortunes by uniting their several properties in one, but that they might have children (as *Ap.* 2.199) who should tend their old age and who should receive from them everything that they needed" (*A.J.* 4.261). Here we see a double disapproval, of marriage for pleasure and of marriage for profit,

---

[230] On the additions see Feldman, *Judean Antiquities Books 1-4*, 429.

[231] Mayer-Schärtel, *Frauenbild*, 170.

[232] So Mayer-Schärtel, *Frauenbild*, 170.

[233] Feldman, *Judean Antiquities Books 1-4*, 430.

but also a clearly functional view of the mutual responsibilities of parents and children at different life stages, essential for the welfare of both in that age.

The brief reference to prohibition of stealing a person (*A.J.* 4.271; Deut 24:7) would have relevance to kidnapping slaves also for sexual purposes, though Josephus adds no specific application. He reports the provision about freeing a slave in the seventh year, but with the provision that a slave may stay on with the fellow slave whom he loves and has borne him children and then they can all be released in the year of jubilee (*A.J.* 4.273). By contrast, the biblical provision speaks of the seventh year and requires that the man stay with the master forever with his ear pierced if he insists he will not go free without his family (Exod 21:2-6; Deut 15:12).

Among other provisions he reports in what follows are the fine for kicking a pregnant woman, when it leads to a miscarriage (*A.J.* 4.278; Exod 21:22-25). Josephus' version makes no mention of the kick being incidental in a fight, and adds that the fine is on the grounds of "having, by the destruction of the fruit of her womb, diminished the population" and that a further sum be paid to the woman's husband, whereas the biblical provision speaks of one and the same fine. Typically Josephus expresses concern about production of children and population.

He has Moses declare: "Shun eunuchs (γάλλους)[234] and flee all dealings with those who have deprived themselves of their virility and of those fruits of generation, which God has given to men for the increase of our race" (*A.J.* 4.290). This is his interpretation of Deut 23:1 which forbids men with crushed testicles or with excised penises from entering the congregation. Josephus is particularly concerned with those who have castrated themselves and goes on to express this by comparing them to "infanticides who withal have destroyed the means of procreation" (*A.J.* 4.290), one of his major emphases, and alleges: "for plainly it is by reason of the effeminacy of their soul that they have changed the sex of their body also. And so with all that would be deemed a monstrosity by the beholders" (*A.J.* 4.291). Josephus clearly assumes that effeminacy is not a neutral state, but a chosen one, and assumes abhorrence not just of physical appearance but also of the behaviour. This coheres with what he reports elsewhere in the history of the behaviour of some eunuchs (cf. *A.J.* 16.229-231).

Finally he notes in relation to the army the provision that "those too who have lately built themselves houses and have not yet had a year to enjoy them, with those who have planted and have not yet partaken of the fruits, must be left on the land, as also the betrothed and recently married, lest regret (better: "desire" πόθῳ)

---

[234] Feldman, *Judean Antiquities Books 1-4*, notes that the word is usually used of the priests of Cybele, who were eunuchs dressed in female clothes and who practised self-mutilation (458). He suggests Josephus may be influenced by Domitian's prohibition of castration, namely that of slaves (459).

for these things should make them chary of their lives" (*A.J.* 4.298; Deut 20:5-7). The biblical rationale for the latter is different: "he might die in the battle and another marry her" (Deut 20:7). It also gives this freedom only to the betrothed. The battle provision also requires total extermination of Canaanites and warns: "Beware, above all in battle, that no woman assume the accoutrements of a man nor a man the apparel of a woman" (*A.J.* 4.300-301). The placement of the prohibition of cross-dressing (cf. Deut 22:5) in the context of battle may target employment of women in war, though this still leaves the man's behaviour without explanation. At least in the first instance it does not appear to be addressing sexual issues.

2.3.3 The Law in *Against Apion*

The other passage where Josephus gives particular attention to laws pertaining to sexual issues is in *Against Apion*. There in the context of expounding, as he puts it, "the precepts and prohibitions of our Law" (*Ap.* 2.190), he notes that the sacrifices are "not occasions for drunken self-indulgence (εἰς μέθην ἑαυτοῖς)" (*Ap.* 2.195; cf. Philo *Spec.* 1.192-193),[235] in which he would doubtless include sexual wrongdoing, but his main discussion of pertinent matters begins with comments about purity. Purifications are prescribed "after a funeral, after child-birth (ἀπὸ λεχοῦς),[236] after conjugal union (ἀπὸ κοινωνίας τῆς πρὸς γυναῖκα) and many others" (*Ap.* 2.198). He then moves to an exposition of marriage laws, declaring: "The Law recognizes no sexual connexions, except the natural union of man and wife (better: "woman"),[237] and that only for the procreation of children (μῖξιν μόνην οἶδεν ὁ νόμος τὴν κατὰ φύσιν τὴν πρὸς γυναῖκα, καὶ ταύτην εἰ μέλλοι τέκνων ἕνεκα γίνεσθαι)" (*Ap.* 2.199). This statement initially enshrines an argument from nature, which focuses here not on what is procreative – that argument immediately follows – but on what happens between man and woman, which Josephus thus affirms as natural in the sense that it is both right order and occurs of its own accord, in contrast to the alternative of same-sex relations which in Josephus' assessment are not natural. This probably has more to do with an innate sense of discomfort common among many heterosexuals combined also

---

[235] Barclay, *Against Apion*, notes the connection which Tacitus makes between Judeans and the cult of Dionysius (*Antiquitates Romanae* 5.5.5) (280).

[236] As Barclay, *Against Apion*, notes the word if accented λέχους from λέχος would mean marriage-bed and so sexual intercourse, but if accented λεχοῦς from λεχώ would indicate childbirth, which is preferable given that reference to sexual intercourse follows (282).

[237] The word γυναῖκα is better translated woman because the focus is gender. So Barclay, *Against Apion*, 282.

with an understanding of order in creation than it has to do, for instance, with the physical complementarity of genitals. The argument about procreation is additional. Marriage and sexual intercourse in marriage is for procreation. It is possible to interpret this as a strict rule that minutely differentiates acts of intercourse in marriage according to the intent at the time of each partner, but as also in Philo on whom Josephus may well depend for this emphasis,[238] this is likely to be over-interpretation and not altogether meaningful in an age where methods of birth control were far from sophisticated and safe. The purpose does, however, carry sufficient weight, to rule out sex during menstruation and during pregnancy, although he does not specify that here (cf. *A.J.* 3.275; *B.J.* 2.161).

In contrast to legitimate sexual intercourse in the context of marriage for procreation Josephus sets same-sex relations: "Sodomy (μίξιν ... τὴν δὲ πρὸς ἄρρενας ἀρρένων) it abhors, and punishes any guilty of such assault (εἴ τισ ἐπιχειρήσειεν lit. "anyone who tries it") with death" (*Ap.* 2.199; Lev 20:13; similarly *Ap.* 2.213). His focus is males. He then addresses the motive for marriage,[239] indicating that the law condemns taking a wife with a view to the dowry (cf. *A.J.* 4.261),[240] by forceful abduction ("not to carry off a woman by force" μηδὲ βιαίοις ἁρπαγαῖς) (cf. Deut 22:28-29),[241] or through guile and

---

[238] So Aryeh Kasher, "Josephus in Praise of Mosaic Laws on Marriage (*Contra Apionem*, II, 199-201)," in *"The Words of a Wise Man's Mouth are Gracious" (Qoh 10,12): Festschrift for Günter Stemberger on the Occasion of his 65th Birthday* (ed. Mauro Perani; Studia Judaica / Forschungen zur Wissenschaft des Judentums 32; Berlin: de Gruyter, 2005) 95-108, who writes: "The fact that Philo Alexandrinus gives a very similar interpretation leads us to believe that he was the direct source of interpretation for Josephus" (97). He sees this emphasis as "Propagandist glorification of the morality embodied in the Torah" (95). Kasher sees Josephus standing under the influence of biblical and postbiblical Jewish authors rather than the *Lex Iulia de maritandis ordinibus* 18 B.C.E. and *Lex Poppaeia* 9 B.C.E., which prescribed punishment for those not marrying by a certain age and producing children (96). On the other hand these may well have influenced Philo and so, indirectly, also Josephus.

[239] Barclay, *Against Apion*, notes that the words, γαμεῖν δὲ κελεύει (lit. "it instructs to marry") (*Ap.* 2.200) could be read as an absolute command to marry (as *Ps.-Phoc.* 175), but are better understood as belonging closely with what follows (283). Similarly Kasher, "Josephus in Praise of Mosaic Laws on Marriage," 99.

[240] On similar concern with marrying for dowries, see Barclay, *Against Apion*, who notes Plato *Leg.* 742E; 774C-E; *Ps.-Phoc.* 199-200. Kasher notes also Plutarch *Solon* 20 (99). Concern with greed for dowries may also inform Luke's reading of the prohibition of divorce and remarriage which it places in the context of greed for wealth (16:18). On this see Loader, *Sexuality and the Jesus Tradition*, 81-82.

[241] Barclay, *Against Apion*, notes the practice of abduction for marriage in Sparta and that Roman listeners might hear an allusion to the rape of the Sabine women, and Jewish, to the abduction of Dinah (283). Similarly Kasher, "Josephus in Praise of Mosaic Laws on

deceit (cf. Exod 22:16-17), and requires approach to the woman's male guardian (cf. on such guardians *A.J.* 4.246, 252; 12.187) and ensuring also that the proposed match does not contravene laws about forbidden marriages: "not ineligible on account of nearness of kin" (κατὰ συγγένειαν τὴν ἐπιτήδειον) (*Ap.* 2.200),[242] where Josephus will have in mind either the provisions of Lev 18:6-18, or concern with intermarriage with foreigners.[243]

Josephus then sets these provisions about marriage within what he portrays as the Law's estimate of woman as "in all things inferior to the man" (γυνὴ χείρων, φησίν, ἀνδρὸς εἰς ἅπαντα) (*Ap.* 2.201; cf. Philo *Hypoth.* 7.3) and so requires her to "be submissive, not for her humiliation, but that she may be directed; for the authority has been given by God to the man" (τοιγαροῦν ὑπακουέτω, μὴ πρὸς ὕβριν, ἀλλ' ἵν' ἄρχηται· θεὸς γὰρ ἀνδρὶ τὸ κράτος ἔδωκεν) (*Ap.* 2.201; similarly Philo *Hypoth.* 7.3). Again Josephus shows some sensitivity to the issue of women's abuse ("not for her humiliation" μὴ πρὸς ὕβριν; similarly πρὸς ὕβρεως μὲν οὐδεμιᾶς Philo *Hypoth.* 7.3), as he did in a limited way on captive wives. Josephus is probably drawing directly or indirectly on Gen 3:16 here,[244] though he omits this from his account of Genesis 1 – 3, where he clearly deems woman as having been inferior from beginning and Adam's heeding her as folly on these grounds, as our discussion above showed (2.2.1). He then depicts the Law as imposing strict sexual limits on the man: "The husband must have union with his wife alone (ταύτῃ συνεῖναι δεῖ τὸν γήμαντα μόνῃ); it is impious to assault (πειρᾶν lit. "try to [have sex with]") the wife [woman] of another" (*Ap.* 2.201). The first half of the statement above might recall the earlier declaration in *Ap.* 2.199 if read as referring to men and their wives, "The Law recognizes no sexual connexions, except the natural union of man and wife", but the focus in that context on gender suggests it is more generic: man and woman. As Barclay notes, the second half about assaulting the wife of another, is best seen as alluding to the two instances he is about address, the first being intercourse with a betrothed woman and the second, adultery,[245] for both of which, Josephus notes, the penalty is death. The restriction, having sex only with one's wife, is probably more far reaching and would include engaging with a prostitute (implied in *A.J.* 4.206), and

---

Marriage," who notes that this is despite the "staged kidnapping" of wives for the Benjaminites (102).

[242] On the alternative and less suitable reading which relates the qualification to the guardian see Barclay, *Against Apion*, 284.

[243] See Barclay, *Against Apion*, 284.

[244] So also Barclay, *Against Apion*, 284.

[245] Barclay, *Against Apion*, 284-85.

with widows,[246] but probably stopped short of forbidding sex with one's slaves (cf. *A.J.* 16.194; 18.340).

Consistent with his concern about procreation and population, Josephus declares that the Law outlaws infanticide and abortion, because a woman doing so "destroys a soul and diminishes the race" (*Ap.* 2.202; cf. *Ps.-Phoc.* 184).[247] This concern would also explain his declaration: "For this same reason none who has intercourse with a woman who is with child can be considered pure (καθαρός)" (*Ap.* 2.202), if this translation were accepted, namely forbidding intercourse during pregnancy (as *B.J.* 2.161). Barclay, however, calls this into question, arguing that the statement is rather to be understood as referring to corpse impurity which applies to anyone who approaches an aborted foetus.[248] The word λέχους or λεχοῦς translated above "woman who is with child" means, respectively, "woman in childbirth or childbirth, itself" or "marriage bed/sexual intercourse". He proposes the former accenting and thus sees here a reference to approaching something at childbirth, namely an aborted or still born foetus. The statement thus remains with the theme of abortion and appropriately deals with the issue of corpse impurity which is also the focus of what follows. Accordingly, ritual purity comes to expression in the requirement of ablution after intercourse (*Ap.* 2.203; cf. already *Ap.* 2.198).

The explanation for the latter, however, imports into the law a particular understanding of sexual intercourse which warrants closer consideration. Josephus states that intercourse entails a partition (μερισμός) of the soul, by which he means that semen carries part of the man's soul into the woman's vagina ("into another place") (*Ap.* 2.203). The theory is articulated in the fifth century philosopher Democritus.[249] Josephus then explains: "For it suffers both when being implanted in bodies, and again when severed from them by death. That is why the Law has enjoined purifications in all such cases". Thus Josephus rationalises the ablution as doing the same as cleansing from corpse impurity (cf. also the parallel expressed in *A.J.* 3.261-262), because in both, death and sexual

---

[246] Cf. Niebuhr, *Gesetz und Paränese*, who argues that Josephus is primarily concerned with adultery (106).

[247] On exposing unwanted infants to die see Barclay, *Against Apion*, who notes its widespread practice and rejection by Jews, as in *Ps.-Phoc.* 185; *Sib. Or.* 3.765-766; Philo *Virt.* 131-132; *Spec.* 3.110-119, and cited by Hecataeus and Tacitus as a reason for the size of Jewish population (285). He notes sensitivity on the issue in Rome and critique of Greeks (285). See also his comments on disapproval of contraception and abortion (285). It is not clear to me that Josephus addresses contraception here.

[248] Barclay, *Against Apion*, 286. The Greek is ambiguous: τοιγαροῦν οὐδ' εἴ τις ἐπὶ λεχους φθορὰν παρέλθοι, καθαρὸς εἶναι τότε προσήκει. λεχους might be accented λέχους or λεχοῦς.

[249] On this see Barclay, *Against Apion*, 286; Mayer-Schärtel, *Frauenbild*, 136.

intercourse, the soul of the man suffers in some sense, in the latter through death of part of himself.

The instructions which follow go beyond marriage, but contain aspects pertinent to our theme. Thus festivities at a birth are not be occasions for drinking to excess (cf. also *Ap.* 2.195) – probably again having in mind that among the outcomes can be sexual wrongdoing (*Ap.* 2.204). Josephus sets limits on relations to aliens when he writes that it was not Moses' "pleasure that casual visitors should be admitted to the intimacies of our daily life (τοὺς δ' ἐκ παρέργου προσιόντας ἀναμίγνυσθαι τῇ συνηθείᾳ οὐκ ἠθέλησεν)" perhaps with sexual implications (*Ap.* 2.210). Josephus is clothing exclusions in language which his hearers might find inoffensive as simply maintaining the values of family privacy. Barclay notes that it foreshadows the exclusions in what is to come: temple access; table fellowship; and intermarriage.[250] On war rules he writes that the law "forbids even the spoiling of fallen combatants", which would include sexual mutilation, and "has taken measures to prevent outrage (ὕβρις) to prisoners of war, especially women" (*Ap.* 2.212), clearly referring to sexual abuse (cf. similarly his addition: "not for her humiliation" μὴ πρὸς ὕβριν in *Ap.*2.201),[251] and prohibits abuse of animals (*Ap.* 2.213), which might include bestiality[252] though that is not specified here.

Josephus makes the claim that "the penalty for most offences against the Law is death: for adultery, for violating an unmarried woman (ἂν μοιχεύσῃ τις, ἂν βιάσηται κόρην), for outrage upon a male (ἂν ἄρρενι τολμήσῃ πεῖραν προσφέρειν), for consent of one so tempted to such abuse (ἂν ὑπομείνῃ παθεῖν ὁ πειρασθείς)" (*Ap.* 2.215). He adds: "The Law is no less inexorable for slaves (ἔστι δὲ καὶ ἐπὶ δούλοις ὁμοίως ὁ νόμος ἀπαραίτητος)" (*Ap.* 2.215). This could be applying the same penalties to abuse by slaves, but it is more probably addressing similar abuse done to them.[253] Further on he cites the exemplary behaviour and discipline of Jews in ways that others would find "difficult to tolerate: I mean personal service, simple diet, discipline which leaves no room for freak or individual caprice (τὸ μηδὲν εἰκῇ μηδ' ὡς ἔτυχεν ἕκαστος ἐπιτεθυμηκώς) in matters of meat and drink, or in the sexual relations (ἢ συνουσίᾳ), or in extravagance, or again the abstention from work at rigidly fixed periods" (*Ap.* 2.234). Again, including in sexual matters, norms are set against "freak or individual caprice".

---

[250] Barclay, *Against Apion*, 292.

[251] So Barclay, *Against Apion*, 293.

[252] So Barclay, *Against Apion*, 294, who notes that the word, χρῆσις used here also occurs in a sexual context in Rom 1:26.

[253] So also Barclay, *Against Apion*, 295.

It has long been recognised that extensive parallels exist among Josephus *Ap.* 2.190-219; Philo *Hypoth.* 6.10 – 7.20 and *Pseudo-Phocylides*. In his review of research and analysis of the relationship Sterling identifies nine clusters of common material and argues that the evidence suggests not dependence between one or other source, nor coinciding extrapolations of pentateuchal law, but a common oral or written tradition based on Leviticus 19 – 20 and Deuteronomy 22, which reflects a common body of instruction in Alexandria and Rome and possibly elsewhere.[254] The table below lists the topics broadly relating to sexuality in the order in which they occur in the three sources.

Josephus *Ap.* 2.190-219	Philo *Hypoth.* 6.10 – 7.20	*Pseudo-Phocylides*
no same-sex relations (199)	pederasty (1)	not remaining unmarried (175)
sex only for procreation (199)	adultery (1)	obligation to procreate (176)
no marrying for dowry (200)	rape of the young female (1)	no prostituting one's wife (177)
no forced abductions (200)	rape of the young male (1)	no adultery (177)
no deceit in marrying (200) approaching male guardian (200)	prostituting oneself (1)	no incest (stepmother/father's concubines/sisters, sisters-in-law (179-183)
no forbidden marriages (incest or intermarriage) (200)	women in submission (3)	no abortion (184)
women inferior and in submission but not for abuse (201)	devoted possessions of wife (5)	no exposure of infants (185) no laying hands on pregnant wife (for sex? for abortion?) (186)
sex only in marriage (201)	no castration men (7)	no castration (187)
no adultery (201)	no aborting women (7)	no bestiality (187)
no violating the betrothed (201)	no separating wife from husband among slaves (8)	no shameful sex with wife (189) no unnatural/same-sex – male and female (190-192)
no abortion (202)		no excessive sex (193)
ablution after sex (203)		no rape of unbetrothed (198)
death penalty for adultery, female rape, same sex acts (both partners) (215)		no marrying bad/wealthy women for dowry (199-200) no multiple marriages (205)

---

[254] Gregory E. Sterling, "Universalizing the Particular: Natural Law in Second Temple Jewish Ethics," *SPA* 15 (2003) 64-80, 69-73. He notes that the severe penalties may reflect influence of Stoics, who propounded severe punishment for contravening natural law, a notion attractive to Jews who identified it with Torah (74-77) and probably used it to counter charges of particularism (79). See also the earlier discussions in Gerber, *Bild des Judentums*,101-16; George P. Carras, "Dependence or Common Tradition in Philo Hypothetica VIII 6.10–7.20 and Josephus Contra Apionem 2.190-219," *SPA* 5 (1993) 24-47.

Among the relevant elements common to Josephus and Philo is the application of the death penalty for rape (Josephus *Ap.* 2.215-217; Philo *Hyp.* 7.1-2, 6). Most common features derive from biblical law, but some reflect common postbiblical tradition: subordination of women (though probably based on Gen 3:16);[255] abortion (probably extrapolating from Exod 21:22-23 LXX which treats the foetus as a human being);[256] the obligation to procreate (probably partly based on Gen 1:28), and not marrying for a dowry.[257] Some are more specific elaborations of biblical law (such as on same-sex relations, rape, and castration/sterilisation). It is unlikely that Josephus depends on Philo's *Hypothetica*. Despite the similarities, too much is different and such dependence would leave unexplained the independent evidence in *Pseudo-Phocylides*.[258]

Much of what Josephus says about attitudes towards sexuality and related matters, including on legal issues, is to be found beyond these specific treatments. These include both legal material and narrative accounts such as we have considered above, but frequently also in minor comments and observations. In the final section of our discussion of Josephus we draw all these together in what then also functions as a summary overview.

2.3.4 The Essenes and Celibacy

The Essenes are a special case of a group applying to themselves a particular application and extension of the Law, and so we consider them here. We have earlier discussed Josephus' portrait of the Essenes in the context of the discussion of celibacy and the Dead Sea Scrolls[259] and also to a limited degree in the treatment of Philo's comments on the Therapeutae and the Essenes (1.3.5 above). Josephus makes reference to Essenes either as individuals or as a group at a number of points in his works. Some of these are of marginal relevance to the issue of attitudes towards sexuality. This is the case in his reference to Judas, the Essene, in *B.J.* 1.78-80, although the fact that he is described as one whose "predictions had never once proved erroneous or false (οὐκ ἔστιν ὅτε πταίσας ἢ ψευσθεὶς ἐν τοῖς προαπαγγέλμασιν)" (*B.J.* 1.78) and as a "seer" (μάντιν) (*B.J.* 1.80) might have some relevance. Josephus, here, takes it as understood that as an Essene Judas might engage in prophecy without necessarily implying that all do. In *B.J.* 2.113 we find reference to an Essene, Simon, who exercises a similar

---

[255] Carras, "Dependence or Common Tradition," 32.

[256] Carras, "Dependence or Common Tradition," 37.

[257] On this see Niebuhr, *Gesetz und Paränese*, 47, 51.

[258] Sterling, "Universalizing the Particular," 72; Carras, "Dependence or Common Tradition," 46.

[259] Loader, *Dead Sea Scrolls on Sexuality*, 369-76.

role as in interpreter of a dream. Other short references in the *Jewish War* include mention of John, the Essene, as a general in the revolt (*B.J.* 2.567; 3.11) and of the Essene gate in Jerusalem (*B.J.* 5.145), probably reflecting their preferred entry point in proximity to their quarters and their particular purity concerns. In the *Antiquities* Josephus refers to an Essene called Manaemus, who similarly exercises the role of a prophet or seer, predicting that the boy Herod would become king of the Jews (*A.J.* 15.373-379).

The other references speak of the Essenes as a group. They can be brief. Thus he lists them beside the Pharisees and Sadducees in *A.J.* 13.171-172, where he differentiates among them on the basis of their understanding of free will and determinism, explaining for his audience in their terms that "the sect of the Essenes (τὸ δὲ τῶν Ἐσσηνῶν γένος), however, declares that Fate is mistress of all things (πάντων τὴν εἱμαρμένην κυρίαν ἀποφαίνεται)" (*A.J.* 13.172). In similar vein he explains in *A.J.* 15.371 that the group "follows a way of life taught to the Greeks by Pythagoras", assuming his hearers will understand the implications. When in *Life* he mentions that at age 16 he "determined to gain personal experience of the several sects" (*Vit.* 10), specifying the three, Pharisees, Sadducees, and Essenes, he probably intends his readers to hear this as matching the best models of learning of his day which entailed engaging the various philosophical schools. Then having "passed through the three courses (τὰς τρεῖς διῆλθον)"[260] and "not content, however, with the experience thus gained (καὶ μηδὲ τὴν ἐντεῦθεν ἐμπειρίαν ἱκανὴν ἐμαυτῷ νομίσας εἶναι)" he went on to spend time with a certain, Bannus in the wilderness, sometimes also identified as an Essene, and so as reflecting Josephus' final standpoint, but wrongly so, since he makes clear that the encounter with Bannus is something different from his previous three engagements.[261]

The more extensive treatments of the Essenes, are to be found in *B.J.* 2.119-161, to which he, himself, sometimes alludes (*A.J.* 15.371; *Vit.* 10), and *A.J.* 18.18-22. The former is the most extensive. It is beyond the present undertaking to consider the full range of detail which Josephus offers here. Generally, some of the tendencies evident in the shorter accounts are clearly again present. Josephus explicitly alludes to the similarities to what he and his audience would affirm of the Greeks, especially the notion of the "Islands of the Blessed" and its counterpart, Hades (*B.J.* 2.155-158) and the underlying anthropology of immortal souls (*B.J.* 2.154). The account clearly idealises them in a way designed to appeal to his hearers, affirming their piety, peaceableness, discipline, engagement with

---

[260] On the problematic claim to have passed through all three in three years, scarcely enough to have completed the first stage of initiation, see Beall, *Josephus' Description of the Essenes*, 34.

[261] On this see Mason, *Life*, 18.

the books of the ancients, shared property, orderliness and discipline. It shows the Jews as anything but troublesome and unstable.[262] At the same time Josephus provides much genuine information, some strikingly similar to detail found in the *Community Rule* at Qumran. The association of the individual Essenes mentioned above with prophecy and prediction finds its explanation in this passage in which he notes that some train especially to this end (*B.J.* 2.159).

With regard to his statement pertaining to sexuality in this report we face the task, noted above more generally, of discerning what might be genuine information and what might be propagandising idealisation. Both, of course, may be taken to reflect his own attitudes. One of his first observations is that "they shun pleasures as a vice and regard temperance and the control of the passions as a special virtue (οὗτοι τὰς μὲν ἡδονὰς ὡς κακίαν ἀποστρέφονται, τὴν δὲ ἐγκράτειαν καὶ τὸ μὴ τοῖς πάθεσιν ὑποπίπτειν ἀρετὴν ὑπολαμβάνουσιν)" (*B.J.* 2.120). Josephus will expect his hearers to share his rejection of a life based on seeking pleasures and his espousal of keeping passions under control.[263] That what he has in mind includes sexual pleasures and passions is suggested by the comments on marriage which immediately follow. "Marriage they disdain (καὶ γάμου μὲν παρ' αὐτοῖς ὑπεροψία)" (*B.J.* 2.120). Here ὑπεροψία means something like giving up or not avail themselves of the opportunity to marry, rather than condemn or despise,[264] since Josephus will soon point out that "they do not, indeed, on principle, condemn wedlock and the propagation thereby of the race" (τὸν μὲν γάμον καὶ τὴν ἐξ αὐτοῦ διαδοχὴν οὐκ ἀναιροῦντες) (*B.J.* 2.121). He has just explained that they adopt the children of others. He then offers the explanation why they choose not to marry: "they wish to protect themselves against women's wantonness, being persuaded that none of the sex keeps her plighted troth to one man (τὰς δὲ τῶν γυναικῶν ἀσελγείας φυλαττόμενοι καὶ μηδεμίαν τηρεῖν πεπεισμένοι τὴν πρὸς ἕνα πίστιν)" (*B.J.* 2.121; cf. Philo: "because a wife is a selfish creature, excessively jealous and an adept at beguiling

---

[262] On this see Mason, "What Josephus Says About the Essenes," 433-35. See also Bilde, "Essenes," who notes of both Josephus and Philo that they "describe Judaism as a sort of ideal 'philosophy', able to compete with Greek philosophical schools and with Hellenistic-Roman religions" and in doing so "present the Essenes as the Jewish elite" (62). McLaren, "Essenes, Pharisees and Sadducees," sees in the statements of *B.J.* 2.119-166 and *A.J.* 18.11-25, successive elaborations of the more neutral description in *A.J.* 13.171-173, and argues that in the former two, Josephus is seeking to distance the Jewish people from Judas as the troublemaker, in the second of them, even depicting him as the leader of a fourth philosophy. Thus Josephus "presents a picture where it is deemed normal not to see Essenes, Pharisees, Sadducees, let alone any other reasonable Jew, as interested in rebellion against Rome" (45).

[263] Mason, "What Josephus says," 434.

[264] Cf. Beall, *Josephus' Description of the Essenes*, who translates: "contempt" (38).

the morals of her husband and seducing him by her continued impostures" *Hypoth.* 11.14). This is typical of Josephus' own views elsewhere, as noted in the previous section.²⁶⁵ Thus the grounds for their espousing celibacy are, according to Josephus, not ascetic nor any hesitation about engaging in sexual intercourse for procreation, nor any taboo about sacred space and time, such as might apply to prophets (a role for which only some of them trained) or the especially holy, but rather their fear of women's infidelity.

At the conclusion of his report Josephus returns to the question of marriage, noting that there is "another order of Essenes" (ἕτερον Ἐσσηνῶν τάγμα) (*B.J.* 2.160), which, while sharing the same mode of life, regulations and customs, "differs from them in its views of marriage" (διεστὼς δὲ τῇ κατὰ γάμον δόξῃ) (*B.J.* 2.160). According to Josephus their argument concerns propagation of the species, matching his own view of its importance: "They think that those who decline to marry cut off the chief function of life, the propagation of the race (μέγιστον γὰρ ἀποκόπτειν οἴονται τοῦ βίου μέρος, τὴν διαδοχήν τοὺς μὴ γαμοῦντας)" (*B.J.* 2.160). Mason suggests that the order may be a deliberate fabrication on Josephus' part to cover the fact that despite lauding these ideals he married.²⁶⁶ This need not be the case, both given other ways in which he also did not share the Essene lifestyle (e.g. concerning property) and that the evidence from writings found at Qumran indicate that among their orders, which seem very close to what Josephus describes as Essene, both celibate and non-celibate orders are to be found.²⁶⁷ The focus on propagation continues in the detail about testing potential wives through three years of probation. They "only marry them after they have by three periods of purification given proof of fecundity (ἐπειδὰν τρὶς καθαρθῶσιν εἰς πεῖραν τοῦ δύνασθαι τίκτειν, οὕτως ἄγονται)", incidentally showing knowledge of the implications of the menstrual cycle for fertility. He then adds that "they have no intercourse with them during pregnancy, thus showing that their motif in marrying is not self-indulgence but the procreation of children (ταῖς δ' ἐγκύμοσιν οὐχ ὁμιλοῦσιν, ἐνδεικνύμενοι τὸ μὴ δι' ἡδονὴν ἀλλὰ τέκνων χρείαν γαμεῖν)" (*B.J.* 2.161). The concern with pursuing pleasure here at the end matches the opening statements and shows Josephus' frame of reference which sees a place for sexual relations only within marriage and only for procreation and never just for pleasure, while not condemning its pleasurableness in the appropriate context. The reference to abstinence during

---

²⁶⁵ See also Mason, "What Josephus says," 434.

²⁶⁶ Mason, "What Josephus says," who suggests that the account of a marrying order of Essenes may be Josephus' invention to account for his own links with the movement and the discrepancy that he had had a number of marriages (448). "He made them up as a device to broaden their representative character to include people such as himself" (449).

²⁶⁷ See my discussion in Loader, *Dead Sea Scrolls on Sexuality*, 369-76.

pregnancy, not attested elsewhere in Josephus, though sometimes read in *Ap.* 2.202, follows logically from his ideals and is probably to be assumed not as a peculiarity to Essenes but as something to apply to all. His closing observation pertains to bathing. Given the preceding context it may well refer to bathing after sexual intercourse (cf. *Ap.* 2.198)[268] and specifies appropriate coverings, presumably because such bathing might be where others might see, and to contrast with the Greek practice of bathing naked (*B.J.* 2.161).

In the much shorter account in *A.J.* 18.18-22 Josephus again depicts the Essenes as being like others who are presumably familiar to his readers, namely the Ctistae[269] among the Dacians (*A.J.* 18.22). He numbers the Essenes at more than 4000, matching Philo's account and perhaps dependent on it or on a common source.[270] He also returns to the theme of marriage: "They neither bring wives into the community (καὶ οὔτε γαμετὰς εἰσάγονται) nor do they own slaves, since they believe that the latter practice contributes to injustice, and that the former opens the way to a source of dissension (τὸ δὲ στάσεως ἐνδιδόναι ποίησιν)" (*A.J.* 18.21). The grounds appear pragmatic: having wives in such a community would cause dissension, on Josephus' assumption that women are contentious, a view shared by his Cynic and Stoic contemporaries.[271] It may be that he is also seeking to differentiate the image of the Essene communities from Plato's ideal of having women in common.[272] Again, not marrying does not relate to asceticism, disapproval of sexual relations, taboos of space and time, or defined roles such as prophets and priests, but simply to the fear that women are troublemakers.

Aside from the Essenes, the issue of celibacy might be reflected in Josephus' etymology of Deborah's name as "bee" (μέλισσαν) (*A.J.* 5.200), used of Delphic celibate priestesses, and related to her prophetic role.[273] Josephus appears to

---

[268] So Mayer-Schärtel, *Frauenbild*, 136.

[269] On the conjecture based on the reference in Strabo to a tribe of the Dacians called Ktistae who lived without wives, see Feldman, *Josephus IX*, 20. The MSS read "from the so-called majority of the Dacians" (Δακῶν τοῖς πλείτοις λεγομένοις). See also the discussion in Beall, *Josephus' Description of the Essenes*, 121-22.

[270] On this see Randal A. Argall, "A Hellenistic Jewish Source on the Essenes in Philo, Every Good Man is Free 75-91, and Josephus, Antiquities 18.18-22," in *For a Later Generation: The Transformation of Tradition in Israel, Early Judaism, and Early Christianity* (ed. Randal A. Argall, Beverly A. Bow, Rodney Alan Werline; Harrisburg: Trinity, 2000) 13-24; and earlier: Bergmeier, *Essener-Bericht des Flavius Josephus*, but also Roland Bergmeier, "Die drei jüdischen Schulrichtungen nach Josephus und Hippolyt von Rom: zu den Paralleltexten Josephus, *B.J.* 2,119-166 und Hippolyt, *Haer.* IX 18,2-29,4," *JSJ* 34 (2003) 443-70.

[271] Feldman, *Interpretation*, 190.

[272] So Taylor, "Philo of Alexandria on the Essenes," 23.

[273] So Brown, *No Longer Be Silent*, 73 in allusion to Sarah Pomeroy, *Goddesses, Whores, Wives, and Slaves* (New York: Schocken, 1975) 49.

associate the prophetic role (*A.J.* 4.330) with his depiction of Moses and his "command of his passions (τῶν παθῶν αὐτοκράτωρ), which was such that he seemed to have no place for them at all in his soul, and only knew their names through seeing them in others rather than in himself" (*A.J.* 4.329; cf. Philo: "For on his belly he bestowed no more than the necessary tributes which nature has appointed, and as for the pleasures that have their seat below [τῶν τε ὑπογαστρίων ἡδονῶν], save for the lawful begetting of children, they passed altogether even out of his memory" *Mos.* 1.28). Josephus' extraordinary statement might indicate that, contrary to much that we have seen elsewhere, he is here espousing total extirpation of the passions and if not marriage along with them, at least passionless sex. More likely, as "command of his passions (τῶν παθῶν αὐτοκράτωρ)" suggests, he has them, but keeps them under control and sees them ruling only in the behaviour of others, not his own. The statement need not imply an assumption that Moses was celibate in his prophetic role, let alone as a model for all.

2.4   Reviewing Josephus on Sexuality

Having reviewed his more systematic statements we can now turn to the scattering of brief relevant allusions throughout his works, which partly illustrate or repeat these claims, but also supplement them. What follows is therefore a synthesis and summary which takes into account both the preceding two sections on narrative and law and also the many minor and incidental details which help complete the picture of attitudes towards sexuality in Josephus' works.

2.4.1   Prisoners, Slaves, and Sexual Abuse

A regular feature of Josephus' accounts is mention of women and children. Sometimes this is positive, as when he reports their presence with the men at Sinai (*A.J.* 3.78; similarly 4.209, 309), or at festivals (*A.J.* 8.123; 11.109), or in Onias' temple (*A.J.* 13.67), or, as permitted by the Senate, in gatherings in community (*A.J.* 14.260). By contrast, he can report their massacre without remainder (*A.J.* 6.133; 14.480//*B.J.* 1.351; 2.253; 7.368; *Vit.* 25); the threat of massacre (*A.J.* 7.291; *B.J.* 3.261); cannibalisation: *B.J.* 6.202-212; *A.J.* 13.345 (cf. 2 Kgs 6:25-29; Deut 28:52-57;[274] and massacre leaving only the unmarried women (*A.J.* 4.162; 5.65). Gruesome scenes of slaughter regularly meet us, such as the killing of the

---

[274] On this see Burton L. Visotzky, "Most Tender and Fairest of Women: A Study in the Transmission of Aggada," *HTR* 76 (1983) 403-18.

wives and children of the 800 crucified Pharisees before their eyes (*A.J.* 13.380), and not least in the capture of Jerusalem by Herod and then by Titus and the bizarre suicides at the caves in *A.J.* 14.429-430 and in the account of Masada (*B.J.* 7.389-398).

At Masada Eleazar partly justifies the suicide pact by declaring that it would be a way of avoiding having the women taken as captives (*B.J.* 7.334). The issue, perhaps even worse than the rape inflicted in the contexts of wholesale slaughter, was the plight of women kept alive and, we may presume, repeatedly sexually abused. Such abuse is to be assumed at some level in most of the many accounts which Josephus gives of women taken captive (*A.J.* 5.48, 164; 9.247; 10.172, 175; 12.251, 329; 13.363; 20.123, 195; cf. also *Vit.* 99, 419; *B.J.* 3.304). They are taken off, sometimes with the children, to be slaves. The assumption of abuse plays itself out in the allegation by the Pharisees against both John Hyrcanus and Alexander Janneus of illegitimacy because they are offspring of a women who had been a captive (*A.J.* 13.289-292, 294; 13.373). It is the reason why Josephus specifies that priests must not marry former war captives (*A.J.* 3.276). It also lies behind Herod's desperate and ultimately successful attempt to block Antigonus from fulfilling his promise to deliver not only 10,000 talents but 500 Jewish women to the Parthians (*A.J.* 14.331, 353-365, 379; *B.J.* 1.257), whereas, when he captured 500 men with their wives and families, he released them (*A.J.* 14.410). Josephus' account of the fall of the first temple has Isaiah warn that refusing surrender would result not only in women being taken captive but also in male offspring being castrated to become eunuchs (*A.J.* 10.33), and has Jeremiah advise that surrender would ensure women and children would not be taken captive (*A.J.* 10.128).

Josephus also recounts the capture of individual women: David's wives whom he then liberates (*A.J.* 6.357, 364-365); Darius' mother, wife and children (*A.J.* 11.316); Simon's wife and two sons by his son-in-law, Ptolemy, producing confrontation of the latter by the third son, John Hyrcanus, but in vain because Ptolemy killed them (*A.J.* 13.228, 230-235); Aristobulus, his mother, wife and children deported to Rome (*A.J.* 14.79, 90; *B.J.* 1.158); and the Zealot's capture of Simon's wife and her subsequent release (*B.J.* 4.538-544). In the aftermath of Pompey's conquest Ptolemy of Chalcis sent for the widow and children of the defeated Aristobulus, and his son, Philippion, fell in love with her daughter, Alexandra, whom he then married, only later to be killed by his own father who took her for himself (*A.J.* 14.126; *B.J.* 1.186). In such high profile political abductions sexual abuse probably did not play a role, but for the common people war brought the threat of sexual abuse of women both in the heat of conquest and through their enslavement (as it still can in today's world).

Sometimes people changed hands not through conquest, but by being given as gifts, equally exploitative. Thus Josephus reports that Hyrcanus bought 100 boys and 100 virgins and gave them as a gift to the Egyptian king and Cleopatra (*A.J.*

12.209, 218), presumably as slaves, who would then be vulnerable to sexual abuse. He also reports Herod's gift to Archelaus of Cappadocia of eunuchs and the concubine Pannychis, clearly for sexual exploitation (*B.J.* 1.511).

Eunuchs were a special category of slaves, who usually served royal courts (e.g. *A.J.* 8.403) and might rise to positions of considerable influence (*A.J.* 9.122; 10.149; 11.200). Josephus shows us that we should not assume they were unengaged sexually, even if by castration they lost (some of) their virility (the threat to exiled boys in *A.J.* 10.33). This is particularly apparent in his note that Herod was inappropriately fond of his eunuchs (*A.J.* 16.229) and outraged when his son Alexander paid them for sex (*A.J.* 16.229-234; *B.J.* 1.488-492), a partially parallel humiliation to Abner's sex with Saul's concubines (*A.J.* 7.23), and Absalom's with David's (*A.J.* 7.213-214). In explaining the banning of eunuchs Josephus associates them with men who have deliberately feminised themselves (*A.J.* 4.290-291).

By regularly mentioning women (and children) in the contexts of war and struggle Josephus shows himself aware of these dangers, including in his own personal involvement, as in helping ward off the threat to women and children in Jopatta (*B.J.* 3.112) and Gama (*Vit.* 58), in contrast to the abuse he alleged was perpetrated by others (*A.J.* 17.309), and in reporting approaches by whole communities with their women and children (*Vit.* 166, 210), even though he can also deem them nuisance value in a siege and so lock them in their homes (*B.J.* 3.263). In his exposition of Law he addresses the issue directly, declaring that it forbids "outrage to prisoners of war, especially women" (*Ap.* 2.212). This single statement floats in a sea of detail depicting unimaginable suffering through sexual abuse, especially of women, directly or indirectly implied.

As noted above, Josephus cites the law about treatment of such captives of war taken by Jews, who are accordingly captive to sexual abuse, but protected to the extent that men must respect their wishes and wait a month before using them for sex and then if dissatisfied must free them and not hold them as slaves (*A.J.* 4.257-259; Deut 21:10-14). Josephus reports that about 32,000 women captives were taken from the Midianites (*A.J.* 4.163) and in the story of Anilaeus reports his use of the context of battle, somewhat like David and Bathsheba, to capture the Parthian commander's wife after killing him, which met with disapproval, not least because she brought her idols with her (*A.J.* 18.342-343). The provision to make wives of foreign captives was potentially problematic, as we shall see, for Josephus' strong emphasis on forbidding intermarriage with foreigners, to which we return below, though it assumes such women were fully assimilated to the religion of their husbands. Related to this was the prohibition of selling or sending Jews to be slaves to foreigners, a provision which Herod transgressed (*A.J.* 16.2).

Captivity and slavery were closely connected, since slavery was the fate of most prisoners of war. Josephus assumes slavery as part of life and cites the biblical provision about married slaves staying together with their wives who have borne them children (*A.J.* 4.273; cf. Exod 21:2-6; Deut 15:12). Slavery laid one open to sexual exploitation. In this regard Josephus may well be very strict if his statement that husbands are to engage in sexual intercourse only with their wives (*Ap.* 2.201) also places household slaves among the forbidden partners, though concubines were an obvious exception.[275] This is, however, unlikely (cf. *A.J.* 16.194; 18.40). He is quite clear, however, in disapproving marriage to slaves by freemen, citing the issue of "decorum and the proprieties of rank" (*A.J.* 4.244).[276] Rank plays a major role in his value system, including in relation to sexual behaviour. Pheroras' falling in love with his slave and marrying her (*A.J.* 16.194, 197-198), whose mother was also a slave, appals Josephus as it did Herod, and the Parthian king's falling in love with the Italian slave, Thumusa, whom he elevated to concubine and then to wife, is equally repugnant (*A.J.* 18.40-44). Josephus is careful to portray Zilpah and Bilhah not as slaves, but as concubines (*A.J.* 1.308). He differentiates legitimate from illegitimate children, i.e. those born of a concubine (*A.J.* 1.153), probably reflecting the concerns of Roman law. He applied rank also in his evaluation of Herod and Mariamme, depicting her superior nobility, so probably having some sympathy with Glaphyra and others who looked down on him (*B.J.* 1.476) and perhaps implying that that Herod's obsessive love for Mariamme, inferior for superior, pathetically reflected his lower status. Notions of hierarchy prompt his addition to the story of Dinah that Jacob was not in a position to refuse because Hamor was his superior (*A.J.* 1.338). Josephus emphasises his own personal claims to rank through noble ancestry (*Vit.* 4) and the similar worthiness of his third wife (*Vit.* 426-427). This stands in contrast to his having been commanded by Vespasian to marry a captive woman from Caesarea,[277] who was a virgin. This was not what one would normally expect among captive women and so is emphasised, making her a valid exception to his understanding of the law about whom a priest may marry (*A.J.* 3.276).[278] She left him when he obtained his release (*Vit.* 414-415).[279]

---

[275] Mayer-Schärtel, *Frauenbild*, 172.

[276] Mayer-Schärtel, *Frauenbild*, notes that Augustan law forbad senatorial ranks marrying freedwomen (173).

[277] Mason, *Life*, notes Josephus' omission of her name, his practice with all his female family members, and that we hear nothing about his being previously married which he considers likely given his being 30 (164), but the latter argument overlooks that this was commonly the age of first marriage.

[278] So Mason, *Life*, 164.

[279] Mason, *Life*, notes that the passive ἀπηλλάγη may suggest "that she was released from imprisonment and *thus* from Josephus" to whom Vespasian had assigned her by direction (165).

2.4.2 Marriages

Marriage features large in Josephus' accounts. Many are political to shore up alliances or achieve political ambitions.[280] Thus Adonijah wants Abishag (*A.J.* 8.5-6); Solomon marries Pharaoh's daughter (*A.J.* 8.21), to whom Pharaoh gives Gazara (*A.J.* 8.151); Joash refuses his daughter to Amaziah, a thistle wanting to marry a cyprus's daughter (*A.J.* 9.197); and Antiochus gives his daughter, a Cleopatra, to Ptolemy (*A.J.* 12.154). In an extreme instance Ptolemy Philometor grants Alexander Balas his daughter in marriage (*A.J.* 13.80), then dissolves the marriage and gives her to his rival Demetrius, who transgresses the loyalty which the match was to ensure (*A.J.* 13.110, 116, 120), and she, in turn, offers herself to Tryphon (*A.J.* 13.222). Herod carefully arranged the marriages of his sons and, after their demise, of their children, to help heal the rift they inherited with his first son, Antipater (*A.J.* 17.15; *B.J.* 1.556-558), but then revised the proposals when Antipater pointed out the political imbalance which would then threaten him (*A.J.* 17.18; *B.J.* 1.561-565). He also arranged the marriages of his siblings, Pheroras (or tried to), and Salome, with empress Julia's help (*A.J.* 17.8-10). Perhaps the most significant alliance is that between Herod and Mariamme which connected him to the Hasmonean dynasty, but this is an instance where the political and personal overlapped, or at least came to do so. The same may be true of Moses and the Ethiopian, at least from her side, and David and Michal, daughter of Saul, though the personal was more significant there (*A.J.* 6.196-210). Marriage was a way for a man to get ahead, but any initiative in this direction by women, Josephus frowned upon.[281] We shall return below to Herod's love for Mariamme and how Josephus might have understood it. His dismissal of his first wife (ἀποπεμψάμενος *B.J.* 1.432), Doris, "a plebeian woman" (γυναῖκα δημότιν *A.J.* 14.300; cf. "a Jewess of some standing" γυναῖκα τῶν ἐπιχωριῶν οὐκ ἄσημον *B.J.* 1.241), was manifestly political as he raised his status by marriage to Mariamme, as was her recall when he faced danger from the latter's sons (*A.J.* 16.85). His marriage to the second Mariamme, son of Simon, appears to have been, rather than political, a judicious means of fulfilling his desire to respond to her sexual attractiveness, which Josephus portrays negatively (*A.J.* 15.319-22). We return to Josephus' assessment of such responses below.

Assumed in such alliances as with all marriage is a dowry (*A.J.* 12.154), which must then be repaid when the marriage is dissolved, and in high flown cases can entail transfer of cities and territory.[282] Thus, Josephus tells us, Herod sent the widow of his son by Mariamme back to her father with her dowry to avoid dispute

---

[280] On this see Mayer-Schärtel, *Frauenbild*, 228-300.

[281] Mayer-Schärtel, *Frauenbild*, 302.

[282] On this see Mayer-Schärtel, *Frauenbild*, 83.

(*A.J.* 17.11). Throughout his accounts Josephus reflects the assumptions which governed marriage, namely that daughters were under the guardianship of the father, or then their male next of kin, and that marriage entailed negotiation between the would-be husband and the guardian (e.g. with Laban for both Isaac and Jacob *A.J.* 1.248, 299), but usually with some consultation with the daughter. It would include a bride price (τὰ ἕδνα), as reflected in Jacob's working for Rachel (*A.J.* 1.302), and David's price for Michal (*A.J.* 6.198, 200).[283] We noted above that Josephus changes the bride price to be paid for a seduced virgin to a punishment (*A.J.* 4.253). In the high profile cases we see consultation; for instance, in Herod's consultation with his sister Salome, over whom he assumed guardianship, about whether she was willing to marry Syllaeus (*A.J.* 16.225-226). As head of the family and as king he wielded such authority among his various offspring, including promising minors in future marriage, presumably with no consultation (*A.J.* 16.11, 97, 131; 17.8-10).[284] Other authorities wielded similar power. Thus, for example, Joash married the two women given him by the high priest (*A.J.* 9.158); Vespasian arranged a wife for Josephus (*Vit.* 414-415)[285] and Caesar arranged marriage for Herod's daughter on his death (*B.J.* 2.99).

Josephus regularly notes the numbers of wives and concubines which kings or rulers had (e.g. Gideon *A.J.* 5.233; David *A.J.* 7.21, 70; Jeroboam *A.J.* 8.249-250, 285), usually without comment (cf. also Joseph Tobias who had two wives; *A.J.* 12.186). In Solomon's case there is a probable implication of disapproval at the excess, beside the clear disapproval of foreign wives (*A.J.* 8.193). With regard to Herod's nine wives (*A.J.* 17.19-23) he explains: "for it is an ancestral custom of ours to have several wives at the same time" (*A.J.* 17.14). In *Jewish War* he has a similar comment, followed by the observation that Herod very much liked the custom (*B.J.* 1.477). Despite this, Josephus appears comfortable with the idea of polygyny notwithstanding the accounts he gives of its potentially chaotic outcomes when rivalry among wives ensues, attested, though more mildly, as early as Sarah and Hagar, Rachel and Leah, Hannah and Peninnah, but especially in the complex intrigues of Herod's wives and their offspring. He cites the law about the rights of the firstborn in polygynous marriages (*A.J.* 4.249-250; Deut 21:15-17), but at no point applies this to the case of Herod's firstborn, Antipater.

---

[283] On this see Mayer-Schärtel, *Frauenbild*, 218.

[284] See further Mayer-Schärtel, *Frauenbild*, 202-203.

[285] Stephen C. Barton, "The Relativisation of Family Ties in the Jewish and Graeco-Roman Traditions," in *Constructing Early Christian Families: Family as Social Reality and Metaphor* (ed. Halvor Moxnes; London: Routledge, 1997) 81-100, notes that Josephus will have been around 30 in 67 C.E. and the late start would reflect his having delayed marriage because of his education (89), but evidence suggests rather that 30 was a common age for men to marry. On this see Satlow, *Jewish Marriage*, 106-109, 132.

2.4.3 Intermarriage

Josephus strongly disapproves of marriage to foreigners.[286] This first surfaces in his history in the case of Esau, having omitted it in relation to Isaac except perhaps the hint that in marrying Rebecca he is honouring his own kin (1.253). It also plays no role in his account of the abduction of Sarah by Pharaoh and then Abimelech. He notes that Isaac would not have approved of Esau's marriages, since he had "no desire to form ties of affinity with the indigenous population" (*A.J.* 1.265). Josephus reports his adding a more acceptable wife, but even in the account of sending Jacob to Laban he omits the prohibition of marrying a Canaanite, probably because he has transformed both accounts of seeking wives, Isaac's and Jacob's, into missions related to specific women. The first specific reference to the prohibition comes in relation to Dinah and Shechem, where Jacob is described as considering it "unlawful to marry his daughter to a foreigner" (*A.J.* 1.338). Josephus does not make it an issue in the attempted seduction of Joseph, nor is it addressed in the accounts of Moses' marriages first to an Ethiopian and then a Midianite, despite Aaron and Miriam's criticism in Num 12:1.

By contrast, it features strongly in his legendary account of Balaam's strategy which has the Midianites' daughters seducing Israel's young men and leading them to idolatry, resulting then in the slaughter of Zimri and his foreign wife and to the slaughter of 14,000 more (*A.J.* 4.129-155).[287] As suggested above, the arguments and counter arguments could well reflect the way Josephus saw the issues being argued in his day. Samson's story reinforces the theme, again linking foreign marriage to the dangers of idolatry, though his first had been divinely sanctioned (*A.J.* 5.286). While he passes over Solomon's marriage to Pharaoh's daughter without comment, his summary assessment of Solomon strongly condemns his having taken many foreign wives, again in part because they led him to idolatry (*A.J.* 8.192-193). Josephus reports the expulsion of priests unable to prove their wives were of Israel, adding that there were 525 of them (*A.J.* 11.71), gives great emphasis to Ezra's ruling about foreign wives both of priests and people (*A.J.* 11.140), and returns to the theme in the account of Manasseh and the many priests who left because of intermarriage with Samaritans (*A.J.* 11.302-307). Here, too, Josephus' glosses suggest contemporary concern, such as when he notes Ezra's fear he may not be given a hearing, and that the ruling "remained fixed for the future" (*A.J.* 11.153). In these contexts the focus is the illicit marriages rather than their potential idolatrous impact, although Josephus would understand the setting up of the Samaritan temple as such. The tale of the Tobiad Joseph's desire to have intercourse with a foreign dancing girl (*A.J.* 12.187) reflects the

---

[286] On this see Feldman, *Interpretation*, 136-39.
[287] Feldman, *Interpretation*, 137.

assumption that foreign liaisons were forbidden, as does the reaction to Anilaeus' taking a Gentile wife (*A.J.* 18.345). It is interesting that in *Against Apion*, having emphasised at the beginning the careful control through genealogies of priests' marriages, Josephus cites the forbidding of intermarriage as a practice also affirmed by others (*Ap.* 1.239, 261, 278) not least by Plato (*Ap.* 2.257-258). The allegation of ἀμιξία by Antiochus VII's advisers may well include allusion to the prohibition of intermarriage, though it is not made explicit (*A.J.* 13.245).

Josephus does not, however, include prohibition of intermarriage within his three main outlines of Jewish law, unless it is implied in his statement that the Law allows no stranger into intimacies of family life (*Ap.* 2.210) or in the reference to marrying (κατὰ συγγένειαν τὴν ἐπιτήδειον) (*Ap.* 2.200). There is some tension which he does not address or attempt to ameliorate in the fact that the stories of Ruth and Esther, to both of which he gives considerable attention, entail intermarriage with foreigners, the latter under duress, but, unlike in the Old Greek text (B), not a significant element in Josephus' account. Indeed his version of Ruth's story has both Jewish parents successively soliciting such intermarriage. He also makes no evaluative comment in relation to other such marriages, including that of Alexander to Glaphyra of Cappadocia (*A.J.* 16.11, 97), and the projected marriage of Salome to Syllaeus, though there the marriage failed to take place because he resisted the requirement of circumcision (*A.J.* 16.225-226). Similarly Antiochus, later, refused in relation to Drusilla, Agrippa's daughter, to be circumcised (*A.J.* 20.139). This was in contrast to "Azizus king of Emesa, who had consented to be circumcised" to marry her (*A.J.* 20.139), though she went off with Felix (*A.J.* 20.141-44), and to Herod of Chalcis' niece and widow, Berenice, who induced Polemo, king of Cilicia to be circumcised and married him to counter an allegation that she had slept with her brother (*A.J.* 20.145). In noting that the marriage did not last Josephus speaks of his being relieved of "adherence to the Jewish way of life" (*A.J.* 20.146), which was obviously to be presupposed in the fact that he undertook circumcision.

The underlying assumption here, and perhaps in the story of Ruth, is that marriage to those who effectively became what are later called proselytes was acceptable. Probably Josephus would have seen captive (and therefore usually foreign) wives in this light.[288] Ironically, therefore, the outcome of the encounter with the Midianite seduction is that Israel takes captive "unmarried women, numbering about 32,000", many of whom, one may assume, became captive wives (*A.J.* 4.163). He notes that Drusilla's marriage to Felix transgressed "ancestral laws", that is the prohibition of intermarriage, and that their son and his wife perished in the eruption of Vesuvius, perhaps as judgement (*A.J.* 20.143-144). The appeal to "ancestral laws" here and elsewhere (Cf. *A.J.* 5.306; 8.190-191; 17.14;

---

[288] Mayer-Schärtel, *Frauenbild*, notes the issue of captive wives as foreigners (133).

18.136) appears to be part of Josephus' attempt to put the prohibition of intermarriage in a positive light as an instance of honouring what Romans honoured, namely the honoured laws of the ancestors.[289]

Sensitivity to the potential offensiveness of forbidding intermarriage to non-Jews may well account for those occasions where Josephus omits reference to it or tones it down. Feldman notes omission of reference to Esau's marrying Hittite women (*A.J.* 1.266; cf. Gen 26:35), the toning down of Joshua's command not to mix with Canaanites (*A.J.* 5.98; cf. Josh 23:12-13), the modification of Samson's parents' objections and his depiction as failing because of human nature (*A.J.* 5.317), the suppression of all but one reference to Ruth as a Moabitess, and the omission of reference to Moabites among Solomon's wives (*A.J.* 8.191 cf. 1 Kgs 11:1) and from the list of forbidden marriages (*A.J.* 3.274-275; 4.244-245; cf. Deut 23:4).[290] As Mayer-Schärtel notes, he also make no comment on Herod's marriage to the Samaritan, Malthace, from whom were born Archelaus and Antipas (*B.J.* 1.562; *A.J.* 17.20).[291] Despite this and Josephus' emphasis, as with Solomon, more on the sin of giving way to passion than on foreignness and idolatry (*A.J.* 8.190-191), Josephus does not compromise on the prohibition, not even in his retelling of Ezra, as we have seen. He depicts it indeed as the reason for the exile (*A.J.* 11.306-307)[292] At best he seeks to dress it up for his Gentile hearers as not outrageous, but comparable to the initiative of Pericles in Athens and the concerns of Plato, and consistent with a worthy commitment to ancestral law and the constitution of the nation, such as, above all, Roman Stoics would know to value.[293]

Often related to the issue of intermarriage but also of broader significance was circumcision, which, as noted, proved a stumbling black for would-be suitors, especially of Herodian Jewish women, and which he explains as designed to keep Abraham's posterity "from mixing with others" (*A.J.* 1.192). Most offensive would have been its use in treachery and aggression, such as in the stories of Dinah and David and Michal, and of that Josephus deletes every trace, also deleting in relation to Samson's parents' objection to his first marriage (*A.J.* 5.268; cf. Judg 14:3).

---

[289] On this see Bernd Schröder, *Die väterlichen Gesetze: Flavius Josephus als Vermittler von Halachah an Griechen und Römer* (TSAJ 53; Tübingen: Mohr Siebeck, 1996) 130. He notes that the concept has featured in the works of Dionysus of Halicarnassus and Thucydides and suggests that this probably inspired its use in Josephus (261) as a term used to evoke understanding and sympathy (264).

[290] Feldman, *Interpretation*, 138. See also p. 192, where he wrirtes: "As we see in his handling of the intermarriages of Esau, Joseph, Moses, Samson and Solomon, among others, Josephus was in a quandary".

[291] Mayer-Schärtel, *Frauenbild*, 134.

[292] Mayer-Schärtel, *Frauenbild*, 134.

[293] Feldman, *Interpretation*, 139.

2.4.4 Incest

Josephus does at times comment on incestuous sexual relations and marriages. As we have seen, he cites incest with one's mother, as "condemned by the law as grossest of sins" and adds stepmother, aunt, sister, and daughter-in-law (*A.J.* 3.274). Turning Sarah into Abraham's niece not his sister (*A.J.* 1.151) probably reflects such concerns. He omits Reuben's incest and rape with Bilhah and also Judah's incest with Tamar, hardly a commendable past for Jewish royalty, and shows no indication of being aware that Jacob's marriage to two sisters and David's son, Amnon's desire to marry his sister, Tamar, breached laws of incest. Ptolemy of Chalcis' (killing and) taking his son's wife was clearly incest (*A.J.* 14.126; *B.J.* 1.186), though Josephus leaves it stand with no comment. Similarly he reports without comment on Ptolemy of Egypt and his wife and sister Cleopatra (*A.J.* 13.69) and Monobazus sleeping with his sister Helena (*A.J.* 20.18). Mention of Gaius having sex with his sister carried strong implications of condemnation (*A.J.* 19.245) and similar disapproval would be expected if the allegations that Herod wanted to sleep with his daughter-in-law (*A.J.* 16.200-219; cf. also 17.309) that Herod of Chalcis' widow, Bernice, slept with her brother (*A.J.* 20.145-147) and that Anilaeus had intercourse with his mother were true (*A.J.* 18.43). He notes that Archelaus transgressed the law by marrying his brother (his stepbrother), Alexander's wife (*A.J.* 17.341). The transgression also comes to expression in a dream he attributes to Glaphyra who is confronted by her first husband, Alexander, both about her remarrying, and then about her offence against the law by marrying his brother. He would take her back to himself, and, accordingly, shortly after she died (*A.J.* 17.349-353; *B.J.* 2.114-116).[294] However he makes nothing of Antipas doing the same, the charge levelled, according to Mark, by John the Baptist. Among the perversions he attributes to the Greeks is that their gods practise the marriage of brother and sister (*Ap.* 2.275; cf. also 2.240). On the other hand marriages to nieces occur frequently in the account (Sarah *A.J.* 1.151; Hyrcanus marries a niece *A.J.* 12.186-187) and Josephus shows no signs of sensing any disapproval in contrast to marriage to nephews.

His brief description of Lot's daughters' initiative to sleep with their father passes without moral comment, except perhaps to excuse what would have been seen as outrageous, on the basis of their mistaken belief (*A.J.* 1.205; similarly Philo *QG* 4.56, 58). Josephus offers no moral evaluation.

---

[294] In *Jewish War*, however, Josephus makes no mention of incest law, so that the focus is solely on Alexander's jealousy. On this see Mason, *Jewish War 2*, 78.

2.4.5 Adultery

Adultery features prominently in Josephus' accounts, both in his exposition of laws, where he cites its prohibition in the Decalogue (*A.J.* 3.92), grounds that prohibition in concern for the interests of both state and family that children be legitimate (*A.J.* 3.274), elaborates it to include that a young man should not seek as his wife a woman already married (*A.J.* 4.244), notes the death penalty (*A.J.* 3.274-275; *Ap.* 2.215), reports the provisions for dealing with accusations of adultery (*A.J.* 3.270-273; Num 5:11-31), and declares that a man should engage in intercourse only with his spouse (*Ap.* 2.201). Josephus can claim condemnation of adultery, at least with fines, in most legislation (*Ap.* 2.276).

Suspicions of adultery fuelled Herod's jealousy on both occasions where those who were set to guard Mariamme, Joseph and then, Soemus, apparently with the best of intentions, reveal his plan that she be executed if he fell into trouble (*A.J.* 15.65, 229). According to *Jewish War* Salome's first husband was executed for adultery and Herod then executed both Joseph and Mariamme when he suspected them (*B.J.* 1.443), though this contradicts what he reports in *Antiquities*. We should read neither as indicating that the death penalty for adultery was generally applied, but rather as reflecting royal prerogative to execute. Syllaeus, who would have been Salome's third husband, faced allegations later of adultery with women both in Arabia and Rome (*A.J.* 16.340). Herod also faced allegations from opponents that he committed adultery (*A.J.* 16.200-219), some of which Josephus declared baseless (*B.J.* 1.438-439), as he does of Nicolas of Damascus' allegations against Mariamme (*A.J.* 16.118-185) and also the allegation from Herod's mother and sister that she initiated sending a portrait of herself to Antony (*B.J.* 1.439), though Josephus does admit that, thinking Herod had met his end, she was wanting to seek union with Antony, presumably including sexual intercourse (*A.J.* 15.73). His final assessment depicts her as having remained faithful to him (*A.J.* 15.219). Josephus also recounts the bizarre story of adultery by Mundus with Paulina through connivance with the priests of Isis (*A.J.* 18.65-80).

The latter constituted adultery by deceit. Josephus insists that sex by deceit or forceful abduction, but also just for the dowry, is forbidden (*Ap.* 2.200). He makes very clear that after Ruth had spent the night in Boaz's bed, "nothing had passed" (*A.J.* 5.330) and also he omitted the potentially ambiguous detail that she uncovered his feet (cf. Ruth 3:7). As noted above, he cites the biblical provision about rape of an unbetrothed virgin, with the modification that the fine be paid only if the father refuses marriage, of a betrothed woman without consent as requiring the man's execution, and with consent as requiring execution of both (*A.J.* 4.251-253). Josephus omits both Reuben's rape and incest with Bilhah and Samson's allegation that the Philistine men had slept with his bride, but brings the account of the rape of the Levite's concubine, now as his wife, without reference to the original intention of male rape (*A.J.* 5.136-155), and Amnon's rape of Tamar (*A.J.* 7.162-180). For the condemnation of adultery he could expect wide support. He reinforces it by reference to the depraved behaviour of Persians who, he alleges, engage in adultery with the neighbours' wives (*Ap.* 2.270) and of the gods of the Greeks (*Ap.* 2.242-247), against whom he is probably citing the fine for adultery (*Ap.* 2.276) as similarly typical of their not taking it seriously.[295]

2.4.6 Female Virginity

Josephus reflects his world's valuing of virginity and the necessary protection of daughters. Beside his citing the biblical provisions protecting and prohibiting virgins from illicit sex, Josephus notes the regulation that the high priest must marry only a virgin from his own tribe (*A.J.* 3.277; as Lev 21:13-14). He notes the gathering of virgins for Ahasuerus, which catches up Esther, but without negative comment (*A.J.* 11.196) and that Abishag remained a virgin (*A.J.* 8.5), but omits the lamentation of Jephthah's daughter that she would die a virgin not having known a man and the annual lamentation in her honour (cf. Judg 11:37-40). We noted above that they were sometimes spared slaughter to be taken off often into forced marriages, effectively sanctioned rape, committed both by opponents and allowed within minimal limits by biblical law. He assures us: "I preserved every woman's honour (γυναῖκα μὲν πᾶσαν ἀνυβρίστον ἐφύλαξα)" (*Vit.* 80), confirmed by the Galileans in his support: "They all swore that the honour of their womenfolk had been preserved (πάντες δ' ὤμνυον ἀνυβρίστους μὲν ἔχειν τας γυναῖκας)" (*Vit.* 259). As Mason notes, "Evidently Josephus intends this as a telling criterion" since the usual assumption was "that any man in a position of authority, especially in a military context, would violate women at will".[296]

2.4.7 Divorce and Remarriage

Divorce features frequently in Josephus' accounts. He expounds the reference in Deut 24:1 to allow it for a wide range of reasons and explains that the certificate guarantees that the first husband will cease having sex with his former wife, thus, in effect, freeing her to engage with someone else (*A.J.* 4.253). This matches what he says that Pheroras agreed to in taking an oath "that he would no longer consort with the woman who had been put away" (*A.J.* 16.198). He also reports its prohibition of a return, even after, as he adds, maltreatment (*A.J.* 4.253). Other

---

[295] Mayer-Schärtel, *Frauenbild*, 256.
[296] Mason, *Life*, 66.

provisions of relevance include the prohibition of priests marrying women separated from their husbands (*A.J.* 3.276), which goes beyond simply the divorced to include any such woman who presumably was likely to have engaged in illicit sex, and the permanent exclusion of divorce for a man forced to marry a raped virgin and for a man making false slander about one's wife's virginity, though he modifies this with an exception clause (*A.J.* 4.247). He reports a number of instances of divorce or intended divorce: the dissolution of marriages to foreigners and, in the case of priests, women of uncertain descent (*A.J.* 11.71, 153; cf. not required of Esau by Isaac: *A.J.* 1.266); Pheroras' agreement to divorce his slave wife, on which he renegs (*A.J.* 16.198; *B.J.* 1.572); Herod's divorce of Mariamme, daughter of Simon (*A.J.* 17.68-78); Archelaus' dissembling threat to divorce Alexander from Glaphyra (*B.J.* 1.508); the divorces of their spouses by Antipas and Herodias to enable them to marry (*A.J.* 18.109-110, 136); Mithridates' wife's threat of divorce (*A.J.* 18.361-362); and his own divorces, first of the captive wife whom Vespasian forced him to marry, which effectively ended in divorce when apparently both were released, she from a forced marriage, and then the woman from Alexandria, "being displeased at her behaviour" (μὴ ἀρεσκόμενος αὐτῆς τοῖς ἤθεσιν), which he does not elaborate (*Vit.* 426-427). If Herod actually divorced Doris, when he married Mariamme (*B.J.* 1.432), then his retrieving her (*A.J.* 16.85) constituted a breach of the law in Deut 24:1-4, as did David's regaining Michal, whom Saul had given to Palti (*A.J.* 7.25-26), but in neither instance does Josephus apply the biblical provision. Josephus also reports Salome's divorce of Costobarus with disapproval on the grounds that she "sent him a document dissolving their marriage" and that only the man could do so and so approve her marrying again (*A.J.* 15.259-260).

The latter has been assumed as evidence that in Josephus' time only the man could divorce. Brooten, however, raised the issue that Salome may have been operating on the basis of an alternative understanding which reflected an older Jewish practice according to which both women and men could initiate divorce. She argued that this was more likely than that she assumed Roman law, against which Herod would hardly have objected.[297] She notes that Josephus also objects to the divorces by Herodias and Drusilla, but points to the evidence from the Babatha archive which provides evidence of a woman issuing a letter of divorce.[298] Jackson reviews subsequent discussion concluding that Salome was probably acting on the basis of Jewish law. He points out that not till later was it Roman

---

[297] Bernadette J. Brooten, "Konnten Frauen im alten Judentum die Scheidung betreiben: Überlegungen zu Mk 10:11-12 und 1 Kor 7:10-11," *EvT* 42 (1982) 65-80, 69, 72. See also Bernadette J. Brooten, "Zur Debatte über das Scheidungsrecht der jüdischen Frau," *EvT* 43 (1983) 466-78.

[298] Brooten, "Scheidung," 70.

practice to issue a letter of divorce.²⁹⁹ While in relation to the Babatha papyrus to which Brooten refers, *P. Hever* 13,³⁰⁰ he writes that "it is generally now agreed that this is not a *get*, but rather an acknowledgement by the wife that the divorce settlement has been paid",³⁰¹ he points out that the husband is the one receiving the notification of abandoning and expulsion. He notes that the Greek papyrus P. Yadin 18 appears to assume a wife divorcing, but that the husband may have procedural initiative,³⁰² and that the Elephantine papyri attest to women initiating divorce without a written document (cf. Isa 50:1; Jer 3:8 which assume one, though Hos 2:4 does not).³⁰³ He also points to what appears to be a Jewish Christian practice attested in Justin who speaks of a woman who gave her husband a bill of divorce and was separated from him, calling it a ῥεπούδιον (*Apol.* 2.6).³⁰⁴ With regard to the desertions by Herodias, Drusilla, Berenice, and Mariamme he considers that these might be considered legitimate in Roman law, but receive Josephus' censure as reckless and contrary to what Jackson describes as palace law, which, he opines, may reflect the lack of institutionalisation of marriage and divorce in the period, where conflicting alternatives were known.³⁰⁵

Josephus' accounts provide numerous instances of remarriage after divorce and also remarriage of widows. In two instances Josephus shows a tendency to see an alternative to this norm. He reports Glaphyra's dream which includes beside the confrontation from her first husband not only of her incest in marrying his step brother but also of her remarrying (*A.J.* 17.349-353; *B.J.* 2.114-116). Then he presents Antonia, widow of Tiberius' brother Drusus, as an ideal depicting her as a "virtuous and chaste woman" who refused to marry again (*A.J.* 18.180).³⁰⁶

2.4.8 Prostitution

Josephus has relatively little to say about prostitutes. The rule that one have intercourse only with one's wife would clearly exclude them for the married (*Ap.* 2.201), if this is to be understood absolutely, but the latter is unlikely. His

---

²⁹⁹ Bernard S. Jackson, "The Divorces of the Herodian Princesses: Jewish Law, Roman Law, or Palace Law?" in *Josephus and Jewish History in Flavian Rome and Beyond* (ed. Joseph Sievers and Gaia Lembi; JSJSup 104; Leiden: Brill, 2005) 343-68, 355.

³⁰⁰ On this see Hannah M. Cotton, and Elisha Qimron, "XHev/Se ar 13 of 134 or 135 C.E.: A Wife's Renunciation of Claims," *JJS* 49 (1998) 108-18.

³⁰¹ Jackson, "Divorces of the Herodian Princesses", 348.

³⁰² Jackson, "Divorces of the Herodian Princesses", 349.

³⁰³ Jackson, "Divorces of the Herodian Princesses", 346-47.

³⁰⁴ Jackson, "Divorces of the Herodian Princesses", 350.

³⁰⁵ Jackson, "Divorces of the Herodian Princesses", 365, 367.

³⁰⁶ On the univira ideal see Mayer-Schärtel, *Frauenbild*, 231.

comment on the law relating to the proceeds of female prostitution (Deut 23:18), however, shows that he does disapprove of prostitution (*A.J.* 4.206) and, had he not read "dog" literally, we would find him similarly expressing the disapproval of male prostitution, which with all same-sex acts meets his disapproval (see the next section). He notes the law forbidding them as wives of priests (*A.J.* 3.276), but then in *A.J.* 4.245 extends that to all and transfers the penalty for a priest's daughter prostituting herself also to when she is found not to be a virgin bride (*A.J.* 4.248; cf. Lev 21:9). His designation of Rahab of Jericho not as a prostitute but as innkeeper (*A.J.* 5.8) may be to remove the offensiveness that such a woman should play a key role in Israel's history, but the expansion of the list of wives forbidden to priests to include innkeepers, though using a different word (*A.J.* 3.276), probably still implies that such a person was liable to have engaged in illicit sex with her guests.[307] Like *LAB* he merges the figure of Delilah with the prostitute whom Samson previously visited (*A.J.* 5.306; cf. *LAB* 43:5) and he repeats with greater elaboration the tale of the two prostitutes disputing before Solomon over a surviving baby (*A.J.* 8.26-34). He reports the anger of the inhabitants of Caesarea and Sebaste against Agrippa, who on his death took images of his daughters and put them up on roofs of brothels in mockery (*A.J.* 19.357, 364). Apart from that we do not hear of prostitutes, who must surely have been a feature of all the periods of history which he covered.

2.4.9 Same-Sex Intercourse

Josephus excludes same-sex relations (along with much else) when he declares that the only place for sexual intercourse is "the natural union of man and wife (woman), and that only for the procreation of children" (*Ap.* 2.199). Here the nature argument stands beside the argument from procreation and in a way that the former is best understood as reflecting both the intellectual belief and the emotional response to same-sex relations as out of order and abhorrent. In his more direct exposition of the prohibitions of Lev 20:10-12 he notes the prohibition "of the practice of sodomy in the pursuit of lawless pleasure" (*A.J.* 3.275), reflecting the common assumption that same-sex behaviour occurred in the context of pursuit of pleasure and excess, rather than as any kind of genuine expression of intimate love. We noted above that in expounding the banning of eunuchs in Deut 23:1 Josephus associates them with people who "by reason of the effeminacy of their soul that they have changed the sex of their body also. And so with all that would be deemed a monstrosity by the beholders" (*A.J.* 4.290-291). Here

---

[307] Mayer-Schärtel, *Frauenbild*, notes that prostitution was a secondary function of many taverns (105).

"effeminacy of their soul" does not indicate espousal of belief that this is natural for some, but rather identifies it as blameworthy. He also compares them with those practising infanticide. We are seeing, then, a parallel to the two arguments present in *Ap.* 2.199. Same-sex relations do not procreate and they are unnatural especially in the sense of being abhorrent to the (heterosexual) beholders. In addition effeminacy rates as shameful for a man, because it makes him less than a man.

Actual practice of same-sex relations appears most directly in his report about Antony and about Herod and the eunuchs. Antony tried to use his power to have the handsome Aristobulus, Mariamme's brother, sent to him for sexual exploitation, which Herod successfully blocked (*A.J.* 15.25, 30). Herod, he reports, was "immoderately fond" of his eunuchs "because of their beauty" (*A.J.* 16.230), whom Alexander lured with money to engage in intimate relations with him (*A.J.* 16.232; cf. also *B.J.* 1.488-492 εἰς τὰ παιδικά), something Josephus deems "disgraceful" (*A.J.* 16.229), but which apparently bothered Herod more for its subversive implications, like Absalom's with David's concubines, and Abner with Saul's. Josephus also reports that the men of Sodom wanted to engage in same-sex relations with Lot's guests, again because of their beauty (*A.J.* 1.200), but changes the account in Judges 19 from a threat of such male rape to a threat carried out of rape of the Levite's beautiful wife (not concubine) (*A.J.* 5.136-155; Judges 19 – 21), though in *Jewish War* he simply alleges their impiety without detail (*B.J.* 4.483). He depicts the Zealots as engaging in violation of women and effeminacy, cross-dressing, and copying women's passions (*B.J.* 4.561-562). This again reflects the view that same-sex acts arise from wayward and excessive sexual passion by people engaging both sexes, and that part of its shame is the effeminacy it entails, including here in cross-dressing. Josephus alleges the latter of Gaius (*A.J.* 19.30) and had cited the biblical provision, but apparently applied it in a different sense in a military context where the sexual associations seem not to be in focus (*A.J.* 4.301).

Same-sex behaviour is targeted in his allusion to the vices of the peoples of Sparta, Elis and Thebes (*Ap.* 2.273-275), speaking of "the unnatural vice so rampant among them (τῆς παρὰ φύσιν καὶ [ἄγαν] ἀνέδην πρὸς τοὺς ἄρρενας μίξεως lit. "unnatural and extremely licentious intercourse with males")"[308] and could be indicated in the disparaging reference to "Greek habits" in *Ap.* 2.269.[309] In that wider context we also find reference to the allegation that Socrates corrupted young men, though Josephus interprets this politically (*Ap.* 2.264), to the people of Elis and Thebes and even to the gods as engaging in same

---

[308] The translation is that of Barclay, *Against Apion*, 323-24.

[309] Roman law forbad what it called *perigraecari* as *stuprum*, sexual intercourse with boys and unmarried women. On this see Skinner, *Sexuality*, 199-200.

sex acts described as "unnatural (παρὰ φύσιν) (*Ap.* 2.273, 275). Josephus may imply same-sex behaviour belonged to Cain's repertoire when "he indulged in every bodily pleasure, even if it entailed outraging his companions ... and became their instructor in wicked practices" (*A.J.* 1.60-61), but it is not explicit. All Josephus' comments pertain to male-male relations. His account of Jonathan and David certainly emphasises their friendship, but without any indication that it may have been of a sexual nature, including lacking the words of David's lament (2 Sam 1:26), which some have read in that way. On female-female relations he is silent but would doubtless have condemned them equally.

2.4.10 Other Prohibitions (Bestiality, Infanticide, Abortion), Fertility Enhancement and Love Potions

Beyond citing law prohibiting bestiality (*A.J.* 3.275) he offers no instances of the practice. He also adds that proceeds from "the mating of a dog, whether hound of the chase or guardian of the flocks" must not be used to pay for sacrifices (*A.J.* 4.206), but this appears to have nothing to do with bestiality, but rather proceeds from breeding, unlike in Deut 23:16 where it represents male prostitution. Josephus similarly cites laws relating to infanticide and abortion (also as subverting the goal of procreation and so an analogy to effeminates engaging in same-sex) (*Ap.* 2.202-203), but without citing instances in his accounts, except the killing of the Hebrew children, an omission which is again surprising given its likely occurrence in the context of his accounts. Josephus retells the story of Rachel and Leah and the mandrake apples (*A.J.* 1.307), perhaps aware that they were meant to enhance fertility,[310] but without evaluative reflection.[311] At some points he notes love-potions or what were alleged to be love potions, to heighten erotic desire (*A.J.* 15.223-229; 17.62-64; cf. also 15.93), but again without evaluative reflection, except by implication on the ill intentions of those employing them. The reversal of miscarriages in the Jericho region through Elisha's miracle (*B.J.* 4.460) belongs to Josephus' idealisation of the region.

---

[310] On the pomegranates or mandrakes, see Kottek, *Medicine and Hygiene*, who notes that they were used for both narcotic anaesthetic and aphrodisiac purposes (132).

[311] On the high mortality rate of infants and of women in childbirth see Mayer-Schärtel, *Frauenbild*, 283, who also notes the stigma of childlessness, which was also a ground for divorce, and then cites the exceptional inscription, *Laudatio Turiae*, which depicts a husband's love in not using that ground to divorce his wife (284). She also observes that in Josephus' list of Herod's wives, the two without offspring come last (285).

2.4.11 Purity Provisions

His exposition of laws notes a number of issues pertaining to purity, such as seclusion from the city of women during menstruation until the seventh day as with corpse impurity (*A.J.* 3.261) (which goes beyond biblical law; cf. Lev 15:19-24),[312] and their exclusion from the Passover meal (*B.J.* 6.426) and from the women's court (*A.J.* 2.103), and impurity after childbirth (*A.J.* 3.269), and their exclusion from the temple during such impurity (*B.J.* 5.227; *Ap.* 2.103-104), and he speaks generally of purifications "after a funeral, after child-birth, after conjugal union, and many others" (*Ap.* 2.198). Regular acts of purification with water had characterised the practice of Bannus with whom Josephus spent time (*Vit.* 11). We noted that he rationalises purification after intercourse on the basis that in implanting his semen in a woman a man gives up part of his life, so that lustration then makes as much sense as it does after a funeral (*Ap.* 2.202-203; cf. also *A.J.* 3.261-262). His exposition of the prohibition of intercourse during menstruation (*A.J.* 3.275, for which he claims the penalty is death; cf. Lev 20:18) and possibly pregnancy (*B.J.* 2.161; but less probably in *Ap.* 2.202), appeals not to purity issues but to the issue of procreation without the possibility of which intercourse is disapproved as self-indulgent.

Only occasionally do purity issues surface in his histories: the requirement of abstinence from intercourse for 3 days before Sinai (*A.J.* 3.78); having Saul account for David's absence on the basis that he will have had intercourse with his wife overnight and so was unclean (*A.J.* 6.235 cf. 1 Sam 20:26); retelling Rachel's feigned menstruation to prevent Laban from recovering his idols (*A.J.* 1.323, 342); and reporting the high priest, Matthias', nocturnal emission during a dream about a woman the night before the fast of Purim, which meant that one of his brothers had to replace him (*A.J.* 17.166). On the other hand, he omits from the Bathsheba story the detail shat she was purifying herself after her period (2 Sam 11:4) and omits the story of David's men and the shewbread, where he assures the priest that his men may eat it because they had not engaged in intercourse (1 Sam 21:5). In addition Josephus mentions the use of menstrual blood and urine in dealing with sticky asphalt from the Dead Sea (*B.J.* 4.480; cf. Tac. *Hist.* 5.6) and with a poisonous root (*B.J.* 7.181), but this has no particular relation to purity or sexual issues, though it reflects some magical aura attached to them.[313]

Related to purity issues are concerns about nakedness. These do not feature large in Josephus. He minimises reference to nakedness and its significance in the Eden narrative, perhaps to avert suggestiveness, perhaps in reaction to naked

---

[312] Mayer-Schärtel, *Frauenbild*, 136.
[313] Mayer-Schärtel, *Frauenbild*, 130.

sculptures of his day. He mentions Ham's being seen naked, and David's misdemeanour in Michal's eyes of dancing naked before the ark in front of the servants (*A.J.* 7.87) and notes the offence caused by the soldier who exposed his genitals (*A.J.* 20.107-108). Mention of the Essenes' covered bathing may be in reaction to naked bathing in his day (*B.J.* 2.161), and he would have been well acquainted with naked sports (cf. *A.J.* 15.268, 270), but aside from these instances he makes nothing of it as an issue, including in relation to sexuality, and does not include it in his depictions of Jewish Law.

2.4.12 Women

Josephus has fairly set views about women. Much of the preceding discussion pertains in particular to women, from the horrors of being enslaved as the sole survivors of massacres to the particular issues of purity. He depicts women as playing major roles, frequently behind the scenes, in the struggles for power, not least, during the reign of Herod: Alexandra, Mariamme, Doris, Salome, and beyond the realm, not least, Cleopatra. In a patriarchal world where men dominated, many women exercised considerable power. Already in the history of the biblical period he notes their initiatives, such as women providing vestments for the tabernacle (*A.J.* 3.107); Rahab's hiding the spies (*A.J.* 5.8); the woman urging reconciliation between David and Absalom (*A.J.* 7.181-186); Michal challenging David over dancing naked in public before the ark in front of inferiors (*A.J.* 7.87); the women hiding the high priest's men (*A.J.* 7.225-226); the wise old woman confronting Joab (*A.J.* 7.289); the visit of the queen of Egypt and Ethiopia to explore Solomon's wisdom (*A.J.* 8.158-159); Belshazzar's (Baltasares) grandmother comforting him (*A.J.* 10.237); Esther's heroic courage (*A.J.* 11.184-296); but also in later periods, women playing key roles as informers (*A.J.* 13.424; 14.369; *B.J.* 1.262); Cypros helping her husband Agrippa cope with depression (*A.J.* 18.148-149, 160); Mithridates' wife challenging him to revenge (*A.J.* 18.361-62); the conversion and generosity of Helena of Adiabene (*A.J.* 20.17-23), to whom Jerusalem's citizens erected a monument (*B.J.* 5.147), and the influential Berenice (*B.J.* 2.310-314; *A.J.* 20.145-147; *Vit.* 119, 343, 355). He repeats the legend of the three youths which includes a sympathetic depiction of women's power, though trimming it of elements which might suggest such respect could override country and of an apparently critical allusion to Gen 2:24 in 1 Esdras 3 – 4 (*A.J.* 11.34-58). Equally he can depict unfavourable acts such as the attempted seduction by Potiphar's wife, who fails with Joseph but succeeds in deceiving her husband because his love blinded him (*A.J.* 2.41-60); the wanton Jezebel (*A.J.* 8.318); the seductive Cleopatra (*A.J.* 15.98); Herodias' spurring Antipas to his downfall (*A.J.* 18.340-353); Claudius' wife poisoning him (*A.J.* 20.148-153); and the wicked wife of Gessius Florus (*A.J.* 20.252). Indeed the ghost of Alexander declares of Glaphyra that women are not to be trusted (*A.J.* 17.352).[314]

Already in his account of the primal couple Josephus shows his hand when he faults Adam "for yielding to a woman's counsel" (*A.J.* 1.49). For, he assumes, a woman's counsel is inferior. Accordingly, in his exposition of the law he declares that woman is "in all things inferior to the man" (*Ap.* 2.201) and is to be "be submissive, not for her humiliation, but that she may be directed; for authority has been given by God to the man" (*Ap.* 2.201). While this view may trace its roots in part to God's judgement on the woman in Gen 3:16, Josephus omits it there, noting only the pains of pregnancy and childbirth. Inferiority and submission to men are not, according to Josephus punishment, as in Gen 3:16, but are grounded in the fact women were created inferior from the beginning.[315] On the other hand, Josephus does not blame women for the angels' transgression in reporting that ancient myth (*A.J.* 1.73-74). Metallurgy, in his account, including its ornaments and instruments of pleasure, came not through fallen angels, but through Lamech's sons, as in *LAB* (*A.J.* 1.64; cf. *LAB* 2:8). Rarely does he blame women for men's sexual wrongdoing or for being beautiful and sexually attractive, something he is happy to recognise and affirm,[316] but where a woman does take the initiative in sexual wrongdoing, as he alleges Egyptian women do, such as Potiphar's wife (*A.J.* 2.41-60) and Cleopatra (*A.J.* 15.97), he identifies this clearly (cf. *A.J.* 1.162 where, conversely Abraham is depicted "fearing the Egyptians' frenzy for women"). Mostly men are portrayed as the predators. He does not depict women

---

[314] As noted above, Ilan, "Josephus and Nicolaus on Women," urges caution in assessing Josephus' attitude towards women, suggesting that aside from where he uses Nicolas of Damascus as his source, who, she claims, delights in inventing intrigues around women, Josephus shows little or no interest in women. Thus she writes: "the '*chercher la femme*' syndrome found in Josephus' descriptions of the Hasmoneans and Herodians is typically Nicolean, and Josephus does not resort to it before, or after he exhausts Nicolaus as a source" (224). Testing her hypothesis by considering material after midway through *Jewish War* Book 2 and in *Life*, she concludes that "Josephus, as a historian, found women to be a topic of little interest" and "found it neither necessary to blame them for negatively affecting the course of history, nor did he see sexual misconduct lurking behind every catastrophe" (233), whereas Nicolas belonged to the Peripatetic school which favoured dressing up history (234). She claims that "all powerful women of the Hasmonean and Herodian dynasties who dominate Josephus' writings are the literary creations of Nicolaus of Damascus, who wrote drama and firmly believed that women were the root of all evil" (262). Such an hypothesis is difficult to test and in doing so one must weigh what Josephus was doing in incorporating such sources – was he oblivious to their values or espousing them? His treatment of earlier biblical material suggests the latter.

[315] On the similar view in Philo see p. 26 above.

[316] Cf. Mayer-Schärtel, *Frauenbild*, who depicts Josephus as seeing women's beauty producing a fatal reaction in men (110-111).

as incapable of controlling their sexual passions and therefore dangerous, even though he strongly affirms control and guardianship of virgin daughters, and does not use Gen 3:16 to portray women as condemned to be forever wanting to return to their men.

Women are, however, not the equal of men, so that in his assessment of Salome Alexandra, he cannot but comment that because she lacked the strength of a man and was too ingenuous she allowed the Pharisees too much room (*B.J.* 1.111) and then when he wants to praise her depicts her as "a woman who showed none of the weakness of her sex" (*A.J.* 13.430). Her son, Aristobulus, perhaps just for his ambition, disparaged her as a woman (*A.J.* 13.147). Assumptions of inferiority surface indirectly in various ways, such as in Nicolas of Damascus' comment, on Herod's behalf, that Antipater's mother spoke "in the frivolous ways of a woman" (*A.J.* 17.121), in the reference to "silly woman" in *A.J.* 19.129-130, and in a qualified sense in the humiliation of Antigonus by calling him Antigone (*A.J.* 14.481; *B.J.* 1.353), which certainly implies inferiority among other more subtle allusions. Warnings about feminisation of men also imply something shameful, not just by making men different but by making them inferior. Josephus' affirmation that even Jewish women folk attend to the Law with piety reflects their inferiority as does his comment that they may not testify in law "because of the levity and temerity of their sex" (*A.J.* 4.219; *Ap.* 2.201; cf. *A.J.* 19.33-36 where we must assume Josephus sneers at Gaius' ally, Timidius, for calling as witness the actress Quintilla). Of Mariamme he declares that she was both "at once womanly and cruel" (*A.J.* 15.219), reflecting a gendered understanding of compassion and cruelty, reflecting stereotypes of softness and hardness. Such stereotypes are reflected in the roles mentioned above in the opening paragraph: providing vestments, hiding spies, urging reconciliation, hiding the high priest's men, comforting Belshazzar, supporting the depressed,[317] as well as challenging and confronting.[318] When Josephus describes Potiphar's wife as seeing her vengeful

---

[317] Mayer-Schärtel, *Frauenbild*, notes Josephus' emphasis on motherly love as natural in depicting the horror at cannibalism (289; similarly 297).

[318] See also Mayer-Schärtel, *Frauenbild*, who traces key terms used by Josephus of women: ἀσθένεια ("weakness") *A.J.* 13.430 linked with lack of understanding: *A.J.* 3.5; μαλακία ("softness, femininity") (*B.J.* 6.211; *A.J.* 19.34), something shameful for men (*B.J.* 4.43; 5.311; 7.338) (185); ἀσέλγεια (of Jezebel: *A.J.* 8.318; alleged of Mariamme: *B.J.* 1.439; *A.J.* 16.185; Cleopatra: *B.J.* 1.568 *A.J.* 17.121; Pheroras' wife; *B.J.* 1.568; *A.J.* 17.121; deemed by Essenes to be characteristic of all women: *B.J.* 2.121; displayed by the Zealots: *B.J.* 4.562; and typical of the Greek deities (185-86); θράσος θάρσος ("boldness, precociousness"; of Salome towards Mariamme: *A.J.* 16.66; cf. also 7.147) (186-87); unfaithfulness, sometimes using ἄπιστος: of Cleopatra: *A.J.* 15.99, and seen as typical of women by the Essenes: *B.J.* 2.120-121; cf. also of Glaphyra *A.J.* 17.352 (187-188); κουφολογία ("levity") linked with γυναικεῖος – of Doris: *A.J.* 17.121; Herodias: *A.J.*

action as "wise and womanly", he probably means something like clever and manipulative.[319] His negative stereotype includes that women are contentious, a view shared with Stoics and Cynics,[320] and, as we shall see below, a primary ground why the Essenes did not want them in their company.

In Josephus' framework of values women are inferior,[321] a view well-entrenched in his society and tradition, and reflected, for instance, already in the unequal purity provisions relating to male and female children (*A.J.* 3.269; as Lev 12:20) and the different price put on redeeming a corban gift (*A.J.* 4.73; Lev 27:3, 4). They are not, however, to be despised nor to be abused, as he emphasises more than once from the context of imprisonment to the context of submission in the household where her being submissive is "not for her humiliation" (*Ap.* 2.201). Women have their place and, like Mariamme, can outshine the most illustrious and powerful of men, and he can speak highly of Poppaea and Domitia (*Vit.* 16, 429; *A.J.* 20.195).[322] On the other hand, he never compares women to men but only to other women.[323] As Bailey notes, "Women are in a category apart from men, although this does not necessarily imply a negative attitude toward females".[324] Women do not really count in the scheme of what is important, so that Josephus can declare that the Hasmonean dynasty would cease to be with the death of Aristobulos and Hyrcanus, even though Mariamme was still alive (*A.J.* 15.164).[325] Josephus clearly affirms them in the place he deems appropriate for them. To the provisions about the rebellious son (Deut 21:18) he adds their role along with fathers (still superior) in oral admonishment (*A.J.* 4.260-265); he expounds

---

18.255; and grounds for not accepting women's testimony: *A.J.* 4.219 (186, 188-89); χείρων ("inferior"); ἀσχημοσύνη ("shamelessness"); and ἀκρασία ("lack of self control") (189-90).

[319] For other negative uses of γυναικεῖος see also *A.J.* 1.49; 15.168, 219; 17.121.

[320] Feldman, *Interpretation*, 190.

[321] As Mayer-Schärtel, *Frauenbild*, notes, Josephus never questions this hierarchical inequality or its effects (68).

[322] Bailey, "Josephus' Portrayal," 156. On highborn women in the world of Josephus and his histories see Shelly Matthews, "Ladies' Aid: Gentile Noblewomen as Saviors and Benefactors in the Antiquities," *HTR* 92 (1999) 199-218. See also Schuller, "Women of the Exodus," who writes: "Undoubtedly it was Josephus' own pragmatic acknowledgement of the power of influential women (such as Poppaea and Domitia) at the Roman court rather than any feminist sentiments that influenced his portrait of Pharaoh's daughter" (188).

[323] Bailey, "Josephus' Portrayal," 156; see also Mayer-Schärtel, *Frauenbild*, 24-25, 372; Feldman, *Interpretation*, 188.

[324] Bailey, "Josephus' Portrayal," 156.

[325] Mayer-Schärtel, *Frauenbild*, 192. The denial may be politically motivated to suggest that thereafter Hasmonean ambitions which might worry the Romans ceased – which was clearly far from the case.

measures that protect them, not least from the sexual abuse of war, but also through such traditional provisions as Levirate marriage, which he explains as, in part, designed to protect women and their rights, not just the household's (*A.J.* 4.254-256; Deut 25:5-10; and on Ruth see 5.318-340), and as measures against physical attack which produces miscarriage (*A.J.* 4.278). But women in the sexual realm are to be passive not active. Their beauty evokes male response which leads through his sexual desire to take the initiative which leads to marriage.[326] Josephus views women who remain unmarried as suspicious,[327] unless they are manifestly upholding chastity in honour of their deceased husband, and those who actively pursue sexual relations, such as Potiphar's wife and Cleopatra, as grossly immoral.[328]

2.4.13 Sexual Love

Love, especially sexual love, features large in Josephus' works and so, alongside the observations above, is central for understanding his attitude toward sexuality.[329] He shows particular interest in the phenomenon, frequently enhancing the erotic and offering psychologising comment.[330] Feldman notes that Josephus "made his narrative more appealing to his Greek readers by introducing romantic motifs reminiscent of Homer in the *Odyssey*, Aeschylus' account (*Choephoroe* 613-22) of Scylla's betrayal of her father out of love for Minos (cf. Ovid, *Metamorphoses* 8.6-151), Xenophon's *Cyropedia*, and Hellenistic novels".[331] Thus he depicts Abraham's fear of "the Egyptians' frenzy for women" (*A.J.* 1.162) and, having doubly emphasised Sarah's beauty, portrays the Pharaoh as "fired with a desire to see her" (*A.J.* 1.163), who then unconvincingly denies that he wanted "to outrage her in a transport of passion" (*A.J.* 1.165). Similarly he notes that the Sodomites were responding to seeing "young men of remarkably fair appearance" and of "youthful beauty" (*A.J.* 1.200). Josephus lis not denying that were sexually attractive. In Sarah's abduction by Abimelech he speaks of the latter's being "too enamoured" of her and having "lustful intent" (*A.J.* 1.207-208). In each of these accounts he enhances the erotic in the context of danger. In depicting Jacob and Rachel, however, he does so in the context of affirmation, describing Jacob's being "overcome with love for the maid" (*A.J.* 1.288) and her beauty and adding:

---

[326] On this see Mayer-Schärtel, *Frauenbild*, 304-305.

[327] So Mayer-Schärtel, *Frauenbild*, 305.

[328] Mayer-Schärtel, *Frauenbild*, 305.

[329] On the words for such love, including στοργή, στέργω, φιλία, φιλέω, ἐπιθυμία, ἐπιθυμέω, ἔρως, ἐράομαι, πάθος, see Mayer-Schärtel, *Frauenbild*, 232-34.

[330] On this see Feldman, *Interpretation*, 185-88, 197-204.

[331] Feldman, *Interpretation*, 185.

"she, as young people are wont to do ... from filial affection burst into tears and flung her arms around Jacob" (*A.J.* 1.291). This is partly because of the family connection but also erotic. "As young people are wont to do" is typical of Josephus' additions. He puts on Jacob's lips a similar kind of comment, speaking of the "affection which wedded wives are wont to have for their husbands" (*A.J.* 1.318).

He removes reference to Shechem's tenderness towards Dinah (cf. Gen 34:3) as a positive trait which he should not be allowed to bear since it might win sympathy from Josephus' hearers (*A.J.* 1.337-341), and enriches the account of Joseph's encounter with Potiphar's wife with astute observation reflective of process (*A.J.* 2.41-60). Thus he has her claim that it might have enhanced his esteem to be solicited by his boss and has him reply about the need to govern passions and with the psychologising observation that with no prospect of fulfilment her passion would eventually dissipate. In the same vein he observes that rejection simply increased the intensity of her feeling. Josephus reveals more of his approach to these things when he has Joseph direct her back to her marriage where she could enjoy sex with her husband, something he sees as appropriate, in contrast to transient enjoyment accompanied by fear of being found out, another astute observation on the dynamics of such relations.

When he reports that the Ethiopian princess fell madly in love with Moses and that he accepted her offer of marriage, this also reflects his affirmation of such love, even though in *A.J.* 4.328-329 he emphasises that Moses was so much in control of his passions that he never saw them in himself out of control but only in others. This does not mean he did not have them.

His rewriting of the rape at Gibeah (*A.J.* 5.136-155) also reflects subtle changes in emphasis. It is no longer homoerotic nor about a concubine, but about a wife, of whom the Levite is "deeply enamoured ... and captivated by her beauty" (*A.J.* 5.136). It is this beauty, which includes sexual attractiveness, which the men of the town see and to which they respond as violent predators. Her sexual attractiveness is not in question, nor is she blamed (cf. *LAB* 47:8).[332] In the account of Samson's parents Josephus enhances the depiction of Manoah's love for his wife, going beyond the biblical account to describe him a "moreover madly enamoured of his wife and hence inordinately jealous" and so unable to cope with his wife's encounter with her account of "the comeliness and stature" of the young man who appeared to her (*A.J.* 5.276-277). This appears to be a favourite motif, and will play itself out dramatically in his account of Herod and Mariamme. Here, again, we find Josephus offering psychologising comment: "he in his jealousy was driven by these praises to distraction and to conceive the suspicion that such passion arouses" (*A.J.* 5.279). Samson's story also emphasises his falling in love

---

[332] On this see Loader, *Pseudepigrapha on Sexuality*, 289.

and in its detail about the wedding may disclose what Josephus could accept on such occasions, when he writes: "when the drinking was far gone and joviality prevailed, as is customary on such occasions" (*A.J.* 5.289), but may not.

There are similar additional touches in his story of David. That not just women, but older and younger women hail his achievements (*A.J.* 6.193), probably prepares the way for Saul's virgin daughter Michal's response, of which he writes that "so overmastering was her passion that it betrayed her and was reported to her father" (*A.J.* 6.196). Again we find Josephus' sexual "expertise" at play when he writes of David and Abishag that "at his age he was too feeble to have sexual pleasure or intercourse with her" (*A.J.* 7.343-344). When he writes of David's response to Bathsheba that "he was captivated by the beauty of the woman and .. was unable to restrain his desire", Josephus means that he could have, but did not because it was hard. In this context we again meet his sexual observations when he has David declare that having sex with their wives "was the natural thing for men to do when they return from abroad" (*A.J.* 7.133). The account of Amnon's rape of Tamar reports that he was "burning with desire and goaded by the spur of passion" (*A.J.* 7.169). On Solomon he declares that "he became madly enamoured of women and indulged in excesses of passion" (*A.J.* 8.190-191) and went astray after the gods of his wives "to gratify his wives and his passion for them" (*A.J.* 8.192) and so was "carried away by thoughtless pleasure" (*A.J.* 8.193).

In the story of Esther he again heightens the erotic describing Ahasuerus as in love with Vashti despite her disobedience and has a steward voice another piece of erotic wisdom, namely that "his affection for her would gradually be diverted to the woman living with him" (*A.J.* 11.196) if he took another wife, then in due course mentioning his falling love with Esther. Josephus reports a number of instances of falling in love with the wrong partner, including Joseph the Tobiad with the dancing girl, from which his brother rescued him with his daughter (*A.J.* 12.186-189); Antony being a captive of love and slave of his passion for Cleopatra (*A.J.* 14.324; *B.J.* 1.243); Ptolemy Chalcis falling in love with son's wife (*A.J.* 14.126); Pheroras' falling in love with his slave girl (*A.J.* 16.194); the Parthian king falling in love with his Italian slave (*A.J.* 18.40); Mundus falling in love with Paulina (*A.J.* 18.65-80); and Linaeus with the Parthian general's wife (*A.J.* 18.342). The latter's brother "excused his brother as mastered by his passion, a vice that he could not resist", which Josephus rejects, as did his contemporaries who saw it as "too great indulgence of fleshly lust" (*A.J.* 18.345). On Syllaeus and Salome's love affair Josephus notes the looks and gestures which gave them away (*A.J.* 16.222) and on Pheroras' passion for his slave wife Josephus has Herod engage in another piece of his erotic wisdom in believing that "his brother's passion had passed its peak" (*A.J.* 16.196) and then describes him playfully as "enslaved to" his slave (*A.J.* 16.198; cf. also his description of Gaius as a slave of pleasure: *A.J.* 19.201).

Pride of place belongs however to the romance and tragedy of Herod and Mariamme, for this, too, is revealing of Josephus' own attitudes or at least of the attitudes reflected in his works. Herod is a tragic figure overwhelmed by love and so losing control and perspective in a way that had him thrashing about in mad jealousy. It coheres with the love stories and erotic encounters we have reviewed that Josephus neither faults Herod's love, including his sexual love, for Mariamme, nor Mariamme's sexual attractiveness, but rather its blinding excess.

Herod's story and the stories of other lovers, licit and illicit, indicate that Josephus had no problem affirming the human sexual experience, and human sexual attractiveness, male and female, but saw its place as belonging only between man and wife and as needing to be controlled by reason. Inside and outside marriage desire for pleasure, in his view, always spelled the potential of danger and irrational or inappropriate response and more: transgression of the law. As he puts it, "our Law holds out no seductive bait of sensual pleasure" (*Ap.* 2.284). He repeatedly condemns lawless, thoughtless and excessive pleasure (*A.J.* 3.274; 8.190-195) and those who are its slaves (such as Antony, *B.J.* 1.243; *A.J.* 14.324; Antipater, *A.J.* 17.121, 235; and Gaius: *A.J.* 19.43, 155, 201). He strongly and consistently affirms procreation as the goal of sexual intercourse between man and wife (*A.J.* 4.259, 261, 290; 5.168; *Ap.* 2.199), despite omitting to take it up directly from Gen 1:28, but emphasises it not in a manner that suggests that sex should be robotic or functional without romance and pleasure – and also not with fear despite his assumption that every issue of semen drains a male's life (*Ap.* 2.203). Joseph's advice to Potiphar's wife to find enjoyment in sex with her husband (*A.J.* 2.51-52) affirms that Josephus sees in sexual intimacy a juxtaposition of pleasure and purpose which enables him, therefore, to value and reflect on romantic love and falling in love with that as the goal.[333] When he depicts Adam, therefore, as "seized with a passionate desire to beget a family" (δεινὸς εἶχεν αὐτὸν γενέσεως ἔρως) (*A.J.* 1.67), we are probably right to see the merging of both aspects. Josephus probably envisioned sexual pleasure as part of the bliss which according to *A.J.* 1.46 God intended in creation. Josephus' accounts may well stand under the influence of romantic literature of his day, but they are set within the strict framework he discerns in the law. In this, procreation is a paramount principle, which necessarily rules out all non-procreative sex, some of which he rejects for other reasons as well, and this includes, therefore, intercourse during menstruation and pregnancy. In his world where understandings

---

[333] So Ellis, *Sexual Desire*, 82.

of conception were primitive, intercourse apart from these times was naturally affirmed.[334]

2.5 Conclusion

Josephus did not set out to write about attitudes to sexuality, but his endeavours to depict the Jewish war and its background, and to give an account of his own people and himself, inevitably included matters pertaining to sexuality. This makes sense both at the level of the material before him and in view of his audience which will at least be acquainted with the titillations of romance. Beyond that, he and his hearers could not avoid being sexual beings themselves and living in communities where regulation of sexually related behaviour was a necessity. Proudly, therefore, Josephus hails his people's constitution and ancestral laws as matching and surpassing the best of his age. The extensive application of the death penalty in his depictions is more designed to impress than to report its execution. His people were not only peace loving, a fact which he asserts should not be seen as contradicted by the revolt, the work of extremists and dysfunctional people on both sides, indeed, of what in the later account he describes as a party or school; they were also people who gave proper deference to law and to the distinction between what and who was honourable and shameful, his own alleged high status not the least of his concerns that people should appreciate.

---

[334] Unlike in Philo and elsewhere we find nothing in Josephus about eschatology which would enable us to see how he saw sexual relations in the future, though he appears to assume God has a future for Israel. On this see Peter Höffken,"Bileams Ratschlag und seine Eigenart bei Josephus: Zu *Antiquitates* 4,126-130," *ETL* 83 (2007) 385-94, who sees Josephus affirming the eternity of Israel, based on Isa 54:7-8 LXX; 57:17 LXX; cf. also Ps 30 and Bar 4:29, arguing that divine providence replaces covenant theology (389-90); Per Bilde, "Josephus and Jewish Apocalypticism," in *Understanding Josephus: Seven Perspectives* (ed. Steve Mason; Sheffield: Sheffield Academic Press, 1998) 35-61, who writes: "it appears that Josephus understood the prophecies in Numbers 23-24 and Daniel (2 and 7-10) to be predictions referring to Josephus's own lifetime. Partly the catastrophe in the year 70 C.E. and partly the approaching eschatological redemption of the Jewish people" (54); and Marianus de Jonge, "Josephus und die Zukunftserwartungen seines Volkes," in *Josephus – Studien: Untersuchungen zu Josephus, dem antiken Judentum und dem Neuen Testament: Otto Michel zum 70. Geburtstag gewidmet* (ed. Otto Betz, Klaus Haacker, and Martin Hengel; Göttingen: Vandenhoeck und Ruprecht, 1974) 205-19, 211-12.

Crass sexual abuse, above all, in the theatre of war, had to be part of his account and he asserts his constitution's sensitivity to its evils in forbidding sexual maltreatment of women prisoners and ameliorates its institutionalisation of abducted foreign women into the household of desirous men. Prohibiting intermarriage with foreigners or at least with those who would not convert, male and female, he makes to sound as inoffensive as possible, while not slipping into compromise. Marriage made alliances among the elite, as Josephus well knew, but, perhaps prompted by the romantic colour of his sources and perhaps by the need for more of the same among his hearers, Josephus depicts most marriages as going far beyond the politically utilitarian.

He stoutly affirmed the equally valid function, procreation, which was for him marriage's fundamental mandate and the goal of sexual union. At the same time his works extol all those elements which contribute to the foreplay of such endeavours, including beauty and attractiveness, mainly in relation to women, sexual passion, falling in love, the standard patterns of male negotiation leading to marriage, and the desirability of continued love between man and wife. Neither sex nor marriage is passionless according to Josephus, but both within and outside marriage, uncontrolled and misdirected passion faces censure in the strongest terms as the flaw which makes the mighty, like Antony and Herod fall.

Excess has no place because of its inevitable propensity to distort good decision making. Desertion of marriages, infidelity, and the like were for Josephus not only breaches of ancestral law, but also manifestations of being ruled by one's passions instead of ruling them. It stood to reason that sexual engagement between males or in contexts which disregarded the mandate of procreation, such as prostitution, during menstruation and pregnancy, not to speak of premarital seduction or violence, had no place, since it both violated what is the natural purpose of sex in his view and exposed one to the shame of having fallen prey to uncontrolled passion. Even more shameful for men acting the female part in such liaisons was to lower one's status by taking on the behaviour of the inferior half of the human race. Throughout his works Josephus assumes such inequality of women. He can trace it to creation: God made women inferior and so Adam was a fool to follow the inferior's advice long before God intervened to put humans under judgement. In relation to sexuality this also meant that it was appropriate for men to take the initiative sexually, not women.

Within this unequal frame of reference Josephus does not fault women's sexuality and attractiveness, but rather what they do with it. He blames women for acting seductively but not in a way that absolves men of their responsibility as if they could not help themselves. Men are to blame who choose to respond to seduction and fail to follow Joseph's chaste behaviour. The preference of what appears to be the main order of Essenes, for all-male communities without women, appears to have little to do with sexuality and most to do with the perception of women as contentious and as prone to infidelity. Not making pleasure, including sexual pleasure one's life goal, which the Essenes dramatically exemplify, but which Josephus sees as a principle for all to follow, need not exclude marriage, as his mention of the marrying order and as his models in history illustrate.

Sexual pleasure, falling in love, being sexually attractive all had their place within the context of coming together in marriage for procreation. It was, therefore, no contradiction, for Josephus to give due deference to his hearers' fondness of the romantic story by embellishing the Bible's love stories accordingly. Both the biblical and the post-biblical sources provided rich opportunity to depict both the positive in this regard and the scandalously negative, from Potiphar's wife to the notorious Cleopatra, both aspects likely to appeal as entertainment mixed with moral instruction.

Josephus' world was one of powerful households, ruled mainly by male heads, subordinate but not unresourceful women, political and social pressures to affirm Roman order, including its hierarchical values of family, and the vicissitudes of imperial rule and its wrangle of regional appointees. Without noting his Jewish heritage we might see him engaged in positioning his people and himself to best advantage in appealing to prevalent values, but Josephus was a conscientious Jew. This not only accounted for his espousal of his people's cause, but also for the governing values which informed his social and religious comment, including his attitudes to sexuality. Beyond the parallels between Rome's rules and Torah, depicted as his people's most noble constitution, are fundamental principles deeply rooted in his tradition. These affirmed divine creation and so could not espouse a total denial of human emotion and passion, let alone sexuality, but had to see it in its place. Even his espousal of what among some was a popular dogma that sex served only for procreation, already taken up by Philo and *Pseudo-Phocylides*, could not expunge its accompaniments and pleasures, but condemn only their excess and misdirection. In this we might let his Joseph have the last word, whose response to his assailant, Josephus summarises as follows:

> He reminded her of her marriage and of sexual intercourse with her husband and urged that she pay more attention to these than to the fleeting pleasure of lust, which would later produce regret leading to distress about her sins but not their correction, and fear of being found out and the evil deed not remaining undisclosed. By contrast, having the enjoyment of engaging in sexual relations with her husband produced no such danger, but rather complete confidence in relation both to God and to people on the basis of having a good conscience. (*A.J.* 2.51-52) (my translation)

PART THREE

Attitudes towards Sexuality in the Testaments of the Twelve Patriarchs

3.1 Introduction

In its present form[1] this writing is clearly a Christian work, possibly from the late second century C.E.[2] It is also clearly a reworking of older material, evident, for

---

[1] In what follows I use the text edition of Marinus de Jonge, in cooperation with H. W. Hollander, H. J. de Jonge and Th. Korteweg, *The Testaments of the Twelve Patriarchs: A Critical Edition of the Greek Text* (PVTG I 2; Leiden: Brill, 1978) and the translation of Harm W. Hollander and Marinus de Jonge, *The Testaments of the Twelve Patriarchs: A Commentary* (SVTP 8; Leiden: Brill, 1985), except where indicated by an asterisk, where I remain as closely as possible to their text, but remove archaisms and consistently replace "impurity" by the more specific "sexual immorality" as the translation for πορνεία.

[2] For what follows see the review of recent research in Marinus de Jonge, "Defining the Major Issues in the Study of the Testaments of the Twelve Patriarchs," in Marinus de Jonge, *Pseudepigrapha of the Old Testament as Part of Christian Literature: The Case of the Testaments of the Twelve Patriarchs and the Greek Life of Adam and Eve* (SVTP 18; Leiden: Brill, 2003) 71-83; and Robert A. Kugler, *The Testaments of the Twelve Patriarchs* (GAP; Sheffield: Sheffield Academic Press, 2001) 31-38. See also Katell Berthelot, "Les parénèses de la Charité dans les Testaments des douze patriarches," *MSRel* 60 (2003) 23-39, 24-26, and her conclusion that in material relating to love, the strong parallels in Jewish literature favour a Jewish origin, in particular from within the wisdom tradition (38-39). On Christian editing of the *Testaments*, see Torleif Elgvin, "Jewish Christian Editing of the Old Testament Pseudepigrapha," in *Jewish Believers in Jesus: The Early Centuries* (ed. Oskar

instance, in the *Testament of Levi*, where traditions found in the 3rd century B.C.E. *Aramaic Levi Document* have been reworked, probably on the basis of a Greek translation,[3] but here the difficulties start and opinions widely diverge. In his reassessment of the evidence for the three main views on the origins of the work, Jewish, Qumran-Jewish, and Christian, Kugler concludes that the failure to "achieve a sufficient consensus on a pre-Christian form of the *Testaments*" counts against taking any one of them as a secure basis for reconstruction and analysis.[4] This, in itself, need not rule out the possibility that the work went through stages of composition over a long period, rather than being composed afresh from various materials by Christian hands. It is also far beyond the task of the current discussion here to revisit the various attempts to reconstruct the pre-history[5] or to mount a new proposal. Even in those sections of the work which contain no explicit

---

Skarsaune and Reidar Hvalvik; Peabody: Hendrickson, 2007) 278-304, esp. 286-92, who inclines towards assuming that behind them is a Jewish work (287).

[3] So Hollander and de Jonge, *Commentary*, who note that *ALD* is the common ancestor of *T. Levi* and MS *e*, a translation which is close to the Aramaic text (23), so that "it remains likely that the present T.L. was modelled upon a Levi-document of some sort" (24). On the relationship see also Michael E. Stone, "Aramaic Levi Document and the Greek Testament of Levi," in *Emanuel: Studies in Hebrew Bible, Septuagint and Dead Sea Scrolls in Honor of Emanuel Tov* (ed. Shalom M. Paul, Robert A. Kraft, Lawrence H. Schiffman and Weston W. Fields; Leiden: Brill, 2003) 429-37; and earlier Robert A. Kugler, *From Patriarch to Priest: The Levi-Priestly Tradition from* Aramaic Levi *to* Testament of Levi (SBLEJL 9; Atlanta: Scholars, 1996).

[4] Kugler, *Testaments*, 38. He affirms the view of de Jonge "that although the testaments are in their present form a Christian work, they probably underwent a long compositional and redactional history that included a lengthy period during which they may have developed in Jewish circles" (36). See also Collins, *Between Athens and Jerusalem*, 175.

[5] They include: Jürgen Becker, *Untersuchungen zur Entstehungsgeschichte der Testamente der Zwölf Patriarchen* (AGSU 8; Leiden: Brill, 1970); Anders Hultgård, *L'Eschatologie des Testaments des Douze Patriarches: 1. Interpretation des Textes* (Acta Universitatis Upsalienses: Historia Religionum 6; Stockholm: Almqvist & Wiksell, 1977); J. H. Ulrichsen, *Die Grundschrift der Testamente der Zwölf Patriarchen: Eine Untersuchung zu Umfang, Inhalt und Eigenart der ursprünglichen Schrift* (AUUHR 10; Uppsala: Almqvist & Wiksell, 1991). See the discussions in Marinus de Jonge, "The Interpretation of the Testaments of the Twelve Patriarchs in Recent Years," in *Studies on the Testaments of the Twelve Patriarchs: Text and Interpretation* (SVTP 3; Leiden: Brill, 1975) 183-92; Marinus de Jonge, "The Testaments of the Twelve Patriarchs: Central Problems and Essential Viewpoints," *ANRW* II 20,1 (1987) 359-420; and Marinus de Jonge, "The Main Issues in the Study of the Testaments of the Twelve Patriarchs," in *Jewish Eschatology, Early Christian Christology and the Testaments of the Twelve Patriarchs* (Leiden: Brill, 1991) 147-63; Hollander and de Jonge, *Commentary*, 4-7, 36-38; Kugler, *Testaments*, 31-34.

Christian references, including nearly all of the passages we shall consider below, we cannot with any certainty assume that they must be non-Christian, let alone pre-Christian in origin, nor that they must be Christian.[6]

At most we can speak of these ethical discourses as reflecting a range of influences, primarily Jewish,[7] including the telling and retelling of biblical stories,[8] now read in the Septuagint, but also philosophical, from the world of popular Stoicism.[9] As Collins notes, these discourses tend "to ignore the distinctive elements of Judaism and to emphasize those which would be acceptable to sophisticated gentiles", thus having no reference to Sabbath, only incidental reference to circumcision, and reference to food laws only for purposes of symbolism.[10] They share with the *Sibylline Oracles* and *Pseudo-Phocylides* a

---

[6] On this see Kugler, *Testaments*, who notes that "the ethics of the *Testaments* compare favourably with those of a number of other Christian didactic works (the *Didache*, the *Epistle of Barnabas*, and the *Shepherd of Hermas*)", that they assume a stance found also in Justin, Irenaeus, Melito and Hippolytus, which saw pre-Mosaic law as God's natural law, still applicable in the Christian dispensation (24). See also Marinus de Jonge, "The Testaments of the Twelve Patriarchs as a Document Transmitted by Christians," in *Pseudepigrapha of the Old Testament as Part of Christian Literature: The Case of the Testaments of the Twelve Patriarchs and the Greek Life of Adam and Eve* (SVTP 18; Leiden: Brill, 2003) 84-106, 101.

[7] So Collins, *Between Athens and Jerusalem*, who writes: "Ultimately the ethics of the *Testaments* cannot be pinpointed as the product of a specific situation. They are of interest for our purpose as material which seems to have accumulated and circulated in Hellenized Jewish circles over two hundred years and which was eventually taken over by Christianity" (177).

[8] Collins, *Between Athens and Jerusalem*, notes that "history is used here as a source of moral examples to an extent which has no precedent in the Bible" but finds its best parallels "in writings of the Hellenistic Diaspora such as 4 Maccabees"(178).

[9] On the merging in the work of Hellenistic Jewish, Christian, and Stoic thought see Kugler, *Testaments*, 17-18, 21-25. De Jonge, "Document Transmitted by Christians," notes that Hollander and de Jonge, *Commentary*, "lists all Hellenistic, Hellenistic Jewish and early Christian parallels that could be found" (102). Collins, *Between Athens and Jerusalem*, observes that the focus on abstract virtues rather than commandments is typical of Greek philosophy rather than the Bible, although catalogues of virtues and vices are found at Qumran, and some parallels can also be found in the biblical tradition" (178). He notes that "Philo also makes frequent use of lists of vices and virtues. The influence of Greek popular philosophy is very probable in the catalogues of vices and virtues in Paul and Philo, and it cannot be dismissed in the *Testaments*" (182).

[10] Collins, *Between Athens and Jerusalem*, 183. See also Marinus de Jonge, "The Two Great Commandments in the Testaments of the Twelve Patriarchs," in *Pseudepigrapha of the Old Testament as Part of Christian Literature: The Case of the Testaments of the Twelve Patriarchs and the Greek Life of Adam and Eve* (SVTP 18; Leiden: Brill, 2003) 141-59, 148; Hollander and de Jonge, *Commentary*, 43.

concern with sexual wrongdoing in particular.[11] Some evidence suggests that testaments of the patriarchs may have appeared as early as the second century B.C.E., at least in the form of patriarchs addressing future generations. *Jubilees* depicts Abraham addressing his descendants on ethical themes, including sexual issues (20:1-10; 21:1-26; 22:10-24), in a way that foreshadows what we find here.[12] Of the fragments at Qumran, de Jonge concludes that "three 'testamentary' writings with priestly instruction by Levi, his son and his grandson, handing down what their fathers told them, plus autiobiographical narratives by Naphtali, Joseph, and perhaps Benjamin, are all we have found" but no "indication of the existence of a writing with the final words of all sons of Jacob directed to their children".[13] The dependence in some parts on earlier material, such as the *Aramaic Levi Document*, makes it more than likely that this occurs where it can no longer be traced, but in any case we are dealing with a Christian composition in its final form.[14] It is therefore with some hesitation that I include this analysis within this study, but do so on the basis of recognising that at present we must be satisfied only with noting tentatively that some, perhaps even much of the material we discuss, will have had its roots in material of our period.

3.2   The Testament of Reuben

Sexual immorality (πορνεία) is the major theme in the first of the testaments, *The Testament of Reuben*.[15] The pre-eminent position of sexual immorality may well reflect the dominant order in the Greek manuscript tradition of the Decalogue.[16]

---

[11] So Collins, *Between Athens and Jerusalem*, 183.

[12] So Nickelsburg, *Jewish Literature*, who draws attention to Deuteronomy as a forerunner (302).

[13] Marinus de Jonge, "The Testaments of the Twelve Patriarchs and Related Qumran Fragments," in *Pseudepigrapha of the Old Testament as Part of Christian Literature: The Case of the Testaments of the Twelve Patriarchs and the Greek Life of Adam and Eve* (SVTP 18; Leiden: Brill, 2003) 107-23, 122.

[14] So de Jonge, "Two Great Commandments," who writes: "To do full justice to the *Testaments*, it seems to me, we have to treat the paraenesis found in them as early Christian, and, particularly, as an example of the continuity in ethical thought between Hellenistic Judaism and early Christianity" (153).

[15] See also my discussion in William Loader, "Sexuality in the Testaments of the Twelve Patriarchs and the New Testament," in *Transcending Boundaries: Contemporary Readings of the New Testament: In Honour of Professor Francis Moloney, S.D.B.* (ed. Rekha M. Chennattu and Mary L. Coloe; Rome: LAS Publications, 2005) 293-309, which includes an earlier version of parts of the following discussion.

[16] On this see Loader, *Septuagint*, 6-7.

On the other hand, Reuben was the firstborn of the twelve and his sin, reported in two slender references (Gen 35:22; 49:4; cf. also 1 Chr 5:1 noting his resultant loss of firstborn status), was sexual immorality. The texts had already spawned elaboration, as evident in *Jub.* 33:1-17.[17] The return to the theme of sexual immorality in the latter part of the final testament (*T. Benj.* 8:2-3) reinforces its major significance for the work.

The testament begins after the pattern with which each of the twelve commences: the claim that this is a copy of what the patriarch said to his sons. Like most it identifies his age here rather than at the end of the testament. Its distinctive element is the depiction of Reuben as weeping. While this may simply refer to grief at departure, one does not find this in other testaments, including in *T. Sim.* 1:1 where the patriarch was also in ill health. It is therefore more likely to relate to the theme of sexual immorality and to reflect Reuben's regret. That is indeed the focus of his opening admonishment to his sons which includes the words:

καὶ ἰδοὺ ἐπιμαρτύρομαι ὑμῖν τὸν θεὸν τοῦ οὐρανοῦ σήμερον
τοῦ μὴ πορευθῆναι ἐν ἀγνοίᾳ νεότητος καὶ πορνείᾳ, ἐν ᾗ ἐξεχύθην ἐγὼ
καὶ ἐμίανα τὴν κοίτην τοῦ πατρός μου Ἰακώβ.
And, see, I admonish you solemnly to-day by the God of heaven,
not to walk in the ignorance of youth and sexual immorality, in which I was poured out and defiled the bed of my father, Jacob.* (1:6)

The allusion is to Reuben's having had sexual intercourse with Jacob's concubine (Gen 35:22; 49:4). It will return in 3:9 – 4:5. The words ἐν ᾗ ἐξεχύθην ἐγώ ("in which I was poured out") reflects the allusion to water found in Gen 49:4 (פחז כמים; "unstable as water", which LXX translates ἐξύβρισας ὡς ὕδωρ; "wanton like water") and here indicates a sense of being controlled or carried along by sexual passion.[18] The words καὶ ἐμίανα τὴν κοίτην τοῦ πατρός μου reflect the LXX of Gen 49:4 ἀνέβης γὰρ ἐπὶ τὴν κοίτην τοῦ πατρός σου τότε ἐμίανας τὴν στρωμνὴν οὗ ἀνέβης ("For you went up upon your father's bed; then you defiled the couch where you went up"). The expression, defiling the bed, serves as a metaphor for sexual immorality. Clearly the bed stands for the marriage. The defilement related, in particular, to Bilhah, who became thereby unclean for Jacob. He never had sexual intercourse with her again: "he touched her

---

[17] On this see the discussion in Loader, *Enoch, Levi, and Jubilees,* 192-200.

[18] So James L. Kugel, "Reuben's Sin with Bilhah," in James L. Kugel, *The Ladder of Jacob: Ancient Interpretations of the Biblical Story of Jacob and his Children* (Princeton: Princeton University Press, 2006) 81-114, 240-44, here: 85, 88-90. Hollander and de Jonge, *Commentary,* note the use of ἐκχεῖν to express being given over to an appetite for food in Sir 37:29 (90).

no more (μηκέτι άψάμενος αυτής) (3:15). The same conclusion is drawn in *Jub.* 33:9. The abstinence recalls Deut 24:1-4, according to which a woman once divorced cannot later return to her former husband because she has been rendered unclean for him, by having slept with another man. While not explicitly cited, the prohibition of incest with one's father's wife (Lev 18:8; 20:11), informs the assumption about Reuben's sin.

In 1:7-10 the author reports God's punishment of Reuben – God struck him with affliction in the same area of the body with which he had sinned: his "loins" which included his genitalia.[19] This follows the principle enunciated in *T. Gad* 5:10: "For by what things a man transgresses, by the same he is also punished". Only Jacob's intercession averted death, which was the punishment required by the Law (Lev 20:11).[20] Reuben mentions his age at the time as thirty, perhaps significant as the age at which men normally married (1:8; cf. *T. Iss.* 3:5; *T. Levi* 11:8 with 12:4;).[21] He describes the deed as "the evil thing" (τὸ πονηρόν) (1:8), his "great sin" (τῇ ἁμαρτίᾳ μου, μεγάλη γὰρ ἦν) (1:10), "the great iniquity" (τὴν ἀνομίαν τὴν μεγάλην) (3:11), "the abominable thing" (τὸ βδέλυγμα) (3:12; cf. *T. Jud.* 12:8), "the impiety" (τὴν ἀσέβειαν) (3:14), "my impiety" (τῆς ἀσεβείας μου) (3:15) and "my sin" (τῆς ἁμαρτίας μου) (4:3; cf. *T. Jud* 14:3).

He spent seven years in repentance and abstinence from wine, strong drink, meat, and, perhaps, "sweet bread" (1:10). None of these relate directly to sexual immorality, although the *T. Judah* makes a strong connection between wine and sexual immorality (14:1-8 and see 15:4) and the author perhaps intends an allusion to sexual passion by word play in the final item: "sweet bread", lit. "bread of desire" (ἄρτον ἐπιθυμίας) (cf. Dan 10:3), which might recall Prov 9:17. There need not be a link between the sin of which one repents and the items from which one abstains. They do, however, all represent physical pleasure. The declaration that "such a thing shall not happen in Israel (καὶ οὐ μὴ γένηται ἐν τῷ 'Ισραὴλ οὕτως)" (1:10) resonates with the account of the rape of Dinah: "because he had done an unseemly thing in Israel by lying with Jacob's daughter, and it shall not be thus (ὅτι ἄσχημον ἐποίησεν ἐν Ισραηλ κοιμηθεὶς μετὰ τῆς θυγατρὸς Ιακωβ καὶ οὐχ οὕτως ἔσται)" (Gen 34:7; cf. also 2 Sam 13:12: "No, my brother, do not humiliate me; for it shall not be done in this way in Israel; do not

---

[19] Renate Kirchhoff, "Die Testamente der zwölf Patriarchen: Über Techniken männlicher Machtausübung," in *Kompendium Feministische Bibelauslegung* (ed. Luise Schottroff, Marie-Theres Wacker, Claudia Janssen, and Beate Wehn; Gütersloh: Chr. Kaiser Gütersloher Verlagshaus, 1999) 474-82, reads this as impotence (481), but the depiction of the illness as endangering his life makes this unlikely.

[20] *Jubilees* explains that the Mosaic law demanding death had not yet been revealed (*Jub.* 33:15-16). Cf. CD 5.2-4 which explains David's taking many wives on the basis that he had no access to the Law.

[21] Satlow, *Jewish Marriage*, 106-109, 132.

do this folly [καὶ εἶπεν αὐτῷ μή ἀδελφέ μου μὴ ταπεινώσῃς με διότι οὐ ποιηθήσεται οὕτως ἐν Ισραηλ μὴ ποιήσῃς τὴν ἀφροσύνην ταύτην] "). *T. Judah* has Judah use similar language of his sin with Tamar: "because I had done this abomination in all Israel (ἀλλ' οὐδὲ ἤγγισα αὐτῇ ἔτι ἕως θανάτου μου, ὅτι βδέλυγμα ἐποίησα τοῦτο ἐν παντὶ 'Ισραήλ)" (12:8)

The Spirits of Creation and the Spirits which Lead Astray (2:1 – 3:8)

In 2:1 – 3:8 the author has Reuben provide an explanation of the basis of sexual immorality. We are thus being taken beyond prohibiting acts to understanding what lies behind them. Reuben claims that he "saw" (εἶδον) these insights during his time of repentance (2:1). Seeing here implies more than simply realising through rational reflection. Rather it expresses a claim to insight through revelation as in 4:3, which refers to angelic revelation about the nature of women. The author begins by mentioning the "seven spirits of deceit (ἑπτὰ πνευμάτων τῆς πλάνης)", which are identified as "given by Beliar against man (ἐδόθη κατὰ τοῦ ἀνθρώπου ἀπὸ τοῦ Βελιάρ)" and described as being "the head of the works of the behaviour of youth (κεφαλὴ τῶν ἔργων τοῦ νεωτερισμοῦ)" (2:1-2). These are elaborated one by one, but not until 3:3-6. The word πλάνη could also be translated "error". Both translations, "deceit" and "error", tend to give more emphasis to one aspect, the former, to being misled or tricked, the latter, to wrong belief. Neither is entirely adequate. Throughout the testaments the meaning is consistently one which indicates going astray from God's commandments.

Before the treatment of the seven spirits of deceit/error, first we have reference to another seven spirits,[22] who are described positively and so set in opposition to the spirits of error: "And seven spirits were given to him at creation that through them should be (done) every work of man (καὶ ἕπτα πνεύματα ἐδόθη αὐτῷ ἐπὶ τῆσ κτίσεως, τοῦ εἶναι ἐν αὐτοῖς πᾶν ἔργον ἀνθρώπου)" (2:3). There follows a list in which each is introduced with an ordinal and the word "spirit" (e.g. πρῶτον πνεῦμα "The first [is] the spirit of") (2:4-8). These spirits are: life, sight, hearing, smell, speech, taste and "procreation and sexual intercourse (σπορᾶς καὶ συνουσίας)". Each item is given an application,

---

[22] As Hollander and de Jonge, *Commentary*, explain, "This list goes back (probably indirectly) to the Stoic division of the soul into eight parts, viz., the five senses and τὸ σπερματικόν, τὸ φωνητικόν, τὸ ἡγεμονικόν ... These parts or functions of the soul are sometimes called πνεύματα and are then pictured as immaterial currents between the ἡγεμονικόν and the parts of the body with which they are connected" (93). See also Howard C. Kee, "Ethical Dimensions of the Testaments of the XII as a Clue to Provenance," *NTS* 24 (1978) 259-70, 266, 269; C. R. Henry, "The Testaments of the XII Patriarchs," *APOT*, 282 – 367, esp. 297; Kugler, *Testaments*, 24.

introduced by μεθ' ἧς. They describe aspects of human psychology in the broadest sense and as positively valued elements of human creation (2:3), but which may be wrongly applied. In only two do we have identification of potential sin and both have direct relevance to the theme of sexual wrongdoing as typified in Reuben's account of his own sin. For the immediate context the other items are superfluous except in the sense that they help the hearer see that sexual desire belongs in this broader context. The author is most likely employing an existing list of categories for his purpose.[23]

Of particular relevance, therefore, are "sight" to which the list adds: "with which comes desire (μεθ' ἧς γίνεται ἐπιθυμία)" (2:4); and especially "procreation and sexual intercourse" (2:8). Here the author adds: "with which sin comes in through love of pleasure (μεθ' ἧς συνεισέρχεται διὰ τῆς φιληδονίας ἡ ἁμαρτία)". Here we find clear indications of the author's value system in relation to sexuality. "Sight" is ethically neutral, as is "desire", but "desire" can be sinful if wrongly directed. Similarly "procreation and sexual intercourse" are affirmed, but, as is evident elsewhere, only when they occur together, as extensively expounded in Philo (see 1.2.2.6.1 above) and asserted in Josephus (*A.J.* 4.259, 261, 290; 5.168; *Ap.* 2.199; and see 2.4.15 above; cf. also *Ps.- Phoc.* 176).[24] In this context sexual intercourse may also be an experience of pleasure, but the desire for sexual intercourse only for pleasure is sin. This is later reinforced in the praise of Rachel for seeking sexual intercourse not for pleasure but only to produce offspring (*T. Iss.* 2:1, 3). In 2:9 the author then elaborates:

διὰ τοῦτο ἔσχατόν ἐστι τῆς κτίσεως
καί πρῶτον τῆς νεότητος,
ὅτι ἀγνοίας πεπλήρωται
καὶ αὕτη τὸν νεώτερον ὁδηγεῖ ὡς τυφλὸν ἐπὶ βόθρον
καὶ ὡς κτῆνος ἐπὶ κρημνόν
Therefore it is the last (in the order) of creation,
and the first (in the order) of youth,
because it is filled with ignorance
and that leads the young man as a blind man to a pit
and as a beast to a precipice. (*T. Reub.* 2:9)

---

[23] Becker, *Untersuchungen*, sees this as reason to consider 2:3 – 3:2 as material secondarily inserted because of the reference to sin in relation to the third spirit (188-89).

[24] Of συνουσία Hollander and de Jonge, *Commentary*, write that "it is mentioned here because of its possible connection with φιληδονία and πορνεία" (94). They go on to mention Philo's criticism of men who have sex not σπορᾶς ἕνεκα τέκνων but pursue τὴν ἐξ ὁμιλίας ἀπόλαυσιν (*Spec.* 3.113) as φιλήδονοι. "Σπορά is the equivalent of σπερματικόν, γεννητικόν, σπέρμα, γόνιμον in Stoic lists" (94). In itself, however, συνουσία is neutral.

In describing the "spirit of procreation and sexual intercourse (πνεῦμα σπορᾶς καὶ συνουσίας)" as the "last of creation", the author may have had the creation of male and female in Gen 1:27 and the command to multiply in Gen 1:28 in mind, but perhaps also the sexual relations implied in Gen 2:24. Coming last may imply that it is of lesser value, although the list does not otherwise suggest a hierarchy. The author plays with contrasts in depicting it as the first of youth, probably implying that it is first among what he sees as the preoccupations of youth, which as already indicated reaches at least to the age of thirty (1:8).

What is "filled with ignorance" (disregard for the Law) is not the spirit of procreation and intercourse, but "youth". Already in his opening remarks Reuben had spoken of the "ignorance of youth and sexual immorality (ἀγνοίᾳ νεότητος καὶ πορνείᾳ)" (1:6). It is important to see that the author does not see the spirit of procreation and intercourse as evil in itself.[25] It is God's gift. It includes pleasure, but love of pleasure makes it a danger. Youth is filled with ἀγνοίας ("ignorance"). ἄγνοια then becomes the subject (thus αὕτη). It, not the spirit, does the leading into the pit or to the brink. Youth are prone to ἄγνοια, which is not, however, innocent ignorance, but the result of turning away from available knowledge. Reuben's discourse is offering that kind of knowledge. Youth's problem is not that it has not yet learned, but that it does not want to learn.[26]

Before proceeding to the list of the seven spirits from Beliar (3:3-6) the author appends an eighth spirit: sleep (3:1). Like the seven spirits of creation it is neutral, but for the author's psychology, particularly in relation to sexuality, it appears significant. The additional comment, "with which the ecstasy of [human] nature and image of death were created (μεθ' οὗ ἐκτίσθη ἔκστασις φύσεως καὶ εἰκὼν τοῦ θανάτου)", appears to be neutral. Both ἔκστασις φύσεως ("ecstasy of [human] nature") and εἰκὼν τοῦ θανάτου ("image of death") seem to be based on observation and speculation about dreaming (which takes one beyond natural experiences) and about death (sleep and death were often compared).[27]

The author now returns to "the spirit of deceit" (cf. 2:1), declaring: "With these spirits is mingled the spirit of deceit (τούτοις τοῖς πνεύμασι συμμίγνυται τὸ πνεῦμα[28] τῆς πλάνης)" (3:2). We then hear how this "spirit of deceit" is to be

---

[25] "Sündig" ("sinful") – so Ulrichsen, *Grundschrift*, 73.

[26] On the vulnerability of youth and its blindness see also *T. Jud.* 11:1 (similarly *T. Sim.* 2:7) and 19:3-4, where it almost reads as an exoneration until one understands that ignorance is culpable (as also in *Jub* 41:25).

[27] See Hollander and de Jonge, *Commentary*, 94. Cf. also Philo on Gen 2:21 in *Leg.* 2.31.

[28] The *lectio difficilior* read by *bkdm*, against the expected reading πνεύματα. See Hollander and de Jonge, *Commentary*, 92.

found in seven spirits (3:3-6).²⁹ The fact that the first list concludes with procreation and sexual intercourse and warnings about abuse makes a neat transition to the list of the spirits from Beliar, for it has sexual immorality as its first item: "The first, that of sexual immorality (πρῶτον τὸ τῆς πορνείας)" (3:3). Its position at the head of the list, as in similar lists in the NT (Mark 7:21-22; 1 Cor 6:9; cf. also Rom 13:9), doubtless reflects its priority as the greatest sin, an emphasis supported by its prominence in the LXX Decalogue where in one strong MS tradition it heads the second table.³⁰

The first three of these spirits are located in the physical body: "in nature and the senses"*, "in the belly", and "in the liver and the gall". The underlying assumption here, too, is that aspects of the human body are not in themselves evil, but evil may inhabit them. Thus the important first spirit of the spirits which lead astray, that of sexual immorality (τὸ τῆς πορνείας) is said to locate itself in one's natural physical make-up (ἐν τῇ φύσει) and in particular in the senses (ταῖς αἰσθήσεσιν). Neither the elements of one's natural physical make-up nor the senses are evil.

Just as the author appended "sleep" to the first list, so he appends "sleep" to the second. This is discordant with the other seven, which are vices. However the author sees a link and speaks of sleep as also one of the spirits of deceit: "the spirit of sleep, the eighth spirit, is connected with deceit and fantasy" (3:7). The focus appears not to be conscious fantasies of committing sin, but impressions created on the mind which appear during sleep in dreams.³¹ The world of dreams was the world where supernatural beings and human beings were believed to connect with each other. Elsewhere the author depicts "daydreaming" such as with the women in relation to the Watchers in 5:6-7 and perhaps in the motif of Reuben's sleeplessness about Bilhah (3:12).³²

One might expect that each item in this list would match an item in the former list and so show how the neutral qualities of the first are subverted. This is not the case except for the first, which matches the seventh in dealing with sexuality, and the eighth. This is therefore an odd juxtaposition of categories, where the spirits of

---

²⁹ On Philo's similar employment of the seven (eight) categories of senses (*Opif.* 62-66; 117; *Abr.* 236; *QG* 1.7; 2.12; 3.4; 4.110; *QE* 2.97; *Leg.* 1.11; *Det.* 168; *Agr.* 30) see the discussion in 1.2.2.4 above. See also Hollander and de Jonge, *Commentary*, 94.

³⁰ On this see Loader, *Septuagint*, 5-8.

³¹ Hollander and de Jonge, *Commentary*, note that φαντασία is a Stoic term ... "primarily used for the impression in the soul caused by what is transmitted through the senses. The term is in itself neutral; only when one emphasizes the deceptiveness of the senses one will value the φαντασίαι negatively" (95-96). Cf. also *T. Sim.* 4:8-9.

³² On the association of sleep and pleasure see Hollander and de Jonge, *Commentary*, 96, who cite *T. Sim* 4:8-9; *T. Jud.* 18:4; Plato *Resp.* 9.571C-572A; Plut *Mor* 129B; Philo *Somn.* 2.147 (96).

creation in the first list refer to neutral capacities, not beings, whereas the spirits from Beliar assume a demonology associated with vices: sexual wrongdoing, insatiate desire, fighting, flattery and trickery, arrogance, lying in destruction and jealousy, and unrighteousness. The author employs both lists to focus only on one aspect, namely "sexual immorality", but having the entire list in each case sets "sexual immorality" in a wider context.[33] The remaining vices, for instance, have some relevance for other testaments, and their similar treatment can, as we shall see, be instructive,[34] but even then they do not correspond to the categories here.[35] Otherwise they have no further relevance in this testament, where the focus of attention is sexual immorality. Both lists show signs of being resources upon which the author has drawn to employ for his purpose.[36] The author of the final document is also thereby combining different streams of thought, Stoic psychology and Jewish demonology. The stream of psychology is more determinative in the discourse than the stream of demonology.[37] This becomes very apparent in the later explanations, where the focus is on processes of the mind, not demonic control. This bears some similarity to Paul's preference for "psychology" and for personifications over demonology, especially in Romans 7, while at the same time employing the language of demonology as, for instance, in his reference to Satan in 1 Cor 7:5 and to Beliar in 2 Cor 6:15.

In 3:8 the author draws the conclusion from his excursus about human beings and the spirits which assail them: "And so every young man perishes (Καὶ οὕτως ἀπόλλυται πᾶς νεώτερος)". This should be read in the light of what follows: "darkening his mind from the truth and not understanding the law of God nor obeying the admonitions of his fathers, as I also suffered in my youth (σκοτίζων τὸν νοῦν ἀπὸ ἀληθείας καὶ μὴ συνίων ἐν τῷ νόμῳ τοῦ θεοῦ μήτε ὑπακούων νουθεσίας πατέρων αὐτοῦ, ὥσπερ κἀγὼ ἔπαθον ἐν τῷ νεωτερισμῷ μου) ". It is exhortatory pessimism, but grounded in the belief that it can motivate other young men not to follow this path – the reason for the testament in the first place. The reason for the hopelessness is youth's "ignorance" (ἄγνοια): they refuse to learn. "The truth", "the law of God" and "the instruction of fathers" are equated. This recalls the exhortation to listen in 2:1 and at the

---

[33] So Niebuhr, *Gesetz und Paränese*, who sees a broad compass indicating that the primary focus is not individual virtues and vices but the will of God as a whole (163-65).

[34] Nickelsburg, *Jewish Literature*, notes that this first testament "functions to lay out the anthropological presuppositions of the entire work" (305).

[35] So Hollander and de Jonge, *Commentary*, 94.

[36] See de Jonge, *Testaments* (1975), 75-77.

[37] Niebuhr, *Gesetz und Paränese*, rightly notes however that one cannot easily separate psychological and demonological understandings of πνεῦμα in the ancient world (90).

beginning of the discourse in 1:5. The assumption is that youth need not be destroyed if it heeds good teaching. Ignorance is no excuse.[38]

Warnings about Sexual Immorality and about Women's Sexuality

In having Reuben conclude his excursus with a reference to himself ("as I also suffered in my youth"), the author returns attention to Reuben's own story and his sin with Bilhah. When Reuben declares to his children, "Love the truth and it will guard you" (3:9), this is to be read in the light of the associated ideas of 3:8, namely, "the truth", "the law of God", and "the instruction of fathers". For the author, part of that truth lies in the primitive psychology which he has just expounded in 2:1 – 3:8. In 3:10 we move to direct exhortation, but to be understood in the light of that exposition.

The first warnings read

μὴ προσέχετε ἐν ὄψει γυναικὸς
μηδὲ ἰδιάζετε μετὰ θηλείας ὑπάνδρου
μηδὲ περιεργάζεσθε πρᾶξιν γυναικῶν
Pay no heed to the face of a woman,
Nor be alone with another man's wife,
Nor meddle with the affair(s) of women. (3:10)

The author has Reuben repeat these warning with some variation after expounding them in the light of the sexual wrongdoing with Bilhah (3:11-15):

μὴ οὖν προσέχετε κάλλος γυναικῶν
μηδὲ ἐννοιεῖσθε τὰς πράξεις αὐτῶν.
Pay no heed, therefore to the beauty of women
And do not set your mind on their affairs. (4:1)

The excursus on spirits had already highlighted the potential misuse of sight "with which desire comes (μεθ' ἧς γίνεται ἐπιθυμία)" (2:4). The warning not to give attention to a woman's face (μὴ προσέχετε ὄψει γυναικός 3:10a) has many parallels both within the testaments (e.g., *T. Jud.* 12:3; 17:1; *T. Iss.* 4:4; 7:2) and beyond (e.g., Sir 9:8-9; 25:21; 42:12; *Pss. Sol.* 4:4-5; 16:7).[39] The verb προσέχω means more than just seeing; it is about intentional gaze. The author will expand

---

[38] There is a tension here between responsibility and blaming ignorance. Judah almost exonerates himself on the basis of ignorance in *T. Jud.* 11:1 and sees the resultant blindness as enough to warrant God's pity (19:3-4; cf. also *T. Sim.* 2:7). On the link between sin and ignorance see also *Jub.* 41:25.

[39] See also Hollander and de Jonge, *Commentary*, who draw attention to Plutarch 769C; Philo *Abr.* 94; *Mos.* 1.296; Justin *Apol.* 2.11.4 (98).

upon these warnings later when he points to women's "gestures" (5:1), "adornment" and "glance" (5:3, 5). The warning about being alone with another man's wife finds an echo in 6:2 which discourages such association and has precedent in Sir 9:9 (cf. also Prov 6:23-29; Clem. *Hom.* 13.18.5). The "affairs" (πράξεις) could mean a range of things, but, given the context, probably indicates their private activities, including bathing.

Accordingly, in 3:11-15 Reuben cites his behaviour as an instance of not heeding such instruction. The detail takes us beyond the terse account in Gen 35:22 and 49:4. Kugel notes that it also relocates it in time so that now Jacob is presented as having already departed to go to see Isaac, with the result that he is not around at that time and so also not in his bed, in contrast to Gen 35:27, according to which the visit to Isaac takes place after this event.[40] As in *Jubilees*,[41] Reuben saw Bilhah bathing[42] discreetly in a covered place.[43] Her bathing would be counted as one of the women's matters/affairs. Her doing so in a sheltered place indicates that she was behaving with appropriate modesty. He sees more than her face (cf. 3:10); he sees her naked (3:12). There is almost a self-distancing in the observation in 3:12: "my mind, comprehending the female nakedness (συλλαβοῦσα γὰρ ἡ διάνοιά μου τὴν γυναικείαν γύμνωσιν)".[44] Bilhah almost disappears as a person: Reuben does not see Bilhah naked; he sees "female nakedness". The author may also be playing with words in speaking of the mind "conceiving" (συλλαβοῦσα) (cf. 5:6; Jas 1:15). This is much more complex than saying: I saw Bilhah naked. It reflects the author's psychology. Somewhat overstated: Reuben's mind became pregnant as a result of female nakedness.[45] The author is not absolving Reuben of responsibility. His fault was that he turned his

---

[40] Kugel, "Reuben's Sin," 91, 93.

[41] The author appears to have known either the account in *Jub.* 33:2-8 or a related tradition, because he shares with it the following details: that Reuben saw Bilhah bathing and that Jacob no longer slept with her. Here, however, she is not drunk, but wakes up and tries to resist. On this see Kugel, "Reuben's Sin," 110-14.

[42] Kugel, "Reuben's Sin," notes this motif may also be derived from the image of water in Gen 49:4, combined with a reading of the word פחז "wanton", which took just its last letters to derive the word חז from חזה "to see" (85-87).

[43] The account recalls the stories of David and Bathsheba and of Susanna (2 Sam 11:2; Susanna), though betrays no linguistic connections. Kugel, "Reuben's Sin," points out Bilhah's virtue in *T. Reuben* in seeking a discreet place to bathe, unlike Bathsheba (90).

[44] In his own way Paul, too, saw danger in some forms of female nakedness for men and for angels, but within the distinctive context of holy worship (1 Cor 11:2-16). See Loader, *Septuagint*, 99-104.

[45] Similarly Kirchhoff, "Testamente," 478.

mind (διάνοια) towards Bilhah.⁴⁶ Once he had done so, the rest followed: "my mind ... did not allow me to sleep until I had done the abominable thing (ἡ διάνοιά μου ... οὐκ εἴασέ με ὑπνῶσαι ἕως οὗ ἔπραξα τὸ βδέλυγμα)" (3:12).

In describing the act, the author exonerates Bilhah completely: she lay in her chamber (her private quarters) "drunk and sleeping" (3:13). It may recall the drunkenness of Lot and his daughters' incest with him (Gen 19:32-33), for which *Jubilees* makes Lot also responsible; and Noah's drunkenness in Gen 9:21, where he lay naked in his tent as a result of which Ham sinned. Here it appears to serve rather to deny her any possible role in what was happening. This is important, given that later the author will lay blame on women who seek to use their sexuality to seduce men and will warn of the dangers of wine. Bilhah had apparently not used wine in an inappropriate way.⁴⁷ The author goes out of his way here to emphasise that Bilhah is not to be blamed, not even for being a woman, as would seem to be the case in other discussions. She even has angelic oversight; an angel tells Jacob,⁴⁸ who, following purity laws, has nothing further to do with her: "he touched her no more (μηκέτι ἁψάμενος αὐτῆς)", for she had become unclean for him (so also *Jub.* 33:9; cf. also Deut 24:1-4).⁴⁹ This contrasts with *Jubilees* where Bilhah herself informs Jacob (33:7).

While Bilhah is depicted as a victim of Reuben's uncontrolled sexual passion, clearly non-consensual sex and incest, the author otherwise shows no direct concern for her nor do Reuben or Jacob. The latter mourns not over her but over Reuben (3:15) and Reuben conceives his sin as primarily against Jacob and God, not as against Bilhah (4:2-4). As an observer of Torah Jacob must not have sexual relations with her. That would be an abomination. This thought informs Deut 24:1-4 and was a widely assumed norm (1QapGen ar/1Q20 2.9-10, 14-16;⁵⁰ *t. Sot.* 5.9; Philo *Abr.* 98; *Lex Iulia de adulteris* of 18 B.C.E.). Poor Bilhah!

While Reuben blames himself for looking and exonerates Bilhah completely, he nevertheless engages in some dissociation from himself in claiming that his mind (διάνοια) did not let him rest until he acted out his sexual passion. This comes close to saying that the first sin of looking set in train the inevitable in which Reuben could not help himself, but clearly the author does not go that far. As the example of Joseph will show, he holds men responsible for their actions.

---

⁴⁶ Hollander and de Jonge, *Commentary*, note that the Stoics sometimes used διάνοια to describe the ruling principle, ἡγεμονικόν (99).

⁴⁷ Kugel, "Reuben's Sin," notes that being drunk she is not even conscious (an angel must inform Jacob), so bears no blame (95-96). Cf. Nickelsburg, *Jewish Literature*, 304.

⁴⁸ This reflects a reading of "Israel" in Gen 35:22 by both our author and *Jubilees* as referring not to the people but to Jacob. See Kugel, "Reuben's Sin," 95.

⁴⁹ Kugel, "Reuben's Sin," sees the cessation of intercourse as helping to explain why no more children were born than the 12 sons, the immediate sequel to the story (97-99).

⁵⁰ On this see Loader, *Dead Sea Scrolls on Sexuality*, 290.

On the other hand the author embraces a psychology that identifies a process which occurs in the mind which is very difficult to control and is best avoided in the first places by such strategies as not looking, not being alone with someone else's wife, and not having to do with their private matters. Unlike, however, the case with Bilhah except in a passive sense – because she was totally incapacitated as woman by being dead drunk! – women's sexuality is, for the author also part of the problem, as his later exposition shows.

After returning to the warnings of 3:10 in 4:1, the author expands them with particular advice for the typical young men. They are to "walk in singleness of heart (ἐν ἁπλότητι καρδίας)", a virtue expounded in *T. Issachar*. Here it means not allowing oneself to be distracted by women, but instead to engage in "labouring in works as well as wandering about in literature (γράμμασι)" and with flocks (4:1). The "literature" will doubtless mean "holy books",[51] passed down through the fathers. The remedy of keeping busy so as not to be overwhelmed by sexual passion, indeed living the lifestyle of a farmer,[52] whose work makes him too tired to be bothered with women, occurs in *T. Iss.* 3:5 (cf. also 4:1, 4; similarly *T. Levi* 9:9-10). Then, Reuben assures them, all in good time "the Lord will give you a wife, whom he wants, that you will not suffer as I did" (4:1) (cf. also Sir 26:1-3, 13-14). This probably assumes monogyny.[53]

In 4:2-4 Reuben returns to the consequences of his action: his shame[54] before his father and brothers and his continuing bad conscience (cf. also *T. Jud.* 13:3 which mentions Judah's rebuke), but also his good behaviour since repenting. Reuben has made himself thus a model for any who have sinned similarly. The author is wielding the familiar weapons of moral exhortation. He returns to direct exhortation in 4:5 where he has Reuben exhort his children to observe his commands (cf. "the admonitions of his fathers" 3:8) so that they might not sin. He declares that "sexual immorality is (leads to) a destruction to the soul (ὄλεθρος γὰρ ψυχῆς ἐστιν ἡ πορνεία)" (cf. Sir 9:7-9; Prov 6:32-35; 7:25-27), explaining

---

[51] So Hollander and de Jonge, *Commentary*, 99; Becker, *Untersuchungen*, 186. See also H. Dixon Slingerland, "The Nature of *Nomos* (law) within the Testaments of the Twelve Patriarchs," *JBL* 105 (1986) 39-48, 42.

[52] Kugler, *Testaments*, notes this as a further link between Reuben and David beyond the allusion to his seeing Bathsheba bathing and suggests that the reference to the study of books is an echo of the royal law in Deut 17:19-20 (90). In this he argues that the author is making the point that "even the most heroic of figures is subject to the temptations of a woman and the force of evil spirits" (91).

[53] So Becker, *Untersuchungen*, 186.

[54] Shame is also a major motif in *T. Judah*, where the patriarch reports his shame, brought on by wine, in having sexual intercourse unawares with his daughter-in-law, Tamar. He uses it to warn future kings about surrendering their power (staff, girdle and diadem) to women (15:1-6).

that it affects the soul by "separating it from God and bringing it near to the idols (χωρίζουσα θεοῦ καὶ προσεγγίζουσα τοῖς εἰδώλοις)" (4:6). The latter assumes sexual wrongdoing leads to idolatry (similarly *T. Sim.* 5:3; *T. Jud.* 23:2; cf. also *T. Dan* 5:5; *T. Benj.*, 10:10),[55] though the reverse, idolatry leading to sexual wrongdoing is also found (*T. Naph.* 2:2 – 3:5).

The psychological theme returns in the claim that "it deceives the mind and the understanding, and leads down young men to the underworld before their time (ὅτι αὕτη ἐστὶ πλανῶσα τὸν νοῦν καὶ τὴν διάνοιαν, καὶ κατάγει νεανίσκους εἰς ᾅδην οὐκ ἐν καιρῷ αὐτῶν)" (4:6; similarly Prov 5:3-5; 7:25-27). Again we see the author asserting that there is a process which sexual desire unleashes which is then hard to control, personifying πορνεία as what drives it. While 4:6 describes death, 4:7 depicts the consequent destructive effects of sexual wrongdoing, for both young and old, in terms of shame and ridicule, even from Beliar. The emphasis on shameful consequences for one's reputation – a long way from any concern about the wrong one might do to others, let alone women – recalls a major emphasis in Ben Sira (7:24-25; 41:14 – 42:8, 9-14).[56]

The author next has Reuben cite the example of Joseph (4:8-10). "Joseph guarded himself from every woman (ἐπειδὴ γὰρ ἐφύλαξεν ἑαυτὸν Ἰωσὴφ ἀπὸ πάσης γυναικός)" (cf. Prov 6:24; 7:5; *Pss. Sol.* 16:7; *Asen.* 7:6). This may appear strange since Genesis recounts a single episode concerned with only one woman, but possibly the author is aware of the kind of tradition that appears in *Joseph and Aseneth*, according to which Joseph had to fight off hoards of female admirers (7:2-3). This is a variation on avoiding their company, on the one hand (3:10b), and keeping oneself from engaging their beauty, on the other (3:10a; 4:1a). The author goes on to explain how this was possible: he "purged his thoughts from all sexual wrongdoing (καὶ τὰς ἐννοίας ἐκαθάρισεν ἀπὸ πάσης πορνείας)" (4:8b). This implies control of the imagination and coheres with the author's psychology.[57] That "he found favour in the sight of the Lord and men (εὗρε χάριν ἐνώπιον κυρίου καὶ ἀνθρώπων)" sets him in contrast to those in 4:7 who brought shame upon themselves. We then hear of the concrete instance: "the Egyptian woman did many things to him and summoned magicians and offered

---

[55] It is quite incidental to Reuben's story, but it looms very large in *T. Judah* in the form of warnings against foreign women (10:6; 11:1, 3; 14:3; 17:1; 23:2) and especially in *T. Levi*, which brings together a range of acts of sexual immorality, including marrying foreign wives and the exposure to idolatry (9:9-10; 14:5-6; see also *T. Dan* 5:5-6).

[56] On attitudes towards sexuality in Sirach, including the importance of issues of honour and shame, see Balla, "Ben Sira," 362-98.

[57] It also gave the testament the title it receives in many manuscripts: περὶ ἐννοιων. Cf. Becker, *Untersuchungen*, who denies the psychological element plays a role in 4:6 – 6:4 and makes it one of his grounds for identifying the block as independent of what precedes (192-93).

him love potions" (4:8),[58] going beyond the Genesis account, but further elaborated in the *T. Jos.* 3:1 – 9:5. This brief reference to Joseph is interesting, because the long narrative in *T. Joseph* about his encounter with the Egyptian woman (3:1 – 9:5) focuses almost entirely on her various manipulations. Only at a very secondary level, almost sounding like an afterthought, do we hear from Joseph about the danger of women's beauty in *T. Jos.* 9:5, where he describes the attractiveness of her bear arms, legs and breasts and adornment.

The key to Joseph's success is: "the disposition of his soul did not admit an evil desire (οὐκ ἐδέξατο τὸ διαβούλιον τῆς ψυχῆς αὐτοῦ ἐπιθυμίαν πονηράν)" (4:9). It is important to see here that ἐπιθυμία is a neutral category, which becomes evil when inappropriately focused. Joseph had the capacity to welcome such desire, but chose not to. From this the author generalises: "For if sexual wrongdoing does not overcome the mind, also Beliar will not overcome you (ἐὰν γὰρ μὴ κατισχύσῃ ἡ πορνεία τὴν ἔννοιαν, οὐδὲ Βελιὰρ κατισχύσει ὑμῶν)" (4:11). We are again at the margins of attributing responsibility, where one might read this as implying that the mind can be overcome by desire and then by Beliar and one cannot then help oneself. It is more likely that the author is arguing preventively, that dealing with wrongly directed desire is the best control, not that somehow actions thereafter are inevitable. The demonic Beliar comes in at a secondary level. In terms of 3:3 one would have to say that the spirit of πορνεία which comes from Beliar seeks control. Reuben is saying: it can and should be resisted.

In 5:1 the author returns to focus on women, declaring: "Women are evil (πονηραί εἰσιν αἱ γυναῖκες)". The statement should not be seen in isolation from its context, from what has gone before – it was not apparently true of Bilhah – and particularly from what follows. There we read that they are evil because, he claims, they compensate for not being as strong as men[59] by acts of trickery, to attract them: "because, having no power or strength over man, they use wiles trying to draw him to them by gestures (ὅτι μὴ ἔχουσιαι ἐξουσίαν ἢ δύναμιν ἐπὶ τὸν ἄνθρωπον, δολιεύονται ἐν σχήμασι, πῶς αὐτὸν πρὸς αὐτὰς ἐπισπάσονται)" (5:1). The word σχήμασι draws attention to form and appearance (cf. also *T. Jud.* 12:1, 3; 13:5), which may encompass more than just "gestures", and include cosmetics and adornment, soon to be addressed directly (5:3, 5). In 5:2 the author begins using the language of struggle and warfare: "and whom she cannot overcome by strength, him she overcomes by craft (καὶ ὃν διὰ δυνάμεως

---

[58] On the use of love potions as a familiar topos see Hollander and de Jonge, *Commentary*, who refer to Homer, Aristophanes, Plutarch, but also 2 Kings 9:22 LXX of Jezebel (100-101).

[59] On women as the weaker sex, cf. also on Philo section 1.2.2.2 and 1.2.2.5 and on Josephus, 2.4.12. See also Hollander and de Jonge, *Commentary*, 102.

οὐκ ἰσχύει καταγωνίσασθαι, τοῦτον δι' ἀπάτης καταγωνίζεται)". While δι' ἀπάτης could mean "by seduction", the whole exercise is about seduction and the focus here is on the means, hence "by craft" or "by deceit". The "Egyptian woman" of 4:8-10 was a prime example and is doubtless still in the author's mind (see also *T. Naph.* 1:6 about Rachel and, in irony, 12:7 about Tamar).

The metaphor of struggle (καταγωνίσασθαι καταγωνίζεται 5:2) evolves into a metaphor of warfare in 5:3, but first in 5:3a the author has Reuben assert that he has received teaching from the angel of the Lord about women's psychology. The previous claim to revelation (2:1) delivered the "psychology" in 2:1– 3:7 and we find a further claim to angelic revelation about women in *T. Jud.* 15:5-6. The revelation about the psychology of women explains why they must fight the way they do. Accordingly, "women are overcome by the spirit of sexual immorality more than man (αἱ γυναῖκες ἡττῶνται τῷ πνεύματι τῆς πορνείας ὑπὲρ τὸν ἄνθρωπον)" (5:3). This reflects a widely attested view that women have less control over their sexual passions (and therefore need men to control them for them).[60] The reference to "the spirit of sexual wrongdoing (τῷ πνεύματι τῆς πορνείας)" is a clear allusion back to 3:3. The same notion comes to expression in 6:2-3, where, in warning against men and women being alone together, the author asserts that continuous meetings are for women "an incurable disease" (νόσος ἀνίατος). Not the meetings themselves, but the desire to have sexual intercourse appears to be the key factor in the disease. They cannot help themselves and are therefore dangerous.

Having explained why women fight, the author then explains how they do so:

καὶ ἐν καρδίᾳ μηχανῶνται κατὰ τῶν ἀνθρώπων,
καὶ διὰ τῆς κοσμήσεως πλανῶσιν αὐτῶν πρῶτον τὰς διανοίας,
καὶ διὰ τοῦ βλέμματος τὸν ἰὸν ἐνσπείρουσι,
καὶ τότε τῷ ἔργῳ αἰχμαλωτίζουσιν.
And in their hearts they plot against men,
And by their adornment they deceive first their minds,
And by their glance they sow the poison,
And then they take them captive by the (accomplished) act. (5:3).

The negative imagery is striking: they plot, deceive, sow poison, take captive.[61] They do so "by their adornment (διὰ τῆς κοσμήσεως)", which can refer to

---

[60] On Gen 3:16 LXX and the notion of insatiable female sexuality, see Loader, *Septuagint*, 47-49.

[61] Cf. Jdt 16:5-6, which celebrates Judith's overcoming of Holofernes as a victory won not by young men, nor sons of titans, nor giants, but "with the hand of a female": "Ioudith the daughter of Merari undid him with the beauty of her face". On this see Loader,

clothing, but also to cosmetics, and "by their glance (διὰ τοῦ βλέμματος)", that is, by catching a man's eye. Women are "evil", therefore, in the sense that they are the enemy when they act in this way. Bringing this section full circle by the inclusio in 5:4 the author reasserts: "For a woman cannot force a man (οὐ γὰρ δύναται γύνη ἄνθρωπον βιάσασθαι)". Men are not bound to face defeat! This means they are also responsible for their actions and can resist the danger such women pose. It also means that for the author women are by nature problematic and always share some of the blame for men's misdeeds because they constantly harass them with their weakly controlled sexual passions, a standpoint which easily plays itself out in blaming the victim in situations of abuse right through to modern times.[62]

In 5:5 the author makes a transition, which on the one hand picks up the issue of adornment from 5:2-3 and at the same time leads into the illustration of the women's seductive impact on the Watchers. Reuben's offspring are told: "Flee, therefore, sexual immorality (φεύγετε οὖν τὴν πορνείαν)". This reiterates the theme running through the testament and probably plays on the account of Joseph's literal flight from the Egyptian woman. Paul uses an identical exhortation in 1 Cor 6:18. Both are probably inspired by Joseph's flight, but Paul's concern is prostitution, Reuben's more generally with women as dangerous.[63] The author then adds that men should therefore control their wives and daughters, who, we have just heard, need to be controlled because of their inherent psychological weakness according to the angel's revelation (5:5). They must not be allowed to engage in such warfare against men. They should not adorn their heads and faces (ἵνα μὴ κοσμῶνται τὰς κεφαλὰς καὶ τὰς ὄψεις αὐτῶν) – otherwise they will face eternal punishment (5:5). This is the other side of the coin from the exhortation to men not to give attention to women's faces, their beauty (3:10; 4:1).

The author then illustrates the danger which such women pose by retelling the myth of the Watchers (5:6-7). "For thus they bewitched the Watchers before the flood (οὕτως γὰρ ἔθελξαν τοὺς ἐγρηγόρους πρὸ τοῦ κατακλυσμοῦ)". He appears to know the version of the myth in the *Book of the Watchers* and to have interpreted the report of Asael's instruction, leading to the situation where men

---

Pseudepigrapha on Sexuality, 185-214, esp. p. 208; also Hollander and de Jonge, *Commentary*, 103.

[62] On this see Kirchhoff, "Testamente," 479, 482; Ulrichsen, *Grundschrift*, 293.

[63] Brian Rosner, "A Possible Quotation of Test. Reuben 5:5 in 1 Corinthians 6,18A," *JTS* 43 (1992) 123-27, argues for Paul's dependence, pointing to three significant parallels. God's indwelling as important for chastity (1 Cor 6:19; cf. *T. Jos.* 10:1-3; glorifying God (1 Cor 6:20; cf. *T. Jos.* 8:5) and this warning about fleeing sexual immorality (1 Cor 6:19; cf. *T. Reub.* 5:5), concluding that they "are surely too remarkable to be written off as sheer coincidence" (126-27), but the parallels are spread and apart from *T. Reub.* 5:5 not linguistically close.

used their new knowledge to create jewellery and cosmetics (*1 Enoch* 8:1-2), as implying that this in turn led to the Watchers' being seduced by the women.[64] The author clearly lays blame on the women, just as he does in the discourse which precedes. And similarly at the same time he does not therefore absolve the Watchers from all responsibility. Accordingly the author recounts of the Watchers' seeing the women: "as these looked at them continually. They lusted after one another (κἀκεῖνοι συνεχῶς ὁρῶντες αὐτὰς ἐγένοντο ἐν ἐπιθυμίᾳ ἀλλήλων)" (5:6). The Watchers should not have kept looking at the women (cf. 3:10; 4:1). The second half of this statement presents some difficulties because it suggests that the effect on the Watchers was that they lusted after each other. This may be understood as the effect of women's sexuality: it awakened their sexual desires and they even directed them towards each other in what would have to be homosexual desire. If so, that is not developed further here (cf. *T. Naph* 3:3-5 and its discussion below). Alternatively, and more probably, the author has both the women and the Watchers in view when he speaks of mutual lust.

The author continues his account with some new psychologising: "and they conceived the act in their mind (καὶ συνέλαβον τῇ διανοίᾳ τὴν πρᾶξιν)" (5:6). As in the account of Reuben's response to "female nakedness" in 3:12, the word συνέλαβον appears with its double meaning which we can express with the English translation, "conceive". As in 3:12, the mind (διάνοια) becomes pregnant with the deed. The account continues: "and they changed themselves into the shape of men,[65] and they appeared to them when they were having sexual intercourse with their husbands (καὶ μετεσχηματίζοντο εἰς ἀνθρώπους, καὶ ἐν τῇ συνουσίᾳ τῶν ἀνδρῶν αὐτῶν συνεφαίνοντο αὐταῖς)". *T. Naph.* 3:5 portrays this change of order as central to their wrongdoing.

Instead of an act of sexual intercourse between the women and the Watchers, however, the author reports that the angels appeared to the women while they were having sexual intercourse (συνουσία) with their husbands. Probably the author meant this to indicate sexual fantasy. Perhaps he envisaged something more supernatural. In any case his account avoids the assumption that acts of sexual intercourse took place between the women and the Watchers. Instead he tells us: "And they, lusting in their mind after their appearances, bore giants; for the Watchers appeared to them as reaching unto heaven (κἀκεῖναι ἐπιθυμοῦσαι τῇ διανοίᾳ τὰς φαντασίας αὐτῶν ἔτεκον γίγαντας· ἐφαίνοντο γὰρ αὐταῖς οἱ ἐγρήγοροι ἕως τοῦ οὐρανοῦ φθάνοντες)" (5:7). The assumption here appears to be that the women became pregnant to the Watchers by fantasising about them while having intercourse with their husbands. The reference to size may refer to size generally (cf. *Sib. Or.* 1 87-103, which depicts them as bigger than giants)

---

[64] See my discussion in Loader, *Enoch, Levi, and Jubilees*, 17-18.
[65] Cf. 2 Cor 11:13-15; *T. Job* 6:4; 17:2; 23:1; *T. Sol.* 20:13; Philo *QG* 1.92.

since angelic figures are sometimes envisaged as being so great their heads touch the sky (*Gos. Pet.* 40), but alternatively it may refer to the size of their penises. Penis length is of interest in describing the Watchers also in *1 Enoch*, but only to the extent of describing them as being like those of horses (88:1).

The psycho-physiology is complicated, given that the child comes from implantation of male seed. The author must imagine that the combination of the women's lusting after these big Watchers and the fact that they were at the time engaging in sexual intercourse, made it somehow easier for the angelic seed to be implanted in them. The notion that an angelic being might implant seed in the womb of a woman without having intercourse with her, provided she is in a receptive state, appears to be assumed in stories of virginal conception of Jesus (Matt 1:18; Luke 1:31, 35) and of Melchizedek (*2 Enoch* 71:30).[66] The author mentions the giants, but says nothing more about them or their activities. His focus is on the dangers which women posed, illustrated by what happened to the Watchers, though without exonerating the Watchers.

In 6:1 the author repeats the exhortation of 5:5 in slightly different terms, thus creating another inclusio which brings this section to a conclusion: "Beware therefore of sexual immorality (φυλάσσεσθε οὖν ἀπὸ τῆς πορνείας)"; cf. "Flee, therefore, sexual immorality (φεύγετε οὖν τὴν πορνείαν)" (5:5). The author reinforces this exhortation with further explanation: "and if you wish to be pure in mind, guard your senses from every woman (lit. female) (καὶ εἰ θέλετε καθαρεύειν τῇ διανοίᾳ, φυλάσσετε τὰς αἰσθήσεις ἀπὸ πάσης θηλείας)". The senses (αἰσθήσεις) are the vehicle through which what is seen or experienced reaches the mind in the author's psychology. In 3:3 the author had described the spirit of sexual immorality as residing in the senses (ταῖς αἰσθήσεσιν). Protecting oneself from woman as "female" (θηλείας), again being used somewhat impersonally, similarly to the reference to nakedness in 3:14, means protecting oneself from danger. By implication that means not doing as the Watchers did: looking continuously at women, nor doing as Reuben: looking at female nakedness. It means not looking at their adorned faces and heads, their beauty, and avoiding being alone with them.

As in 5:5, the author makes this exhortation in association not only with avoiding the danger which women pose, but also with concern about controlling women, so that 6:2 returns to what men should tell women and for a moment the author even seems concerned that women, too, be pure in mind: "And command the women likewise not to associate with men that they, too, may be pure in mind

---

[66] David R. Jackson, *Enochic Judaism: Three Defining Paradigm Exemplars* (Library of Second Temple Studies 49; London: T&T Clark, 2004) notes Egyptian mythological tradition about such impregnation by an angel (65). See also Loader, *Pseudepigrapha on Sexuality*, 55.

(κἀκείναις δὲ ἐντείλασθε μὴ συνδυάζειν ἀνθρώποις, ἵνα καὶ αὐταὶ καθαρεύωσι τῇ διανοίᾳ)". Women should not be alone with men, nor men with women. The author then offers further explanation, based on his assumptions about women's psychology: "For the continuous meetings, even though the impious deed is not performed are to them an irremediable disease and to us an eternal reproach of Beliar (αἱ γὰρ συνεχεῖς συντυχίαι, κἂν μὴ πραχθῇ τὸ ἀσέβημα, αὐταῖς μὲν ἐστι νόσος ἀνίατος, ἡμῖν δὲ ὄνειδος τοῦ Βελιὰρ αἰώνιον)" (6:3). Here, again, we find the notion that women in such situations cannot help themselves if they keep meeting with men. They will want to sleep with them. On the male side, the author is equally pessimistic: such constant meetings will inevitably lead to people having sex and that will bring shame, including being ridiculed by Beliar, a motif already used in 4:7.

In 6:4 the author summarises his argument: "for sexual wrongdoing has neither understanding nor piety in itself, and all jealousy dwells in its desire (ὅτι ἡ πορνεία οὔτε σύνεσιν οὔτε εὐσέβειαν ἔχει ἐν ἑαυτῇ, καὶ πᾶς ζῆλος κατοικεῖ ἐν τῇ ἐπιθυμίᾳ αὐτῆς)" (cf. Sir 25:2 on the adulterer lacking understanding). As in 4:6, we return in 6:4 to the personification of πορνεία ("sexual immorality"): it has no understanding or piety. In other words sexual immorality is foolishness and disobedience towards God and the Law. In 6:4b the author shifts rather abruptly to another possible subtheme: "jealousy" (ζῆλος), but, rather than exploit it, the author appears to have introduced it only as a point of transition to jealousy in a general sense, directed in future towards the sons of Levi (6:5). It will become the theme of the following testament. With that the author moves away from the theme of sexual immorality and does not return to it in this testament.

Conclusion

This testament is of major significance for understanding attitudes towards sexuality in the work as a whole. It employs popular psychology to explain why one should keep the commandments and not engage in sexual immorality. While it employs a demonological framework in speaking of spirits from Beliar that lead people astray, the actual leading astray is explained psychologically.[67] In this the body and body parts are good or neutral, as are its senses, and desires, including sexual desire. Sexual intercourse and procreation belong together and seeking

---

[67] Similarly Kirchhoff, "Testamente," who notes that the author is employing not mythology but metaphor and dealing with causal processes (479). See also Niebuhr, *Gesetz und Paränese*, who notes the tendency to objectivise (156), and also to differentiate and to internalise (157), the inner person being the basis for good behaviour.

sexual intercourse just for pleasure is sin.[68] The author depicts a process that is set off by the sexual gaze which corrupts the mind, making control difficult. It is further complicated by the fact that, unless totally incapacitated (such as when drunk or asleep), women are always wanting men to have sex with them and have less capacity to control their sexual desires and so are dangerous. This means women are always liable to blame. This goes beyond negative statements about women in wisdom literature hitherto and also arguably beyond what we find in Philo and Josephus, which see women as weak and inferior, in that it attributes propensity to evil not just to some, but to all women.[69]

Men do not need to be overcome by the combination of women's attractiveness and wiles, and their own inner dynamic, but they are best to avoid allowing the process to begin in the first place and should avoid looking at women in this way. As Kugler notes, "self-control and sexual constraint were highly prized virtues" in the socio-historical context of the Graeco-Roman world "and the way to achieve them was generally thought to be through self-discipline and education of the mind and soul".[70] Though employing Stoic ideas the author still sets them within the broader overarching framework of the will of God, informed by Jewish presuppositions grounded in Torah and illustrated by examples drawn from Genesis. The testament says little that is positive about human sexuality, though its brief mention of marriage as a norm and its listing of sexual intercourse and procreation as gifts of creation indicate that sexual relations and sexual desire are positive within their defined place and purpose.

---

[68] Marinus de Jonge, "Rachel's Virtuous Behavior in the Testament of Issachar," in *Greeks, Romans, and Christians: Essays in Honor of Abraham J. Malherbe* (ed. David L. Balch, Everett Ferguson, and Wayne A. Meeks; Minneapolis: Fortress, 1990) 340-52, notes that Josephus' comments on the Essenes reflect very similar values to those found in *T. Reuben* 5 (348). See also the discussion of Philo and pleasure and procreation, 1.2.2.6.1-2, and on the Essenes and Therapeutai, 1.2.3.5, and of Josephus on the place of sexual experience 2.4.13, and on the Essenes 2.3.4 above. De Jonge notes that the view was also widespread in early Christianity that procreation was the sole purpose of sexual intercourse (350).

[69] So Max Küchler, *Frühjüdische Weisheitstraditionen: Zum Fortgang weisheitlichen Denkens im Bereich des frühjüdischen Jahweglaubens* (OBO 26; Fribourg: Universitätsverlag; Göttingen: Vandenhoeck und Ruprecht, 1979), citing as parallels: Prov 11:16; 12:4; Sir 25:13 – 26:18, 19-27 (446). Similarly Reinhard Weber, *Das Gesetz im hellenistischen Judentum: Studien zum Verständnis und zur Funktion der Thora von Demetrios bis Pseudo-Phokylides* (ARGU 10; Frankfurt: Peter Lang, 2000) 157.

[70] Kugler, *Testaments*, 91, illustrating his point with reference to Isocrates, *On the Peace* 119 and Musonius, *Fragments* 12.

3.3 The Testament of Simeon

This testament concerns itself with envy, citing Simeon's envy of Joseph. It employs the language of "spirits of deceit (τῶν πνευμάτων τῆς πλάνης)" (3:1; 6:6) and identifies envy as one of its spirits which blinded Simeon (2:7) and should be guarded against (3:1; 4:5, 7). However in the conclusion to the ethical exhortations it somewhat abruptly touches on the theme of sexual immorality: "And guard against committing sexual immorality, because sexual immorality is the mother of all evils, separating from God and bringing near to Beliar (καὶ φυλάσσεσθε τοῦ μὴ πορνεύειν· ὅτι ἡ πορνεία μήτηρ ἐστὶ πάντων τῶν κακῶν, χωρίζουσα θεοῦ καὶ προσεγγίζουσα τῷ Βελιάρ)" (5:3). This recalls *T. Reub.* 4:6 which also speaks of sexual immorality as "separating from God" (χωρίζουσα θεοῦ) and in the next verse depicts its consequences as becoming a laughingstock before Beliar (*T. Reub.* 4:7). The new element here in *T. Simeon* is the claim that sexual immorality is the mother of all evil. This may well connect to what immediately follows, where Simeon cites the writing of Enoch (5:4). There it comes at the beginning of the predictive section, which, as in *T. Reuben*, enjoins among other things respect for Levi and his successors, but it also happens to be the case that the *Book of the Watchers* depicts the origin of all evil as brought about by the Watchers' sexual immorality, a theme exploited in *T. Reub.* 5:6-7. It also continues the theme of sexual immorality: "For I have seen in the writing of Enoch that your sons will be destroyed with you in sexual immorality (ἑώρακα γὰρ ἐν χαρακτῆρι γραφῆς Ἐνὼχ ὅτι υἱοὶ ὑμῶν μεθ' ὑμῶν ἐν πορνείᾳ φθαρήσονται)" (*T. Sim.* 5:4). It is not clear to which event this refers. Beyond this brief focus on sexual immorality, sexual themes do not appear elsewhere in the work.

Somewhat surprisingly, given the attention to Levi and Simeon's exploits in response to the abduction of Dinah in the *Testament of Levi* (see immediately below), we find no reference to the event in Simeon's testament, perhaps because it was less suited to its theme of ζῆλος as envy, though it was certainly relevant to ζῆλος as zeal! As Kugel observes, *T. Sim.* 5:4-6 appears to reflect an interpretation of Gen 49:5-7 as referring not to the Shechem incident at all but to a later conflict between the brothers themselves in a manner which marginalises the Simeonites, though it also assumes the brothers' deed was fully vindicated.[71] In this he sees this testament reflecting a hard line on intermarriage with gentiles such as we find in *Jubilees* and Judith, in contrast to the more moderate position of the

---

[71] On this see James L. Kugel, "The Rape of Dinah, and Simeon and Levi's Revenge," in James L. Kugel, *The Ladder of Jacob: Ancient Interpretations of the Biblical Story of Jacob and his Children* (Princeton: Princeton University Press, 2006) 36-80, 231-39, 70-73.

T. Levi and *Theodotus* which have Jacob genuinely make such an offer.[72] This remains, however, an interpretation of silence, but a silence which Kugel argues "is almost deafening".[73]

3.4 The Testament of Levi

This testament assumes great importance because of the status given to Levi within the testaments, even though in its Christian redaction Levi's role has been superseded. The testament appears to have drawn on parts of *Aramaic Levi Document*. In passages where material runs parallel, sometimes the author has greatly expanded, sometimes greatly abbreviated. We shall note the relevant parallels.

In 2:2 Levi declares: "I was a young man of about twenty years of age (ὡσεῖ ἐτῶν εἴκοσιν), when, with Simeon, I avenged our sister Dinah on Hamor". Later in 12:5 he says more precisely that he was eighteen when he killed Shechem, but this is a context in which the author appears to be drawing on older material focused on genealogy and dates. The Dinah episode comes into focus again near the end of Levi's first heavenly vision and sojourn (2:5 – 5:6). In 2:3 Levi speaks of seeing "all men corrupting their way (πάντας ... ἀνθρώπους ἀφανίσαντας τὴν ὁδὸν αὐτῶν)"; cf. "for all flesh had corrupted its ways upon the earth (κατέφθειρεν πᾶσα σὰρξ τὴν ὁδὸν αὐτοῦ ἐπὶ τῆς γῆς)" (Gen 6:12); καὶ ἠφάνισαν τὰς ὁδοὺς αὐτῶν (*1 Enoch* 8:2 Syncellus). The allusion is thus probably to the aftermath of the Watchers' sin, but without specific reference to sexual wrongdoing.

In the vision the angel gives Levi a shield and sword (5:3; similarly: Jdt 9:2-4)[74] and instructs him about avenging Dinah: "Execute vengeance on Shechem because of Dinah, and I will be with you, because the Lord has sent me" (5:3). This clearly mandates the act as something appropriate. Accordingly Levi notes his compliance: "And I destroyed the sons of Hamor at that time, as it is written in the heavenly tables" (5:4), perhaps an allusion to the account in *Jubilees*, though

---

[72] Kugel, "Rape of Dinah," 74-75, 79.

[73] Kugel, "Rape of Dinah," 73.

[74] Kugel, "Rape of Dinah," observes the notion of being given a heavenly sword may derive originally from the attempt to explain how two kill a whole town and possibly because of Gen 49:5 (40-41). On the other hand, the reference here to Shechem is probably not to the city, Shechem, but to the individual and accordingly Levi kills only Shechem. So T. Baarda, "The Shechem Episode in the Testament of Levi: A Comparison with Other Traditions," in *Sacred History and Sacred Texts in Early Judaism: A Symposium in Honour of A. S. van der Woude* (CBET 5; ed. J. N. Bremmer and F. García Martínez; Kampen: Pharos, 1992) 11-73, 26.

elsewhere "heavenly tables" can refer to the pentateuch.[75] After the vision we then hear of the action itself. As in *ALD* 1c Levi takes the initiative in advising his father and Reuben (the firstborn), that Jacob would tell the Shechemites to be circumcised (6:3), thus, unlike in Genesis, taking sole initiative (cf. Gen 34:13) and doing so with a view to his plan; hence the explanation: "because I was zealous because of the abomination (βδέλυγμα – cf. *T. Reub.* 3:12; *T. Jud.* 12:8; *T. Dan* 5:5) which they had wrought in Israel" (6:3). This contrasts with Jdt 9:2 and *Theod.* 6, where it is Judith's ancestor, Simeon, who takes the lead role, and with *Jubilees* and Philo (*Migr.* 224; *Mut.* 199-200; and see 1.3.2.7), where both do so but are listed in order of age. Reference to the circumcision is absent in Judith, *LAB*, Philo, and Josephus (see 2.2.6 above), and in the initial account in *Jubilees*, making an appearance only indirectly in later reflection (30:17).

According to MS *c*, Graecus 731, Levi's advice is that the Shechemites *not* be circumcised and both Baarda and Kugel independently have argued on internal grounds for this as the preferred reading, and that it was omitted to bring the narrative into conformity with the Genesis account.[76] It would effectively eliminate the image of Levi from having slaughtered circumcised people and have him instead embody a stance which opposes intermarriage through circumcision as espoused here (and in Theodotus) by Jacob.[77] Simeon and Levi "must have been from the start opposed to circumcision as a means of allowing intermarriage between the two groups".[78] This, they argue, is more plausible than having the text depict Levi deceiving his father.[79] The internal grounds taken on their own are strong. The problem is that this is is the sole attestation among the quite extensive body of external witnesses.

Also going beyond Genesis, but reflected in the account of Theodotus (8), Levi tells us that he killed Shechem and Simeon killed Hamor (6:4), but goes beyond all extant accounts in reporting that the rest of the brothers, not Levi and Simeon, then slaughtered all in the city (6:5; cf. Gen 34:27-29; *Jub.* 30:4; Demetrius; Theodotus; Josephus *A.J.* 1.340; *LAB* 8:7). The author does not ignore Jacob's disapproval in Gen 34:40, concerned with consequences for his security,

---

[75] See the discussion in Baarda, "Shechem Episode," who notes *Jubilees'* mention of the recording of Levi's deed on heavenly tablets in 30:19-20, 23, Levi's seeing heavenly writings in *Asen.* 22:13, and the view that in effect it alludes to the pentateuchal account which may well have been understood as existing in heaven before it was later given to Moses (44-45).

[76] Baarda, "Shechem Episode," 36-40; Kugel, "Rape of Dinah," 43-49. Similarly H. C. Kee, "Testaments of the Twelve Patriarchs," *OTP* 1.775-828, 790. Bader, *Tracing the Evidence*, 92.

[77] Kugel, "Rape of Dinah," 45.

[78] Kugel, "Rape of Dinah," 46.

[79] So Kugel, "Rape of Dinah," 47.

but redefines its grounds: Jacob was concerned about the killing of people after they had received circumcision, *de facto* Israelites, and Levi acknowledges also that Jacob's blessing expresses disapproval (6:6; cf. Gen 34:30; 49:6-7; *Jub.* 30:25-26). The author even has Levi acknowledge the act as sin for acting against their father and making him ill (6:7).[80] The hearer knows, however, from the report of the vision, that there was an overriding factor: divine instruction mediated by the angel (5:3).

At one level the execution went far beyond what Torah required in the case of abduction and rape (Deut 22:28-29). The advice offered in sincerity by Jacob (as in *Theod.* 4), seems reasonable in a context where a Gentile is involved, notwithstanding that one text has Levi advise the opposite and the rest have him propose the suggestion insincerely. Jacob's response here and in Theodotus is important evidence for a flexible approach to intermarriage[81] such as we see espoused in *Aseneth*.[82] In the light of this the slaughter clearly needs further explanation. This comes to expression in what follows. Thus in 6:8 the testament speaks of God's sentence.[83] It also provides further justification by lumping together the actions of the people of Hamor with those of Pharaoh and Abimelech who abducted Sarah ("because they wished to do to Sarah also as they did to Dinah our sister, but the Lord prevented them") (6:8),[84] and citing inhospitable behaviour towards Abraham (6:9).[85] In 6:10 the author generalises even further:

---

[80] Baarda, "Shechem Episode," notes that the day on which 6:7 reports that Jacob became ill may refer to the day of blessing, thus alluding as a parenthesis to Gen 48:21, or even, as some MSS read, to Levi's becoming ill (52). See also Hollander and de Jonge, *Commentary*, 147.

[81] So Kugel, "Rape of Dinah," 78.

[82] On this see Loader, *Pseudepigrapha on Sexuality*, 300-34, esp. 327-34. See also William Loader, "The Strange Woman in Proverbs, LXX Proverbs and *Aseneth*," in *Septuagint and Reception: Essays Prepared for the Association for the Study of the Septuagint in South Africa* (ed. Johann Cook; SVT 127; Leiden: Brill, 2009) 97-115, 222-27.

[83] On God's involvement in the act of vengeance see also *Jub.* 30:5, 23; Jdt 9:2-4 where God gives the sword to Simeon; similarly *Asen.* 23:13; *ALD* 1c2; 78; and *Theod.* 6, which also connects it to the mandate to conquer the Canaanites and take their land. Kugel, "Rape of Dinah," notes that Jdt 9:2 reads the words "such a thing ought not to be done" (Gen 34:7) as God's own words (68).

[84] Baarda, "Shechem Episode," notes that the *a*-recension adds Rebecca in 6:8, reflecting Gen 26:1-11, and that in the words: καὶ κύριος ἐκώλυσεν αὐτούς ("but the Lord prevented them") is an echo of God's words to Abimelech about Sarah: ἐφεισάμην ἐγώ σου τοῦ μὴ ἁμαρτεῖν σε ("and I spared you from sinning"*) (Gen 20:6) (28).

[85] Kugel, "Rape of Dinah," suggests that the background is Gen 13:7-8, where intolerance towards Abraham from Lot's people is linked with the Canaanites and Perizzites, mentioned also in Gen 34:30 (60).

"And in the same way they did to all strangers, taking their wives with force (ἐν δυναστείᾳ ἁρπάζοντες τὰς γυναῖκας)[86] and banishing them" (cf. Josephus *A.J.* 1.164, 200-201, 208). At this point the author declares: "But the wrath of the Lord came upon them finally* (ἔφθασε δὲ ἡ ὀργὴ κυρίου ἐπ' αὐτοὺς εἰς τέλος)" (6:11).[87] As Fisk notes, this connects their fate to the previous incidents in a way that sees in the slaughter a punishment for all of them.[88] The Shechemites are treated in 7:1 as representative of "the Canaanites" (cf. 12:5) who are to be driven from their land by Jacob's seed (similarly *Theod.* 6). The focus is not Gentiles *per se*, with whom one may intermarry on the basis of circumcision according to the patriarch Jacob, but more specifically, Canaanites.[89] Indeed, the Shechemites warrant not sympathy but mockery according to 7:2, which then returns to the deed which such violence is to be seen as having rightly avenged: "because also they had wrought folly (ἀφροσύνην) in Israel to defile our sister (μιᾶναι τὴν ἀδελφήν)" (7:3; cf. "They had defiled their sister Dinah" [ἐμίαναν Διναν τὴν ἀδελφὴν αὐτῶν] (Gen 34:13, 27; cf. also 34:5; *Asen.* 23:13). As Kugel notes, behind the assertion of folly may lie the dual meaning of נבל which can refer also to sexual wrongdoing. This is probably also the case in the anti-Samaritan note in Sir 50:25-26 which singles out the people of Shechem as foolish (μωρός) and as "non-people" (Deut 32:21).[90] Levi reports that they then took their sister from there and departed (7:4), a sequence also found in *Theod.* 8, but differing from Gen 34:26, which has her taken before the pillaging of the city.

---

[86] Both *Jub.* 13:11, 13 and 1QapGen ar/1Q20 report that Sarah was not only taken, but taken by force, though not violated as is assumed in the accounts of Dinah's abduction. Baarda, "Shechem Episode," notes the depiction of violence in *Theod.* 4, humiliation in *LAB* 8:7 and Gen 34:2 LXX, and in *Tg. Jon.* Gen 34:2 the rendering of ויקח אתה (Gen 34:2) by ודבר יתה באונסא ("and he took her by force [or robbery]") (16).

[87] This is closely parallelled in 1 Thess 2:16, ἔφθασεν δὲ ἐπ' αὐτοὺς ἡ ὀργὴ εἰς τέλος ("but upon them the wrath came finally"*), MSS *g d m* even preserving the same order. On the possible relationship between the two, including his preference for a common source in tradition, see Baarda, "Shechem Episode," 61-72. Cf. Marinus de Jonge, "Light on Paul from the Testaments of the Twelve Patriarchs? The Testaments and the New Testament," in *Pseudepigrapha of the Old Testament as Part of Christian Literature: The Case of the Testaments of the Twelve Patriarchs and the Greek Life of Adam and Eve* (SVTP 18; Leiden: Brill, 2003) 160-77, who favours seeing a dependence on Paul (173-75).

[88] Bruce N. Fisk, "One Good Story Deserves Another: The Hermeneutics of Invoking Secondary Biblical Episodes in the Narratives of Pseudo-Philo and the Testaments of the Twelve Patriarchs," in *Interpretation of Scripture in Early Judaism and Christianity* (Sheffield: Sheffield Academic Press, 2000) 217-38, 233-35.

[89] So rightly Kugel, "Rape of Dinah," 54-55.

[90] Kugel, "Rape of Dinah," 62-64.

This account is clearly designed to deal with the problem of Jacob's disapproval and does so without denying it, but by overriding it on the one hand with divine mandate and on the other by associating the deed with other potential acts of sexual violence and with divine mandate of the conquest, and if the attestation of one MS is correct, by reporting that Levi had sought to dissuade his father from proposing circumcision. It also explains why the vengeance was taken not just against Shechem, but also against his people, as Canaanites.[91] The designation of the sin as an expression of hostility to strangers, breach of hospitality, is similar to Theodotus (7)[92] and may imply a connection with the breach of hospitality through sexual violence by the inhabitants of Sodom and Gomorrah. The focus of Levi's account is not on the act itself or even any wrong done to Dinah, but primarily on the wrong done to the family. In this sense the sexual element is incidental in the narrative. If *ALD* 1c indicated that Dinah bore some responsibility and herself defiled her family,[93] nothing of that view remains in this testament.[94]

After reporting a second vision (8:1-19), in which he is ordained,[95] Levi speaks of instructions given him by his father, Isaac. These include the words:

πρόσεχε, τέκνον, ἀπὸ τοῦ πνεύματος τῆς πορνείας·
τοῦτο γὰρ ἐνδελεχιεῖ, καὶ μέλλει διὰ τοῦ σπέρματός σου μιαίνειν τὰ ἅγια.
Beware, child, of the spirit of sexual immorality,
for this will continue and will defile the holy things by your seed. (9:9)

The expression πνεύματος τῆς πορνείας ("spirit of sexual immorality") recalls the excursus in *T. Reub.* 2 – 3. The statement is both an instruction, and a prediction of sexual wrongdoing by future priests which will bring defilement on τὰ ἅγια, which could mean "holy things" or even the temple, itself.

---

[91] As Baarda, "Shechem Episode," notes, the generalising of the guilt occurs already in Gen 34:27, and is reflected in *Jub.* 30:2-3; Jdt 9:2; and *Asen.* 23:13 (14-15).

[92] Kugel, "Rape of Dinah," notes that "the resemblance between the interpretation of the Dinah incident underlying the Testament of Levi and that attributed to Theodotus in Eusebius is most striking" and must "represent a common source or tradition" (76).

[93] On this see Loader, *Enoch, Levi, and Jubilees*, 88-89.

[94] On the use of *Aramaic Levi Document* here Marinus de Jonge, "Levi in the Aramaic Levi Document and in the Testament of Levi," in *Pseudepigrapha of the Old Testament as Part of Christian Literature: The Case of the Testaments of the Twelve Patriarchs and the Greek Life of Adam and Eve* (SVTP 18; Leiden: Brill, 2003) 124-39, writes: "The Christian authors of T. Levi would not have dwelt at such length on Levi's role at Shechem, both in 5:1-6:2 and in 6:3-7:4, if this had not been in their *Vorlage*" (137).

[95] The sequence of his deed against Shechem followed by his ordination is similar to *Jub.* 30:4-17, 18, though that account suppresses Jacob's disapproval, mentioning only some discussion of his fears (30:25).

The fact that this is immediately followed in 9:10 by a word about marriage should be understood in the sense that appropriate marriage is the alternative to sexual immorality and, as in Paul, a safeguard against it (1 Cor 7:2).[96] This makes sense of the instruction to marry while one is young (11:1), which in this case includes at age 28, in contrast to the more usual 30 (9:10). The requirement that Levi (representative of his descendants) is to marry someone without blemish, not defiled (that is, a virgin), and a fellow Jew ("one who has no blemish and has not been defiled and is not of a race of strangers or Gentiles" μὴ ἔχουσαν μῶμον μηδὲ βεβηλωμένην μηδὲ ἀπὸ γένους ἀλλοφύλων ἢ ἐθνῶν), matches the provisions of Lev 21:7, 13-14 according to which a priest may not marry a prostitute, a woman not a virgin, nor a divorcee, and must marry someone of his own kin or race (ἐκ τοῦ γένους αὐτοῦ).

In 9:9-10 the author appears to be reworking earlier material similar to that found in *Aramaic Levi Document*. The comparisons are set out in the table below, using the Athos text, MS *e*, which has a long interpolation 18:2 which appears to be a Greek translation of *ALD*.[97]

Aramaic Levi Document	*Testament of Levi*
14 τέκνον Λευί, πρόσεχε σεαυτῷ ἀπὸ πάσης ἀκαθαρσίας (טומאה)· ἡ κρίσις σου μεγάλη ἀπὸ πάσης σαρκός	
16 πρόσεχε σεαυτῷ ἀπὸ παντὸς συνουσιασμοῦ (פחז) καὶ ἀπὸ πάσης ἀκαθαρσίας (טומאה) καὶ ἀπὸ πάσης πορνείας (זנו). 17 σὺ πρῶτος ἀπὸ τοῦ σπέρματος λάβε (סב) σεαυτῷ καὶ μὴ βεβηλώσης (חלל) τὸ σπέρμα σου μετὰ πόρνων (זנין) ἐκ σπέρματος γὰρ ἁγίου εἶ, καὶ τὸ σπέρμα τοῦ ἁγιασμοῦ σου ἐστίν. 18 ἐγγὺς εἶ κυρίου καὶ σὺ ἐγγὺς τῶν ἁγίων αὐτοῦ, γίνου καθαρὸς ἐν τῷ σώματί σου ἀπὸ πάσης ἀκαθαρσίας (טומאה) παντός ἀνθρώπου	9:9 πρόσεχε, τέκνον, ἀπὸ τοῦ πνεύματος τῆς πορνείας· τοῦτο γὰρ ἐνδελεχιεῖ, καὶ μέλλει διὰ τοῦ σπέρματός σου μιαίνειν τὰ ἅγια. 9:10 λάβε οὖν σεαυτῷ γυναῖκα, ἔτι νέος ὤν, μὴ ἔχουσαν μῶμον μηδὲ βεβηλωμένην μηδὲ ἀπὸ γένους ἀλλοφύλων ἢ ἐθνῶν

---

[96] So Ulrichsen, *Grundschrift*, 293.

[97] I cite the text as emended in Henryk Drawnel, *An Aramaic Wisdom Text from Qumran: A New Interpretation of the Levi Document* (JSJSup 86; Leiden: Brill, 2004) 118-24. See also the table of comparison of the contents of the two works in overview in Kugler, *Testaments*, 50. See also de Jonge, "Levi," on what he sees as Christian use of *ALD* in abbreviated form at this point (137).

14 Levi, beware, my son, of every impurity; your judgement is greater than all flesh	9:9 Beware, son, of the spirit of sexual immorality. For this will continue, and will defile holy things (or: the temple) through your seed.
16 First of all, beware, my son, of every act of illicit sexual intercourse and impurity and of every act of sexual wrongdoing.	9:10 Take, therefore, for yourself a wife. While you are still young, one who has no blemish and has not been defiled and is not of a race of strangers or Gentiles.
17 And you, take for yourself a wife from my family so that you may not defile your seed with illicit sexual partners, because you are a holy seed. And holy is your seed like the Holy One, for a holy priest you are called for all the seed of Abraham.	
18 You are close to God and close to all his holy ones, now be pure in your flesh from every impurity of any man. (Drawnel adapted)[98]	

Here the author of the testament appears to have used material from *Aramaic Levi Document*, but, as in other discourse material, modified it significantly. He prefers his own terminology, "spirit of sexual immorality", reworks the warning about judgement into a prediction, and revises the instruction about marriage so that it applies now to any Israelite, but adding the qualifications that she not be blemished, defiled, or from another race or a Gentile, and has omitted the rationale related to Levi's holiness and closeness to the angels.

In 11:1 we then hear that Levi took Melcha as his wife, when aged 28. The marriage of his daughter Jochebed to her nephew Amram (12:4) was problematic, because it contravened Lev 18:12, though it is clearly attested in Exod 6:19. The account seeks to ameliorate this breach to some extent by informing hearers that "they were born on the same day" (12:4). Here we learn also that Levi was in fact 18 when he killed Shechem (12:5), and, as 11:1 had already informed us, 28 when he married (12:5). Between the instruction about sexual immorality and marriage in *ALD* 14, 16-18, and its detail about Levi's genealogy (62-81), is extensive instruction which Isaac went on to add about sacrifices and their preparation (19-61) of which the testament has preserved only a summary in 9:11-14. The author returns to *ALD* in 11:1 – 12:7, reproducing much of the significant detail found in 62-81, including the material discussed above, and omission of any reference to Aaron, and without significant differences.

Directly addressing his children Levi cites Enoch to predict future impiety of his descendants (14:1-2). They will "rob from the offerings of the Lord and steal

---

[98] See my discussion in Loader, *Enoch, Levi, and Jubilees*, 95-103.

from his portions and before sacrificing to the Lord take the choice things, eating contemptuously with prostitutes* (καὶ πρὸ τοῦ θυσιάσαι κυρίῳ λήψεσθε τὰ ἐκλεκτά, ἐν καταφρονήσει ἐσθίοντες μετὰ πορνῶν)" (14:5). The catalogue continues with reference to greed (πλεονεξίᾳ) and the prediction:

> τὰς ὑπάνδρους βεβηλώσετε,
> καὶ παρθένους 'Ιερουσαλὴμ μιανεῖτε,
> καὶ πόρναις καὶ μοιχαλίσι συναφθήσεσθε,
> θυγατέρας ἐθνῶν λήψεσθε εἰς γυναῖκας,
> καθαρίζοντες αὐτὰς καθαρισμῷ παρανόμῳ,
> καὶ γενήσεται ἡ μεῖξις ὑμῶν Σόδομα καὶ Γόμορρα ἐν ἀσεβείᾳ.
> you will pollute married women,
> defile virgins of Jerusalem,
> be joined with prostitutes and adulteresses,
> take to wives daughters of the Gentiles,
> purifying them with unlawful purification,
> and your union will be like Sodom and Gomorrah in ungodliness.* (14:6)

This catalogue resembles accusations made elsewhere against corrupt priesthood. Here the sins are adultery, illicit sex with virgins, prostitutes, and adulterous women, and marrying Gentiles. The comparison with Sodom and Gomorrah focuses on sexual immorality there, which would be understood either as homosexual acts or as homosexual violence, though references elsewhere suggest it is the former. Here the accusation need not be understood as indicating that the future descendants would engage in homosexual acts, but their sexual immorality would be on a par in seriousness with that of the people of Sodom and Gomorrah.

One finds similar accusations in *Pss. Sol.* 2:11 about openly engaging in prostitution in the light of day and in 2:13 about profaning daughters who engaged in illicit intercourse, probably also referring to prostitution, and in *Pss. Sol.* 8:9-10 about incest and adultery and coming to priestly service unclean through contact with menstrual blood. *Pss. Sol.* 16:7-8 contains a prayer which closely matches the *Testament*' concerns:

> ἐπικράτησόν μου ὁ θεός ἀπὸ ἁμαρτίας πονηρᾶς
> καὶ ἀπὸ πάσης γυναικὸς πονηρᾶς σκανδαλιζούσης ἄφρονα
> 8 καὶ μὴ ἀπατησάτω με κάλλος γυναικὸς παρανομούσης
> καὶ παντὸς ὑποκειμένου ἀπὸ ἁμαρτίας ἀνωφελοῦς
> Keep me back from wicked sin
> and from every wicked woman who makes the foolish stumble (sexually)
> 8 and let not the beauty of a woman who transgresses the Law deceive me
> nor anyone subject to useless sin.* (16:7-8).

The only other reference pertinent to sexuality comes in the list of wicked priests who are to come in the seventh week of the seventh jubilee, in other words, at the end of time, where the author apparently places himself. They are described as "idolators, contentious, lovers of money, arrogant, lawless" and then also as "lascivious, abusers of children and beasts (ἀσελγεῖς, παιδοφθόροι καὶ κτηνοφθόροι)" (17:11), a clear allusion to pederasty and bestiality.

3.5   The Testament of Judah

Like the *Testament of Levi*, this testament carries great significance because, as the former, itself, indicated, Judah (together with his royal descendants) is second ranked among the sons of Jacob after Levi (and his priestly descendants). The *Testament of Judah* begins with Judah's many exploits in face of danger from animals, armies, and giants (1 – 7; but cf. 13:2). Then in 8:2 it has Judah report his marriage to Bath-shua, the daughter of the Adullamite king: "He made a feast for us and persuading (παρακαλέσας) me he gave me his daughter Bath-shua to wife". At this point the information seems unproblematic except for hearers who knew the story well, for he had thereby married a Canaanite, contrary to divine instruction (cf. Gen 28:1 to Jacob), but nothing of that comes to expression here. In 8:3 the mention of their children, Er, Onan, and Shelah, and that "two of them the Lord killed" signals a problem. But first we hear of the battle between Jacob and Esau (9). Then 10:1-6 reports the scheming of Bath-shua, who as a Canaanite sought to prevent Er having children by his wife Tamar of Mesopotamia, daughter of Aram (cf. *Jub.* 41:1-2 which reports that Judah chose Er's wife against his will, since he had wanted to marry a Canaanite). Accordingly an angel of the Lord (cf. Gen 38:7; *Jub.* 41:3 "the Lord") killed him on the third day (an element unique to this retelling) (10:2). Onan, to whom she was given by levirate marriage still during the days of the wedding feast (presumably set for seven days, also an element unique to this account), also colluded with his mother, initially not engaging in intercourse with her for a year and then doing so under threat from Judah, but on his mother's advice spilling his semen on the ground, and was also killed (10:4-5).[99] As in Genesis, what is envisaged was probably *coitus*

---

[99] Esther Marie Menn, *Judah and Tamar (Genesis 38) in Ancient Jewish Exegesis: Studies in Literary Form and Hermeneutics* (JSJSup 51; Leiden: Brill, 1997), notes that, unlike in Gen 38:8, the author does not have Judah instruct him to produce children from the beginning (145) nor have him promise Tamar the third son, thus making him less culpable (149). De Jonge, "Rachel," notes that Tamar's legitimate wish to have children, denied to her by her husband and his family (Genesis 38), receives no attention in the testament (345).

interruptus, since Judah reports that "he had sexual intercourse with her" (συνῆλθε μὲν αὐτῇ) (cf. *Jubilees* which rewrites the story in a way that implies no intercourse has taken place and so implies masturbation) (41:5).[100]

The account in Genesis 38 gives no such prominence to Bath-shua, so that it is very likely that in this the author stands under the influence of the account in *Jubilees*, where she is behind these events and is described as hating Tamar because she is not a Canaanite, as here (41:2, 7). There, as here, it is Bath-shua who prevented Judah from giving Tamar to Shelah when he came of age (10:6; cf. *Jub.* 41:7). The report that she found a Canaanite wife for Shelah (11:3) is a distinctive element in the account. The fact that this is assumed to obviate Shelah's taking Tamar in addition on the basis of levirate law may well indicate that the author assumes monogyny as a norm, as Menn suggests.[101] As in *Jubilees*, the wickedness of Bath-shua enhances the severity of Judah's sin in marrying her in the first place, because, as he knew, "the race of Canaan is wicked" (11:1; cf. *Jub.* 25:1-2). Ironically, as Menn notes, "the ideal of marriage within one's own race is held most strongly not by any member of Abraham's family, but rather by a member of the very Canaanite race that Israel is advised to avoid in biblical law".[102]

Judah's foolishness in marrying a Canaanite becomes a major motif in what follows. Like Reuben, he blames "the disposition of youth (τὸ διαβούλιον τῆς νεότητος)" for blinding his heart (11:1; cf. *T. Reub.* 3:8; 2:9;1:6; also *T. Jud.* 18:3, 6; 19:4; *T. Sim.* 2:7). Thus we return to Judah's own marriage in the first place, reported without explicit evaluation in 8:2. Already in 11:2 Judah begins his analysis: "When I saw her pouring wine, I was deceived owing to the intoxication of wine, and I fell for her* (καὶ ἰδὼν αὐτὴν οἰνιχοοῦσαν ἐν μέθῃ οἴνου ἠπατήθην, καὶ συνέπεσα πρὸς αὐτήν)". συνέπεσα appears also in 13:3, 7; *T. Jos.* 9:5. But first the author continues the story of the disasters which ensued from Bath-shua's wickedness, especially her preventing Tamar finding a husband in Shelah.

The account of Judah's sin with Tamar has distinctive features. Instead of simply depicting Tamar as deciding to act as prostitute, it elaborates, indicating that "she adorned herself in bridal array,[103] and sat in the city of Enan by the

---

[100] See Loader, *Enoch, Levi, and Jubilees*, 180-81.

[101] Menn, *Judah and Tamar*, 148. She notes that Deut 25:5-10 loses its prescriptive force and becomes an event in *T. Zeb.* 3:4 (148).

[102] Menn, *Judah and Tamar*, 146.

[103] Menn, *Judah and Tamar*, suggests that this motif may derive from the fact that כלה (Gen 38:11) can mean "daughter-in-law" or "bride" and that LXX translates νύμφη ("bride") (151).

gate",[104] adding the explanation: "For it was a law of the Amorites that she who was about to marry should sit in prostitution by the gate for seven days"* (νόμος γὰρ 'Αμορραίων, τὴν γαμοῦσαν προκαθίσαι ἐν πορνείᾳ ἕπτα ἡμέρας παρὰ τὴν πύλην) (12:2).[105] This may well derive from an interpretation of the Hebrew word used in the Genesis account, קדשה, meaning cult prostitute (Gen 38:21-22)[106] and reflect practices like the one Herodotus records of Assyrian women offered their virginity to goddess Mylitta (= Aphrodite).[107]

The author further embellishes the account depicting Judah as having become drunk at the waters of Kozebah (12:3). The mention of Kozebah, identified with Khezib in 1 Chr 4:22, related to where Shelah born (Gen 38:5), may reflect an etymological play since כזב means "to deceive", thus alluding to what will take place.[108] The drunkenness may well be inspired by Gen 49:11-12.[109] It might to some degree ameliorate Judah's guilt (cf. also the depiction of Bilhah as drunk in *T. Reub.* 3:13), but it serves the author's purpose well to develop his teaching about abuse of wine. His drunken state, which might recall the infamous drunkenness of Noah and Lot, impaired his ability both to recognise Tamar and to resist her attraction: "I did not recognize her because of the wine, and her beauty deceived me through the fashion of the adorning (οὐκ ἐπέγνων αὐτὴν ἀπὸ τοῦ οἴνου· καὶ ἠπάτησέ με τὸ κάλλος αὐτῆς διὰ τοῦ σχήματος τῆς κοσμήσεως)" (12:3). Here we find echoes of the instruction about κάλλος in *T. Reub.* 4:1 and the excursus in 5:1-4, which speaks of women's σχήματα.

---

[104] Menn, *Judah and Tamar*, notes that the LXX translates ותתעלף ("wrapped herself up") Gen 38:14 by ἐκαλλωπίσατο ("beautified her face") which has influenced the account here (153).

[105] Menn, *Judah and Tamar*, notes that the reference to the Amorites recalls Judah's own deception in posing as an Amorite with Dan when entering Gaash (7:2-3) (152).

[106] Menn, *Judah and Tamar*, observes that Deut 23:18 forbids sexual relations with a "consecrated woman" τελεσφόρος or "consecrated man" τελισκόμενος (151).

[107] Herodotus *Hist.* 1.199. So Weigand Naumann, *Untersuchungen über den apokryphen Jeremiasbrief* (BZAW 25; Giessen: Töpelmann, 1913) 1-31. See also Loader, *Pseudepigrapha on Sexuality*, 80-81 and the critical discussion of this passage in Herodotus in Stephanie Lynn Budin, *The Myth of Sacred Prostitution in Antiquity* (Cambridge: Cambridge University Press, 2008) 105-11.

[108] So James L. Kugel, "Judah and the Trial of Tamar," in James L. Kugel, *The Ladder of Jacob: Ancient Interpretations of the Biblical Story of Jacob and his Children* (Princeton: Princeton University Press, 2006) 169-85, 256-57, 177-78. Similarly, Menn, *Judah and Tamar*, 152.

[109] So Kugel, "Judah and the Trial of Tamar," 173; his greed he sees inspired by Gen 37:26. In neither instance does the LXX supply these motifs. Menn, *Judah and Tamar*, suggests the motif of greed may derive from Samuel's prediction in 1 Sam 8:11-18 and the account of Solomon's excesses (140).

Judah's offer does not include the promise of a kid, as in Gen 38:17 (and *Jub.* 41:12 where it comes up after offering the pledges), but only the pledges listed as: "my staff and my girdle and the diadem of kingship" (τὴν ῥάβδον μου καὶ τὴν ζώνην καὶ τὸ διάδημα τῆς βασιλείας) (12:4). This contrasts with "ring, neck chain, and staff (Gen 38:18; *Jub.* 41:11). The author has shaped the detail to fit his metaphorical exposition in 15:1-6. He adds further distinctive elements: instead of reporting Tamar's trial (Gen 38:24), the author reports that Judah planned to kill her.[110] She had not only sent the pledges, but also revealed "secret words" (τοὺς ἐν μυστηρίῳ λόγους) spoken during intercourse while he was drunk (οὓς καθεύδων σὺν αὐτῇ ἐν τῇ μέθῃ μου ἐλάλησα) (12:6).[111] In 12:7 the author rather awkwardly has Judah wonder if the pledge had been retrieved from another woman, but in his narrative the preceding verse had already shown that this would make little sense. There is also some disorder in his mentioning in 12:8 that he never again had sexual intercourse with her: "I did not again come near her until my death, because I had done this abomination in all Israel (ἀλλ' οὐδὲ ἤγγισα αὐτῇ ἔτι ἕως θανάτου μου, ὅτι βδέλυγμα ἐποίησα τοῦτο ἐν παντὶ Ἰσραήλ)"; (cf. Gen 38:26 "And he did not lie with her again" [καὶ οὐ προσέθετο ἔτι τοῦ γνῶναι αὐτήν]) before giving the detail in 12:9 that he had searched for her and thought no one knew.[112]

The narrative then breaks off to report Judah's entering Egypt with Jacob and his brothers (12:11-12). At this point Judah addresses his children, drawing moral lessons from his behaviour: "Do not walk after your lusts, nor in the devices of your dispositions, in the arrogance of your heart (καὶ μὴ πορεύεσθε ὀπίσω τῶν ἐπιθυμιῶν ὑμῶν μηδὲ ἐν ἐνθυμήσεσι διαβουλίων ὑμῶν, ἐν ὑπερηφανίᾳ καρδίας ὑμῶν)" (13:2). This clearly includes a sexual reference. He then tells them: "do not boast of the deeds of strength of your youth" (13:2), which must call into question the first seven chapters of his testament, at least as something to be

---

[110] So Menn, *Judah and Tamar*, who notes that it confirms the image of Judah seeking to remain in control (155).

[111] Kugel, "Judah and the Trial of Tamar," argues the addition of secret words is to add proof, but that it creates inconsistencies in the narrative (180-82). Menn, *Judah and Tamar*, adds: "The repetition of Judah's disclosure of esoteric lore received from worthy male ancestors and God to licentious women emphasizes the grievous nature of his sin" (156).

[112] Menn, *Judah and Tamar*, notes that the author includes nothing of Judah's searching for the mysterious woman (154). See also Cecilia Wassen, "The Story of Judah and Tamar in the Eyes of the Earliest Interpreters," *Literature and Theology* 8 (1994) 354-66, who writes: "The dramatic undercurrent of uncertainty in the biblical narrative regarding the fate of Tamar following the disclosure of her 'illegitimate' pregnancy has completely disappeared in the Testament of Judah. Here, Judah quickly changes the subject in his speech from the description of the seduction scene to his own problematic situation following the disclosure of his fatherhood" (358).

admired. He then focuses on a particular instance of boasting relating to sexual wrongdoing: "in wars no comely woman's face had deceived me (ὅτι ἐν πολέμοις οὐκ ἠπάτησέ με πρόσωπον γυναικὸς εὐμόρφου)", possibly a reference to not having engaged in the common practice of sexual violence in war,[113] and "(I) reproved Reuben my brother because of Bilhah my father's wife (ὠνείδιζον Ῥουβὴμ τὸν ἀδελφόν μου περὶ Βάλλας γυναικὸς πατρός μου)" (13:3). As a consequence he observes: "the spirit of jealousy and sexual immorality arrayed itself in me, until I met Bath-shua the Canaanite and Tamar who was espoused to my sons (τὸ πνεῦμα τοῦ ζήλου καὶ τῆς πορνείας παρετάξατο ἐν ἐμοί, ἕως συνέπεσα εἰς Βησσουὲ τὴν Χαναναίαν καὶ εἰς Θαμὰρ τὴν νυμφευθεῖσαν τοῖς υἱοῖς μου)" (13:3).

The author then revisits each of these two foolish acts. Instead of following his initial inclination, expressed to his future father-in-law, that he consult with Jacob about his marriage to Bath-shua, Judah allowed himself to be persuaded first by the size of the dowry (13:4),[114] then by his father-in-law's strategy of adorning Bath-shua with gold and pearls and having her serve wine at their meal "with the beauty of women" (13:5).[115] Female adornment came under fire already in *T. Reub.* 5:3, 5. Now the author returns to the theme of wine, itself, which, as with Tamar, clouded his vision: "And the wine distorted my vision [lit. turned away my eyes] and pleasure blinded my heart* (καὶ ὁ οἶνος διέστρεψέ μου τοὺς ὀφθαλμούς, καὶ ἠμαύρωσέ μου τὴν καρδίαν ἡ ἡδονή)" (13:6). As a result, he declares: "I became enamoured with her and fell for her* (ἐρασθεὶς αὐτῆς συνέπεσα)" (13:7; similarly 11:2). Judah is quite clear that in taking her as wife he transgressed the commandment of his fathers (13:7; cf. 14:6; *T. Reub.* 3:8). That commandment was about prohibition of intermarriage, implied in Gen 28:1 and everywhere emphasised in *Jubilees*.

The author then connects sexual immorality and abuse of wine. "Wine turns the mind away from the truth and puts into (it) the passion of lust and leads the eyes into error* (ὅτι ὁ οἶνος διαστρέφει τὸν νοῦν ἀπὸ τῆς ἀληθείας, καὶ ἐμβάλλει ὀργὴν ἐπιθυμίας καὶ ὁδηγεῖ εἰς πλάνην τοὺς ὀφθαλμούς)"

---

[113] On this see the discussion of Josephus above (2.4.1).

[114] On the dangers of marrying for dowries see Plato *Leg.* 742E; 774C-E; *Ps.-Phoc.* 199-200; Josephus *Ap.* 2.200.

[115] Kugler, *Testaments*, notes the possible intertextual link with David's fateful marriage to a Bath-shua (1 Chr 3:5; cf. 1 Chr 2:3), which produced a child fated by God to die (2 Sam 12:14, 18) (97). "So not only is the recipient of the *Testaments* compelled to see in the biblical David an example of the tragedies that befall anyone who is afflicted by the Graeco-Roman vice of inordinate desire; he or she is also encouraged to understand that it is God who punishes the human who gives in to unrestrained lust" (97).

(14:1).[116] The exposition which follows unpacks this claim, using the author's psychology. Thus in 14:2 we read of "the spirit of sexual immorality (τὸ ... πνεῦμα τῆς πορνείας)" (cf. *T. Reub.* 3:3), "the pleasures of the mind" (τὰς ἡδονὰς ... τοῦ νοός), and wine as minister or servant (τὸν οἶνον ὡς διάκονον). On the author's construction wine serves to draw together what might be seen as itself neutral, namely "the pleasures of the mind", with a particular way of finding such pleasure: sexual immorality. When he then writes that "the spirit of sexual immorality" and wine "take away the strength of man", the thought appears to be that they lower his resistance. Alternatively the author may reflect the view that excessive engagement in intercourse weakens a man by his losing so much semen.[117] In 14:3 the author goes into further detail about what wine does when a man becomes drunk: "it disturbs the mind with filthy thoughts [leading to] sexual immorality (ἐν διαλογισμοῖς ῥυπαροῖς συνταράσσει τὸν νοῦν εἰς πορνείαν)". This is a somewhat unsophisticated explanation, since the mind itself has the thoughts, the wine if anything lowering the inhibitions. He continues along similar lines: "it heats up the body for sexual intercourse* (καὶ ἐκθερμαίνει τὸ σῶμα πρὸς μεῖξιν)", giving expression to effects of alcohol, often sensed as warming, but which need have nothing to do with directing sexual appetite – if anything, it has to do with level of control. Then he adds: "and if the object of desire is present (καὶ εἰ πάρεστι τὸ τῆς ἐπιθυμίας αἴτιον)", that is, if the woman is present towards whom the sexual desire is directed, "he performs the sin and is not ashamed (πράσσει τὴν ἁμαρτίαν καὶ οὐκ αἰσχύνεται)" (14:3). Here we find the typically dual focus: sin and shame, loss of honour.

This then becomes the focus in what follows, where Judah attributes to drinking too much wine that he disregarded what others would think when he turned to Tamar (14:5), on the one hand, and that he sinned "a great sin" (ἁμαρτίαν μεγάλην). The explication of the sin, "I uncovered the covering of my sons' shame (ἀνεκάλυψα κάλυμμα ἀκαθαρσίας υἱῶν μου)" reflects the prohibition in Lev 18:15, "the shame of your daughter-in-law you shall not uncover for she is the wife of your son; you shall not uncover her shame (ἀσχημοσύνην νύμφης σου οὐκ ἀποκαλύψεις γυνὴ γὰρ υἱοῦ σού ἐστιν οὐκ ἀποκαλύψεις τὴν ἀσχημοσύνην αὐτῆς)". Instead of ἀσχημοσύνη the author uses ἀκαθαρσία (lit. "impurity"). By describing it in this way the author puts the emphasis on contravention of a biblical prohibition, and wrong done to his sons (though they are no longer alive), not on wrong done to Tamar. In 14:6 he similarly turns attention to breaching the divine commandment, which he assumes

---

[116] On the dangers of wine and women see also Hos 4:10-11 LXX; Sir 9:9; 19:2; 26:8-9; Philo *Spec.* 1.148, 150, 192; *Somn.* 2.165; *Mos.* 2.185; *QG* 2.12; *Flacc.* 136; *Agr.* 37-38; Plutarch *Mor.* 12B 496F.

[117] On loss of semen as loss of vitality see Josephus *Ap.* 2.203 and p. 364 above.

applies as much to him as to Jacob, namely not to intermarry outside his own people (Gen 28:1): under the influence of too much wine he agreed to marry a Canaanite (14:6; cf. 13:7).

The author completes this section of his excursus on the dangers of wine with a clarification. He is not promoting abstinence, but moderation in drinking wine (14:7). Recalling the opening thesis, he explains that excess "puts the spirit of deceit into the mind* (ἐμβάλλει εἰς τὸν νοῦν τὸ πνεῦμα τῆς πλάνης)" (14:8) (cf. "it puts the passion of desire into it* [ἐμβάλλει ὀργὴν ἐπιθυμίας]") (14:1). In 14:2 he had singled out the first of the seven spirits which belong to the repertoire of the "spirit of deceit", namely "the spirit of sexual immorality (τὸ ... πνεῦμα τῆς πορνείας)". He then summarises its effects: it produces filthy talk (αἰσχρορρημονεῖν 14:8; cf. διαλογισμοῖς ῥυπαροῖς 14:3), transgression of the law, lack of shame and even belief that what one is doing is good (14:8).

The author then elaborates the obliviousness to appropriate shame of the one "who engages in sexual wrongdoing (ὁ πορνεύων)" (15:1), applying it also to "when someone is a ruler and engages in sexual wrongdoing* (κἂν γὰρ τις βασιλεύσῃ πορνεύων)", who ends up "being stripped naked of his kingship (γυμνούμενος τῆς βασιλείας)" – a neat play on sexuality, nakedness, and shame – "having become the slave of sexual immorality (δουλωθεὶς τῇ πορνείᾳ)" (15:2). The dramatic imagery of kingship, but also of the contrast between slave and king is appropriate on the lips of Judah whose descendants would be Israel's kings. The author does not make specific reference to David and Bathsheba or to Solomon and his wives, but remains general, preferring to illustrate his point by referring to his own deed, which he has previously narrated in a manner which fits his metaphorical application here. Thus his staff represents the stay of his tribe (τὸ στήριγμα τῆς ἐμῆς φυλῆς); his girdle, his power (τὴν δύναμιν); and his diadem, the glory of his kingship (τὴν δοξαν τῆς βασιλείας μου) (15:3). Like Reuben, he repented by abstaining till his old age from wine and meat (15:4; cf. *T. Reub.* 1:10, which adds sweet bread, lit. bread of desire, and strong drink). The statement that he also saw no joy (καὶ πᾶσαν εὐφροσύνην οὐκ εἶδον) (15:4) may well have a sexual reference (cf. ἄρτον ἐπιθυμίας *T. Reub.* 1:10; Esther C 29/14:18). Like Reuben, he, too, receives an angelic revelation and also about women (15:5; cf. *T. Reub.* 5:3; Dan 10:3):

καὶ ἔδειξέ μοι ὁ ἄγγελος τοῦ θεοῦ
ὅτι ἕως τοῦ αἰῶνος καὶ βασιλεῖ καὶ πτωχῷ, αἱ γυναῖκες κατακυριεύουσιν
6 καὶ τοῦ μὲν βασιλέως αἴρουσι τὴν δόξαν,
τοῦ δὲ ἀνδρείου τὴν δύναμιν,
καὶ τοῦ πτωχοῦ τὸ τῆς πτωχείας ἐλάχιστον στήριγμα.
The angel of God showed me
that women have dominion over king and beggar alike forever;

and from the king they take away the glory
and from the valiant man the power
and from the beggar even that little which is the stay of his poverty. (*T. Jud.* 15:5-6)

In *T. Reub.* 5:3 the author already warned against this possibility, so that here the claim means something like: all too often women exercise such dominion. In the author's view this is not just a statement about women as potentially dangerous for men, but also about men's foolishness in acquiescing in such servitude. Rather than portray men as hapless victims, the author is constantly asserting that men need to take responsibility to ensure this does not happen. The author employs his imagery in reverse in a neat chiasm to illustrate what happens when it does, here associating glory with king, power with the valiant man, not previously introduced, and "the stay" with the poor man, set in contrast with the king in 15:5. While men need to take responsibility, clearly the author is expressing the view depicted already in the *T. Reuben*, namely, that when women behave seductively, they are a grave danger to men and that danger is being drawn into sexual wrongdoing by beings who are less able to control their passions. As Menn notes, "Whether the problem is promiscuity or irresponsible avoidance, women are blamed for the sexual misconduct of men in the *Testament of Judah*".[118] The focus is not the man responsible for Tamar's situation but the woman who seduced the patriarch.[119]

In 16:1-5 the author continues his discourse about appropriate use of wine, identifying it as containing "four evil spirits: of lust, of burning desire, of profligacy, of filthy lucre (τέσσαρα πνεύματα πονηρά· ἐπιθυμίας, πυρώσεως, ἀσωτίας, αἰσχροκερδίας)" (16:1). The first two have relation to sexuality. The word ἐπιθυμία featured strongly in the warning against sexual immorality in *T. Reuben* (1:10; 2:4; 4:9; 6:4) and in this context refers to inappropriate sexual desire, hence, lust. The motif of fire (πυρώσεως) in relation to sexual desire was common. We saw it in 14:3 (ἐκθερμαίνει τὸ σῶμα πρὸς μεῖξιν "heats up the body for sexual intercourse"*; cf. also Prov 6:27; 1 Cor 7:9). The focus in 16:2-3 is moderate use of wine as opposed to drunkenness and shamelessness, with the author even commending abstinence for some (16:3). According to 16:4 Judah sinned by sharing "the mysteries of God and men" (καίγε μυστήρια θεοῦ καὶ ἀνθρώπων) with aliens, in this instance, Bath-shua, recalling the author's earlier innovation of the story of Tamar according to which during sexual intercourse he

---

[118] Menn, *Judah and Tamar*, 146.

[119] Menn, *Judah and Tamar*, 156. Wassen, "Story of Judah and Tamar," writes: "the implied author encourages a sense of revulsion towards Tamar and Saba [Bath-shua] by using them to represent seductive women who make men powerless by their snares" (359).

revealed secrets (τοὺς ἐν μυστηρίῳ λόγους 12:6). Nothing indicates what these were.[120]

Next the author connects greed (ἀγαπᾶν ἀργύριον) and gazing on women's beauty (ἐμβλέπειν εἰς κάλλος ... εὐμορφίαν), citing them as reasons for his falling for Bath-shua (17:1; so 13:4-5) and predicting that they will be the downfall of Judah's descendants (17:2-3), referring also to "the books of Enoch the righteous" (18:1). Accordingly they should beware "of sexual immorality and love of money* (ἀπὸ τῆς πορνείας καὶ τῆς φιλαργυρίας)" (18:2). In 18:2-5 he lists a range of outcomes, apart from being drawn away from the law of God, none of which, however, pertains to sexual wrongdoing, concluding in summary that they make a person into someone who "being a slave of two passions contrary to the commandments of God: he cannot obey God, because they have blinded his soul and he walks in the day as in the night* (δύο γὰρ πάθη ἐναντία τῶν τοῦ θεοῦ δουλεύων θεῷ ὑπακούειν οὐ δύναται, ὅτι ἐτύφλωσαν τὴν ψυχὴν αὐτοῦ, καὶ ἐν ἡμέρᾳ ὡς ἐν νυκτὶ πορεύεται)". Again, the psychology of impotence here is to be noted. Passion is so strong, whether lust or greed, that one loses control and does not know what one is doing, a motif earlier connected with wine, but here directly with passions.

The application of this understanding comes to expression in 19:3-4, where, having deplored the fact that love of money led to idolatry (19:1) and having noted the repentance of his flesh (his abstinence from meat and wine and possibly sexual intercourse; similarly 15:4), humiliation of his soul, and his father's intercession, he declares that God forgave him and why:

ἀλλ' ὁ θεός τῶν πατέρων μου, ὁ οἰκτίρμων καὶ ἐλεήμων, συνέγνω ὅτι ἐν ἀγνοίᾳ ἐποίησα.
4 ἐτύφλωσε γάρ με ὁ ἄρχων τῆς πλάνης,
καὶ ἠγνόησα ὡς ἄνθρωπος,
καὶ ὡς σὰρξ ἐν ἁμαρτίαις φθαρείς·
καὶ ἐπέγνων τὴν ἐμαυτοῦ ἀσθένειαν,
νομίζων ἀκαταμάχητος εἶναι.
but the God of my fathers, the compassionate and merciful, knew that I had done it in ignorance.
For the prince of deceit blinded me
and I was ignorant as a man
and as flesh corrupted through sins,
and I recognized my own weakness
while thinking myself invincible.* (19:3-4)

Ignorance here is not a plea of innocence, but something blameworthy (similarly *Jub.* 41:25). It unleashed a sequence of effects, however, which the

---

[120] Kee, *OTP*, sees this as indicating that the *Testaments* are sectarian (1.799 n. 16a).

author describes as blinding (similarly 11:1), attributing this in his psychological demonology to "the prince of deceit" (cf. also *T. Sim.* 2:7), and corrupting of his flesh, probably referring to his senses, and sufficiently debilitating to win God's pity. It reads almost as fatalistically as *T. Reub.* 3:8 which suggests the young man doesn't have a chance! The author's discourse further unpacks his understanding of the human predicament in a manner which recalls the discussion in *T. Reub.* 2 – 3. Here he reports: "two spirits devote themselves to man, the spirit of truth and the spirit of deceit, and in the midst is the spirit of understanding of the mind, which inclines in whatever direction it wishes to* (ὅτι δύο πνεύματα σχολάζουσι τῷ ἀνθρώπῳ, τὸ τῆς ἀληθείας καὶ τὸ τῆς πλάνης καὶ μέσον ἐστὶ τὸ τῆς συνέσεως τοῦ νοός, οὗ ἐὰν θέλῃ κλῖναι)" (20:1-2). This is similar to the contrast in 1QS/1Q28 3.13 – 4.26, but our author employs the contrast in the context of his distinctive anthropology. Thus the understanding mind is crucial in choosing to respond to these spirits and the sets of works which they engender. "The spirit of truth" is not directly identified as God, but functions on God's side, testifying and accusing before God about people, much as the spirit is understood in the fourth gospel. This discussion does not touch on matters of sexual wrongdoing, although that has featured previously and is to be assumed as among "the works of deceit".

The remaining chapters which, like *T. Reub.* 6:8-10; *T. Naph.* 8:2; *T. Gad* 8:1; *T. Jos.* 19:6, tell the descendants to love Levi, have predictions about the future, in particular about behaviour of kings. Among these we find specific accusations of sexual wrongdoing in 23:1-2, "because of the lewdness and witchcrafts and idolatries that you will practise against the kingdom, following mediums, soothsayers and demons of deceit (διὰ τας ἀσελγείας καὶ γοητείας καὶ εἰδωλολατρείας ἃς ποιήσετε εἰς τὸ βασίλειον, ἐγγαστριμύθοις ἐξακολουθοῦντες, κληδόσι καὶ δαίμοσι πλάνης)". The word ἀσελγείας probably encompasses sexual wrongdoing. This is made more likely in the light of what follows: "you will make your daughters singing girls and prostitutes and you will mingle in the abominations of the Gentiles (τὰς θυγατέρας ὑμῶν μουσικὰς καὶ δημοσίας ποιήσετε, καὶ ἐπιμιγήσεσθε ἐν βδελύγμασιν ἐθνῶν)" (23:2). The "abominations of the Gentiles" in 23:2 probably include the sorcery and idolatry mentioned in 23:1. Idolatry and sexual wrongdoing are commonly associated. Thus Hos 4:11-14 associates idolatry with daughters engaging in prostitution and adultery and *Pss. Sol.* 2:11-13 brings accusations about prostitution and daughters engaging in sexual wrongdoing. Among the afflictions which Judah's descendants will suffer is that Gentiles will castrate some of them to be eunuchs for their wives (23:4). In its image of resurrection life it may be significant "that in the closing apocalyptic hymn (*TJud* 25.3-4) sexuality plays no role in the vision of the world to come", as Eron observes,[121] though that remains an argument from silence. It is true, however, of the testaments as a whole in contrast to eschatological images of abundance and fertility present in *1 Enoch* and many documents in Qumran.

Conclusion

Overall in this testament the author has exploited and expanded the accounts of Judah's marriage to Bath-shua and his sin with Tamar, not only on the basis that they breach two prohibitions which he upholds, marrying a foreigner and engaging in prostitution, but also in order to reinforce previous teaching about the processes unleashed by looking in combination with women's powers of seduction and sexual attractiveness. He manipulates the stories then further to underline the role which excessive consumption of wine can have on perception and control in the first place, making it servant to the spirit of sexual immorality and bringing men into its servitude, dramatically portrayed through symbolic depiction of Judah's pledges through which a king is made a slave.

The author describes this as servitude, in particular, servitude to women and to sin, for which men are responsible in having starting on the slippery slope but for which they also have some sympathy from the author and his God, and from which they can be delivered (as Judah reminds us in his own case, and Reuben in his).[122] A new element in his portrayal of the human condition is the spirit of truth, which as counterpart of the spirit of deceit, also appeals to the mind and reports to God its responses. As earlier, while the author employs the language of demonology, he primarily describes the moral danger in psychological terms as about having a properly informed and sober mind which can deal with visual and

---

[121] Lewis John Eron, "'That Women Have Mastery Over Both King and Beggar' (TJud. 15,5)—The Relationship of the Fear of Sexuality to the Status of Women in Apocrypha and Pseudepigrapha: 1 Esdras (3 Ezra) 3–4, Ben Sira and the Testament of Judah," *JSP* 9 (1991) 43-66, 62.

[122] Menn, *Judah and Tamar*, notes the parallels between Judah and Heracles, a king with heroic successes sexual adventures and falling under spell of women and wine, a figure not of failure like Judah, but exemplary, especially in Cynic and Stoic philosophical discourse (177-211). She concludes: "The Testament of Judah redefines kingship in moral terms, much as Greek philosophy does. While the patriarch ostensibly addresses the royal descendants who will govern after him, he also addresses the common man, who similarly experiences threats to his sovereignty over life and the passions. But whereas Heracles presents a positive model for how a person may be a 'king' in everyday life through control of his passions, Judah presents a negative model of how even a king may fall due to the wiles of women and warns that all classes of men are similarly endangered (*T. Jud.* 15:5-6)" (211).

other stimuli and so not initiate the process which all too easily leads to lack of control and to sin.

3.6   Testament of Issachar

In this testament Issachar begins by recalling the encounter between Rachel and Leah over two mandrakes (μανδραγόρων) as a result of which he was conceived by his mother Leah (1:2 – 2:5; Gen 30:14-16). Reuben, her son, had brought them in from the field, but contrary to Gen 30:14, where he first gave them to Leah, Issachar's account has Rachel seize them directly (1:3). Leah comes out to see what has happened only when she hears Reuben weeping (1:4). Unlike in Genesis, Rachel addresses Leah declaring: "I shall not give them to you, for they shall be to me instead of children (ἀντὶ τέκνων [possibly: as a means of getting children])" (1:6).[123] The background which the author's hearers are assumed to have known from Genesis is that Rachel had been infertile and had given her maid Bilhah to Jacob, whereas Leah had been fertile and after she became infertile gave him her maid, Zilpah, who also bore children, leaving Leah very happy and Rachel distressed. Rachel's seizure of the mandrakes might at one level seem like simply compensation for not having children, but the hearers would also know that mandrakes were widely believed to enhance fertility,[124] so that she hoped thereby to be able to conceive.

The author's imagination takes us inside a polygynous marriage and builds on the picture of Rachel's envy and frustration depicted earlier in the Genesis narrative (30:1-2). She had already been cheated by her father Laban, who engineered that Jacob first marry Leah. In Issachar's account, as in Genesis, Leah protests: "Let it suffice that you have taken the husband of my virginity; would you take these also?" (1:7; cf. Gen 30:15). Again the hearer must fill in the gaps, knowing that Jacob loved Rachel more than Leah, and presumably slept with her, not Leah. The account stays close by the original in naming Rachel's compromise: she would vacate Jacob's bed that night for Leah (1:8; cf. Gen 30:15). The author then embellishes the conflict in a way that recalls the unhappy beginning of the marriage, with Leah declaring that Jacob is hers and that she is the wife of his youth and Rachel countering that she was first betrothed to him and he had served fourteen years for her, alleging that Leah was not really his wife but by her father's deceit had usurped her (1:9-13). Rachel then compromises, giving back one mandrake, but declaring that the other would be deemed payment by which Leah

---

[123] So Kee, *OTP*: "they shall be mine as a means of getting children" (1.802 n. 1b).

[124] Kee, *OTP*: "a herb with a large forked root, considered to be a love philter and an aid to pregnancy" (1.802 n 1a).

could hire Jacob for the night (1:14). The hearers are presumed to have known enough Hebrew to understand the play on words, when Leah called the son, whom she bore as a result of this stormy encounter, Issachar, from שכר "to hire" (1:15). One could at first think that the one mandrake helped her regain fertility, but the author later tells us that she never consumed it, but used it to hire one more night with Jacob (2:2).

The author then uses this story[125] in order to have Issachar propound to his descendants what he claims an angel of the Lord declared (2:1). It is interesting that this is a third angel revelation dealing directly with women's issues (cf. *T. Reub.* 5:3; *T. Jud.* 15:5), though here it consists of only a brief statement which Issachar then expands: "Two children will Rachel bear, because she has despised intercourse with a man and has chosen continency (δύο τέκνα 'Ραχὴλ τέξεται, ὅτι διέπτυσε συνουσίαν ἀνδρὸς καὶ ἐξελέξατο ἐγκράτειαν)". The author is twisting the narrative to use Rachel's trade-off to imply abstention from intercourse. He then has Issachar explain that the mandrakes had nothing at all to do with Rachel later becoming fertile, since she offered them to the priest in the house of the Lord (2:5). God made her fertile, he claims, because "he saw that for the sake of children she wished to have intercourse with Jacob and not for the love of pleasure* (εἶδε γὰρ ὅτι διὰ τέκνα ἤθελε συνεῖναι τῷ 'Ιακώβ, καὶ οὐ διὰ φιλοδονίαν)" (2:3). Here the author is expounding a widely held view, held by Stoics among others,[126] and not least Philo and Josephus (see 1.2.2.6.1-2 and 2.4.13 above), that sexual intercourse is to serve procreation, never pleasure alone, implied already in *T. Reub.* 2:8. He may also imply disapproval of using such fertility enhancements. Rachel doesn't even want the mandrakes.[127]

The quality associated continually with Issachar in the rest of his address is ἁπλότης. It includes the notion of singleness of purpose as well as simplicity. Issachar was ideal, a farmer (γεωργός 3:1; he is pictured as a farmer in Gen 49:14-15 LXX).[128] Accordingly he married at the age of thirty, explaining: "for my labour wore away my strength, and I did not think of pleasure with a woman (καὶ οὐκ ἐνενόουν ἡδονὴν γυναικός), but because of my toil sleep overcame me"

---

[125] On the parallels with the account in *Gen. Rab.* 72.3, 5, which in contrast affirms Leah and blames Rachel, see Marinus de Jonge, *The Testaments of the Twelve Patriarchs: A Study of their Text, Composition and Origin* (2d ed.; Assen: van Gorcum, 1975) 78-80.

[126] On this see de Jonge, "Rachel", who cites Musonius Rufus fr. 12, 13A, 13B, Ocellus Lucanus *De Universi Natura* 44-45; Seneca, *De Matrimonio* (341). See also Hierocles, *On Duties*, 4.28.21; Justin *Apol.* 1.29. See also Kee, "Ethical Dimensions," 265.

[127] So Kirchhoff, "Testamente," 480.

[128] de Jonge, "Rachel," notes "that Musonius advocates the life of a farmer or shepherd as the ideal occupation of a philosopher" (342). It is a theme also in Philo *Leg.* 1.80; *Migr.* 221. Kugel, "Judah and the Trial of Tamar," notes it need not derive from LXX, but is implied already in the Hebrew text (174-76).

(3:5). This coheres with the author's advice at *T. Reub.* 4:1 and contrasts with Reuben's sleeplessness before assaulting Bilhah (*T. Reub.* 3:12). Then in *T. Iss.* 4:4 Issachar declares of the single minded man: "and the spirits of deceit have no power against him. For he does not look to welcome the beauty of a woman lest he would pollute his mind with perversion (καίγε τὰ πνεύματα τῆς πλάνης οὐδὲν ἰσχύουσι πρὸς αὐτόν. Οὐ γὰρ εἶδεν ἐπιδέξασθαι κάλλος θηλείας, ἵνα μὴ ἐν διαστροφῇ μιάνῃ τὸν νοῦν αὐτοῦ)". This fits the author's psychology. It comes close to saying: looking in a particular way. The eyes are a potential vehicle for evil (as also 3:4). In 4:6 the author repeats this emphasis: "and looks at all things in simplicity, not welcoming with the eyes bad things that come from the deceit of the world, lest he see anything in the commandments of the Lord in a perverted way (καὶ πάντα ὁρᾷ ἐν ἁπλότητι, μὴ ἐπιδεχόμενος ὀφθαλμοῖς πονηρίας ἀπὸ τῆς πλάνης τοῦ κόσμου, ἵνα μὴ ἴδῃ. διεστραμμένως τι τῶν ἐντολῶν τοῦ κυρίου)". The reference to seeing the commandments in a perverted way may allude to misinterpretations of the commandments to suit one's immoral ends, such as is alleged in CD 4.12b – 5.19 and elsewhere. He had controlled his eyes and not married till he was 30 (3:4). Simplicity of eyes will include keeping them from lustful looks.

In 7:2 Issachar similarly reports that he has not known another woman beside his wife, nor committed sexual immorality by lifting up his eyes (πλὴν τῆς γυναικός μου οὐκ ἔγνων ἄλλην. Οὐκ ἐπόρνευσα ἐν μετεωρισμῷ ὀφθαλμῶν μου), adding that he also "did not drink wine to be led astray thereby" (7:3), echoing the discourse of Judah. Among the more general predictions are the statements in 6:1 that in the last days his sons "will forsake (καταλείψουσιν) simplicity and will cleave to insatiable desire (κολληθήσονται τῇ ἀπληστίᾳ), leaving guilelessness they will draw near to wickedness (προσπελάσουσι τῇ κακουργίᾳ) and forsaking (καταλιπόντες) the commandments of the Lord they will cleave to Beliar (κολληθήσονται τῷ Βελιάρ)". The language may well play with sexual metaphors, recalling the language of Gen 2:24 (ἕνεκεν τούτου καταλείψει ἄνθρωπος τὸν πατέρα αὐτοῦ καὶ τὴν μητέρα αὐτοῦ καὶ προσκολληθήσεται πρὸς τὴν γυναῖκα αὐτοῦ).

The testament reflects the author's psychology evident in the earlier testaments, speaking of Beliar and the spirit of deceit, the danger of woman's sexuality, and making men responsible for how women look. It makes explicit what was previously implied: the desire for sexual intercourse except for procreation is sin. This then sets in perspective all his statements about sexual desire, which he must accordingly see as something positive not in itself, but only when directed to procreation in marriage. Correspondingly the testament has Issachar imply his faithfulness in marriage as an ideal.

3.7 Testament of Zebulon

This testament, concerned with the theme of compassion and mercy has little pertaining directly to our theme. The one exception is in relation to the brothers' treatment of Joseph where Zebulon reports that Simeon and Gad with the six other brothers used the money received from the sale of Joseph to buy sandals for themselves and their familes.[129] Zebulon then adds: "Therefore it is written in the writing of the law of Enoch that whoever does not want to raise up offspring to his brother, his sandal should be pulled off his foot and he should be spat upon on the face* (διὰ τοῦτο ἐν γραφῇ νόμου Ἐνὼχ γέγραπται, τὸν μὴ θέλοντα ἀναστῆσαι σπέρμα τῷ ἀδελφῷ αὐτοῦ ὑπολυθήσεσθαι τὸ ὑπόδημα καὶ ἐμπτύεσθαι εἰς τὸ πρόσωπον)" (3:4). This refers to the provision in the regulation of levirate marriage that the widow whose husband's brother refuses to take her as wife is to pull off his sandal and spit in his face (Deut 25:5-10; cf. also Ruth 4:1-11).[130] Strangely he continues: "The Lord pulled off their feet the sandal of Joseph" (3:5) and then reports that at their entry to Egypt their sandals were pulled off and people spat in their faces (3:6-7). Here it is used symbolically against the brothers for wanting to kill Joseph and thereby ensuring he has no seed. It coheres with the author's emphasis on the importance of bearing offspring, which matches the emphasis in the previous testament on procreation.

3.8 The Testament of Dan

This testament is a striking exposition of anger. Its only allusion to sexual wrongdoing comes in 5:5 where Dan predicts that his descendants will turn away from the Lord and "walk in all evil, working the abominations of the Gentiles (βδελύγματα ἐθνῶν), engaging in sexual immorality with women of the lawless ones, and in all wickedness (ἐκπορνεύοντες ἐν γυναιξὶν ἀνόμων καὶ ἐν πάσῃ πονηρίᾳ), while the spirits of deceit (τῶν πνευμάτων τῆς πλάνης) are working in you". As Kugler notes,[131] the prime example of his somewhat unexpected reference to intermarriage with Gentiles is Samson's marriage to Timnah (Judg 14:1 – 15:20), his engagement with a prostitute (16:1-3), and his fateful alliance with Delilah (16:4-31). Dan then adds what he claims to have read "in the book of Enoch, the righteous one", namely that his descendants' "prince is Satan and that all the spirits of sexual immorality and arrogance will obey Levi, to attend upon the sons of Levi to make them sin before the Lord" (5:6). The descendants of Dan

---

[129] On the brothers not involved see Hollander and de Jonge, *Commentary*, 260.

[130] Attributed to Enoch because pre-Mosaic, so Kugler, *Testaments*, 65.

[131] Kugler, *Testaments*, 98.

and Levi will sin in all things and the sons of Judah will be covetous. The prediction of sexual wrongdoing is complicated by being committed with "the lawless ones" (5:5), probably an allusion to Gentiles (cf. Wis 17:2; 3 Macc 6:9). "In all wickedness (ἐν πάσῃ πονηρίᾳ)" qualifies "engaging in sexual immorality" (ἐκπορνεύοντες) which indicates extensive sexual wrongdoing, but without further specification. The depiction of the behaviour of the descendants in 5:7 has no further sexual references. "The abominations of the Gentiles (βδελύγματα ἐθνῶν)" (5:5) may already have sexual wrongdoing in mind. The word βδέλυγμα describes the sin of Reuben (*T. Reub.* 3:12), Shechem (*T. Levi.* 6:3), and Judah (*T. Jud.* 12:8) and is used in relation to the sexual sins of the nations in Lev 18:22, 26-27, 29; 20:13. The prediction recalls that of Judah in in *T. Jud.* 23:1, where the same phrase, "abominations of the Gentiles (βδελύγματα ἐθνῶν)" occurs in connection with sexual sin (there, in relation to behaviour of daughters). The reference to "the spirits of deceit (τῶν πνευμάτων τῆς πλάνης)" (5:5) recalls the exposition in *T. Reub.* 2 – 3 where the spirit of sexual immorality comes first in the list (cf. also "Satan and his spirits" 6:1).

Most of this testament is taken up, however, with "the spirit of anger" (τὸ πνεῦμα τοῦ θυμοῦ) (1:8), identified as "one of the spirits of Beliar" (1:7) and sometimes described as "the spirit of lying and anger (τὸ πνεῦμα τοῦ ψεύδους καὶ τοῦ θυμοῦ)" (2:1). The author's treatment of anger parallels his treatment of sexual lust. Thus anger, too, blinds (2:2, 4), darkens the mind (2:4), disturbs the mind (4:2, 7), leading to Beliar's domination of it (4:7) and to sinful behaviour. We see here a similar psychological approach, to which the apparent demonology is subordinated. Thus anger "becomes a soul to the soul itself (3:1), gaining dominion over it (3:2), and justifies its acts (3:3). The author describes the means used by anger for its violence (3:4-6) and recommends strategies for its management, primarily at the level of avoiding expectations which might cause disappointment and frustration (4:3-6), but also straight obedience to the commandments (5:1-3).

3.9 The Testament of Naphtali

This testament begins with Naphtali giving an account of his birth to Rachel's maid, Bilhah (1:4-12). Rachel is described as acting craftily (ἐν πανουργίᾳ – here apparently not used negatively as in *T. Jud.* 10:3; *T. Iss.* 1:11) in giving Bilhah to Jacob (1:6). Naphtali then tells us that he was born on Rachel's knees (1:7). As Hillel notes, "'On Rachel's knees' reflects a widely used sign of legitimization acknowledging either parenthood or adoption.[132] The author places great emphasis on enhancing Bilhah's status, first as born on the same day as Rachel (1:9), but especially in tracing her lineage through to Abraham's family through Rotheus "a Chaldean, god-fearing, freeborn and noble", who was Zilpah's father, who was thus Bilhah's elder sister (1:10-11). The point of this explanation is in part to remove any suggestion that Jacob would have slept with a Gentile woman, since for our author intermarriage with Gentiles is clearly prohibited. It coheres with the positive depiction of Bilhah in *T. Reuben* where any suggestion that she may have been implicated in Reuben's sin is avoided (see the discussion above). Her genealogy, thus Naphtali's genealogy, legitimises also his status "as Jacob's son of equal status or rank with the sons of Leah and Rachel" and as like Joseph "in all things" (1:8)[133] all the more important because such claims are not made about Dan, Gad, and Asher.[134]

The theme of 2:2 – 3:5 is balance and order in creation, beginning with the image of God as a potter. Accordingly bodies are made after the likeness of the spirit and the spirit given in relation to the body's capacity, capacity determines performance, people are as different from each other as light from darkness or seeing and hearing, and the body has its five senses and various functions related to various body parts (2:2-8). The author is displaying more of his learning about human psychology. The point of the excursus is to underline the sense of order: "for God made all things good, in order" (2:8). Hence, the exhortation in 2:9, "So then, my children, be in order for good, in the fear of God and do nothing disorderly in scorn or out of its due season"*. As further support for this sense of order the author reminds them that "the sun and moon and stars do not change their order" (3:2). Similar appeal to order in the heavens in relation to upholding God's will on earth are found in *1 Enoch* 2:1 – 5:3.[135]

The author then points to examples of disorder: "The Gentiles changed their order, having gone astray and having forsaken the Lord and they followed after

---

[132] Vered Hillel, "Naphtali, a Proto-Joseph in the *Testaments of the Twelve Patriarchs*," *JSP* 16 (2007) 171-201, 187.

[133] Hillel, "Naphtali," 186-87. He also shows the similarity between the portraits of Naphtali and Joseph, including physical beauty matching inner goodness (*T. Naph.* 2:2, 6; *T. Jos.* 18:4; *T. Sim.* 5:1) (172).

[134] Hillel, "Naphtali," 190. He notes that Tobit was of the tribe of Naphtali (Tob 1:1, 4, 5; 7:3) (186). De Jonge, *Testaments*, argues that the common source behind this testament and the Medieval *Heb. Naph* will have contained such a genealogy (197-98). See also Gabriele Boccaccini, *Roots of Rabbinic Judaism: An Intellectual History, from Ezekiel to Daniel* (Grand Rapids: Eerdmans, 2002) 125; Betsy Halpern-Amaru, "Bilhah and Naphtali in Jubilees: A Note on QTNaphtali," *DSD* 6 (1999) 1-10; Loader, *Enoch, Levi, and Jubilees*, for discussion of the possibility that Jubilees' interest in Naphtali may be related to the legitimation of the Tobiads (177).

[135] On this see also Küchler, *Weisheit*, 510-12.

stones and sticks, having followed after spirits of deceit" (3:3), the standard accusation of idolatry expounded as failing to recognise God's true nature, similar to Paul's exposition in Rom 1:18-23. Next he turns to Sodom, warning that his sons should not become "as Sodom which changed the order of its nature (ἵνα μὴ γένησθε ὡς Σόδομα, ἥτις ἐνήλλαξε τάξιν φύσεως αὐτῆς)" (3:4). This focuses not on the breach of hospitality, but on the homosexual actions, which it understands, like Paul, as deliberate perversion of one's true nature (which is heterosexual).[136] This receives further confirmation in the reference to the Watchers which immediately follows: "In like manner also the Watchers changed the order of their nature (ὁμοίως δὲ καὶ οἱ ἐγρήγοροι ἐνήλλαξαν τάξιν φύσεως αὐτῶν)" (3:5).

The prediction, based typically on "the holy writing of Enoch", indicates that the descendants would not only "depart from the Lord, walking according to all the wickedness of the Gentiles", but would also "do according to all the lawlessness of Sodom (ποιήσετε κατὰ πᾶσαν ἀνομίαν Σοδόμων)" (4:1); it thus returns to the example of Sodom, and again by the "wickedness of the Gentiles" must allude to homosexual activity here, though without further specification.[137] The focus on "nature" suggests that the primary focus is not the violence but the perversion which our author sees entailed in any homosexual activity, so not restricted here to just some aspects such as pederasty or male prostitution, but homosexual acts in general.

Compared with the constant warnings about heterosexual immorality, allusions to homosexual acts are rare in the *Testaments*, this being the most direct reference. The author gives it scant attention, but enough to help us see a frame of reference for dealing with the issues that is similar to what we find in Romans 1: as people deny God's true nature in engaging in idolatry, so in engaging in homosexual acts they deny their own. Eron notes that the comparative lack of interest is indicated also by the absence of the usual vocabulary attached to the issue.[138] He suggests that its lack of prominence may reflect the situation of the hearers in urban contexts where adultery posed a much greater risk and

---

[136] So Lewis John Eron, "Early Jewish and Christian Attitudes toward Male Homosexuality as Expressed in the Testament of Naphtali," *Homophobia and the Judaeo-Christian Tradition* (Dallas: Monument, 1990) 25-49, who cautions in relation to early Christian and Jewish texts that "concepts such as (1) an individual's sexual orientation and (2) sexuality as being inherent in a person are foreign to these texts ... In other words, there are no gay men for the early Church and the early Synagogue; there are only men who engage in sexual relations with other men" (25).

[137] So Eron, "Male Homosexuality," 35-36. "The condemnation of male-male sexual relations is a blanket condemnation. No distinctions are made between the active and passive partner" nor about age or sexual predilections (38).

[138] Eron, "Male Homosexuality," 27-28.

homosexual behaviour, condemned also by philosophers such as Musonius Rufus, was seen as something in which outsiders, idolaters, engaged.[139]

Much of the remainder of the testament is taken up with exhortations to support Levi and Judah and reassurance of hope in the future. Near the end of the testament we then return to exhortation which includes the following statement:

> 7 Καὶ γὰρ αἱ ἐντολαὶ τοῦ νόμου διπλαῖ εἰσι
> καὶ μετὰ τέχνης πληροῦνται.
> 8 Καιρὸς γὰρ συνουσίας γυναικὸς αὐτοῦ
> καὶ καιρὸς ἐγκρατείας εἰς προσευχὴν αὐτοῦ.
> 9 Καὶ δύο ἐντολαί εἰσιν·
> καὶ εἰ μὴ γένωνται ἐν τάξει αὐτῶν, ἁμαρτίαν παρέχουσιν.
> Οὕτως ἐστὶ καὶ ἐπὶ τῶν λοιπῶν ἐντολῶν.
> 10 γίνεσθε οὖν σοφοὶ ἐν θεῷ καὶ φρόνιμοι,
> εἰδότες, τάξιν ἐντολῶν αὐτοῦ καὶ θεσμοὺς παντὸς πράγματος,
> ὅπως ὁ κύριος ἀγαπήσει ὑμᾶς.
> 7 The commandments of the law are twofold
> and they must be fulfilled through prudence.
> 8 For there is a season (for a man) to have sexual intercourse with his wife
> and a season to abstain therefrom for his prayer:
> 9 so there are two commandments
> and if they are not done in their order, they bring sin.
> So also is it with the other commandments.
> 10 Be, therefore, wise in God and prudent,
> understanding the order of his commandments and the laws of every activity,
> that the Lord will love you. (8:7-10)

The "twofold" commandments in 8:7 refer to the commandment to love God and love one's neighbour,[140] a common theme in the *Testaments* (e.g., *T. Iss.* 5:1-2; 7:6; *T Zeb.* 5:1; *T. Dan* 5:3; *T. Benj.* 3:3-5).[141] The same thought recurs in 8:9, which speaks of the "two commandments". μετὰ τέχνης (v.7), translated here as "prudence", probably focuses on deliberate planning and attention. Verse 8 somewhat suddenly introduces sexual intercourse. In v. 8 the use of καιρός ("season", "time") echoes Eccles 3:1-8 LXX and the two "times" relate here to the two commandments. Devoting oneself to prayer is a way of fulfilling the first commandment to love God; having sexual intercourse with one's wife is a way of fulfilling the second commandment to love one's neighbour as oneself. Verse 9 makes it clear that there is a priority of loving God over loving one's wife and all

---

[139] Eron, "Male Homosexuality," 38-39.

[140] So Kee, *OTP*, 1.814 n. 8c. See also Loader, "Sexuality in the Testaments," 294-98.

[141] See de Jonge, "Two Great Commandments," who does not, however, cite *T. Naph.* 8:7 in this context nor do Hollander and de Jonge make this connection in dealing with the passage in their *Commentary*, 318-19.

other commandments. It is a matter of getting the priority, the order (τάξιν), right (8:10; cf. also 2:9).[142]

Implied then within the exposition of the order of the commandments is a very positive statement about sexual intercourse in marriage as an act of love. It may include also something more than that, namely that sexual intercourse with one's wife also belongs within the category of what is commanded. Elsewhere the author also implies that sexual intercourse for purposes other than procreation is sin, but here sexual intercourse comes within the sphere of loving one's neighbour. Perhaps the author thought of the two together, making a distinction between sexual intercourse as an expression of love which is also procreative, fulling the command of Gen 1:28 to multiply, and sexual intercourse just for pleasure. The passage is frequently footnoted in relation to Paul's instruction in 1 Cor 7:5 that married couples not deprive one another of sexual love except by mutual agreement for a time, to make room for prayer, but then should return to "the same", lest Satan tempt them because of their likely lack of self control (1 Cor 7:5). The assumption behind both is that abstinence from sexual intercourse in some way benefits or is appropriate to prayer. The issue is not time spent in sexual intercourse, but rather a longer period of time which is to be devoted to prayer and that sexual intercourse during that period is to be avoided. We are probably dealing with long established and widely held beliefs which saw holy space (and time) needing to be kept free from sexual activity. We find comparable instances when Moses asks that the people abstain from sexual intercourse before the holy encounter at Sinai and when David reassures the priest that his men may enter the Temple because they had not engaged in sexual intercourse with women in the preceding days (Exod 19:15; 1 Sam 21:5).[143]

The testament is important in providing both the first clear indication of the author's stance towards homosexual acts and the philosophy which underpins it, namely that it represents a denial of one's nature, all people being understood as heterosexual. It is also interesting for its employment of the Sodom tradition in this way, which is frequently interpreted in relation to hospitality or violent rape elsewhere, and of the Watcher tradition, also not usually employed in this context. Its statement about sexual intercourse within marriage as an expression of the the second great commandment is a high point in the work.

---

[142] On τάξις and καιρός as an allusion to Eccles 3:11 LXX, see Hollander and de Jonge, *Commentary*, 319. Cf. Ulrichsen, *Grundschrift*, who sees 8:7-10 as a secondary gloss because, he argues, it completely misunderstands the point of 8:4, 6 ("die Pointe in 8:4,6 völlig missverstanden hat" 161; similarly 332); likewise Becker, *Untersuchungen*, 217. Its appeal to order does, however, cohere well with the earlier discourse in 2 – 3.

[143] On sex and sacred space and time see also Loader, *Dead Sea Scrolls on Sexuality*, 363-76; William Loader, "Attitudes towards Sexuality in Qumran and Related Literature – and the New Testament," *NTS* 54 (2008) 338-54, 347-48.

3.10 The Testament of Gad

This testament makes no reference to sexual issues, but in expounding hatred continues the same kind of psychological explanation found elsewhere, along with strategies to counter it (5:3-11; 6 – 7), speaking also of the "spirit of hatred" (τῷ πνεύματι τοῦ μίσους) (3:1) as residing in the liver (5:9-11; cf. *T. Reub.* 3:3) and connecting it with Satan (4:7), and concluding with exhortations to support Levi and Judah (8:1). Predictions of future generations abandoning them and engaging "in all wickedness" (8:2) remain at the level of generality.

3.11 The Testament of Asher

This testament focuses on two ways, good and evil (cf. Prov 4:10-14; Ps 1:6; Deut 30:15),[144] but characteristically of the author, treats them systematically as representing not only actions, but dispositions (1:3-9), connected also with the rule of Beliar (1:8), but explained psychologically using the image of the poisoned disposition. In 2:1 – 3:2 the author describes people who are two-faced, appearing to do good, but really intending wickedness as their goal. Among the illustrations we find one pertaining to sexuality:

> ἄλλος μοιχεύει καὶ πορνεύει,
> καὶ ἀπέχεται ἐδεσμάτων, καὶ νηστεύων κακοποιεῖ,
> καὶ τῇ δυναστείᾳ καὶ τῷ πλούτῳ πολλοὺς παρασύρει,
> καὶ ἐκ τῆς ὑπερόγκου κακίας ποιεῖ ἐντολάς·
> Another commits adultery and engages in sexual immorality,
> and he abstains from food, and fasting he does evil
> and by his power and his wealth he sweeps away many,
> and from his excessive wickedness he does the commandments. (2:8)

---

[144] On the Christian parallels (e.g. Didache 1 – 6; Barnabas 18 – 20; *Doctrina Apostolorum*; and the *Apostolic Church Order*), see Marinus de Jonge, "The *Testaments of the Twelve Patriarchs* and the 'Two Ways'," in *Biblical Traditions in Transmission: Essays in Honour of Michael A. Knibb* (ed. Charlotte Hempel and Judith M. Lieu; JSJSup 111; Leiden: Brill, 2006) 179-94, 181-83, who also offers a critical assessment of attempts to trace a Jewish "two ways" document (184-88). Comparing the two ways metaphor in the testaments and in the *Shepherd of Hermas*, he concludes that "neither presents an elaborate 'Two-Ways' instruction, though in both, the "pneumatology/angelology is certainly related to the notion of the 'Two Angels' in *Barnabas* and, earlier, that of the 'instruction of the two Spirits' in 1Q28/1QS 3:13 – 4:26, but each of the two writings has developed this basic theme in its own way" (194). See also the discussion of the "Treatise on the Two Spirits" in the Community Rule in Loader, *Dead Sea Scrolls on Sexuality*, 189-95.

The author employs food laws further in categorising all such two faced evildoers as being like pigs and hares, which, on the basis of Lev 11:5, 7; Deut 14:7-8, described as belonging to "the tables of heaven" (2:10), means: "they are half clean, but in reality they are unclean" (2:9), and "good single-faced men" as "stags and hinds", which though they seem to be unclean, ... are altogether clean" (so Deut 14:5) (4:5). The "single-faced men" include the man who hates the two faced man cited earlier in 4:3 as "the one who commits adultery and fasts. These are the only specific references to sexual wrongdoing. In 7:1 we hear the warning: "Do not become, my children, as Sodom", but unlike in the *Testament of Naphtali*, the focus here is not homosexual actions, but lack of hospitality: they "did not know the angels of the Lord and perished forever" (7:1).

3.12 The Testament of Joseph

This testament falls into two main sections: the account of Joseph's resisting seduction (3:1 – 9:5) and the account of his purchase from slavery (11:2 – 16:6). The latter is a separate elaboration, probably drawing from a different source, of what is briefly and poetically retold at the beginning of Joseph's speech, namely how God supported him from his brothers' selling him into slavery through to "Photimar (Petephres, according to the account in 12:1), the chiefcook of Pharaoh" (2:1) setting him, over his house (1:3 – 2:1). This leads immediately to the statement: "And I struggled against a shameless woman, urging me to transgress with her; but the God of Israel my father guarded me from the burning flame (ἀπὸ φλογὸς καιομένης)" (2:2). Imagery of the struggle in relation to seduction occurred already in *T. Reub.* 5:2-3, shortly after reference to Joseph's resistance (4:8-9). "Burning flame" is best heard as alluding to sexual passion (as in *T. Jud.* 14:2-3; 16:1, linked to wine), rather than to future punishment, though there may be a metaphorical intertextual reference to the plight of the three in Dan 3:88 LXX.[145] According to 2:7 Joseph faced ten temptations or trials, which he understands as having occurred as a result of God "departing for a short time to try the inclination of the soul (εἰς τὸ δοκιμάσαι τῆς ψυχῆς τὸ διαβούλιον)" (2:6).[146] These recall the ten temptations which Abraham faced according to *Jub.* 19:8.

---

[145] Cf. Harm W. Hollander, *Joseph as an Ethical Model in the Testament of the Twelve Patriarchs* (SVTP 6; Leiden: Brill, 1981), who notes only Dan 3:88 (also 3:51) LXX and Sir 8:10 (24, 37). See also Kirchhoff, "Testamente," 480.

[146] Marinus de Jonge, "Sidelights on the Testaments of the Twelve Patriarchs from the Greek Catena on Genesis," in *Things Revealed: Studies in Early Jewish and Christian Literature in Honor of Michael E. Stone* (ed. Esther G. Chazon, David Satran, and Ruth A. Clements; JSJSup 89; Leiden: Brill, 2004) 303-15, draws attention to a similar claim that

The author describes these trials extensively. They are not narrated as single events but as instances that occurred "often" (3:1). First "the Egyptian woman" threatened to kill or punish Joseph if he did not "have intercourse with her" (συνελθεῖν αὐτῇ) (3:1), promising him headship of her and the household (3:2), as befitted a man in the author's world. Joseph tells us: "I, then, remembered the words of my father Jacob" (3:3), but cites none (cf. *Jub.* 39:6; *Asen.* 7:5). He prayed and fasted for seven years from wine and food, which he distributed to the poor and sick (3:4-5),[147] weeping for "the Egyptian woman from Memphis, for very unceasingly she troubled me and in the night she came to me under the pretence of visiting me" (3:6).

Next Joseph reports that she treated him as her own male child, until by his prayers she had her own (3:7), but then Joseph reports: "I was ignorant. Finally she drew me towards (into?) sexual immorality* (κἀγὼ ἠγνόουν· ἔσχατον εἰς πορνείαν με ἐφελκύσατο)" (3:8). The Greek could mean not only "towards, in the direction of" but directly "into", the more common meaning of εἰς. Against the latter reading is the unlikelihood that the author, who praises Joseph's chastity throughout this testament and elsewhere, would report here that he failed.[148] The following words, "When I perceived it, I sorrowed unto death, and when she had gone out, I came to myself and I lamented for her many days" (3:9), are not an expression of repentance but of grief in recognising her guile and deceit. He then seeks to persuade her "from her evil desire (ἀπὸ τῆς ἐπιθυμίας αὐτῆς τῆς πονηρᾶς)" by quoting "the words of the Most High" (3:10), perhaps the prohibition of adultery (cf. 3:3 and *Jub.* 39:6; *Asen.* 7:5).

Her fourth strategy was to affirm to her husband Joseph's chastity (σωφροσύνη) (cf. ὁ σώφρων Ιωσηφ 4 Macc 2:2), hoping thereby to deflect her husband's concerns about their being together and so take advantage of the opportunity (4:1-2), in response to which Joseph lay on the ground in sackcloth praying for deliverance. Then, fifthly, she tried persuading Joseph that she would take instruction from him if he slept with her, including abandoning idolatry and persuading her husband to do the same, to which Joseph replied by declaring that

---

Joseph faced ten temptations, in fr. 1852 in the collection of Greek parallels to Genesis compiled in F. Petit, *La chaîne sur la Genèse: Édition integrale* (4 vols.; Traditio Exegetica Graeca 1-4; Leuven: Peeters, 1991-1996), though its list of ten covers other events in Joseph's life as well (307-308).

[147] Fisk, "One Good Story," poimts to the interplay here with Dan 1:8-16, which similarly describes the four Israelites slaves as preferring vegetables and water to the palace food, and then despite that becoming handsome (236-37). He notes the probable role of Gen 39:6-7 in making the connection.

[148] Implied in the comment of Hollander and de Jonge, *Commentary*: "it refers to the woman's open attempts to seduce Joseph" (376). Similarly Hollander, *Joseph*: "she sought to draw me into fornication" (36).

God "does not want those who reverence him (to be) in uncleanness (ἐν ἀκαθαρσίᾳ), nor does he take pleasure in those who commit adultery (ἐν τοῖς μοιχεύσουσιν)" (4:6) and gave himself to more prayer and fasting.

Next, sixthly, she offered to kill her husband and legally marry Joseph, who in response threatened to report her (5:1-2). She then plied him with gifts, including fine food, but laced with witchcraft and contaminated with idolatry (5:3 – 6:1, 5). On her return he confronted her with it, eats it in the confidence that God protects those who worship him "in chastity" (ἐν σωφροσύνῃ) (6:7), bringing her to her knees with a promise to desist (6:2-9). Thereupon, seventh, she became sick, but rushed back to Joseph threatening suicide, which Joseph recognised as a sign "that the spirit of Beliar was troubling her", confronted her blindness through sin and pulled her back from the brink by alerting her to the consequences for her children if the concubine, her rival, should usurp her place (7:1-5). This, in turn, persuaded her, eighthly, that Joseph really did love her after all (7:6), which the author through Joseph then explains as typical of the self-deception which occurs when "someone has submitted to the passion of an evil desire (ἐπιθυμίας πονηρᾶς) and become a slave of it as she" and twists to suit that passion's goal (7:8), typical of the author's psychology. Again Joseph prayed for release – for twenty-four hours (8:1).

In 8:2-5 we return to the biblical account, ninthly, of her grabbing his clothes and Joseph fleeing naked, falsely accused by her, and subsequently landing in prison. But there too, tenthly, the Egyptian woman, sick with grief, heard him in good spirits (because God has finally delivered him), and promised to secure his release from prison if he would consent to fulfil her desire (9:1) and even came by at midnight to listen. Joseph gave her no attention and reminds his children how God prefers chastity in a den of darkness to licentiousness in luxury (9:2). Finally, out of sequence, and as an eleventh trial the author has Joseph report that when he was in her house she would bare her arms and breasts and legs "so that I might fall for her"* (ἵνα συμπέσω εἰς αὐτήν), and make herself beautiful "to seduce me" (πρὸς ἀπάτησίν μου) (9:4-5). If the ten stratagems focused on wiles, this one returns to the author's emphasis on women's bodies, in particular, the power of their physical attractiveness and naked sexuality.

The section 3:1 to 9:5 is thus a narrative focusing on the Egyptian woman and her attempts to get Joseph to sleep with her. Many of its elements have parallels in the Phaedra tradition and are not well organised.[149]. Here the episodes are joined

---

[149] On the extent to which one might call this account a romance see the discussion in Richard I. Pervo, "The Testament of Joseph, and Greek Romance," in *Studies on the Testament of Joseph* (ed. George W. E. Nickelsburg; SBLSCS 5; Missoula: Scholars, 1975) 15-23. He offers a critical assessment of Martin Braun *History and Romance in Greco-Oriental Literature* (Oxford: Basil Blackwell, 1938), who identified numerous parallels

rather arbitrarily, mostly with the help of transitional phrases or key-words, often just πολλάκις, ποσάκις, πάλιν δὲ ἐν ἑτέρῳ χρόνῳ or just καί or δέ.[150] They were "probably taken from a (Jewish) source in which hellenistic romantic traditions were connected with and applied to biblical tradition".[151]

When the author has Joseph draw conclusions for his children, he has him declare: "if you follow after chastity and purity (τὴν σωφροσύνην καὶ τὴν ἁγνείαν) with patience and humility of heart, the Lord will dwell in you because he loves chastity (τὴν σωφροσύνην)" (10:2) and God will deliver them "from evils for the sake of his chastity" (διὰ τὴν σωφροσύνην) (10:3). It is most probable that σωφροσύνη ("chastity") here includes avoidance both of adultery and of any other sexual relations before marriage.

The second major story (11:2 – 16:6) takes us back in time before the seduction scenes to the time when Joseph was delivered as a slave into Egypt by the Ishmaelites. It also concerns the seductress, introduced in 12:1, "About that time the Memphian woman (ἡ Μεμφία) passed by in a chariot, the wife of Petephres, with great pomp, and she cast her eyes on me (καὶ ἐπέβαλεν ἐπ' ἐμὲ τοὺς ὀφθαλμοὺς αὐτῆς)". She had been identified as from Memphis already in 3:6, but her husband as Photimar. In this story eunuchs play a role as informers and agents, including one who was "head of all the eunuchs, having a wife and children and concubines" (13:5), indicating the technical use of the term for an official, clearly not using it to describe someone who could not be sexually active. "The Memphian woman" (ἡ Μεμφία) persuades Petephres, her husband, to fetch Joseph to become his steward (12:2), which leads at one stage to Joseph being beaten naked and her looking at him through the window (14:1), a common stance of women in such stories (cf. *Asen*. 7:2). Joseph is then imprisoned, but, he tells us, "she wanted to see me out of a desire for sin; and I was ignorant concerning all these things" (14:4). She has a eunuch unsuccessfully try to purchase him, but a second succeeded, making a small profit for himself on the side, whom Joseph kindly did not expose (16:1-6). The account ends there, which is where the first begins.

In his closing words Joseph mentions his marriage to "the daughter of my masters" from whom he received an enormous dowry (18:3), and like his brothers, urges that Judah and Levi be honoured (19:6). The marriage to a Gentile receives no comment, though it stands in tension with what is demanded elsewhere. It

---

between the account of the attempted seduction of Potiphar's wife in *T. Joseph* and contemporary romantic literature (44-93). Pervo argues that *T. Jos.* 3 – 9, in contrast to Genesis 39, a novella, is "a longer narrative with much in common with what we call Romance" (89-90), pointing to parallels in Plato, *Phaedo* 107D – 108C; *Resp.* 10.614-21.

[150] Hollander and de Jonge, *Commentary*, 373.

[151] Hollander and de Jonge, *Commentary*, 373.

appears that the author has identified the Potiphar of Gen 37:36; 39:1 with the Potiphera of Gen 41:45, 50; 46:20, as do the author of Jubilees (*Jub.* 40:10) and the LXX, which translates both as Petrephres.[152]

For all its detailed elaboration of Joseph's encounter with the Egyptian woman through both stories, this testament offers relatively little that is new on the author's attitudes towards sexuality. The seductive strategies are mechanisms and tricks, but underlying both stories is the assumption that seductive women pose a danger, cannot help themselves at times, are desperate to the point of irrationality, in a manner which the author also uses to entertain his hearers, and that a man should avoid being alone with a married woman, must have an alert and sober mind to see what is happening and not fall to her wiles, and so to avoid adultery and probably, by implication, sexual relations before marriage. As Gur-Klein notes, "In the *Testament of Joseph* the basic story is extended to capture femininity as a dark evil dream of men the beauty of whom is reluctantly admitted".[153] Only somewhat as an appendage to the first story do we hear of the woman's physical sexual attractiveness, added by the author because this is usually his concern. Of incidental interest is the author's not making anything of Joseph's marriage to a Gentile, which could hardly be contradicted, and the reference to sexually active eunuchs.

3.13   The Testament of Benjamin

The testament begins with brief reference to Benjamin's birth, emphasising that he was born to Rachel after she prayed to the Lord with fasting for twelve days, having been barren for twelve years after giving birth to Joseph, and that he was then suckled by Bilhah (1:3-4), already established as most worthy in *T. Naph.* 1:6-8.[154] The figures are probably symbolic; at a literal level they contradict information elsewhere. According to Gen 30:32 God responded to Rachel's prayer in enabling her to conceive Joseph after having been barren. Genesis says nothing of subsequent barrenness and prayer, but for the author prayer is assumed to help the infertile.

The author's psychology is again apparent in his emphasis in this testament on the "good mind" (ἀγαθὴ διάνοια) (3:2; 5:1; 6:5), or "good disposition" (τὸ διαβούλιον τοῦ ἀγαθοῦ) (6:1, 4), which produces good behaviour according to

---

[152] See also de Jonge, "Sidelights," drawing attention to further discussion in a fragment of Origen which even has Aseneth inform her father about her mother's false accusation (308-309).

[153] Thalia Gur-Klein, "Potiphar's Wife and the Cultural Template of Sacred Sexuality," *Lectio difficilior* 2.1 (2001) (http://www.lectio.unibe.ch/01_1/inhalt_e.htm).

[154] See also de Jonge, "Sidelights," 310-11.

the commandments (4:3-5) because it sees well and so can resist the spirits of Beliar (3:3-4; 6:1). Accordingly, the good man "does not gaze passionately upon corruptible things", "does not delight in pleasure" (φιληδονίαν) and "does not err in the uplifting of the eyes" (μετεωρισμοῖς ὀφθαλμῶν) (6:2-3), the latter possibly with reference to sexual wrongdoing. The author employs the image of conception to describe the link between evil idea and evil action: for "first the mind conceives through Beliar" (πρῶτον συλλαμβάνει ἡ διάνοια διὰ τοῦ Βελιάρ) (7:2) (cf. similar usage in *T. Reub.* 3:12; 5:6).

Sexual themes appear in 8:2:

2 ὁ ἔχων διάνοιαν καθαρὰν ἐν ἀγάπη οὐχ ὁρᾷ γυναῖκα εἰς πορνείαν
οὐ γὰρ ἔχει μιασμὸν ἐν καρδίᾳ
ὅτι ἀναπαύεται ἐν αὐτῷ τὸ πνεῦμα τοῦ θεοῦ.
3 ὥσπερ γὰρ ὁ ἥλιος οὐ μιαίνεται προσέχων ἐπὶ κόπρον καὶ βόρβορον,
ἀλλὰ μᾶλλον ἀμφότερα ψύγει καὶ ἀπελαύνει τὴν δυσωδίαν,
οὕτω καὶ ὁ καθαρός νοῦς ἐν τοῖς μιασμοῖς τῆς γῆς συνεχόμενος μᾶλλον οἰκοδομεῖ,
αὐτὸς δὲ οὐ μιαίνεται.

He who has a pure mind in love does not look at a woman with a view to sexual immorality; for he has no defilement in his heart,
because the spirit of God rests upon him.
3 For as the sun is not defiled though in contact with dung and mire,
but rather dries up both and drives away the evil smell,
so also the pure mind though encompassed by the defilements of the earth rather builds up, but is not itself defiled. (8:2-3)

Apparently the author compares the danger which women pose, with dung and mire. The good mind can accordingly cope with the danger and does not become defiled by looking at a woman with a view to sexual immorality. The qualification is significant since it envisages that men do look at women, but are not to do so for the wrong reasons and at the same time will be able to ward off dangers from the woman's side. This fits the author's psychology elsewhere, illustrated by Joseph's success in dealing with what the author would see as the dung and mire which she represented. The offensiveness of the imagery is all the more because the author is not simply singling out what some women might do, but what he assumes all women have a tendency to do and be, namely seductive, as the exposition in *T. Reuben* shows. In this sense it fits that this passage functions as a closure of the author's paraenetic expositions, which began warning against sexual wrongdoing and women in particular, and so end on the same note.[155]

In this testament the predictions of Enoch relate specifically to sexual sin: "you will engage in sexual immorality (following) the sexual immorality of

---

[155] On this see also Menn, *Judah and Tamar*, 169.

Sodom* (πορνεύσετε γὰρ πορνείαν Σοδόμων)" (9:1). This is to be taken as a reference to homosexual acts (already *T. Naph.* 3:4; 4:1). The author adds: "you will renew wanton deeds with women (καὶ ἀνανεώσεσθε ἐν γυναιξὶ στρήνους)" (cf. *T. Dan* 5:5). These are not specified, but most likely refer to prostitution, given the references elsewhere (*T. Levi* 14:5-6). Then within what is clearly an element of Christian composition we read that God "will convict Israel through the chosen ones of the Gentiles, even as he convicted Esau through the Midianites, who refused to be their brothers through sexual immorality and idolatry (διὰ τῆς πορνείας καὶ τῆς εἰδωλολατρείας); and they were alienated from God"*(10:10). The latter reference is unclear, though its power is evident in having even the Midianites, notorious for sexual wrongdoing and idolatry (cf. Num 25:6-18), reject Esau's people on grounds of sexual immorality.

Apart from the link between prayer and fertility this testament reinforces the author's view that a sound mind produces right behaviour and in that context underlines that this is particularly true of encountering women where on the one hand it prevents one from looking lustfully and on the other disempowers the danger which women present because of the uncontrolled sexuality. The author again notes homosexual acts in the context of predictions of sexual wrongdoing beside hetersosexual immorality.

3.14 Conclusion

In relation to sexuality the author addresses appropriate sexual behaviour from two major starting points. Throughout we find allusions to the divine Law. Mostly we can identify the source, such as for the prohibitions of adultery, incest, homosexual acts, and bestiality, but given the fictional setting of pre-Mosaic patriarchs, we should not expect to find direct references to the written law.[156] Sometimes appeal is made to commandments which existed already at the alleged time of the speeches, such as the prohibition of marrying a Canaanite (Gen 28:1; *T. Jud.* 13:7; 14:6) and the requirement of circumcision (Gen 17:9-14), which is a key element in the story of Shechem. Frequently the author has recourse to the strategy of referring to the books of Enoch, for instance, on levirate marriage in *T. Zeb.* 3:4, which we know from Deut 25:5-10. Such references are best understood as mostly[157] alluding not to the Enochic corpus which we know, but to the teachings believed to be passed down through Enoch and his successors. Sometimes the author employs the alternative strategy of appealing to heavenly tablets, on the

---

[156] Slingerland, "Nature of *Nomos*," 41, 43.

[157] The myth of the Watchers as depicted in *1 Enoch* 8:1-2, is assumed, for instance, in the account of their engagement with women. See also Jackson, *Enochic Judaism*, 68.

assumption that what was revealed to Moses on Sinai already pre-existed in the heavenly world, a view likely to have been espoused by the author, who apparently knew the book of *Jubilees*. As in *Jubilees*, therefore, pentateuch laws are assumed, but portrayed as pre-Mosaic,[158] but many, especially those related to the cult and cult purity, go unmentioned.

On the other hand, for instance, notions of defilement of a woman through sexual intercourse with someone other than her husband, rendering her unclean in relation to her husband, reflected in Deut 24:1-4, inform the author's explanation of Reuben's sin with Bilhah. Unlike *Jubilees* it lacks reference to the Sabbath, but, as Slingerland points out,[159] a number of other elements are present including such concerns as idolatry (*T. Reub.* 4:6; *T. Levi* 17:11; *T. Jud.* 19:1; 23:1; *T. Zeb.* 9:5; *T. Benj.* 10:10), witchcraft (*T. Jud.* 23:1; *T. Jos.* 6:1), burial rites (*T. Sim.* 9:1), fasting (*T. Reub.* 1:10; *T. Sim.* 3:4; *T. Jos.* 4:8; 10:1; *T. Benj.* 1:4), levirate marriage (*T. Jud.* 10:4-5); food laws (*T. Levi* 9:13); sacrifices (*T. Reub.* 6:8; *T. Levi* 2:12; 9:4 9:7); and firstfruit offerings and gifts (*T. Iss.* 3:6 2:5; 5:3-4).[160] Some elements, such as levirate marriage (*T. Zeb.* 3:4) and food laws (*T. Ash.* 4:5) are employed also symbolically. *T. Iss.* 4:6 also points to possible perversion of the commandments in the interests of sexual wrongdoing. *T. Iss.* 6:1 appears to use sexual imagery from Gen 2:24 to depict future sins.

Biblical accounts of sexual wrongdoing, by Reuben against Bilhah, Shechem against Dinah (though the focus there is on exonerating Levi), Judah against Tamar (embellished by Amorite tradition about communal induction of brides; *T. Jud.* 12:2), the men of Sodom and Gomorrah, the Watchers, Judah in marrying Bath-shua, or of its avoidance, pre-eminently by Joseph, but also by Rachel, inform the author's values, who brings all such sin under the category of πορνεία.

The author goes, however, far beyond enjoining obedience to commandments and illustrating them positively or negatively with biblical accounts and their embellishments. For he relates behaviour to attitudes, which he describes as spirits. He identifies processes and appeals to his hearers to understand them. In relation to sexual immorality this means understanding how it begins. He affirms human embodiedness, including what he lists as its created senses, including sexual desire, which he sets in the context of procreation within marriage as its solely appropriate sphere. Not sexual desire but its misdirection beyond that context constitutes the beginning of sexual wrongdoing. Here he identifies the importance

---

[158] Hollander and de Jonge, *Commentary*, note that this was also a widespread view in late second century C.E. Christianity (83).

[159] Slingerland, "Nature of *Nomos*," 45-47.

[160] Kee, "Ethical Dimensions," speaks of the cultus as "taken for granted" (260). Similarly Slingerland, "Nature of *Nomos*," 47; Matthias Konradt, "Menschen- und Bruderliebe? Beobachtungen zum Liebesgebot in den Testamenten der Zwölf Patriarchen," *ZNW* 88 (1997) 296-310, 296-97 n. 2.

of another sense or spirit, sight, as the vehicle through which stimuli are received in response to which desire might be aroused in a way that is inappropriate. In this, two key elements play a role. The subject, exclusively male and primarily as the young male (*T. Reub.* 2:1-2), though not exclusively so (*T. Reub.* 4:7), needs to know what he sees and be well informed about it and needs to resist responding to it by desirous looking. Ignorance is failure to know these things and to observe instruction from "the law of God" and from "the admonitions of his fathers" (*T. Reub.* 3:8; cf. *T. Jud.* 19:3-4); its effects are blinding or blurring of vision.

The "law of God", strongly rooted in Jewish understandings of God's will and the commandments, finds expression in this document, as many have recognised, in the language of virtues and vices and the processes of ethical thought and behaviour familiar from Stoic discourse. As Kee notes, "the moral exhortations of the Test XII are expressed pervasively in abstract terms ... the virtues that are extolled are expressed not in terms of legal precepts quoted from Torah, but in the commonplaces of Stoicism".[161] The focus is not on obedience to individual commandments given to Israel in the covenant, but on following divine order mirrored in creation, so that "the Jewish term for 'law', in its Greek translation, νόμος, is being interpreted under the perspective of universal law developed by the Stoics".[162] This is the path followed by Jewish wisdom in its engagement with Hellenistic philosophical world. "The most important, most common and most revealing terms in Test XII ... are σύνεσις, σωφροσύνη, and ἁπλότης."[163] Kee's claim, however, that "the framework of decision-making is not the precepts of Torah, but the goal of achieving integrity as the highest virtue",[164] does not do justice to the overall framework which remains theological and rooted in Jewish tradition, any more than it does to those writings which he rightly cites as comparable, the Wisdom of Solomon and 4 Maccabees.[165] Strikingly, however, the author's most authoritative claims, namely to revelation through angels, relate above all to the nature of women and despite their theological gloss seem fairly clearly derived from popular prejudice of the Greco-Hellenistic world, rather than Jewish biblical tradition. A similar claim to revelation is made for the author's foundational psychology set out in *T. Reub.* 2:1 – 3:8.

The need to understand what one sees leads the author, therefore, to warn his male hearers about women. While the problem is not seeing women *per se*, the author (or the patriarch whose speech he creates) claims that such angelic revelation has informed him that women have less ability than men to control their sexual desires (*T. Reub.* 5:3), even at one point identifying this as a sickness (*T.*

---

[161] Kee, "Ethical Dimensions," 263.
[162] Kee, "Ethical Dimensions," 262.
[163] Kee, "Ethical Dimensions," 263.
[164] Kee, "Ethical Dimensions," 266.
[165] Kee, "Ethical Dimensions," 269.

Reub. 6:3). It makes them dangerous, all the more so because they are so intent on having intercourse that they adorn themselves and practise other strategies to achieve their goal, the Egyptian woman confronting Joseph being a prime example. They are even blamed for seducing the Watchers (*T. Reub.* 5:6-7). Another angelic revelation informs him that they can even conquer kings (*T. Jud.* 15:5-6) and yet another, that the only proper approach to sexual activity (for both men and women) is to be like Rachel and engage in sexual intercourse only for procreation (*T. Iss.* 2:1-3). Armed with this knowledge, one should, accordingly, not gaze at their beauty, should shun interest in their affairs, not keep regular company with them, and especially avoid being alone with a married woman, because of the sexual pressure they exert. In this, women are to be blamed as "evil", and are depicted as mire and dung. Even women whose sexuality is not engaged and are totally passive, such as Bilhah who was dead drunk, and later depicted positively also in *T. Naph* 1:9 as born the same day as Rachel, pose a danger because of their appearance. Bilhah was stark naked. Reuben's seeing her is the author's illustration for exhortations not to pay heed to a woman's face or beauty (3:10; 4:1). If a man recognises these dangers, then he can resist responding with illicit desire.

This ability, the author tells us, can be seriously inhibited, however, by the effects of drinking excessive wine, a theme extensively treated in *T. Judah*, but also by being combined with other allurements such as greed (*T. Jud.* 18:2). Being drunk can also lead one to divulge secrets (*T. Jud.* 12:6; 16:4). In the author's analysis wine becomes sexual immorality's servant, troubling the mind with "filthy thoughts", warming the body up for sex (*T. Jud.* 14:2-3; cf. also 16:1), though the author sees sexual desire as a burning flame even without wine (*T. Jos.* 2:2), and desensitising one's sense of shame (*T. Jud.* 14:5). Unlike in Genesis, wine is portrayed as playing a key role in both Judah's failures: marrying Bathshua and having sex with Tamar.

Once a man has decided to look sexually and become involved, a process is set in motion, according to the author, which can easily lead to action in which a man is described as offending God and harming himself by bringing shame on himself before other men, but also before Beliar (*T. Reub.* 4:7; 6:3), but rarely as wronging the woman. The author even speaks of the beginning of the process as conception, one's mind falling pregnant to women's sexuality, as he describes sleeplessness once desire is awakened, and a corruption of the mind (*T. Reub.* 3:12; cf. also 5:6; *T. Benj.* 7:2). The author assures his hearers, however, that women need not control men. Men can resist (*T. Reub.* 5:4), but the mix of engendered passion especially with excessive drinking of wine makes it difficult, often leading to entrapment and servitude. This is developed especially in the case of Judah where on the basis of the alleged angelic revelation Judah turns his pledges into symbols and shows how the king, the valiant, and even the poor, fall victim to women (*T. Jud.* 15:5), so much so that even the author's God responds with some sympathy (*T. Jud.* 19:3). The author expounds the nexus between anger and violence similarly in *T. Gad*, including the need to manage initial responses and do the best one can not to have strong emotional responses, when thinking one has been wronged.

Surrounding what is effectively a psychological explanation of a process leading from misdirected sexual desire—in response to the dangerous stimuli of female sexuality—to sexual wrongdoing, is a framework of demonology and a pneumatology. Thus the author not only personifies sexual immorality (*T. Reub.* 4:6; 6:4; *T. Sim.* 5:3), but also speaks of the spirit of sexual immorality as one of the spirits of Beliar, also identified as Satan. Conversely, at one point he can also speak of the "spirit of truth" appealing to the mind and reporting to God (*T. Jud.* 20:1-5). The merging with demonology also explains how bodily location of vices in various parts of the body (*T. Reub.* 3:2-4) leads to the notion that God afflicted Reuben in his loins for sexual wrongdoing (*T. Reub.* 1:7) and Gad in his liver for hatred (5:9-11; cf. *T. Reub.* 3:3). What governs the author's understanding of the processes which lead from desire to action, however, is not demonology, perceiving the activities of demons, nor, when speaking positively, of the spirit of God, pneumatology, but psychological dynamics. We are in the realm of appropriating philosophies of how to live, being applied to biblical values.[166] While the author mentions food laws at least symbolically, like the author of *2 Enoch* and the *Testament of Abraham*, he shows no interest in traditional boundary markers such as Sabbath and circumcision laws.

Sexual wrongdoing is the pre-eminent sin. Reuben, its chief perpetrator, still weeps (1:5), unlike any of his brothers. This sin is described as the great sin. Coincidentally linked with the first born, Reuben, it is the first addressed, and it is the first of Beliar's spirits (*T. Reub.* 3:3) and the anticlimax of the seven spirits of creation (*T. Reub.* 2:8-9). Matching its prominence in the first testament is its featuring in the closing chapters of the last (*T. Benj.* 8:2-3). Sexual immorality is portrayed as leading to the downfall of several tribes (Simeon, Issachar, Dan, Benjamin), and the degradation of both the priesthood and kingship.[167] Joseph is the countermodel to Reuben and Judah.[168] Yet, as Menn, observes, "Ironically, in this work that ostensibly endeavours to suppress immoral sexuality, there is a

---

[166] Kee, *OTP*, notes: "Although the Law is the declared norm for ethical behaviour in T12P, the details of moral obligation and the overall framework in which obedience to the Law is enjoined are shaped by Stoic virtues and by Stoic anthropological conceptions, and also by the dualistic notions of Jewish apocalypticism" (1.782 n 1c). "Sexual misdeeds are not linked to specific commandments; rather, they are handled by injunctions to temperance or asceticism, for which there is no basis in Torah" (1.770).

[167] So Menn, *Judah and Tamar*, 169-70.

[168] So Menn, *Judah and Tamar*, 172.

florid development of biblical stories containing irregular sexual encounters, obsessive in its detail".[169]

The range of sexual wrongdoing, in the exhortations, in their illustrative material and in the predictions, is extensive, but not comprehensive nor coextensive. Thus sometimes what is said in the exhortations and predictions is closely linked, as in the general warning in *T. Sim.* 5:3 and general prediction in 5:4; and the allusion to Sodom and homosexual acts in *T. Naph.* 3:4-5 and, immediately following, the prediction about walking in the wickedness of the Gentiles and doing according to the lawlessness of Sodom (4:1). Generally, however, the range of specific acts of sexual wrongdoing is broader in the predictions. It includes unique elements not addressed in the exhortations nor present in their illustrations, such as making singing girls or prostitutes of one's daughters (*T. Jud.* 23:2); pederasty (*T. Levi* 17:11); and bestiality (*T. Levi* 17:11). It also includes elements present in the illustratory material of the exhortations, though not addressed directly in the exhortations, themselves, such as going to prostitutes (*T. Levi* 14:5-6; probably also *T. Benj.* 9:1); defiling virgins (*T. Levi* 14:6); and homosexual acts (*T. Levi* 14:6; *T. Naph.* 4:1; *T. Benj.* 9:1). Some elements in the predictions are present in both the illustrations and the exhortations, themselves, such as adultery (*T. Levi* 14:6) and intermarriage, to which we return below. The range expressed in the illustrative material of the exhortations is also broad: rape and incest with Bilhah (*T. Reub.* 1:6-10; 3:11-15; 4:2-4), the Egyptian woman's seductive behaviour (*T. Reub.* 4:8-11; *T. Jos.* 3 – 9), the illicit relations between women and angels (*T. Reub.* 5:6-7), the abduction and rape of Dinah (*T. Levi* 5:3-4; 6:3 – 7:4), Judah's marrying a Canaanite (*T. Jud.* 8:1-2; 11:1-5; 13:3-8; 14:6; 17:1-2), his going to Tamar as a prostitute and committing incest (*T. Jud.* 12:1-12; 15:1-6), *coitus interruptus* (*T. Jud.* 10:4-5), and Sodom's homosexual acts (*T. Naph.* 3:4).

On the other hand the exhortatory material, itself, apart from its illustrations remains fairly general, with its warnings against sexual immorality also sometimes linked to idolatry, shame, greed, and abuse of alcohol. It seems, however, to envisage a more limited range of concerns than those in the predictions and those present in its illustrative material. It certainly includes adultery (sometimes specifically as in *T. Ash.* 2:8; 3:3; *T. Jos.* 4:4-7), any kind of extra-marital or premarital sex (implied in Joseph's story and the defiling of Dinah but also in the exhortation to wait for God to supply a wife), and also any sexual intercourse just for pleasure and not for procreation. On the other hand, it never addresses incest or prostitution. Thus in its warnings about the apparel of wives and daughters (*T. Reub.* 5:5) it makes no mention of the possibilities named in the predictions of their becoming singing girls or prostitutes. It also includes no warnings about

---

[169] Menn, *Judah and Tamar*, 170.

homosexual acts, pederasty, and bestiality, nor, of course, about sex with angels. The exhortations envisage the likely dangers faced by the work's first hearers, themselves. The wider range found in the predictions (which also function in some respects as warnings) reflect the broader range of sexual wrongdoing associated in particular with the gentile world: such as prostitution, but also homosexual acts, and, in one reference, pederasty and bestiality.

Prohibited intermarriage features in all three categories. Thus intermarriage with Gentiles is predicted of Levi's descendants in *T. Levi* 14:6, including breaches of purity laws in relation to them. The account of the slaughter at Shechem may well embody diverse stances: Jacob's compromise of intermarriage after circumcision of males and possibly Levi's rejecting such intermarriage, a stance which may also be reflected in *T. Simeon*. As in *Jubilees*, a source used by the author, Judah's marriage to a Canaanite, seen as flouting patriarchal law represented in Gen 28:1 (*T. Jud.* 13:7; 14:8), is one of the root causes of his problems (*T. Jud.* 14:6), whereas ironically Bath-shua lives out a hard line stance from the opposite side of the fence. Establishing an Abrahamic pedigree for Bilhah and Zilpah may even be designed to protect Jacob from having slept with a foreign woman (*T. Iss.* 1:10-11). Then both *T. Jud.* 23:2 and *T. Dan* 5:5 predict sin through connection with "the abominations of the Gentiles" in a context which implies sexual relations though not necessarily marriage. At the level of Christian readership, forbidding intermarriage would make little sense, unless perhaps transferred to marriage with unbelievers, but in some instances it would have been easy to read what once doubtless addressed this live issue of early Judaism as historical comment not about Gentiles in general but about marriage to Canaanites in particular (relevant for both *T. Levi* and *T. Judah*).[170] As in *Jubilees*, which otherwise champions a hard line on intermarriage, nothing is made of Joseph marrying a Gentile Egyptian, negatively or positively (as in *Aseneth*).

The author links sexual immorality and idolatry, sometimes seeing the former leading to the latter (*T. Reub.* 4:6; *T. Sim.* 5:3; *T. Jud.* 23:2; cf. also *T. Dan* 5:5; *T. Benj.* 10:10), sometimes the reverse (*T. Naph.* 2:2 – 3:5). While incest is deplored (applicable to both Reuben's and Judah's sins, explicitly *T. Jud.* 14:5-6 alluding to

---

[170] Cf. Hollander and de Jonge, *Commentary*, who argue that "Marriage with gentile women is forbidden in the case of Levi (T.L. 9,10) and predicted among the sins of the sons of Levi (14,6) – both passages may ultimately go back to the Levi-document which was used here-, and Judah emphasizes the troubles which he experienced when he married the Canaanite Bath-shua (T. Jud. 8; 10–12)" (43-44). Similarly de Jonge, "Rachel," 345, who argues also that "Judah does not explicitly warn against marrying non-Israelite women" (345); Marinus de Jonge, "Die Paränese in den Schriften des Neuen Testaments und in den Testamenten der Zwölf Patriarchen:. Einige Überlegungen," in *Jewish Eschatology, Early Christian Christology and the Testaments of the Twelve Patriarchs* (Leiden: Brill, 1991) 277-89, 288-89. Cf. Kugel, "Rape of Dinah," 79.

Lev 18:15), nothing is made of Jochabed's marrying her nephew in contravention of Lev 18:12, though the author adds that they were born the same day (*T. Levi* 12:4; cf. Exod 6:19), something he notes positively also of Bilhah and Rachel in *T. Naph.* 1:9, nor of Jacob's marrying two sisters (cf. *T. Iss.* 1 – 2), nor in the latter case of any heavenly sanction for the sequence as in *Jub.* 28:6 (cf. Gen 29:26).

Homosexual acts are understood to be the result of denying God's created order according to *T. Naph.* 2:2 – 3:5, and illustrated both with the Watchers (in regard to denying natural order) and with the people of Sodom (3:4-5). As in Rom 1:18-23, 24-28, it is also seen as a consequence of failing to observe God's true nature (3:3). While at one point depicted as breach of hospitality and violence (*T. Ash.* 7:1), the sin of Sodom and Gomorrah is elsewhere understood as illicit sexual union, thus as adult male to male homosexual acts (*T. Levi* 14:6; *T. Naph.* 4:1; *T. Benj.* 9:1). It is possibly alleged against even the Watchers (*T. Reub.* 5:6). Their sin, in which women were complicit, is rewritten, perhaps to placate sensitivities of the author and his hearers, so that now the women fall pregnant not through directly engaging in sex with the Watchers, but by remote fantasy (*T. Reub.* 5:6-7). Their sin may be alluded to in the reference to sexual immorality as the mother of all evils in *T. Sim.* 5:3. There are two references to eunuchs, one to castrated eunuchs, the fate of some of Judah's male descendants at the hands of the Gentiles (*T. Jud.* 23:5), and in the story of Joseph the eunuch who is married and has a family, clearly not castrated (*T. Jos.* 13:5). Neither implies value judgements about being a eunuch except for the shame entailed in the former.

On the positive side, the author affirms human sexual desire and its fulfilment in sexual intercourse for procreation within marriage (implied already in *T. Reub.* 2:9) and therefore affirms marriage.[171] Within this valid context he even depicts sexual relations with one's wife as an expression of the second commandment to love one's neighbour, as long as it stays second (*T. Naph.* 8:7-10). Monogyny is probably assumed as the norm (*T. Reub.* 4:1; cf. also *T. Iss.* 7:2), probably accounting for why the author seems not to reckon with the possibility of Shelah taking Tamar in levirate marriage (cf. *T. Jud.* 11:3). The author makes Rachel into a model of desiring sexual intercourse only for procreation (*T. Iss.* 2:3) and perhaps also of rejecting fertility enhancements. The author understands marriage on the basis of the common household model where the male rules (*T. Jos.* 3:2), and men marry around the age of 30 (*T. Iss.* 3:5; *T. Levi* 11:8 with 12:4; cf. Reuben, who was 30 when he raped Bilhah: *T. Reub.* 1:8). Thus when Levi married at 28 (*T. Levi* 9:10; 11:1; 12:5), he is consistent with his own instruction of *T. Levi* 9:10 that his descendants marry early. In the mean time young men should keep busy reading literature (*T. Reub.* 4:1), and working ideally as farmers, labouring so hard they are too tired even to think about sex let alone respond to

---

[171] So Ulrichsen, *Grundschrift*, 291.

women and so can wait for the God-appointed woman at the due time (*T. Reub.* 4:1; similarly *T. Iss.* 3:5; 4:1, 4; *T. Levi* 9:9-10). The major theme of Joseph's premarital chastity gives the same message.

Men are to keep strict control over their wives and daughters and prevent them from equipping themselves with the weaponry of adornment and cosmetics (*T. Reub.* 5:5). Marriage appears at one point as valued because it served as an appropriate alternative to sexual immorality (*T. Levi* 9:9-10). Issachar preserved fidelity all his life (*T. Iss.* 7:2). When the author applies the commandment to love one's neighbour to marital love, expressed in sexual intercourse, this assumes a cultic value system which sees sexual relations as inappropriate in the sphere of the holy and so at times and probably places, to be avoided (*T. Naph.* 8:7-10). In its images of the age to come, the work makes no reference to marriage, sexual relations, fertility or abundance,[172] despite the promise of re-entry into paradise (cf. *T. Levi* 18:10-11; *T. Dan* 5:12-13).

Nothing indicates that the author sees the body as dirty or evil. His statements about women as evil and as comparable to dung (*T. Benj.* 8:2) should not be understood as a generalisation about women *per se*, although his belief that women are less able to control their sexuality means that he must see most women as dangerous and evil in this way, the only positive model mentioned being a woman incapacitated by alcohol, dead drunk, but even then posing a danger because she was naked! He sees youth as especially vulnerable to the dangers of sexual passion, almost to the point of hopelessness (*T. Reub.* 2:9; 3:8; *T. Jud.* 11:1; 18:3, 6; 19:4; *T. Sim.* 2:7), but believes in the possibility of forgiveness and rehabilitation through prayer and fasting and possibly sexual abstinence if the references to "bread of desire" (1:10) and "joy" (*T. Jud.* 15:4; 19:3-4) mean this.

The *Testaments* share much in common with Philo and Josephus, including a view of women as weak and inferior, but exhibit greater pessimism and fear in relation to women's sexuality and while not absolving men of responsibility virtually depict every woman as a potential danger on the assumption that she cannot control her sexual urges. Otherwise the commonality extends to the appropriation of Stoic ideals, in particular the psychology of seven faculties common to the Testaments and Philo. In Philo and Josephus sex has a chance: there are good lovers and good women and men as partners. By contrast, the *Testaments* largely ignore good women. Matriarchs are largely invisible with the exception of Rachel, whose chief virtue appears to have been not wanting pleasure from sex but only procreation.

---

[172] As Hollander and de Jonge, *Commentary*, note the reference in *T. Sim.* 6:2 to abundance is about his tribe's future (123).

Conclusion

The bodies of writing considered in this volume stand individually on their own, so that it makes little sense to seek to provide a synthesis of all three together. A comparative discussion lies within a broader assessment taking all writings considered in this series into account. The works of Philo, Josephus, and the *Testaments*, are, however, different from most of those considered in previous volumes, in that, at least with regard to the first two, we are dealing with known individual authors. The closest comparable writings in this respect are Ben Sira's work and those fragmentary remains of Hellenistic Jewish writers. But of none do we have as much information about the authors as of Philo and Josephus. Furthermore, it is clear that Josephus knows of Philo and has probably met members of his family.

Both share a number of common values, including that procreation is the justification for engaging in sexual intercourse, that passions, especially sexual passions, are dangerous, and need be held in control, though they are not in essence wrong if serving the right end in the right context. Nothing suggests a wooden calculated commitment to procreation of a kind that would calculate days of fertility with a view to avoiding sexual engagement at all other times, notwithstanding the clear avoidance of intercourse during menstruation, a prohibition for which there were also other grounds. Both consider women inferior to men, based probably both on their reading of Genesis and on widespread assumptions of their day. Such assumptions of inferiority of intellect and body need not, however, imply misogynism. Indeed in different ways both can envisage very positive relations between men and women, each with defined roles engaged in harmony for the good of the household and the community. These instances of shared values do not require that Josephus derives them from Philo, since they are well attested elsewhere both in Judaism and in various forms of Hellenistic philosophy. Even the quite specific parallels in rules relating to the household are best seen as the result of drawing on common Jewish tradition, as attested also in *Pseudo-Phocylides*.

The third body of material, the *Testaments*, might have found a place in the previous volume on the Pseudepigrapha, a place they had in the initial stages of planning of this series, but both on grounds of space, and, more importantly, content, they belong appropriately beside Philo and Josephus with whose attitudes to sexuality and ethical philosophy they share most in common. Their rhetoric is much more negative concerning women, deeming them as evil and dangerous for men, not simply because of their inferiority, but also because of their inability to exercise control over their passions, a kind of permanent disease and disability, and, even more blatantly, because of their deliberate engagement in deceit and seduction. Again, it would be wrong to turn rhetoric into definition, as though this must be the case with all women, who are thus all permanently evil, since the author knows of women who are not, like Rachel, or who are victims, like Dinah. Similarly, the author can contemplate marital partnership, including sexual engagement and love, in very positive terms.

In the next volume we turn to those writings which emerged from that distinctive Jewish movement which became Christianity, preserved primarily in the New Testament.

Bibliography

Attridge, Harold W. *The Interpretation of Biblical History in the* Antiquitates Judaicae *of Flavius Josephus* (HDR 7; Missoula: Scholars, 1976)

Aune, David E. "Mastery of the Passions: Philo, 4 Maccabees and Earliest Christianity," in *Hellenization Revisited: Shaping a Christian Response within the Greco-Roman World* (ed. Wendy E. Helleman; Lanham: University Press of America, 1994) 125-58

Avioz, Michael. "Josephus's Portrayal of Lot and His Family," *JSP* 16 (2006) 3-13

Baarda, T. "The Shechem Episode in the Testament of Levi: A Comparison with Other Traditions," in *Sacred History and Sacred Texts in Early Judaism: A Symposium in Honour of A. S. van der Woude* (ed. J. N. Bremmer and F. García Martínez; CBET 5; Kampen: Pharos, 1992) 11-73

Bader, Mary Anna. *Tracing the Evidence: Dinah in Post-Hebrew Bible Literature* (Studies in Biblical Literature 102; New York: Peter Lang, 2008)

Baer, Richard L. *Philo's Use of the Categories Male and Female* (ALGHJ 3; Leiden: Brill, 1970)

Bailey, James L. "Josephus' Portrayal of the Matriarchs," in *Josephus, Judaism and Christianity* (ed. Louis H. Feldman and Gohei Hata; Leiden: Brill, 1987) 154-79

Balla, Ibolya. "Ben Sira / Sirach," in William Loader, *The Pseudepigrapha on Sexuality: Attitudes Towards Sexuality in Apocalypses, Testaments, Legends, Wisdom, and Related Literature* (Grand Rapids: Eerdmans, forthcoming) 362-98

Barclay, John M. G. *Against Apion* (Flavius Josephus: Translation and Commentary 10; Leiden: Brill, 2007)

Barton, Stephen C. "The Relativisation of Family Ties in the Jewish and Graeco-Roman Traditions," in *Constructing Early Christian Families: Family as Social Reality and Metaphor* (ed. Halvor Moxnes; London: Routledge, 1997) 81-100

Baynes, Leslie. "Philo, Personification and the Transformation of Grammatical Gender," *SPA* 14 (2002) 31-47

Beall, Todd S. *Josephus' Description of the Essenes Illustrated by the Dead Sea Scrolls* (SNTSMS 58; Cambridge: Cambridge University Press, 1988)

Beavis, Mary Ann. "Philo's Therapeutai: Philosopher's Dream or Utopian Construction?" *JSP* 14 (2004) 30-42

Becker, Jürgen. *Untersuchungen zur Entstehungsgeschichte der Testamente der Zwölf Patriarchen* (AGSU 8; Leiden: Brill, 1970)

Becker, Jürgen. *Die Testamente der zwölf Patriarchen* (JSHRZ 3.6; 2d ed.; Gütersloh: Gütersloher Verlagshaus, 1980) 15-163

Begg, Christopher T. "David, Object of Hate and Love According to Josephus," *REJ* 166 (2007) 395-410

Begg, Christopher T. "Josephus' Retelling of Genesis 34," in *Studies in the Book of Genesis* (ed. A. Wénin; Leuven: Peeters, 2001) 599-605

Begg, Christopher T. "Samson's Final Erotic Escapades According to Josephus," *Hermenêutica* 6 (2006) 39-63

Begg, Christopher T. *Judean Antiquities Books 5-7* (Flavius Josephus: Translation and Commentary 4; Leiden: Brill, 2005)

Begg, Christopher T. "The Josephan Judge Jephthah," *SJOT* 20 (2006) 161-88

Begg, Christopher T. and Paul Spilsbury. *Judean Antiquities Books 8-10* (Flavius Josephus: Translation and Commentary 5; Leiden: Brill, 2005)

Belkin, Samuel. *Philo and the Oral Law: The Philonic Interpretation of Biblical Law in Relation to the Palestinian Halakah* (Cambridge, Mass.: Harvard University Press, 1940)

Bergmeier, Roland. "Die drei jüdischen Schulrichtungen nach Josephus und Hippolyt von Rom: zu den Paralleltexten Josephus, *B.J.* 2,119-166 und Hippolyt, *Haer.* IX 18,2-29,4," *JSJ* 34 (2003) 443-70

Bergmeier, Roland. *Die Essener-Bericht des Flavius Josephus: Quellenstudien zu den Essenertexten im Werk des Jüdischen Historiographen* (Kampen: Kok Pharos, 1993)

Berthelot, Katell. "Les parénèses de la Charité dans les Testaments des douze patriarches," *MScRel* 60 (2003) 23-39

Bilde, Per. "Josephus and Jewish Apocalypticism," in *Understanding Josephus: Seven Perspectives* (ed. Steve Mason; Sheffield: Sheffield Academic Press, 1998) 35-61

Bilde, Per. "The Essenes in Philo and Josephus," in *Qumran between the Old and New Testaments* (ed. Frederick H. Cryer and Thomas L. Thompson; JSOTSup 290; Sheffield: Sheffield Academic Press, 1998) 32-68

Bilde, Per. *Flavius Josephus between Jerusalem and Rome: His Life, His Works, and Their Importance* (JSPSup 2; Sheffield: JSOT Press, 1988)

Birnbaum, Ellen. "Allegorical Interpretation and Jewish Identity Among Alexandrian Jewish Writers," in *Neotestamentica et Philonica: Studies in Honor of Peder Borgen* (ed. David E. Aune, Torrey Seland, and Jarl H. Ulrichsen; NovTSup 106; Leiden: Brill, 2003) 307-29

Boccaccini, Gabriele. *Roots of Rabbinic Judaism: An Intellectual History, from Ezekiel to Daniel* (Grand Rapids: Eerdmans, 2002)

Böhm, Martina. *Rezeption und Funktion der Vätererzählungen bei Philo von Alexandria: Zum Zusammenhang von Kontext, Hermeneutik und Exegese in frühen Judentum* (BZNW 128; Berlin: de Gruyter, 2005)

Bonhöffer, A. *Epiktet und die Stoa* (Stuttgart: Ferdinand Enker, 1890)

Booth, A. Peter. "The Voice of the Serpent: Philo's Epicureanism," in *Hellenization Revisited: Shaping a Christian Response within the Greco-Roman World* (ed. Wendy E. Helleman; Lanham: University Press of America, 1994) 159-72

Borgen, Peder. "'There Shall Come Forth a Man': Reflections on Messianic Ideas in Philo," in *The Messiah: Developments in Earliest Judaism and Christianity* (First Princeton Symposium on Judaism and Christian Origins; ed. James H. Charlesworth; Minneapolis: Augsburg Fortress, 1992) 341-61

Borgen, Peder. *Philo of Alexandria: An Exegete for his Time* (NovTSup 86; Leiden: Brill, 1997; Atlanta: SBL, 2005)

Boyarin, Daniel. *Carnal Israel: Reading Sex in Talmudic Culture* (Berkeley: University of California Press, 1993)

Braun, Martin. *History and Romance in Greco-Oriental Literature* (Oxford: Blackwell, 1938)

Brooten, Bernadette J. "Konnten Frauen im alten Judentum die Scheidung betreiben: Überlegungen zu Mk 10:11-12 und 1 Kor 7:10-11," *EvT* 42 (1982) 65-80

Brooten, Bernadette J. "Zur Debatte über das Scheidungsrecht der jüdischen Frau," *EvT* 43 (1983) 466-78

Brown, Cheryl A. *No Longer Be Silent: First Century Jewish Portraits of Biblical Women* (Louisville: Westminster John Knox, 1992)

Brunschwig, J. "The Cradle Argument in Epicureanism and Stoicism," in *The Norms of Nature: Studies in Hellenistic Ethics* (ed. M. Schofield and G. Striker; Cambridge: Cambridge University Press, 1995) 69-112

Budin, Stephanie Lynn. *The Myth of Sacred Prostitution in Antiquity* (Cambridge: Cambridge University Press, 2008)

Calabi, Francesca. *God's Acting, Man's Acting: Tradition and Philosophy in Philo of Alexandria* (Studies in Philo of Alexandria 4; Leiden: Brill, 2008)

Carras, George P. "Dependence or Common Tradition in Philo Hypothetica VIII 6.10–7.20 and Josephus Contra Apionem 2.190-219," *SPA* 5 (1993) 24-47

Cazeaux, Jacques. "'Nul n'est prophète en son pays' – contribution à l'étude de Joseph d'après Philon," in *The School of Moses: Studies in Philo and Hellenistic Religion: In Memory of Horst R. Moehring* (ed. John Peter Kenney; BJS 304; SPM 1; Atlanta: Scholars, 1995) 41-81

Charles, Robert Henry. "The Testaments of the XII Patriarchs," in *The Apocrypha and Pseudepigrapha of the Old Testament in English with Introductions and Critical and Explanatory Notes to the several Books. Vol. II: Pseudepigrapha* (ed. R. H. Charles; Oxford: Clarendon, 1913) 282-367.

Cohen, Naomi G. "The Mystery Terminology in Philo," in *Philo und das Neue Testament: Wechselseitige Wahrnehmungen: 1. Internationales Symposium zum Corpus Judaeo-Hellenisticum 1.-4. Mai 2003* (ed. Roland Deines and Karl Wilhelm Niebuhr,; Tübingen: Mohr Siebeck, 2004) 173-87

Cohn L. and P. Wendland, ed., *Philonis Alexandrini opera quae supersunt* (Berlin: Reimer, 1896-1814)

Collins, John J. *Between Athens and Jerusalem: Jewish Identity in the Hellenistic Diaspora* (2d ed., Grand Rapids: Eerdmans, 2000)

Colson F. H., G. H. Whittaker (and R. Marcus), *Philo in Ten Volumes (and Two Supplementary Volumes)* (12 vols.; LCL; London: Heinemann; Cambridge, Mass.: Harvard University Press, 1929–62)

Conway, Colleen M. "Gender and Divine Relativity in Philo of Alexandria," *JSJ* 34 (2003) 471-91

Cotton, Hannah M. and Elisha Qimron, "XHev/Se ar 13 of 134 or 135 C.E.: A Wife's Renunciation of Claims," *JJS* 49 (1998) 108-18

D'Angelo, Mary Rose. "Εὐσεβεία: Roman Imperial Family Values and the Sexual Politics of 4 Maccabees and the Pastorals," *BibInt* 11 (2003) 139-65

D'Angelo, Mary Rose. "Gender and Geopolitics in the Work of Philo of Alexandria: Jewish Piety and Imperial Family Values," in *Mapping Gender in Ancient Religious Discourses* (ed. Todd Penner and Caroline Vander Stichele; BIS 84; Leiden: Brill, 2007) 63-88

de Jonge, Marinus, in cooperation with H. W. Hollander, H. J. de Jonge and Th. Korteweg, *The Testaments of the Twelve Patriarchs: A Critical Edition of the Greek Text* (PVTG I 2; Leiden: Brill, 1978)

de Jonge, Marinus. "Defining the Major Issues in the Study of the Testaments of the Twelve Patriarchs," in *Pseudepigrapha of the Old Testament as Part of Christian Literature: The Case of the Testaments of the Twelve Patriarchs and the Greek Life of Adam and Eve* (SVTP 18; Leiden: Brill, 2003) 71-83 de Jonge, Marinus. "Die Paränese in den Schriften des Neuen Testaments und in den Testamenten der Zwölf Patriarchen: Einige Überlegungen," in *Jewish Eschatology, Early Christian Christology and the Testaments of the Twelve Patriarchs* (Leiden: Brill, 1991) 277-89

de Jonge, Marinus. "Josephus und die Zukunftserwartungen seines Volkes," in *Josephus – Studien: Untersuchungen zu Josephus, dem antiken Judentum und dem Neuen Testament: Otto Michel zum 70. Geburtstag gewidmet* (ed. Otto Betz, Klaus Haacker, Martin Hengel; Göttingen: Vandenhoeck und Ruprecht, 1974) 205-19

de Jonge, Marinus. "Levi in the Aramaic Levi Document and in the Testament of Levi," in *Pseudepigrapha of the Old Testament as Part of Christian Literature: The Case of the Testaments of the Twelve Patriarchs and the Greek Life of Adam and Eve* (SVTP 18; Leiden: Brill, 2003) 124-39

de Jonge, Marinus. "Light on Paul from the Testaments of the Twelve Patriarchs? The Testaments and the New Testament," in *Pseudepigrapha of the Old Testament as Part of Christian Literature: The Case of the Testaments of the Twelve Patriarchs and the Greek Life of Adam and Eve* (SVTP 18; Leiden: Brill, 2003) 160-77

de Jonge, Marinus. "Rachel's Virtuous Behavior in the Testament of Issachar," in *Greeks, Romans, and Christians: Essays in Honor of Abraham J. Malherbe* (ed. David L. Balch, Everett Ferguson, and Wayne A. Meeks; Minneapolis: Fortress, 1990) 340-52

de Jonge, Marinus. "Sidelights on the Testaments of the Twelve Patriarchs from the Greek Catena on Genesis," in *Things Revealed: Studies in Early Jewish and Christian Literature in Honor of Michael E. Stone* (ed. Esther G. Chazon, David Satran, and Ruth A. Clements; JSJSup 89; Leiden: Brill, 2004) 303-15

de Jonge, Marinus. "The future of Israel in the Testaments of the Twelve Patriarchs," in *Jewish Eschatology, Early Christian Christology and the Testaments of the Twelve Patriarchs* (Leiden: Brill, 1991) 164-79

de Jonge, Marinus. "The Interpretation of the Testaments of the Twelve Patriarchs in Recent Years," in *Studies on the Testaments of the Twelve Patriarchs: Text and Interpretation* (SVTP 3; Leiden: Brill, 1975) 183-92

de Jonge, Marinus. "The Testaments of the Twelve Patriarchs and Related Qumran Fragments," in *Pseudepigrapha of the Old Testament as Part of Christian Literature: The Case of the Testaments of the Twelve Patriarchs and the Greek Life of Adam and Eve* (SVTP 18; Leiden: Brill, 2003) 107-23

de Jonge, Marinus. "The *Testaments of the Twelve Patriarchs* and the 'Two Ways'," in *Biblical Traditions in Transmission. Essays in Honour of Michael A. Knibb* (ed. Charlotte Hempel and Judith M. Lieu; JSJSup 111; Leiden: Brill, 2006) 179-94 de Jonge, Marinus. "The Testaments of the Twelve Patriarchs as a Document Transmitted by Christians," in *Pseudepigrapha of the Old Testament as Part of Christian Literature: The Case of the Testaments of the Twelve Patriarchs and the Greek Life of Adam and Eve* (SVTP 18; Leiden: Brill, 2003) 84-106

de Jonge, Marinus. "The Testaments of the Twelve Patriarchs: Central Problems and Essential Viewpoints," ANRW II 20,1 (1987) 359-420

de Jonge, Marinus. "The Testaments of the Twelve Patriarchs: Christian and Jewish," *Jewish Eschatology, Early Christian Christology and the Testaments of the Twelve Patriarchs* (Leiden: Brill, 1991) 233-43

de Jonge, Marinus. "The Two Great Commandments in the Testaments of the Twelve Patriarchs," in *Pseudepigrapha of the Old Testament as Part of Christian Literature: The Case of the Testaments of the Twelve Patriarchs and the Greek Life of Adam and Eve* (SVTP 18; Leiden: Brill, 2003) 141-59

de Jonge, Marinus. *Testamenta XII Patriarcharum Edited According to Cambridge University Library MS Ff1.24 fol.203a-262b, with Short Notes* (2d ed., PVTG 1; Leiden: Brill, 1970)

de Jonge, Marinus. *The Testaments of the Twelve Patriarchs: A Study of their Text, Composition and Origin* (2d. ed.; Assen: van Gorcum, 1975)

Deutsch, Celia. "The Therapeutae, Text Work, Ritual, and Mystical Experience," in *Paradise Now: Essays on Early Jewish and Christian Mysticism* (SBLSym 11; ed. April D. DeConick; Atlanta: SBL, 2006) 287-311

Dillon, John M. "Philo's Doctrine of Angels," in *Two Treatises of Philo of Alexandria: A Commentary on De Gigantibus and Quod Deus Sit Immutabilis* (ed. David Winston and John Dillon; BJS 25; Chico: Scholars, 1983) 197-205

Dillon, John M. "The Pleasures and Perils of Soul-Gardening," SPA 9 (1997) 190-97

Donaldson, Terence L. *Judaism and the Gentiles: Jewish Patterns of Universalism (to 135 CE)* (Waco: Baylor University Press, 2007)

Elgvin, Torleif. "Jewish Christian Editing of the Old Testament Pseudepigrapha," in *Jewish Believers in Jesus: The Early Centuries* (ed. Oskar Skarsaune and Reidar Hvalvik; Peabody: Hendrickson, 2007) 278-304

Ellis, J. Edward. "Philo's View of Homosexual Activity," PRSt 30 (2003) 313-23

Ellis, J. Edward. *Paul and Ancient Views of Sexual Desire: Paul's Sexual Ethics in 1 Thessalonians 4, 1 Corinthians 7 and Romans 1* (LNTS 354; London: T&T Clark, 2007)

Engberg-Pedersen, Troels. "Philo's De Vita Contemplativa as a Philosopher's Dream," JSJ 30 (1999) 40-64

Eron, Lewis John. "Early Jewish and Christian Attitudes toward Male Homosexuality as Expressed in the Testament of Naphtali," *Homophobia and the Judaeo-Christian Tradition* (Dallas: Monument, 1990) 25-49

Eron, Lewis John. "That Women Have Mastery Over Both King and Beggar" (TJud. 15,5)—The Relationship of the Fear of Sexuality to the Status of Women in Apocrypha and Pseudepigrapha: 1 Esdras (3 Ezra) 3-4, Ben Sira and the Testament of Judah," *JSP* 9 (1991) 43-66

Feldman, Louis H. "Flavius Josephus Revisited: The Man, His Writings, and his Significance," ANRW 2.21, 2 (1984) 763-805

Feldman, Louis H. "Josephus (CE 37—c. 100)," in *CHJ* 3 (1999) 901-21

Feldman, Louis H. "Josephus' Portrayal (Antiquities 5.136-174) of the Benjaminite Affair of the Concubine and its Repercussions (Judges 19-21)," *JQR* 90 (2000) 255-92

Feldman, Louis H. "Josephus's Biblical Paraphrase as a Commentary on Contemporary Issues," in *Interpretation of Scripture in Early Judaism and Christianity: Studies in Language and Tradition* (ed. Craig A. Evans; JSPSup 33; Sheffield: Sheffield Academic Press, 2000) 124-201

Feldman, Louis H. "Philo, Pseudo-Philo, Josephus, and Theodotus on the Rape of Dinah," *JQR* 94 (2004) 253-77

Feldman, Louis H. "Philo's Interpretation of Jethro," *ABR* 51 (2003) 37-46

Feldman, Louis H. "Questions about the Great Flood, as Viewed by Philo, Pseudo-Philo, Josephus, and the Rabbis," *ZAW* 115 (2003) 401-22

Feldman, Louis H. "The Portrayal of Phinehas by Philo, Pseudo-Philo, and Josephus," *JQR* 92 (2002) 315-45

Feldman, Louis H. *Josephus and Modern Scholarship (1937-1980)* (Berlin: de Gruyter, 1984)

Feldman, Louis H. *Josephus: A Supplementary Bibliography* (New York: Garland, 1986)

Feldman, Louis H. *Josephus's Interpretation of the Bible* (Berkeley: University of California Press, 1998)

Feldman, Louis H. *Judean Antiquities Books 1-4* (Flavius Josephus: Translation and Commentary 3; Leiden: Brill, 2000)

Feldman, Louis H. *Studies in Josephus' Rewritten Bible* (JSJSup 58; Leiden: Brill, 1998)

Fisk, Bruce N. "One Good Story Deserves Another: The Hermeneutics of Invoking Secondary Biblical Episodes in the Narratives of Pseudo-Philo and the Testaments of the Twelve Patriarchs," *Interpretation of Scripture in Early Judaism and Christianity* (Sheffield: Sheffield Academic Press, 2000) 217-38

Fossum, J. "Gen. 1,26 and 2,7 in Judaism, Samaritanism, and Gnosticism," *JSJ* 16 (1985) 202-39

Fraade, S. "Ascetical Aspects of Ancient Judaism," in *Jewish Spirituality: From the Bible through the Middle Ages* (ed. A. Green; New York: Crossroads, 1986) 1.253-88

Franxman, Thomas W. *Genesis and the "Jewish Antiquities" of Flavius Josephus.* (BibOr 35; Rome: BIP, 1979)

Frazier, Françoise. "Les visages de Joseph dans le De Josepho," *SPA* 14 (2002) 1-30

Fredrickson, David. "Passionless Sex in 1 Thessalonians 4:4-5," *WW* 23 (2003) 23-30

Gaca, Kathy L. *The Making of Fornication: Eros, Ethics, and Political Reform in Greek Philosophy and Early Christianity* (Berkeley: University of California Press, 2003)

Gerber, Christine. *Ein Bild des Judentums für Nichtjuden von Flavius Josephus: Untersuchungen zu seiner Schrift Contra Apionem* (AGJU 40; Leiden: Brill, 1997)

Golberg, Shari. "The Two Choruses Become One: The Absence/Presence of Women in Philo's *On the Contemplative Life*," *JSJ* (2008) 459-70

Goodblatt, David. *Elements of Ancient Jewish Nationalism* (Cambridge: Cambridge University Press, 2006)

Goodenough, Erwin R. *An Introduction to Philo Judaeus* (2d ed.; New York: Barnes & Noble, 1962)

Grabbe, Lester L. *A History of the Jews and Judaism in the Second Temple Period: Volume 1: Yehud: A History of the Persian Province of Judah* (London: T&T Clark, 2004)

Grabbe, Lester. "Eschatology in Philo and Josephus," in *Judaism in Late Antiquity; Volume 3.4: Death, Life-after-Death, Resurrection and the World-to-Come in the Judaisms of Antiquity* (ed. A. J. Avery-Peck and J. Neusner; Leiden: Brill, 2001) 163-85

Gur-Klein, Thalia, "Potiphar's Wife and the Cultural Template of Sacred Sexuality," *Lectio difficilior* 2.1 (2001) (http://www.lectio.unibe.ch/01_1/inhalt_e.htm)

Haaland, Gunnar. "Jewish Laws for a Roman Audience: Toward an Understanding of Contra Apionem," in *Internationales Josephus-Kolloquium, Brüssel 1998* (Münster: Lit, 1999) 282-304

Halpern-Amaru, Betsy. "Bilhah and Naphtali in Jubilees: A Note on QTNaphtali," *DSD* 6 (1999) 1-10

Halpern-Amaru, Betsy. "Flavius Josephus and The Book of Jubilees: A Question of Source," *HUCA* 72 (2001) 15-44

Halpern-Amaru, Betsy. "Portraits of Biblical Women in Josephus's Antiquities," *JJS* 39 (1988) 143-70

Halpern-Amaru, Betsy. *The Empowerment of Women in the Book of Jubilees* (JSJSup 60; Leiden: Brill, 1999)

Harl, M. "Adam et les deux arbres du Paradis (Gen. II-III) ou l'homme milieu de la doctrine du libre-arbitre," *RecSR* 50 (1962) 321-88

Harrison, Verna E. F. "The Allegorization of Gender: Plato and Philo on Spiritual Childbearing," in *Asceticism* (ed. Vincent L. Wimbusch and Richard Valantasis; New York: Oxford University Press, 1995) 520-34

Hay, David M. "Foils for the Therapeutae: References to Other Texts and Persons in Philo's 'De vita contemplativa'," in *Neotestamentica et Philonica: Studies in Honor of Peder Borgen* (ed. David E. Aune, Torrey Seland, and Jarl H. Ulrichsen; NovTSup 106; Leiden: Brill, 2003) 330-48

Hay, David M. "Philo of Alexandria," in *Justification and Variegated Nomism: I: The Complexities of Second Temple Judaism* (ed. D. A. Carson, P. T. O'Brien and M. A. Seifrid; Tübingen: Mohr Siebeck; Grand Rapids: Baker, 2001) 357-79

Hay, David M. "Philo's Anthropology, the Spiritual Regimen of the Therapeutae, and a Possible Connection with Corinth," in *Philo und das Neue Testament: Wechselseitige Wahrnehmungen: 1. Internationales Symposium zum Corpus Judaeo-Hellenisticum 1.-4. Mai 2003* (ed. Roland Deines and Karl Wilhelm Niebuhr; Tübingen: Mohr Siebeck, 2004) 127-42

Heinemann, Isaac. *Philons Griechische und Jüdische Bildung: Kulturgleichende Untersuchungen zu Philons Darstellung der Jüdischen Gesetze* (Hildesheim: Olms, 1973)

Henry, C. R. "The Testaments of the XII Patriarchs," *APOT*, 282-367

Hilgert, Earle. "A Survey of Previous Scholarship on Philo's *De Josepho*," *SBLSP* (1986) 262-70

Hillel, Vered. "Naphtali, a Proto-Joseph in the *Testaments of the Twelve Patriarchs*," *JSP* 16 (2007) 171-201

Höffken, Peter. "Bileams Ratschlag und seine Eigenart bei Josephus: Zu Antiquitates 4,126-130," *ETL* 83 (2007) 385-94

Hollander, Harm W. *Joseph as an Ethical Model in the Testament of the Twelve Patriarchs* (SVTP 6; Leiden: Brill, 1981)

Hollander, Harm W. and Marinus de Jonge. *The Testaments of the Twelve Patriarchs: A Commentary* (SVTP 8; Leiden: Brill, 1985)

Horowitz, Maryanne Cline. "The Image of God in Man—Is Woman Included?" *HTR* 72 (1979) 175-206

Horsley, Richard A. "Spiritual Marriage with Sophia," *VC* 33 (1979) 30-54

Hultgård, Anders. *L'Eschatologie des Testaments des Deuze Patriarches: 1. Interpretation des Textes* (Acta Universitatis Upsalienses: Historia Religionum 6; Stockholm: Almqvist & Wiksell, 1977)

Ilan, Tal. "Josephus and Nicolaus on Women," in *Geschichte-Tradition-Reflexion: Festschrift für Martin Hengel zum 70. Geburtstag: Bd 1: Judentum* (ed. Hubert Cancik, Hermann Lichtenberger, and Peter Schafer; Tübingen: Mohr Siebeck, 1996) 221-62

Jackson, Bernard S. "The Divorces of the Herodian Princesses: Jewish Law, Roman Law, or Palace Law?" in *Josephus and Jewish History in Flavian Rome and Beyond* (ed. Joseph Sievers and Gaia Lembi; JSJSup 104; Leiden: Brill, 2005) 343-68

Jackson, David R. *Enochic Judaism: Three Defining Paradigm Exemplars* (Library of Second Temple Studies 49; London: T&T Clark, 2004)

Jervell, Jacob. "Imagines und Imago Dei: Aus der Genesis-Exegese des Josephus," in *Josephus – Studien: Untersuchungen zu Josephus, dem antiken Judentum und dem Neuen Testament: Otto Michel zum 70. Geburtstag gewidmet* (ed. Otto Betz, Klaus Haacker, and Martin Hengel; Göttingen: Vandenhoeck und Ruprecht, 1974) 197-204

Jobling, David. "And Have Dominion: The Interpretation of Genesis 1:28 in Philo Judaeus," *JSJ* 8 (1977) 50-82

Kasher, Aryeh. "Josephus in Praise of Mosaic Laws on Marriage (*Contra Apionem*, II, 199-201)," in *"The Words of a Wise Man's Mouth are Gracious" (Qoh 10,12): Festschrift for Günter Stemberger on the Occasion of his 65th Birthday* (ed. Mauro Perani; Studia Judaica / Forschungen zur Wissenschaft des Judentums 32; Berlin: de Gruyter, 2005) 95-108

Kee, Howard C. "Ethical Dimensions of the Testaments of the XII as a Clue to Provenance," *NTS* 24 (1978) 259-70

Kee, Howard C. "Testaments of the Twelve Patriarchs," *OTP*, 1.775-828

King, Karen L. "The Body and Society in Philo and the Apocryphon of John," in *The School of Moses: Studies in Philo and Hellenistic Religion: In Memory of Horst R. Moehring* (ed. John Peter Kenney; BJS 304; SPM 1; Atlanta: Scholars, 1995) 82-97

Kirchhoff, Renate. "Die Testamente der zwölf Patriarchen: Über Techniken männlicher Machtausübung," in *Kompendium Feministische Bibelauslegung* (Luise Schottroff, Marie-Theres Wacker, Claudia Janssen, and Beate Wehn; Gütersloh: Chr. Kaiser Gütersloher Verlagshaus, 1999) 474-82

Kokkinos, Nikos. "Which Salome did Aristobulus Marry?" *PEQ* 118 (1986) 33-50

Konradt, Matthias. "Menschen- und Bruderliebe? Beobachtungen zum Liebesgebot in den Testamenten der Zwölf Patriarchen," *ZNW* 88 (1997) 296-310

Kottek, Samuel S. *Medicine and Hygiene in the Works of Flavius Josephus* (Leiden: Brill, 1994)

Kraemer, Ross S. "Implicating Herodias and her Daughter in the Death of John the Baptizer: A (Christian) Theological Strategy?" *JBL* (2006) 321-49

Kraemer, Ross S. "Monastic Jewish Women in Greco-Roman Egypt: Philo Judaeos on the Therapeutrides," *Signs: Journal of Women in Culture and Society* 14 (1989) 342-59

Kraemer, Ross S. "Typical and Atypical Jewish Family Dynamics: The Cases of Babatha and Berenice," in *Early Christian Families in Context: An Interdisciplinary Dialogue* (ed. David L. Balch and Carolyn Osiek; Grand Rapids: Eerdmans, 2003) 130-56

Kraft, Robert A. "Philo (Josephus, Sirach and Wisdom of Solomon) on Enoch," *SBLSP* (1978) 1.253-57

Krieger, Klaus-Stefan. "Berenike, die Schwester König Agrippas II, bei Flavius Josephus," *JSJ* 28 (1997) 1-11

Küchler, Max. *Frühjüdische Weisheitstraditionen: Zum Fortgang weisheitlichen Denkens im Bereich des frühjüdischen Jahweglaubens* (OBO 26; Fribourg: Universitätsverlag; Göttingen: Vandenhoeck und Ruprecht, 1979)

Kugel, James L. "Judah and the trial of Tamar," in James L. Kugel, *The Ladder of Jacob: Ancient Interpretations of the Biblical Story of Jacob and his Children* (Princeton: Princeton University Press, 2006) 169-85, 256-57

Kugel, James L. "Reuben's Sin with Bilhah," in James L. Kugel, *The Ladder of Jacob: Ancient Interpretations of the Biblical Story of Jacob and his Children* (Princeton: Princeton University Press, 2006) 81-114, 240-44

Kugel, James L. "The Rape of Dinah, and Simeon and Levi's Revenge," in James L. Kugel, *The Ladder of Jacob: Ancient Interpretations of the Biblical Story of Jacob and his Children* (Princeton: Princeton University Press, 2006) 36-80, 231-39

Kugler, Robert A., *From Patriarch to Priest: The Levi-Priestly Tradition from* Aramaic Levi *to* Testament of Levi (SBLEJL 9; Atlanta: Scholars, 1996)

Kugler, Robert A. *The Testaments of the Twelve Patriarchs* (GAP; Sheffield: Sheffield Academic Press, 2001)

Lassen, Eva Marie. "The Roman Family: Ideal and Metaphor," in *Constructing Early Christian Families: Family as Social Reality and Metaphor* (ed. Halvor Moxnes; London: Routledge, 1997) 103-20

Le Boulluec, Alain. "La place des concepts philosophiques dans la réflexion de Philon sur le plaisir," in *Philon d'Alexandrie et le langage de la philosophie, Monothéismes et Philosophie* (ed. Carlos Lévy; Turnhout: Brepols, 1998) 129-52

Leonhardt-Balzer, Jutta. *Jewish Worship in Philo of Alexandria* (TSAJ 84; Tübingen: Mohr Siebeck, 2001) 256-72

Leoni, Tommaso. "The Text of Josephus's Works: An Overview," *JSJ* 40 (2009) 149-84

Lévi, Carlos. "Philo's Ethics," in *The Cambridge Companion to Philo* (ed. Adam Kamesar; Cambridge: Cambridge University Press, 2009) 146-71

Levine, Daniel B. "*Hubris* in Josephus' *Jewish Antiquities* 1-4," *HUCA* 64 (1993) 51-87

Levison, John R. "Josephus' Version of Ruth," *JSP* 8 (1991) 31-44

Lloyd, Genevieve. *The Man of Reason: "Male" and "Female" in Western Philosophy* (2d ed.; London: Routledge, 1995)

Loader, William. "Attitudes towards Sexuality in Qumran and Related Literature – and the New Testament," *NTS* 54 (2008) 338-54

Loader, William. "Sexuality in the Testaments of the Twelve Patriarchs and the New Testament," in *Transcending Boundaries: Contemporary Readings of the New Testament: In Honour of Professor Francis Moloney, S.D.B.* (ed. Rekha M. Chennattu and Mary L. Coloe Rome: LAS Publications, 2005) 293-309

Loader, William. "The Strange Woman in Proverbs, LXX Proverbs and *Aseneth*," in *Septuagint and Reception: Essays Prepared for the Association for the Study of the Septuagint in South Africa* (ed. Johann Cook; SVT 127; Leiden: Brill, 2009) 97-115

Loader, William. *Enoch, Levi, and Jubilees on Sexuality: Attitudes towards Sexuality in the Early Enoch Literature, the Aramaic Levi Document, and the Book of Jubilees* (Grand Rapids: Eerdmans, 2007)

Loader, William. *Sexuality and the Jesus Tradition* (Grand Rapids: Eerdmans, 2005)

Loader, William. *The Dead Sea Scrolls on Sexuality: Attitudes Towards Sexuality in Sectarian and Related Literature at Qumran* (Grand Rapids: Eerdmans, 2009)

Loader, William. *The Pseudepigrapha on Sexuality: Attitudes Towards Sexuality in Apocalypses, Testaments, Legends, Wisdom, and Related Literature* (Grand Rapids: Eerdmans, forthcoming)

Loader, William. *The Septuagint, Sexuality and the New Testament: Case Studies on the Impact of the LXX in Philo and the New Testament* (Grand Rapids: Eerdmans, 2004)

Mack, Burton L. "Wisdom and Apocalyptic in Philo," *SPA* 3 (1991) 21-39

Martens, John W. *One God, One Law: Philo of Alexandria on the Mosaic and Greco-Roman Law* (Studies in Philo of Alexandria and Mediterranean Antiquity 2; Leiden: Brill, 2003)

Mason, Steve. "'Should Any Wish to Enquire Further' (Ant. 1.25): The Aim and Audience of Josephus's *Judean Antiquities/Life*," in *Understanding Josephus: Seven Perspectives* (ed. Steve Mason; Sheffield: Sheffield Academic Press, 1998) 64-103

Mason, Steve. "The *Contra Apionem* in Social and Literary Context: An Invitation to Judean Philosophy," in *Josephus'* Contra Apionem: *Studies in Its Character and Context with a Latin Concordance to the Portion Missing in Greek* (ed. Louis H. Feldman and John R. Levison; AGJU 34; Leiden: Brill, 1996) 187-228

Mason, Steve. "What Josephus Says About the Essenes in his Judean War," in *Text and Artifact in the Religions of Mediterranean Antiquity: Essays in Honour of Peter Richardson* (ed. S. Wilson and M. Desjardins; Waterloo: Wilfrid Laurier University Press, 2000) 423-55

Mason, Steve. *Flavius Josephus on the Pharisees: A Composition-Critical Study* (SPB 39; Leiden: Brill, 1991)

Mason, Steve. *Josephus and the New Testament* (2d ed.; Peabody: Hendrickson, 2003)

Mason, Steve. *Judean War 2* (Flavius Josephus: Translation and Commentary 1b; Leiden: Brill, 2008)

Mason, Steve. *Life of Josephus* (Flavius Josephus: Translation and Commentary 9; Leiden: Brill, 2001)

Matthews, Shelly. "Ladies' Aid : Gentile Noblewomen as Saviors and Benefactors in the Antiquities," *HTR* 92 (1999) 199-218

Mattila, Sharon Lea. "Wisdom, Sense Perception, Nature, and Philo's Gender Gradient," *HTR* (1996) 103-29

Mayer-Schärtel, Bärbel. *Das Frauenbild des Josephus: Eine sozialgeschichtliche und kulturanthropologische Untersuchung* (Stuttgart: Kohlhammer, 1995)

McArthur, Harvey. "Celibacy in Judaism at the time of Christian Beginnings," *AUSS* 25 (1987) 163-81

McLaren, James S. "Josephus' Summary Statements regarding the Essenes, Pharisees and Sadducees," *ABR* 48 (2000) 31-46

Mendels, Doron. "Hellenistic Utopia and the Essenes," *HTR* 72 (1979) 207-22

Menn, Esther Marie. *Judah and Tamar (Genesis 38) in Ancient Jewish Exegesis: Studies in Literary Form and Hermeneutics* (JSJSup 51; Leiden: Brill, 1997)

Milgrom, Jacob. "Philo the Biblical Exegete," *SPA* 9 (1997) 79-83

Moehring, Horst. "Arithmology as an Exegetical Tool in the Writings of Philo of Alexandria," in *The School of Moses: Studies in Philo and Hellenistic Religion: In Memory of Horst R. Moehring* (ed. John Peter Kenney; BJS 304; SPM 1; Atlanta: Scholars, 1995) 141-76

Morris, Jenny "The Jewish Philosopher Philo," in Emil Schürer, *The History of the Jewish People in the Age of Jesus Christ (175 B.C. – A.D. 135): Vol. III.2* (3 vols; ed. Geza Vermes; Fergus Millar, and Martin Goodman; Edinburgh: T&T Clark, 1987) 808–89

Najman, Hindy. "A Written Copy of the Law of Nature: An Unthinkable Paradox?" *SPA* 15 (2003) 54-63

Najman, Hindy. "The Law of Nature and the Authority of Mosaic Law," *SPA* 11 (1999) 55-73

Naumann, Weigand. *Untersuchungen über den apokryphen Jeremiasbrief* (BZAW 25; Giessen: Töpelmann, 1913)

Newman, Judith H. "Lot in Sodom: The Post-Mortem of a City and the Afterlife of a Biblical Text," in *The Function of Scripture in Early Jewish and Christian Tradition* (JSNTSup 154; ed. Craig A. Evans and James A. Sanders; Sheffield: Sheffield Academic Press, 1998) 34-44

Nickelsburg, George W. E. *Jewish Literature Between the Bible and the Mishnah: A Literary and Historical Introduction* (2d ed.; Minneapolis: Fortress, 2005)

Niebuhr, Karl-Wilhelm. *Gesetz und Paränese: Katechismusartige Weisungsreihen in der frühjüdischen Literatur* (WUNT 2.28; Tübingen: Mohr Siebeck, 1987)

Niehoff, Maren. "Mother and Maiden, Sister and Spouse: Sarah in Philonic Midrash," *HTR* 97 (2004) 413-44

Niehoff, Maren. *Philo on Jewish Identity and Culture* (TSAJ 86; Tübingen: Mohr Siebeck, 2001)

Niehoff, Maren. *The Figure of Joseph in Post-Biblical Literature* (AGJU 16; Leiden: Brill, 1992)

Niese, Benedictus. *Flavii Iosephi Opera* (7 vols.; Berlin: Weidmann, 1885-95)

Nikiprowetzky, Valentin."Sur une lecture démonologique de Philon d'Alexandrie, De Gigantibus 6-18," in Hommage à Georges Vajda: Études d'histoire et de pensé juives (ed. G. Nahon et C. Touati; Louvain: Peeters, 1980) 43-71

Nikiprowetzky, Valentin. *Le commentaire de l'Écriture chez Philon d'Alexandrie: Son caractère et sa portée: Observations philologiques* (ALGHJ, 11; Leiden: Brill, 1977) 117-55

Noack, Christian. *Gottesbewusstsein: Exegetische Studien zur Soteriologie und Mystik bei Philo von Alexandrien* (WUNT 2.116; Tübingen: Mohr Siebeck, 2000) 182-203, 226-47

Pearce, Sarah J. K. *The Land of the Body: Studies in Philo's Representation of Egypt* (WUNT 2.208; Tübingen: Mohr Siebeck, 2007)

Pearson, Birger A. "Philo and Gnosticism," ANRW II.21.1 (1984) 295-342

Pervo, Richard I. "The Testament of Joseph, and Greek Romance," in *Studies on the Testament of Joseph* (ed. George W. E. Nickelsburg; SBLSCS 5; Missoula: Scholars, 1975) 15-23

Petit, F. *La chaîne sur la Genèse: Édition integrale* (4 vols.; Traditio Exegetica Graeca 1-4; Leuven: Peeters, 1991-1996)

Pomeroy, Sarah. *Goddesses, Whores, Wives, and Slaves* (New York: Schocken, 1975)

Rajak, Tessa. *Josephus: The Historian and His Society* (London: Duckworth, 2002)

Ranocchia, Graziano. "Moses against the Egyptian: The Anti-Epicurean Polemic in Philo," in *Philo of Alexandria and Post-Aristotelian Philosophy* (ed. Francesca Alesse; SPA 5; Leiden: Brill, 2008) 75-102

Reinhartz, Adele. "Parents and Children: A Philonic Perspective," in *The Jewish Family in Antiquity* (ed. Shaye J. D. Cohen; Atlanta: Scholars, 1993) 61-88

Reinhartz, Adele. "Philo on Infanticide," *SPA* 4 (1992) 42-58

Reydams-Schils, Gretchen. "Philo of Alexandria on Stoic and Platonist Psycho-Physiology: The Socratic Higher Ground," in *Philo of Alexandria and Post-Aristotelian Philosophy* (ed. Francesca Alesse; SPA 5; Leiden: Brill, 2008) 169-95

Riedweg, Christoph. *Mysterienterminologie bei Platon, Philon und Klemens von Alexandrien* (Berlin: de Gruyter, 1987)

Roncace, Mark. "Josephus' (Real) Portraits of Deborah and Gideon: A Reading of *Antiquities* 5.198-232," *JSJ* 31 (2000) 247-74

Rosner, Brian. "A Possible Quotation of Test. Reuben 5:5 in 1 Corinthians 6,18A," *JTS* 43 (1992) 123-27

Royse, James R. "The Works of Philo," *The Cambridge Companion to Philo* (ed. Adam Kamesar; Cambridge: Cambridge University Press, 2009) 32-64

Runia, David T. "A Neglected Text of Philo of Alexandria: First Translation into a Modern Language," in *Things Revealed: Studies in Early Jewish and Christian Literature in Honor of Michael E. Stone* (ed. Esther G. Chazon, David Satran, and Ruth A. Clements; JSJSup 89; Leiden: Brill, 2004) 199-207

Runia, David T. "Eudaimonism in Hellenistic-Jewish Literature," in *Shem in the Tents of Japhet: Essays on the Encounter of Judaism and Hellenism* (ed. James L. Kugel; JSJSup 7; Leiden: Brill, 2002) 131-57

Runia, David T. "The Place of *De Abrahamo* in Philo's *Oeuvre*," *SPA* 20 (2008) 133-50

Runia, David T. *On the Creation of the Cosmos according to Moses: Introduction, Translation and Commentary* (Leiden : Brill, 2001)

Runia, David T. *Philo of Alexandria and the* Timaeus *of Plato* (Philosophia Antiqua 44; Leiden: Brill, 1986)

Satlow, Michael L. *Jewish Marriage in Antiquity* (Princeton: Princeton University Press, 2001)

Schenck, Kenneth. *A Brief Guide to Philo* (Louisville: Westminister John Knox, 2005)

Schoedel, William R. "Same-Sex Eros: Paul and the Greco-Roman Tradition," in *Homosexuality, Science, and the "Plain Sense" of Scripture* (ed. David L. Balch; Grand Rapids: Eerdmans, 2000) 43-72

Schreckenberg, Heinz. "Text, Überlieferung und Textkritik von Contra Apionem," in *Josephus'* Contra Apionem*: Studies in Its Character and Context with a Latin Concordance to the Portion Missing in Greek* (ed. Louis H. Feldman and John R. Levison; AGJU 34; Leiden: Brill, 1996) 49-82

Schröder, Bernd. *Die väterlichen Gesetze: Flavius Josephus als Vermittler von Halachah an Griechen und Römer* (TSAJ 53; Tübingen: Mohr Siebeck, 1996)

Schuller, Eileen M. "Women of the Exodus in Biblical Retellings of the Second Temple Period," in *Gender and Difference in Ancient Israel* (ed. Peggy Day; Minneapolis: Fortress, 1989) 178-94

Schwartz, Daniel R. "Composition and Sources in Antiquities 18; The Case of Pontius Pilate," in *Making History: Josephus and Historical Method* (ed. Zuleika Rodgers; JSJSup 110; Leiden: Brill, 2007) 125-46

Schwartz, Daniel R. "Did the Jews Practice Infanticide in Antiquity?" *SPA* 16 (2004) 61-95

Schwartz, Daniel R. "Doing Like Jews or Becoming a Jew? Josephus on Women Converts to Judaism," in *Jewish Identity in the Greco-Roman World / Jüdische Identität in der griechisch-römischen Welt* (ed. Jörg Frey, Daniel R. Schwartz, and Stephanie Gripentrog; AGJU 71; Leiden: Brill, 2007) 93-109

Schwartz, Daniel R. "Philo, His Family and His Times," in *The Cambridge Companion to Philo* (ed. Adam Kamesar; Cambridge: Cambridge University Press, 2009) 9-31

Scott, James M. "Dionysus in Philo of Alexandria: A Study of *De Vita Contemplativa*," *SPA* 20 (2008) 33-54

Seland, Torrey. "Philo and the Clubs and Associations of Alexandria," in *Voluntary Associations in the Graeco-Roman World* (ed. John S. Kloppenborg and Stephen G. Wilson; London: Routledge, 1996) 110-27

Siegert, Folker, and Jean Laporte. "The Philonian Fragment De Deo: First English Translation," *SPA* 10 (1998) 1-33

Siegert, Folker, Heinz Schreckenberg, and Manuel Vogel, *Flavius Josephus: Aus meinem Leben (Vita)* (Tübingen: Mohr Siebeck, 2001)

Sievers, Joseph. "The Role of Women in the Hasmonean Dynasty," in *Josephus, the Bible, and History* (ed. Louis H. Feldman and Gohei Hata; Leiden: Brill, 1989) 132-46

Sievers, Joseph. *Synopsis of the Greek Sources for the Hasmonean Period: 1-2 Maccabees and Josephus, War 1 and Antiquities 12-14* (Rome: PBI, 2001)

Skinner, Marilyn B. *Sexuality in Greek and Roman Culture* (Oxford: Blackwell, 2005)

Slingerland, H. Dixon. "The Nature of *Nomos* (law) within the Testaments of the Twelve Patriarchs," *JBL* 105 (1986) 39-48

Slingerland, H. Dixon. *The Testaments of the Twelve Patriarchs: A Critical History of Research* (SBLMS 21; Missoula: Scholars, 1977)

Sly, Dorothy. "Philo's Practical Application of Dikaiosynē," *SBLSP* (1991) 298-308

Sly, Dorothy. *Philo's Perception of Women* (BJS 209; Atlanta: Scholars, 1990)

Spilsbury, Paul. *The Image of the Jew in Flavius Josephus' Paraphrase of the Bible* (Tübingen: Mohr Siebeck, 1998)

Sterling, Gregory E. "'The Jewish Philosophy': The Presence of Hellenistic Philosophy in Jewish Exegesis in the Second Temple Period," in *Ancient Judaism in its Hellenistic Context* (ed. Carol Bakhos; JSJSup 95; Leiden: Brill, 2005) 131-53

Sterling, Gregory E. "'Wisdom among the Perfect': Creation Traditions in Alexandrian Judaism and Corinthian Christianity," *NovT* 37 (1995) 355-84

Sterling, Gregory E. "The Invisible Presence: Josephus's Retelling of Ruth," in *Understanding Josephus: Seven Perspectives* (ed. Steve Mason; Sheffield: Sheffield Academic Press, 1998) 104-71

Sterling, Gregory E. "Universalizing the Particular: Natural Law in Second Temple Jewish Ethics," *SPA* 15 (2003) 64-80

Stone, Michael E. "Aramaic Levi Document and the Greek Testament of Levi," in *Emanuel: Studies in Hebrew Bible, Septuagint and Dead Sea Scrolls in Honor of Emanuel Tov* (ed. Shalom M. Paul, Robert A. Kraft, Lawrence H. Schiffman and Weston W. Fields; Leiden: Brill, 2003) 429-37

Stuckenbruck, Loren. "To What Extent did Philo's Treatment of Enoch and the Giants Presuppose a Knowledge of the Enochic and Other Sources Preserved in the Dead Sea Scrolls?" *SPA* 19 (2007) 131-42

Szesnat, Holger. "'Mostly Aged Virgins': Philo and the Presence of the Therapeutrides at Lake Mareotis," *Neot* 32 (1998) 191-201

Szesnat, Holger. "'Pretty boys' in Philo's De vita contemplativa," *SPA* 10 (1998) 87-107

Szesnat, Holger. "Philo and Female Homoeroticism: Philo's Use of γύvανδρος and Recent Work on *Tribades*," *JSJ* 30 (1999) 140-47

Taylor, Joan E. "Philo of Alexandria on the Essenes: A Case Study on the Use of Classical Sources in Discussions of the Qumran-Essene Hypothesis," *SPA* 19 (2007) 1-28

Taylor, Joan E. *Jewish Women Philosophers of First Century Alexandria: Philo's 'Therapeutae' Reconsidered* (London: Oxford University Press, 2004)

Terian, Abraham. *Philonis Alexandrini De Animalibus: The Armenian Text with an Introduction, Translation, and Commentary* (SHJ 1; Chico: Scholars, 1981)

Termini, Cristina. "Philo's Thought within the Context of Middle Judaism," *The Cambridge Companion to Philo* (ed. Adam Kamesar; Cambridge: Cambridge University Press, 2009) 95-103

Thackeray, H. St. John, Ralph Marcus, Allen Wikgren, and Louis H. Feldman, *Josephus* (LCL 10 vols.; London: Heinemann; Cambridge, Mass.: Harvard University Press, 1926–1965)

Tobin, Thomas H. "Interpretations of the Creation of the World in Philo of Alexandria," in *Creation in the Biblical Traditions* (CBQMS 24; Washington: CBA, 1992) 108-28

Tobin, Thomas H. "Philo and the Sibyl: Interpreting Philo's Eschatology," *SPA* 9 (1997) 84-103

Tobin, Thomas H. "Tradition and Interpretation in Philo's Portrait of the Patriarch Joseph," *SBLSP* (1986) 271-77

Tobin, Thomas H. *The Creation of Man: Philo and the History of Interpretation* (CBQMS 14; Washington: CBA, 1983)

Ulrichsen, J. H. *Die Grundschrift der Testamente der Zwölf Patriarchen: Eine Untersuchung zu Umfang, Inhalt und Eigenart der ursprünglichen Schrift* (AUUHR 10; Uppsala: Almqvist & Wiksell, 1991)

van den Hoek, Annewies. "Endowed with Reason or Glued to the Senses: Philo's Thought on Adam and Eve," in *The Creation of Man and Woman: Interpretations of the Biblical Narratives in Jewish and Christian Traditions* (Themes in Biblical Narrative: Jewish and Christian Traditions I; ed. G. P. Luttikhuizen; Leiden: Brill, 2000) 63-75

van der Horst, Pieter W. "Celibacy in Early Judaism," *RB* 109 (2002) 390-402

van der Horst, Pieter W. "Images of Women in Ancient Judaism," in *Female Stereotypes in Religious Traditions* (ed. Ria Kloppenborg and Wouter J. Hanegraaff; SHR 66; Leiden: Brill, 1995) 43-60

van der Horst, Pieter W. *Philo's* Flaccus*: The First Pogrom: Introduction, Translation and Commentary* (Leiden: Brill, 2003)

van Henten, Jan W. "Cleopatra in Josephus: From Herod's Rival to the Wise Ruler's Opposite," in *Wisdom of Egypt* (Leiden: Brill, 2005) 115-34

van Unnik, Willem Cornelis. "Josephus' Account of the Story of Israel's Sin with Alien Women in the Country of Midian (Num 25:1ff)," in *Travels in the World of the Old Testament: Studies Presented to Prof. Mabveek on the Occasion of his 65th Birthday* (ed. M. S. H. G. Heerma van Voss et al.; Assen: Van Gorcum, 1974) 241-61

VanderKam, James C. *From Joshua to Caiaphas: High Priests after the Exile* (Minneapolis: Fortress; Assen: Gorcum, 2004)

Vermes, Geza. *Jesus the Jew: A Historian's Reading of the Gospels* (London: Collins, 1973)

Visotzky, Burton L. "Most Tender and Fairest of Women: A Study in the Transmission of Aggada," *HTR* 76 (1983) 403-18

Völker, Walther. *Fortschritt und Vollendung bei Philon von Alexandrien: Eine Studie zur Geschichte der Frömmigkeit* (TU 49.1; Leipzig: Hinrichs, 1938)

von Gemünden, Petra, and Pierre Magne de la Croix, "La femme passionnelle et l'homme rationnel? Un chapitre de psychologie historique," *Bib* 78 (1997) 457-80

Wassen, Cecilia. "The Story of Judah and Tamar in the Eyes of the Earliest Interpreters," *Literature and Theology* 8 (1994) 354-66

Weber, Reinhard. *Das "Gesetz" bei Philon von Alexandrien und Flavius Josephus: Studien zum Verständnis und zur Funktion der Thora bei den beiden Hauptzeugen des hellenistischen Judentums* (ARGU 11; Frankfurt: Peter Lang, 2001)

Weber, Reinhard. *Das Gesetz im hellenistischen Judentum: Studien zum Verständnis und zur Funktion der Thora von Demetrios bis Pseudo-Phokylides* (ARGU 10; Frankfurt: Peter Lang, 2000)

Wegner, Judith Romney. "Philo's Portrayal of Women: Hebraic or Hellenic?" in *"Women Like This": New Perspectives on Jewish Women in the Greco-Roman Period* (ed. A. J. Levine; Atlanta: Scholars, 1991) 41-66

Wevers, John William. *Notes on the Greek Text of Deuteronomy* (SBLSCS 39; Atlanta: Scholars, 1995)

Williamson, G A. *Josephus: The Jewish War* (Harmondsworth: Penguin, 1959)

Wilson, Walter T. "Pious Soldiers, Gender Deviants, and the Ideology of Actium: Courage and Warfare in Philo's *De Fortitudine*," SPA 17 (2005) 1-32

Wilson, Walter T. "Sin as Sex and Sex with Sin: The Anthropology of James 1:12-15," *HTR* 95 (2002) 147-68

Winslow, Karen Strand. *Early Jewish and Christian Memories of Moses' Wives: Exogamist Marriage and Ethnic Identity* (Lewiston: Edwin Mellen, 2005)

Winston, David, "Philo and the Rabbis on Sex and the Body," in *The Ancestral Philosophy, Hellenistic Philosophy in Second Temple Judaism: Essays of David Winston* (ed. Gregory E. Sterling; BJS 331; SPM 4; Providence: Brown University Press, 2001) 199-219

Winston, David. "Philo of Alexandria on the Rational and Irrational Emotions," in *Passions and Moral Progress in Greco-Roman Thought* (ed. John T. Fitzgerald; London: Routledge, 2008) 201-20

Winston, David. "Philo's Ethical Theory," *ANRW* II.21.1 (1984), 372-416

Winston, David. "Sage and Super-Sage in Philo of Alexandria," in *The Ancestral Philosophy, Hellenistic Philosophy in Second Temple Judaism: Essays of David Winston* (ed. Gregory E. Sterling; BJS 331; SPM 4; Providence: Brown University Press, 2001) 171-80

Winston, David and John Dillon, *Two Treatises of Philo of Alexandria: A Commentary on De Gigantibus and Quod Deus Sit Immutabilis* (BJS 25; Chico: Scholars, 1983)

Winter, Bruce W. *Philo and Paul among the Sophists: Alexandrian and Corinthian Responses to a Julio-Claudian Movement* (2d ed.; Grand Rapids: Eerdmans, 2002)

Wolfson, Harry A. *Philo* (2 vols.; Cambridge, Mass.: Harvard University Press, 1962)

Wright, Archie T. "Some Observations of Philo's *De Gigantibus* and Evil Spirits in Second Temple Judaism," *JSJ* 36 (2005) 471-88

Index of Modern Authors

Attridge	286	Borgen	2, 4, 96, 99, 102, 132, 135
Aune	43, 44, 89, 96, 102		153, 154
Avioz	275	Boyarin	6, 24, 46, 76
Baarda	392, 393, 394, 395, 396	Braun	283
Bader	280, 393	Brooten	351
Baer	4, 5, 8, 12, 13, 15, 16, 17, 18, 19	Brown	264, 289, 290, 295, 338
	20, 22, 23, 24, 26, 43, 44, 48, 50, 52	Brunschwig	68
	53, 54, 68, 72, 84, 98, 105, 137, 139	Budin	402
	216	Calabi	72, 73, 74, 76
Bailey	263, 274, 277, 279, 360	Carras	333, 334
Balla	137, 383	Cazeaux	173
Barclay	262, 328, 329, 330, 331, 332	Cohen	137, 203
	354	Cohn	4
Barton	344	Collins	369, 370, 371
Baynes	138	Colson	4, 184, 209, 210, 242
Beall	263, 335, 336, 338	Conway	8, 9, 47, 50, 52
Beavis	102	Cotton	352
Becker	369, 375, 382, 383, 419	D'Angelo	5, 33, 196, 272
Begg	262, 281, 282, 287, 288, 289	de Jonge	365, 368, 369, 370, 371, 372
	290, 291, 292, 295, 296, 297, 298		374, 375, 376, 377, 378, 379, 381
Belkin	30, 199, 219, 224, 225, 229		382, 384, 386, 390, 394, 395, 396
Bergmeier	263, 338		397, 412, 414, 418, 419, 420, 421
Berthelot	368		422, 424, 425, 428, 433, 435
Bilde	259, 263, 336, 365	de la Croix	54
Birnbaum	96	Deutsch	104, 107
Boccaccini	416	Dillon	85, 88, 89, 143
Böhm	103, 152, 153, 196, 225	Elgvin	368
Bonhöffer	86	Ellis	57, 62, 77, 78, 84, 205, 213, 364
Booth	43, 60, 67	Engberg-Pedersen	102

INDEX OF MODERN AUTHORS

Eron 410, 417, 418
Feldman 146, 175, 176, 177, 182, 259
  260, 261, 262, 263, 265, 267, 268
  269, 270, 272, 273, 274, 275, 277
  278, 279, 280, 281, 282, 285, 286
  287, 288, 289, 290, 291, 292, 293
  294, 295, 296, 298, 299, 300, 302
  321, 322, 323, 325, 326, 327, 338
  345, 347, 360, 361
Fisk 395, 422
Fossum 17
Fraade 100
Franxman 265, 266, 268, 269
Frazier 173
Fredrickson 77
Gaca 6, 7, 8, 47, 55, 62, 63, 64, 246
Gerber 260, 333
Golberg 104, 106
Goodblatt 188
Grabbe 132, 135, 301
Gur-Klein 425
Haaland 260
Halpern-Amaru 263, 266, 269, 271
  272, 274, 276, 277, 279, 280, 283
  284, 286, 288, 291, 292, 293, 294
  295, 296, 301, 302, 416
Harl 66
Harrison 12
Hay 14, 15, 102, 103, 107, 135
Heinemann, 34
Henry 374
Hilgert 172
Hillel 415, 416
Höffken 365
Hollander 368, 369, 370, 372, 374
  375, 376, 377, 378, 379, 381, 382
  384, 386, 394, 414, 418, 419, 421
  422, 424, 428, 433, 435
Horowitz 6, 24
Horsley 100, 101, 102
Hultgård 369
Ilan 126, 261, 264, 265, 305, 319
  320, 358
Jackson, B. 351, 352
Jackson, D. 388, 427
Jervell 265, 266

Jobling 99
Kasher 329
Kee 374, 393, 408, 411, 412, 418
  428, 429, 431
King, 84
Kirchhoff 373, 380, 386, 389, 412, 421
Kokkinos 318
Konradt 428
Kottek 278, 355
Kraemer 103, 105, 107, 318, 319, 320
Kraft 142
Krieger 319, 320
Küchler 390, 416
Kugel 372, 380, 381, 391, 392, 393
  394, 395, 396, 402, 403, 412, 433
Kugler 368, 369, 370, 374, 382, 390
  397, 404, 414
Lassen 299, 323
Le Boulluec 19
Leonhardt-Balzer 184, 236
Leoni 262
Lévi 42
Levine 274
Levison 260, 262, 292, 293, 294
Lloyd 35, 50
Loader 1, 18, 28, 56, 75, 101, 109, 137
  165, 189, 200, 226, 229, 267, 268
  270, 271, 280, 302, 303, 304, 324
  329, 334, 337, 362, 371, 372, 377
  380, 381, 385, 387, 388, 394, 396
  398, 401, 402, 416, 418, 419, 420
Mack 132, 134, 135
Marcus 4, 160, 262, 287, 319
Martens 11
Mason 260, 262, 263, 292, 335, 336
  337, 342, 348, 350, 365
Matthews 360
Mattila 8, 9, 16, 42, 46, 48, 49, 52
  53, 54, 76, 98, 136
Mayer-Schärtel 264, 269, 296, 302
  303, 312, 314, 315, 316, 319, 325
  326, 331, 338, 342, 343, 344, 346
  347, 350, 352, 353, 355, 356, 358
  359, 360, 361
McArthur 101
McLaren 263, 336

Mendels	102	Seland	96, 102, 146
Menn	400, 401, 402, 403, 407, 410 426, 431, 432	Sievers	304, 306, 352
		Skinner	323, 324, 325, 354
Milgrom	199	Slingerland	382, 427, 428
Moehring	38, 84, 120, 173	Sly	5, 6, 8, 9, 22, 23, 26, 32, 33, 46 47, 48, 49, 50, 51, 52, 53, 54, 55, 68 81, 82, 83, 86, 87, 121, 137, 150 151, 152, 153, 161, 164, 165, 177 178, 179
Morris	84		
Najman	11		
Naumann	402		
Newman	274		
Nickelsburg	259, 371, 378, 381, 423	Spilsbury	262, 281, 284, 287, 298
Niebuhr	14, 107, 137, 331, 334 378, 389	Sterling	6, 13, 15, 89, 292, 293 294, 333, 334
Niehoff	33, 34, 57, 64, 65, 103, 108 137, 149, 150, 151, 152, 153, 167 172, 194, 196, 197, 198, 204, 211 273, 274, 283, 284	Stone	369, 421
		Stuckenbruck	142, 143
		Szesnat	64, 103, 104, 105, 107, 204 207, 209, 211, 215, 216
Niese	262	Taylor	102, 103, 104, 105, 106, 107 108, 109, 338
Nikiprowetzky	11, 13, 143, 172		
Noack	96	Terian	33, 62, 127, 192, 212
Pearce	87, 130, 183, 185	Termini	24, 116
Pearson	17	Thackeray	262, 287
Pervo	423	Tobin	13, 15, 132, 134, 135, 172
Petit	422	Ulrichsen	369, 376, 386, 397, 419, 434
Pomeroy	338	van den Hoek	23, 26
Qimron	352	van der Horst	101, 126, 146
Rajak	259	van Henten	308
Ranocchia	60, 67	van Unnik	286
Reinhartz	203, 244	VanderKam	301
Reydams-Schils	42	Visotzky	339
Riedweg	137	Völker	18, 85
Roncace	289	von Gemünden	54
Rosner	386	Wassen	403, 407
Royse	3	Weber	229, 390
Runia	10, 13, 15, 17, 18, 21, 22, 23, 24 25, 26, 30, 35, 38, 41, 42, 44, 46, 54 63, 67, 68, 69, 70, 78, 86, 93, 110 117, 120, 121, 122, 123, 135, 147	Wegner	6, 35, 47
		Wendland	4
		Wevers	219
		Whittaker	4
		Wikgren	262
Satlow	119, 151, 163, 226, 227, 272 324, 344	Wilson	44, 45, 146, 215
		Winslow	101, 180
Schenck	2	Winston	6, 7, 13, 19, 24, 27, 30, 41 42, 43, 46, 47, 55, 63, 84, 85, 86 87, 89, 90, 91, 93, 94, 143
Schoedel	208		
Schreckenberg	262		
Schröder	347		
Schuller	263, 264, 360	Winter	67
Schwartz	2, 3, 244, 261, 300, 320	Wright	143
Scott	107		

Index of Ancient Sources

OLD TESTAMENT

Genesis

1:1-5	11, 13
1:1 – 2:15	21
1:2 – 4:1	141
1:11, 12, 21, 24, 25	11
1:26	11, 12, 253
1:26-27	12, 16, 242
1:27	11, 13, 14, 15, 52, 107, 376
1:28	99, 144, 271, 334, 364, 376, 419
2:4	12
2:4-6	266
2:6	12
2:7	11, 12, 14, 15, 16, 17, 22, 246, 246
2:8-17	267
2:16	267
2:17	130
2:18	27, 267
2:18-19a	266
2:18, 20	21, 29, 42
2:20	266
2:20-24	20, 29, 31
2:21	16, 376
2:21-22	27, 249
2:21-24	22, 125
2:22-23	267
2:23	28, 29, 56, 58, 122
2:24	28, 29, 59, 267, 300, 357, 376, 413, 428
2:25 (MT 3:1)	146, 267
2:25 – 3:6	66
3:1	72
3:8	74
3:12, 13	75
3:14	111, 112, 114
3:14 – 4:1	110
3:15	113
3:16	31, 51, 110, 113, 125, 269, 330, 334, 334, 358, 359, 385
3:17-19	110
3:18	113
3:19	129
3:19-20	17
3:20	129, 267
3:24	141
3:24 – 10:9	141
4:1	136, 141
4:1, 2	114
4:2-4, 8, 16	141
4:17	141, 142
4:24	270
5:1-3	265
5:18	142
6:1-2	143
6:1-12	141
6:7	79
6:12	392
6:13	271
7:11	120
9:1	99
9:1-2	144
9:6-7	271
9:20-27	141, 144
9:21	381
9:22	271
11:1-9	141
11:29	271
12:1-4, 6	148
12:10	151
12:16	273
12:17	272
13:7-8	394
14:5	273
15:2-18	148
15:7 – 28:9	148
16:1-6	154
16:2	152
16:6-9	154
16:6-12	148
16:7	120
17:1-5, 15-22	148
17:9-14	427
17:16	152
18:1-15	152
18:11	149
18:12	274
18:15	152
19:5	156, 209
19:8, 14	275
19:32-33	381
20:1-18	275
20:3	276
20:6	276, 394
20:12	151, 272, 276

24:2	160	39:9	283	15:19-24	356
24:3, 16, 50	277	41:45, 50; 46:20	425	15:24	201
25:21, 22	278	42:2	62	17:10-16	246
25:28	161, 162	48:15-16	17	17:11	15, 247
26:1-11	394	48:21	394	18:1-6	118, 195
26:2	160	49:3-4	179, 372, 380	18:6-18	330
26:6-11	277	49:5-7	175, 282, 391	18:7	195, 321
26:8	60		392, 394	18:8	194, 373
26:34	278	49:11-12	402	18:8, 9, 12, 15	321
26:35	278, 347	49:14-15	412	18:9	194, 297
27:28	94	49:16-18	73, 114, 116	18:10, 12	194
27:46	277			18:11	297
28:1	399, 404, 406	**Exodus**		18:12	398, 434
	427, 433	1:19	181	18:15	405, 434
28:9	278	2:11-12, 20	285	18:18	194, 279
28:11	163	4:1-5	73	18:19	201
29:2, 11, 23	279	6:19	398, 434	18:19, 22, 23	193
29:26	279, 434	12:2-23	180	18:20	204, 216
29:27	280	13:2	233	18:22	204, 415
29:31	164	15:1	114	18:26-27, 29	415
29:31 – 30:24	164, 280	15:1, 21	97	19:19	248
30:1	164	19:15	101, 419	19:20-22	323
30:14-15	164, 411	20:25 – 28:34	180	20:10	191, 200
30:32	425	21:2-7	327, 342	20:10-12	321, 353
31:35	120, 165, 280	21:5	183, 232	20:11	373
32:10	73	21:10	94, 249	20:13	193, 205, 216
34:2	395	21:22	243		322, 415
34:3	176, 280, 362	21:22-23	334	20:17	297
34:5, 13, 27	281	21:22-25	327	21:7	322, 323, 397
34:7	281, 373, 394	22:16-17	193, 217, 225	21:9	324, 353
34:8	281		226, 330	21:13-14	322, 329, 350
34:13	393, 395	22:19	193, 217		397
34:26	395	22:29	233	21:14	232
34:27-29	393, 395, 396	23:5	79, 249	20:15-16	193, 217, 322
34:30	175, 394	23:26	133	20:18	120, 201, 202
34:31	221	23:28	132		322, 356
34:40	393	30:12-16	231	20:21	204
35:22	179, 372, 380, 381	33:7	72, 146, 185	21:7	198, 221, 232
35:27	380	34:16	193, 195	21:13-14	198, 199, 232
37:7	172				304
37:26	402	**Leviticus**		22:4-7	233
37:36	425	8:21	91	22:5-8	234
38:5	402	8:29	89, 112, 236	22:13	233
38:7, 8	399-400	10:1-2	184	24:10-16	183
38:11	401	11:5, 7	421	25:23-55	293
38:13-14	178, 402	11:22	69	26:6	131
38:17, 18	403	12:2-5	249	26:8	132
38:21-22	402	12:20	321, 360	27:2-8	237
38:24, 26	403	13:46; 14:3	321	27:3-4	360
39:1	168, 425	15:1-5, 19	321	30:10	201
39:6-7	422	15:18	224		

INDEX OF ANCIENT SOURCES

Numbers	
5:12-31	193, 224, 349
5:27	224, 321
7:20	132
11:4	184, 214
12:1	101, 285, 345
18:15-16	233
19:11	321
21:6	73
24:3-9	132
25:1, 6	286
25:6-9	187
25:6-18	427
27:3	172
27:8-11	239
30:3-15	237
31:15-16	77, 187
31:19	321
36:1-12	239

Deuteronomy	
7:3	193, 195, 298
10:9	29
14:5, 7-8	421
15:12	327, 342
16:16	36, 249
17:15-16	115, 249
17:19-20	382
20:5-7	60, 247, 328
20:14	247
21:10-13	240, 248, 326, 341
21:14	326
21:15-17	81, 164, 222, 240, 249, 324, 344
21:18-21	250, 326, 360
21:27-30	187
22:5	328
22:9-11	247
22:13-21	193, 324
22:16-17	228
22:17	201, 226
22:19	229
22:21	324
22:22	191
22:22-23	227
22:23-24	325
22:23-27	193, 227, 325
22:28-29	193, 225, 226, 227, 325, 329, 394
23:1-2	147, 158, 174

	204, 206, 213, 223, 250, 327, 353
23:4	294, 347
23:13	91, 236, 251
23:16	355
23:17	193, 218, 221
23:18	221, 222, 232, 323, 353, 402
23:21	395
24:1	228, 325, 350
24:1-4	192, 193, 199, 200, 201, 257, 296, 313, 325, 351, 373, 381, 428
24:7	327
25:3	324
25:5-10	293, 325, 361, 401, 414, 427
25:11-12	245
27:17, 18	111, 251
27:19	251
27:29	112
28:7	132
28:52-57	339
30:15	420
32:13	229
32:32	157, 209
33:8	177

Joshua	
23:12-13	347

Judges	
2:11-15	288
4:9	289
11:2	290
11:37-40	290, 350
14:1 – 15:20	414
14:3	291, 347
14:9	291
14:18, 15:6, 16:1-3, 4	292
19:4-8	288
19:22, 24	288

Ruth	
1:3-4, 22	293
2:8-9	294
3:4	293
3:7	349
3:7-15	293
4:1-13	293, 414

1 Samuel	
1:6-7	294
8:11-18	402
18:6, 16-20, 25	295
20:26	356
21:5	356, 419
25:3	296

2 Samuel	
1:19-27	295
1:26	296, 355
11:2	380
11:4	356
12:11	297
12:14, 18	404
13:1-22	297
13:12	373
13:13, 18; 16:20-22	297

1 Kings	
1:4	296
2:3	297
3:1, 16-28	298
10	298
11:1	294, 347
11:1-13	298

2 Kings	
6:25-29	339
23:18-30	273

1 Chronicles	
2:3; 3:5	404
4:22	402
5:1	372

2 Chronicles	
35:20-27	274

Ezra	
9:1, 3-4; 10	299, 300

Nehemiah	
10:1-30	300
13:23-29	300
13:28	301

Esther	
2:5	301
2:7, 16-18	302

Index of Ancient Sources

Psalms	
1:6	420
30	365
80 [79]:7	80

Proverbs	
4:10-14	420
5:3-5	383
6:23-29	380
6:24	383
6:27	407
6:32-35	382
7:5, 25-27	382, 383
8:22	123, 136
9:17	373
11:16; 12:4	390
18:8; 19:15	216

Ecclesiastes	
3:1-8, 11	419

Isaiah	
50:1	352
54:1	132
54:7-8, 57:17 LXX	366

Jeremiah	
3:4	136
3:8	352

Ezekiel	
16:49	274
44:22	304

Daniel	
1:8-16	422
3:51, 88 LXX	421
10:3	373, 406

Hosea	
2:4	352
4:10-11	405
4:11-14	409

OLD TESTAMENT APOCRYPHA AND PSEUDEPIGRAPHA

Additions to Esther	
14:18 (C 29)	406

Aramaic Levi Document	
1c	393, 394 396
2	394
14, 16-18; 62-81	398

Aseneth (Joseph and)	
7:2	424
7:2-3, 6	383
7:5	422
23:13	395

Baruch	**81-85**
4:29	366

Ben Sira / Sirach	
4:11-19	137
6:18-31	137
8:10	421
9:8-9	379, 380, 382 405
14:20 – 15:10	137
19:2	405
24	137
25:2	389
25:21	379
25:13 – 26:27	390
26:1-3, 13-14	382
26:8-9	405
37:29	372
42:12	379
44:16	142
47:20	298
50:25-26	395
51:13-30	137

Demetrius	393

1 Enoch	
2:1 – 5:3	416
6 – 16	199
8:1-2	143, 271, 387, 392 427
10:9-10	272
106:2-3	159

2 Enoch	
71:17-18	159
71:30	388

Jubilees	
3:1, 3	266
3:3-9, 12, 18	267
5:7	271
10:29-34	271
12:9	271
13:11, 13	396
25:1-2	401
30:2-3	396
30:4	393
30:4-18	396
30:5, 23	394
30:7	324
30:25-26	394, 396
33:1-17	372
33:2-8	380
33:9	373, 381
33:15-16	374
41:1-3	400
41:2, 5, 7	401
41:11, 12	403
41:25	279, 408

Judith	
9:2-4	392-394, 396
16:5-6	385

Liber Antiquitatum LAB (Pseudo-Philo)	
2:6-10	270
2:8	146, 270, 358
8:7	393, 395
9:5	179
12:7	185
18:13-14	77, 187, 286
43:5	292, 353
47:8	362

1 Maccabees	
1:11-15	304

2 Maccabees	
2:2	422
3:19	126

3 Maccabees	
1:18	126
6:9	415

4 Maccabees	
1:6; 2:6	98
15:5	121
18:7	126

INDEX OF ANCIENT SOURCES

Psalms of Solomon
2:11	399
2:11-13	409
8:9-10	399
4:4-5	379
16:7-8	379, 383, 399

Pseudo-Eupolemus
9.17.7-8	272-273

Pseudo-Phocylides
175	329
176	375
184, 185	331
199-200	329, 404
215-216	126

Sibylline Oracles
1:87-300	387
3:765-766	331

Testament of Job
6:4; 17:2, 23:1	387

Testament of Solomon
20:13	387

Theodotus
4 7-9	280, 394-396

Tobit
1:1, 4, 5; 7:3	416
4:12	196

Wisdom of Solomon
2:24	267
7:1	17
8:2	137
10:1	22
12:8	132
14:6	271
17:2	415
19:13-14	274

TESTAMENTS OF THE TWELVE PATRIARCHS

Testament of Reuben
1:6	372, 376, 401
1:7	431
1:7-10	373, 432
1:8	376, 434
1:10	406, 428
2:1	385
2:1-2	429
2:1 – 3:9	41, 374-379, 385, 396, 409, 415, 429
2:8	25, 412, 431
2:9	401, 431, 434, 435
3:2-4	431
3:3	385, 388, 405, 420, 431
3:8	401, 404, 409, 429, 435
3:9 – 4:5	372, 379-383
3:10	386
3:11, 12	373, 387, 393, 413, 415, 426, 430
3:11-15	432
3:13	279, 402
3:14	388
3:15	373
4:1	386, 402, 413, 434, 435
4:2-4	432
4:3	374
4:6	383, 391, 428, 431, 433
4:7	391, 429, 430
4:8-11	383-384, 385, 432
5:1-5	380, 384-386, 388, 402, 404
5:2-3	421
5:3	406, 407, 412, 429
5:4	430
5:5	386, 432, 435
5:6-7	377, 386-388, 391, 426, 430, 432, 434
6:1-5	388-389
6:2-3	380, 385, 430
6:4	431
6:8-10	409, 428

Testament of Simeon
1:1	372
2:7	376, 379, 391, 401, 409, 435
3:1	391
3:4	428
4:8-9	377
5:1	416
5:3	383, 391, 431, 432, 433, 434
5:4-6	391
5:5, 7	391
6:2	435
9:1	428

Testament of Levi
2:2-3	392
2:5 – 5:6	392
2:12	428
5:2-3	392, 394
5:3-4	432
6:4-8, 10, 11	393-395
7:1-4	394
8:1-19	396
9:4, 7	428
9:9-10	382, 396, 397-398, 434, 435
9:11-14	398
9:13	428
11:1	397, 398
11:8	373, 434
12:4	373, 398, 434
12:5	395, 398, 434
14:1-2	398
14:5, 6	399, 427, 432, 433, 434
17:11	428, 432
18:10-11	435

Testament of Judah
1 – 7	400
8:1-2	432
8:2-3	400
10:1-6	400-401
10:3	415
10:4-5	428, 432
11:1- 3	376, 379, 401, 435
11:1-5	432
11:3	434
12:1	383
12:1-12	432
12:2	402, 428
12:3	379, 383, 402
12:4, 6-12	403
12:6	408, 430
12:7	385
12:8	373, 393, 415
13:2-7	403-404
13:3	382
13:3-8	432
13:3, 7	401, 406
13:4-5	408

13:5	383		*Testament of Dan*			18:4	416
13:7	427, 433		1:7, 8; 2:1-4; 3:1-6	415		19:6	409, 424
14:1-8	405-406		4:2-7; 5:1-3	415		*Testament of Benjamin*	
14:2-3	421, 430		5:5	383, 393, 418		1:3-8	425
14:5	430, 433			427, 433		1:4	428
14:6	404, 427, 432, 433		5:5-7; 6:1	414-415		3:2; 5:1	425
14:8	433		5:12-13	435		3:3-4	418, 426
15:1-6	432		*Testament of Naphtali*			6:1-3	426
15:4	408, 435		1:4-12	415-416		6:1, 4, 5	425
15:5-6	385, 407, 403		1:6	385		7:2	426, 430
	407, 412, 430, 431		1:6-8	425		8:2-3	372, 426, 431
16:1	421, 430		1:9	434			435
16:1-5	407		2:2 – 3:5	383, 416-417		9:1	427, 432, 434
16:4	430			433, 434		10:10	428
17:1	379		2:2, 6	416			
17:1-3	408, 432		2:9	419		**DEAD SEA SCROLLS**	
18:1-5	408		3:4	427, 432			
18:2	430		3:5	387		*CD (Damascus*	
18:3, 6	401, 435		4:1	417, 427, 432, 434		*Document)*	
18:4	377		8:2	409		4.12b – 5.19	413
19:1	428		8:7-10	418-419, 434, 435		5.2-4	373
19:1-4	408		*Testament of Gad*			4QD^f/4Q271 3 12b-15	324
19:3-4	429, 431, 435		3:1; 4:7; 5:3-11	420			
19:4	401, 435		5:19	373		*1Q20 (Genesis*	
20:1-2	409		6 – 7; 8:1-2	420		*Apocryphon)*	
20:1-5	431		8:1	409		2.9-10, 14-16	56, 381
23:1	415, 428		*Testament of Asher*			2.12-16	152
23:1, 2, 4	409		1:3-9	420		20.19	272, 395
23:2	383, 432, 433		2:8	420, 432			
23:5	434		2:9-11; 4:3, 5	421		*1Q28 (Rule of the*	
Testament of Issachar			3:3	432		*Community)*	
1:2 – 2:5	411-412, 434		4:5	428		3.13 – 4.26	409, 420
1:11	415, 433		7:1	421, 434			
2:1, 3	375, 430, 434		*Testament of Joseph*			*4Q159 (Ordinances^a)*	
2:5	428		1:3 – 2:1	421		2-4+8 8-10	229, 324
3:1	412		2:2, 6, 7	421, 430			
3:4	413		3:1-10	422		*4QMMT (Halakhic*	
3:5	373, 382, 413		3:1 – 9:5	384, 424, 432		*Letter)*	199
	434, 435		3:2	434			
3:6	428		4:1-6	422-423		*11Q19 (Temple Scroll^a)*	
4:1, 4	382, 435		4:4-7	432		66.1-8a	226
4:4	379, 413		4:8	428			
5:1-2	418		5:3 – 9:5	423			
5:3-4; 6:1	428		6:1	428		**NEW TESTAMENT**	
7:2	379, 413, 434, 435		8:5	386			
7:3	414		9:5	401		**Matthew**	
7:6	418		10:1	428		1:18-19	119, 388
Testament of Zebulon			10:2-3	424, 386			
3:4	401, 427, 428		11:2 – 16:6	424		**Mark**	
3:4-7	414		13:5	434		6:17-18, 21-29	318
9:5	428		18:3	424			

7:8-13	238	1.114,134, 141	271	3.274	349, 364
7:21-22	377	1.151	271, 348	3.274-275	294, 329, 347
		1.153	272		348
Luke		1.154	285	3.275	353, 355, 356
1:31, 35	388	1.161-165	272-273, 361	3.276	264, 287, 289
12:36	101	1.162	358		340, 342, 349, 351, 353
16:18	329	1.164	275, 276, 395	3.277	350
		1.174, 183	273	4.73	360
Acts		1.186, 188, 192	274, 347	4.129-144	187, 286, 345
21:9	101	1.194, 197-198	274	4.145-155	286
25:13, 23; 27:30	319	1.200-201	275, 354, 361	4.162	339
			395	4.163	287, 346
Romans		1.202, 204, 205	275	4.176-319	323-328
1:18-23	417, 434	1.205	158, 348	4.206	323, 330, 353
1:24-28	434	1.207-212	275-276, 361		355
1: 26	332	1.208	275, 395	4.209, 309	339
13:9	377	1.239, 261, 278	346	4.219	360
		1.242, 248, 253	277, 344	4.244-245	289, 294, 342
1 Corinthians		1.253, 265	345		347, 349, 353
6:9	377	1.265, 266, 276-278	278	4.246, 252	330
6:18	386	1.266	347, 351	4.247	351
7:2	397	1.288	361	4.248	353
7:5	378, 419	1.288-292	278-279	4.249-250	344
7:9	407	1.291	362	4.251-253	349, 350
11:2-16	380	1.299-302	279-280, 344	4.254-256	361
		1.301	303	4.257-259	341, 364, 375
2 Corinthians		1.305-308	280, 342	4.260-265	360, 364
6:15	378	1.307	355	4.261	329, 331, 375
11:1-3	75	1.315, 318, 322-323	280	4.273	342
11:13-15	387	1.318	362	4.278	361
		1.323, 342	35	4.290-291	342, 353, 364
Ephesians		1.337-341	280-282, 342		375
5:32	137		362	4.301	354
		1.338	345	4.330	339
1 Thessalonians		1.340	393	4.328	284, 462
2:16	395	2.41-60	282-284, 357	4.329	339, 462
			358, 362	5.8	287, 353, 357
James		2.51-52	364, 367	5.48	340
1:15	129, 380	2.218	269	5.65	339
		2.232	285	5.98	247
		2.252-263	285-286	5.136-155	287-288, 289
JOSEPHUS		2.269	347		350, 354, 362
		3.5	359	5.164	340
Antiquitates judaicae		3.78	339, 356	5.165, 168, 171	288
1.27-51	265-270	3.83-286	321-322	5.168	375
1.46	364	3.92	349	5.200	338
1.49	360	2.103	356	5.201, 203, 209	289
1.60-64	270, 355	3.107	357	5.233	244
1.64	146, 358	3.261-262	356	5.259	290
1.67, 69	271, 364	3.269	360	5.276-285	290-291, 311
1.73-74	79, 271, 358	3.270-273	349		362

Index of Ancient Sources

5.276-313	290-292	9.122	341	14.351	305
5.286	345	9.158	344	14.369	357
5.289	363	9.197	343	14.410	340
5.306	346, 353	9.247	340	14.429-430	340, 359
5.317	347	10.33, 128	340, 341	14.467	305
5.318-340	292-294	10.149	341	14.480	339
5.324-325	294	10.172, 175	340	14.481	359
5.330	349	10.237	357	15.22-35	306
5.335	294	11.34-58	357	15.25, 30	354
5.341-347	294-295	11.34-38, 52, 71, 140	299	15.26	307
6.133	339	11.71	345, 351	15.40	312
6.193, 198	295, 344, 363	11.109	339	15.63-67	306-307, 349
6.196-210	343, 363	11.140	345	15.72-73, 81-87	307-308
6.200	344	11.140, 142, 152-153	300	15.73	340
6.206, 241, 275	295	11.146-151	300	15.93, 97, 98, 103	308-309
6.235	356	11.153	345, 351	15.97	358
6.296-308	296	11.184-296	301-303, 357	15.98	357
6.309 .330-340	296	11.196	250, 363	15.99	359
6.357, 364-365	296, 340	11.200	341	15.164	360
7.5, 111	295	11.234-242	302	15.167-178, 185-186	309
7.21, 70	244	11.302-324	301, 345	15.168	360
7.25-26, 87	296, 351	11.306-307	347	15.203, 207, 209-220	310
7.87	357	12.154	343	15.219	79, 349, 359, 360
7.130-158	296-297	12.186-189	303, 348, 363	15.220	349
7.133	363	12.187	330, 345	15.222-240	310-311
7.147	359	12.251, 329	340	15.223-229	355
7.162-180	297, 350	13.67	339	15.240	291
7.169	363	13.69	348	15.241-242	312
7.170	297	13.80, 110, 116, 120	343	15.259	314, 351
7.181-187	357	13.147	359	15.268, 270	357
7.190-191	363	13.171-172	335	15.318-340	361
7.213-214	297, 316, 341	13.222	343	15.319, 321	312, 343
7.225-226, 289	357	13.228, 230-235	340	15.371, 373-379	335
7.291	339	13.245	346	16.2	341
7.343-344	296, 363	13.276-277, 292, 373	304	16.11, 97, 131	344, 346
7.384	297	13.389-393, 394, 373	340	16.66	359
7.391	296	13.345	339	16.85	313, 343, 351
8.5, 21, 24-34	298, 343	13.363, 380	340	16.118-185	349
8.27	298	13.401	304	16.185	359
8.26-34	353	13.417	291, 304	16.194	291, 311, 331
8.128	339	13.430-431	304, 359		342, 363
8.151	343	13.424	357	16.194-199	313, 342
8.158-159	357	14.79, 90, 126	340	16.196	363
8.165-178	298	14.126	348, 363	16.198	79, 351, 364
8.190-191	291, 311, 346	14.260	339	16.201-219	314, 348, 349
	347	14.297-299	305	16.220-231	315-316, 341
8.190-193, 197	298, 345	14.324	364	16.222	363
	363, 364	14.300	343	16.225-226	344, 346
8.249-250, 285	344	14.324	363	16.229, 230, 232	354
8.318	357, 359	14.325	305	16.257, 263, 340	315
8.402	341	14.331, 353-365, 379	340	16.340	349

17.8-10, 15, 18	343, 344	1.158	340	4.561-562	354, 359
17.11	344	1.186	340, 348	5.145	335
17.14, 19-23	344, 346, 347	1.240, 243, 262, 264	305	5.147	357
17.42, 52, 58, 62-64	314	1.241	343	5.227	356
17.62-64	355	1.243	308, 363, 364	5.311	359
17.68, 78, 121	314, 351	1.257	340	6.202-212	339
17.121	359, 360, 364	1.262	357	6.211	359
17.134-145	315	1.344	305	6.426	356
17.166	356	1.351	339	7.181	356
17.235	364	1.353	359	7.334	340
17.309	341, 348	1.432	305, 343, 351	7.338	359
17.341, 349-353	348, 352	1.436	312	7.368	339
17.352	358, 359	1.437, 439	306, 310, 311, 349	7.389-398	340
18.18-22	335, 338			7.399	298
18.21	108	1.439	359	*Contra Apionem*	
18.40, 43-44	316, 342, 363	1.441-443	307-308	1.216	280
18.65-80	316-317, 349, 363	1.443	298, 349	1.239, 261, 278	346
		1.444	312	2.103-104	356
18.109-119, 136	318, 347, 351	1.475	315	2.190	328
		1.476	342	2.190-219	249, 333-334
18.148-149, 160	357	1.477	344	2.195	332
18.180	352	1.486	314	2.195, 198-199	328
18.240-256	318	1.487	315	2.198	331, 338, 356
18.255	360	1.488-492	316, 341, 354	2.199	326, 329, 330, 353, 354, 364, 375
18.340	331	1.500	315		
18.340-353	357	1.508	351	2.199-203	294
18.342, 345	363	1.511	341	2.200	329, 330, 346, 349, 404
18.342-343	341, 363	1.556-558, 561-565	343		
18.342-370	317-318	1.562	347	2.201	32, 269, 330, 342, 349, 352, 358, 359, 360
18.345	346	1.568	359		
18.361-362	351, 357	1.572	351	2.202-203	331, 338, 355, 356, 364, 405
19.30	354	2.99	344		
19.33, 34, 129-130	359	2.113	334	2.204, 210, 212, 213	332
19.43, 55	364	2.114-116	348, 352	2.210	346
19.201	79, 364	2.119-161	335-338	2.212	341
19.245	348	2.121	359	2.213	329
19.354-355	319	2.161	329, 331, 357	2.215	322, 332, 349
19.357, 364	353	2.253	339	2,234	332
20.17-23	357	2.310-314	320, 357	2.242-247	350
20.18	348	2.567	335	2.257-258	346
20.107-108	357	3.11	335	2.264, 269	354
20.123, 195	340	3.112	341	2.270	350
20.139-147	319-320, 346, 348	3.261	339	2.273-275	354-355
		3.263	241	2.275	348
20.145-153	357	3.304	340	2.276	349, 350
20.195	360	3.380-381	273	2.284	364
20.252	358	4.43	359	*Vita*	
Bellum judaicum		4.460	355	4	342
1.78-80	334	4.480	356	10	335
1.108, 111, 113	304	4.483	354	11	356
1.111	359	4.538-544	340	16	360

Index of Ancient Sources

25	339
58	341
80	350
99	340
119, 343, 355	357
166, 210	341
259	350
345, 355	320
414-415	264, 342, 344
419	340
426-427	342, 351
429	360

PHILO

De Abrahamo

1-47	141
20	146
24	142
29	41, 76, 144
48	142, 154, 161
52	159
90-98	192
93	151
94	155, 379
95	155
98	155, 381
99-101	149, 150
100	56
101-102	121, 138, 139
103, 105	140
107	155
109	32, 126
116	32, 126
133-141	156, 206, 209
135	192, 204
135-136	211
148	76, 94
149	76, 159
150	35
164	159
168	197
195	121
219	96
226-235	93
236	41, 94, 159, 377
237, 240-241	94
244	94, 159
245-246	32, 150, 151
246	126

248	61, 154
249-260	61
250	154
250-251	197
253	61, 154, 203
256-257	85, 88
257-258	155

De aeternitate mundi

12	8
65, 66	123
67	124
69	121
97	41
100	124

De agricultura

6	88
17	88, 89, 144
24	145
30	41, 377
34	80, 145
35, 37-38	146, 405
43	182
56, 59	170
73	98
80	97
80-81	49
83	97, 115
84	115, 250
88	115
89	142
94	98, 115
94-98	115
97-98	145
101, 103	115
104-105	145
107-109	116
109	145
122	116
148, 153	60, 248
157, 158	248
160	146
166	248

De animalibus

2	127
11.1	33, 35
48	62
49	192, 212, 220
66	218, 220

De cherubim

1-39	141
3	154
8	114, 129
10	114, 129, 149, 154
12	20, 114, 142
17	224
40	114, 136
40-130	141
41	149, 150, 160
43	30, 62
45-47	161
46-47	136
48-49	137
50	54, 122, 137, 139, 149, 150
51-52	137
52	101, 140, 216
57	140
59, 60, 62	29, 60
67	140, 163
71	79
72	183
82	35
92	146
109-112	30
113	60
115	201
124, 128	140

De confusione linguarum

15, 27	147
27-28, 40	157, 209
42	187
44	147
52	43
61	20
70	181
71	170
81	160, 181
82, 88, 90, 91	181
117	192
144	223, 250
163	97, 192
165	98
178, 179	17
198	147

De congressu eruditionis

2	150
3	181
4	149
5	154
7	150
9	154
12	62, 149, 154

23	128	*insidari soleat*		111	98, 114
26-33	164	15	155	164	37, 157
36	160	19-21	100	164-169, 203	158
59	140	26	174	211	121, 174
71, 77	154	28	139, 149	212	213
81	148	38	182	212-213	174
81-87	118, 195	46	161, 162	213	223, 250
109	157, 208, 209	80-86	15	214-215, 220	97
124-126	178, 221	102	99, 192	222	157, 208
129, 131	181	105	88	*In Flaccum*	
136	122	110	79	89	126
136-138	244	112	81	136	146, 405
152	154	119	270	*De fuga et inventione*	
162-163	184	127	123, 129, 140, 201	1	154
180	154	147	138	3	128, 213
De vita contemplativa		168	41, 377	16-18	165
2	81, 107	169, 172, 173	44	18	163
6	81	174, 176	81	28	220
18	128, 158	*Quod Deus sit immutabilis*		29	127
25	97	3	140, 144	32	145
33	34, 82, 107, 126	4	159	33-34, 36, 38	100
38	97	14	123	35	43
50-63	209-211	14-15	140	36	131
58	107	15	43	46	96, 162
63	16	16-19	177	46-47	163
66	104	67	85	50, 511	36, 138, 161
68	105	71	43	51-53	139
68-69	107	111	174, 250	52	138, 161
73, 81	104	136	140	67-72	17
De decalogo		137	123, 179	73	165
2	183	*De ebrietate*		114	80, 136, 138, 199
8-9	223, 250	13-98	250		201, 223, 232
45	184	21	213	117-210	120
102	238	30-31	123	128	149
106-107	242	31	136	142, 144	157, 208-209
110	57, 242	33	37, 139	148	182
112, 119	242	36	37, 182	149-156	179
121-122	78	47	163	153	83, 179, 221
122-131	189-190	54	120, 165	154	179
123	188, 191	55	37	167	153, 159
126-131	127	59	150	168	181
131	167, 188	59-60	37, 123, 139	188-189	120, 139, 202
142	78	60	149	190	202
142-145	43	64	154	192	120, 144
149	78, 81	65	188	193	195
150, 151, 153	78	73	187	204	123, 154
168	188	75	80	*De gigantibus*	
173	78	95, 97-98	185	4-5	37, 135, 140, 216
De Deo		98	80	32-33	195
3	35, 136	101-102, 104	80, 185	34-35	97
Quod deterius potiori		105	159	35	79

44	83	42-44	166	2.59	148, 160, 162
55	89	43	118, 127, 220	2.60-61	147
60-61	130	44	188, 191	2.63	201, 238
62-64	149	44-45, 48	167, 192	2.65-59	72
65	29, 143	51	128, 167	2.67	196
Quis rerum divinarum		56	37, 167, 192	2.70, 75-77	72
heres sit		58-59, 61	173	2.71-74	59, 72
36	173	63	77, 173	2.77	182
38	138, 173	64-65	37	2.77, 79, 81, 84-85, 89	73
40	155	79	43, 77	2.88-102	73
42	96, 155	80	166, 167	2.94	197
47-49	164, 240	84, 87	167, 192	2.97	35
51	164	121	127, 167	2.103-105, 107-108	74
52	130	146	131	2.105	247
52-53	155	148	169	3.1	75
54-57	247	151-152	167	3.1-2	162
56	15	153	168	3.3	181
61	246	201-203, 206	127	3.11	36, 259
62	38, 150	202	168	3.13	182
63-64	247	246	168	3.16, 23	163
71, 73	96, 148	264	168	3.24	159
77	157, 209	*Legum allegoriae*		3.26	170
109	221, 223	1.9	123	3.28-36	75
139	30	1.10	118	3.37-39	182
164	16, 30, 47, 62	1.11	41, 377	3.40	126
171-172	125, 243	1.13	120	3.44	148, 183
175	165	1.31, 39	14	3.50	36, 75
186	183, 231	1.51, 54, 69, 70, 71	14, 20	3.56-57, 60-64	75
192	241	1.70	41, 42	3.66-67	180
245	80	1.72-73	19, 98	3.67	44, 111
255	241	1.76	123, 140	3.68	64, 79, 111
269	81, 181	1.80	412	3.69	129, 177
272	181	1.105-106	130	3.74	138, 179
274	213, 215, 216	2.4, 5	19	3.76	111
293-299	119	2.5	43, 59	3.77	144
316	182	2.5-9	29	3.77-105	114
Hypothetica		2.8	19	3.79-80	159
6.10 – 7.20	249, 333	2.11	79	3.81	158, 183
7.1	191, 192, 213, 220	2.13	16	3.85-87	159
	227	2.19, 21, 25	29	3.107	79, 111, 112
7.3	32, 126, 330	2.29	145, 251	3.108-109	111, 351
7.5	238	2.31	376	3.109-115	112
7.7	174, 244	2.38	29, 35	3.111	79
7.8	249	2.42-43	29	3.113, 114	43, 81
7.14	32, 106, 126	2.47-48	164	3.115	42, 48
11.3	108	2.48	240	3.118	98, 112
11.14	108, 337	2.49, 51	29	3.125-159	130
11.17	109	2.53-62	72	3.129	85, 112
De Iosepho		2.54-55	185	3.129-132	88, 89, 90, 236
40-41	77, 166	2.55-60	146	3.132	98
42	118	2.57	184	3.134, 140	89, 130

3.140-142, 145, 147	90	95-100	39	2.193	196
3.147	131	100	97, 165	2.193-208	183
3.148	224	105	94, 249	2.210	38, 239
3.153, 154	91	119	94	2.233-245	172, 240
3.153-158	251	142	149, 159, 181	*De mutatione nominum*	
3.159	91, 131, 236	144-145	196	30-31	17
3.160, 162-178	112, 184	154	183	38-39	142
3.165, 172	141	155	184, 214	72	80
3.175	183	158	184	81	162
3.179	170	158-162	169	89-91	169
3.181	136, 164	192	201	96	165, 169
3.182, 184	112	195	96, 148	98	179
3.185-190	113	203	169	104	182
3.197	159	205-206	172, 240	107-111	182, 187
3.198-199	183	214	162	111-118	95
3.213	157	215	181	120	182
3.200	113	217	60	132	159, 192, 195
3.220	126	219	94	133-134	149
3.220-224	98, 113	221, 223	175, 412	134-136	179
3.223	98	223	174	144	140
3.225-227	187	224	175, 221, 393	171-174	170
3,234	187	224-225	175-176	173	173
3.236-242	168-169	*De vita Mosis I, II*		193-200	176
3.242	187, 188	1.3	92	199-200	393
3.243	181, 188	1.7-9	180, 196	205	223, 250
3.244-245	154	1.8	35	214-215	170
3.246, 250-251	113, 129	1.25-26	93, 181	223	15
3.248	129	1.28	43, 61, 91, 93	223-225	174-176
Legatio ad Gaium			181, 339	226	170
14	214	1.59	196	255	136, 139, 154, 164
39	35	1.52-59	180	261	124, 139, 154, 159
54, 55, 56	122-123	1.147	183, 196	*De opificio mundi*	
72	127	1.154	91, 180	3	10
312	146	1.155	151	13, 14	35, 40, 239
319-320	35	1.289-291	132	25	12
De migratione Abrahami		1.295-297	77, 185-186	29-35	11
2, 7, 9	87-88, 148		222, 286, 379	36	123, 136
13	157	1.299-305	186	38	124
19-21	168	1.300	192	43	123, 124, 136
25-26	241	1.301-302	187, 220	62-66	41, 377
28	163	1.311	186	65, 66, 68, 69	11
33	121, 123, 140, 239	2.23-24	43, 235	67	121
33-37	20, 138	2.44	135	69, 72-76	12, 16
35-36	184	2.55	157, 209	76	13
62	114	2.58	157	77	18
66	98, 114	2.68-69	101, 104	79	43, 239
67	89, 91	2.84	123	80	110, 129, 214
69	223, 250	2.137	39	82-88	12
89-93	224, 230, 239	2.162	185	89-128	120
92	85	2.183, 184	184, 201	100	38, 239
95, 99	164, 165	2.185	144, 145, 406	103-105	117, 118

123	121	133	161	2.12	79, 145, 249
124	120, 122, 123	134	120, 122, 140	2.13	59
132	120		149, 150	2.97	41, 377
133	12, 124	135	136, 164	2.112	35
134	13, 15, 16	137-139	154, 162	2.115	95, 98, 129
135	14	146	162	2.119	203
135-139	17	155	146, 184	*Quaestiones et solutiones*	
136-147	18	156	181	*in Genesin*	
151	16, 21, 25, 55, 56	158-159	185	1.4	14
	66, 68, 71	166	185, 212	1.6, 8	20
151-152	4, 7, 24, 30, 56	175	158	1.7	42, 377
152	26, 61	175-176	145	1.10	58
153	22	176	123	1.12	20, 43
153-155	20, 66	177	158	1.17	27
157-159	67	179	164	1.25	16, 27
158	71, 112, 115, 145	180-181	177	1.26-29	27-28, 126
160, 161	56, 67	182	188	1.27	203
161	65, 68, 121, 124	*De praemiis et poenis*		1.28	123
161-163	70	1-3	10	1.28-29	58
162	68, 69, 74	14-51	131	1.29	36
164	129	48	92	1.31	71
164-166	69-70	52-65, 66-78, 79-92	131	1.33, 37, 45-46	36, 71
165	40, 46, 71	93-110	132-133	1.41	58, 71
166	46, 75, 222	118-119	133	1.47-48	71
167	31, 110, 117	124	146	1.48-51	111
	125, 129, 268	139, 140	220, 247	1.49	117, 125
169-170	110, 129	157-160	133-134, 149	1.51	129
170	66, 18	159	129	1.57	42
De plantatione		164, 168, 170	134	1.92	143, 387
15	124	*Quod omnis probus liber*		1.94	79
29	41	*sit*		2.5	118, 119
38	20	17-18	79	2.9	144
43	20, 144	18	43	2.12	42, 43, 129, 145
104-105	220	38	128		377, 405
145	145	75-91	108	2.13	59
158	213	117	35	2.13-14	35
162	145	124	128, 212	2.14	40
166, 169	160	151	79	2.26	32
169	60	159	43, 79	2.34, 39	144
171-172	145	*De providentia I, II*		2.46	58, 144
De posteritate Caini		2.59	122	2.49	35, 58, 59, 62, 95
22	142	*Quaestiones et solutiones*			139, 140, 144, 215
31	163	*in Exodum*		2.56	99, 144
33	141	1.2	236	2.69	146, 147
40-43	142	1.4	241	2.82	143, 218
52	142, 209, 212	1.7	35	2.115	129
60-61	155, 156	1.8	35, 37	3.3	35, 120
62	165	1.15, 17, 19	241	3.4	42, 377
71	81	2.2	231	3.10	181
73-74	129, 140	2.3	39, 87, 101, 121	3.13	35
74	123		122, 137, 138	3.18	31, 125

3.20	150, 151	4.241, 243	161, 246	2.17	172
3.21	30, 128	4.245	162	2.30, 43-65	172
3.41	79	*De sacrificiis Abelis et*		2.33	180, 209
3.47	49, 119, 121, 230	*Caini*		2.68	245
3.48	39, 58, 121, 230	16	80	2.69-70	246
3.54	136	17-18	162	2.93, 105	172
3.61	118, 230	19	240	2.105, 106, 109	168
4.11	138	20-34	139	2.147	43, 80, 81, 192, 377
4.15	37, 41, 43, 91, 120	21	222, 82	2.165	145, 405
	126, 149, 150	21-23	70	2.184	173, 174, 250
4.18	38, 139	21-44	81-83, 240	2.185	37, 122, 139
4.22	153	26, 28-29	82		150, 233
4.23	157, 208, 209	32	216	2.191-192	157, 208, 209
4.27	122, 123	45	83	2.202	174
4.31	157, 208	48	97, 163	2.204	124
4.37, 41-42	156, 209	49	43, 98, 99	2.269	114
4.38	37	63	241	2.276, 278, 281	114, 115
4.39	209	81	162	*De specialibus legibus*	
4.53	157	100-101	31, 216	1.9	57, 58, 330
4.56, 58	158, 275, 348	101	121	1.24	3
4.59	123	103	38, 123, 125, 126	1.44	92, 94, 96, 231
4.60	150, 195	105	80, 99	1.51-53	231
4.60-61, 63, 66-67	155	115	97	1.56-57	187, 196, 231
4.68	38, 139, 149, 150	121	187	1.77	231
	155	121-122	157, 209	1.101	198, 232
4.73	155, 192	134	183	1.102	324
4.83	155	*De sobrietate*		1.102-104	221
4.86	62, 127, 160	6	146	1.105-112	232
4.88	118, 160	13, 14	170	1.107-112	198-199
4.90	196	21	240	1.112	61
4.95	161	28	172	1.118-119	233
4.97	160, 161	44, 65	147	1.129-130	201, 233
4.99	79, 221	*De somniis I, II*		1.137-139	233
4.110	42, 377	1.25-37	41	1.138	27
4.119	87	1.37	164	1.148, 150	146, 234, 405
4.122, 128	159	1.44, 46-47	96, 148, 154	1.171	15
4.132	127		162	1.172-176	234
4.142	161	1.55-57	96, 148, 163	1.173	92
4.145	160	1.74	12	1.186-188	234, 242
4.147	155	1.88-89	158	1.191	80
4.148	37, 38, 159	1.122-125	163, 212	1.192	43, 79, 146, 328
4.154	58, 62, 118, 122	1.200	122, 138, 140		405
	160	1.215-227	171	1.200	35
4.159, 166	161	1.246	36, 171	1.200, 201	235
4.167-170	162	1.247	157	1.206	236
4.185-188, 200		2.9	213	1.228, 233	235
4.215	94	2.9-11	171	1.236	250
4.220	95	2.10	159	1.257, 270	236
4.224, 229	162	2.13-14	80	1.280-282	223
4.234	79	2.15-16	169, 171	1.305	231
4.238	162	2.16	165	1.325	213

Index of Ancient Sources

1.326, 331-332	223, 150	3.63	224	112	57, 220
1.343	92	3.64-65	64, 193	131-133	244, 331
2.24-25	237	3.65-71	57, 64, 201	182	43, 78
2.25, 31	201		225-226	203-205	15
2.29	121, 140	3.67	196	207	61
2.29-30	138	3.71	127	208	43, 162
2.29-34	237	3.72	119	222	178
2.30	43	3.72-78	227	223	163, 197
2.39	238	3.79-82	228-229		
2.44, 46	238	3.80	57, 119, 201		
2.46	92		221, 324	**OTHER WRITINGS**	
2.49	238	3.82	193		
2.50	192, 213, 238	3.104	138	**Aristotle**	
2.54	149, 238	3.105, 108	201	*De generatione animalium*	
2.56	38, 238	3.108, 109	243	2.3-4	121
2.58	35, 239	3.109	123	*Metaphysica*	
2.108, 124	239	3.110-113	244	986A25	35
2.126	196, 239	3.110-119	331	*Historia animalium*	
2.135-139, 145-148	240	3.112-113	61, 375	584A36-B14	123
2.147	241	3.117-118	244		
2.157	43, 241	3.125	185, 244	**Pseudo-Aristotle**	
2.160	18, 241	3.159	236, 244	*Problemata*	
2.161	234	3.169	33, 126, 345	879A36-880A5	208
2.163	43, 92, 163, 98, 242	3.170-173	34, 126, 345		
2.170	157, 209	3.175-176	34, 147, 345	**Pseudo-Clementines**	
2.191-193	235	3.178-180	35, 345	*Hom.* 13.18.5	380
2.193	234, 242	3.190	36		
2.195	43, 235	4.79	93, 98, 115	**Dionysius of**	
2.201, 203	235	4.79-85	78	**Halicarnassus**	
2.225	243	4.81	81	*Antiquitates romanae*	
3.7-11	193	4.84	79, 192	5.5.5	328
3.8-9	57, 64, 77, 93, 167	4.87	246		
	188, 189, 190, 199	4.89	78, 214	**Epictetus**	
3.10-11	191	4.95	92	*Diatribai*	
3.12-28	193-195	4.96-97	64	2.8.12; 3.22.67-69, 77	86
3.12-82	193	4.123	246		
3.25	196	4.130, 132	247	**Herodotus**	
3.27	201	4.203	191, 214, 247	*Histories* 1.199	402
3.29	195	4.223	247		
3.30-31	199, 200	*De virtutibus*		**Hesiod**	
3.31	192	1-50	215	*Opera et dies* 90-93	68
3.32	201, 202, 211	13	41, 93	*Theognis* 924	150
3.33	123, 202, 211, 243	18-21	36, 214-215, 216		
3.34-36	202-203	19	33	**Hierocles**	
3.37-42	204-208	20-21	36	*On Duties* 4.28.21	412
3.39	208, 216	28-31	60, 247		
3.43-45, 48-49	217, 218	35-36	187, 192	**Homer**	463
3.47-48	230	35-40	222	*Odyssea*	
3.51	218-219	36, 39, 40	77	6.198-210	277
3.52-63	224	40	187	11.436-439	269
3.61	230	110-115	240, 248		

Pseudo-Iamblichus
61.2-4   120
61.2-63.5.   122
63.1-5   123

Justin
Apologia
1.29.   412
2.11.4   379

Laudatio Turiae   355

Macrobius
1.6.62-70   120, 122

Musonius Rufus   418
Frag. 12   390
Frag. 13A, 13B   412

Ocellus Lucanus
De Universi Natura
44-45   412

Plato
Leges
742E; 774C-E   329, 404
838A-B   194
Phaedo
107D–108C   424
Phaedrus
245A   138
Respublica
509C5-D6   153
571C-572A   377
575B 6-9   246
Symposium   16, 106, 210
189-193   26
Timaeus
40C   265
42D 2-4   17
70E   78
87C-89C   18
98A 2-7   67

Gospel of Peter
40   388

Plutarch
Solon 20   329
De liberis educandis
Mor. 12B   405
De tuenda sanitate praecepta
Mor. 129B   377
De amore prolis
Mor. 496F   405
An seni respublica gerenda sit
Mor. 796C   379
Bruta animalia
Mor. 988F-991D   62

Seneca
Ad Helviam 19.6   34, 126
De Matrimonio   412

Tacitus
Historiae
2.2.1   320
5.5.2   286
5.6   357

Theon
104.1-5   122

Xenophon
Memorabilia 2.1   81
Symposium 2   210

RABBINIC LITERATURE

Mishnah
Gittin 9.3   325

Tosefta
Sotah 5.9   381

Babylonian Talmud
Megillah 14b   126
Yevamot 77a   126

Midrash Rabbah
Genesis Rabbah
72:3, 5   412
Exodus Rabbah
1:27   285

www.ingramcontent.com/pod-product-compliance
Lightning Source LLC
Chambersburg PA
CBHW031540300426
44111CB00006BA/122